OXFORD PRIVATE INTERNATIONAL
LAW SERIES

GENERAL EDITOR: JAMES J FAWCETT
Professor of Law
University of Nottingham

CROSS-BORDER CONSUMER CONTRACTS

OXFORD PRIVATE INTERNATIONAL LAW SERIES

General Editor: James J Fawcett

The aim of the series is to publish work of quality and originality in a number of important areas of private international law. The series is intended for both scholarly and practitioner readers.

ALSO IN THIS SERIES

Agreements on Jurisdiction and Choice of Law
ADRIAN BRIGGS

Conflict of Laws Within the UK
KIRSTY J HOOD

Civil Jurisdiction Rules of the EU and their impact on Third States
THALIA KRUGER

Insolvency in Private International Law: National and International Approaches Main Work (Second Edition) and Supplement
IAN FLETCHER

The Transfer of Property in the Conflict of Laws
JANEEN M CARRUTHERS

International Sale of Goods in the Conflict of Laws
JAMES J FAWCETT, JONATHAN M HARRIS and MICHAEL BRIDGE

Choice of Law for Equitable Doctrines
T M YEO

Procedural Law in International Arbitration
GEORGIOS PETROCHILOS

Foreign Law in Civil Litigation
SOFIE GEEROMS

Shares and Other Securities in the Conflict of Laws
MAISIE OOI

Forum Shopping and Venue in Transnational Litigation
ANDREW S BELL

Cross-Border Enforcement of Patent Rights
MARTA PERTEGAS SENDER

Res Judicata, Estoppel and Foreign Judgments
PETER R BARNETT

Corporations in Private International Law
STEPHAN RAMMELOO

The Enforcement of Judgments in Europe
WENDY KENNETT

Claims for Contribution and Reimbursement in an International Context
KOJI TAKAHASHI

The Hague Convention on International Child Abduction
PAUL BEAUMONT and PETER McELEAVY

Autonomy in International Contracts
PETER NYGH

Intellectual Property and Private International Law
JAMES J FAWCETT and PAUL TORREMANS

Foreign Law in English Courts
RICHARD FENTIMAN

Declining Jurisdiction in Private International Law
J J FAWCETT

CROSS-BORDER CONSUMER CONTRACTS

JONATHAN HILL

LLB, LLM
Professor of Law, University of Bristol

OXFORD
UNIVERSITY PRESS

OXFORD
UNIVERSITY PRESS

Great Clarendon Street, Oxford OX2 6DP

Oxford University Press is a department of the University of Oxford.
It furthers the University's objective of excellence in research, scholarship,
and education by publishing worldwide in

Oxford New York

Auckland Cape Town Dar es Salaam Hong Kong Karachi
Kuala Lumpur Madrid Melbourne Mexico City Nairobi
New Delhi Shanghai Taipei Toronto

With offices in

Argentina Austria Brazil Chile Czech Republic France Greece
Guatemala Hungary Italy Japan Poland Portugal Singapore
South Korea Switzerland Thailand Turkey Ukraine Vietnam

Oxford is a registered trade mark of Oxford University Press
in the UK and in certain other countries

Published in the United States
by Oxford University Press Inc., New York

First published 2008

British Library Cataloguing in Publication Data
Data available

Library of Congress Cataloging in Publication Data
Data available

ISBN 978–0–19–927654–7

1 3 5 7 9 10 8 6 4 2

Typeset by Cepha Imaging Private Ltd, Bangalore, India
Printed in Great Britain
on acid-free paper by
CPI Antony Rowe, Chippenham, Wilts

General Editor's Preface

Private international lawyers in Europe are familiar with the special jurisdictional rules for consumer contracts set out in the Brussels Convention/ Brussels I Regulation and the corresponding choice of law rules in the Rome Convention/Rome I Regulation. A considerable amount has already been written on these rules, particularly in relation to their application in cases of electronic commerce. Jonathan Hill's book, *Cross-Border Consumer Contracts*, provides a definitive analysis of these rules, along the way debunking some of the more fanciful notions in relation to e-commerce. Not only is private litigation examined but also litigation in the public interest. The private international implications of various EC consumer protection Directives are discussed. All of this is very welcome. But the book goes much further than this. It points out the unreality of much of the private international law discussion. It asks the fundamental question: is litigation the best way of solving cross-border consumer disputes? It points out that there are very few reported cases on the special private international law rules for consumer contracts and, using statistical evidence, explains why this is so. The author comes to the conclusion that litigation is not the answer and that some form of alternative dispute resolution would be better. The various forms that this can take, including online dispute resolution, are examined and their limitations exposed.

Any exercise in applied private international law has to be carried out with a proper understanding of the substantive law background. The numerous consumer protection measures and initiatives in Europe are considered, so this book should be of interest not just to the private international lawyer but to anyone interested in consumer protection.

The aim of the Oxford Private International Law Series is to publish work of high quality and originality in a number of important areas of private international law. *Cross-Border Consumer Contracts* certainly meets these criteria and is a very welcome addition to the Series.

James Fawcett
Nottingham
30 April 2008

Preface

THE AIM OF THE WORK

The main purpose of this book is to assess the extent to which adequate avenues are available for the effective resolution of disputes arising out of cross-border consumer contracts. The work is premised on the notion that, in certain respects, the legal regime that seeks to regulate the problems generated by cross-border consumer contracts is (and should be) different from the legal regime applicable to international contracts in general. This is not to say, however, that all consumer contracts are (or should be) entitled to different treatment from commercial contracts. Inevitably, there are areas where there is overlap between the regimes applicable to cross-border consumer contracts and international commercial contracts. In view of the fact that there is a rich and varied literature addressing the legal problems generated by international commercial contracts, it would be largely pointless in the context of the present work to devote a large number of pages to a detailed analysis of matters which are fully explored elsewhere. Nevertheless, it is important for the reader to be aware not only of the point at which the 'special' consumer contract rules end and the 'general' contract rules take over but also of the significance of that dividing line. Accordingly, there are passages where a brief account of the 'general' rules has been necessary—so that the discussion of international consumer contracts can be put into some sort of context. These passages are also important for any non-specialist reader who is not familiar with the general framework within which the special regime governing consumer contracts operates. Only the reader can decide whether these passages are sufficient for the non-specialist without unduly trying the patience of the expert.

TERMINOLOGICAL ISSUES

With a view to achieving a degree of linguistic simplicity, I have taken the decision to use a number of phrases (not all of them intrinsically desirable) in particular ways; this is particularly the case in the discussion of e-commerce. Throughout the text, phrases which include the word 'electronic' are abbreviated and the prefix 'e-' is used. So, electronic commerce becomes e-commerce, electronic mail becomes e-mail etc. Although this is not always elegant, such abbreviations make the text easier to manage. It is also necessary to be able to draw a distinction between events which occur through the medium of computer systems and equivalent events which do not involve such technology. In this regard, it has become common to contrast 'cyberspace' (where e-contracts or online contracts take place) with the 'real world' or 'real space' (where offline contracts are concluded). It should, perhaps, be added that use of the term 'cyberspace' should not be taken to imply that a distinct space—separated in any way from the real world—actually exists.[1]

As this book is concerned with consumer contracts, it is helpful to have simple terms to describe the parties to such contracts. Whereas some legal regimes refer to 'the consumer' and 'the other party to a contract',[2] the latter expression becomes clumsy when used repeatedly. Throughout the text, 'the other party' to a consumer contract is referred to as 'the supplier' (regardless of the type of contract involved).

In the context of the Brussels I Regulation, the Rome Convention, and the Rome I Regulation, a distinction has to be drawn between, on the one hand, consumer contracts in general and, on the other, consumer contracts to which special jurisdictional and choice-of-law rules apply. In this work, the latter are referred to as 'protected consumer contracts'.

As regards the recognition and enforcement of foreign judgments and arbitral awards, the court which granted the judgment is referred to as the 'court of origin' or the 'original court'; the country (or state) in which the court of origin sits or in which the arbitral tribunal has its seat is referred to as the 'country of origin' (or 'state of origin'). The court in which recognition or enforcement of a foreign judgment or arbitral award is sought is referred to as the 'court addressed'; the country (or state) in which the court addressed sits is referred to as the 'country addressed' (or 'state addressed').

Various acronyms are used throughout the text. Hopefully, they are either obvious to the reader or the text provides sufficient explanation. One less well-known organization which makes an appearance at various junctures is 'ECC-Net'. The European Consumer Centre Network is a network of advice centres designed to assist consumers with disputes which arise out of cross-border contracts; the network covers the EU Member States (except Bulgaria and Romania), Norway, and Iceland. For further discussion see paras 10.15–10.29.

[1] Some argue, however, that 'from the angle of international law, cyberspace should be categorised as international space' (like the high seas, Antarctica, and outer space): Y Zhao (2005: 226).

[2] See, eg, Brussels Convention, art 14.

Throughout the text, 'England' is used to signify 'England and Wales' and 'he', 'his', and 'him' to signify 'he or she', 'his or her', and 'him or her'.

A significant part of the material discussed in several chapters of this work is to be found in Regulation (EC) No 44/2001 ('the Brussels I Regulation') and the Lugano Convention (which was originally signed in 1988, but was revised in 2007 to bring it into line with the Brussels I Regulation).[3] In substance, the Brussels I Regulation and the revised Lugano Convention are almost identical. However, there are some differences in terminology which mean that it is difficult to deal with both instruments together: for example, whereas the Brussels I Regulation is divided into 'Chapters', the Lugano Convention is divided into 'Titles'; the states bound by the Brussels I Regulation are 'member states', but the Lugano Convention refers to 'States bound by this Convention'. Where it is necessary to refer collectively to member states and states bound by the Lugano Convention, this work uses the phrase 'EU-Lugano states'; countries which are not EU-Lugano states are referred to as 'third states'.

With regard to civil jurisdiction and the recognition and enforcement of judgments, the text discusses the Brussels I Regulation. Any relevant substantive differences between the Regulation and the Lugano Convention are identified in footnotes. If the footnotes are silent, the reader should assume that the substance of the Lugano Convention is identical to that of the Brussels I Regulation. If, for example, the text states that 'the Brussels I Regulation provides that a person domiciled in a member state may be sued in that member state', the reader can assume that the Lugano Convention provides that a person domiciled in a state bound by the Convention may be sued in that state. And so on.

REFERENCES AND CITATIONS

A significant number of footnotes and the bibliography lists refer to material which is (or was) available in electronic form via the Internet. One of the problems with Internet sources is their re-location and disappearance. While researching this book I have attempted to follow up many web references which have frustratingly led to a dead-end, often signposted by the message 'Error 404'. Where the text or a footnote refers to material which is (or was) available at a particular URL, after the web address I have added a date in square brackets—for example, [15/11/07]. This date

[3] See Council Decision [2007] OJ L339/1 and the revised text of the Lugano Convention at [2007] OJ L339/3.

indicates the last time that I accessed that particular document at the URL in question. I can only apologize if the material referred to can no longer be found at the URL which is indicated. For anyone interested in pursuing such matters, material which is no longer available at the cited URL can often be found through the web archive: <http://www.archive.org>.

Throughout the text, citation of academic literature in the footnotes is by reference to the author's name (or authors' names), the date and, where appropriate, the page, section, or chapter number(s). So, page 200 of J Hill, *International Commercial Disputes in English Courts* (Oxford: Hart Publishing, 3rd edn, 2005) would be cited in the footnotes as: J Hill (2005: 200). The full reference to works cited in the footnotes is to be found in the Bibliography.

The text refers to several cases decided by the European Court of Justice. As the full citations tend to be rather long, an abbreviated case name is frequently employed. The full case names are set out in the Table of Cases.

ACKNOWLEDGEMENTS

As always, many people have provided invaluable help at various stages of the project. Thanks go to James Fawcett, the General Editor of the series, and the staff of OUP for their patience, encouragement, and assistance. Andrew Charlesworth was a mine of useful knowledge on issues relating to the Internet. Sheila was, as always, helpful and supportive.

Thanks are also due to the Arts and Humanities Research Council. Completion of this book was assisted by a grant made under the AHRC Research Leave Scheme.

Arts & Humanities
Research Council

As far as possible, I have tried to state the law as on 1 April 2008, although it has been possible to incorporate some later material. Between completion of the manuscript and publication of this work, the UK government (as predicted on p 374, n 7) decided to opt into the Rome I Regulation (Reg (EC) No 593/2008, [2008] OJ L177/6).

Jonathan Hill
23 April 2008

Summary Table of Contents

Contents

Table of Cases

(1) English courts

(2) European Court of Justice

(3) Scottish courts

(4) Courts of other EU member states

Table of Legislation

(1) UK Legislation

(a) Statutes

(b) Statutory Instruments

(2) EU Legislation

(a) Regulations

(b) Directives

(c) Treaties and Conventions

(d) Decisions, Recommendations and Declarations

(3) National Legislation

(a) France

(b) New Zealand

(c) Sweden

(d) United States

(4) International Legislation

1

Introduction

I. PRELIMINARY ISSUES

1. The Starting Point

Since the second half of the twentieth century it has been acknowledged that there are significant practical and legal obstacles confronting consumers who seek redress for defective goods or substandard services. There is a considerable body of evidence to suggest that, in a significant proportion of cases, consumers do not obtain satisfactory outcomes to their complaints. One of the major weaknesses of many contemporary legal systems is that they fail to provide effective mechanisms for the vindication of consumers' contractual rights. The problems which consumers face in domestic cases are substantial; such problems are significantly greater in the cross-border context. **1.01**

1.02 The basic thesis of the present work is that, if the obstacles facing consumers who have complaints arising out of cross-border contracts are to be significantly reduced or eliminated, there are several policy objectives which need to be pursued in parallel. First, to the extent that this is possible, the legal framework for the resolution of cross-border disputes should seek to ensure that, in appropriate cases, consumers have a real opportunity to enforce their legal rights by means of litigation. Secondly, since it has to be recognized that litigation is ill-suited to the resolution of most consumer disputes and is, in any event, a last resort, effective alternative modes of dispute resolution, whereby consumers can obtain redress without having to go to court, are needed. Thirdly, the function of the legal system is not only to facilitate the resolution of disputes as and when they arise; it can also play an important role in establishing an environment in which disputes do not occur in the first place. The policy of preventing disputes can be advanced through various strategies for educating consumers and raising standards among suppliers, thereby reducing the incidence of consumer complaints.

1.03 It also needs to be recognized that not all disputes arising out of consumer contracts result from a failure by suppliers to comply with their contractual obligations. In cases where consumers are in breach of contract (typically, by failing to pay for the goods or services they have ordered), suppliers have a legitimate interest in being able to take action (whether through the courts or some other appropriate channel) against a consumer in order to recover the money which they are owed.

2. What is a 'Consumer Contract'?

1.04 There is no universally applicable definition of 'consumer contract' for the purposes of the law; different legal regimes and statutory schemes draw the dividing line between commercial contracts, on the one hand, and consumer contracts, on the other, in different places. For example, at the domestic level there is no very clear picture in English law as to who exactly qualifies as a consumer and much depends on the precise scope of the particular legislation involved.[1] For the purpose of the current work, it is the approach adopted by instruments which operate at the European level (such as the Brussels I Regulation and the Rome I Regulation) which is the most relevant. This approach—which is considered in greater detail in subsequent chapters[2]—turns on a number of elements: the characteristics of the parties to the contract and the subject-matter of the contract itself.

[1] See D Oughton and J Lowry (2000: ch 1).

[2] See chs 3, 4, and 12.

The Parties to the Contract

To the extent that the law makes special provision for consumer contracts—in contrast to commercial contracts or contracts in general—such special provision is motivated by the policy of seeking to protect consumers because of a perceived economic inequality between the parties. Accordingly, the characteristics of the parties to the contract are relevant to the question of which contracts are to be regarded as consumer contracts. **1.05**

It is possible to imagine a legal system which attempted to define the scope of the law's protective provisions by reference to the subjective characteristics of the parties to the contract in question. For example, protection could (in theory) be extended to all cases in which there was an inequality of bargaining power between the parties—and leave it to the courts to decide on a case-by-case basis whether such inequality existed in any particular case. Not surprisingly, the law does not adopt such an approach; the rules relating to consumer contracts do not apply to 'any contract, irrespective of its subject-matter and purpose, in which an economically weaker party is faced by a party in a position which is objectively superior or superior by reason of the circumstances'.[3] Instead, the law determines the scope of consumer protection by reference to objective factors with a view to identifying *types* of contract in relation to which there is deemed to be an inequality between the contracting parties. According to such an approach, if the relevant conditions are satisfied, it does not matter whether or not there is actually an inequality between the parties. **1.06**

For a contract to be regarded as a consumer contract, one party to the relationship (the consumer) must be an individual (rather than a legal person) and must be acting otherwise than in the course of his trade or profession. Secondly, the other party (the supplier), who may be either a natural or legal person, must be acting in the course of business. **1.07**

Contracts which satisfy these very general criteria are often referred to as business-to-consumer contracts (or b2c contracts) and are to be distinguished not only from business-to-business (b2b) contracts but also from consumer-to-consumer (c2c) contracts. So, the sale of a car from A, a car manufacturer, to B, a car dealer, is a b2b contract; the sale of the car by B to C, a private purchaser, is a b2c contract; a sale by C of the (now second-hand) car to D, another private purchaser, is a c2c contract. Of these three contracts, this work is concerned only with that between B and C. **1.08**

[3] Case C-269/95 *Benincasa* [1997] ECR I-3767, 3781 (para 50) (Ruiz-Jarabo Colomer AG).

The Subject-matter of the Contract

1.09 The paradigm consumer contract is a contract for the supply of goods (such as a contract for the sale of a toaster, a CD player, or a set of golf clubs) or a contract for the provision of services (such as a contract for the repair of a motor car or an insurance contract). However, there is a question whether all b2c contracts, regardless of the subject-matter of the contract, should be treated as consumer contracts.

Contracts for the sale of immovable property

1.10 A contract for the sale of land will normally not be a consumer contract. Many contracts for the sale of land are private sales (c2c contracts) between two individuals, neither of whom is in the business of buying and selling land. However, there is no reason why, in principle, a case which involves a b2c contract (for example, where an individual buys a house directly from a property developer) should not be regarded as a consumer contract—at least as regards issues relating to consumer redress. The counter-argument is that consumer protection is premised (at least in part) on the consumer's 'information deficit'—that is, the fact that consumers are typically at a disadvantage vis-à-vis suppliers in terms of the amount of information at their disposal (relating to the subject-matter of the contract and its terms and conditions). However, wherever a contracting party may be expected to have the benefit of specialist advice (typically legal and financial advice), there is less need for special rules to seek to overcome the information deficit which consumers normally experience. In a purchase of immovable property from a developer, there is an argument for saying that the economic weakness of the purchaser is offset by the fact that the buyer can be expected to be in receipt of legal advice.

Tenancies, timeshares, and holiday contracts

1.11 Certain types of tenancy agreement have all the hallmarks of consumer contracts (for example, where an individual tenant rents an apartment for residential use from a commercial landlord). This is not to say that a b2c tenancy should be treated in the same way as other consumer contracts. Most legal systems have complex and elaborate schemes which govern residential tenancies—typically with the intention of providing residential tenants with a measure of rent control and/or protection from eviction; it may be inappropriate to try to apply in tandem both substantive consumer protection legislation and specific housing legislation. Nevertheless, there are good reasons for treating b2c tenancies, timeshare contracts, and holiday contracts which involve the letting of immovable property as consumer contracts for the purposes of the current work—whose main focus is on methods of consumer redress as opposed to substantive consumer protection. One of the contexts in which cross-border consumer contracts have given rise to significant problems concerns contracts for holiday-based products falling outside the scope of the Timeshare Directive;[4] problems have included the non-availability of accommodation at the consumer's chosen resort, onerous contractual terms, and the like.[5]

Contracts for high-value goods and services

According to one view, not all b2c contracts for goods and services should be regarded as consumer contracts for the purposes of the law. For example, the category of contracts governed by consumer contract provisions could be restricted to contracts for the supply of 'a consumer good'[6] or 'goods for personal, family or household use'.[7] This raises questions over the extent to which rules designed to protect consumers should be applied to contracts where the purchaser of goods or services is (or is likely to be) a sophisticated economic agent, even though he is not acting in the course of business. Should consumer rules apply to investment contracts (for example, where a private individual enters speculative currency transactions) or to contracts for the sale of high-value goods (such as works of art, yachts, and luxury cars)? If the rationale for the application of special rules to consumer transactions is the relative inexperience and economic weakness of the consumer, it may be questioned whether protection should be afforded to sophisticated consumers who might reasonably be thought capable of looking after their own interests.[8] **1.12**

There are, however, severe difficulties in drawing coherent dividing lines between different types of contract based either on the value of the subject-matter of the contract or on the nature of the goods or services involved. Although one may feel that one can intuitively distinguish consumer goods from luxury goods, it is not easy to devise a workable legal test. Although some legal regimes may seek to draw these kinds of distinction, for the purposes of the current work, a contract for the purchase of a yacht or a contract for financial services is no less capable of being a **1.13**

[4] Dir 94/47/EC [1994] OJ L280/83.

[5] ECC-Net (December 2002: 10). Because the Timeshare Directive does not apply to various holiday products which resemble timeshares there are proposals to replace the existing directive with a new instrument: see European Commission, COM (2007) 303.

[6] Case 150/77 *Bernard* [1978] ECR 1431, 1451 (Capotorti AG).

[7] Vienna Convention on the International Sale of Goods, art 2(a).

[8] For example, it has been suggested by A Vahrenwald (May 2000: 17) that 'Internet consumers are often persons with higher education [who] speak several languages and [who] are used to conclude contracts for trade, business and professional purposes over the Internet. Whether such persons need consumer protection at all may be questionable.'

consumer contract than a contract for the purchase of a bicycle or a contract for the repair of a personal computer.

3. The Rise of Cross-border Consumer Contracts

1.14 Traditionally, consumer contracts were almost invariably domestic in nature. In the past, if a consumer bought foreign goods, he would normally do so through a seller in his own country which represented the foreign manufacturer in the distribution chain.[9] However, changes in consumer lifestyles and new technologies have brought about significant changes in consumers' buying patterns.[10] In Europe, the creation of the internal market has made goods and services from member state A much more accessible in member state B: 'The continuing expansion of economic activity within the Internal Market means that more and more consumers' activities are not confined to their own Member State.'[11] In the global marketplace, foreign travel (especially through cheap flights) has made it much easier for consumers physically to access distant markets. Perhaps most significantly, the development of e-commerce has provided consumers with the opportunity to purchase goods and services via the Internet from foreign suppliers without leaving their home country.

1.15 According to a 2006 survey of European consumers, more than a quarter of the sample had made at least one cross-border purchase over the course of the previous year; in the United Kingdom a third of consumers had made a cross-border purchase in the survey period.[12] It is reasonably clear that cross-border purchasing is becoming more widespread; a previous survey (in 2003) had found that only 12 per cent of European consumers had participated in cross-border commerce in the previous year.[13]

1.16 For the purposes of these surveys, cross-border purchases include not only those made while on holiday or during a business trip abroad ('in-person shopping') but also 'distance contracts'[14] concluded by traditional

[9] JP Nehf (1999: 459).

[10] Having said that, it is worth noting that 'cross-border sales directly to consumers have not progressed as expected. According to a recent study . . . cross-border sales are still insignificant, around 3 per cent': EMOTA (September 2003: 1–2).

[11] European Commission, COM (2001) 161, p 2.

[12] Eurobarometer (September 2006: 4–5).

[13] Eurobarometer (September 2006: 5).

[14] A distance contract is a contract 'concluded between a supplier and a consumer under an organized distance sales or service-provision scheme run by the supplier, who, for the purpose of the contract, makes exclusive use of one or more means of distance communication up to and including the moment at which the contract is concluded': Dir 97/7/EC, art 2(1).

means of communication (such as telephone or post) or via the Internet.[15] Although some commentators seem to assume that, without the Internet, b2c commerce between parties from different countries would be extremely limited,[16] surveys indicate that, notwithstanding increased use of the Internet, European consumers are still more likely to enter a cross-border contract as a result of in-person shopping while abroad than via the Internet. According to the 2006 survey of consumer behaviour in the European Union, over the course of the previous year, 19 per cent of consumers had made cross-border purchases when they were physically in another country (while on holiday or during a business trip),[17] whereas only 7 per cent had concluded cross-border distance contracts.[18]

4. Consumer Protection: The Cross-border Dimension

In broad terms, there are three strands to consumer protection in modern legal systems. First, the law seeks to redress the information deficit which consumers typically face. One of the reasons for the inequality of power between consumers and suppliers is that consumers do not normally have access to accurate information relating to the goods and services which are available for them to buy. Consequently, steps have been taken to ensure that consumers are better informed—and not misinformed by misleading advertising—so that consumers can more readily make properly considered purchasing decisions. It has come to be accepted that consumers have the right to be given the facts they need in order to be able to make an informed choice.[19] Secondly, the law seeks to redress the imbalance of power which flows from the information deficit by providing the consumer with substantive rights[20]—by overriding, if necessary, unfair terms in the standard-form contract between the parties. Whereas parties to a commercial contract are generally bound by the terms of that contract once the contract has been concluded, in the consumer context, certain types of contractual term (such as exclusion clauses) may be unenforceable and consumers may, in certain situations, have the right to change **1.17**

[15] The purchase of foreign goods from a supplier established in the consumer's country is not a cross-border transaction.

[16] HH Perritt Jr (2000: 675).

[17] Eurobarometer (September 2006: 7). For the United Kingdom, the figure was 27 per cent of the sample.

[18] Eurobarometer (September 2006: 11). For the United Kingdom, the figure was 9 per cent of the sample.

[19] MJ Trebilcock (1971: 276).

[20] See, eg, MI Meyerson (1990). See the Unfair Commercial Practices Directive, Dir 2005/29/EC [2005] OJ L149/22.

their mind and to withdraw from a contract after its conclusion (during the so-called cooling-off period). It is widely recognized that 'justice requires that a distinction be drawn between freely negotiated contracts and standard form contracts'.[21] Thirdly, consumers need to be given better means of recourse when their rights are infringed. This links into the broader concerns of the access-to-justice movement—which has been described as comprising three 'waves': (i) attempts to make the legal system more accessible to the poor (for example, by the provision of legal aid); (ii) efforts to provide legal representation for unrepresented or under-represented groups (for example, through public interest litigation) and (iii) the creation of alternatives to 'ordinary' litigation for the resolution of disputes (such as small claims procedures and extra-judicial dispute resolution).[22] As regards improving consumers' access to justice, there is a collective dimension as well as the more obvious individual one. Even in the field of private law, society has a collective interest in the application and enforcement of the law:

> If one claimant foregoes his legal right, little damage is done to the rule of law, which provides that right, but if many forego their legal rights, *a fortiori* if no one asserts his legal rights, the very rule which provides the right withers and dies, being reduced to the status of a mere paper rule, perhaps descriptively accurate in historical terms but wholly out of touch with the realities of social practice.[23]

1.18 Furthermore, if the legal system fails to address the access-to-justice problems which consumers experience when they seek to vindicate their contractual rights, a situation arises in which suppliers can ignore consumers' rights with impunity:

> If there are no effective [dispute-resolution] procedures, cases of non-performance will proliferate, and eventually the market system will suffer; conversely, the existence of appropriate procedures for settling disputes encourages the 'spontaneous' performance of contractual obligations.[24]

1.19 In Europe, although the development of consumer law in these three areas originated in national legal systems, in more recent years, the focus has shifted from national regulation towards transnational regulation at the EU level.

[21] *Couch v First Guaranty Ltd* 578 F Supp 331, 333 (ND Texas, 1984).
[22] See M Cappelletti and B Garth (1978: 21–54); M Cappelletti (ed) (1981: vi–vii).
[23] R von Ihering (trans P Ashworth) *The Battle for Right* (1883), cited by RHS Tur (1982: 143).
[24] European Commission, COM (93) 576, p 7.

5. The Role of Private International Law

As regards consumer's substantive rights and access to justice, it is not wholly unreasonable to imagine that the framework established by choice-of-law and jurisdiction rules should seek to ensure that, in certain circumstances, consumers not only have the benefit of a law which provides an appropriate level of substantive protection but also, in jurisdictional terms, do not find themselves at a significant disadvantage vis-à-vis suppliers established in other countries. **1.20**

Many commentators start from the premise that litigation is the primary mode of dealing with disputes which arise out of consumer contracts. For example, one author states: **1.21**

> The private international law on consumer contracts . . . has to provide solutions to the question of which is the applicable law to consumer contracts made over the World Wide Web, and it must determine which courts have jurisdiction to hear the case. These questions are not only of academic interest, but their answers imply dramatic practical consequences both for the courts and for people conducting business on the Web. If the consumer receives defective goods or if he regrets having made the purchase, he will want to know where to sue the supplier and which law governs his right to damages or to cancel the contract. The supplier, on the other hand, might find himself confronted with foreign consumer protection law which he is not aware of.[25]

Similar statements are to be found throughout the literature: questions of private international law are central because they provide the framework which shapes cross-border consumer litigation. This view is really not much more than an extension of the lawyer's assumption that courts provide the primary forum in which disputes are resolved; it is all to easy for lawyers to become blinkered into seeing judicial means of redress as all important.[26] **1.22**

In the context of consumer disputes, any picture of dispute resolution which takes litigation as the central element runs the risk of presenting an extremely distorted picture. Although parts of this book provide an analysis of the private litigation model in the context of cross-border consumer contracts, it has to be recognized at the outset that the litigation of disputes arising out of cross-border consumer contracts is extremely unusual; all the evidence points to private international law being largely irrelevant in all but a tiny proportion of situations involving cross-border **1.23**

[25] R Schu (1997: 194).

[26] G Howells and S Weatherill (2005: 606).

consumer contracts.[27] From this point of view, the access-to-justice movement has failed to bring about an environment in which consumers are able to vindicate their contractual rights through the courts. This also means that, in practical terms, there is a real danger that all the reforms and policy initiatives designed to make consumer litigation less complicated and burdensome will prove to be of little more than symbolic significance. Indeed, one of the dominant themes of this work is that court-based systems of redress have failed to provide an effective channel for the resolution of complaints arising from cross-border consumer contracts. To a large extent, this failure is an inevitable concomitant of the fact that legal systems have not been able to resolve the central problems at the domestic level. If litigation does not provide an effective mechanism for the resolution of complaints arising from domestic consumer contracts, it is almost inconceivable that the position in relation to cross-border contracts will be any better.

II. E-COMMERCE ISSUES

1.24 Although this book deals with aspects of the law relating to e-commerce, e-commerce is not the work's only focus. The Internet is unique in terms of its power and global reach, but it is fundamentally no more than a different (albeit extremely effective) means of communication. Essentially, this book argues that, as regards the topics under consideration, there may be rather less to the legal issues surrounding e-commerce than is sometimes suggested. It is easy to be blinded by the technological wizardry which lies behind the Internet and to reach the conclusion that the uniqueness of cyberspace gives rise to a range of complex and unique problems.

1. What is E-commerce?

1.25 For the purposes of the current work e-commerce is taken to encompass transactional activity which, in one way or another, is mediated by computer technology. A useful definition is provided by the Organisation for Economic Co-operation and Development in the following terms:

> Electronic Commerce refers generally to all forms of transactions relating to commercial activities involving both organisations and individuals, that are based upon the processing and transmission of digitised data, including text, sound and visual images. It also refers to the effects that the electronic exchange of commercial

[27] See ch 2.

information may have on the institutions and processes that support and govern commercial activities.[28]

Rather more simply it has been suggested that an e-commerce transaction is one which 'involves computer-to-computer communication in [an] open or a closed network'.[29]

E-commerce includes contracts for the sale of goods or for the provision of services where some method of computer-mediated communication is used by at least one of the parties for entering into the contract. Of course, within the broad scope of e-commerce, the electronic aspect of any contract may range from the substantial to the relatively trivial. At the relatively trivial end of the spectrum, there are contracts where the only electronic aspect is the use of e-mail as a method of communication. At the other end of the spectrum are contracts concluded for digitized products (such as computer software) which are concluded via an active website and where the subject-matter of the contract is delivered to the purchaser in digital format online. Between these two extremes there are many permutations. In the consumer context, one of the commonest types of e-commerce transaction is the purchase of goods (such as books or CDs) or services (such as the use of a hotel room or an airline flight) through an active website—where the conclusion of the contract takes place in cyberspace and performance of the payment obligation by the consumer is effected online, but performance of the characteristic obligation of the contract (delivery of the goods or provision of the services) occurs in the real world in exactly the same way as in relation to offline contracts. For the purposes of this work, the terms 'e-commerce' and 'online' or 'Internet shopping' are used interchangeably: the key feature of Internet shopping is that the consumer is able to place an order for goods or services online (whether or not payment by the consumer and/or performance by the supplier takes place online).[30] **1.26**

2. Why is Consumer E-commerce (Potentially) Important?

Within the institutions of the European Union, there is a stated policy of seeking to encourage cross-border activity at the consumer level. This policy is a facet of the development of the internal market and is based on the view that cross-border economic activity will promote healthy competition between suppliers established in different member states. It is for this **1.27**

[28] Organisation for Economic Co-operation and Development (1997: 20).
[29] L Biukovic (2002: 330).
[30] See Office of Fair Trading (June 2007: 11).

reason that e-commerce is thought to be of such significance; the Internet greatly extends the opportunities for consumers to engage in cross-border shopping on a regular basis (as opposed to only occasionally, such as while on holiday or during a business trip). However, the role of the Internet in promoting an efficient and fully competitive market is significantly curtailed if consumers are discouraged from participating in e-commerce—whether because of legal, technical, or psychological factors.

1.28 An important element which potentially inhibits consumer involvement in e-commerce is lack of trust. It has been argued that:

> If consumers are unwilling to experiment with unknown vendors, then the Internet fails to create competitive pressures that serve to erode online price dispersions between vendors. When competitive pressures are relaxed, consumers pay more for their products, and consumer welfare is thus not maximized.[31]

1.29 This is a major theme among policy makers and in the literature. Many commentators see lack of consumer trust as a major obstacle to the development of consumer-based e-commerce[32] and research shows that lack of trust plays a significant role in discouraging consumers from engaging in Internet shopping.[33] It has also been suggested that the lack of a clear legal framework for b2c e-commerce deters many consumers from purchasing luxury and other expensive items online; instead, consumers tend to buy high-value goods and services from 'bricks and mortar' businesses that are established in the country in which the consumer is resident.[34] According to this view, a more effective mechanism for the resolution of cross-border consumer disputes arising out of e-commerce could help to promote consumer confidence[35] and make the internal market more of a reality at the consumer level.

3. How Widespread is Consumer E-commerce?

1.30 Research conducted in the European Union indicates that consumers are much less likely to make online purchases from foreign suppliers than from local suppliers. For example, a 2006 survey of European consumers indicated that whereas more than 40 per cent of UK consumers had made

[31] EA O'Hara (2005: 1897).

[32] See, eg, LM Ponte (2002); JEJ Prins (2003); MD Powell and PM Turner-Kerr (2000); LA Reisch (2003).

[33] See Office of Fair Trading (June 2007: ch 3). According to LM Ponte (2002: 442, n 3), more than 80 per cent of consumers do not trust the Internet.

[34] K Stewart and J Mathews (2002: 1114).

[35] See, eg, C Rule (2002: 92–3, 97–100). But, see L Edwards and A Theunissen (2007) whose research questions the dominant view.

an Internet purchase from a 'local' website in the previous year, only 7 per cent had made a cross-border purchase online.[36] These figures are supported by evidence from credit card companies which indicates that 92 per cent of the money spent on Internet shopping by UK consumers is derived from purchases from UK e-traders, with only 5 per cent being paid to e-traders based in other EU member states and 3 per cent to e-traders based in the rest of the world.[37]

It has also been found that, even when making cross-border purchases via the Internet, consumers remain relatively conservative. British consumers who buy goods and services from foreign suppliers are more likely to buy from other European countries than from further afield. According to research conducted on behalf of the Department for Trade and Industry in 2002, whereas three quarters of cross-border shoppers made purchases from other EU countries, only one fifth purchased goods or services from suppliers based in North America.[38] It also seems that, if an online purchase is not made from a local supplier, the tendency is for consumers to buy from e-traders established in neighbouring and/or same-language countries;[39] only about one third of EU consumers are willing to make a purchase in a foreign language.[40] So, as regards disputes arising out of cross-border e-contracts, complaints by Austrian consumers tend to **1.31**

[36] Eurobarometer (September 2006:14); the figures for the European Union as a whole were 23 per cent and 6 per cent. See, also, the figures set out in a recent OFT report, which suggests that 44 per cent of UK adults have shopped online and (somewhat improbably) that 47 per cent have made at least one purchase from a non-UK site within the previous 12 months: Office of Fair Trading (June 2007: 16, 150). As with all surveys, the accuracy of the data (which is provided by members of the public on the basis of their recollections, opinions, etc) is unreliable. For example, consumers may not be aware whether or not they have made cross-border online purchases; indeed, in the OFT research, over a third said that they were unable to tell whether or not an e-trader is based in the United Kingdom: Office of Fair Trading (June 2007: 16, 150). This is not very surprising: five percent of websites with a *.co.uk* domain name are registered to overseas locations (Office of Fair Trading (June 2007: 150)); unless they have read the 'small print' carefully, many British consumers who purchase goods via the *amazon.co.uk* website are likely to imagine that they have made a domestic purchase; however, as *amazon.co.uk* is the trading name of two Luxembourg companies, *Amazon EU Sàrl* and *Amazon Services Europe Sàrl*, both of which are subsidiaries of Amazon.com Inc, the US parent, a British consumer who makes a purchase via *amazon.co.uk* is party to a cross-border contract. A similar source of potential confusion is the fact that a business with a *.com* domain name may be based either within or outside the United Kingdom.

[37] Office of Fair Trading (June 2007: 150).

[38] Department for Trade and Industry (November 2002).

[39] A Fielder (May 2007: 9).

[40] See the factsheet: 'The European Consumer Centres Network: ECC-Net': <http://ec.europa.eu/consumers/publications/factsheet-ECC-Net_en .pdf> [12/7/07].

concern German suppliers; complaints by Belgian consumers concern French and Dutch suppliers; complaints by Irish consumers concern suppliers based in the United Kingdom; and so on.[41]

1.32 Furthermore, research indicates that many e-traders do not offer cross-border sales. For example, according to a recent report on the e-commerce market in the United Kingdom, nearly two thirds of UK e-traders are not aiming to sell abroad.[42] The authors of a Europe-wide study published in 2003 noted:

> We knew that most e-commerce companies operate mainly in their domestic market, however it still came as a bit of a surprise to learn that it's only a very small minority of the EU based webtraders that offered their products and services to the whole of the internal market . . . . The webtraders that did not sell to foreign consumers could be divided into two categories. The first relates to those that limited their market by language and the second to those that explicitly informed the consumer that they did not deliver abroad or to certain specified countries. Several of the webtraders that did not offer cross-border sales failed to inform the consumer about this.[43]

4. How Valuable is E-commerce?

1.33 Notwithstanding the extensive literature devoted to consumer e-commerce, its significance needs to be kept in proportion—in terms of not only the balance between commercial e-commerce and consumer e-commerce but also the balance between online and offline shopping. Although global e-commerce is estimated at billions of dollars,[44] it is important to remember that the vast majority of e-commerce involves business-to-business transactions. Estimates as to the balance between b2b e-commerce and b2c e-commerce vary; it seems likely that, globally, b2b transactions account for at least 80 per cent of all e-commerce transactions,[45] though the proportion could be as much as 85 per cent[46] or even more.[47] In the United Kingdom, a country which has a high rate of consumer access to the Internet and which, therefore, is likely to see an above average level of b2c e-commerce, b2c sales accounted for 21 per cent of online sales made by

[41] See ECC-Net (June 2006: 6–16).
[42] Office of Fair Trading (June 2007: 151).
[43] ECC-Net (May 2003: 6).
[44] For example, it was estimated that by the end of 2003, b2c e-commerce was worth $250 billion: LJ Gibbons (2002: 2).
[45] Organisation for Economic Co-operation and Development (March 2001: 14).
[46] G Pearce and N Platten (2000: 364).
[47] T Puurunen (2002: 136).

UK businesses in 2005—with the remaining 79 per cent being b2b transactions.[48]

A 2001 OECD report indicates that b2c e-commerce accounts for a very small share of all retail trade in OECD countries—typically less than 1 per cent.[49] Nevertheless, use of the Internet by consumers for buying goods and services is undoubtedly growing. The value of Internet sales by UK businesses to households rose from £5 billion in 2002 to more than £21 billion in 2005;[50] UK online sales were estimated at £40 billion in 2007 with it being predicted that the figure will rise to £162 billion by 2020.[51] Notwithstanding the prediction of growth in b2c e-commerce, it is thought that, in the medium term, it will continue to account for significantly less than 10 per cent of the total retail market. Figures for 2005 suggest that online shopping accounted for a little over 3 per cent of all retail sales in the United Kingdom.[52] One of the more upbeat predictions for e-commerce growth in the United Kingdom suggests that by 2011 online retailing will still be worth less than 9 per cent of the United Kingdom's total retail sales.[53] Having said that, it seems clear that online sales are growing at a faster rate than offline sales.[54] **1.34**

Although there is potential for a wide range of different consumer transactions to be conducted online, it seems that a high proportion of online consumer sales are for relatively low-value goods and services. As regards consumer e-commerce in the United Kingdom, it is estimated that, in 2005, one quarter of online sales were of electrical items, flights, music, and videos.[55] According to a 2007 survey, on average, UK consumers who bought goods and services via the Internet in the 12 months prior to the **1.35**

48 Office of Fair Trading (June 2007: 31).

49 Organisation for Economic Co-operation and Development (March 2001: 14).

50 Office of Fair Trading (June 2007: 16).

51 See<http://www.computing.co.uk/computing/news/2203184/online-shopping-rise-40bn> [1/2/08].

52 Office of Fair Trading (June 2007: 18). Although this figure seems modest, the United Kingdom is at the forefront of b2c e-commerce within Europe (in terms of overall value of online sales, ratio of online to offline sales, and value of online sales per capita).

53 See <http://news.bbc.co.uk/1/hi/business/6690397. stm> [25/5/07], which cites a report compiled by retail analysts, Verdict Research. The full report can be purchased online (at <http://www.verdictonline.co.uk/Selection/VSelRep.asp?Rep=549> [15/4/08]) for £1,850.

54 It has been estimated that online sales are growing at 20 times the rate of offline sales: <http://www.computing.co.uk/computing/news/2204573/online-spend-reach-15bn-3681370> [1/2/08].

55 Office of Fair Trading (June 2007: 13).

survey, made 14 online 'shopping trips' and spent £763.[56] Based on these figures, the average value of each Internet 'shopping trip' is £55. This figure is not inconsistent with other market research: in 2005, a survey estimated that the average value of each online purchase was £42.[57] Of course, these figures do not mean that there are no high-value b2c contracts concluded via the Internet and there is some evidence to suggest that a small percentage of Internet shoppers in the United Kingdom occasionally make cross-border purchases whose value exceeds £5,000.[58] However, such high-value transactions are very much the exception.

5. What Kinds of Dispute Arise out of Consumer E-commerce?

1.36 In e-commerce cases, the supplier will normally have no problems with the consumer's performance, as the consumer will usually be required to pay in advance (typically by credit or debit card). Various studies have confirmed that credit card is far and away the most common payment method for cross-border transactions.[59] In more than 70 per cent of Internet transactions, payment is made by credit cards.[60] Although a majority of European websites offer more than one method of payment, in most cases the supplier requires payment from the consumer prior to dispatching goods or performing services. There are, however, variations between different countries. For example, in certain countries there are many websites which allow consumers to pay cash on delivery: either the consumer pays directly to the person delivering the goods or the consumer pays at the post office when collecting the goods.[61] So, even in these cases, where the supplier dispatches goods before payment is made, the consumer cannot actually obtain the goods without paying for them. It seems, therefore, that, except in cases where payment is deferred or the consumer pays by instalments,[62] if there is a dispute, it will arise because the consumer is

[56] Office of Fair Trading (June 2007: 19).

[57] Office of Fair Trading (June 2007: 63). As regards sales through online auction websites, in cases in which problems arose, the median value of the items involved is even lower (£35): Office of Fair Trading (June 2007: 142).

[58] Department for Trade and Industry (November 2002).

[59] ECC-Net (May 2003: 21).

[60] M Turner and D Callaghan (2006: 334), citing data supplied by the Office of Fair Trading.

[61] This latter method of payment is very common in the Nordic countries: ECC-Net (May 2003: 20).

[62] Such as in *Océano Grupo Editorial and Salvat Editores* Joined Cases C-240/98 to C-244/98 [2000] ECR I-4941 (offline contracts for the purchase of encyclopaedias; payment in instalments).

unhappy in some way about the supplier's performance (rather than because the supplier is unable to secure payment).

Across the whole of the European Union, in 2005 the network of European Consumer Centres (ECC-Net) handled over 42,000 requests for information, complaints and disputes;[63] fewer than 10 per cent (3,780) of these cases concerned cross-border online shopping.[64] As in previous years, in 2005 the non-delivery of ordered products was the greatest area of complaint: 46 per cent of complaints concerned problems with delivery; 25 per cent related to problems with the product (such as defects or non-conformity with the order); only 8 per cent of complaints were concerned with contract terms (of which most problems related to the cooling-off period conferred by the Distance Selling Directive[65]).[66] What is clear is that, in the consumer context, most complaints arising from e-commerce relate to allegations of non-performance or defective performance by the supplier and rarely raise complex questions of law. **1.37**

In formal legal terms, European consumers are generally well protected by substantive rules. In addition to general principles of contract law, according to which a supplier is bound to perform in conformity to the agreement between the parties, the Distance Selling Directive makes provision for a cooling-off period (of at least seven days) in which the consumer has a right to withdraw from the contract[67] and the Unfair Terms in Consumer Contracts Directive[68] outlaws the use by suppliers of unfair terms in standard-form contracts. **1.38**

As regards a typical online sale of goods, a consumer may be faced by one or more of the following problems: **1.39**

(i) the consumer places an order; nothing is delivered;
(ii) the consumer places an order; although nothing is delivered, the supplier takes payment (normally from the consumer's credit card);
(iii) the wrong goods are delivered;

[63] See 'Factsheet: The European Consumer Centres Network: ECC-Net' <http://ec.europa.eu/consumers/publications/factsheet-ECC-Net_en.pdf> [12/7/07].

[64] The situation in the United Kingdom was fairly typical; the ECC (UK) handled 1,834 cases, of which fewer than 200 involved e-commerce: ECC-Net (June 2006: 17).

[65] Dir 97/7/EC on the protection of consumers in respect of distance contracts [1997] OJ L144/19.

[66] ECC-Net (June 2006: 20). Figures for years after 2005 are not available.

[67] Art 6.

[68] Dir 93/13/EEC on unfair terms in consumer contracts [1993] L95/29.

(iv) the ordered goods are delivered, but when the consumer changes his mind and exercises his right of withdrawal the supplier refuses to provide a refund;

(v) the right goods are delivered but, after the cooling-off period has elapsed, the consumer finds that the goods are defective in some way.

1.40 Although each of these situations involves a breach of the consumer's rights, some of them are likely to give rise to frustration, rather than to engender significant problems for which some form of redress is expected or required. Both anecdotal evidence and more systematic surveys suggest that problems with Internet shopping are quite frequent, though the true extent of these problems is quite difficult to assess.

1.41 Several years ago, *Consumers International* carried out a worldwide survey of Internet shopping.[69] This research was based on 412 orders (of which 255 were domestic and 146 were cross-border). In a small number of cases (6 per cent), goods that were ordered did not arrive (even though in nearly all of these cases the order had been confirmed); but in around a third of these cases of non-delivery (2 per cent), the customer was charged for the goods and had to request a refund.[70] There were only three cases (less than 0.5 per cent) in which there were problems with the delivered goods. Where the purchaser returned the goods and claimed a refund, refunds were not received in 9 per cent of cases. In nearly half of these cases the purchaser had to pay for both the delivery and return postage; in a third of cases, the purchaser had to pay for return postage. (As regards e-commerce in Europe, suppliers are required by the Distance Selling Directive to refund both the cost of the goods and all delivery costs.[71]) The researchers did not come across a single case of free returns within the United States.[72]

1.42 A comparable study carried out by ECC-Net a couple of years later paints, if anything, an even less encouraging picture.[73] The first part of the survey involved the researchers (who were based in different member states)

[69] Consumers International (September 2001).

[70] Consumers International (September 2001: 27).

[71] Dir 97/7/EC, art 6.

[72] Consumers International (September 2001: 28). In principle, where a European consumer buys goods online from a US e-trader, the consumer is entitled to rely on the terms of the Distance Selling Directive (see ch 12). In practice, however, many US e-traders who sell in Europe may fail to comply with the Directive's requirements and consumers will not take steps to enforce their right to a full refund if the e-trader does not provide this voluntarily.

[73] ECC-Net (May 2003).

making 114 cross-border online purchases. These purchases fell into six categories:

(i) in nine cases (8 per cent), the e-trader did not respond at all to the order;
(ii) in six cases (5 per cent), although the e-trader did not confirm the order (as required by article 5 of the Distance Selling Directive), the goods were delivered and the consumer was charged for them;
(iii) in 21 cases (18 per cent), the order was confirmed, but the goods were not delivered and the consumer was not charged;
(iv) in nine cases (8 per cent), the order was confirmed and a charge was made, but there was no delivery;
(v) in four cases (3.5 per cent), the order was confirmed and the goods were delivered, but no charge was made;[74]
(vi) in 65 cases (57 per cent), the order was confirmed, the goods were delivered and the consumer was charged.[75]

So, in not much more than half of the cases (57 per cent) did things work out exactly as they should have done (category (vi)). However, in many of the cases in which the supplier's processing of the order was defective in some way, there was no harm done: category (i) is frustrating, but the consumer does not suffer any real harm; as regards category (ii), the consumer is left in some uncertainty, but he will probably be content when the order is fulfilled; although category (iii) cases involve a clear breach of contract and are a cause of vexation for the consumer, (again) no real harm is done; category (v) is not problematical from the consumer's perspective. Obviously, category (iv)—which accounts for 8 per cent of the cases—is the major cause for concern as, in these cases, the consumer paid for the goods, but there was no delivery. It is not clear how serious this problem is in practice as the research does not indicate whether or not, once the supplier had been informed of the error, the wrongly taken payment was refunded.[76] 1.43

The second part of the research sought to test whether e-traders act in accordance with the consumer's right to cancel the contract (under article 6 1.44

[74] As the research also involved returning goods during the cooling-off period, it is possible that in these cases the e-trader would have taken payment for the goods after the expiry of the cooling-off period.

[75] ECC-Net (May 2003: 10–11).

[76] The results of the similar survey conducted by *Consumers International* suggest that there is rarely any problem in obtaining a refund in this type of case: Consumers International (September 2001: 27).

of the Distance Selling Directive).[77] A total of 57 products were returned during the cooling-off period, but reimbursements were obtained in only 39 cases (68.5 per cent). As regards these cases, a full refund was obtained in only 21 cases (37 per cent); in the other 18 cases (31.5 per cent), the supplier did not reimburse the original delivery cost (as required by article 6). So, the customer's rights were respected in full in significantly fewer than half of the cases.

1.45 The authors of the report considered that the overall picture was fairly bleak; only two thirds of the goods ordered online were delivered; one-in-twelve were charged for, but not delivered; where goods are returned during the cooling-off period, full refunds were obtained in fewer than four tenths of cases. In sum: 'Cross-border e-commerce in the EU is a good shopping alternative unless something goes wrong, which it frequently does.'[78]

1.46 In the United Kingdom, research into cross-border shopping conducted in 2002 reported that only 3 per cent of cross-border shoppers had experienced the non-delivery of goods ordered online.[79] Similarly, a recent survey conducted by the Office of Fair Trading in the United Kingdom (which was more focused on domestic e-commerce than on cross-border Internet shopping) suggests a far less negative picture than that painted by international surveys—though this does not mean that there are not plenty of problems. The UK research indicates that 23 per cent of Internet shoppers had experienced some form of problem in an online transaction in the previous year.[80] This is estimated to equal one problem experienced for every 58 transactions. This statistic is much less troubling than the ECC-Net data—which suggests a rate of nearly one problem for every two transactions or the *Consumers International* research which suggests a ratio of roughly 1:16.

1.47 It is not easy to provide a simple explanation for such divergences in data. One possibility is that cross-border e-contracts throw up more problems than domestic transactions. Another possibility is that whereas *Consumers International* and ECC-Net conducted online transactions and recorded the number of times that certain things happened or did not happen, the UK research was based on consumer perceptions and recollections. It is not impossible that various situations which ECC-Net would record as examples of where things did not work out exactly as they should have done (for example, where the consumer attempts to order goods, but receives

[77] ECC-Net (May 2003: 13–14).
[78] ECC-Net (May 2003: 16).
[79] Department for Trade and Industry (November 2002).
[80] Office of Fair Trading (June 2007: 63).

no response at all from the e-trader) would not be regarded as a problem by a consumer.

Research also shows that website information (about the consumer's rights etc) is generally poor on a significant proportion of sites and that there is widespread flouting of the laws providing for consumer protection.[81] The number of fully compliant websites (in terms of the provision of legally required information and respect for consumers' rights—such as to return goods in the cooling-off period and receive a full refund) is low, probably less than 50 per cent.[82] **1.48**

6. Approaches to E-commerce

There are various possible approaches which the law might adopt to cyberspace—and to events and actions which are considered to take place there: 'These are reflected in the differing decisions on which legal metaphors and analogies are appropriate to solve the problems'.[83] At one extreme, there is the view that cyberspace is a different place from the real world and, as a result, to the extent that cyberspace should be regulated by law at all, rather than by consensual relations, different laws are required. The logical extension of this approach is that the rules governing online contracts should be different from those governing offline contracts: **1.49**

> International law is founded on the premise that physical space is divided into geographical units, states, each of which is sovereign and can exercise control over persons and things within its physical territory. It can be argued that since e-commerce transcends physical and political space, it could be recognized as a separate community with its own definition of jurisdiction.[84]

There is an argument that, given that no country has a more compelling claim than any other to regulate events which take place in cyberspace, existing jurisdictional rules must be abandoned and a distinct law of cyberspace should be developed.[85] **1.50**

At the other end of the spectrum, there is the view that existing rules can apply and, if necessary, be developed or refined to deal with problems thrown up by e-commerce. According to this view, the notion of cyberspace as a separate place is rejected and the need for rules to regulate specifically e-contracts is doubted. Just as the law adapted, in the middle **1.51**

[81] Consumers International (September 2001: 8).
[82] Office of Fair Trading (June 2007: 83).
[83] U Kohl (1999: 129).
[84] P Naarajärvi and JV Koivisto (2002: 28).
[85] DR Johnson and DG Post (1996: 1379). See also GI Zekos (2007).

of the twentieth century, to the development of new communication technologies (such as telephone and telex) it is not excessively optimistic to suppose that the challenges posed by the Internet can be met by the application (and, where appropriate, adaptation) of existing legal doctrines.[86]

1.52 Nevertheless, it has to be conceded that transactions in cyberspace potentially present particular challenges to private international law. One of the aims of jurisdiction and choice-of-law rules is to link transactions and events to one place rather than another. In view of the global and borderless architecture of the Internet, it is easier to identify the location of events which occur within real space than it is to localize equivalent phenomena generated within a network of computers, the location of which may be significantly separated from the natural or legal persons on whose behalf they operate.

1.53 With regard to b2c contracts, the argument for 'cyberlaw' is weak as the similarities between offline and online contracts are much more striking than their differences. A contract concluded by an exchange of e-mails is not substantially different from a contract concluded by an exchange of letters; the fact that the parties communicate via computer technology rather than by another method of communication changes neither the fundamentals of the legal relationship nor the legal issues to which it gives rise.[87] Accordingly, it is important that the potential problems generated by the borderless and global nature of the Internet are kept in proportion.

1.54 Notwithstanding the close parallels between offline and online contracts, there may be particular situations in which approaches devised for the real world prove to be incapable of producing rational solutions to cyberproblems and the application of established doctrine to e-commerce may reveal weaknesses in that established doctrine. Although there are certain contexts in which the application of traditional approaches to jurisdiction may be thought to lead to potentially arbitrary results[88] and there may need to be some minor adaptations to take account of specific aspects of the new technology, any suggestion that the advent of contracting via the Internet requires the creation of a wholly new set of legal rules and principles grossly exaggerates the potential difficulties. If existing principles are not satisfactory, the most promising answer is the re-assessment of the

[86] RS Zembek (1996). See also R Stevens (2003: 116).

[87] See, eg, *Thoresen & Co (Bangkok) Ltd v Fathom Marine Company Ltd* [2004] 1 Lloyd's Rep 622.

[88] See U Kohl (2002).

application of doctrines across the range of communication media,[89] rather than the formulation of a new 'cyberlaw': 'Rather than requiring its own standard, the Internet really only necessitates novel applications of existing jurisdictional principles.'[90] It follows that the proper approach of the legal system is one of 'technological neutrality'—which enables relevant principles to be adapted (as necessary) to changing technologies.[91]

A third view is that the solution to the international dimensions of e-commerce cannot be adequately resolved by national legal systems and that the only solution is the conclusion of an international convention. Such a convention would have the aim of achieving a high level of uniformity across a significant number of countries. In the absence of such a convention, national systems are likely to develop along different lines and the longer this process continues (and the further national systems diverge from each other), the harder it will be to achieve international consensus at some later date.[92] Although there have been developments at the regional level (such as within the European Union) and there are several NGOs and private-sector organizations which have attempted to find consensus between the major players in the world of e-commerce, any kind of binding international instrument remains little more than a far-off dream.[93] **1.55**

7. Where are Online Contracts Concluded?

Notwithstanding some views to the contrary,[94] English private international law rarely has to address the question of where a contract is concluded. Although the place of contracting is a connecting factor which, in certain contexts, may help to localize a contract for jurisdictional or choice-of-law purposes, it is a weak connecting factor. As regards e-contracts, the place of contracting is a particularly weak connecting factor. **1.56**

[89] See, generally, the Reports of the New Zealand Law Commission on aspects of e-commerce: NZLC R50 (1998); R58 (1999); R68 (2000).

[90] M Traynor and L Pirri (2002: 127).

[91] MA Geist (2001: 1360).

[92] P Naarajärvi and JV Koivisto (2002: 48).

[93] At one stage there was a chance that the worldwide judgments convention project—which was initiated under the auspices of the Hague Conference in the 1990s—could have produced general consensus on jurisdictional questions relating to, inter alia, cross-border e-commerce. However, the project ran into difficulties and was re-focused; the result of the negotiations was the Convention on Choice of Court Agreements of 2005 (which excludes consumer contracts from its scope): see <http://www.hcch.net/index_en.php?act=conventions. text&cid=98> [10/8/07].

[94] See, eg, L Davies (1997: 99).

Accordingly, the *locus contractus* cannot play a significant role in assisting the court's decision whether or not England is the most closely connected forum for the purposes of the doctrines of *forum conveniens* and *forum non conveniens* or in determining the country with which an online contract is most closely connected for the purposes of the choice-of-law regime (whether the Rome Convention or the Rome I Regulation). Having said that, it should be noted that one of the bases on which the English court may assume jurisdiction over a foreign defendant who is not domiciled in an EU-Lugano state is that the contract was made within the jurisdiction.[95] As a result, there may be situations in which the court has to decide where an e-contract was concluded—though, if such cases arise, they will almost invariably involve b2b contracts rather than b2c transactions.[96] As, in the context of the current work, the practical significance of the question where an e-contract is concluded is strictly limited, the discussion in the rest of this section has been kept as brief as possible.

1.57 In the 1990s there was a lot of discussion by commentators on the question of when and where e-contracts are concluded. In the European context, the Draft E-Commerce Directive[97] sought to determine the moment when an online contract is concluded,[98] but the final version of the Directive[99] was very different from the draft. The Directive is concerned with the regulation of business practice in the area of e-commerce; it leaves it to national legal systems to determine the legal effect of such practice. Article 11 of the Directive, in its final version, merely deems certain acts ('the order' and 'the acknowledgment of receipt') to take place at certain times ('when the parties to whom they are addressed are able to access them').

1.58 The Directive does not determine where such acts take place. Furthermore, the final text of the Directive deliberately uses legally neutral terms and avoids the language of offer and acceptance. So, whether an 'order' takes effect as an invitation to treat or an offer and whether an 'acknowledgment of receipt' is legally to be regarded as an offer or an acceptance is a question which turns on the way the particular website is constructed, the contractual terms and the applicable law. Having said that, in legal terms, the terms of a commercial website will normally constitute an invitation to treat, the buyer's order will usually be an offer, and the e-trader's acknowledgement of receipt is likely to constitute the acceptance. As a

[95] CPR r 6.20(5)(a). See para 3.11.
[96] For discussion of why consumer litigation is so exceptional, see ch 2.
[97] See art 11 the draft: European Commission, COM (98) 586, pp 26–7.
[98] J Dickie (1999: 28–9).
[99] Dir 2000/31/EC [2000] OJ L178/1.

result, an e-contract will normally be concluded when the person to whom the acknowledgement of receipt is addressed is able to access it.

In principle, it should not be too difficult to determine where an online contract is concluded. As long as it is remembered that the parties to an online contract are natural or legal persons (rather than computers and other computing hardware), the localization of an e-contract should not present significant difficulties—however artificial the localization of e-contracts may seem at first glance. An online contract concluded between people located in different countries does not generally involve more jurisdictions than an equivalent offline contract;[100] just as a contract concluded by post between an offeror in England and an offeree in Malta can only be regarded as having been concluded in England or in Malta (or in both places), the same is true with regard to an online contract concluded between a Maltese consumer and an e-trader established in England. The most that can be said is that, as regards online contracts, the process of localization may have to be slightly different from that which operates for transactions in real space. The suggestion that 'contractual relationships in electronic commerce are far more complicated than in traditional international commerce'[101] almost certainly overstates the case. There are two different scenarios to consider: first, contracts concluded by e-mail; secondly, contracts concluded via an interactive or active website. **1.59**

E-mail Contracts

One of the difficulties is that e-mail contracts fall somewhere between contracts concluded by post and contracts concluded by a simultaneous method of communication.[102] English law is unusual in adhering to the postal rule or 'sending rule' for the conclusion of contracts formed by correspondence; the more usual approach is the 'receipt rule'.[103] If one takes the sending rule as the starting point for the formation of e-mail contracts, such contracts are formed when the offeree sends his acceptance (by clicking on 'send'). If the receipt rule is applied, the contract is **1.60**

[100] U Kohl (2002: 559, n 12).

[101] Y Zhao (2005: 127).

[102] M Chissick and A Kelman (2002: 89). For an inconclusive discussion which considers some of the arguments surrounding the application of the postal and receipt rules to contracts concluded by e-mail, see M Chissick and A Kelman (2002: 87–9).

[103] Less common (and more extreme) is the 'cognizance rule' according to which a contract is concluded when the offeror has knowledge of the offeree's acceptance: see H Snidjers (2003).

concluded when, in the normal course of events, the offeror would be expected to be able to access the message of acceptance.

1.61 Given that either approach produces an arguably arbitrary result, which approach is the more appropriate? There is a good case for saying that, notwithstanding the fact that e-mail is not, strictly speaking, an instantaneous means of communication, it does not make sense to apply the postal rule to contracts concluded by e-mail. Although an Internet link does not involve a direct physical link between the parties, a contract concluded by e-mail has much more in common with a contract concluded by telephone than with a contract concluded by post.[104]

1.62 The postal rule was formulated in order to achieve a degree of contractual certainty (for the offeree) at a time when post not only was the sole method of long-distance communication but also was, by modern technological standards, rather slow. Although there are occasions when an e-mail may take hours or even days to arrive at its intended destination, such delays are rare. Furthermore, if an offeree wishes to know whether or not his acceptance has been received, the available technology enables the offeree to arrange for e-mail confirmation when the message containing the acceptance has been accessed by the offeror.[105] In terms of legal policy, the arguments for treating contracts concluded by e-mail as analogous to contracts concluded by telephone, telex, and fax (rather than as analogous to contracts concluded by post) are overwhelming.[106] While some commentators have suggested that the postal rule should apply to contracts concluded by e-mail,[107] the opposing view is more convincing and seems to command more widespread support.[108]

1.63 If the correct analysis is that an e-mail acceptance is to be treated as effective *when* it is received (which under the E-Commerce Directive means when it is available to be accessed by the offeror), it would seem to follow that the contract is concluded *where* the acceptance is received. As regards contracts concluded by telephone, fax, or telex, there can be no doubt as to where the acceptance is received by the offeror. The same is not true for e-mail messages; a consumer may access his e-mail messages through a computer at home or through another computer in a different place.

104 L Davies (1997: 111).
105 See D Capps (2004: 208–9).
106 See SWB Hill (2001).
107 See, eg, AD Murray (2000).
108 J Dickie (1998).

There are several possible approaches. The first is to follow the analogy with other instantaneous (or almost instantaneous) forms of communication and decide that the place of conclusion is where, in the normal course of business, the offeror would be expected to access the message. So, where a consumer orders goods by e-mail and the supplier replies (also by e-mail) accepting the order, the contract is concluded at the consumer's home address (where the supplier would normally expect the consumer to access the message). It should not be relevant for the purposes of localizing the contract that the offeror happens to access the message of acceptance at some other place (for example, where the consumer accesses a message from an Internet café in another country while on holiday). The second is to have regard to the place where the offeror physically is when he accesses the offeree's acceptance. A third possibility is to treat the contract as simultaneously concluded both at the place from where the acceptance is sent and the place where it is received (or deemed to be received). As between these alternative solutions, the first is the most convincing and is the one which finds favour with commentators.[109] **1.64**

Contracts Concluded via an Active or Interactive Website

It is acknowledged that, as a general rule, the offering of goods or services for sale on a website is not an offer, but an invitation to treat.[110] In addition, the terms of the supplier's website may make it clear that the consumer's order is an offer and that the supplier's acknowledgement of the order constitutes acceptance of the consumer's offer.[111] It is also widely recognized that the location of the computer hardware through which a contract is concluded is irrelevant for determining where a contract is concluded.[112] For example, the UNCITRAL Model Law on Electronic Commerce provides that a data message is dispatched at the sender's **1.65**

[109] See J Dickie (1998); SWB Hill (2001).

[110] L Davies (1997: 115). However, depending on the structure of the website in question, the purchaser's order of goods or services may constitute an acceptance of an offer contained in the website: S Christensen (2001: 28). For example, where a supplier offers goods for sale via an auction site (such as *eBay*), the structure of the site means that the supplier is the offeror and the purchaser is the offeree: see J Meuser (2005: N13–14). Although the issue is not expressly addressed by the Singapore Court of Appeal in *Chee Kin Keong v Digiland.com Pte Ltd* [2006] 1 LRC 37, the judgment seems to be based on the premise that, where goods are advertised for sale on a website, the buyer's order is an offer and the supplier's confirmation is the acceptance.

[111] See, eg, <http://www.amazon.co.uk/gp/help/customer/display.html?nodeId=1040616#sale> [13/9/07].

[112] The contrary view suggested by some authors (such as L Davies (1997)) cannot be accepted.

place of business and received at the addressee's place of business; if a person does not have a place of business, the connecting factor is that party's habitual residence.[113] It is perhaps unfortunate that the E-Commerce Directive deals only with the timing of electronic messages and not with where such messages are deemed to be sent and received.

1.66 Where a contract is concluded via an active or interactive website, the rule which applies to other forms of instantaneous methods of communication should apply.[114] If the website is constructed so that the consumer's communication is regarded as an offer (in response to the e-trader's invitation to treat), rather than as an acceptance (in response to the e-trader's offer) the receipt rule means that the contract is concluded at the consumer's place of residence (where the e-trader's acceptance is received).

8. Contracts Involving 'Digitized' Products

1.67 In the context of the current discussion, there can be no doubt that a b2c contract for the acquisition of 'digitized' products (such as a computer program) should be capable of being a consumer contract. To the extent that problems may arise, this is a consequence of the fact that some rules apply to contracts for the supply of goods, but not to contracts for services (or to contracts for the supply of goods and services, but not to other contracts), and the fact that the proper classification of contracts relating to digitized products is controversial.[115] There are three possible approaches.

1.68 First, some commentators refer to 'digital goods'[116] and argue that contracts for digitized products should be seen as contracts for the sale of goods.[117] The idea underlying this approach is there is no obviously good reason why the mode of delivery of a product should be the most important factor when deciding how the contract should be classified. According to this approach, in a situation where a product may be delivered either offline or online, the same classification should be used for both transactions.[118] So, a contract for downloading recorded music in electronic format from the Internet should be treated as a contract for the sale

[113] Art 15(4). See <http://www.uncitral.org/pdf/english/texts/electcom/05-89450_Ebook.pdf> [2/11/07].

[114] M Chissick and A Kelman (2002: 89).

[115] M Chissick and A Kelman (2002: 69–71).

[116] See JL Goldsmith (1998: 1224); R Debusseré (2002: 350).

[117] M Chissick and A Kelman (2002: 71). See also S Green and D Saidov (2007). Arguably, some support for this view may be derived from *St Albans City and District Council v International Computers Ltd* [1995] FSR 686 (High Court); [1996] 4 All ER 481 (CA).

[118] M Foss and LA Bygrave (2000: 109).

of goods as the same product can be purchased in the form of a CD. One of the problems with this approach is that the apparently similar online and offline transactions are structured in different ways—and may, in fact, have different contents. If a consumer purchases an encyclopaedia, this transaction is obviously a sale of goods. However, if the same consumer pays for online access to a database (such as *Encyclopaedia Britannica*[119] or the *New Grove Dictionary of Music and Musicians*[120]), the contract appears to have all the hallmarks of a contract for the provision of services.[121]

Secondly, there is a case for saying that, as a general rule, it is probably better to classify a contract relating to digitized products as either a contract for the supply of goods and services (for example, where a consumer buys a computer program on a computer disk) or a contract for the supply of services (for example, where a consumer buys software which is delivered electronically through the Internet). The essence of a contract relating to digitized products is the licence granted to the 'buyer' to use the product in question (often coupled with an obligation not to copy the product or allow others to use it). Although one may refer colloquially to 'buying software', the core of the contract is the licence from the copyright owner to the 'buyer'. Although contracts of this type are different from traditional real space contracts for the supply of services, it makes sense for contracts for the acquisition of digitized products to be classified as contracts for the supply of services. **1.69**

The third possibility is that contracts for digitized products are neither contracts for the sale of goods nor contracts for the provision of services; they are *sui generis*. There is some case law authority that can be invoked to support this analysis.[122] **1.70**

Although the neatest solution would be to decide on a classification of digitized products for all purposes, such a solution may not be realistic. Because much of the legislation which deals with contracts for the sale of goods and for the provision of services pre-dates the online delivery of digitized products, it may have to be accepted that, if rational results are to be reached, different classifications need to be employed in different contexts. **1.71**

As regards jurisdictional questions considered in his book, to a large extent, the relevant consumer contract provisions of the Brussels I Regulation **1.72**

[119] <http://www.britannica.com/>.
[120] <http://www.grovemusic.com>.
[121] M Foss and LA Bygrave (2000: 111).
[122] *Beta Computers (Europe) Ltd v Adobe Systems (Europe) Ltd* [1996] FSR 367 (Court of Session).

sidestep the issue by replacing the phrase used in the Brussels Convention ('any other contract for the supply of goods or a contract for the supply of services'[123]) with the words 'all other cases'.[124] However, there are (in theory) two contexts in which the classification of contracts relating to digitized products may be relevant.

1.73 First, the problem of classification could arise under paragraphs (a) and (b) of article 15(1) of the Brussels I Regulation (which, for jurisdictional purposes, confer protected status on contracts for the sale of goods on instalment credit terms and other credit contracts financing the sale of goods, but do not cover contracts for the provision of services). For the purposes of these paragraphs it makes sense to treat digitized products as 'goods' (rather than as services or as neither). In policy terms, the purchase of digitized products on credit raises exactly the same issues as the purchase of material goods on credit. There is no good reason to extend jurisdictional protection in one case, but not in the other.[125]

1.74 Secondly, the classificatory question may arise in the context of choice of law. Article 5 of the Rome Convention on the law applicable to contractual obligations (which lays down special choice-of-law rules for protected consumer contracts) applies to contracts for 'the supply of goods or services'. Although article 6 of the Rome I Regulation (which will replace article 5 of the Convention) follows the approach of the Brussels I Regulation and refers to 'a contract' (without qualification), the Regulation applies only to contracts concluded after the expiry of eighteen months following its publication in the Official Journal; furthermore, the Regulation will apply in England only if the UK government decides to opt in (which, at the time of writing, remains uncertain).

1.75 For the purposes of article 5 of the Convention, it does not matter whether digitized products are treated as goods or services. If, however, digitized products were regarded neither as goods nor as services, a contract for the sale of digitized products would fall outside the scope of article 5 entirely. Although a case can be made for regarding a contract for digitized products as *sui generis* for certain purposes, it would be perverse to take such a view in the context of choice of law under the Rome Convention. In the unlikely event of the question arising for decision, a contract involving digitized products would surely be regarded as a contract for 'the supply of goods or services' for the purposes of article 5.[126]

[123] Art 13.
[124] Art 15(1)(c).
[125] M Foss and LA Bygrave (2000: 112).
[126] See C Riefa (2004: 63).

III. SOME IMPORTANT LEGAL BACKGROUND

There are various international legal regimes which have an important impact on some of the issues considered in this book. The most important of them operate at the European level: (i) the Brussels I Regulation and the Lugano Convention (which deal with jurisdiction and the recognition and enforcement of judgments in civil and commercial matters); and (ii) the Rome Convention and the Rome I Regulation (which concern choice of law with regard to contractual obligations). As part of this introductory chapter, it is worth outlining their general scheme and saying something about their history. Readers who are already familiar with private international law in the European Union may wish to skip this section of the book. **1.76**

1. The Brussels I Regulation and the Lugano Convention

The origins of Regulation (EC) No 44/2001 ('the Brussels I Regulation') are to be found in the Brussels Convention of 1968. The purpose of the Convention was two-fold: first, the allocation of jurisdiction in civil and commercial matters between the contracting states; secondly, the mutual recognition and enforcement of judgments between those states. **1.77**

The Brussels Convention on jurisdiction and the enforcement of judgments in civil and commercial matters was signed by the original six member states of the European Economic Community[127] in 1968. As more countries joined the European Community, the new member states acceded to the Brussels Convention by means of accession conventions in 1978,[128] 1982,[129] 1989,[130] and 1996.[131] Although there was no major revision of the Brussels Convention during this period, substantive amendments to various provisions were made by some of the accession conventions, in particular by the convention of 1978. In 1988 the EC member states concluded the parallel Lugano Convention with the six countries which were then members of the European Free Trade Area.[132] **1.78**

[127] Belgium, France, Germany, Italy, Luxembourg, and the Netherlands.

[128] Denmark, Ireland, and the United Kingdom.

[129] Greece.

[130] Portugal and Spain.

[131] Austria, Finland, and Sweden.

[132] Austria, Finland, Iceland, Norway, Sweden, and Switzerland. As regards Austria, Finland, and Sweden, the Lugano Convention was partly superseded on their accession to

1.79 In the 1990s it was decided to reform the Brussels and Lugano Conventions in tandem. However, the process of reform did not follow the course which had been originally envisaged. As a result of the Treaty of Amsterdam conferring legislative competence on the European Community in relation to judicial cooperation in civil matters,[133] the decision was taken to translate the Brussels Convention into a Community instrument. The Brussels I Regulation[134] came into force on 1 March 2002[135] and superseded the Brussels Convention for all the EU member states except Denmark, which did not participate in the adoption of the Regulation. However, Denmark subsequently entered an agreement with the European Community so that, under international law, the provisions of the Regulation apply to relations between Denmark and the other EC member states.[136] The Brussels I Regulation is directly applicable throughout the participating member states and automatically extended to the ten states[137] which acceded to the European Community in May 2004 and the two member states which acceded in January 2007.[138]

1.80 Although the envisaged process for amending the Lugano Convention in line with the Brussels I Regulation stalled for a while (for constitutional reasons), early in 2006, in response to a request for an opinion by the Council of the European Union, the Court of Justice ruled that the conclusion of the new Lugano Convention was within the exclusive competence of the European Community.[139] Negotiations between the European Community, Denmark, and the Lugano contracting states[140] were concluded in March 2007; the Commission made a proposal for a Council Decision concerning the revised Lugano Convention in July of that year;[141] and the revised Convention was signed in October.[142] The renegotiated

the Brussels Convention. The Lugano Convention was also extended to Poland a few years prior to Poland's accession to the European Community.

133 Arts 61 and 65.

134 Reg (EC) No 44/2001, [2001] OJ L12/1.

135 Art 76.

136 See Council Decision (EC) No 2005/790 and the attached agreement: [2005]OJ L299/61–70. The agreement entered into force on 1 July 2007.

137 Czech Republic, Cyprus, Estonia, Hungary, Latvia, Lithuania, Malta, Poland, Slovakia, and Slovenia.

138 Bulgaria and Romania.

139 Opinion 1/03 [2006] ECR I-1145.

140 Iceland, Norway, and Switzerland.

141 European Commission, COM (2007) 387.

142 See Council Decision [2007] OJ L339/1 and the revised text of the Lugano Convention [2007] OJ L339/3. The Convention will enter into force six months following its ratification by the European Community, on the one hand, and one of Iceland, Norway, and Switzerland, on the other: Lugano Convention, art 69(4). Until the revised Convention comes into force in

text aligns the Lugano Convention with the Brussels I Regulation (both as regards jurisdiction and the recognition and enforcement of judgments) subject to some minor amendments and clarifications.[143]

Provision is made for national courts to make references to the Court of Justice on questions of interpretation under the Brussels I Regulation.[144] Rulings from the Court of Justice are binding on national courts. Some guidance on the interpretation of the Brussels I Regulation is offered by the official reports which accompany the various conventions[145] and by the *travaux préparatoires* relating to the Brussels I Regulation.[146] **1.81**

The Brussels I Regulation is divided into blocks of provisions ('Chapters') which are further divided into 'Sections'. For the purposes of the issues addressed in this book Chapter II, which lays down uniform jurisdiction rules for the member states, is of prime importance. However, something also ought to be said about Chapters I and III. **1.82**

The material scope of the Brussels I Regulation is defined by Chapter I (which comprises a single provision—article 1). Article 1 provides that the Regulation applies in 'civil and commercial matters', but goes on to exclude various matters: family law; bankruptcy and insolvency; social security; and arbitration. In the overwhelming majority of cases concerned with disputes relating to consumer contracts, there will be no doubt that the case is covered by article 1, although there may be cases where the situation involves arbitration and is, therefore, excluded from the Regulation's scope. According to the jurisprudence of the Court of Justice, civil proceedings are covered by article 1 unless they involve 'a public authority which acted in the exercise of its public authority powers'.[147] Even proceedings brought by a consumer protection organization (on behalf of consumers generally) with a view to obtaining an injunction restraining the defendant from using unfair terms in standard consumer contracts are covered by article 1 as the subject-matter of the proceedings is not an exercise of public powers.[148] **1.83**

accordance with art 69(4), the 1988 Convention will continue to apply. This work, however, does not address the issues raised by the original text of the 1988 Convention.

[143] European Commission, COM (2007) 387, p 3.

[144] Art 234 EC. The House of Lords can refer questions of interpretation under the Brussels I Regulation: art 68 EC.

[145] In particular, the Jenard Report, [1979] OJ C59/1 (Brussels Convention 1968). the Schlosser Report [1979] OJ C59/71 (Accession Convention 1978) and the Jenard-Möller Report, [1990] OJ C189/57 (Lugano Convention 1988).

[146] See European Commission, COM (99) 348.

[147] See, eg, Case C-172/91 *Sonntag v Waidmann* [1993] ECR I-1963, 1996 (para 20).

[148] Case C-167/00 *Henkel* [2002] ECR I-8111.

1.84 Although the overriding objective of the Brussels I Regulation is the free flow of judgments, this is only made possible by uniform rules for the allocation of jurisdiction, thereby (largely) obviating the need for the court addressed to review the basis on which the court of origin assumed jurisdiction. The basic scheme of Chapter II of the Brussels I Regulation is to draw a distinction between defendants who are domiciled in a member state and other defendants. Broadly speaking, a natural person is domiciled where he resides[149] and a legal person is domiciled where it has (i) its statutory seat (which in the United Kingdom normally means the registered office or, where there is no such office anywhere, the place of incorporation) or (ii) its central administration or (iii) its principal place of business.[150]

1.85 As regards defendants who are not domiciled in a member state, article 4 provides that, as a general rule, the jurisdiction of a member state court is determined by the law of that member state. So, whether a New York corporation can be sued in England is normally to be decided by reference to English traditional rules. However, the general rule is subject to some exceptions. First, the Brussels I Regulation contains certain jurisdiction rules which apply 'regardless of domicile'.[151] These exclusive jurisdiction rules apply to various types of proceedings relating to immovable property, aspects of company law, public registers, intellectual property rights, and the enforcement of judgments; except in relation to proceedings relating to certain types of tenancy agreement, the exclusive jurisdiction rules will not normally be relevant in situations involving consumer contracts. Secondly, a jurisdiction clause in favour of the courts of a member state confers jurisdiction on the chosen courts even where the party against whom proceedings are brought is not domiciled in a member state.[152] However, in the context of disputes relating to consumer contracts, this rule is largely overridden by other provisions.[153] Thirdly, as regards proceedings relating to insurance and to certain consumer contracts, a defendant who is not domiciled in member state, but who has a branch, agency, or other establishment in a member state, is deemed to be domiciled in that member state with regard to disputes arising out of the operation of the branch, agency, or other establishment.[154]

[149] For the relevant UK law see Civil Jurisdiction and Judgments Order 2001, sched 1, para 9.

[150] Art 60.

[151] Art 22.

[152] Art 23.

[153] In particular by art 17.

[154] Arts 9(2) and 15(2).

1.86 If the defendant is domiciled in a member state, the courts have jurisdiction only in accordance with the provisions of Chapter II of the Brussels I Regulation[155] (or in accordance with a convention to which the member state in question is party and which in relation to particular matters governs jurisdiction[156]). The general rule under the Brussels I Regulation is that a person domiciled in a member state should be sued in that member state.[157] However, as regards disputes arising out of certain types of consumer contract, there are special rules to be found in Section 3 (which applies to matters relating to insurance) and Section 4 (which applies to protected consumer contracts). If jurisdiction is not determined by the exclusive jurisdiction rules (article 22) or by a valid jurisdiction agreement (article 23) and neither Section 3 nor Section 4 applies, it is provided that jurisdiction in matters relating to a contract may be brought in the courts for the place of performance of the obligation in question.[158]

1.87 It should also be noted that there are various provisions designed to reduce the circumstances in which there is fragmentation of proceedings involving the same (or related) matters. In situations involving multiple parties domiciled in different member states, there are certain circumstances in which related proceedings can be consolidated in the same court.[159] The courts of a member state must decline jurisdiction if proceedings involving the same parties and the same cause of action are pending in the courts of another member state[160] and may stay the proceedings (or in certain circumstances decline jurisdiction) if there are related proceedings pending in the courts of another member state.[161] These rules apply regardless of the domicile of the parties and regardless of the basis on which the courts in question assumed jurisdiction.[162]

1.88 There are two further facets of the jurisdictional code established by the Brussels I Regulation which must be considered. Whereas some jurisdiction rules in Chapter II allocate jurisdiction to a place in a member state, others allocate jurisdiction to a member state. In the context of the United Kingdom, a rule of the first type confers jurisdiction on the courts of England, Scotland, or Northern Ireland (as the case may be). However, as

155 Arts 2 and 3.
156 Art 71.
157 Art 2.
158 Art 5(1).
159 Art 6.
160 Art 27.
161 Art 28.
162 Case C-351/89 *Overseas Union Insurance Ltd v New Hampshire Insurance Co* [1991] ECR I-3317.

regards rules of the second type, there is nothing in the Brussels I Regulation to determine whether it is the English courts or the courts of another part of the United Kingdom which have jurisdiction. Accordingly, the Brussels I Regulation has to be read in conjunction with schedule 4 to the Civil Jurisdiction and Judgments Act 1982.[163] Where, for example, article 16(2) allocates jurisdiction over a claim brought against a consumer domiciled in England to the courts of the United Kingdom (because the consumer is domiciled in the United Kingdom), it is rule 8(2) of schedule 4 which determines that it is the English courts which have jurisdiction.

1.89 Schedule 4 to the 1982 Act is also important in situations which are not domestic (in the sense that they have connections with more than one country), but are internal to the United Kingdom. In this type of case, the Brussels I Regulation has no application, because all the connections are with one member state. Where, for example, an English supplier sells goods to a Scottish consumer, rule 8(2) allocates jurisdiction to the Scots courts in relation to a claim by the supplier against the consumer—and article 16(2) of the Brussels I Regulation is irrelevant.

1.90 Chapter III of the Brussels I Regulation concerns recognition and enforcement of judgments granted by member state courts. In order for Chapter III to apply, the judgment must fall within the material scope of the Regulation as defined by article 1. Chapter III provides for the (almost) automatic recognition of judgments granted by the courts of other member states[164] and sets out a uniform procedure for their enforcement.[165] The range of potential defences to recognition or enforcement is narrowly circumscribed.[166] Subject to one minor exception,[167] the regime for the recognition and enforcement of judgments relating to consumer contract disputes is the same as that applicable to judgments in general.

1.91 The final point to consider in this brief account of EC rules relating to jurisdiction and the recognition and enforcement of judgments is the relationship between the Brussels I Regulation and the Lugano Convention. As regards questions of jurisdiction, the general rule is that the dividing lines between the two instruments are determined by the domicile of the defendant: if the defendant is domiciled in a member state, the Brussels I Regulation applies; if the defendant is domiciled in Iceland, Norway, or

[163] As substituted by Civil Jurisdiction and Judgments Order 2001, SI 2001 No 3929.
[164] Art 33.
[165] Art 35(1).
[166] Arts 34–36.
[167] Art 35(1). See ch 6.

Switzerland, the Lugano Convention is relevant.[168] This general rule yields in cases where a rule which applies regardless of domicile allocates jurisdiction to the courts of a member state or a state bound by the Lugano Convention.

With regard to the recognition and enforcement of judgments, everything turns on the court of origin: if the judgment is granted by a member state, Chapter III of the Brussels I Regulation applies; recognition or enforcement of a judgment granted by the courts of Iceland, Norway, or Switzerland is governed by Title III of the Lugano Convention. **1.92**

2. The Rome Convention, the Rome I Regulation, and the Rome II Regulation

In the European Community, harmonization of the choice-of-law rules relating to contractual obligations was first achieved through the Rome Convention of 1980 (which was implemented into the law of the United Kingdom by the Contracts (Applicable Law) Act 1991). A few years ago, following the entry into force of the Treaty of Amsterdam, it was proposed that the Convention should be replaced by a Community instrument (which has become known as the Rome I Regulation).[169] In its original form, the Rome I proposal departed from the Convention in a number of fundamental respects and the UK government decided not to opt into the Regulation. However, over the course of the legislative process, many of the more controversial differences between the Convention and the proposed Regulation were eliminated or eroded; although some significant differences between the Convention and the Regulation remain, there is a case for saying that the Regulation improves on the Convention in a number of ways. The final text of the Rome I Regulation[170] was approved at a meeting of the Council of Ministers in June 2008. Early in April 2008, the Ministry of Justice launched a consultation exercise on the question whether the UK government's decision not to opt into the Regulation should be reconsidered; the government's provisional view was that it should seek the approval of the European Commission to opt into the Regulation.[171] Nevertheless, in the short to medium term the Rome Convention will continue to apply throughout the contracting states as **1.93**

[168] Art 68; Civil Jurisdiction and Judgments Act 1982, s 1(4).

[169] See European Commission, COM (2005) 650. This proposal followed a green paper dating from 2002: European Commission, COM (2002) 654.

[170] Reg (EC) No 593/2008 [2008] OJ L177/6.

[171] See Consultation Paper CP05/08 'Rome I—Should the UK opt in?': <http://www.justice.gov.uk/docs/cp0508.pdf> [5/4/08].

the Regulation will apply only to contracts entered into after 17 December 2009.[172] Moreover, the Regulation will not apply in Denmark[173] and, if the UK government does not opt in, the Rome Convention will continue to apply in England for the indefinite future.

1.94 As regards contracts in general, the core elements of the choice-of-law regime contained in both the Convention and the Regulation are to be found in articles 3 and 4—which determine the applicable law. The starting point is the principle of party autonomy: parties to a contract may choose the law applicable to their contract; such choice must be made expressly or clearly demonstrated by the terms of the contract or the circumstances of the case.[174]

1.95 In cases where a contract does not include a choice of law, the Regulation takes a slightly different approach from the Convention. Under article 4 of the Convention, in the absence of choice, an international contract is governed by the law of the country with which it is most closely connected.[175] For the purposes of this rule, there is a presumption that a contract is most closely connected with the country in which the characteristic performer (for example, as regards a contract of sale, the seller) has a particular territorial connection (normally, the principal place of business).[176] However, the law of another country is the applicable law if the contract is more closely connected with that country.[177]

1.96 Under the Regulation, article 4(1) provides that contracts of various types are governed by the law of the country in which one of the parties to the contract is habitually resident;[178] for example, a contract for the sale of goods

[172] Art 28.

[173] It seems quite likely that, in due course, another international agreement will be concluded between Denmark and the European Community enabling the Rome I Regulation to apply in Denmark under international law.

[174] Art 3(1).

[175] The complications generated by this provision are well documented. See, eg, CMV Clarkson and J Hill (2005: 185–94).

[176] Art 4(2).

[177] Art 4(5).

[178] For the purposes of the Regulation, the habitual residence of companies and other bodies, corporate or unincorporated, is normally the place of central administration and that of a natural person acting in the course of his business activity is his principal place of business (art 19(1)); where the contract is concluded in the course of the operations of a branch, agency, or any other establishment, or if, under the contract, performance is the responsibility of such a branch, agency, or establishment, the place where the branch, agency, or any other establishment is located is the place of habitual residence (art 19(2)).

is governed by the law of the country where the seller has his habitual residence;[179] a contract for the provision of services is governed by the law of the country where the service provider has his habitual residence;[180] a franchise contract is governed by the law of the country where the franchisee has his habitual residence;[181] and a distribution contract is governed by the law of the country where the distributor has his habitual residence.[182] It is also provided that a contract relating to a right *in rem* in immovable property is governed by the law of the country where the property is situated.[183] In cases not covered by article 4(1), it is provided by article 4(2) that the contract is governed by the law of the country in which the characteristic performer is habitually resident.[184] However, these rules are subject to the proviso that where it is clear from all the circumstances of the case that the contract is *manifestly* more closely connected with a country other than that indicated by the foregoing rules, the law of that other country applies.[185] Finally, if the applicable law cannot be determined pursuant to article 4(1) or (2), the contract is governed by the law of the country with which it is most closely connected.[186]

The applicable law is the law which is primarily relevant for determining whether a contract is valid or not; this law also governs questions such as interpretation, performance, and the limitation of actions.[187] In certain cases, rules which are not part of the applicable law have a bearing on the rights of contracting parties. Under the Rome Convention, the applicable law may be overridden by the overriding mandatory rules of the forum (ie, rules which cannot be derogated from by contract and which apply regardless of the law applicable to the contract).[188] The Regulation contains the same rule,[189] but also defines overriding mandatory provisions as **1.97**

[179] Art 4(1)(a).
[180] Art 4(1)(b).
[181] Art 4(1)(e).
[182] Art 4(1)(f).
[183] Art 4(1)(c).
[184] In an ordinary bilateral contract under which one party pays money in return for the other party's contractual performance, the other party is the characteristic performer: Giuliano-Lagarde Report, [1980] OJ C282/20.
[185] Art 4(3).
[186] Art 4(4).
[187] See Rome Convention, arts 8–10; Rome I Regulation, arts 10–12.
[188] Rome Convention, art 7(2).
[189] Art 9(2).

'provisions the respect for which is regarded as crucial by a country for safeguarding its public interests, such as its political, social or economic organization, to such an extent that they are applicable to any situation falling within their scope, irrespective of the law otherwise applicable to the contract under this Regulation'.[190]

1.98 One of the controversial provisions of the Rome Convention allows for the application of the overriding mandatory rules of a country with which the situation has a close connection.[191] However, this rule was not implemented into English law[192] (nor into the laws of several of the other contracting states). The Regulation takes a less controversial approach and the equivalent provision stipulates that the overriding mandatory rules of a country where the obligations arising out of the contract have to be or have been performed, in so far as those overriding mandatory provisions render the performance of the contract unlawful, may override the applicable law.[193] Under both the Convention and the Regulation, the application of any rule specified by the relevant choice-of-law rules may be refused if such application is manifestly incompatible with the public policy of the forum.[194]

1.99 The general choice-of-law rules are modified with regard to specific types of contract. Of particular importance for the current work is article 5 of the Convention and article 6 of the Regulation, both of which lay down special choice-of-law rules for certain consumer contracts.[195]

1.100 Running slightly ahead of the proposal to replace the Rome Convention with a Regulation, there was also a project to harmonize choice-of-law rules in the field of non-contractual obligations. The original proposal for the so-called Rome II Regulation was made in 2003.[196] The Regulation[197]—which addresses choice of law with regard to tort, unjust enrichment, *negotiorum gestio*, and *culpa in contrahendo*—was finally agreed in July 2007.

[190] Art 9(1).

[191] Art 7(1).

[192] Contracts (Applicable Law) Act 1991, s 2(2).

[193] Art 9(3).

[194] Rome Convention, art 16; Rome I Regulation, art 21.

[195] Under the Rome Convention, there are similar provisions for individual contracts of employment (art 6). The Rome I Regulation sets out special choice-of-law rules for insurance contracts (art 7) as well as employment contracts (art 8); it also contains provisions dealing with contracts of carriage (art 5).

[196] European Commission, COM (2003) 427.

[197] Reg (EC) No 864/2007 on the law applicable to non-contractual obligations (Rome II) [2007] OJ 199/40.

Notwithstanding the legislative process having come to an end, there will be a period of transition as the Regulation does not apply to events occurring prior to 11 January 2009. Accordingly, in the short term, choice of law in tort in English law will continue to be primarily regulated by Part III of the Private International Law (Miscellaneous Provisions) Act 1995.

2

The Incidence of Cross-border Consumer Litigation

Before the discussion turns to the legal framework which regulates cross-border consumer litigation, it is worth considering why this type of litigation is such a rare phenomenon. The first and most obvious point is that there are far fewer cross-border consumer contracts than there are domestic consumer contracts; if consumers tend not to make purchases from abroad, there will be few cross-border contracts and less scope for cross-border disputes. However, even as regards those cross-border contracts which do occur, there are three 'filters' each of which has a role to play in preventing cross-border consumer litigation from occurring. First, there are various factors which prevent complaints arising from cross-border consumer contracts. Secondly, even if complaints do arise, there are factors which prevent a significant number of those complaints developing into full-blown disputes. Thirdly, there are factors which have the result that, even as regards full-blown disputes arising from cross-border consumer contracts, litigation is rarely seen as offering a solution to the problem. **2.01**

I. FACTORS THAT REDUCE THE NUMBER OF CROSS-BORDER CONTRACTS

2.02 Notwithstanding changes in recent years in terms of lifestyles (such as foreign travel becoming more prevalent) and new technology (in particular, the development of the Internet), it is still the case that a minority of European consumers buy goods or services from suppliers established in other countries. Over the course of a 12-month period, only about a quarter of EU consumers buy goods or services from abroad either through in-person shopping while away from home or via the Internet or some other mode of distance communication (such as telephone or post).[1]

2.03 There is an argument that the weaknesses and inefficiency of mechanisms for solving cross-border disputes is a significant disincentive for consumers to engage in cross-border commerce.[2] One of the ways of avoiding cross-border disputes is simply by not entering cross-border transactions. Consumers may choose to buy locally in order to avoid the risks posed by the difficulties (whether real or imagined) surrounding the resolution of disputes with suppliers established in another country; suppliers may choose not to sell outside their domestic market. To the extent that this phenomenon poses a socio-economic problem, the problem operates at the level of the failure to establish an environment in which consumers enjoy the economic benefits (in terms of competition and consumer welfare) which the internal market promises—rather than at the level of consumer redress as such. That is to say, at the European level, the fact that problems surrounding cross-border dispute resolution may discourage cross-border economic activity represents a failure to achieve market integration.

2.04 This is why one of the recurrent themes in the international context is the importance of attempts to promote consumer confidence. For example, lack of consumer confidence is identified as a key issue by the Organisation for Economic Co-operation and Development: one of the reasons why the potential for cross-border b2c e-commerce has yet to be realized is the fact that consumers continue to have concerns about shopping online.[3] Part of the background to the approach taken in the Brussels I Regulation, the Rome Convention, and the Rome I Regulation is the desire to create a legal framework which does not discourage consumers from entering

[1] Eurobarometer (September 2006: 4–5). There are variations between member states.
[2] U Kohl (1999: 147).
[3] See Organisation for Economic Co-operation and Development (February 2003: 4).

cross-border contracts.[4] Whether any step taken at the level of private international law could be effective to make consumers feel comfortable about contracting with foreign suppliers about whom they have little or no relevant information is debatable.

As things currently stand, although there are some sectors (such as air travel and music) where obstacles to an integrated EU retail market have largely been removed, retail markets, in general, remain predominantly fragmented along national lines.[5] For example, notwithstanding attempts to create a single market in the field of insurance services, the reality is that, in the consumer context, cross-border insurance contracts are encountered very infrequently. Writing in 2001, the Director of the Max Planck Institute for foreign private law and private international law noted that 'most of the European insurance companies prefer to organize their activities in other Member States by means of subsidiaries or branches, instead of directly acquiring transborder business from their headquarters'.[6] Matters do not seem to have changed in recent years and the single market for insurance has yet to become a reality; as regards consumer risks, insurance companies still choose not to solicit cross-border business.[7] A recent European survey revealed that, in the previous 12 months, only 1 per cent of European consumers had entered into a contract relating to financial services with a supplier based in another EU member state.[8] **2.05**

Although the Internet has created far more opportunity for cross-border shopping, most consumers continue to shop locally or nationally rather than internationally: **2.06**

> The advent of the e-commerce revolution . . . has transformed the potential for integration of retail markets in the EU to give a major stimulus to competitiveness and expand the opportunities for EU citizens. While the technological means are increasingly in place, business and consumer behaviour lags far behind, restrained respectively by internal market obstacles and lack of confidence in cross-border shopping.[9]

A survey conducted in 2006 revealed that a significant minority (more than 40 per cent) of EU consumers feel less confident buying goods or **2.07**

[4] For an American view of issues surrounding consumer trust and the Internet, see EA O'Hara (2005).

[5] European Commission, COM (2007) 99, p 4.

[6] J Basedow (2001: 500); the author reports that cross-border transactions contribute only 0.13 per cent of the total turnover of German non-life companies.

[7] G Rühl (2007: 879).

[8] Eurobarometer (September 2006: 108). Another 1 per cent of the sample had entered transactions with non-EU suppliers.

[9] European Commission, COM (2007) 99, p 2.

services from other member states than from local suppliers. The mode of shopping does not seem to be a critical factor; the proportion of consumers admitting to such feelings of lack of confidence was largely the same with regard to shopping in person (44 per cent),[10] buying goods or services via the Internet (45 per cent),[11] or making purchases by some other means of distance communication, such as telephone or post (44 per cent)[12]. In the United Kingdom, lack of confidence was even more widespread, with a narrow majority (55 per cent) expressing concerns about cross-border Internet shopping.[13]

2.08 The most significant reasons for the lack of consumer confidence appear to be: concerns about difficulties in resolving problems; greater risks of fraud; greater delivery problems; more problems when returning goods; lack of trust in the safety of goods bought from other countries; and concern that foreign sellers are less likely to respect consumer protection laws.[14] Of course, relatively few of the consumers who participated in the survey had experienced any problems with goods or services purchased from another member state and, indeed, many had not made any purchases from abroad in the 12-month period immediately prior to the survey. Accordingly, as the authors of the report note, although levels of mistrust are high, attitudes are, to a large extent, based on preconceptions and prejudice, rather than personal experience.[15] There are also other factors which provide obstacles to cross-border economic activity at the consumer level. Nearly two thirds of EU consumers consider that having to use a foreign language constitutes a barrier to buying goods and services from a supplier based in another member state and a similar number feel that they do not know where they can get information and advice about cross-border shopping.[16]

2.09 Even as regards consumers who, in principle, are perfectly willing to make purchases from foreign suppliers via the Internet, the way some businesses organize themselves reduces the potential for genuinely cross-border contracts to arise. One of the factors which limit the cross-border nature of e-commerce is the so-called 'bricks and clicks' model. That is to say, a supplier established in country A not only sells goods online to

[10] Eurobarometer (September 2006: 49).
[11] Eurobarometer (September 2006: 44).
[12] Eurobarometer (September 2006: 47).
[13] Eurobarometer (September 2006: 44).
[14] Eurobarometer (September 2006: 79). Whether perceived difficulties in solving problems really have the effect of undermining consumer confidence has been (tentatively) questioned: see L Edwards and A Theunissen (2007).
[15] Eurobarometer (September 2006: 55–61).
[16] Eurobarometer (September 2006: 69–71).

consumers in country B, but also establishes a physical presence in that country. As a result, any dispute between the supplier and a consumer resident in country B will be, to all intents and purposes, domestic in nature: contracts between the supplier and consumers resident in country B will normally be governed by the law of country B and there can be no question of litigation (or any other dispute-resolution mechanism) taking place outside that country. This phenomenon—which is quite widespread—can be illustrated by the US greeting card manufacturer, *Hallmark*: although *Hallmark* makes online sales both in the United States and the United Kingdom, the UK website refers to a UK company, a subsidiary of the US parent, as the seller.[17] Furthermore, it is also worth reiterating that a majority of e-traders choose not to sell to consumers other than those who are resident in the country in which the e-trader is established.

II. FACTORS THAT REDUCE THE INCIDENCE OF COMPLAINTS AND PREVENT COMPLAINTS DEVELOPING INTO FULL-BLOWN DISPUTES

Much of the material considered in this book is focused on legal strategies and policies for dealing with cases where things have gone wrong—typically, cases where the consumer feels aggrieved (for example, because he has not received what he paid for). In view of the fact that consumer complaints are fairly widespread, each legal system needs to have in place mechanisms for enabling legitimate complaints to be handled quickly, cheaply, simply, and effectively. Furthermore, national legal systems should, ideally, be no less accessible to consumers based in other countries than they are to local consumers. **2.10**

However, a coherent strategy for dealing with consumer complaints cannot be directed solely at the resolution of disputes; it also needs to find ways of trying to prevent such disputes arising. Although this chapter does not attempt to address all the myriad of ways in which cross-border consumer disputes can be avoided, it does seek to draw attention to various developments (some of which are considered in greater detail in later chapters) which aim to nip certain types of problem in the bud, as it were. In simple terms, an effective strategy of dispute avoidance reduces the pressure placed on dispute-resolution processes. So, it is important to consider some of the techniques for preventing (cross-border) disputes from arising in the first place. **2.11**

[17] See <http://www.hallmarkuk.com/pages/terms_of_use.php> [26/11/07].

1. Promoting Sensible Shopping

2.12 A lot of potential consumer disputes—at least, those arising from e-commerce—can be avoided by sensible shopping. Consumers can, to a large extent, prevent problems arising by making online purchases from e-traders which have good policies on complaints handling and dispute resolution. The Organisation for Economic Co-operation and Development has offered the following advice:

> Some businesses provide information about their policies on dispute settlement. Enquire about the company's in-house customer complaint services or money-back guarantees. At the very least, you should make sure the site has a phone number or e-mail address so you can contact the company if something goes wrong. In addition, some online businesses are part of 'seal' or 'trustmark' programmes that certify that a business meets certain minimum standards. Click on the seal or trustmark for more information. Some companies offer escrow services, through which a third party can hold your money until you get the goods or services you ordered. Other companies offer insurance programmes through which you can get your money back if you don't get the products or services you ordered.[18]

2.13 This advice is eminently sensible. However, since this passage is contained in a report of the Working Party on Information Security and Privacy of the OECD Committee on Consumer Policy it seems inherently unlikely that many consumers have read it or will ever do so. Nevertheless, the basic point is that, if consumers are educated to make better purchasing decisions when buying goods and services online,[19] many of the access-to-justice problems which consumers encounter (or fear encountering) in the e-commerce context could be effectively avoided.

2. Payment Methods

2.14 As regards the potential for cross-border consumer contracts to generate complaints which might develop into litigable disputes, there are two important issues (one practical, the other legal) concerning the way in

[18] Organisation for Economic Co-operation and Development (June 2002: 3).

[19] See, for example, ECC-Net's online shopping assistant ('Howard') which can be found on the UK ECC's website (<http://ready21.dev.visionteam.dk/index.php?id=7&L=23&type=99> [15/1/08]) (as well as on the websites of the ECCs of several other states, including Denmark, Hungary, Ireland, Norway, and Sweden). 'Howard' gives easy access to some basic information about e-traders, thereby helping consumers to make a better assessment of the risks involved in purchasing from a particular website. As with all initiatives of this type, one of the major challenges is to find ways of educating consumers to use such tools *before* they enter an online contract.

which consumers discharge their payment obligations under contracts for the purchase of goods or services.

A Factual Issue: Pre-payment

Although the main focus of this work is consumer access to justice and redress, it is important not to lose sight of the fact that any bilateral contract can (in theory) give rise to a claim by either party. A buyer of goods will have a claim if the goods are not delivered or are defective; a seller will have a claim if the buyer fails to pay the purchase price. In the cross-border context, the supplier, no less than the consumer, has an interest in the other party to the contract performing his side of the bargain. However, the risk of non-performance by the consumer can normally be eliminated by structuring the transaction in such a way that the consumer is required to make payment in full before the supplier performs his obligations under the contract.[20] **2.15**

In the e-commerce context, because e-traders normally require pre-payment (by a debit or credit card), there is hardly any scope for the supplier to have a claim against the consumer. As a result, disputes arising from cross-border e-contracts are almost bound to result from the consumer being unhappy with the supplier's contractual performance.[21] As regards offline contracts which result from in-person shopping, there is, perhaps, greater variation in terms of the way in which consumers discharge their payment obligations. Nevertheless, in relation to real world contracts, the supplier will normally structure the deal so that payment is received from the consumer when the contract is concluded. **2.16**

A Legal Issue: Payment Cardholder Protection

In some legal systems,[22] a consumer who pays for goods or services by means of a payment card is entitled to claim reimbursement from the card issuer in cases where the supplier fails to comply with its obligations under the contract. In the United Kingdom, as regards a transaction whose value is more than £100 but not more than £30,000, the consumer is protected by section 75 of the Consumer Credit Act 1974 if he uses a credit **2.17**

[20] In a minority of consumer contracts (both offline and online) which allow the consumer to defer payment or to pay by instalments, there is a risk that, although the supplier performs his side of the bargain, the consumer fails to comply with his payment obligations.

[21] European Consumer Law Group (2000: 15).

[22] For example, Finland, Greece, Japan, Korea, Norway, the United Kingdom, and the United States: Organisation for Economic Co-operation and Development (2006: 13). For discussion of the role of payment cards and consumer protection, see AS Rosenberg (2006).

card (but not a debit card)[23] to purchase goods or services. By virtue of section 75, if the consumer has a valid claim against the supplier for breach of contract or misrepresentation, he will have a like claim against the card issuer, who is jointly and severally liable with the supplier. As long as the contract between the consumer and the card issuer is a UK credit agreement, section 75 applies to overseas supply transactions (typically, cases where a consumer has purchased goods or services from a foreign supplier) as well as to domestic supply transactions (where the supplier is established in the United Kingdom).[24] Section 75 covers foreign transactions including where:

- a consumer uses a UK credit card to buy goods or services while abroad;
- a consumer orders goods or services from a foreign supplier while abroad for delivery into the UK;
- a consumer in the UK buys goods or services from overseas by telephone, mail order, or over the Internet which are delivered to a UK address; or
- there are face-to-face pre-contract dealings with a foreign supplier temporarily in the UK, or with a UK agent of a foreign supplier, but the contract is not completed in the UK.[25]

2.18 Consider a case where a consumer orders and pays for a computer from a US e-trader. Where the value of the transaction exceeds £100 (which it invariably will) and the consumer pays by credit card (which is more likely than not), if the supplier fails to deliver the goods, the consumer can claim a refund from the card issuer. In this type of case, the dispute between the consumer and the e-trader is effectively resolved by the fact that the credit card company is liable for the e-trader's default.

2.19 Of course, a large number of consumer transactions concluded by UK consumers—both those concluded offline and online—have a value of less than £100.[26] If, in such cases, the consumer has paid by credit card, the card issuer is not liable for any breach of contract by the supplier; similarly, if the consumer pays by debit card or prepaid card, there is no recourse against the card issuer for the supplier's contractual breach, regardless of the value of the transaction. Accordingly, if the consumer is unable to resolve such cases amicably with the supplier, the only choice is

[23] Research conducted a few years ago revealed that only a minority of British consumers are aware that the protection offered by credit cards does not also apply to debit cards: see Scottish Consumer Council (March 2001: 7).

[24] *Office of Fair Trading v Lloyds TSB Bank plc* [2008] 1 AC 316. For discussion of the decision of the Court of Appeal ([2007] QB 1), see S Saxby (2006).

[25] This advice is provided by the ECC (UK)'s website: <http://www.ukecc.net/sub.asp?id=200> [2/11/07].

[26] See para 1.35.

between 'lumping it' or pursuing some more formal dispute-resolution process.

3. Raising Standards

Codes of Practice and Transparency

In the consumer sphere, dispute avoidance is as important as, if not more important than, dispute resolution.[27] Where consumer complaints arise, it is often because of misunderstandings, rather than as a result of a breach of contract by the supplier. One of the important functions of consumer law is to promote good business practices, so that consumers are better informed about the deals they are making and complaints by consumers are handled in a way that prevents their escalating into disputes whose resolution requires the intervention of a third party. In the context of e-commerce, Internet service providers (including e-traders) based in the European Union are required by the E-Commerce Directive[28] to include various types of information on their websites: not only should a supplier furnish potential customers with details such as its name, geographic address, and e-mail address,[29] but also, in the process of contracting, the supplier should provide clear information on matters such as the different technical steps for the conclusion of the contract and the technical means for identifying and correcting input errors prior to the placing of the order.[30] **2.20**

There are also good business practices—which tend to boil down to suppliers treating their customers fairly—which can have a significant preventative role: **2.21**

> [M]isunderstandings can be avoided by transparency and playing by the rules, as well as monitoring customer behaviour and collecting feedback. An extensive after-sales service . . . can also go a long way towards preventing problems.[31]

In this context, it is important to note the role played by codes of practice and trustmarks (which indicate that an organization agrees to comply with some code of practice). When a supplier is a member of a trade association which has a code of practice (such as *ABTA*) or joins a trustmark **2.22**

[27] For example, it has been suggested that, '[i]n the sector of financial markets it is more practical to prevent conflicts rather than trying to somehow remedy the same': G Alpa (2001: 249).

[28] Dir 2000/31/EC [2000] OJ L178/1.

[29] Art 5.

[30] Art 10.

[31] C Schulze and J Baumgartner (2001: 33).

scheme (such as *Internet Shopping is Safe*[32]), the supplier has to abide by certain minimum standards. These normally include requirements as to transparency etc. An important aspect of b2c contract dispute resolution (at the domestic level) is through codes of practice which must contain suitable means of handling consumer complaints and may contain an arbitration scheme. Several trade organizations have codes which provide for the arbitration of consumer disputes.

2.23 Code approval operates at different levels. For example, in the United Kingdom, there are seven codes[33] which not only are approved by the trade organization itself, but also are accredited at the level of the Office of Fair Trading under its Consumer Codes Approval Scheme.[34] Such codes confer on consumers rights greater than those established by law: for example, whereas under the Consumer Protection (Distance Selling) Regulations 2000[35] consumers must be given a cooling-off period of seven days (in which to withdraw from the contract and to obtain a refund), the approved codes of practice include a cooling-off period of 14 days. One of the conditions for OFT approval is that the organization must demonstrate that the code is working in practice and delivering on its promises by monitoring its members' compliance with the code and the experiences of consumers. Other codes are internal to particular trade organizations and do not have accreditation from any outside or independent body. The extent to which these codes ensure that consumer complaints are handled properly depends on a variety of factors.

2.24 Although a code of practice does not prevent disputes arising, it provides a framework in which consumer complaints should be handled quickly and cheaply. First, codes of practice normally require suppliers to have an effective complaints handling system. As most consumer disputes result from misunderstandings, direct communication between the parties often results in the problem being resolved.[36] Secondly, an important feature of codes of practice is that they set out an ADR process (normally arbitration)

[32] A code of practice for e-traders: <http://www.internetshoppingissafe.co.uk>.

[33] Operated by Carpet Foundation; *DSA* (Direct Selling Association); Ombudsman for Estate Agents; Robert Bosch Ltd; *SMMT* (Society of Motor Manufacturers and Traders); *BAR* (British Association of Removers); and *VBRA* (Vehicle Builders & Repairers Association): <http://www.oft.gov.uk/advice_and_resources/resource_base/approved-codes/codes-search/cons_trade_search.aspx> [14/4/08]. There are also several other organizations part-way through the accreditation process: Office of Fair Trading (June 2007: 90).

[34] The power to approve codes of practice is conferred on the Office of Fair Trading by the Enterprise Act 2002, s 8. See <http://www.oft.gov.uk/oft_at_work/consumer_initiatives/codes/> [14/4/08]; G Howells and S Weatherill (2005: 586–91).

[35] SI 2000 No 2334.

[36] For further consideration of complaints handling, see ch 9.

for cases where complaints by consumers are not handled satisfactorily by the supplier's internal complaints procedure. From the consumer's point of view, these schemes are either free or involve very low costs.[37]

There are certain parallels between trustmark schemes and the operation of the medieval guilds. Membership of the scheme requires suppliers to abide by the specified code of practice. Although the organization responsible for trade standards does not enjoy the coercive powers of the state, it controls membership of the organization. The ultimate sanction against the member for failure to comply with the code of practice is expulsion from the scheme. If membership of the trustmark scheme brings sufficient benefits (as did membership of a trade guild in the Middle Ages), the threat of expulsion may be enough to ensure that the standards required by the code of practice are adhered to. **2.25**

It is important, however, to recognize the limits of codes of practice; the most significant limitation is the fact that codes of practice are normally voluntary and extend only to suppliers who choose to submit to their terms or to join the sponsoring organization. As regards those traders who do not participate in such schemes, consumers are protected only to the extent that the legal framework operates to vindicate their legal rights. In the cross-border context—even more than in domestic cases—the protection provided by the legal framework may be largely theoretical. Furthermore, codes of practice have had a relatively low impact on Internet shopping to date, both in terms of business take-up and consumer awareness.[38] **2.26**

User Groups and Feedback Systems

One of the methods of dispute avoidance is through the emergence of user groups. Such groups are primarily found in the information technology sector—though they also occur in some other industries. User groups bring together users of a product or a service for an exchange of views and experiences: **2.27**

> The exchange of information with other users improves the understanding of the product or service by the users. It provides manufacturers or sellers with suggestions for improvements in their products or services, and assists them in setting their priorities and in communications with users. Such communication between suppliers and users allows for early identification of problems, and thus the avoidance of disputes. Once disputes arise, the user group can cause

[37] For further discussion of dispute resolution under codes of practice, see ch 11.

[38] Office of Fair Trading (June 2007: 90).

pressure to be put on the supplier and can contribute to the search for creative solutions.[39]

2.28 More generally, there are websites which enable consumers to complain about specific suppliers (sometimes referred to as 'Corporate Complaint Websites');[40] many suppliers monitor such websites to ensure that public relations problems do not occur.[41]

2.29 There are also websites that incorporate feedback systems which allow consumers to rate the service provided by the supplier in question; such mechanisms seem to be particularly important in the context of online auction websites (such as *eBay*[42]). Empirical studies suggest that the feedback systems operated by auction websites provide a reasonable guide to consumers as to whether sellers are reliable.[43]

2.30 Nevertheless, one needs to be aware of the limitations which are inherent in mechanisms such as feedback systems: the Office of Fair Trading has observed that while they 'have a valuable role to play in raising consumer confidence', they do not 'provide a mechanism for monitoring or enforcing compliance with a set of standards or regulatory obligations'.[44] Accordingly, these open-textured mechanisms, although helping to promote higher standards among suppliers (and encouraging consumers to buy from more reputable suppliers), go no way towards providing mechanisms for dealing with problems as and when they arise.

Litigation in the Public Interest

2.31 One of the problems faced by consumers is presented by rogue traders who deliberately engage in 'scams' and other types of unfair commercial practice (such as misleading advertising, bogus prize draws, and unfair contractual terms). When a consumer falls victim to such practices, there is often very little, if anything, that the consumer can do to secure redress. This type of problem can, however, be tackled by public regulation and enforcement. Public and quasi-public bodies which have a responsibility

[39] ME Schneider and C Kuner (1997: 26).

[40] See, eg, 'The Unofficial American Express and American Express Financial Advisors consumer opinion site' <http://www.amexsux.com/>.

[41] Y Zhao (2003: 75).

[42] For a brief discussion of how the *eBay* feedback system operates, see L Edwards and A Theunissen (2007).

[43] Office of Fair Trading (June 2007: 142).

[44] Office of Fair Trading (June 2007: 94).

for promoting the essential fairness of the consumer market are best placed to take legal action against rogue traders—not with the aim of obtaining redress for individual consumers whose interests have been harmed, but in order to put an end to inappropriate business behaviour.

In recent years, one of the strands of consumer policy has been to give consumer protection agencies powers which enable them to put a stop to unfair commercial practices. Enforcement at this level does nothing to solve individual disputes that have arisen. However, the theory is that, if suppliers who engage in unfair commercial practices are brought to book, consumers in general will be less likely to find themselves in dispute with a rogue trader: 'the more effectively collective cross-border litigation works, the fewer individual actions will be necessary'.[45] **2.32**

Substantive Consumer Rights: The Right of Withdrawal

One of the ways of enabling consumers to obtain some form of redress without having to initiate a formal dispute-resolution process is by providing them with self-help remedies if they encounter problems with the supplier's contractual performance. If consumers are allowed to take the law into their own hands, as it were, the onus is then placed on suppliers (rather than consumers) to initiate some form of action if the situation is not to their liking. For example, in the field of distance contracts, consumers in Europe have a right under the Distance Selling Directive[46] (as transposed into national law by appropriate implementing legislation[47]) to withdraw from a contract within the cooling-off period (which, as regards a sale of goods, must be at least seven days after the goods have been received) and to obtain a full refund.[48] In cases involving the sale of goods, many consumer complaints can be simply resolved by the consumer being able to return the goods to the supplier and, if the goods have been paid for in advance, to recover the purchase price and delivery costs. So, by striking the right balance between the rights of suppliers and consumers, **2.33**

[45] European Consumer Law Group (April 1998: para 8 n 3). For further discussion, see ch 8.

[46] Dir 97/7/EC [1997] OJ L144/19.

[47] For detailed consideration of how the Directive has been transposed into the national laws of the various member states, see European Commission, COM (2006) 514. For the UK legislation, see Consumer Protection (Distance Selling) Regulations 2000, SI 2000 No 2334 (as amended).

[48] Similar rights of withdrawal are conferred under other European legislation, such as the Doorstep Selling Directive (Dir 85/577/EEC [1985] OJ L372/31) and the Timeshare Directive (Dir 94/47/EC [1994] L280/83).

the law can go some way towards reducing the circumstances in which consumers are left with a grievance against the supplier.

2.34 However, this type of solution is effective only as long as the supplier is prepared to play by the rules and to comply with its legal obligations. In cases where the consumer has been required to pay in advance for goods, if the consumer exercises his right of withdrawal, but the supplier fails to provide the refund as required by the law, the consumer is faced with a choice between pursuing the dispute or 'lumping it'. Unfortunately, research suggests that a significant minority of European suppliers fail to act in accordance with the terms of the Distance Selling Directive. In a small-scale cross-border shopping survey in 2003, suppliers failed to provide any refund in more than 30 per cent of cases and among the 70 per cent or so who did refund the purchase price, nearly half failed to refund the delivery charge (as required by the Directive).[49]

III. THE EXCEPTIONAL NATURE OF CONSUMER CONTRACT LITIGATION: WHY DISPUTES ARE NOT FREQUENTLY LITIGATED

1. Alternative Dispute Resolution

2.35 A partial explanation for why consumer complaints do not progress to the courts is that, for certain types of dispute, an alternative dispute resolution mechanism is available.[50] For example, in the United Kingdom, many complaints arising from holiday contracts are handled by alternative dispute resolution under the *ABTA* code of practice,[51] rather than by litigation. If ADR mechanisms are widespread and easily accessible, there will be a tendency for consumer disputes to be channelled away from litigation—which, in any event, is normally seen as a last resort. However, as the availability of ADR is very patchy, there are many situations in which, unless the consumer's dispute is resolved by the parties themselves by negotiation, the consumer's only choice is between dropping the matter or litigating the claim.

[49] ECC-Net (2003: 13–14).

[50] For a full discussion of ADR in the consumer context, see chs 9 to 11.

[51] See para 11.56.

2. 'Lumping it'

How Often do Consumers Choose to 'Lump it'?

In the consumer sphere, there are many occasions where, although a consumer is dissatisfied with the goods or services he has purchased from a supplier (in legal terms, it is alleged that the supplier is in breach of contract), he decides not to pursue a complaint: 'A universally encountered response to a perceived wrong is to do nothing—to "lump it".'[52] Research conducted in England in the late 1990s found that more than one eighth of consumers who experience problems with faulty goods or services did nothing.[53] In the cross-border context, the proportion of consumers who do not pursue complaints against suppliers may be considerably higher. In a 2004 survey of more than 15,000 consumers across the European Union, nearly a quarter of those who had a complaint about something they had bought from abroad did not even contact the supplier.[54] However, a different study carried out in the United Kingdom in 2005 suggested that only 11 per cent of those in a position to seek international redress had failed to do so.[55] **2.36**

In cases involving the purchase of low-value goods or services, a consumer who decides to 'lump it' will also normally decide that, for the future, the appropriate strategy is 'exit'—that is to say, the next time he buys goods or services of the same or a similar type, he will buy them from another supplier.[56] Although this phenomenon is perfectly rational from the point of view of each consumer—who decides that the costs of pursuing the complaint (in any way) will outweigh any possible redress and that the best way of registering his dissatisfaction is to buy from another supplier in future—it is not necessarily desirable in broader socio-economic terms. There are three strands to the argument. First, if consumers fail to seek redress for breaches of contract committed by suppliers, the rule of law is weakened. Suppliers who sell low-value goods can fail to comply with their contractual obligations with impunity. The European Consumer Centre in Dublin cites, as an example, a situation where an Irish retailer, who was in dispute with an English consumer, informed the **2.37**

52 S Roberts and M Palmer (2005: 81).

53 H Genn (1999: 39).

54 Eurobarometer (October 2004: 56). In a US study in 1975 around two thirds of consumers who perceived a problem with goods they had purchased did not take any form of action: A Best and AR Andreasen (1977: 729).

55 Office of Fair Trading (June 2007: 154).

56 I Ramsay (1981: 124).

Inspector from the Office of the Director of Consumer Affairs (ODCA) that he had no respect for the ECC or for the ODCA or for consumer legislation.[57] The English consumer, when informed of the option of bringing proceedings in the Small Claims Court in Ireland, decided, in view of the travel costs, to drop the matter. Secondly, consumer complaints have a role to play in enhancing the efficiency of the market; if consumers do not seek to enforce their legal rights, there are fewer incentives for suppliers to maintain (or improve) the quality of the goods and services which they provide. Thirdly, in moral terms, it is wrong if suppliers are able to avoid their responsibilities at the expense of consumers: 'when complaints go unaddressed, producers are in effect stealing small amounts from large numbers of people and escaping sanctions for such behaviour'.[58]

2.38 Whatever may be the downsides of consumers choosing to 'lump it', if consumers fail to take any form of action against defaulting suppliers, there is, in legal terms, no dispute. As well as being undesirable in socio-economic terms, such cases expose significant access-to-justice questions. Not surprisingly, empirical research indicates that the likelihood of dissatisfied consumers considering formal legal action decreases as the amount of money at stake falls.[59] There will always be a category of cases in which the monetary value of the claim is so low that it is simply not worth the consumer's while pursuing an individual complaint against a supplier who is in breach of contract. More troubling is the category of complaints which are not valuable enough to justify the expense and hassle which a formal dispute-resolution process would entail, but which are more than merely trivial. This is the area in which, unless effective dispute-resolution mechanisms are available, there will continue to be a significant shortfall in terms of the vindication of consumers' contractual rights.

2.39 Another point to note is that some problems with consumer sales are a direct result of fraud or deliberate wrongdoing by the trader; recent years have seen plenty of instances of 'scams' (such as in the timeshare industry). Most problems of this type are never going to be resolved in a way which is satisfactory for the consumers who have been swindled; standard dispute-resolution processes are rarely going to produce a solution in cases where the supplier is a fraudster. These are cases where consumers have little choice but to put the whole thing down to experience—and seek to learn from the mistake they made for the future.

[57] ECC (Dublin) (June 2004: 4).
[58] L Nader (1979: 1000).
[59] See Eurobarometer (October 2004: 28, 53).

In cases involving 'scams' and systematic fraud or deception, public bodies (such as the Office of Fair Trading) may take action to deal with the rogue trader.[60] In this type of case, the CPC Regulation[61] has a role to play in the cross-border context. Such action will not normally produce anything by way of compensation for individual consumers who have been swindled or defrauded; the function of public enforcement is to make the market (as a whole) more consumer-friendly and hopefully to reduce the possibility of consumers being defrauded in the future. **2.40**

Why do Consumers Choose to 'Lump it'?

As regards disputes which arise from cross-border contracts, even if the consumer is able to litigate in his home forum (rather than having to bring the claim in the supplier's forum), the fact that the consumer and the supplier are domiciled in different countries inevitably presents problems for the consumer over and above those that would be experienced in the context of wholly domestic litigation. **2.41**

First, there are psychological barriers which manifest themselves in a general reluctance on the part of members of the public to get involved in processes which involve lawyers and the courts. It has been observed that: **2.42**

> For large sections of the population, the courts are seen as uninviting, even forbidding institutions to be visited only in extreme circumstances. They are places to which they are 'taken'; not somewhere they use to settle disputes.[62]

Another commentator suggests that 'most citizens with a legal grievance . . . have a strong aversion to entanglement either with lawyers or courts, or anything that looks like lawyers and courts, not only because of costs and delays but because of the stress and general unpleasantness associated with a structured adversarial process'.[63] This aversion which is evident in purely domestic cases is likely to be even more pronounced in cross-border situations.

Secondly, even if these psychological barriers can be overcome, there are major practical obstacles to cross-border litigation. As the European Commission has observed: 'If things are complex enough in national disputes, they are even more complicated when more than one country is involved.'[64] As a result, disputes arising out of cross-border consumer **2.43**

[60] See ch 8.

[61] Reg (EC) No 2006/2004 on cooperation between national authorities for the enforcement of consumer protection laws [2004] OJ L364/1.

[62] G Howells and R James (2002: 21).

[63] MJ Trebilcock (2003: 85).

[64] European Commission, COM (98) 198, p 5.

contracts are even less likely to be litigated than domestic disputes. The fact that service of process has to be effected abroad adds an additional level of complication—which is not present in domestic proceedings. Because, at the national level, some attention has been directed to making small claims procedures more user-friendly, consumers who decide, in purely domestic cases, to pursue a claim through the courts often choose to litigate in person—without incurring the costs of legal representation. However, when a consumer contemplates bringing proceedings against a foreign defendant, it is much harder to imagine that the consumer will be able to proceed without professional assistance. Furthermore, where the supplier is a foreign company without a place of business and/or assets in the country in which the consumer resides, there is a significant danger that, if the dispute is to be brought to a successful conclusion (from the consumer's perspective), the litigation process will involve two phases: the pursuit of the substantive claim in the consumer's home forum; then, if the consumer obtains a judgment in his favour, proceedings abroad to enforce the judgment in the foreign country where the supplier's assets are located. The possibility of the added expense of enforcement proceedings abroad reduces the likelihood of a case being litigated in the first place.[65]

2.44 A third disincentive for consumers to seek to vindicate their rights through the courts is that cross-border litigation is almost bound to take longer than domestic litigation:

> Whereas some Member States offer proceedings which take a year or less, the courts with jurisdiction over small claims in Ireland and in particular Italy need several years for resolving the dispute. The average duration of a cross-border civil law suit in Europe is almost 2 years at the defendant's residence and six months more at the plaintiff's residence (where service of process and the procedure for recognition and enforcement add to the duration).[66]

2.45 Although some efforts have been made recently to simplify the cross-border enforcement of judgments pronounced in the context of uncontested claims,[67] order for payment procedures,[68] and small claims,[69] it is too early to tell whether these developments will, in practical terms, make very much difference to the realities of cross-border consumer litigation.[70]

[65] TP Lester (2003: 472).

[66] European Commission, COM (2002) 746, p 59.

[67] Reg (EC) No 805/2004 creating a European Enforcement Order for uncontested claims [2004] OJ L143/15.

[68] Reg (EC) No 1896/2006 creating a European order for payment procedure [2006] OJ L399/1.

[69] Reg (EC) No 861/2007 establishing a European Small Claims Procedure [2007] OJ L199/1.

[70] For further discussion, see chs 5 and 6.

Even at the domestic level: 'One of the main deterrents to litigation is likely to be the thought of the effort involved, especially when set against the value of the claim.'[71] There is a level of commitment in terms of time, effort, and money needed on the consumer's part to make the litigation process work. Even if court fees are quite modest, one of their effects is to discourage all but relatively large claims.[72] The consumer has to decide—once informal attempts to produce a solution to the problem have failed—that it is worth spending time and a certain amount of money on the litigation process. **2.46**

Where X has a claim worth £200 (for example, because electrical goods bought from an e-trader are faulty), if settlement with the supplier cannot be reached, X has to decide whether to pursue a claim through formal channels or to buy replacement goods from another supplier. Any court-based procedure will require the filling in of forms and/or the writing of letters/e-mails, responding to questions etc. As many small claims procedures require a hearing and are traditionally premised on the parties attending the proceedings, X may have to take time off work and travel to attend the hearing. These types of costs and expenses will often exceed the amount in dispute and will normally make commencing legal proceedings totally unrealistic.[73] **2.47**

While it is difficult to assess scientifically the extent to which consumers sue for breach of a cross-border contract, it would seem that, if the claim is for less than €2,000, litigation against a foreign supplier (either in the consumer's home forum or in the country in which the supplier is established) is, from an economic perspective, not a rational option. Research conducted for the European Commission in the mid-1990s revealed the extent to which the costs of cross-border litigation effectively prevent consumers from seeking redress through the courts. The basic message was that, even as regards a claim for around €2,000, the average cost of suing across borders in the European Union exceeds the value of the claim; in addition, legal proceedings could take as long as five years: **2.48**

3. Summarising in cost/benefit terms the perspectives of a 'standard' court case, the study shows that for a 'simple' inter-Community dispute the situation is as follows:

- a party who has suffered damage in the amount of ECU 2000 must, in order to have 'access to justice', first pay an 'entrance fee' of ECU 2500 (court cost +

[71] Lord Chancellor's Department (1986: 31).

[72] AJ Duggan (2003: 48).

[73] See European Commission, COM (93) 576, p 62. As far back as the 1970s it was considered not worth taking a *domestic* case to court if the value of the claim was less than £150: *The Times*, 25 January 1972, cited by S Prince (2007: 331).

lawyer's fees, exclusive of VAT), in the (uncertain) perspective of recovering his loss within 12 to 64 months (depending on the country)—all this on the assumption that the defendant will (still) be solvent when the court makes its decision.

- If the second condition is not (or no longer) met at the time of judgment, the plaintiff (while 'winning' the case) will have lost ECU 4500 (his initial loss + expenses).
- If the condition is met, and if the court finds for the plaintiff, he will be awarded damages; in most of the Member States (11 out of 15 according to the study) he will however recover only a part of his outgoings (in addition, certain legal orders simply rule out compensation for the fees charged by 'foreign' lawyers).
  Since these costs amount to ECU 2500 on average, the plaintiff's 'balance' (damages minus non-reimbursed outgoings) will often be close to zero if not indeed negative.

4. Bearing the above points in mind, the study's fourth conclusion is hardly surprising: very few intra-Community disputes involving consumers come to court.[74]

The obvious conclusion from this data is that, unless considerable sums of money are at stake, a rational actor would not choose to litigate a cross-border consumer claim within Europe.[75]

2.49 When faced with the possibility of cross-border litigation, the choice confronting the consumer is not an attractive one. On the one hand, the consumer may consider that he needs to hire a lawyer to assist him. This course of action is not, however, free from difficulty. The first problem is that the consumer may simply be unable to find a lawyer who is willing to take on the case. A report from the late 1990s noted that:

> Most lawyers from the outset refuse to take on international cases. Those few lawyers with an international practice deal with business disputes. They have very little experience with consumer cases, either because consumers do not turn up in their offices or because lawyers refuse to represent them for economic reasons. If fees are calculated on an hourly basis, they quickly surpass the average amount of a consumer claim. If fees follow guidelines or statutory regulations, the lawyer's time investment for a consumer claim is not profitable.[76]

2.50 In England, conditional fee agreements (which have become the principal market mechanism for funding civil litigation in England) are inappropriate

[74] See European Commission, COM (96) 13, pp 9–10.

[75] H von Freyhold, V Gessner, EL Vial, and H Wagner (October/November 1995: 117). See also B Feldtmann, H von Freyhold, and EL Vial (June 1998); this later report concluded that 'in most member states a dispute value of 50,000 ECU might be a reasonable value to pursue a cross-border dispute' (June 1998: 276–7).

[76] European Consumer Law Group (April 1998: Annex II, para 4).

for small claims, which are inherently unattractive for private sector lawyers.[77]

Secondly, if a lawyer can be found to take on the case, there is the question of funding. Changes to legal aid eligibility are such that, in practice, public funds are not available for the vast majority of consumer claims.[78] It has been concluded that 'whilst consumers should have access to information and advice through the Consumer Gateway[79] and the networks of CABx and debt advisers, they will usually be expected to act without legal assistance taking their cases to arbitration, ombudsmen or in person before the small claims courts'.[80] The obtaining of legal aid in cross-border cases is equally problematical. Although the European Legal Aid Directive[81] aims to ensure that member states make legal aid available to litigants who are resident in other member states (to assist, for example, a French consumer who wishes to sue an English supplier in England), its impact, in England, is non-existent. The Directive was implemented in the United Kingdom by the addition of regulation 5D to the Community Legal Service (Financial) Regulations 2000. However, by the end of 2007, no money had been paid out under regulation 5D; in June 2006, there was one application (which, in all probability, did not involve a consumer matter), but it was refused.[82] **2.51**

So, in practice, a consumer who requires the services of a lawyer (and can find one to represent him) will have to pay the fees charged by the lawyer out of his own pocket. In such a case, even if the consumer is successful in the proceedings, there is a significant risk that he will be unable to recover the money that he has expended on lawyers' fees. As regards English small claims proceedings under the Civil Procedure Rules, the **2.52**

[77] Citizens Advice (October 2005).

[78] The low priority currently given to claims arising out of consumer contracts is well illustrated by the Legal Services Commission's website. In the webpage devoted to 'civil areas of work' (<http://www.legalservices.gov.uk/civil/civil_areas_work.asp> [24/5/07]), the five headings are: (i) Family; (ii) Immigration and asylum; (iii) Social welfare; (iv) Mental health and other civil areas; (v) Specialist support. One of the sub-headings under 'Mental health and other civil areas' is 'consumer general contract'. In 2005/06 only £50 million of the total legal aid budget of more than £2 billion (ie, less than 0.25 per cent) was devoted to cases that come under the heading 'civil low volume categories' (which covers clinical negligence, consumer general contract, education, miscellaneous, personal injury, and public law).

[79] See <http://www.consumerdirect.gov.uk>.

[80] G Howells and S Weatherill (2005: 612).

[81] Dir 2002/8/EC [2003] OJ L26/41.

[82] Data provided by the Legal Services Commission in response to a request made under the Freedom of Information Act 2000.

'no costs' rule means that successful claimants are unable to recover the costs they have incurred as a result of hiring a lawyer. (By the same token, claimants do not face a huge bill if their claim is unsuccessful, because they do not have to pay the costs of the other side.) The effect of the 'no costs' rule is, of course, to discourage the use of lawyers. The position under the European Small Claims Procedure (ESCP), which comes into operation (as an alternative procedure) in January 2009, is different.[83] As regards costs, the general rule under the European Small Claims Procedure Regulation[84] is that 'the unsuccessful party shall bear the costs of the proceedings'.[85] While, at first glance, this rule might be thought not to discourage consumers from litigating cross-border claims under the ESCP (because, if successful, they will be able to recover their lawyer's fees from the supplier), the rule may, in fact, have the opposite effect—as it exposes the consumer-claimant to the risk of having to pay not only his own lawyer's fees, but also, if the claim fails, the fees charged by the supplier's lawyer.

2.53 On the other hand, if the consumer either is unable to find a lawyer to help him or baulks at incurring the costs involved, he is faced with the prospect of trying to advance the claim on his own. However, in view of the inherent complexity of cross-border litigation, it will be almost impossible for the consumer to pursue a claim successfully without some professional assistance. It has been observed that '[i]f lawyers do not normally represent consumers in cross-border cases, it is no surprise that these cases are rarely found in court files.'[86]

What Type of Consumer Claims do Generate Litigation?

2.54 It follows from the foregoing that, as a general rule, the only types of cross-border consumer contracts which might generate litigation are those which involve high-value goods or services. In Europe, such contracts are unusual, but they are not unheard of: there are some cross-border consumer transactions whose value exceeds €50,000. The kinds of situation which might lead to cross-border consumer litigation include cases involving the purchase of immovable property (including holiday homes and timeshares), building work, bank loans, life insurance contracts, investment contracts, and contracts for luxury goods (such as cars, boats, and works of art).

[83] For consideration of the ESCP, see ch 5.
[84] Reg (EC) No 861/2007 [2007] OJ L199/1.
[85] Art 16.
[86] European Consumer Law Group (April 1998: Annex II, para 5).

Although there are very few reported English cases concerning cross-border consumer contracts, the few that can be found relate to works of art, financial services, and yachts. *Maharanee of Baroda v Wildenstein*[87] involved a dispute over the sale of a painting, allegedly by Boucher, a French nineteenth-century master; the painting had been sold in 1965 for nearly £33,000.[88] The second case is *Standard Bank London Ltd v Apostolakis*,[89] which involved a foreign exchange agreement; the claimants' losses were in excess of $1 million. Although the English court regarded this as a consumer contract, this classification is not uncontroversial; in parallel Greek proceedings, the Greek court considered that the agreement was a commercial contract rather than a consumer contract.[90] In *Rayner v Davis*[91] a dispute arose between a buyer of a yacht and the defendant, a marine surveyor, who had allegedly conducted a pre-purchase survey of the yacht negligently.[92] **2.55**

In addition to the rare cases in which there is a significant sum of money at stake, there may also be court cases in which consumers have decided to bring a claim on a point of principle, rather than for economically rational reasons. **2.56**

IV. CONCLUSION

Although, for obvious reasons, lawyers tend to focus on the way in which disputes are resolved by formal processes, in particular through litigation, and much of the literature proceeds on the assumption that the emergence of online shopping will generate litigation arising out of cross-border consumer contracts, the economic reality is that, in the vast majority of situations, litigation will not provide a solution to disputes which arise from such contracts.[93] For the various reasons considered in this chapter, when a problem arises from a cross-border b2c contract (whether concluded online or offline), the most likely outcomes are: (i) the consumer does nothing (ie, he 'lumps it'); or (ii) the consumer obtains some form of **2.57**

87 [1972] 2 QB 283.

88 As a result of inflation since 1965, this sum would be worth something in the region of £450,000 today.

89 [2000] ILPr 766; *(No 2)* [2001] Lloyd's Rep Banking 240.

90 [2003] ILPr 499 (Multi-Member First Instance Court, Athens). For further discussion, see ch 3.

91 [2003] ILPr 258.

92 The report indicates neither the purchase price nor the amount of the claim.

93 V Heiskanen (1999: 38).

redress either directly from the supplier or, if payment was made by credit card, from the card issuer; or (iii) the matter is handled by an applicable ADR mechanism.

2.58 In the domestic context, an OFT report from 1988 estimated that, in the United Kingdom, there were 12 million consumer complaints per year where the average price was above £100 (for example, situations involving contracts for the sale of goods such as furniture, white goods, and cars or contracts for services such as car servicing, building work, and holidays); fewer than 2 per cent of consumers who took some form of action threatened legal proceedings and none of those who participated in the survey actually took court action.[94] Further research dating from the late 1990s indicated that less than 1 per cent of consumer complaints end up in court.[95] Recent Europe-wide research paints a similar picture: in a 2004 survey of European consumers, 8 per cent of the sample reported that, over the previous five-year period, they had had problems with a product or service that they had been unable to resolve amicably with the supplier; of this group only 13 per cent (ie, 1 per cent of the total sample) litigated their claim.[96] The number of consumers pursuing cross-border complaints appears to be even lower: whereas around one eighth of domestic consumer contracts generate a formal complaint, complaints are made in relation to cross-border consumer contracts in a very small proportion of cases (1 per cent)[97] and, although reliable statistical data is hard to come by, it seems clear that litigation arising from such contracts is extremely rare.

2.59 In the Netherlands, an examination of around 5,000 cases involving a private international law element (over a five-year period in the late 1980s and early 1990s) revealed that only, at most, two could be regarded as consumer cases.[98] A similar picture emerges from the absence of reported cases in England. Of course, there is not a guaranteed correlation between the number of reported cases in a particular field and the volume of litigation in that field. Nevertheless, the lack of reported cases involving disputes arising out of consumer contracts is striking. As noted already, over the course of the last half century, the English law reports contain only three cases involving a cross-border consumer contract.[99] Furthermore, recent

[94] R Thomas (1991: 160). The survey was based on a sample of 5,000 consumers.

[95] H Genn (1999: 156).

[96] Eurobarometer (October 2004: 26). These figures relate to domestic (rather than cross-border) contracts.

[97] Eurobarometer (September 2006: 30).

[98] CAJFM Hensen (1992).

[99] *Maharanee of Baroda v Wildenstein* [1972] 2 QB 283; *Standard Bank London Ltd v Apostolakis* [2000] ILPr 766; (*No* 2) [2001] Lloyd's Rep Banking 240; *Rayner v Davis* [2003] ILPr 258.

research into the operation of the Brussels I Regulation throughout the member states found that, in most member states, there is *no* published case law of national courts with regard to cross-border consumer contracts.[100] As regards b2c e-commerce in Europe, litigation arising from cross-border contracts is unheard of.[101]

It is, therefore, surprising that some commentators proceed on the assumption that consumers might be prepared to engage in cross-border litigation over the price of a CD[102] or a pair of shoes.[103] One author uses the example of a Belgian domiciliary who, having purchased a book from a Swedish e-trader and a computer game from a French e-trader, 'decides to sue both sellers'.[104] To suggest that this example has little point of contact with anything that might conceivably happen would be something of an understatement. Needless to say, one should not go to the other extreme and suggest that cross-border consumer litigation never occurs. Moreover, the pattern across different EU member states may not be uniform. A member state which is both geographically relatively isolated and has high litigation costs is likely to see less cross-border consumer litigation than a country which shares borders with other member states that speak the same language and has relatively low litigation costs. It would, therefore, not be altogether surprising to discover that consumer litigation in the regions adjacent to, say, the Austro-German or Franco-Belgian borders is less uncommon than in England.[105] **2.60**

Nevertheless, when thinking about consumer redress in relation to cross-border disputes, it is important that the relative significance and relevance of the private litigation model is kept clearly in perspective. **2.61**

[100] B Hess, T Pfeiffer, and P Schlosser (September 2007: 144). It is interesting that the authors considered that published case law of national courts in this field 'is not as frequent as one would be inclined to consider due to the extent of cross-border consumer-directed marketing': B Hess, T Pfeiffer, and P Schlosser (September 2007: 144). In view of the factors considered in this chapter, the lack of reported case law is exactly what might reasonably be expected.

[101] See ECC-Net (2005: 29).

[102] Z Tang (2007a: 124–5).

[103] D Svantesson (2001: 323).

[104] F Debusseré (2002: 349).

[105] But note that the absence of reported litigation involving cross-border consumer contracts (admittedly, not necessarily an accurate measure of the volume of cross-border consumer litigation) seems to be pan-European: B Hess, T Pfeiffer, and P Schlosser (September 2007: 144).

3

Cross-border Consumer Litigation: Jurisdiction Rules

This chapter considers the principles which determine whether or not the English courts may assume jurisdiction in relation to disputes which arise from cross-border consumer contracts—but excluding specific e-commerce issues[1] and the potential impact of dispute-resolution clauses.[2] For reasons already considered,[3] cross-border litigation involving consumer contracts is very unusual and arises only in exceptional circumstances—for example, when significant sums of money are at stake. **3.01**

For the purposes of the current chapter, the most important legal instrument is the Brussels I Regulation,[4] which allocates jurisdiction to the courts **3.02**

[1] See ch 4.

[2] See ch 7.

[3] See ch 2.

[4] Reg (EC) No 44/2001 [2001] OJ L12/1.

of EU member states in civil and commercial matters. However, the scope of the Brussels I Regulation is not unlimited and there are other sets of rules and principles which have a bearing on the courts' jurisdiction.

I. COMMON LAW BACKGROUND

3.03 Prior to the entry into force of the Brussels Convention in the United Kingdom in the 1980s,[5] there were no special jurisdiction rules directed to consumer contracts; in jurisdictional terms, consumer contracts—to the extent that they gave rise to litigation at all—were treated in exactly the same way as commercial contracts. These 'traditional' rules continue to apply in situations which are not governed by the Brussels I Regulation (or the Lugano Convention).[6] In *Maharanee of Baroda v Wildenstein*,[7] for example, a dispute arose out of a contract (concluded in 1965) for the sale of a painting, allegedly by Boucher, a nineteenth-century French master. When the buyer, an Indian princess who resided in Paris, started English proceedings against the seller, a French art dealer, the defendant applied for a stay of the proceedings (on the basis that the case had an insufficiently close connection with England). Since the seller was a dealer and the buyer was not in the business of buying and selling works of art, the contract was a b2c contract. There is nothing in the decision of the Court of Appeal (which did not accede to the defendant's application for a stay) to suggest that the fact that the scenario involved a consumer contract, rather than a commercial contract, had any bearing on how the jurisdictional issue should be handled. This is not very surprising for a number of reasons: (i) the case pre-dates the development of much of modern thinking about consumer issues; (ii) the contract in question (which concerned a painting which had been purchased for nearly £33,000) was a very atypical consumer contract; (iii) in any event, it is very difficult for a common law system (whose development is derived from decided cases, rather than legislation) to formulate doctrines which apply specifically to consumer contracts, rather than to contracts in general.[8] Apart from the *Maharanee of Baroda* case, there seems to be no reported litigation in which

[5] The Brussels Convention (on which the Brussels I Regulation is based) was implemented into the law of the United Kingdom by the Civil Jurisdiction and Judgments Act 1982, which brought the Convention into force in January 1987.

[6] For a general introduction to the Brussels I Regulation and the Lugano Convention, see paras 1.77–1.92.

[7] [1972] 2 QB 283.

[8] D Oughton and J Lowery (2000: 89).

the courts have had to consider the operation of the traditional jurisdiction rules in the context of a consumer contract.

Where, for example, an English consumer buys goods from a New York supplier which does not have a branch, agency, or other establishment in an EU member state, the Brussels I Regulation does not normally determine the English court's jurisdiction in relation to a claim brought by the consumer against the supplier (although it would apply to a claim brought by the supplier against the consumer). Article 4 of the Brussels I Regulation provides that, where the defendant is not domiciled in a member state, the court's jurisdiction is (subject to articles 22 and 23) determined by the law of the member state in question. There are very few disputes arising from b2c contracts which give rise to exclusive jurisdiction under article 22 and it seems very unlikely that a consumer contract involving a supplier with no place of business in a member state would include a jurisdiction clause in favour of the courts of one of the member states, thereby potentially bringing article 23 into play. Accordingly, the traditional rules apply to a claim brought by a consumer against a supplier not domiciled in an EU-Lugano state. **3.04**

In very broad outline, under the traditional rules (which apply to consumer contracts as well as to commercial contracts), the English court has jurisdiction in three types of situation: (i) if the defendant can be served with the claim form in England (as in *Maharanee of Baroda v Wildenstein*[9]); (ii) if the defendant submits to the court's jurisdiction; (iii) if the claim comes within CPR rule 6.20 and the court gives permission for service of the claim form out of the jurisdiction. In the first category of case, the court may stay the proceedings on the basis of *forum non conveniens* if the court of another country is a more appropriate forum; in the third category, the court will only give permission to serve out if the English court is the most appropriate forum or *forum conveniens*.[10] In addition, by virtue of the Brussels I Regulation and the Lugano Convention the court may be under a duty (or have a discretion) to stay proceedings if there are parallel or related proceedings in another member state or in a state bound by the Convention.[11] **3.05**

In cases where a supplier seeks legal redress against a consumer in England, it will normally be because the consumer resides in England. **3.06**

[9] Were the facts of this case to occur today, the case would be governed by the Brussels I Regulation, under which the English court would not have jurisdiction.

[10] For further discussion of the court's jurisdiction under the traditional rules, see J Hill (2005: ch 7).

[11] See J Hill (2005: section 9.1).

In these cases, the English court's jurisdiction is founded on the Brussels I Regulation and the traditional rules are wholly irrelevant. While it is perfectly possible for a supplier to invoke the English court's jurisdiction against, say, a Japanese consumer by serving a claim form on the consumer while he is physically present in England, it is doubtful whether such cases ever occur in practice. Even if service were effected in this way, the consumer would normally be entitled to a stay of proceedings on the basis of *forum non conveniens*—unless, perhaps, the contract had been concluded by the parties in England.

3.07 The one type of case in which a supplier might conceivably think of invoking the English court's jurisdiction under the traditional rules in a claim arising out of a contract with a consumer not domiciled in an EU-Lugano state is where, as a result of the contract having been made in England or being governed by English law, the claim falls within the scope of CPR rule 6.20(5). However, even if the court were prepared to give permission for service out in such a case (on the basis that England was the *forum conveniens*), the supplier would, if successful, normally be faced with the difficulty of having to apply to a foreign court to have the judgment enforced—as the foreign consumer is unlikely to have assets in England. Accordingly, it is not difficult to see why, in the context of contractual claims against consumers, cases involving the English court's jurisdiction under the traditional rules do not figure more prominently in the law reports.

3.08 What about cases where an English consumer has a claim against a foreign supplier not domiciled in an EU-Lugano state? Where, in relation to a cross-border consumer contract, a foreign supplier fails to comply with its obligations under the contract, an English consumer might, if enough money were at stake, wish to bring proceedings against the foreign supplier in England. If the supplier is domiciled in a third state, the traditional rules normally apply. However, if the supplier has a branch, agency, or other establishment in an EU-Lugano state, the supplier is deemed to be domiciled in that state as regards disputes arising out of the operations of that branch, agency, or other establishment.[12] So, if a dispute arises out of a contract concluded between an English consumer and the English branch of a New York supplier, the English courts have jurisdiction under the Brussels I Regulation.[13]

[12] Brussels I Regulation, art 15(2).

[13] Arts 2 and 15(2); Civil Jurisdiction and Judgments Act 1982, sched 4, r 1.

3.09 Under the traditional rules, if the supplier does not have a place of business in England, service normally cannot be effected in England.[14] However, service on a foreign supplier is possible if the supplier is an individual who is (even temporarily and for a purpose unrelated to his business) physically present in England at the time of service[15] or if the supplier has a place of business (not amounting to a branch, agency, or other establishment for the purposes of the Brussels I Regulation), regardless of whether the dispute has any connection with England.[16] However, even if, under the traditional rules, the foreign supplier can be served personally in England or at a place of business in England, the supplier can apply for a stay of proceedings if there is another more appropriate forum.

3.10 As regards contractual claims, the circumstances in which a consumer can rely on the long-arm jurisdiction of the English court under CPR rule 6.20 are quite limited. The jurisdictional bases which are potentially relevant are the following:

CPR rule 6.20(5)(a)

3.11 The court may give permission for service out of the jurisdiction in cases where the contract was made within the jurisdiction. For the purposes of CPR rule 6.20, English law determines the place where the contract was concluded, whether or not the contract is governed by English law. Obviously, where an English consumer purchases goods or services while on holiday or during a business trip abroad, CPR rule 6.50(5)(a) is not satisfied. However, the rule may be satisfied as regards distance contracts (such as contracts concluded by post or via the Internet). The position in relation to contracts concluded by post is fairly clear: the contract is made in the country where the acceptance is posted.[17] This means that the place where a mail-order contract is concluded turns on how the ordering process is constructed. The most likely structure is that the consumer's order is the offer and the supplier's confirmation is the acceptance. Accordingly, where an English consumer purchases goods from a foreign supplier through a mail-order catalogue, the contract is made abroad. Conversely, if virtually instantaneous means of communication, such as telephone, are used the contract is made in the country where the acceptance is received.[18]

[14] CPR r 6.5(6).

[15] As in *Maharanee of Baroda v Wildenstein* [1972] 2 QB 283.

[16] CPR r 6.5(6); *Sea Assets Ltd v PT Garuda Indonesia* [2000] 4 All ER 371.

[17] *Benaim & Co v Debono* [1924] AC 514.

[18] *Entores Ltd v Miles Far East Corpn* [1955] 2 QB 327; *Brinkibon Ltd v Stahag Stahl und Stahlwarenhandelsgesellschaft mbH* [1983] 2 AC 34.

So, if an English consumer orders goods by telephone from a foreign supplier, the contract is made in England—as long as the order is the offer and the supplier's confirmation is the contractual acceptance. As regards e-commerce, for reasons already considered,[19] online consumer contracts will normally be regarded as having been concluded at the consumer's place of residence.

CPR rule 6.20(5)(b)

3.12 Under this rule, the English court may assume jurisdiction if the contract 'was made through an agent trading or residing within the jurisdiction'. Although it could be argued that, where an online contract is concluded via computer hardware located in England, the conditions of this rule are satisfied, such an argument cannot be accepted. It is widely recognized that the physical location of computers through which online communications pass is irrelevant for jurisdictional purposes.[20]

CPR rule 6.20(5)(c)

3.13 The English court may give permission to serve out of the jurisdiction if the contract is governed by English law.[21] Consumer contracts are normally concluded on the supplier's terms and conditions. If such terms and conditions contain a choice of law, the chosen law will almost invariably be the law of the supplier's home country. However, if there is no choice of law, the applicable law will—in certain circumstances—be the law of the country in which the consumer is habitually resident. Where an English consumer enters an in-person contract while abroad, it is obvious that the contract will be governed by a foreign law. However, in the absence of a choice of law, a distance contract (such as a contract concluded by telephone or via an interactive website) between an English consumer and a foreign supplier will normally be governed by English law.[22]

CPR rule 6.20(6)

3.14 Under this rule, jurisdiction can be exercised where 'a claim is made in respect of a breach of contract committed within the jurisdiction'. It is not

[19] See paras 1.56–1.66.

[20] See, eg, M Chissick and A Kelman (2002: 119); HA Deveci (2006: 44); LE Gillies (2001); LE Gillies (2001a); LE Gillies (2003: 367–8); M Schaub (2004: 151); PA Stone (2002: 128). See also R Schu (1997: 204, 221–2) (in a discussion of choice-of-law rules).

[21] It is also provided that the English court may give permission to serve out if the contract contains an English jurisdiction clause: CPR r 6.20(5)(d). However, for most purposes this rule is superseded by provisions of the Brussels I Regulation and there is no plausible scenario in which the rule might be of relevance in a case involving a consumer contract.

[22] See ch 12.

difficult to imagine circumstances involving consumer contracts in which rule 6.20(6) might be satisfied—though much will depend on the precise terms of the contract. For example, if a supplier, having undertaken to deliver goods to an English consumer's home address, fails to do so, rule 6.20(6) would appear to be satisfied.

If the consumer can bring his claim within one of these jurisdictional bases, he can apply to serve a foreign defendant out of the jurisdiction. The court will give permission for service out if two further requirements are satisfied: there is a serious issue to be tried[23] and England is the most appropriate forum (*forum conveniens*).[24] However, in view of the fact that these principles also apply to commercial contracts—and that there is no reported case in which a consumer has sought to establish the English court's jurisdiction against a foreign supplier under CPR rule 6.20 (or its predecessors)—further discussion is not appropriate. **3.15**

II. THE INTRODUCTION OF JURISDICTION RULES FOR CONSUMER CONTRACTS

From an early stage it was recognized within the European Community that the application of the normal private international law rules to consumer contracts would exacerbate the problems faced by consumers who seek redress through the courts for problems resulting from cross-border contracts. The special treatment of consumer contracts in private international law—to the extent that such treatment exists at all—has the same starting-point as 'substantive' consumer protection; it is concerned with trying to find a suitable balance between the interests of consumer and suppliers. **3.16**

The Brussels Convention of 1968 introduced special jurisdiction rules for matters relating to insurance[25] and for matters relating to instalment sales and loans.[26] As will be seen, the rules relating to instalment sales and loans evolved into the current rules relating to consumer contracts—which can be found in Section 4 of Chapter II of the Brussels I Regulation. As regards protected consumer contracts, the key features of the jurisdictional scheme introduced by the Convention—and reproduced in the Brussels I Regulation—are as follows. First, proceedings against a consumer domiciled **3.17**

[23] *Seaconsar Far East Ltd v Bank Markazi Jomhouri Islami Iran* [1994] 1 AC 438.

[24] *Spiliada Maritime Corpn v Cansulex Ltd* [1987] AC 460.

[25] Arts 7–12.

[26] Arts 13–15.

in a member state can be brought only in the member state of the consumer's domicile.[27] Secondly, a consumer domiciled in a member state may bring proceedings against a supplier domiciled in another member state, either in the member state in which the consumer is domiciled or the member state in which the supplier is domiciled.[28] Thirdly, jurisdiction clauses in protected consumer contracts are not normally enforceable.[29] Fourthly, these jurisdiction rules are bolstered by a rule which provides that a judgment which is given in breach of Section 4 shall be refused recognition and enforcement in other member states.[30] In the consumer context, the same basic approach is adopted in Section 3 of Chapter II in relation to disputes arising out of insurance contracts.[31]

3.18 These rules are in stark contrast to both the general jurisdictional basis of the Convention (namely that proceedings should normally be brought in the courts for the place where the defendant is domiciled)[32] and the strict enforcement of jurisdiction agreements.[33] The Jenard Report, which accompanied the 1968 Convention and is a guide to its interpretation, states that the jurisdiction rules in Section 4 'are similar to those applicable in the national law of several of the Member States and, like them, stem from a desire to protect certain categories of persons'.[34] Jenard also refers to 'social considerations for the protection of certain categories of persons'[35] and suggests that the rules relating to instalment sales and loans 'are dictated by social considerations and are aimed in particular at preventing abuses which could result from the terms of contracts in standard form'.[36]

3.19 When Denmark, Ireland, and the United Kingdom acceded to the Brussels Convention in the 1970s, the accession convention was accompanied by the Schlosser Report. The Schlosser Report explains that, in view of the growth of consumer protection in the domestic laws of the member states in the preceding decade, there would be tension between national legislation and the Brussels Convention 'if the Convention did not afford the consumer much the same protection in the case of transfrontier contracts

[27] Art 16(2) of the Brussels I Regulation (replacing art 14(2) of the Convention).
[28] Art 16(1) of the Brussels I Regulation (replacing art 14(1) of the Convention).
[29] Art 17 of the Brussels I Regulation (replacing art 15 of the Convention).
[30] Arts 35(1) and 45(1) of the Brussels I Regulation (replacing arts 28(1) and 34(1) of the Convention). See ch 6.
[31] See, generally, F Seatzu (2003).
[32] Art 2.
[33] Art 23 of the Brussels I Regulation (replacing art 17 of the Convention).
[34] [1979] OJ C59/33.
[35] [1979] OJ C59/28.
[36] [1979] OJ C59/29.

as he received under national legislation'.[37] There is, however, nothing in the report which explains how the jurisdiction provisions are capable of mirroring the protection provided by national law. Indeed, there is a good argument for saying that choice-of-law rules—rather than jurisdiction rules—are more likely to translate the protection provided by national law into the cross-border context. So, in terms of the background to the jurisdiction rules contained in the Brussels Convention, the explanation for the introduction of special jurisdiction is rather unspecific.

III. AN IRRATIONAL STRUCTURE?

In jurisdictional terms, the Brussels I Regulation (like the Brussels Convention before it) divides consumer contracts into three groups. In the first category, the consumer is able to bring proceedings against the other party to the contract ('the supplier') in the consumer's home forum (and cannot be sued by the supplier in any other forum) irrespective of the connection (or lack of connection) between the contract and that forum. This category comprises insurance contracts,[38] contracts for the sale of goods on instalment credit terms[39] and contracts for loans repayable by instalments, or for any other form of credit, made to finance the sale of goods.[40] Secondly, the consumer has the same jurisdictional privileges as regards other consumer contracts[41] if the contract has 'a sufficiently strong connection with the place where the consumer is domiciled'.[42] Thirdly, any consumer contract which does not fall within the other two categories is subject to the jurisdiction rules which apply to contracts in general. **3.20**

Although the structure of the Brussels I Regulation can be explained historically, the current situation exposes a degree of schizophrenia within the rules. It appears that, in the original Brussels Convention, it was accepted that, to offset the fact that, vis-à-vis suppliers, consumers are in a weak position economically, consumers should not be expected to incur the extra trouble and expense of litigating (whether as claimant or defendant) in a country other than that in which they are domiciled. As a general rule, consumers would find fighting litigation in a foreign country more difficult than a supplier (who might be expected to have more experience, **3.21**

37 [1979] OJ C59/117 (para 153).
38 Art 12.
39 Art 15(1)(a).
40 Art 15(1)(b).
41 Art 15(1)(c).
42 Schlosser Report [1979] OJ C59/118 (para 158).

better access to legal advice, and a deeper pocket). Accordingly, as regards the types of contract specified in the 1968 Convention (insurance contracts, instalment sales, and loans), no territorial connection with the consumer's domicile was required for the application of the special jurisdiction rules.

3.22 However, when the scope of the special consumer contract provisions was extended to a wider range of contracts, this was thought justified only if the contract was closely connected with the consumer's domicile. This approach was adopted from the preliminary draft of the Rome Convention on the law applicable to contractual obligations.[43] In the final version of the Rome Convention, the special choice-of-law regime which applies to protected consumer contracts (article 5) does not follow the approach of the original Brussels Convention: the application of article 5 depends on there being a sufficient connection with the contracting state in which the consumer is habitually resident and there is no special provision for instalment sales and loans on deferred terms.[44] The current text of the Brussels I Regulation is, therefore, a mixture of two different approaches—one derived from the original 1968 Convention, the other derived from the Rome Convention. At the time of the accession of Denmark, Ireland, and the United Kingdom to the Brussels Convention in the 1970s, no attempt was made either to reconcile these two approaches or to justify the different treatment of different types of consumer contract; the differently inspired provisions were simply put side by side in a redrafted article 13. When the Brussels Convention was replaced by the Brussels I Regulation, this aspect of the jurisdictional regime applicable to consumer contracts was not changed. Accordingly, the overall scheme is somewhat arbitrary.

3.23 For example, if an English consumer makes a shopping trip to Paris and, while there, purchases goods on instalment credit terms, any proceedings relating to a dispute arising from that contract would have to take place in England. However, if the goods are bought for cash, the English court would not have jurisdiction over a claim brought by the consumer against the supplier and the Parisian court would have jurisdiction over any claim brought by the supplier against the consumer on the basis that, for the purposes of article 5(1)(b), Paris was the place where, under the contract, the goods were delivered.

3.24 Underlying the approach to insurance contracts, instalment sales, and loans is the paternalistic idea that consumers should not be discouraged from seeking to enforce their rights when those rights have been infringed.[45]

[43] Schlosser Report [1979] OJ C59/118 (para 158).
[44] Giuliano-Lagarde Report [1980] OJ C282/24.
[45] Case C-89/91 *Shearson Lehman Hutton* [1993] ECR I-139, 187 (para 18).

Although jurisdiction rules on their own cannot ensure that, in practical terms, consumers are able to litigate contractual claims against suppliers, if the jurisdictional balance is not tilted in the consumer's favour, general jurisdiction rules which require a consumer to take legal proceedings in a country other than that in which he resides may operate as an insurmountable obstacle to consumer litigation. This approach ties in with the importance of upholding the rule of law and von Ihering's view that 'if no one asserts his legal rights, the very rule which provides the right withers and dies'.[46] Providing consumers with the opportunity of enforcing their rights is a prerequisite for the upholding of the rule of law in this sense. The logic of this approach is to allow consumers to bring proceedings in their home forum whether or not the contract is closely connected with that forum.

However, the approach of the Rome Convention—and the Brussels I Regulation's approach to consumer contracts other than contracts of insurance, instalment sales, and loans—is premised on a distinction between 'passive' consumers and 'active' consumers. This distinction grows out of the idea of legitimate expectations. An active consumer is one who travels from his home country and, while abroad, purchases goods or services. The hypothesis is that an active consumer cannot reasonably expect that, if a dispute arises out of the contract which he concluded in another country, he will be able to sue the supplier in the consumer's home forum. It is the consumer, rather than the supplier, who has entered the international arena. Accordingly, there is no basis on which to displace the usual jurisdiction rules which apply to international contracts. By contrast, the passive consumer is targeted by the supplier in the consumer's country of domicile; the supplier, rather than the consumer, has entered the international arena. In such circumstances, the consumer who has not ventured abroad in the process of entering the contract has a legitimate expectation that any litigation arising from the contract will take place in his home forum. **3.25**

IV. PROTECTED CONSUMER CONTRACTS UNDER THE BRUSSELS I REGULATION

As has been seen already, under the Brussels I Regulation, the jurisdiction rules relating to protected consumer contracts are very simple. To the extent that difficulties of interpretation arise, they concern the field of application of these rules, rather than the rules themselves. **3.26**

[46] R von Ihering (trans P Ashworth) *The Battle for Right* (1883), cited by RHS Tur (1982: 143).

1. Introduction

Background

3.27 As originally drafted, the Brussels Convention of 1968 did not establish special jurisdiction rules for consumer contracts as such. Section 4 of Title II was headed 'Jurisdiction in matters relating to instalment sales and loans' and did not explicitly refer to consumers at all; article 13 of the 1968 Convention referred only to 'the sale of goods on credit terms' and to 'loans expressly made to finance the sale of goods and repayable by instalments'. When, however, the scope of this provision was considered in *Bertrand*[47] the Court of Justice decided that Section 4 did not apply to a commercial contract, even if, on a literal reading, it appeared to satisfy the criteria of article 13. The reference from the French courts arose out of a contract between two commercial undertakings for the sale of machinery. Under the terms of the contract the buyer undertook to pay for the machinery by means of two bills of exchange payable at 60 and 90 days. When the German seller, having obtained a German judgment against the French buyer, applied to enforce the judgment in France, the buyer sought to resist enforcement on the basis of article 28(1) of the 1968 Convention,[48] which provides that recognition of a judgment shall be refused if the court of origin assumed jurisdiction in contravention of Section 4. The buyer's argument was that the proceedings concerned a sale of goods on credit terms and that the German court had misapplied Section 4 by assuming jurisdiction over a defendant domiciled in France (in contravention of the second paragraph of article 14). Having regard to the purpose of Section 4, the Court of Justice decided that the provisions relating to instalment sales should be restricted to cases involving 'buyers who are in need of protection, their economic position being one of weakness in comparison with sellers by reason of the fact that they are private final consumers and are not engaged, when buying the product acquired on instalment credit terms, in trade or professional activities'.[49]

3.28 On the accession of Denmark, Ireland, and the United Kingdom in 1978, the Brussels Convention was amended in various ways; two significant changes were made to Section 4 of Title II. First, the Court of Justice's ruling in *Bertrand* was effectively incorporated into the revised text. The new Section 4 was labelled 'Jurisdiction over consumer contracts' and article 13

[47] Case 150/77 [1978] ECR 1431.
[48] Art 35(1) is the corresponding provision of the Brussels I Regulation.
[49] Case 150/77 [1978] ECR 1431, 1446 (para 21).

was expressly restricted to cases involving 'a contract concluded by a person for a purpose which can be regarded as outside his trade or profession, hereinafter called "the consumer"'. Secondly, the range of contracts to which the special jurisdiction rules applied was extended beyond instalment sales and loans to other consumer contracts for the supply of goods or services which satisfied two conditions: (a) the conclusion of the contract was preceded by a specific invitation addressed to the consumer or by advertising in the state of the consumer's domicile; and (b) the consumer took in that state the steps necessary for the conclusion of the contract.[50] The amended Section 4 was also included in the Lugano Convention of 1988.

When, in the 1990s, it was decided that the Brussels and Lugano Conventions should be amended, further attention was directed to Section 4—in particular, to the third category of consumer contracts added by the 1978 accession convention. The problem was that the two conditions which a contract for the supply of goods or services must satisfy in order to be a protected consumer contract were drafted with only real-world sales in mind. In view of the expansion of e-commerce, it was considered appropriate to redraft those conditions in a way which would satisfactorily cover online contracts as well as offline contracts. Article 15(1)(c) of the Regulation brings within the scope of Section 4 contracts which have been concluded with 'a person who pursues commercial activities in the Member State of the consumer's domicile or, by any means, directs such activities to that Member State or to several States including that Member State, and the contract falls within the scope of such activities'. **3.29**

The Proper Approach to Questions of Interpretation

Although there are general trends in the area of consumer law throughout Europe and there has been some measure of harmonization of consumer law within the European Community, it is still the case that there are substantive differences in the consumer laws of different member states. This presents a challenge for the Brussels I Regulation—which is designed to create a uniform system for the allocation of jurisdiction and the reciprocal recognition and enforcement of judgments throughout the member states. If, for example, each national court were to determine what constitutes a consumer contract in accordance with its own national law, the scope of Section 4 would be broader in some EU member states than in others. From the outset, the Court of Justice established that the concepts which **3.30**

[50] Art 13(1).

determine the boundaries of Section 4 must be given an autonomous interpretation, independent from national laws.

3.31 In *Bertrand*[51] the Court of Justice was asked to decide whether a contract was a 'sale of goods on instalment credit terms' for the purposes of what is now article 15 of the Brussels I Regulation. Having noted that the concept under consideration 'varies from one Member State to another,'[52] the Court decided to 'consider that concept as being independent and therefore common to all the Member States'.[53] When it comes to fixing the substantive content of the Brussels I Regulation's key concepts, the Court's interpretation is guided by the system and objectives of the Regulation to ensure that it is fully effective.[54] The same approach can be seen in *Shearson Lehman Hutton*,[55] a case in which one of the questions referred to the Court of Justice was the meaning to be given to the concept 'consumer' for the purposes of the Brussels Convention. In the course of its judgment, the Court relied upon 'the principle . . . according to which the concepts used in the Convention, which may have a different content depending on the national law of the Contracting States, must be interpreted independently . . . in order to ensure that the Convention is uniformly applied in all the Contracting States'.[56] Again, in *Gabriel* the Court of Justice reiterated that article 13 of the Brussels Convention must be 'interpreted independently . . . in order to ensure that it is fully effective'.[57]

3.32 The general basis of jurisdiction in the Brussels I Regulation is the defendant's domicile.[58] While there is a significant number of provisions which either supersede or supplement this general rule, it is important not to lose sight of the fact that the starting point for the allocation of jurisdiction in civil and commercial matters is the principle *actor forum sequitur rei* (the claimant must sue the defendant in the jurisdiction to which the defendant is subject). Accordingly, the Court of Justice has repeatedly expressed the view that exceptions to the general principle should be

[51] Case 150/77 [1978] ECR 1431.

[52] Case 150/77 [1978] ECR 1431, 1444 (para 12).

[53] Case 150/77 [1978] ECR 1431, 1445 (para 14).

[54] See, eg, Case 34/82 *Peters* [1983] ECR 987, 1002 (para 10); Case 9/87 *Arcado* [1988] ECR 1539, 1554 (para 11).

[55] Case C-89/91 [1993] ECR I-139.

[56] Case C-89/91 [1993] ECR I-139, 187 (para 13). See also Case C-269/95 *Benincasa* [1997] ECR I-3767, 3794 (para 12); Case C-27/02 *Engler* [2005] ECR I-481, 513 (para 33).

[57] Case C-96/00 [2002] ECR I-6367, 6399 (para 37). See also Case C-99/96 *Mietz* [1999] ECR I-2277, 2310 (para 26).

[58] Art 2.

interpreted 'restrictively'[59] or 'strictly'.[60] Such statements must, however, be taken with a healthy pinch of salt. It is certainly not the case that, as between a narrow and broader interpretation of an exception to the domicile rule, the Court of Justice will always choose the narrower interpretation; a restrictive interpretation of an exception to the general rule may not be appropriate.[61]

The overriding approach of the Court of Justice to questions of interpretation is purposive, rather than literal. In its response to references made by national courts on the interpretation of provisions of the Brussels Convention, the Court of Justice has littered its judgments with references to 'the objectives of the Convention'; the proper interpretation of a particular provision may conflict with its literal wording.[62] It is universally accepted that a provision should be interpreted in a way which is consistent with the jurisdictional scheme and its objectives and its interpretation should not extend its scope beyond that which is required by the objectives it was designed to achieve.[63] **3.33**

2. Consumer Contracts—General

Contract

Article 5(1) allocates jurisdiction in 'matters relating to a contract'; article 15 refers to 'proceedings concerning a contract . . .'. Article 5(1) relates to contractual matters in general, whereas article 15 relates specifically to various types of contracts concluded by consumers.[64] Neither provision attempts to define what is meant by 'contract'. Although it is reasonable to assume that the word 'contract' bears the same meaning in article 5(1) and article 15,[65] the wording of the two provisions is different and article 15 limits the range of circumstances falling within its scope. Accordingly, it cannot be assumed that a situation which does not concern a contract **3.34**

[59] See, eg, Case 189/87 *Kalfelis* [1988] ECR 5565, 5585 (para 19).

[60] See, eg, Case 33/78 *Somafer* [1978] ECR 2183, 2191 (para 7); Case C-89/91 *Shearson Lehman Hutton* [1993] ECR I-139, 169 (para 39) (Darmon AG).

[61] See Case C-96/00 *Gabriel* [2002] ECR I-6367, 6379 (para 46) (Jacobs AG); Case C-167/00 *Henkel* [2002] ECR I-8111, 8120 (para 33) (Jacobs AG).

[62] See, eg, Case 150/77 *Bertrand* [1978] ECR 1431.

[63] See, eg, Case 150/77 *Bertrand* [1978] ECR 1431, 1445 (para 17); Case C-115/88 *Reichert* [1990] ECR I-27, 41 (para 9); Case C-26/91 *Handte* [1992] ECR I-3967, 3994 (para 14); Case C-89/91 *Shearson Lehman Hutton* [1993] ECR I-139, 187 (para 16); Case C-269/95 *Benincasa* [1997] ECR I-3767, 3794 (para 13). See also Case 73/77 *Sanders v Van der Putte* [1977] ECR 2383, 2391 (para 18).

[64] Case C-27/02 *Engler* [2005] ECR I-481, 513 (para 31).

[65] Case C-96/00 *Gabriel* [2002] ECR I-6367, 6398–9 (paras 35–6).

concluded by a consumer for the purposes of article 15 necessarily falls outside the scope of article 5(1)—on the basis that it does not concern matters relating to a contract.[66]

3.35 In the context of article 5(1) the Court of Justice has ruled that the phrase 'matters relating to a contract' does not extend to 'a situation where there is no obligation freely assumed by one party towards another'.[67] The context of this ruling was the drawing of the dividing line between article 5(1) ('matters relating to a contract') and article 5(3) ('matters relating to tort, delict or quasi-delict'). The jurisprudence of the Court of Justice establishes a number of important qualifications to this principle. First, the scope of article 5(1) covers situations involving consensual dealings between the parties, even though the situation does not fall squarely within the classical conception of contract.[68] Secondly, article 5(1) applies in cases where, even though the defendant denies the existence of a contractual relationship, the claimant alleges that the defendant is in breach of contract.[69] Thirdly, the operation of article 5(1) does not depend on there being a concluded contract between the parties.[70]

3.36 In *Engler*[71] the Court of Justice ruled that, where a supplier writes to a consumer offering a cash prize and, to claim the prize, the consumer merely has to return a 'payment order' (without thereby assuming any obligation to buy goods from the supplier), a claim by the consumer for payment of the prize falls within the scope of article 5(1). In this type of case, even though there is no concluded contract between the supplier and the consumer, the letter sent by the supplier may give rise to an obligation 'freely assumed' by the supplier to the consumer within the meaning of the Court of Justice's jurisprudence.[72] Whether, in any particular case, the offer of a prize does give rise to a binding obligation on the part of the offeror is to be determined by the *lex causae*;[73] nevertheless, for jurisdictional purposes, the consumer's (disputed) claim that such an obligation

[66] Case C-27/02 *Engler* [2005] ECR I-481, 517 (para 49).

[67] Case C-26/91 *Handte* [1992] ECR I-3967, 3994 (para 15); Case C-51/97 *Réunion Européenne* [1998] ECR I-6511, 6542 (para 17).

[68] See, eg, Case 34/82 *Peters* [1983] ECR 987.

[69] Case 38/81 *Effer* [1982] ECR 825.

[70] Case C-334/00 *Tacconi* [2002] ECR I-7357, 7393 (para 22).

[71] Case C-27/02 [2005] ECR I-481.

[72] Case C-27/02 [2005] ECR I-481, 518 (para 53).

[73] Under Austrian law, undertakings which send prize notifications to specific consumers and give the impression that the consumer has won a particular prize must give that prize to the consumer and may be sued for the prize in legal proceedings: see Case C-27/02 *Engler* [2005] ECR I-481, 486 (para 10) (Jacobs AG).

has arisen is a matter relating to a contract for the purposes of article 5(1). If, under the applicable law, the place of performance of the supplier's (disputed) obligation is the place where the consumer is domiciled, article 5(1) allows the consumer to bring proceedings claiming payment of the prize in his home forum.[74]

However, the fact that, with regard to a dispute between a consumer and a supplier, the situation involves matters relating to a contract for the purposes of article 5(1) does not necessarily mean that the case falls within article 15. The jurisprudence of the Court of Justice establishes that the conditions of article 15(1) of the Regulation are not satisfied if the relations between the parties are pre-contractual. In *Gabriel*[75] the question was whether the case involved 'proceedings concerning a contract concluded by a [consumer]' within the scope of what is now article 15(1) of the Brussels I Regulation. The dispute arose out of a direct-selling technique whereby the supplier (in this case, domiciled in Germany) wrote personally to the consumer (in this case, domiciled in Austria) informing him that, if he ordered goods of a certain value from the supplier, he would receive a cash prize. When the consumer, having ordered the goods, did not receive the anticipated prize, he started proceedings for breach of contract in Austria. There was no doubt that, if the proceedings were 'proceedings concerning a contract', the contract in question was a protected consumer contract and the Austrian courts had jurisdiction. However, the supplier argued that the dispute over the alleged obligation to pay the prize did not come within the concept 'proceedings concerning a contract' as, under the supplier's terms and conditions, the original 'offer' to the consumer was legally an invitation to treat (rather than an offer) and the consumer's order was legally an offer (rather than an acceptance). According to this analysis, although there was a contract for the sale of the goods ordered by the consumer (because the supplier had accepted the consumer's offer), there was no contract in relation to the anticipated prize. In the proceedings before the Court of Justice both the German government and the European Commission supported the supplier's position on the basis that the consumer jurisdiction rules apply only if the dispute relates to an obligation arising from a contract between the parties; in a case like *Gabriel* this depends on whether the supplier's 'offer' was, in legal terms, an offer or only an invitation to treat.[76] **3.37**

[74] *Re Jurisdiction in a Claim Based on a Prize Draw Notification* [2007] ILPr 243 (Federal Supreme Court, Germany).

[75] Case C-96/00 [2002] ECR I-6367.

[76] See Case C-96/00 [2002] ECR I-6367, 6377 (para 34) (Jacobs AG).

3.38 Both the Advocate General and the Court rejected the supplier's argument; they emphasized the importance of reaching an interpretation which is consistent with the aim of protecting the interests of consumers and both noted that it would be contrary to such interests if jurisdiction over different disputes arising out of a unitary relationship between the consumer and the supplier were allocated to the courts of different states.[77] The policy arguments pointed strongly towards treating the litigation relating to the cash prize as 'proceedings concerning a contract' so that the courts with jurisdiction over any dispute relating to the supply of the goods (in *Gabriel*, the Austrian courts) also had jurisdiction over the dispute relating to the unpaid prize. The Court of Justice concluded that, notwithstanding the fact that the consumer's claim for the unpaid prize was not contractual in nature, the issue in dispute fell within the scope of what is now article 15(1) because it was related to a contract between a consumer and supplier which had given rise to reciprocal and interdependent obligations between the two parties.[78]

3.39 The limits of this decision are, however, illustrated by the later ruling by the Court of Justice in *Engler*.[79] The facts of this case were superficially similar to those in *Gabriel*: the defendant (a German company) wrote to the claimant (a consumer domiciled in Austria) sending her a mail-order catalogue and informing her that she had won a prize. However, there are important differences between *Gabriel* and *Engler*: whereas in *Gabriel* receipt of the prize was said to be dependent on the claimant ordering goods from the defendant, in *Engler* all the claimant had to do was to return a 'payment notice'. So, although the purpose of the defendant's conduct in *Engler* was to encourage the claimant to order goods from the defendant, only pre-contractual relations existed between the parties.

3.40 In an earlier case, in which a Dutch mail-order company had written to a German consumer informing her that she had been awarded a cash prize, the German Federal Supreme Court had held that, in this type of case, the court for the place where the consumer is domiciled has jurisdiction under Section 4.[80] However, in *Engler*, the Court of Justice reached the opposite conclusion. This conclusion was primarily based on the wording of the relevant provision. Whereas article 5(1) refers to 'matters relating to a contract', article 15 uses the expression 'proceedings concerning a contract

[77] Case C-96/00 [2002] ECR I-6367, 6380 (para 50) (Jacobs AG); [2002] ECR I-6367, 6404 (paras 57–8) (ECJ).

[78] See the Court of Justice's summary of its decision in Case C-27/02 *Engler* [2005] ECR 481, 513–14 (para 34).

[79] Case C-27/02 [2005] ECR I-481.

[80] *Re Claim for Payment of Prize Money* [2005] ILPr 222.

concluded by a [consumer]'.[81] In *Engler* no contract had been concluded, because the claimant had chosen not to order goods from the defendant's catalogue.[82]

It may be questioned whether policy arguments point conclusively in the same direction. In favour of the result in *Engler* is the point made by the defendant that the purpose of Section 4 is to protect consumers, not to facilitate their enrichment.[83] If the purpose of Section 4 is only to remove the difficulties which a consumer might face by having to litigate a dispute over an onerous contract for the supply of goods or services in a state other than that of the consumer's domicile, there is no policy reason to extend the scope of Section 4 to the circumstances which arose in *Engler*. In a case like *Engler* there is no possibility of the consumer being sued in a foreign forum (as the consumer does not undertake obligations for the breach of which he could be sued by the supplier) and, although the supplier has withheld an anticipated benefit from the consumer, the latter has not suffered any loss. **3.41**

However, there are good reasons for tilting the jurisdictional balance in favour of consumers. One of them is not to discourage consumers from enforcing their rights. It must be remembered that the importance of consumer rights being enforced is not simply that the rights of individual consumers are vindicated; of equal significance are the educative and deterrent functions that litigation of this type can perform. Consumer litigation both publicizes abusive marketing practices and can play a role in deterring such practices being used in the future—not only by the defendant, but also by other suppliers. From this point of view, in *Engler*, a case can be made for allowing the consumer to sue the supplier in the state of her domicile. Advocate General Jacobs acknowledged that the facts of *Engler* involved 'predatory conduct' by the supplier towards the consumer[84] but considered that Section 4 could not be extended in a way which ran counter to the clear wording of the relevant provision. Arguably, it would have been better, in policy terms, if the claimant in *Engler* could have sued in Austria on the basis of her Austrian domicile.[85] **3.42**

[81] Emphasis added.

[82] See also *Re Jurisdiction in a Claim Based on a Prize Draw Notification* [2007] ILPr 243 (Federal Supreme Court, Germany).

[83] See Case C-27/02 [2005] ECR-I 481, 490 (para 29) (Jacobs AG).

[84] Case C-27/02 [2005] ECR I-481, 489 (para 22).

[85] Article 5(1) would confer jurisdiction on the Austrian courts in *Engler* only if Austria had been the place of performance of the supplier's obligation to pay the prize.

The Consumer: A Person Acting for a Purpose Outside his Trade or Profession

3.43 A key element of all contracts falling within the scope of Section 4 is that the contract is concluded by a 'consumer', a concept which is defined as 'a person [acting] for a purpose which can be regarded as being outside his trade or profession'.[86] The Court of Justice has been called upon to consider the significance of this formula on several occasions—and the jurisprudence of the Court of Justice has been considered and applied by national courts.

Natural and legal persons

3.44 Whether a legal person can qualify as a consumer is not explicitly addressed by any of the provisions of Section 4. Article 15 of the Brussels I Regulation refers only to 'a person' (without qualification) and some commentators have suggested that legal persons 'can be consumers within Section 4 just as natural persons may be'.[87] The case law of the Court of Justice, however, makes it clear that only natural persons can claim the jurisdictional protection offered by Section 4. In *Bertrand* the Court of Justice rejected the argument that a b2b contract (between two economic operators) could be an instalment sale for the purposes of article 13 of the Brussels Convention: only 'private final consumers' qualify for protection.[88] Furthermore, in *Benincasa* the Court of Justice indicated that the provisions designed to protect consumers apply to an 'individual',[89] a term which necessarily implies that a natural person is involved.[90]

3.45 It is also worth noting that some other Community legislation in the field of consumer protection explicitly defines 'consumer' in a way which excludes legal persons. For example, article 2 of the Directive on unfair terms in consumer contracts[91] defines 'consumer' as 'any *natural person* who . . . is acting for purposes which are outside his trade, business, or profession'.[92] In view of this definition it is, perhaps, surprising that

86 Brussels I Regulation, art 15.

87 P Kaye (1997: 829).

88 Case 150/77 [1978] ECR 1431, 1446 (para 21).

89 Case C-269/95 [1997] ECR I-3767, 3795 (para 17).

90 See Joined Cases C-541/99 and C-542/99 *Cape Snc* [2001] ECR I-9049, 9064 (para 17) (Mischo AG).

91 Dir 93/13/EEC [1993] OJ L95/29.

92 The same definition is found in art 2 of the Directive on doorstep selling: Dir 85/577/EEC [1985] OJ L372/31. Other consumer legislation adopts different definitions depending on the subject-matter of the legislation; see, eg, the Directive on package travel, package holidays and package tours: Dir 90/314/EEC ([1990] OJ L158/59), art 2(4).

in *Cape Snc*[93] the Italian courts made a reference to the Court of Justice asking whether a company can be regarded as a consumer for the purposes of the Directive; the unambiguous wording of the Directive made it inevitable that the question posed by the Italian court would be answered in the negative.[94] What is significant about the decision in the context of the current discussion is that, in the course of his opinion, the Advocate General expressly linked the Court's interpretation of 'consumer' in the context of the jurisdictional regime with the definition of 'consumer' in article 2 of the Directive.[95] It is legitimate to conclude that, unless the drafting of particular provisions requires a different interpretation, the concept 'consumer' should have the same meaning throughout the field of Community law. In a situation involving a contract between two legal persons, it is impossible to regard one of the contracting parties as a 'consumer', even if that party is in an economically weaker position than the other.

A purpose outside the consumer's trade or profession

It is important to stress at the outset that 'consumer' is not a status which **3.46** a person carries with him throughout his contractual dealings: whether a person is a 'consumer' cannot be determined in the abstract; the question has to be examined in the context of the particular contract in question. It is perfectly possible for an individual to enter two apparently identical contracts, but for only one of them to be a consumer contract: '[T]he selfsame person may be regarded as a consumer in relation to certain transactions and as an economic operator in relation to others.'[96] For example, where A, a restaurant owner, buys an oven for use in the kitchen of his restaurant, the contract is not a consumer contract—because the purpose of the contract is related to A's business activity. However, if A buys exactly the same type of oven from the same supplier for use in his kitchen at home, the contract is a consumer contract because the purpose of the contract is outside A's trade or professional activities. As regards the second contract, the fact that A has relevant business experience and may be thought not to need the protection of Section 4 is irrelevant to the proper classification of the contract: '[I]n order to determine whether a person has the capacity of a consumer, . . . reference must be made to the position of the person concerned in a particular contract, having regard to the nature

[93] Joined Cases C-541/99 and C-542/99 [2001] ECR I-9049.

[94] Joined Cases C-541/99 and C-542/99 [2001] ECR I-9049, 9064 (para 16).

[95] Joined Cases C-541/99 and C-542/99 [2001] ECR I-9049, 9064 (paras 17–18).

[96] Case C-269/95 *Benincasa* [1997] ECR I-3767, 3795 (para 16). See also Case C-269/95 *Benincasa* [1997] ECR I-3767, 3778 (para 38) (Ruiz-Jarabo Colomer AG); Case C-361/89 *Di Pinto* [1991] ECR I-1189, 1201 (para 19) (Mischo AG).

and aim of that contract, and not to the subjective situation of the person concerned.'[97]

3.47 This proposition must, however, be read subject to the possibility that a contracting party may, in certain circumstances, be estopped from claiming that he is a consumer with regard to a particular contract. On the basis of the Giuliano-Lagarde Report's discussion of article 5 of the Rome Convention,[98] it is reasonable to suppose that, in a case where the consumer has acted in a way which indicates that he is concluding the contract for business or professional purposes, Section 4 does not apply.[99] For example, if a lawyer buys a computer for home use (rather than for use in connection with his profession), but enters the contract by correspondence and uses his business stationery, the supplier has every reason to think that the contract is an ordinary b2b contract and it would be contrary to the supplier's reasonable expectations if the buyer were able to claim that, as he was acting as a consumer, he should be able to rely on the jurisdiction rules applicable to protected consumer contracts.

3.48 The trade or professional purpose which determines whether or not a contract is a protected consumer contract will normally be an existing trade or profession. However, a contract concluded by a person who is not, at the time of the conclusion of the contract, carrying on a trade or profession, is not a consumer contract if the contract relates to an anticipated or future trade or profession. *Benincasa*[100] involved disputes arising out of a franchise agreement, the purpose of which was to enable the claimant to set up a shop selling dental hygiene products. The Court of Justice held that Section 4 did not apply because the contract was for the purpose of trade or professional activity: the fact that such activity 'is in the nature of a future activity does not divest it in any way of its trade or professional character'.[101]

3.49 In many ways, the situation in *Benincasa* was fairly straightforward as the purpose of the franchise agreement was to set the claimant up in business. The position is less clear where a person whose normal activities do not involve trade acquires goods with the intention of selling them at a profit. If X buys a CD for personal use, the contract is a consumer contract. What if X, as a one-off transaction, buys ten copies of a CD (or a hundred copies or a thousand) with the intention of re-selling them? There is an argument

[97] Case C-269/95 *Benincasa* [1997] ECR I-3767, 3795 (para 16).
[98] [1980] OJ C282/23.
[99] M Foss and LA Bygrave (2000: 107–8).
[100] Case C-269/95 [1997] ECR I-3767.
[101] Case C-269/95 [1997] ECR I-3767, 3795 (para 17).

for saying that where a purchaser of goods has the intention of reintroducing those goods into the market with a view to making a profit, the contract should not be classified as a consumer contract.[102]

'Exceptional' activities within a business context

Can a person be regarded as a consumer if he concludes a contract which is not a usual, day-to-day business transaction and which is not closely connected to his trade or profession? This question arose in *Di Pinto*,[103] in the context of the Doorstep Selling Directive.[104] The defendant ran a company which published a periodical in which businesses were advertised for sale. The defendant sold advertising space in this periodical to a businessman (A) who was planning to sell his business; the contract failed to inform A of his right to withdraw from the contract—which, if A had been a consumer, was required by the Doorstep Selling Directive and the implementing French legislation—and the defendant was convicted of an offence. The defendant appealed against enforcement of the judgment on the basis that, as A was not a consumer, the contract did not fall within the scope of the Doorstep Selling Directive. One of the questions referred by the Paris court of appeal to the Court of Justice was whether a trader canvassed at home in connection with the sale of his business is entitled to the protection accorded to consumers by the Doorstep Selling Directive. **3.50**

Advocate General Mischo, accepting the arguments of the Commission and the French government, considered that, in the circumstances of the case, A should be regarded as a consumer: the rules relating to consumer protection are designed not only to protect the average consumer, but also to protect 'the trader who unexpectedly finds himself in the position of a consumer in so far as he is required to perform an act in which, in the majority of cases, he will be involved only once in his life'.[105] Although his opinion does not spell out in detail how the dividing line between contracts for 'day-to-day' business purposes and contracts for 'unusual' business purposes (which he would treat as consumer contracts) should be drawn, the Advocate General thought that a contract for advertising the sale of a business is sufficiently unusual to justify the application of consumer protection legislation. **3.51**

The Court of Justice, however, adopted the opposite position. Central to the Court's analysis was the rejection of the idea that it is possible, in the **3.52**

[102] A Lopez-Tarruella (2001: 245).

[103] Case C-361/89 [1991] ECR I-1189.

[104] Dir 85/577/EEC [1985] OJ L372/31.

[105] Case C-361/89 [1991] ECR I-1189, 1202 (para 23).

context of contracts with a business connection, to draw a meaningful distinction between 'normal' acts and acts of an 'exceptional' nature.[106] Where a contract is connected with the professional activity of the trader (even if the contract relates to the sale of the business) the contract is not concluded for a purpose which is outside that person's trade or profession. Even so-called 'exceptional' acts (such as steps taken to advertise the sale of a business) are 'managerial acts performed for the purpose of satisfying requirements other than the family or personal requirements of the trader'.[107] The Court's ruling is clearly preferable to the opinion of the Advocate General. The problem with the Advocate General's approach is that it would leave the way open for a person with very substantial business experience to argue that he should be treated as a consumer whenever he enters into a contract which does not fall directly within his business activities even though there can be no possibility of his being in an economically weaker position than the other contracting party.[108]

3.53 The approach taken by the Court of Justice in *Di Pinto* is not limited to the interpretation of the Doorstep Selling Directive;[109] it applies generally across the field of EC consumer legislation. Accordingly, where a trader enters any contract for a purpose which is within the scope of his business activity, but for a purpose which is wholly unconnected with his normal trade or business (such as where A, a lawyer, enters a contract with B, a catering firm, for the provision of catering services for A's clients and employees), the contract cannot be a protected consumer contract for the purposes of Section 4. The significance of the *Di Pinto* ruling is illustrated by a couple of cases decided by the Scots courts in the context of the Civil Jurisdiction and Judgments Act 1982.[110] In *Semple Fraser WS v Quayle*[111] the claimant solicitors sought payment of fees from the defendant client whom the claimants had represented in proceedings brought by the Secretary of State for Trade and Industry for disqualification of the defendant as a

[106] Case C-361/89 [1991] ECR I-1189, 1211 (para 15).

[107] Case C-361/89 [1991] ECR I-1189, 1211 (para 16).

[108] The suggestion in *Semple Fraser WS v Quayle* [2002] SLT (Sh Ct) 33 (Sheriff Court, Glasgow and Strathkelvin) that even 'the largest of corporations' would be able to claim that they were consumers in relation to 'exceptional' contracts is false in view of the Court of Justice's jurisprudence, according to which legal persons cannot be consumers.

[109] See Joined Cases C-541/99 & C-542/99 *Cape Snc* [2001] ECR I-9049, 9055 (paras 25–6) (Mischo AG).

[110] In view of the ruling in Case C-361/89 *Di Pinto* [1991] ECR I-1189, the cases of *Chris Hart* (Business Sales) Ltd v Niven 1992 SLT (Sh Ct) 53 (Sheriff Court, Glasgow and Strathkelvin) and *BJ Mann (Advertising) Ltd v Ace Welding & Fabrications Ltd* 1994 SCLR 763 (Sheriff Principal) were wrongly decided.

[111] 2002 SLT (Sh Ct) 33 (Sheriff Court, Glasgow and Strathkelvin).

company director. The court held that, even though the defendant was not in the business of buying legal services, the contract for services was not a protected consumer contract; the purpose of the contract between the parties was to further the defendant's business interests. Similarly, in *Prostar Management Ltd v Twaddle*[112] it was held that a management agreement between a company and a professional footballer under the terms of which the company undertook to act on the footballer's behalf in relation to the negotiation and/or management of any business relating to his football career was not a protected consumer contract, notwithstanding the fact that the contract was not directly connected with playing football.

Secondary trades and professions

Although article 15 of the Brussels I Regulation refers to the consumer's 'trade or profession' in the singular, it is perfectly possible for a person to carry out more than one trade or profession. If the purpose of a contract is within A's commercial or professional activities, Section 4 cannot apply and the fact that the contract relates to a secondary activity, rather than A's principal trade or profession is irrelevant. In many situations, it is perfectly obvious that someone is carrying on two types of business activity. So, where A not only practices as a veterinary surgeon but also owns a stud farm, a contract whose purpose is related to either type of commercial activity is excluded from the scope of Section 4. **3.54**

There are, however, circumstances where it may be difficult to draw the dividing line between someone who runs two businesses, on the one hand, and someone who has one trade or profession and a hobby which has the potential to generate income, on the other. X, a second-hand car dealer, obviously carries on a trade; Y, an accountant, whose hobby is collecting classic cars and who, in the course of pursuing his hobby, occasionally sells a classic car at a profit does not. If X contracts to sell a second-hand car to Y, Y concludes the contract for a purpose outside his trade or profession and the contract falls within the scope of Section 4. Nevertheless, if Y buys and sells classic cars with a sufficient degree of regularity, there comes a point at which, although Y's principal economic activity is his professional work as an accountant, it is proper to regard his buying and selling of classic cars as a secondary trade. **3.55**

The same kind of demarcation issues can arise in the financial sector. If X, a restaurant owner, invests in a unit trust or in futures and options deals, there is no reason to think that X is acting in the context of a trade **3.56**

[112] 2003 SLT (Sh Ct) 11 (Sheriff Court, Glasgow and Strathkelvin).

or profession.[113] However, in a case where Y, using his own money, makes his living solely through trading stocks and shares or commodity futures, individual trading contracts entered into by Y cannot be classified as consumer contracts. Somewhere between these two extremes a dividing line has to be drawn.

3.57 The nature of the problem is revealed by *Standard Bank London Ltd v Apostolakis*, a case which came before the courts in both England[114] and Greece.[115] The dispute arose out of foreign exchange agreements concluded between the claimant, the English subsidiary of a South African bank, and the defendants, a wealthy married couple domiciled in Greece: the husband was a civil engineer; the wife was a lawyer. One of the questions which the courts had to decide was whether the agreements between the parties were protected consumer contracts for the purposes of what is now article 15 of the Brussels I Regulation. In the English proceedings, Longmore J concluded that, notwithstanding the very large sums invested by the defendants in the scheme (more than $1 million), the umbrella agreements and the individual transactions concluded under those agreements were consumer contracts—as the defendants were acting outside their trade or profession: 'It is certainly not part of a person's trade as a civil engineer or a lawyer to enter into foreign exchange contracts.'[116] Furthermore, the defendants were not 'engaging in the trade of foreign exchange contracts as such' as they 'were not trading in foreign exchange contracts in the sense that a bank or dealer can be said to trade'.[117] Longmore J's view was that the defendants were using their money 'in a way which they hoped would be profitable but merely to use money in a way one hopes would be profitable is not enough . . . to be engaging in trade'.[118] In effect, Longmore J thought that the defendants were simply investing (in the hope of making a profit) and rejected the idea that the defendants' involvement in foreign exchange contracts was sufficiently extensive to give rise to the conclusion that they were engaging in a secondary trade or profession.

3.58 The Greek court's analysis was coloured by the fact that Greek law (like the laws of many civil law countries and unlike English law) draws a distinction between traders, on the one hand, and non-traders, on the other. The reason for this distinction is relevant for both substantive and

[113] See *Re Futures Transactions* [1998] ILPr 327 (Court of Appeal, Düsseldorf).
[114] [2000] ILPr 766.
[115] [2003] ILPr 499 (Multi-Member First Instance Court, Athens).
[116] [2000] ILPr 766, 771 (at [15]).
[117] [2000] ILPr 766, 771 (at [15]).
[118] [2000] ILPr 766, 771 (at [15]).

procedural law.[119] From the perspective of Greek law, the fact that the defendants repeatedly carried out 'objectively commercial acts [ie, the sale and purchase of foreign exchange for the purpose of profiting] reaching tens or hundreds of millions of drachmas each time, gave them, . . . irrespective of any other primary professional activity, the additional capacity of traders'.[120] Once the Greek court had decided that the defendants were to be regarded as traders under Greek domestic law, it was a short step to the conclusion that the foreign currency agreements were not concluded for a purpose which could be regarded as outside the defendants' trade or profession and were, therefore, not consumer contracts.

Which of these conflicting views is correct? In terms of analysis, there are certain question marks over the decision of the Greek court. Whether a contract is a consumer contract or not is a question of EC law (rather than the domestic law of any of the member states).[121] So, the fact that the defendants were regarded as traders under Greek domestic law cannot be conclusive on the question whether the agreements were consumer contracts for the purposes of Section 4. Having said that, the decision of the Greek court does highlight an issue to which the High Court could have given more attention. It must be correct that there are circumstances in which a person can be regarded as carrying out more than one trade or profession. Accordingly, the fact that it is not part of a civil engineer's (or lawyer's) profession to conclude foreign currency transactions does not necessarily mean that the defendants' agreements with the claimant were consumer contracts. Moreover, the fact that the defendants were not trading as a bank or dealer trades does not necessarily mean that they were not trading. A classic car enthusiast does not trade in used cars as a second-hand car dealer trades, but if the enthusiast's buying and selling activities are sufficiently extensive, it is reasonable to conclude that the enthusiast is carrying on a secondary trade. **3.59**

Even if the Greek court was right to consider the possibility that the defendants were carrying on a secondary trade or profession, the question **3.60**

[119] For example, under French law, disputes arising out of contracts concluded by traders (*commerçants*) are referred to the commercial court (*tribunal commercial*), whereas litigation in respect of contracts not involving traders takes place in the ordinary civil courts (*tribunaux d'instance* and *tribunaux de grande instance*); similarly, the rules on insolvency which apply to traders are different from those which apply to non-traders. And so on. See J Bell, S Boyron, and S Whittaker (1998: ch 11).

[120] [2003] ILPr 499, 507 (at [22]).

[121] See, eg, Case C-89/91 *Shearson Lehman Hutton* [1993] ECR I-139, 187 (para 13); Case C-269/95 *Benincasa* [1997] ECR I-3767, 3794 (para 12); Case C-27/02 *Engler* [2005] ECR I-481, 513 (para 33).

which its decision does not satisfactorily resolve is how to determine when a person's economic activity counts as a trade or profession for the purposes of Section 4 even though it is not that person's principal business. Since the answer has to depend on the quality and quantity of the economic activity in question, it is difficult to see how, if the issue were ever to be referred to the Court of Justice, the Court would be able to give clear guidance to national courts.[122]

Mixed purposes

3.61 What is the position where goods are purchased partly for use in connection with a business and partly for domestic or private use? This question was considered by the Court of Justice in *Gruber*,[123] a reference from the Austrian Supreme Court. The claimant, an Austrian farmer, decided to replace the roof tiles on his farm building and purchased a quantity of tiles from the German defendant. About 60 per cent of the floor space of the farm building was used by the claimant as his home; the remainder was given over to agricultural use. When disputes arose under the contract the claimant started proceedings in Austria. The defendant contested jurisdiction on the basis that the contract was not a protected consumer contract and, therefore, the claimant was not entitled to rely on what is now article 16(1) of the Brussels I Regulation to bring proceedings in his home forum. One of the claimant's arguments was that, since the farm building was used principally for domestic rather than farming purposes, the contract should be regarded as a consumer contract.

3.62 Although some commentators, relying on a passage in the Giuliano-Lagarde Report (discussing article 5 of the Rome Convention),[124] had taken the view that Section 4 applies in cases when the main purpose of the contract lies outside the purchaser's trade or profession,[125] neither the Advocate General nor the Court of Justice was prepared to accept the defendant's argument. As Advocate General Jacobs noted, it is the contract as a whole which must be classified: 'There is in fact . . . no such thing as a "mixed contract", there are only consumer contracts and other contracts.'[126] This proposition follows logically from the fact that the policy of

[122] As the dividing line is a question of European law, questions of national law (such as whether an individual is liable to pay income tax on the profits of a secondary economic activity) cannot be decisive.

[123] Case C-464/01 [2005] ECR I-439. See E Gambaro and N Landi (2006).

[124] [1980] OJ C282/23.

[125] M Foss and LA Bygrave (2000: 107). See also K Hertz (1998: 195); C Wild, S Weinstein, and C Riefa (2005: 14).

[126] Case C-464/01 [2005] ECR I-439, 472–3 (para 35).

Section 4 is to protect contracting parties who are deemed to be economically weaker than the other party to the contract; a buyer of goods cannot simultaneously be in a weaker position vis-à-vis the seller in so far as the contract relates to goods intended for domestic purposes but on an equal footing with the seller as regards the remainder. If a contract is partly for trade or professional purposes, the buyer cannot be entitled to the protection afforded to consumers because he is deemed to be on an equal footing with the seller and this conclusion cannot be undermined by the fact that the contract also serves a private purpose—whether it is the trade purpose or the private purpose which is the more significant.[127] Accordingly, arguments based on policy point towards contracts for a dual purpose being excluded from Section 4—even if the private purpose is predominant.[128] Textual analysis of the relevant provision points in the same direction. The definition of a consumer contract adopts a negative turn of phrase ('for a purpose . . . outside [a person's] trade or profession');[129] a contract which is partly for trade purposes and partly for private or domestic purposes does not satisfy this definition as the contract is (partly) concluded for a purpose which is not outside that person's trade or profession.

There may, however, be an exception to this general approach. If, as regards a contract for mixed purposes, the trade or professional purpose is negligible or *de minimis*, the contract should be classified as a consumer contract.[130] The burden of proof to show that the business purpose is negligible is on the party who claims that a contract for mixed purposes should be classified as a consumer contract.[131] **3.63**

The consumer as party to the litigation

The terms of Section 4 make it clear that, at the time of the conclusion of the contract, one of the parties must be a consumer. It is also implicit that one of the parties to the litigation must be a consumer in order for Section 4 to apply;[132] it is provided that '[a] consumer may bring proceedings' in certain courts[133] and that 'proceedings may be brought against a consumer' in a particular forum.[134] In view of the fact that the purpose of Section 4 is 'to protect the consumer as the party deemed to be economically **3.64**

[127] Case C-464/01 *Gruber* [2005] ECR I-439, 450 (para 41) (Jacobs AG).
[128] Case C-464/01 *Gruber* [2005] ECR I-439, 474 (para 42).
[129] Case C-464/01 *Gruber* [2005] ECR I-439, 475 (para 43).
[130] Case C-464/01 *Gruber* [2005] ECR I-439, 474 (para 41).
[131] Case C-464/01 *Gruber* [2005] ECR I-ECR 439, 475 (para 46).
[132] See Case C-89/91 *Shearson Lehman Hutton* [1993] ECR I-139, 167 (para 26) (Darmon AG).
[133] Brussels I Regulation, art 16(1).
[134] Brussels I Regulation, art 16(2).

weaker and less experienced in legal matters than the other party',[135] it would be strange if a commercial undertaking were able to rely on the consumer contract provisions.

3.65 *Shearson Lehman Hutton*[136] concerned litigation arising out of an agency contract under the terms of which a German investor had instructed the defendant brokers to carry out currency, security, and commodity futures transactions. After the investor had lost nearly all of his investments, he assigned his claims against the defendant to the plaintiff, a German trust company. The plaintiff started proceedings against the defendant in Germany and a question arose whether the plaintiff, as assignee of claims from a consumer, could rely on the jurisdiction rules relating to consumer contracts. The Court of Justice had no hesitation in concluding that 'a plaintiff who is acting in pursuance of his trade or professional activity and who is not, therefore, himself a consumer party . . . may not enjoy the benefit of the rules of special jurisdiction . . . concerning consumer contracts'.[137]

3.66 It is not clear whether the position would be the same if the claimant, although not an original party to the contract, was not acting in the course of trade or professional activity (where, for example, the litigant had, on the consumer's death, succeeded to his rights under the contract). In terms of policy, there is a strong argument for saying that Section 4 ought to apply in these circumstances. Where, for example, the successor is the original consumer's widow, the successor is no less deserving of the protection of Section 4 than the original contracting party. However, the opinion of the Advocate General in *Shearson Lehman Hutton* suggests the opposite conclusion: the special jurisdiction rules relating to consumer contracts can be invoked 'only by a consumer in relation to a contract which he himself concluded'.[138] Of course, this statement was made in the context of a case in which the party seeking to rely on the consumer contract rules was a company bringing legal proceedings within the ambit of its corporate objects. Nevertheless, later in his opinion the Advocate General repeated the view that 'an initiator of legal proceedings who is not himself a party to [a consumer contract] is not a consumer'[139] and there is nothing in the rest of the opinion to suggest that this principle is limited to the type of factual scenario which arose in *Shearson Lehman Hutton*.

[135] Case C-89/91 *Shearson Lehman Hutton* [1993] ECR I-139, 187 (para 18).
[136] Case C-89/91 [1993] ECR I-139.
[137] Case C-89/91 [1993] ECR I-139, 189 (para 24).
[138] Case C-89/91 [1993] ECR I-139, 168 (para 28).
[139] Case C-89/91 [1993] ECR I-139, 169 (para 35).

'Reverse' consumer contracts

The paradigm consumer contract is where a consumer buys goods or services from a supplier. A question arises whether the provisions of Section 4 apply to a 'reverse' consumer contract—where it is the consumer, rather than the supplier, who is undertaking the characteristic performance of the contract. While such situations are less frequent than the paradigm case, they arise not infrequently. Where, for example, a consumer sells his second-hand car to a car dealer, the basic conditions of a consumer contract are met as the consumer is acting for a purpose which is outside his trade or profession. Although this issue has not been directly addressed in the jurisprudence of the Court of Justice, it seems reasonably clear that 'reverse' consumer contracts are outside the scope of Section 4. In *Bertrand* the Court of Justice stated that the purpose of Section 4 required the consumer contract provisions to be limited to cases involving parties who are 'private, final consumers'.[140] The Court's choice of words strongly suggests that Section 4 is restricted to cases where the consumer is the buyer of goods or services, rather than the seller. It is worth noting, however, that some commentators take the opposite view.[141] **3.67**

The Other Party ('The Supplier')

Although the question is not completely free from doubt, it seems that Section 4 does not apply to c2c contracts (for example, where a consumer sells second-hand goods to another individual who is acting outside his trade or profession). Various reasons support this interpretation. **3.68**

First, the Brussels I Regulation expressly provides that a contract is outside article 15(1)(c) unless the contract falls within the scope of the supplier's 'commercial or professional activities'.[142] It is reasonable to suppose that the same condition applies to all categories of consumer contract. Secondly, the jurisprudence of the Court of Justice indicates that Section 4 applies only to b2c contracts (and not c2c contracts). For example, it is implicit in *Bertrand*[143] that Section 4 is limited to cases where one party is a 'final private consumer' and the other is engaged 'in trade or professional activities'. Later cases have been more explicit. In *Gruber* the Court of Justice refers to a consumer being economically weaker and less experienced than 'the other, commercial, party to the contract'.[144] Thirdly, the **3.69**

140 Case 140/77 *Bertrand* [1978] 1431, 1446 (para 21).
141 See, eg, P Kaye (1997: 829); K Hertz (1998: 206).
142 Art 15(1)(c).
143 Case 150/77 [1978] ECR 1431, 1446 (para 21).
144 Case C-464/01 [2005] ECR I-439, 472 (para 34).

Giuliano-Lagarde Report (on the Rome Convention of 1980) indicates that the majority view was that the consumer contract provisions apply only if the party other than the consumer is acting in the course of his trade or profession.[145] Fourthly, most commentators argue that both the policy and drafting of Section 4 strongly suggest that the consumer contract provisions do not apply to c2c contracts.[146]

Economic Inequality

3.70 One of the key reasons for treating consumer contracts differently from other contracts is the fact that consumer contracts typically display economic inequality between the contracting parties. However, in order for a contract to fall within the scope of Section 4, it is not necessary for the consumer to show that he actually was economically weaker than the supplier. By the same token, the fact that there is a significant inequality between two parties to a commercial contract does not turn the contract into a consumer contract for the purposes of Section 4: 'Contracting parties are not normally in a position of equality in the area of business relationships, but that does not mean that contracts of that kind, including standard-form contracts, entered into by businessmen benefit from the [rules in Section 4].'[147]

The *Benincasa* Formula: 'satisfying an individual's own needs in terms of private consumption'

3.71 As already noted, the concept of 'consumer contract' under the Brussels I Regulation requires the contract to have been concluded by a person for a purpose which can be regarded as being outside his trade or profession.[148] This is an 'exclusive definition' as opposed to an 'inclusive definition'.[149] Whereas an inclusive definition seeks to identify in a positive way the types of contract that qualify for consumer protection (such as the purchase of goods 'for personal, family or household use'), an exclusive definition identifies consumer contracts in a negative way (for example, by reference to the absence of a business purpose). Although, in purely textual terms, the Brussels I Regulation's definition of consumer contracts is exclusive in nature, it is not clear that *all* contracts which literally satisfy

145 [1980] OJ C282/23.
146 See, eg, P Kaye (1987: 830–1).
147 Case C-269/95 *Benincasa* [1997] ECR I-3767, 3781 (para 51) (Ruiz-Jarabo Colomer AG).
148 Brussels I Regulation, art 15(1).
149 See P Nygh (1999: 146).

the negative definition are to be regarded as consumer contracts for the purposes of Section 4. This uncertainty is, to a large extent, caused by a passage in the Court of Justice's judgment in *Benincasa* ('the *Benincasa* formula'), in which the Court said that:

> only contracts concluded for the purpose of satisfying an individual's own needs in terms of private consumption come under the provisions designed to protect the consumer as the party deemed to be the weaker party economically.[150]

In the context of *Benincasa* the significance of this statement was perfectly clear. In that case, the defendant was an Italian company which promoted a chain of franchise shops specializing in the sale of dental hygiene products. The defendant concluded a franchise agreement with the plaintiff (who was resident in Munich), under the terms of which the latter was to open and operate a shop in Germany. After making various payments due under the franchise agreement, the plaintiff started proceedings in Munich for a declaration that the franchise agreement was void and for repayment of the sums paid. When the defendant contested the German court's jurisdiction (on the basis of a contractual jurisdiction clause in favour of the Italian courts), the plaintiff claimed that, as the contract was a protected consumer contract, the jurisdiction clause was of no effect and he was entitled to sue the defendant in the courts of his domicile. **3.72**

As, when the contract was concluded, the plaintiff was not carrying out a trade or profession, it could be argued that the contract was concluded for a purpose which was outside his trade or profession. However, the contract was for the purpose of an *anticipated* business. So, the context of the *Benincasa* formula was the Court of Justice's attempt to draw a clear dividing line between business contracts (whether the business is existing or in the future) and contracts with no business purpose at all. The use of the phrase 'for the purpose of satisfying an individual's own needs in terms of private consumption' made it clear that a contract for the purpose of trade or professional activity cannot be classified as a consumer contract even if the trade or professional activity 'is only planned for the future'.[151] **3.73**

But, what is the significance of the *Benincasa* formula in contexts other than the one which arose in that particular case? There would appear to be three possible answers to this question and determining which answer is the correct one is not entirely straightforward. In practice, the first two are substantively the same; only the third answer produces different outcomes. **3.74**

[150] Case C-269/95 [1997] ECR I-3767, 3795 (para 17).
[151] Case C-269/95 [1997] ECR I-3767, 3795 (para 17).

3.75 The first possibility is that the *Benincasa* formula was unnecessary for the decision and is an unhelpful gloss on the words of the relevant provision which refers only to contracts concluded 'for a purpose which can be regarded as outside [the consumer's] trade or profession'. This view has been favoured by the English courts. In *Standard Bank London Ltd v Apostolakis*[152] Longmore J did not think that 'the European Court of Justice can have intended the words "for the purpose of satisfying an individual's own needs in terms of private consumption" as a substitute for the words of . . . the Brussels Convention'.[153] According to this view, if the contract was concluded for a purpose outside that person's trade or profession, the contract is a consumer contract—and the question whether the contract was 'concluded for the purpose of satisfying an individual's own needs in terms of private consumption' does not have to be addressed as a separate issue.

3.76 The second way of approaching the *Benincasa* formula is to accept that the passage is an authoritative interpretation of the relevant provision, but that it does not require the idea of 'needs in terms of private consumption' to be interpreted too narrowly.[154] In *Standard Bank London Ltd v Apostolakis*,[155] a case involving foreign exchange contracts, Longmore J considered that, even if the *Benincasa* formula had to be applied literally, the purpose of the foreign exchange agreements satisfied the test. According to Longmore J, the purpose of the agreement was to satisfy the defendants' needs—in the sense that the agreement was an appropriate use for their income—and those needs were needs in terms of private consumption: 'Consumption cannot be taken as literally consumed so as to be destroyed but rather consumed in the sense that a consumer consumes, viz he uses or enjoys the relevant product.'[156]

3.77 The third way of approaching the *Benincasa* formula is to see it as an interpretation which has the effect of narrowing the range of contracts to which Section 4 applies—by turning the exclusive definition of consumer contract in article 15 of the Brussels I Regulation into an inclusive definition (which requires a positive condition to be satisfied). This third approach was taken by the Greek court in *Standard Bank of London v Apostolakis*;[157] the court concluded, contrary to the view taken by Longmore J in the related English proceedings, that the foreign exchange agreements were

152 [2000] ILPr 766.
153 [2000] ILPr 766, 773 (at [20]).
154 See K Hertz (1998: 195).
155 [2000] ILPr 766.
156 [2000] ILPr 766, 773 (at [21]).
157 [2003] ILPr 499 (Multi-Member First Instance Court, Athens).

not consumer contracts.[158] One of the strands in the Greek court's decision was the observation that the contracts did not aim at 'satisfying . . . needs in terms of consumption'.[159] According to the Greek court, a foreign exchange agreement is excluded from Section 4 by the *Benincasa* formula: 'It is clear that the increase of one's wealth and indeed by assuming considerable entrepreneurial risks without investing one's own funds does not constitute a "consumption need", since it does not aim at satisfying any natural or intellectual demand of human life.'[160] In reaching this conclusion, the Greek court suggested that Longmore J's contrary decision was wrong and had failed to apply the *Benincasa* formula properly.[161]

Both in terms of policy and authority the conclusion of the Greek court is **3.78** hard to support. The Greek court's judgment was based partly on the fact that the investors' experience of investment contracts was such that they were 'not in need of the protection afforded to inexperienced and ignorant consumers'.[162] However, according to the jurisprudence of the Court of Justice, the application of Section 4 is based on the presumed inequality between a consumer and a supplier, rather than proof of actual inequality between the parties. The fact that, in a particular contractual situation, a consumer may not be in need of legal protection does not mean that the contract falls outside the scope of Section 4. In *Mietz* Advocate General Léger considered that, in a case where a businessman (who runs a construction business and trades in construction materials) purchases a boat for DM 250,000,[163] the contract is a consumer contract for the purpose of Section 4 if the purpose of the acquisition is 'totally separate from the business activity of the [buyer]'.[164] The fact that the subject-matter of the contract is a valuable, luxury item and that the buyer has business experience are irrelevant considerations.[165]

[158] This had the result that, although the English court considered that the Greek court had jurisdiction (on the basis that the consumer-defendants were domiciled in Greece), the Greek court declined jurisdiction (on the basis that the jurisdiction clause in favour of the English courts was binding). To the bank, this situation 'must have seemed like the work of Kafka': A Briggs (2006: 128). The most logical way of avoiding this type of impasse would be for it to be accepted that the decision of the first court to render judgment on the question of its jurisdiction creates an issue estoppel (binding on all other member state courts) on the question whether or not the contract is a protected consumer contract for the purposes of Section 4.

[159] [2003] ILPr 499, 506 (para 19).

[160] [2003] ILPr 499, 507 (para 24).

[161] [2003] ILPr 499, 509 (para 27).

[162] [2003] ILPr 499, 506 (para 18).

[163] The equivalent of around £85,000.

[164] Case C-99/96 [1999] ECR I-2277, 2291 (para 42).

[165] There are some, however, who think that the inclusion of high-value transactions within the scope of Section 4 means that protection is extended too widely: 'It could . . . be questioned

3.79 Although the Court of Justice has not ruled specifically on whether investment contracts fall within Section 4, it is generally accepted that they may. As long as an individual does not enter investment contracts on such a regular or extensive basis that he can be regarded as carrying on a business (albeit not necessarily his principal business), investment contracts should be regarded as contracts concluded both for a purpose outside the consumer's trade or profession and for the purpose of satisfying the individual's own needs in terms of private consumption.[166] Notwithstanding the Greek court's decision in *Apostolakis*, the dominant view of national courts seems to be that investment contracts are capable of being consumer contracts for the purposes of Section 4.[167] Furthermore, in both *Shearson Lehman Hutton*[168] and *Brenner and Noller*[169] the German courts made a reference on the question whether Section 4 applies to 'contracts on a commission basis for the purpose of carrying out commodity futures transactions'. In both cases, the Court of Justice decided that it was not necessary for it to provide an answer to this question. However, in *Shearson Lehman Hutton* Advocate General Darmon took the view that an agency contract concerning futures dealings is capable of being a consumer contract for the purposes of Section 4[170] and the Advocate General repeated this opinion in *Brenner and Noller*.[171] Notwithstanding the Court of Justice's side-stepping of the issue, in *Standard Bank of London v Apostolakis* the Greek court acknowledged that 'it can be convincingly established from the relevant case law of the European Court of Justice that the conclusion of a banking or investment transaction does not *ab initio* preclude the application of Art 13 of the Brussels Convention'.[172] Furthermore, the Greek court drew attention to '[a] number of investment transactions (eg, unit trusts, investments in the stock exchange)' which 'are addressed to the general public' and seemed to accept that contracts of this type would normally be consumer contracts.[173]

3.80 There appears, therefore, to be an inconsistency in the Greek court's judgment. If the foreign exchange contracts concluded by the defendants

whether someone who buys something at a price of DEM 250,000 for recreational use needs the special protection of the rules on jurisdiction over consumer contracts': German Federal Supreme Court in Case C-99/96 *Mietz* [1999] ECR I-2277, 2291 n 29 (cited by Léger AG).

166 See K Hertz (1998: 195).
167 See K Hertz (1998: 195 n 11).
168 Case C-89/91 [1993] ECR I-139.
169 Case C-318/93 [1994] ECR I-4275.
170 Case C-89/91 [1993] ECR I-139, 175 (para 79).
171 Case C-318/93 [1994] ECR I-4275, 4283 (para 29).
172 [2003] ILPr 499, 505–6 (para 15).
173 [2003] ILPr 499, 506 (para 16).

in *Standard Bank of London v Apostolakis* did not satisfy the *Benincasa* formula (because the purpose of such transactions was not to satisfy 'any natural or intellectual demand of human life'), it is not clear how any investment contract which is designed to make a profit but involves a risk of making a loss can be said to do so; in each case, the purpose of the investment contract is the same—to make a profit. In view of the fact that the predominant view of commentators and the courts of other member states[174] is that investment contracts are not excluded from the scope of Section 4, it is difficult to see how the Greek court's view of the significance of the *Benincasa* can be accepted.[175]

Consumer Contracts Excluded from Section 4

Contracts of transport

It is expressly provided that Section 4 does not apply to contracts of transport.[176] However, article 15(3) of the Brussels I Regulation goes on to say that Section 4 does apply to 'a contract which, for an inclusive price, provides a combination of travel and accommodation'. The rationale for excluding contracts of transport from the consumer contract provisions seems to be that such contracts are covered by other international conventions.[177] These conventions do not, however, apply to package holiday contracts; so, it is reasonable for package holiday contracts to come within Section 4. This conclusion is supported by the fact that the European Community has legislated in the field of package holidays.[178] **3.81**

Contracts relating to immovable property

Article 22(1)(a) of the Brussels I Regulation provides that 'in proceedings which have as their object rights *in rem* in immovable property . . ., the courts of the Member State in which the property is situated' shall have 'exclusive jurisdiction, regardless of domicile'. The same rule applies to **3.82**

[174] See, eg, *Re Futures Transactions* [1998] ILPr 327 (Court of Appeal, Düsseldorf). See also A Vahrenwald (1994).

[175] This does not necessarily mean that the conclusion of the Greek court—that the foreign exchange transactions were not consumer contracts—is wrong; if the defendants' investment activities constituted a secondary trade, the foreign exchange transactions were not concluded for a purpose outside the defendants' trade or profession.

[176] Brussels I Regulation, art 15(3).

[177] Because of the existence of such conventions, the effect of which is, in any event preserved by art 71 of the Brussels I Regulation, the express exclusion of contracts of transport from Section 4 appears to be largely redundant.

[178] Directive on package travel, package holidays and package tours (Dir 90/314/EEC [1990] OJ L158/59).

'proceedings which have as their object . . . tenancies of immovable property'—though it is also provided that, in certain circumstances, alternative exclusive jurisdiction in respect of disputes arising from short-term lettings is conferred on the member state in which the defendant is domiciled.[179] If article 22(1) applies, it takes precedence over all other jurisdictional bases in the Regulation.

The purchase of houses and apartments

3.83 In *Reichert v Dresdner Bank*[180] the Court of Justice ruled that the phrase 'proceedings which have as their object rights *in rem* in immovable property' must be given an autonomous interpretation[181] and decided that the exclusive jurisdiction rule covers only proceedings which:

> seek to determine the extent, content, ownership or possession of immovable property or the existence of other rights *in rem* therein and to provide the holders of those rights with the protection of the powers which attach to their interest.[182]

3.84 It follows from this approach that purely contractual disputes (rather than disputes over ownership) fall outside the scope of article 22(1). This is consistent with the Schlosser Report, according to which claims based on contracts for the transfer of ownership or other rights *in rem* affecting immovable property do not fall within the exclusive jurisdiction rules.[183] This analysis was confirmed in *Gaillard v Chekili*:[184] the Court of Justice ruled that a claim for rescission of a contract for the sale of land and for consequential damages does not involve rights *in rem* for the purposes of what is now article 22(1) of the Brussels I Regulation. Accordingly, a contract for the sale of immovable property may constitute a consumer contract for the purposes of Section 4.

3.85 However, under the Brussels Convention, proceedings relating to contracts for the sale of immovable property or an interest in such property were largely excluded from Section 4. This follows from the fact that article 13 of the Convention (as amended) was drafted exclusively with contracts for the sale of goods or the supply of services in mind. Under the Regulation, however, article 15 (the provision which has replaced article 13 of the Convention) is not so limited. Assuming that the other conditions are satisfied, there is no reason why contracts for the sale of immovable property

179 Art 22(1)(b).
180 Case C-115/88 [1990] ECR I-27.
181 Case C-115/88 [1990] ECR I-27, 41 (para 8).
182 Case C-115/88 [1990] ECR I-27, 41–2 (para 11).
183 [1979] OJ C59/122 (para 172).
184 Case C-518/99 [2001] ECR I-2771.

and similar contracts (such as mortgages of immovable property) should not fall within the scope of article 15(1)(c), which refers to 'all other cases'—rather than 'any other contract for the supply of goods or a contract for the supply of services' (the phrase employed by article 13 of the Brussels Convention). So, in principle, a contract for the purchase of a holiday apartment is capable of being a consumer contract for the purposes of Section 4.[185] Similarly, it seems clear that, unless they constitute tenancies of immovable property, timeshare contracts fall within Section 4.[186]

Having said that, it should be noted that relatively few contracts for the sale of land will be protected consumer contracts within Section 4. First, most contracts for the sale of immovable property are private sales (c2c contracts) between two individuals, neither of whom is in the business of buying and selling land. Secondly, even as regards cross-border b2c contracts for the sale of land—such as where a consumer domiciled in member state A purchases a house from a property developer domiciled in member state B—the contract will be a protected consumer contract only if the supplier pursues commercial activities in member state A or directs such activities to that member state and the contract falls within the scope of such activities.[187] **3.86**

Tenancies of immovable property

The position in relation to tenancies of immovable property is potentially more problematical. In relation to disputes arising out of tenancies, exclusive jurisdiction is allocated by article 22(1)(a) of the Brussels I Regulation to the member state in which the immovable property is situated. As regards tenancies for temporary private use for a maximum period of six consecutive months, alternative exclusive jurisdiction is conferred on the member state in which the defendant is domiciled if the tenant is a natural person and the landlord and tenant are domiciled in the same member state.[188] The exclusive jurisdiction rule applies regardless of domicile and prevails over all other jurisdictional bases in the Regulation. In the consumer context, there are two issues to consider: first, timeshares; secondly, holiday contracts (such as package holidays). **3.87**

Timeshares

Timeshare contracts are on a spectrum; the degree to which the accommodation or the period of use is specified varies considerably. At one end of **3.88**

[185] Case C-361/89 *France v Di Pinto* [1991] ECR I-1189, 1203 (para 26) (Mischo AG).
[186] COM (99) 348, p 16.
[187] For further consideration of art 15(1)(c), see paras 3.115–3.118.
[188] Art 22(1)(b).

the spectrum, there are contracts which clearly take the form of a lease of immovable property. For example, the 'classical' timeshare contract might, for example, give the right to spend week 13 in apartment X in Resort A each year for 21 years. At the other end of the spectrum, there are timeshare contracts based on 'point clubs': different types of accommodation in different resorts are allocated a certain number of points; the consumer buys a number of points which can be used for booking accommodation etc. Between these two extremes there are forms of agreement which are less specific than a 'classical' timeshare, but more specific that a 'points club'. For example, a timeshare contract may leave the location of the apartment to be decided in the future and only specify the duration (such as one week) and the general timing (for instance, in the low season) and the category of accommodation (for example, a two-bedroom apartment in a specific type of resort). Furthermore, the legal form adopted varies from legal system to legal system. For example, in some member states (such as Italy, Spain, and Portugal) timeshare is regarded as a real property right (right *in rem*); in Greece, timeshare is regarded as a type of tenancy; under French law a timeshare is deemed a personal right (under the system of *société civile d'attribution*). In the United Kingdom and Ireland the dominant mode of holding is the 'trustee-club system';[189] membership of the club entitles the member to spend a number of weeks in the club's resorts. Such contracts do not take the form of a lease; they do not specify the apartment for which the buyer acquires a right of use (or even its location); for each of the weeks that the member has 'bought', the member has to make a booking.

3.89 In recent years, timeshares and analogous contracts have given rise to major problems for consumers. The market for timeshares and timeshare-like products is very significant; it is estimated that, throughout Europe, there are nearly 1.5 million households holding rights in timeshare resorts. However, recent figures indicate that growth in the market has slowed down considerably—partly because, as a result of predatory marketing practices and such like, consumers have a poor opinion of standards in the industry and negative attitudes towards timeshares.[190] In the 1990s the Timeshare Directive[191] attempted to tackle problems posed by aggressive marketing; the Directive confers certain rights on consumers—in particular, the right to withdraw from the contract within a cooling-off period. However, following the enactment of the Timeshare Directive, different

[189] See European Commission (June 2006: 9).

[190] European Commission (June 2006: 5).

[191] Dir 94/47/EC on the protection of purchasers . . . of a right to use immovable properties on a timeshare basis [1994] OJ L280/83.

types of contract designed to avoid the consumer protection provisions of the Directive were developed. In several EU member states, there is a significant market in products resembling timeshares (such as the 'holiday club membership contract').[192] The Directive does nothing to stem the problems surrounding the marketing of such holiday-based products.[193]

Between 2000 and 2004 the annual number of complaints concerning timeshare-type contracts that were handled by ECC-Net rose from 500 to 1,883.[194] However, these complaints do not give a full picture of the extent of the problem. The Spanish police authorities estimate that 50,000 tourists across Europe have been swindled by one of the fraudulent timeshare companies.[195] Although most of the problems in the 1990s and the first few years of the 2000s were generated by Spanish timeshares, there are indications that the same problems have spread to Greece, Portugal, Malta, and Cyprus.[196] ECC-Net[197] (and others[198]) recommended that the Timeshare Directive should be amended so that the full range of timeshare-type contracts would benefit from the Directive's consumer protection rules.[199] A consultation paper relating to a review of the Timeshare Directive was published in 2006[200] and the European Commission made a formal proposal for a new Directive in June 2007.[201] It is anticipated that a new directive may be enacted in 2008 or 2009. **3.90**

Although it may be tempting to try to find an interpretation of article 22(1)(a) which would provide a uniform jurisdictional solution to litigation arising out of timeshare contracts, the use of different legal forms in different European legal systems means that it would be very difficult to find an interpretation which would achieve uniformity in terms of the allocation of jurisdiction. The Court of Justice has not attempted to find a global solution; instead it has adopted a case-by-case approach to timeshare contracts. This first became evident in the context of the Doorstep Selling Directive.[202] In the *Travel-Vac* case[203] the primary question was **3.91**

192 ECC-Net (December 2002: 10).
193 See ECC-Net (December 2002).
194 See European Commission (June 2006: 12).
195 See ECC-Net (December 2002: 5).
196 European Commission (June 2006: 12).
197 ECC-Net (December 2002).
198 See, eg, European Consumer Law Group (November 2004a).
199 See also European Commission (June 2006: 22–3).
200 See European Commission (June 2006).
201 European Commission, COM (2007) 303.
202 Dir 85/577/EEC [1985] OJ L372/31.
203 Case C-423/97 [1999] ECR I-2195.

whether or not the Directive applied to a Spanish timeshare contract.[204] According to article 3(2)(a), the Directive does not apply to 'contracts for the construction, sale and rental of immovable property or contracts concerning other rights relating to immovable property'. Although, under the contract, the consumer acquired rights to use immovable property, the major part of the costs of the timeshare was for services. The Advocate General suggested that the contract had to be characterized as a whole[205] and that the contract was not excluded from the scope of the Directive. The Court of Justice agreed: the Directive applied to 'a contract relating to the acquisition of a right to use immovable property on a time-share basis and to the provision of services whose value is higher than that of the right to use the immovable property'.[206] Both the Advocate General and the Court emphasized that because, in different European legal systems, timeshare contracts take different legal forms, they were not concerned with timeshare contracts in general, but with the specific contract in that case.

3.92 The same case-by-case approach has been adopted in the context of the European jurisdictional system. In the *Klein* case[207] the claimants, a married couple domiciled in Germany, entered into a timeshare contract with the defendant, a company established in the Isle of Man. Under the terms of the contract, the claimants acquired the right to the use of an apartment of a specified type in a hotel complex in Greece for a specified week of each year for 40 years. However, it was a requirement that, in order to acquire this right to use the apartment, the claimants had also to enter a contract whereby they became members of a club. As members of the club, the claimants were also able to exchange holiday 'slots' for other times and for other apartments. The total price was DM 13,300. The greatest part of this sum represented the membership fee (DM 10,153); the fee for use of the apartment was DM 2,048 and there were small sums for maintenance (DM 317) and for membership of the organization which coordinated the exchange of holiday slots (DM 317). In fact, the claimants paid a deposit of DM 2,640 when the contract was signed and a further DM 13,300 (which represented an overpayment of DM 2,640). Subsequently, the claimants alleged that the contract was void and started proceedings in Germany for the refund of DM 15,490. The defendants challenged the German court's jurisdiction, arguing that the Greek courts had exclusive jurisdiction

[204] The contract was concluded before the implementation of the Timeshare Directive (Dir 94/47/EC on the protection of purchasers . . . of a right to use immovable properties on a timeshare basis [1994] OJ L280/83) into Spanish law.

[205] Case C-423/97 [1999] ECR I-2195, 2207 (para 29).

[206] Case C-423/97 [1999] ECR I-2195, 2226 (para 26).

[207] Case C-73/04 *Klein v Rhodos Management Ltd* [2006] ILPr 29.

because the dispute related to a tenancy of immovable property situated in Greece.

Although the UK government tried to encourage the Court of Justice to give a ruling on the question whether timeshares in general fall within the scope of what is now article 22(1) of the Brussels I Regulation, neither the Advocate General nor the Court of Justice attempted a formulation that would provide a general test for determining jurisdiction in relation to disputes arising out of timeshares. For Advocate General Geelhoed, a powerful reason for not attempting such a formulation is the fact that, as already noted, 'the content and legal nature of time-share arrangements vary greatly across Member States'.[208] Although the interpretation of the exclusive jurisdiction rule cannot depend on the way in which timeshare arrangements are characterized by national law, 'the differences in the legal nature of these arrangements between Member States are so substantial that an attempt to formulate a uniformly applicable rule would be artificial and counter-productive'.[209] **3.93**

According to the Advocate General, it is the substance of the contract (rather than its form) which should determine whether or not proceedings concern a tenancy of immovable property: **3.94**

> [I]t is not decisive that the time-share arrangement . . . took the form of participation in a 'club', that the title of the contract was 'Request for and Contract of Membership', and that, according to the terms of the contract, most of the contractual sum due was in the form of a 'membership fee' . . . . If it were otherwise, this would enable circumvention of [the exclusive jurisdiction rules], which would compromise the consistency of their application.[210]

In the Advocate General's view, 'the substance, and principal object, of the contract . . . was, albeit via membership of the [club], the right to use an apartment on a time-share basis.'[211] Given that the arrangement displayed sufficient characteristics of a lease of immovable property, the Advocate General's conclusion was that the dispute between the parties fell within the scope of the exclusive jurisdiction rule[212]—with the result that the Greek courts (rather than the German courts) had jurisdiction. **3.95**

[208] Case C-73/04 [2006] ILPr 29, 35 (para 20).

[209] Case C-73/04 [2006] ILPr 29, 36 (para 22) (Geelhoed AG).

[210] Case C-73/04 [2006] ILPr 29, 36 (para 25).

[211] Case C-73/04 [2006] ILPr 29, 37 (para 27).

[212] Case C-73/04 [2006] ILPr 29, 37–8 (paras 29–30). However, the Advocate General considered that the claim for return of the overpayment was outside the scope of the exclusive jurisdiction rule: Case C-73/04 [2006] ILPr 29, 39 (para 39).

3.96 The Court of Justice, however, did not accept the Advocate General's analysis. The Court emphasized that, in the context of disputes relating to immovable property, the purpose of the exclusive jurisdiction rule is to allocate jurisdiction to the courts which 'are the best placed, for reasons of proximity, to ascertain the facts satisfactorily, by carrying out checks, inquiries and expert assessments on the spot, and to apply the rules and practices which are generally those of the State in which the property is situated'.[213] However, the dispute in the *Klein* case—which concerned a claim for repayment of the whole of the amount paid by the claimants under the contract—was not within this objective. Whereas the Advocate General considered that the main substance of the contract was a right to use an apartment on a timeshare basis, the Court of Justice did not seek to look behind the form of the agreement. So, the Court, having noted that, under the contract, the membership fee constituted the major part of the total price and that the amount the claimants paid for the right to the use of an apartment was a small proportion of the overall payment, concluded that 'the value of the right to use the property is of only secondary economic importance, in the construction of the contract at issue, compared with the right to membership'.[214] Furthermore, the Court of Justice noted that, under the terms of the contract, the claimants did not acquire a right to the use of a specific apartment (as opposed to a right to the use of an apartment of a specified type). Accordingly, 'the link between the club membership contract . . . and the property to be actually used by the member is not sufficiently close to warrant classifying it as a tenancy'[215] for the purposes of the exclusive jurisdiction rule. The Court's final conclusion was that the exclusive jurisdiction rule 'does not apply to a club membership contract which, in return for a membership fee which represents the major part of the total price, allows members to acquire a right to use on a time-share basis immovable property of a specified type in a specified location and provides for the affiliation of members to a service which enables them to exchange their right of use'.[216]

3.97 On the one hand, from the perspective of consumer protection, the Court of Justice's solution is more beneficial than the approach adopted by the Advocate General. If timeshare contracts are classified as 'tenancies of immovable property' for the purposes of article 22(1) of the Brussels I Regulation, the practical problems for a consumer who wishes to pursue litigation against a foreign holiday company will normally be overwhelming.

[213] Case C-73/04 [2006] ILPr 29, 42 (para 16).
[214] Case C-73/04 [2006] ILPr 29, 43 (para 20).
[215] Case C-73/04 [2006] ILPr 29, 43 (para 26).
[216] Case C-73/04 [2006] ILPr 29, 43–4 (para 28).

The claimants in *Klein* would have been less prepared to contemplate proceedings in Greece (where the property was located) than in Germany (where they were domiciled). On the other hand, the approach of the Court of Justice is not without its problems—as it fails to give clear guidance for future cases. In its conclusion the Court of Justice refers to a number of the elements of the contract which was the subject-matter of the proceedings: (i) the membership fee was the major part of the total price: (ii) the right of use related to an immovable property of a particular type (rather than specific property); and (iii) membership permitted holiday slots to be exchanged. What would have been the position if one or more of these characteristics were not present? The judgment of the Court of Justice does not provide a clear answer. It is, however, implicit in the approach taken by the Court of Justice that there are types of timeshare contract which provide for a close link between the consumer's right of use and a specific apartment which would have to be classified as 'tenancies of immovable property' for the purposes of article 22(1)(a). Disputes arising out of such contracts would be within the exclusive jurisdiction of the member state in which the immovable property is situated.

An open-textured approach to timeshare contracts—which turns not only **3.98** on the relative value of the right to use the property as against the services but also the specific characteristics of the contract in question—is rather unsatisfactory. One of the few areas in which cross-border consumer litigation is a serious possibility is in the field of timeshare contracts—because the amount of money at stake is invariably much higher than in the vast majority of consumer contracts. In many ways, it would be much more satisfactory if the Court of Justice were to lay down a simple rule that timeshare contracts are outside the scope of article 22(1) and are capable of being protected consumer contracts for the purposes of article 15(1)(c). This would give consumers the benefit of the consumer jurisdiction rules and would mean that there would be little incentive for further litigation concerning the dividing line between article 22 and Section 4 in the timeshare context.

Package holidays

There are also potential problems concerning the dividing line between **3.99** tenancies of immovable property (to which article 22(1) of the Brussels I Regulation applies) and package holiday contracts (within the scope of Section 4). This dividing line is not always easy to draw in practice.[217] If the contract is regarded as a tenancy, it will be unusual for the tenant to be able bring proceedings in his home forum; if the contract is truly international,

[217] B Dahl (1977: 107).

the landlord will not normally be domiciled in the same member state as the tenant and the conditions of article 22(1)(b) will not be satisfied. If, on the other hand, the contract is classified as a contract for a package holiday—and it satisfies the criteria of article 15(1)(c) of the Brussels I Regulation—a consumer would be able to ensure that any legal proceedings took place in his home forum.

3.100 It is clear that a contract for the renting of a holiday home is a tenancy of immovable property for the purposes of article 22(1)[218] and cannot be a consumer contract within Section 4.[219] Conversely, 'a contract which, for an inclusive price, provides for a combination of travel and accommodation'[220] is capable of being a protected consumer contract. The Court of Justice has ruled that, where proceedings relate to a holiday contract which includes not only accommodation, but also other services, such as information and advice, the reservation of transport, reception on arrival, and insurance against cancellation, the object of such proceedings is not a tenancy of immovable property for the purposes of article 22(1).[221] Similarly, even in cases involving the renting of a holiday home, article 22(1) does not apply to proceedings which are only indirectly related to the use of the property let, such as those concerning the loss of holiday enjoyment and travel expenses.[222] In cases not covered by article 22(1), the contract is capable of being a consumer contract within the scope of Section 4.

3.101 It is worth noting that, in the UK context, the fact that a holidaymaker can make use of the consumer contract provisions as regards a dispute arising from a package holiday contract is normally of little practical significance. Although contracts for package holidays are one of the types of consumer contract which generates disputes, most English holidaymakers purchase their holidays from local travel agents which are members of the Association of British Travel Agents (*ABTA*). *ABTA* promotes a code of practice which makes provision for disputes between consumers and *ABTA* members to be resolved through ADR.[223] So, from the perspective

[218] Case 241/83 *Rösler* [1985] ECR 99.
[219] C Joustra (1992: 432).
[220] Art 15(4).
[221] Case C-280/90 *Hacker* [1992] ECR I-1111.
[222] Case 241/83 *Rösler* [1985] ECR 99.
[223] See ch 11. Of course, not all disputes between English holidaymakers and travel companies which are members of *ABTA* are referred to *ABTA* arbitration: see, eg, *Watson v First Choice Holidays and Flights Ltd* [2001] 2 Lloyd's Rep 339. As between the holidaymaker and the travel company no significant jurisdictional issues arise—as both parties are domiciled in England; in *Watson* the jurisdictional question was whether a Spanish co-defendant could be joined to the English proceedings.

of the English courts, the consumer contract provisions would generally only be relevant where an English consumer, having purchased a package holiday from a travel company domiciled in another member state, wishes to bring proceedings against that company in England. With the increased availability (via the Internet) of holidays from foreign travel companies, this scenario may well be on the increase.

Credit agreements

There are potential problems concerning the dividing line between article 22 and Section 4 in the field of credit agreements. In principle, a consumer credit agreement is a consumer contract which may fall within the scope of Section 4. However, where a credit agreement forms part of a secured transaction (where, for example, a loan to purchase a house is secured by a charge over the house), a demarcation problem arises. The case law of the Court of Justice in the context of the Doorstep Selling Directive[224] suggests that, in principle, secured transactions are to be regarded as consumer contracts. In *Heininger*[225] the Court of Justice held that the fact that a credit agreement is secured by a charge on immovable property does not deprive the consumer of the protection provided by the Directive.[226] If this approach were adopted in the context of the Regulation, such agreements would be capable of falling within Section 4. **3.102**

3. Three Categories of Consumer Contract

The fact that a contract displays the general characteristics of a consumer contract is not sufficient for the application of the consumer jurisdiction rules to apply. In addition, the contract must fall within one of the three subparagraphs of article 15(1) of the Regulation. **3.103**

Instalment Sales and Loans

There are several types of contract in the consumer field which clearly display an imbalance of power between the contracting parties. Consumer credit agreements are perhaps one of the most obvious examples. Where a consumer, for economic reasons, is unable to pay outright for the purchase of goods, he may be induced to make such a purchase by the offer of **3.104**

[224] Dir 85/577/EEC [1985] OJ L372/31.
[225] Case C-481/99 [2001] ECR I-9945.
[226] Case C-481/99 [2001] ECR I-9945, 9980 (para 33).

payment by instalments.[227] Whereas many disputes arising from cross-border sales result from the consumer's dissatisfaction with the supplier's performance,[228] as regards credit agreements, problems will arise if the consumer fails to keep up with the contractual instalments.[229] Because one of the consequences of the imbalance between supplier and consumer is the imposition of harsh and potentially misleading terms in the agreement, there is a good argument for seeking to redress the balance by ensuring that, if litigation does take place, the consumer is not required to defend away from his home forum.

3.105 The first two categories of protected consumer contracts originated in article 13 of the Brussels Convention of 1968. Although the consumer contract provisions have been amended, as regards these two categories, article 15(1)(a) and (b) of the Brussels I Regulation follows the text of the Brussels Convention.

3.106 The first and second paragraphs of article 15(1) are limited to contracts involving the sale of goods: article 15(1)(a) applies to contracts 'for the sale of goods on instalment credit terms'; article 15(1)(b) covers contracts 'for a loan repayable by instalments, or for any other form of credit, made to finance the sale of goods'. Taken together, these two paragraphs are intended to cover the purchase of goods on credit, regardless of the form which the provision of credit takes.

3.107 The wording of article 15(1) means that paragraphs (a) and (b) do not apply to contracts whereby a consumer buys services on credit. Such contracts are outside the scope of Section 4 unless they fall within the third paragraph of article 15(1). In view of the shift in the consumer market from goods to services, there is no reason, in policy terms, why paragraphs (a) and (b) should apply to credit agreements to facilitate the sale of goods, but not the provision of services (such as luxury holidays). Furthermore, because these paragraphs refer to the sale of goods, they do not cover the sale of shares, bonds or other forms of intangible property.[230] Similarly, neither a 'pure' consumer credit agreement (ie, one not connected with the purchase of goods) nor a contract to finance the acquisition of a lease (such as a timeshare lease) is covered by article 15(1)(a) or (b).

[227] See Case 140/77 *Bertrand* [1978] 1431, 1450 (para 3) (Capotorti AG).

[228] As the supplier will normally secure payment from the consumer before performing his side of the bargain, in the cross-border consumer context, claims by suppliers against purchasers of goods are very uncommon.

[229] See, eg, Joined Cases C-240/98 to C-244/98 *Océano Grupo Editorial SA and Salvat Editores SA* [2000] ECR I-4941.

[230] K Hertz (1998: 197).

One possible justification for seeking to protect consumers in cases where goods are paid for by instalments or purchased on credit is that such transactions are likely to involve a relatively significant sum of money.[231] If this is a partial explanation of the rules, it is hard to see why their scope should be limited to credit related to the purchase of goods—as opposed to services, financial instruments (such as bonds), and rights in immovable property. **3.108**

Contract for the Sale of Goods on Instalment Credit Terms

A 'contract for the sale of goods on instalment credit terms' is an independent concept which has the same meaning throughout the member states.[232] In *Bertrand* the Court of Justice provided the following basic definition: 'a transaction in which the price is discharged by way of several payments or which is linked to a financing contract'.[233] If this definition were applied literally, it would cover a situation where a consumer buys goods by instalments, but only takes possession of the goods on payment of the final instalment. However, in *Mietz*[234] the Court of Justice ruled that a consumer contract does not fall within paragraph (a) unless the supplier extends credit to the consumer: Section 4 protects the consumer only 'where the vendor has transferred to the purchaser possession of the goods in question before the purchaser has paid the full price'.[235] **3.109**

There are two reasons for restricting instalment sales in this way. The first concerns the potentially misleading nature of credit agreements: 'the purchaser may, when the contract is concluded, be misled as to the real amount which he owes, and . . . will bear the risk of loss of those goods while remaining obliged to pay any outstanding instalments'.[236] Secondly, as the purpose of Section 4 is to protect the weaker contracting party, there is no reason to adopt a broad definition of instalment sales which would extend to contracts where the consumer does not require any special protection. Whereas a buyer who is granted credit is in a position of weakness vis-à-vis the supplier, there is no such weakness in a case 'where the buyer is billed for the total price *before* the delivery of the good, even if the obligation to pay is spread over several instalments'.[237] However, as the concept of an instalment sale does not imply 'that ownership of the article **3.110**

[231] A Lopez-Tarruella (2001: 247).
[232] Case 140/77 *Bertrand* [1978] 1431, 1445 (para 14).
[233] Case 140/77 [1978] 1431, 1446 (para 20). See also Jenard Report [1979] OJ C59/33.
[234] Case C-99/96 *Mietz* [1999] ECR I-2277.
[235] Case C-99/96 [1999] ECR I-2277, 2311 (para 31).
[236] Case C-99/96 [1999] ECR I-2277, 2311 (para 31).
[237] Case C-99/96 [1999] ECR I-2277, 2293 (para 52) (Léger AG).

must necessarily pass to the purchaser at the same time as physical possession, hire purchase is in practice tantamount to an instalment sale'[238] and falls within article 15(1)(a).

3.111 The central feature of a sale on instalment credit terms is that the contract makes provision for the buyer to make payment of instalments for the goods on successive, predetermined dates.[239] The mere fact that a contract makes provision for one of the parties to perform successive obligations does not mean that the contract falls within the first category. Where a franchisee undertakes to buy goods from the franchisor and to make, at regular intervals, payment of 3 per cent of his annual turnover for use of the franchisor's business name, the contract is not within the scope of article 15(1)(a).[240]

Loans to finance the sale of goods

3.112 Article 15(1)(b) refers to credit 'made to finance the sale of goods'. There is, however, a lack of precision over the degree of linkage which is needed between the sale of goods and the 'related' loan. At one end of the spectrum, there is the standard case where the seller who offers to sell goods on credit effectively acts as agent for the lender. In this type of case there can be no doubt that the contract between the consumer and the lender falls within article 15(1)(b). At the other end of the spectrum are cases where there is no contractual relationship between the seller and the lender.

3.113 It is not difficult to imagine different scenarios. One possibility is that the consumer has represented to the lender that the purpose of the loan is to purchase specific goods (such as a car) and the borrowed money is applied to such a purchase. This situation would appear to be covered by article 15(1)(b). A second situation is where the lender has not enquired as to the purpose of the loan, but the borrowed money is in fact used for the purchase of goods. Although the dividing line between this example and the previous one is narrow, this type of case prima facie falls outside article 15(1)(b): although a loan has been made and the consumer has purchased goods with the borrowed money, it cannot reasonably be said that that the loan was *made to finance* the sale of goods.[241]

3.114 There is no reported case law on the proper interpretation of article 15(1)(b) (or the provision of the Brussels Convention which it replaced) and these problems of interpretation are likely to remain more theoretical

238 Schlosser Report [1979] OJ C59/118 (para 157(a)).

239 Case C-269/95 *Benincasa* [1997] ECR I-3767, 3782 (para 59) (Ruiz-Jarabo Colomer AG).

240 Case C-269/95 [1997] ECR I-3767, 3783 (para 63) (Ruiz-Jarabo Colomer AG).

241 See K Hertz (1998: 200).

than practical. This is presumably because, although the buying of goods on credit is not uncommon, such cases tend to be domestic rather than international in nature; if they do have an international dimension and a dispute arises, it must be remembered that cross-border consumer litigation is very rare.

'All Other Cases'

Article 15(1)(c) of the Brussels I Regulation differs in two significant respects from the provision of the Brussels Convention which it replaced. First, whereas the Brussels Convention limited the third category to 'any other contract for the supply of goods or a contract for the supply of services', article 15(1)(c) refers simply to 'all other cases' in which a 'contract has been concluded'. Secondly, the territorial requirements under article 15(1)(c) are drawn less narrowly than those under the Convention. **3.115**

'All other cases' in which a 'contract has been concluded'

The use of the phrases 'contract for the supply of goods' and 'contract for the supply of services' in article 13 of the Brussels Convention potentially gave rise to questions of classification. Although it made no difference whether a contract was for the supply of goods or for the supply of services, article 13 of the Convention did not cover a contract falling within neither category. Under the Brussels Convention there were questions over whether a 'pure' consumer credit agreement is a contract for services[242] and whether a contract for the sale of digitized products is a contract for the sale of goods or for the provision of services (or neither).[243] It was also thought that a contract for the sale of securities or bonds was outside the scope of Section 4.[244] Problems of this type can no longer arise under article 15(1)(c), which applies to 'all other cases'. Nevertheless, it is important to stress that, for article 15(1)(c) to apply, a contract (as broadly defined by the Court of Justice) must have been 'concluded'.[245] **3.116**

Territorial connections: 'marketing' and 'contracting' criteria[246]

When the Brussels Convention was replaced by the Brussels I Regulation, the territorial requirements of the third category of protected consumer **3.117**

[242] Compare 'Credit contracts are not . . . contracts for the supply of services' (Schlosser Report, [1979] OJ C59/118 (para 157(a)) with 'The grant of a credit facility is indeed the provision of a service . . .' (Case C-45/96 *Dietzinger* [1998] ECR I-1199, 1221 (para 18)).

[243] See paras 1.67–1.75.

[244] See Giuliano-Lagarde Report [1980] OJ C282/23.

[245] See Case C-96/00 *Gabriel* [2002] ECR I-6367 and Case C-27/02 *Engler* [2005] ECR I-481.

[246] For further discussion (in the context of the Rome Convention and the Rome I Regulation), see ch 12.

contract were reworded 'to take account of developments in marketing techniques',[247] in particular marketing through the Internet.[248] Whereas article 13 of the Convention required either a specific invitation to the consumer or advertising in the state of the consumer's domicile (the 'marketing' criteria), article 15(1)(c) of the Brussels I Regulation requires only that the supplier 'pursues commercial or professional activities in the Member State of the consumer's domicile or, by any means, directs such activities to that Member State or to several Member States including that Member State'. In terms of offline contracts, the most obvious ways in which a supplier can carry out commercial activities in a particular place is either through direct marketing techniques (such as door-to-door selling, individually addressed advertising, or telephone sales) or through general advertising (through newspapers, magazines, radio and television etc). As regards such activities, the 'marketing' requirements of article 13 of the Convention and article 15(1)(c) of the Regulation overlap completely.

3.118 The 'contracting' criterion of article 13 of the Convention was that the consumer should have taken the steps necessary for the conclusion of the contract in the state in which he is domiciled. Article 15(1)(c) is potentially broader; it requires only that the contract should fall within the scope of the supplier's commercial activities undertaken in or directed to the member state of the consumer's domicile. Accordingly, special consumer contract rules apply regardless of where the consumer takes the steps necessary for the conclusion of the contract. This means that, under the Brussels I Regulation, if an English consumer, having received a catalogue from a German supplier in England, orders goods from the catalogue while on holiday in Spain, the consumer can rely on the provisions of Section 4. More significantly, the consumer can rely on Section 4 when he has been induced, at the supplier's instigation, to leave the state in which he is domiciled to conclude the contract. The requirements of article 15(1)(c) are satisfied where a consumer domiciled in England is invited by a Spanish supplier to travel to Spain to attend a timeshare presentation and, while in Spain, enters a timeshare contract with the suppler. Article 15(1)(c) also applies to 'border-crossing excursion-selling' (for example, where a storekeeper in state A arranges one-day bus trips for consumers in neighbouring state B with the main purpose of encouraging the consumers to buy goods in his store[249]).

[247] European Commission, COM (99) 348, p 16.

[248] The e-commerce aspects of art 15(1)(c) of the Brussels I Regulation are considered in ch 4.

[249] See Giuliano-Lagarde Report [1980] OJ C282/24.

V. THE JURISDICTION RULES

The basic scheme of the jurisdictional regime applicable to protected consumer contracts under the Brussels I Regulation has already been noted: as regards such contracts, article 16(1) provides that the consumer may sue a supplier domiciled in another member state in the courts of the member state in which the consumer is domiciled (or in which the supplier is domiciled); by virtue of article 16(2), the supplier may sue a consumer domiciled in a member state only in the courts of the member state in which the consumer is domiciled; article 17 renders jurisdiction clauses in such contracts unenforceable in most circumstances.[250] With regard to the jurisdiction rules set out in article 16, a question arises as to the moment at which the consumer's domicile is to be determined. The obvious alternatives are the place of domicile at the time of the conclusion of the contract or the place of domicile when the proceedings are commenced. 3.119

The arguments in favour of the place of domicile when the contract is concluded are overwhelming. This interpretation makes sense in policy terms and is favoured by commentators.[251] Article 15(1)(c) is based on the notion that any proceedings should take place in the consumer's home forum because, whereas the consumer has not entered the international arena, the supplier has done so by promoting its goods or services across borders. In these circumstances, the supplier has a reasonable expectation of having to sue (or of being sued) in that member state; the supplier has metaphorically entered the consumer's country and cannot legitimately complain if he is sued there. However, the rationale of article 15(1)(c) does not justify jurisdiction being allocated to the consumer's home forum in a situation where the consumer moves from state A (to which the supplier directs commercial activities) to state B (to which the supplier does not direct such activities) after the contract has been concluded.[252] 3.120

In addition to the jurisdiction rules contained in the first two paragraphs of article 16, for the sake of completeness, there are a few other provisions which ought to be noted. 3.121

[250] A similar scheme, albeit with certain modifications, operates in relation to b2c insurance contracts; see arts 9, 12(1), 13, and 14.

[251] See, eg, K Hertz (1998: 204).

[252] It should be noted, however, that in relation to other jurisdictional provisions the relevant time for determining the defendant's domicile is when the claim form is issued: *Canada Trust Co v Stolzenberg (No 2)* [2002] 1 AC 1 (a decision concerning art 6).

'Deemed Domicile' of Defendants Domiciled in Third States

3.122 If the supplier is domiciled in a third state, the jurisdiction of the English court will normally be determined by the so-called traditional rules.[253] However, by virtue of article 15(2) of the Brussels I Regulation, where a supplier is domiciled in a third state, but has a branch, agency, or other establishment in a member state, the supplier is deemed to be domiciled in that state 'in disputes arising out of the operations of the branch, agency or establishment'.[254] Although it may appear, at first glance, that this rule creates a general basis of jurisdiction against defendants who have a branch etc in a member state, jurisdiction is 'special' in that it covers only disputes arising out of the operations of the branch etc. In terms of its effect, this rule extends, in the context of consumer contracts, article 5(5)—which applies only to defendants who are domiciled in a member state—to defendants who are domiciled in third states. As the key concepts used in article 15(2) are borrowed *verbatim* from article 5(5), they should be interpreted in the same way.[255]

3.123 In *Shearson Lehman Hutton* the Advocate General took the view that what is now article 15(2) does not apply in a case where the dispute arises from the operations of a branch which is located in the member state in which the consumer is domiciled (for example, where the dispute arises from a contract concluded between an English consumer and the English branch of a New York company). Advocate General Darmon thought that, in this type of case, there is not a sufficient international element to bring the Brussels Convention into play. This view, however, almost certainly does not represent the law. In *Owusu*[256] the Court of Justice ruled that article 2 applied in a case where both the claimant and the defendant were domiciled in the same member state (viz the United Kingdom). This approach leads to the conclusion that where an English consumer deals with the English branch of a New York company and a dispute arises out of the

[253] Art 4.

[254] The same rule applies to insurance contracts: Brussels I Regulation, art 9(2).

[255] cf M Foss and LA Bygrave (2000: 131–3). In broad terms, a 'branch, agency or other establishment' normally has the following characteristics: it is subject to the direction and control of the parent body; it has a place of business which has the appearance of permanency; it is able to transact business with third parties: Case 14/76 *De Bloos* [1976] ECR 1497; Case 33/78 *Somafer* [1978] ECR 2183; Case 139/80 *Blanckaert* [1981] ECR 819; see also the opinion of Advocate General Darmon in Case C-89/91 *Shearson Lehman Hutton* [1993] ECR I-139, 185 (para 7). See, however, the exceptional case of Case 218/86 *Schotte* [1987] ECR 4905 in which it was ruled that a parent company may be regarded as a 'branch' of one of its subsidiaries if it appears to third parties that the parent is acting on behalf of the subsidiary. For further discussion, see J Hill (2005: 154–8).

[256] Case C-281/02 [2005] ECR I-1383.

operations of the branch, the consumer may bring a claim against the New York company in the English court on the basis of article 15(2) of the Brussels I Regulation.

Counter-claims

As regards protected consumer contracts, proceedings against a consumer domiciled in a member state must be brought in the state of the consumer's domicile.[257] However, if the supplier is sued by a consumer in a state in which the consumer is not domiciled (for example, if the consumer brings proceedings in the state in which the supplier is domiciled), the supplier is able to bring a counter-claim against the consumer in the court in which the original claim is pending.[258] This rule is the same as that which applies to other types of case governed by the Brussels I Regulation[259] (including situations involving insurance contracts[260]). **3.124**

Submission

Although Section 4 is silent on this point, it is widely assumed that, if proceedings are commenced in the court of a member state and the defendant (whether a supplier or a consumer) takes part in those proceedings without challenging the jurisdiction of the court, article 24 of the Brussels I Regulation entitles that court to assume jurisdiction on the basis of the defendant's submission. The Jenard Report suggests that the parties may 'derogate from the provisions of Section . . . 4' by submission[261] and the majority of commentators are agreed that submission (probably) takes precedence over Section 4.[262] Although the position cannot be regarded as definitively determined one way or the other,[263] the arguments in favour of article 24 prevailing over Section 4 are more convincing than those pointing in the other direction. In particular, it is provided that a jurisdiction agreement concluded between a supplier and a consumer after the dispute has arisen is enforceable (even if it deprives the consumer of the right to bring proceedings in the courts of his domicile).[264] In policy terms, **3.125**

[257] Art 16(2).

[258] Art 16(3).

[259] See Art 6(3).

[260] See Art 12(2).

[261] [1979] OJ C59/29.

[262] See, eg, L Collins *et al* (2006: 442); PM North and JJ Fawcett (1999: 228–9); A Briggs and P Rees (2005: 104); A Layton and H Mercer (2004: 575); P Kaye (1987: 841); A Lopez-Tarruella (2001: 236). See also the literature from mainland Europe to which the Regional Court of Appeal (Koblenz) referred in *Re Jurisdiction in a Consumer Contract* [2002] ILPr 157, 160 (para 11). But note the equivocation of L Collins (1983: 76, n 1).

[263] See Case C-99/96 *Mietz* [1999] ECR I-2277, 2287–9 (paras 28-32) (Léger AG).

[264] Art 17(1).

if prorogation of jurisdiction by contractual agreement after a dispute has arisen is permitted, there is no reason why prorogation of jurisdiction by the defendant's submission should not also be allowed.[265]

3.126 The only circumstance in which submission does not confer jurisdiction on the court before which the defendant enters an appearance is where the courts of another member state have exclusive jurisdiction under article 22 of the Regulation. So, where a dispute arises out of a letting in respect of premises situated in Spain concluded between an English consumer and a German company, the German courts do not have jurisdiction over proceedings brought by the German company against the consumer even if the consumer purports to submit to German jurisdiction.

VI. B2C INSURANCE CONTRACTS UNDER THE BRUSSELS I REGULATION

3.127 In principle, a contract of insurance is a contract for services[266] which, if the relevant conditions were satisfied, could fall within the scope of Section 4 on consumer contracts. However, the Brussels I Regulation contains separate jurisdictional rules for 'matters relating to insurance' (in Section 3 of Chapter II) and it has never been doubted that Section 3 takes precedence over the consumer contract provisions in Section 4.[267] So, where an insured concludes a contract of insurance for a purpose which can be regarded as being outside his trade or profession, Section 3 (rather than Section 4) applies.[268]

3.128 In the context of disputes arising out of b2c insurance contracts, the jurisdiction rules in Section 3 broadly mirror those in Section 4. So, the consumer can sue an insurer domiciled in a member state in the country in which the consumer is domiciled[269] and, as a general rule, the insurer is permitted to sue the consumer only in the country of the latter's domicile.[270] In order for these rules to apply there are no conditions relating to the process

[265] See Case C-99/96 *Mietz* [1999] ECR I-2277, 2289 (para 31) (Léger AG).

[266] Giuliano-Lagarde Report [1980] OJ C282/23.

[267] Schlosser Report [1979] OJ C59/117 (para 156).

[268] Sched 4 to the Civil Jurisdiction and Judgments Act 1982 does not contain provisions corresponding to Section 3, whereas it does contain provisions corresponding to Section 4. This means that, in a case which is internal to the United Kingdom, the consumer contract provisions apply to consumer insurance contracts (as long as the relevant conditions are satisfied).

[269] Art 9(1)(a).

[270] Art 12(1).

whereby the contract was concluded corresponding to those of article 15(1)(c). In substance, insurance contracts involving consumers are treated in the same way as contracts for the sale of goods on instalment credit terms (under article 15(1)(a)) and loans and other credit contracts which finance the sale of goods (under article 15(1)(b)). There is an extra basis of jurisdiction where a dispute relates either to liability insurance or insurance of immovable property; in such cases, a consumer can sue the insurer in the courts for the place where the harmful event occurred.[271] As a general rule, jurisdiction agreements in insurance contracts are unenforceable—though article 13 specifies certain circumstances in which such agreements are binding.[272]

As regards an insurer which is not domiciled in a member state, jurisdiction is, subject to article 23 (which gives effect to jurisdiction agreements in favour of the courts of a member state), governed by the traditional rules.[273] However, an insurer which is not domiciled in a member state, but has a branch in a member state, may be sued in that state in relation to disputes arising out of the operations of the branch.[274] This rule has the same function as article 15(2). So, if a consumer enters a contract of insurance through the English branch of a New York insurance company, the consumer may bring proceedings in England in relation to any claim arising out of the contact. **3.129**

VII. CONSUMER CONTRACTS GOVERNED BY SPECIALIZED CONVENTIONS: CONTRACTS OF TRANSPORT

The Brussels I Regulation provides that contracts of transport (other than package holidays) are excluded from Section 4.[275] This means either that these excluded contracts are covered by the ordinary contract rules or that such contracts are governed by specialized conventions, the operation of which is preserved by the Brussels I Regulation. In view of the range of international conventions in the field of transport which contain special jurisdictional provisions [276] the number of contracts of transport falling **3.130**

[271] Art 10.
[272] In the consumer context, art 13 largely adopts the same basic approach as art 17. See ch 7.
[273] Art 4.
[274] Art 9(2).
[275] Art 15(3).
[276] See L Collins *et al* (2006: ch 15).

within the scope of the ordinary contract rules (rather than the rules of specialized conventions) is very small or non-existent.

3.131 Article 71 of the Brussels I Regulation provides that it 'shall not affect any convention to which the Member States are parties and which in relation to particular matters, govern jurisdiction or the recognition or enforcement of judgments'. Conventions which are preserved by this rule include: the Warsaw and Montreal Conventions (on travel by air), the Berne Convention (on travel by rail), and the Athens Convention (on carriage by sea). Each of these international conventions contains similar jurisdictional regimes. This section considers only that relating to carriage by air; one of the areas generating a large number of consumer complaints is air transport.[277]

3.132 In the consumer context, any litigation arising out of contracts of transport will invariably result from claims by the passenger (or their relatives) against the carrier. Such claims typically relate either to the passenger's death or personal injury or to losses suffered as a result of damage to or the loss of their baggage. Where such litigation is contemplated, the main question will be whether the passenger can bring proceedings in his home forum.[278]

3.133 Under the Montreal Convention[279] (which came into force in England in 2004 and replaces the Warsaw Convention) a claimant may bring proceedings in a number of different fora, including the place where the carrier is domiciled or has its principal place of business.[280] In cases where a consumer enters a contract with a foreign carrier, these options will normally be relatively unattractive to the consumer. However, the claimant may also bring proceedings where the carrier has a place of business through which the contract was made or at the place of destination.[281] This means that where an English consumer buys a ticket through the English agent of a foreign carrier, as long as the agent's office is regarded as the carrier's place of business, the consumer can litigate claims against the carrier in England. In addition, as regards disputes relating to homeward journeys

[277] See ECC-Net (October 2006: 4). See also European Consumer Law Group (February 2005a).

[278] In cases involving air disasters and the like, there may be cases where passengers (or their families) collectively seek to bring a class action in a sympathetic forum (such as one of the states of the United States of America), rather than in their home forum. As England is not the forum of choice for class actions of this type, issues surrounding class actions resulting from transport disasters are outside the scope of the current discussion.

[279] Cm 4651; Carriage by Air Act 1961, sched 1B. See B Cheng (2004).

[280] Art 33(1).

[281] Art 33(1).

(where the destination is England), an English consumer can litigate in England.[282]

VIII. CONCLUSION

1. What Can 'Protective' Jurisdiction Rules Achieve?

Even though the majority of European consumers always (or nearly always) buy locally, the evidence suggests that there is a significant number of cross-border contracts—both contracts which result from in-person shopping (for example, where holidaymakers or business people buy goods and services while abroad) and distance contracts (for example, where a consumer domiciled in one member state enters a distance contract for the purchase of goods or services from a supplier established in another member state). Research suggests that nearly a quarter of the citizens of the member states sporadically buy goods or services in other EU member states; 10 per cent of these consumers are dissatisfied and some of them want to pursue a claim against the supplier.[283] **3.134**

The approach of the Brussels I Regulation is based on the idea that consumers should be able to sue at home because the claim will not normally be worth all the trouble of suing abroad.[284] If, from the consumer's perspective, litigation in his home forum is a complex and expensive prospect, cross-border litigation is worse. As noted by the European Commission: 'Cross-border disputes tend to result in even more lengthy proceedings and higher court costs than domestic disputes.'[285] The factors which make cross-border litigation more problematical include: (i) the applicable law is always foreign for one of the parties; (ii) the forum is always foreign for one of the parties; (iii) documents need to be transmitted across borders; and (iv) documents may need translating.[286] **3.135**

282 A new basis of jurisdiction was added by art 33(2) of the Montreal Convention in personal injury cases: in the event of a passenger's death or injury, if certain (complex) conditions are satisfied, a claim may be brought against the carrier in the country of the passenger's principal and permanent residence at the time of the accident. If, for example, an English passenger is injured on an internal flight in the United States, the passenger can litigate any claim against the carrier in England if the carrier also operates flights to and from the United Kingdom; the fact that the contract itself has no connection with England is irrelevant. See I Kilbey (2005: 129–30).

283 See European Commission, COM (2002) 746, p 59.

284 C Joustra (1992: 432).

285 COM (2002) 196, p 7 (para 1.2.6).

286 European Commission, COM (93) 576, p 99.

3.136 Of course, often the claim will not be worth the trouble of litigating at all and, even if the claim is, in principle, worth pursuing, the decision whether or not to take formal legal action needs to take into account the risks surrounding cross-border enforcement. Even where a consumer is successful in litigation in his home forum against a foreign supplier, if the supplier does not satisfy the judgment, the consumer who wants actually to recover the money owed under the judgment (rather than simply to make a legal point or to enjoy the dubious satisfaction of obtaining a judgment in his favour) will have to take enforcement proceedings abroad; the recognition and enforcement procedure under the Brussels I Regulation 'takes far too long and costs too much'.[287]

3.137 So, the choice facing a consumer who is contemplating litigation of a dispute arising from a protected consumer contract against a foreign supplier is between, on the one hand, suing abroad (where the defendant has assets) and (if successful) proceeding directly to enforcement of the judgment in that country or, on the other, suing at home and (if successful) seeking to enforce the judgment abroad if the supplier fails to honour the judgment. The crucial point is that, even though under the Regulation the jurisdictional dice are loaded in the consumer's favour, the consumer has to face the prospect of foreign proceedings—either at the merits stage or the enforcement stage.

3.138 The Jenard Report and the case law of the Court of Justice seem to be premised on the idea that, if the law provides consumers with jurisdictional protection, obstacles to consumer litigation will be swept away. However, the jurisdictional issues which the Brussels I Regulation's consumer contract provisions seek to address are a very small part of the access-to-justice problems faced by consumers. The reality is that there is only so far (that is, not very far) that private international law can go in alleviating the obstacles which confront consumers who find themselves in dispute with a foreign supplier. A rule such as article 16(1) of the Brussels I Regulation, which permits a consumer to sue a foreign supplier in the former's home forum, is beneficial only to the extent that the *domestic* procedural rules of the consumer's home state (and the enforcement procedures of the supplier's home state) are effective in providing consumers with realistic means of redress through the courts; the domestic procedural law of the country in which the consumer is domiciled and the costs of pursuing litigation in that country may well produce a situation where it is not a practical option for a consumer to seek to vindicate his rights by means of litigation. If a legal system does not have an efficient

[287] European Commission, COM (97) 609, p 6. See also M Andenas (2006).

and accessible small claims procedure, the effect of article 16(1) of the Regulation is simply to translate consumers' access-to-justice problems from the domestic situation into the cross-border context. Jurisdiction rules cannot, in themselves, overcome access-to-justice problems; the most they can do is to take away the *further* obstacles which would otherwise be placed in the consumer's way as a result of the fact that the contract, rather than being domestic, arises from cross-border activity.

It is hard to see how consumers can be encouraged to see litigation as an **3.139** effective means of obtaining redress in cross-border situations unless and until small claims procedures and methods of cross-border enforcement are made much more user-friendly. In addition to the technical issues, there is the underlying economic reality that, as regards small claims, court-based redress mechanisms involve too much time, effort, and money for the process to be worth pursuing by consumers—even on the assumption that they will be successful in that process. So, if any progress is to be made in terms of consumers' access to court-based justice at the cross-border level,[288] the minimum requirements include: (i) a simple, cheap small claims procedure; (ii) a jurisdiction rule which enables consumers to sue foreign suppliers in the consumers' home forum; and (iii) a simple, cheap method whereby consumers can enforce judgments in other countries. The problem with the Brussels I Regulation is that it only addresses point (ii) and that it applies to some cross-border consumer contracts, but not to others. Until the European Small Claims Regulation[289] comes into force, point (i) is left to national procedural law—which may (or may not) be effective. Point (iii) is covered by the Brussels I Regulation, but the enforcement regime places almost insuperable financial and practical obstacles in the way of consumers and it remains to be seen whether the recent developments in European civil procedure (including the European Small Claims Regulation)[290] will do anything to reduce cross-border enforcement problems in the consumer context. So, the idea that the Brussels I Regulation 'solves' consumer access-to-justice problems is not much more than wishful thinking. It is for this reason that, in recent years, there have been initiatives at the European level which focus on the reform of civil

[288] Access to justice through litigation is only one part of the access-to-justice equation (and almost certainly not the most important part); alternative dispute resolution (ADR) has more potential for finding practical solutions, particularly as regards disputes arising out of e-commerce. See chs 9 to 11.

[289] Reg (EC) No 861/2007 [2007] OJ L199/1.

[290] See also the European Enforcement Order Regulation (Reg (EC) No 805/2004 [2004] OJ L143/15) and the European Order for Payment Procedure Regulation (Reg (EC) No 1896/2006 [2006] OJ L399/1).

procedure, rather than simply providing an apparently consumer-friendly framework at the private international law level.[291]

2. How Important are Jurisdiction Rules in the Context of Disputes Arising out of Consumer Contracts?

3.140 Because the jurisdiction rules relating to consumer contracts have generated a number of references to the Court of Justice and have spawned a significant body of case law, it might appear, at first sight, that the Brussels I Regulation plays an important role in the field of consumer litigation. However, nothing could be further from the truth.

3.141 Nearly all the jurisprudence surrounding Section 4 focuses on the characteristics of a 'consumer contract' for the purposes of the jurisdiction rules and, in the majority of the reported cases, the court's conclusion has been that the contract in question either was not a consumer contract at all (either because the person seeking to rely on the pro-consumer rules was not a 'consumer'[292] or because there was no concluded contract[293]) or was not a protected consumer contract (because the conditions of what is now article 15(1) were not satisfied[294]). From the point of view of consumer litigation (rather than proceedings in which non-consumers have attempted to take advantage of the jurisdictional provisions which apply to protected consumer contracts), the Court of Justice has handed down only one relevant judgment.[295] In short, to the extent that questions of interpretation have been raised under the consumer contract provisions, nearly all the questions have concerned the scope of the provisions and the cases have primarily been about what *is not* a protected consumer contract.

3.142 The fact that the case law discussed in this chapter is mainly about the boundary between consumer contracts and commercial contracts—and that nearly all the reported cases involve abortive attempts to persuade the court that a commercial situation should fall under the consumer contract provisions—should hardly come as a surprise. As already noted,

[291] See ch 5.

[292] Case 150/77 *Bertrand* [1978] ECR 1431; Case C-89/91 *Shearson Lehman Hutton* [1993] ECR I-139; Case C-269/95 *Benincasa* [1997] ECR I-3767; Case C-464/01 *Gruber* [2005] ECR I-439.

[293] Case C-27/02 *Engler* [2005] ECR I-481.

[294] Case C-99/96 *Mietz* [1999] ECR I-2277.

[295] Case C-96/00 *Gabriel* [2002] ECR I-6367. One other significant ECJ decision (Case C-318/93 *Brenner and Noller* [1994] ECR I-4275) involved a genuine consumer contract, but Section 4 was not directly relevant as the defendant was neither domiciled nor deemed to be domiciled in a member state.

for the vast majority of genuine consumer contracts, the costs of litigation far exceed the sums in dispute; in the contractual sphere, reported litigation nearly always involves cases in which the value of the claim is serious enough to justify legal proceedings; such cases are almost invariably commercial cases.

As regards the material considered in this chapter there appears to be a very significant gap between the law as it appears in much of the literature and the realities of cross-border dispute resolution in the consumer context. When it comes to discussions of the Brussels I Regulation, there is often a significant dislocation between the way in which the consumer contract provisions are discussed and their practical significance. One finds scholarly discussion of the relevant jurisdiction rules accompanied by statements about how important the rules are in ensuring the protection of consumer interests. However, in practice, the jurisdiction rules relating to consumer contracts are largely irrelevant—except in the rare cases in which the value of the claim is high enough to make it worthwhile for the consumer to bring an action.[296] **3.143**

Although a variety of interesting doctrinal questions are raised by the consumer contract provisions of the Brussels I Regulation, it has to be recognized that private international law does not have a high degree of practical significance in the field of cross-border consumer contracts. In 1999, during the debate on the Electronic Commerce Bill, Patricia Hewitt pointed out that '[t]he Brussels convention has existed for 31 years and, in that time, almost no consumer has used it to sue for breach of contract.'[297] At around the same time, the European Consumer Law Group concluded that: 'The Brussels Convention . . . does not seem to have any positive influence as regards access to court for consumers or the enforcement of judgements'[298] and that '[c]ross-border small claims fall *de facto* outside the Brussels Convention.'[299] **3.144**

If, in the cross-border context, there is little or no prospect of the vast majority of consumer complaints ever leading to litigation, it would be legitimate to conclude that changes to private international law rules are unlikely to bring about a significant change in the way in which disputes arising out of consumer contracts are handled in practice. This is not to say **3.145**

[296] K Vasiljeva (2004: 142).

[297] Hansard, 29 November 1999, col 48: <http://www.publications.parliament.uk/pa/cm199900/cmhansrd/vo991129/debtext/91129-14.htm> [14/7/06].

[298] European Consumer Law Group (April 1998: Annex II, para 5).

[299] European Consumer Law Group (April 1998: para 7).

that efforts to develop a rational framework for handling cross-border consumer disputes should not be taken seriously; there could be no justification for the preservation of an inappropriate set of rules.[300] Nevertheless, the development of the jurisdiction rules in Section 4 is of more symbolic and theoretical significance, than of practical value.

[300] See T Puurunen (2003: 791) in the context of choice-of-law rules.

4

Consumer E-commerce: Jurisdiction Rules

I. INTRODUCTION

E-commerce presents certain challenges to the traditional, territorial approach to questions of jurisdiction. While it is important that the enormity of these challenges is not exaggerated, there is an argument for saying that 'cyberspace radically undermines the relationship between a particular transaction and a specific physical location'.[1] Whereas it is normally easy to identify the territorial connections of the various elements of a real-world contract, the Internet enables people to enter into contracts without knowing (and, in many cases, without being able to know) the physical location of the other party.[2] **4.01**

1. Pro-consumer or Pro-supplier?

How one approaches e-contracts from a jurisdictional point of view depends in part on how such contracts are articulated in terms of language: **4.02**

> [T]he impulse to assert jurisdiction over an outsider who 'invades' a community via the Internet is tied to the need to assert dominion in order to domesticate

[1] M Berlini (2003a: 48).
[2] M Berlini (2003a: 48).

external chaos. On the other hand, the jurisdictional puzzle will look quite different if online interaction is conceived not as foreign websites 'sending' information into a community, but rather as members of a community choosing to 'travel' to a foreign site to obtain information. Accordingly, linguistic metaphors for conceptualizing online interaction may also help determine the way people develop intuitions about jurisdictional questions.[3]

4.03 Those who equate online shopping with in-person shopping favour a so-called country-of-origin approach, according to which disputes arising from online transactions should be subject to the jurisdiction of the courts of the country in which the e-trader is established (and governed by the law of that country). This approach is supported by two strands of reasoning. First, some consider that, in a cross-border consumer contract, the consumer should be the party who runs the risk of being sued in a foreign jurisdiction on the ground that the consumer is more likely than the supplier to know that the other party to the contract is based in another country.[4] Secondly, it can be argued that a country-of-destination approach—which makes an e-trader potentially subject to the jurisdiction of the courts of every country in the world—places an unfair burden on sellers; so much so that such an approach would have the effect of impeding the growth of e-commerce.[5]

4.04 By contrast, other commentators deny the parallel between offline and online shopping: 'It is not fair to think of the consumer who logs on to the Net as if he or she were going for a weekend shopping spree to London or New York. Virtual shopping is not real travelling, and therefore it should not entail submission to a foreign sovereign's courts of law.'[6] Those who see online transactions as the result of e-traders marketing their goods and services globally via the Internet prefer a country-of-destination approach according to which the courts of the country in which the buyer is located have jurisdiction over e-commerce disputes (and the buyer's law is the applicable law). Not everyone is convinced that the growth of e-commerce is dependent on jurisdiction over disputes arising from online contracts being allocated to the courts of the e-trader's country (and the application of the e-trader's law to such contracts).[7] In the b2c context, the growth of e-commerce depends on the willingness of both suppliers and consumers to enter online contracts. It can, therefore, be argued that the building of consumer confidence—by ensuring that consumer protection policies are

[3] PS Berman (2002: 435).
[4] C Chen (2004: 444–5).
[5] M Cordera (2001: 245).
[6] F Dessemontet (2000: 71).
[7] A Briggs (2002: 68).

not undermined in relation to e-commerce transactions—is no less important than the fostering of a legal environment in which e-traders are happy to trade.

2. Approaches to Jurisdiction over Internet Activity

Over the course of the last decade there has been a lot of discussion of the problems surrounding jurisdiction over Internet activity. These problems exist at two levels. The first level, which might be termed 'legislative jurisdiction', relates to the question of which state is entitled to regulate Internet activity. The dominant approach to this question, as exemplified by the E-Commerce Directive,[8] is the country-of-origin approach according to which a person who is authorized in one member state to carry out certain activities may carry out those activities in other member states without further authorization. Recital 22 to the Directive states: **4.05**

> Information society services should be supervised at the source of the activity, in order to ensure an effective protection of public interest objectives; to that end, it is necessary to ensure that the competent authority provides such protection not only for the citizens of its own country but for all Community citizens; in order to improve mutual trust between Member States, it is essential to state clearly this responsibility on the part of the Member State where the services originate; moreover, in order to effectively guarantee freedom to provide services and legal certainty for suppliers and recipients of services, such information society services should in principle be subject to the law of the Member State in which the service provider is established.

The country-of-origin approach is implemented through Article 3, which provides: **4.06**

> (1) Each Member State shall ensure that the information society services provided by a service provider established on its territory comply with the national provisions applicable in the Member State in question . . .
> (2) Member States may not . . . restrict the freedom to provide information society services from another Member State.

The second level, which one might call 'adjudicative jurisdiction', concerns the question of which courts are entitled to hear and determine private law disputes which result from Internet activity. It is this second level with which this chapter is concerned.[9] **4.07**

[8] Dir 2000/31/EC [2000] OJ L178/1.

[9] Throughout this work, the word 'jurisdiction', when used without any adjectival qualification, signifies 'adjudicative jurisdiction'.

4.08 Because the development of the Internet started in the United States, it is hardly surprising that questions concerning Internet jurisdiction were encountered in America before those questions arose in Europe. Accordingly, the earliest judicial attempts to grapple with the jurisdictional issues posed by the Internet are to be found in cases decided by the US courts. In some ways, this may be unfortunate, because it is not immediately obvious that answers to questions posed within the unique context of the jurisdictional framework of the US constitution offer a wordwide solution to the problems of Internet jurisdiction. Furthermore, for the purposes of the current work—which is concerned with certain types of transaction, namely consumer contracts—it is important that the US jurisprudence is not misunderstood and that decisions which answer question A are not necessarily thought to provide the solution to question B.

4.09 If questions relating to contractual dispute-resolution clauses are put to one side,[10] the key jurisdictional question concerning online consumer contracts is whether jurisdiction may be assumed by the courts of the country in which the consumer resides and/or by the courts of the country in which the supplier is established. (There have been suggestions that, as regards online contracts, the courts of other countries might be able to assume jurisdiction either on the basis of the location of computer equipment which supports the supplier's website or on the basis of the location of computers through which data is exchanged between the parties. Such suggestions are, however, largely fanciful and it is generally accepted that, in the e-commerce context, the location of the computer hardware through which electronic messages are transmitted is not jurisdictionally relevant.[11]) A factor which runs the risk of obscuring the real issues under discussion is the tendency for commentators[12] (and some judges also[13]) to talk about jurisdiction 'over websites'. In the context of adjudicative jurisdiction, the idea of jurisdiction 'over websites'—even if an understandable shorthand—is largely meaningless; websites do not have legal personality and cannot sue or be sued. Discussion of jurisdiction 'over websites' may generate confusion between two different kinds of case: first, there are situations where the question is whether the court has general jurisdiction over the business entity which is responsible for a particular website (often referred to as the 'website owner'); secondly, there are situations where

[10] See ch 7.

[11] See, eg, M Chissick and A Kelman (2002: 119); HA Deveci (2006: 44); LE Gillies (2001); LE Gillies (2001a); LE Gillies (2003: 367–8); M Schaub (2004: 151); PA Stone (2002: 128). See also R Schu (1997: 204, 221–2) (in a discussion of choice-of-law rules).

[12] See, eg, BD Boone (2006: 248).

[13] See, eg, *Amberson Holdings LLC v Westside Story Newspaper* 110 F.Supp.2d 332, 336 (2000).

the question is whether the court has specific jurisdiction with regard to a particular dispute which has arisen out of a transaction concluded via a website (typically, an online contract). It is important that this fundamental distinction is kept in mind when thinking about the significance of the early US jurisprudence.

The obvious starting point for any discussion of American approaches to jurisdiction over Internet activity is *Zippo Manufacturing v Zippo Dot Com Inc*,[14] a case decided in 1997. In the course of his judgment Judge McLaughlin drew a distinction between different types of website: **4.10**

At one end of the spectrum are situations where a defendant clearly does business over the Internet. If the defendant enters into contracts with residents of a foreign jurisdiction that involve the knowing and repeated transmission of computer files over the Internet, personal jurisdiction is proper. At the opposite end are situations where a defendant has simply posted information on an Internet Web site which is accessible to users in foreign jurisdictions. A passive Web site that does little more than make information available to those who are interested in it is not grounds for the exercise of personal jurisdiction. The middle ground is occupied by interactive Web sites where a user can exchange information with the host computer. In these cases, the exercise of jurisdiction is determined by examining the level of interactivity and commercial nature of the exchange of information that occurs on the Web site.[15]

An important point to note is that the issue facing the court in this case was not whether it had jurisdiction over a dispute arising out of a contract concluded via a website, but whether the court had jurisdiction over a dispute relating to trademark infringement (ie, a dispute which was wholly independent from any transactional activity associated with the website in question). The court's discussion of different types of website activity was directed at trying to identify what level of online commercial activity (having some connection with the forum) justified the assumption of jurisdiction over tortious conduct which allegedly resulted from the operation of the website through which such commercial activity was conducted. The fact that in the *Zippo* case the court considered that, where an e-trader regularly transacts online business with residents of state A, the courts of state A are entitled to assume jurisdiction over a trademark action against the e-trader is not directly relevant to the question whether the courts of state A are entitled to exercise jurisdiction over disputes arising out of e-contracts concluded by an e-trader with residents of state A. Accordingly, much of the literature—both in the United States and in Europe—which **4.11**

[14] 952 F Supp 1119 (WD Pa, 1997).

[15] 952 F Supp 1119, 1124 (WD Pa, 1997). Citations omitted.

discusses the *Zippo* case as part of a comparison between the US approach to Internet jurisdiction and the European approach to jurisdiction over online consumer contracts is, to a significant extent, failing to compare like with like.[16] Indeed, the *Zippo* case has been used as a starting point for a lot of unfocused analysis and discussion.[17]

4.12 Although the *Zippo* sliding-scale has been applied by US courts in numerous cases, the paradigm cases are disputes about tortious wrongs; the vast majority of the reported US cases in the e-commerce field have been concerned with online defamation and the alleged infringement of intellectual property rights.[18] Indeed, the pattern is the same in other common law jurisdictions, such as England,[19] Canada,[20] and Australia;[21] in Commonwealth jurisdictions, there seems to be no reported litigation concerned with jurisdiction questions relating to disputes arising out of e-contracts.

4.13 The *Zippo* test is by no means the end of the story of Internet jurisdiction in the United States. The appropriateness of the *Zippo* sliding-scale has come under attack[22] on the basis that its application tends towards excessively broad jurisdiction over Internet activity.[23] By 1999 there was already a shift away from the *Zippo* test and by 2001 some courts were looking to fix jurisdictional boundaries over Internet activity in alternative ways, such as by means of an effects-based analysis or targeting approach.[24]

[16] See, eg, BD Boone (2006); C Chen (2004); DT Rice (2001).

[17] Another problem to be found in the literature is the fact that several commentators attempt to make use of the French *Yahoo!* case (*Association Union des Étudiants Juifs en France c Yahoo! Inc*) in the context of their discussion of e-commerce jurisdiction. The *Yahoo!* case concerned the question whether criminal liability can be imposed in state A against a website owner established in state B on the basis that the website infringes the law of state A; although the case involves the Internet, it addresses neither questions of civil jurisdiction in relation to e-commerce nor adjudicative jurisdiction in general.

[18] See, eg, trademark infringement cases: *CompuServe Inc v Patterson* 89 F 3d 1257 (6th Cir, 1996); *Cybersell Inc v Cybersell Inc* 130 F 3d 414 (9th Cir, 1997); *Bensusan Rest Corp v King* 126 F 3d 25 (2d Cir, 1997); *ALS Scan Inc v Digital Serv Consult Inc* 293 F 3d 707 (4th Cir, 2002); *Toys "R" Us Inc v Step Two SA*, 318 F 3d 446 (3d Cir, 2003); *Minnesota Public Radio v Virginia Beach Educational Broadcasting Foundation* 519 F Supp 2d 970 (D Minn, 2007); defamation cases: *Young v New Haven Advocate* 315 F 3d 256 (4th Cir, 2002); *Best Van Lines Inc v Walker* 490 F 3d 239 (2d Cir, 2007).

[19] See, eg, *King v Lewis* [2005] ILPr 185.

[20] See, eg, *Braintech v Kostiuk* (1999) 171 DLR (4th) 46 (Court of Appeal, British Columbia).

[21] See, eg, *Gutnick v Dow Jones* (2002) 210 CLR 575 (High Court, Australia).

[22] See, eg, TD Leitstein (1999).

[23] See M Traynor and L Pirri (2002).

[24] See MA Geist (2001); T Puurunen (2002: 202); BD Boone (2006).

Some US courts have applied the 'effects doctrine' of *Calder v Jones*[25] which looks at whether intentional tortious conduct was expressly aimed at the forum or the plaintiff. In the online environment, an effects-based approach looks at the effect of a website within a particular country, whereas the *Zippo* test is based primarily on the characteristics of the website itself. An effects-based test can work in the context of tort claims and in cases in which it is alleged that the defendant infringed the claimant's intellectual property rights, but it is not well adapted to disputes arising out of contracts (and it does not seem that courts have been tempted to try to apply the effects doctrine in the contractual context).

Although there is only a small number of reported cases concerning disputes arising out of online contracts, there are a few examples where the American courts have considered the *Zippo* test in such cases.[26] These authorities support the view that, in a case involving an online contract whereby a resident of state A buys goods or services from an e-trader established in state B via the e-trader's website, it is legitimate for the courts of state A to exercise jurisdiction over a dispute which arises from that contract. In such cases, the assumption of jurisdiction does not turn on whether performance of the e-trader's obligation takes place in the real world (for example, by delivering physical goods to the buyer) or in cyberspace (such as where, in the context of a contract for the sale of software, the supplier transfers electronic data to the buyer's computer via the supplier's website). Furthermore, the position appears to be the same even if the transaction between the e-trader and the buyer is a one-off and does not form part of a pattern of business with the state in which the buyer resides.[27] **4.14**

It has been said that, because of the diversity of approaches taken by the US courts in e-commerce cases and the inconsistencies in the case law, 'predicting whether a Web site operator will be subject to jurisdiction in a particular forum is almost impossible'.[28] Notwithstanding the problems with the US case law and the interesting legal questions to which it gives rise, in the context of the current work, further discussion of the US position—and the literature generated by the *Zippo* case and its aftermath—is hardly justified. Whatever problems there may be in finding the proper approach to jurisdiction over Internet-based torts, in relation to which the **4.15**

[25] 465 US 783 (1984).

[26] See, eg, *Brown v AST Sports Science Inc* WL 32345935 (ED Pa, 2002); *All Enthusiast Inc v Gunter* WL 1869395 (ND Cal, 2005).

[27] See, eg, *Thompson v Handa-Lopez Inc* 998 F Supp 738 (WD Tex, 1998).

[28] RA Bales and S van Wert (2001: 22).

US courts have attempted a variety of different doctrinal approaches, there is little disagreement about which courts are entitled to exercise jurisdiction over disputes arising from online contracts. It seems to be widely accepted that, unless there is a binding jurisdiction clause in the contract, the courts of state A have jurisdiction over a contractual dispute arising from an online contract concluded between a consumer from state A and an e-trader established in state B.[29]

3. The Need for International Agreement?

4.16 It is sometimes suggested that the international community should attempt to establish a convention addressing questions of jurisdiction in relation to Internet activity.[30] It is tempting to see the harmonization of private international law rules as the solution to what appear to be problems which exist at a global level and no doubt a case can be made for trying to create a worldwide regime for the allocation of jurisdiction with regard to disputes arising from b2b contracts. Indeed, the project which ultimately resulted in the Hague Convention on Choice of Court Agreements[31] had started with the objective of creating a worldwide convention something along the lines of the Brussels Convention.[32] Had the final convention been similar to the preliminary draft convention of 1999,[33] the wishes of those who would like to see worldwide solutions to questions of Internet jurisdiction may have been fulfilled.

4.17 However, the work undertaken by the Hague Conference shows how difficult it is to achieve international consensus on jurisdictional questions relating to cross-border business activity. Furthermore, even if it is thought that effort should be directed at the unification of jurisdiction rules in the commercial context, it may be doubted whether, in view of the very limited incidence of cross-border consumer litigation, the practical benefits which might flow from a worldwide jurisdictional regime for disputes arising from b2c contracts would justify the effort which would be required to create it.

[29] M Cordera (2001: 250). See also TD Leitstein (1999: 585); JS Burns and RA Bales (2001). Compare LM Ponte (2002: 486).

[30] See, eg, AM Sachdeva (2007).

[31] See <http://www.hcch.net/index_en.php?act=conventions.pdf&cid=98> [8/1/08].

[32] The preliminary documents, which show the way in which the project was significantly narrowed in scope, are available from the Hague Conference's website: <http://www.hcch.net/index_en.php?act=conventions.publications&dtid=35&cid=98> [8/1/08].

[33] See <http://www.hcch.net/upload/wop/jdgmpd11.pdf> [8/1/08].

II. E-CONTRACTS AND THE BRUSSELS I REGULATION

1. Article 15(1)(c)

Introduction

Background: article 13 of the Brussels Convention

The text of article 13 of the Brussels Convention was drafted before the development of the Internet and the rise of e-commerce. Because article 13 was drafted with real-world contracts in mind, it employs concepts which cannot be applied straightforwardly to online situations. As a result, it was considered that the operation of article 13 in the context of e-commerce was uncertain.[34] As regards the 'marketing' criterion of article 13 (which requires the supplier either to address a 'specific invitation' to the consumer or to engage in 'advertising' in the member state of the consumer's domicile), it is reasonably clear that the maintenance of a website (which is accessible from anywhere in the world by anyone who has a computer linked to the Internet) is not a 'specific invitation' addressed to the consumer; by contrast, an e-mail solicitation is a 'specific invitation'—as it is directed to an individual.[35] Whether such a website amounts to 'advertising' is more controversial.[36] Because a website owner does not have to take active steps to bring the site's existence to the attention of the potential customer—web pages are never 'directed' at a particular jurisdiction, but are passively visible across the world—there is an argument for saying that a website is not advertising for the purposes of article 13. If this analysis were correct, the consumer jurisdiction rules of the Convention would not apply to online consumer contracts. **4.18**

As regards the 'contracting' criterion of article 13 (which requires the consumer to take 'the steps necessary for the conclusion of the contract' in the member state of his domicile), it may be difficult in online situations to say with accuracy where the consumer took the relevant steps. For example, there may be problems in determining where the consumer was located when he clicked on the 'Buy now' icon on the e-trader's website. Nevertheless, it would seem that, in principle, where a consumer domiciled in country X enters an online contract while visiting country Y, the **4.19**

[34] M Cordera (2001: 241).

[35] M Chissick and A Kelman (2002: 118); T Puurunen (2002: 158).

[36] See, eg, F Debusseré (2002: 352–3); M Foss and LA Bygrave (2000: 114–17).

contracting criterion of article 13 is not satisfied.[37] This might be thought to illustrate the extent to which article 13 of the Brussels Convention was not well adapted to the realities of e-commerce.

The aim of article 15(1)(c) of the Regulation

4.20 In view of the uncertainties surrounding the interaction of e-commerce with the Brussels Convention's provisions relating to consumer contracts, in the negotiations which ultimately led to the Brussels I Regulation, it was considered essential that both the 'marketing' and 'contracting' criteria should be reformulated—with a view to ensuring that the consumer's home forum has jurisdiction where a consumer purchases goods or services online from a supplier domiciled in another member state.[38] On the one hand, the revised wording of article 15(1)(c) of the Regulation is designed to make sure that 'consumer contracts concluded via an interactive website accessible in the State of the consumer's domicile'[39] are protected consumer contracts for the purposes of Section 4 of Chapter 2. On the other, it is not intended that article 15(1)(c) should extend to situations simply by virtue of the fact that, prior to entering an offline contract, the consumer acquires knowledge of a service or of the possibility of buying goods via a passive website.[40]

A domicile question

4.21 Article 15(1)(c) applies only if the defendant is domiciled in a member state. Domicile for the purposes of the Brussels I Regulation must be where the natural or legal person in question is located; the place where an e-trader sets up his computer systems is irrelevant for the determination of the e-trader's domicile.[41] So, a corporate e-trader whose principal place of business is situated in a member state is domiciled in that state even if all the relevant computing activity takes place through hardware located in other countries.[42]

[37] M Foss and LA Bygrave (2000: 125–6).

[38] For discussion of the various steps leading to the introduction of the Brussels I Regulation, see LE Gillies (2001).

[39] European Commission, COM (99) 348, p 16.

[40] European Commission, COM (99) 348, p 16. See K Vasiljeva (2004). Nevertheless, such situations may well give rise to protected consumer contracts on the basis that the supplier directs commercial or professional activities to the member state of the consumer's domicile by means other than the website.

[41] A Lopez-Tarruella (2001: 242).

[42] M Chissick and A Kelman (2002: 119).

Article 15(1)(c): Analysis

There has been a lot of discussion over exactly when it should be possible for a consumer, domiciled in member state A, to sue in that state an e-trader established in member state B. It would not be unfair to say that some of this discussion involves paper tigers and suggests possible interpretations which are highly implausible; the operation of article 15(1)(c) in relation to e-commerce is not as problematical as some commentators have suggested. However, while the bulk of situations are easy enough to analyse, there are some less mainstream scenarios which could, in theory, pose more difficult questions of interpretation. **4.22**

The effect of the revised consumer contract provisions in the Brussels I Regulation is that, where the consumer concludes an online contract with an e-trader domiciled in another member state, the consumer will have the choice of suing in his home forum. Article 15(1)(c) applies in cases where a consumer enters 'a contract with a person who pursues commercial or professional activities in the Member State of the consumer's domicile or directs such activities to that Member State or to several States including that Member State, and the contract falls within the scope of such activities'. This formula is wide enough to include contracts concluded via active or interactive websites. **4.23**

'Marketing' criterion: 'pursues' or 'directs'

Whereas article 13 of the Brussels Convention was based on the distinction between 'active' and 'passive' consumers, article 15 of the Brussels I Regulation adopts a slightly different approach (albeit one which, for the most part, achieves very similar results). As regards the marketing criterion, article 15(1)(c) contains two alternatives: first, where the supplier 'pursues' commercial activities in the member state of the consumer's domicile; secondly, where the supplier 'directs' such activities to that member state. It is possible that cases of 'pure' electronic commerce (ie, where the supplier has no physical presence at all in the consumer's home forum) do not come within the first alternative on the basis that, without some tangible sign of a pattern of activity, it cannot be said that the supplier 'pursues' activities in the member state of the consumer's domicile.[43] However, it hardly matters whether the first alternative should be interpreted strictly or more broadly as, in the context of e-commerce, it is the second marketing criterion ('directs') under article 15(1)(c) which is more relevant.[44] **4.24**

43 JST Øren (2003: 677).
44 For the legislative history of the 'directing' test, see JST Øren (2003: 679–83).

4.25 In the context of e-commerce, the key element in article 15(1)(c) is that the supplier 'directs [commercial or professional] activities' to the country in which the consumer is domiciled. The use of the phrase 'by any means' in the amended text of the Brussels I Regulation is specifically intended to cover e-commerce transactions and to give consumers the ability to proceed in their home forum as regards contracts concluded via the Internet—at least when the contract is concluded via an interactive or active website accessible in the state in which the consumer is domiciled. This is made clear by the *travaux préparatoires* to the Brussels I Regulation; according to the European Commission: 'the very existence of [an online consumer contract] would seem to be a clear indication that the supplier has directed his activities towards the state where the consumer is domiciled'.[45] Furthermore, the Joint Statement of the Council and the Commission on articles 15 and 73 of the Regulation is in the following terms:

> The Council and the Commission point out that . . . for Article 15(1)(c) to be applicable it is not sufficient for an undertaking to target its activities at the Member State of the consumer's residence, or at a number of Member States including that Member State; a contract must also be concluded within the framework of its activities. . . . In this context, the Council and the Commission stress that the mere fact that an Internet site is accessible is not sufficient for Article 15 to be applicable . . .[46]

4.26 Notwithstanding criticisms of this interpretation of article 15[47] and the fact that some commentators think that the conclusion of a contract via a website is not enough to satisfy the 'directing' requirement,[48] this aspect of the joint statement should be uncontroversial. Arguments based on both the text of article 15(1)(c) and its policy support the view that, where a consumer domiciled in member state A enters a contract with an e-trader domiciled in member state B via the e-trader's website, the e-trader should be treated as directing its activities to member state A.

4.27 First, the way in which article 15(1)(c) is drafted suggests that 'pursues' and 'directs' have different meanings and it appears from the *travaux préparatoires* that the 'directing' requirement is intended to broaden the scope of article 15(1)(c). Secondly, if the goal of 'protecting' consumers (by enabling them to sue in their home forum) is to mean anything, it makes

[45] COM (2000) 689, p 6 (para 2.2.2).

[46] The Joint Statement can be found at more than one online location. See <http://ec.europa.eu/civiljustice/homepage/homepage_ec_en_declaration.pdf> [2/11/07] or pp 5–6 of the document to be found at <http://register.consilium.eu.int/pdf/en/00/st14/14139en0.pdf> [2/11/07].

[47] See F Debusseré (2002: 359–61).

[48] JST Øren (2003: 687).

no sense artificially to interpret 'directs' narrowly; a broad interpretation is more consistent with the provision's purpose.[49] Thirdly, article 15 is not a basis of general jurisdiction; it is a basis of special jurisdiction for disputes arising out of consumer contracts. It goes without saying that, in order for article 15 to apply, there must be a contract between the consumer and the supplier. This means that, in analytical terms, the requirement that the supplier 'directs [commercial or professional] activities' largely disappears as an independent criterion in a case where the consumer buys goods or services through an interactive or active website. If the supplier's website is accessible in the member state of the consumer's domicile and the consumer enters a contract with the supplier through that website, the conditions of article 15(1)(c) are satisfied: the combination of accessibility of the website and online contracting satisfies the 'directs activities' criterion. Accordingly, in cases where the supplier is domiciled (or deemed to be domiciled) in a member state, litigation relating to a dispute which arises from an online consumer contract will take place in the country of the consumer's domicile (unless the consumer chooses to litigate elsewhere).[50]

If a website makes it clear that it is intended only for consumers from a particular country, the supplier should not be regarded as directing activities to other countries: 'where prominent disclaimers are displayed stating that a web site is targeting English consumers . . . only, then it is reasonable to assume that the particular web site is not directing activities to other EU member states'.[51] Some commentators would go further: it has been argued that, to determine whether a website is 'directed' to a particular member state, one should have regard to matters such as the language in which the site is written, the currency in which the supplier's prices are expressed, and the suffix of the supplier's web address (such as *.de* for Germany or*.uk* for the United Kingdom); if all such factors point to a particular member state, the supplier should not be treated as directing activities to other member states.[52] This view cannot be supported—for several reasons. First, this approach is contrary to the Joint Statement of the Council and Commission which indicates that 'the language or currency **4.28**

[49] It is perhaps worth reiterating that, because of the obstacles to consumer litigation, it is doubtful whether even a broad interpretation of the 'directing' requirement can make much of a contribution, in practical terms, to the attainment of the general goal of promoting consumer welfare.

[50] N Reich and A Halfmeier (2001: 120).

[51] M Chissick and A Kelman (2002: 137).

[52] JST Øren (2003: 690).

which a website uses does not constitute a relevant factor'.[53] Secondly, such an approach would be very difficult to apply as many elements of a website may point equally to several member states. For example, prices may be denominated in euros; the website may be drafted in languages which are spoken in more than one member state (such as English, French, or German); the supplier's web address may be jurisdiction-neutral (such as *.com* or *.org*). Thirdly, even if these practical issues were put to one side, this type of approach is likely to generate an unacceptable degree of uncertainty.

The 'contracting' criterion

4.29 Article 15(1)(c) also requires that the contract 'falls within the scope of' the professional or commercial activities directed to the member state of the consumer's domicile. There is no requirement that the consumer should actually take the steps necessary for the conclusion of the contract in the member state in which he is domiciled. So, a consumer who is domiciled in Belgium, but works in the Netherlands, may access the supplier's website while at home in Belgium, but place an online order for goods or services from his work PC during his lunch hour in the Netherlands. In this situation, the requirements of article 15(1)(c) are satisfied.

4.30 It is less clear that these conditions should be treated as satisfied if the consumer had never accessed the website while at home in Belgium. Arguably, the mere fact that the website is accessible in Belgium should not bring article 15 into the picture if the consumer's contract with the supplier has no connection with Belgium. If the Belgian consumer, while in the Netherlands, orders the goods online, it is arguable that the consumer should not be entitled to expect that he could sue the supplier in Belgium.[54] However, the wording of article 15(1)(c) suggests that the relevant conditions are satisfied in this type of case. If the supplier's website is accessible in both Belgium and the Netherlands and the supplier habitually contracts with consumers domiciled in both countries, it can be said that the supplier directs commercial activities to 'several States including [the State of the consumer's domicile]' and that, regardless of whether the consumer first accesses the website while at home in Belgium or at work in the Netherlands, the contract 'falls within the scope of those activities'. Having said that, the precise operation of article 15(1)(c) in this type of situation could have been made clearer.

[53] See <http://ec.europa.eu/civiljustice/homepage/homepage_ec_en_declaration.pdf> [2/11/07].

[54] M Foss and LA Bygrave (2000: 137).

Potential problems of interpretation

The preceding paragraphs have dealt with the paradigm case in which a consumer accesses a supplier's website and enters a contract with the supplier via that website. In these cases, the intended operation of article 15(1)(c) is normally easy enough to discern. As regards some less straightforward factual situations, the proper interpretation of article 15(1)(c) is less certain. Only time will tell whether the courts will ever be called upon to consider such scenarios. One commentator has expressed the hope that 'the European Court of Justice will be given the opportunity to clarify what is meant by "directing such activities" to consumers'[55] and to define 'other establishment' for the purposes of article 15(2).[56] Given the low value of the vast majority of b2c e-contracts, the likelihood of such issues being referred to the Court of Justice under article 234 EC is extremely small. Such a reference can be made only by a member state's final court of appeal.[57] How many cross-border online consumer contracts are likely to generate jurisdictional litigation which progresses to the apex of a member state's court system? **4.31**

There is disagreement over whether the requirements of article 15(1)(c) are satisfied in a case where the consumer learns about the supplier's products via a website—and then concludes the contract offline.[58] For example, a consumer may, having looked at the supplier's website, order goods by post or telephone. There is a view that, as a website is akin to a mere advertisement, it should not be possible for jurisdiction to be established in the consumer's home forum if the website does not entitle the consumer to contract online with the business via the site.[59] According to this view a purely passive website which is accessible from the consumer's country is not, in itself, a sufficiently strong connection with that country to justify the assumption of jurisdiction by its courts. However, the Joint Statement of the Council and the Commission can be read as supporting a broader view; according to the statement, for the purposes of determining whether a contract is concluded within the scope of the professional or commercial activities directed by the supplier to the member state in which the consumer is domiciled, a relevant factor is that the supplier's website 'solicits the conclusion of distance contracts and . . . a contract has actually been concluded at a distance, *by whatever means*'. [60] This statement strongly **4.32**

[55] LE Gillies (2001a: 397). See also F Debusseré (2002: 360, 365).

[56] LE Gillies (2003: 367).

[57] See arts 65, 68, and 234EC.

[58] See the discussion of Z Tang (2007: 44–5).

[59] LE Gillies (2001a: 397).

[60] See <http://ec.europa.eu/civiljustice/homepage/homepage_ec_en_declaration.pdf> [2/11/07]. See also M Berliri (2003a: 50).

suggests that, in the situation where the supplier has a passive website which is accessible in the member state of the consumer's domicile, an offline distance contract between a consumer and the supplier will satisfy the conditions of article 15(1)(c). *A fortiori* the conditions of article 15(1)(c) are satisfied in a case where a supplier promotes its goods through an interactive website, but the consumer, having learned about the supplier's products through the website, contracts with the supplier offline—rather than via the website.[61]

2. Article 15(2)

4.33 As has been seen already,[62] article 15(2) deals with cases where a supplier who is not domiciled in a member state has a branch, agency, or other establishment in a member state; where a dispute arises out of the operations of the branch between a consumer and the supplier, the supplier is deemed to be domiciled in the member state in which the branch is located as regards that dispute. So, if a New York company has a branch in Germany, the company can be sued in Germany in relation to a dispute arising out of the operations of the German branch. In the context of e-commerce, there is a question whether a website can constitute a 'branch' for the purposes of article 15(2). This question must be answered in the negative.

4.34 It is widely assumed that 'branch' should bear the same meaning in both article 15(2) and article 5(5)[63] and it must be doubtful whether a website could, in itself, satisfy the criteria laid down by the Court of Justice (in the context of article 5(5)) in the cases of *De Bloos*,[64] *Somafer*,[65] and *Blankaert*.[66] Since, in these cases, the Court of Justice emphasized the tangible nature of a 'branch', it seems clear that a 'virtual office' cannot be a branch for the purposes of article 5(5).[67]

4.35 However, it has been argued that the term 'branch, agency or other establishment' should be interpreted more broadly for the purposes of article 15(2) than in the context of article 5(5)—and that, under article 15(2), it might be appropriate to treat a highly-localized 'virtual office' as a branch.[68]

[61] T Puurunen (2002: 176).
[62] See paras 3.122–3.123.
[63] cf M Foss and LA Bygrave (2000: 131–3).
[64] Case 14/76 [1976] ECR 1497.
[65] Case 33/78 [1978] ECR 2183.
[66] Case 139/80 [1981] ECR 819.
[67] cf Y Zhao (2005: 111).
[68] See, eg, M Foss and LA Bygrave (2000: 125–31).

If, as regards disputes arising out of the operations of a US supplier's French 'bricks-and-mortar' branch, a consumer can sue the supplier in France, it is not obvious why, in policy terms, it should not be possible for the consumer to sue a US supplier in France as regards disputes arising from sales made through the supplier's 'French' website—even though the supplier is not domiciled in a member state. A consumer would have a reasonable expectation that a supplier who operated a 'national' website (such as a website which is drafted in the Danish language, is denominated in Danish krone, and has a domain name ending *.dk*) would be amenable to the jurisdiction of the courts of the country in question. However, whatever merit this argument may have in policy terms, it is legally unconvincing—and not only because of the Court of Justice's case law concerning article 5(5).

The majority view among commentators is that the location of computer hardware (such as a server or an electronic agent) either owned or used by the defendant in a particular member state is not a relevant factor for jurisdictional purposes.[69] This view is supported by the E-Commerce Directive, according to which 'the place of establishment of a company providing services via an Internet website is not the place at which the technology supporting its website is located'.[70] In addition, article 2(c) of the Directive states that '[t]he presence and use of the technical means and technologies required to provide [information society services] do not, in themselves, constitute an establishment.' Accordingly, it seems reasonably clear that what is jurisdictionally important for the purposes of article 15(2) is the physical office from which a website is administered: an electronic presence, in the form of a server containing a website or handling e-mail, cannot constitute a branch, agency, or other establishment.[71] **4.36**

III. CONCLUSION

1. E-commerce: The Emperor's New Clothes?

In the context of cross-border consumer contracts, there is considerably less to e-commerce, from a legal point of view, than meets the eye. For all the talk of paradigm shifts, the uniqueness of cyberspace, and the **4.37**

[69] See, eg, M Chissick and A Kelman (2002: 119); HA Deveci (2006: 44); LE Gillies (2001); LE Gillies (2001a); LE Gillies (2003: 367–8); M Schaub (2004: 151); PA Stone (2002: 128). See also R Schu (1997: 204, 221–2) (in a discussion of choice-of-law rules).

[70] Dir 2000/31/EC, recital 19.

[71] PA Stone (2002: 128). See also M Schaub (2004: 151).

inappropriateness of applying the rules designed for the real world to e-contracts, in jurisdictional terms, online b2c contracts present relatively few problems in terms of analysis. This is not to say that there are no interesting questions or potentially tricky doctrinal issues. Nevertheless, for the most part, jurisdiction rules designed for the real world can be relatively easily adapted for the online environment. In the United States it has been observed that:

> although Internet transactions might appear to pose novel jurisdictional issues, traditional jurisdictional standards have proved to be sufficient to resolve all civil Internet jurisdictional issues raised to date, refuting the view of [those who] . . . believe a new body of jurisprudence is needed.[72]

4.38 Even in the European Union, in which it was thought necessary to amend the consumer contract provisions in the Brussels I Regulation, the effect of the Regulation is to clarify the position, rather than to bring about a significant change in the law. The practical difference between article 13 of the Brussels Convention and article 15 of the Regulation seems small; it has plausibly been suggested that the only real difference is where a consumer orders goods online while in a country other than that in which he is domiciled (for example, where an English consumer places an online order from an Internet café while on holiday in France)—which is a protected consumer contract under article 15 of the Regulation, but would not have been within the scope of article 13 of the Convention.[73]

2. How Controversial is Article 15(1)(c)?

4.39 In the context of e-commerce, the net result of article 15(1)(c) is that an e-trader can, in principle, be sued in any of the member states in which he sells goods or services to consumers. It has been suggested that:

> Since any website is almost always accessible in all EU Member States, . . . any website holder who is domiciled in an EU Member State can be sued in any EU Member State, irrespective of whether or not he wished to do business in the Member State concerned.[74]

4.40 This passage—by adding the words 'irrespective of whether or not he wished to do business in the Member State concerned'—runs the risk of overstating the case. Under the Brussels I Regulation, there are various strategies which an e-trader can adopt to avoid being sued in a forum which is considered uncongenial. There are both legal and practical aspects to consider.

[72] *New York v Lipsitz* 663 NYS 2d 468, 473 (NYC, 1997).

[73] PA Stone (2002: 125).

[74] F Debusseré (2002: 358).

From a legal perspective, there is a view that if companies were to restrict themselves to particular jurisdictions and to deny access to their goods or services for consumers based in other jurisdictions, such practice would be contrary to EC rules relating to the common market.[75] However, the better view is that, notwithstanding the desire of the EC institutions to promote a single market, it is legitimate for an e-trader to confine his business to countries with whose legal systems he is familiar and willing to engage.[76]

From a technical point of view, it is relatively easy for e-traders to ring-fence their commercial activities and it seems clear that a significant proportion of e-traders choose either not to enter cross-border contracts at all or not to sell to consumers from certain countries.[77] Most e-contracts are structured in such a way that the website is an invitation to treat, the consumer's order is an offer to buy, and the contract is concluded only when the consumer's order is accepted by the e-trader. The supplier can indicate on the website's homepage that transactions will not be concluded with consumers from certain countries (where the supplier does not want to run the risk of being sued). Moreover, the consumer can also be required to indicate his home address when contracting via the website and, if the address is in an 'unacceptable' country, the supplier can choose not to proceed with the transaction. If, in order to be able to transact with the supplier, a consumer who is domiciled in an 'unacceptable' country misrepresents that he is domiciled in an 'acceptable' country[78] there is a very strong argument for saying that the consumer should be treated as estopped from seeking to rely on his domicile as a basis for suing the supplier in the consumer's home forum.[79] **4.41**

Although the e-commerce lobby complained about the country-of-destination approach to consumer jurisdiction in the Brussels I Regulation,[80] the fact that an EU consumer can sue an e-trader domiciled in another **4.42**

[75] K Vasiljeva (2004: 134).

[76] PA Stone (2002: 125).

[77] See Consumers International (September 2001: 20).

[78] It would, of course, make little sense for a consumer to make such a misrepresentation in a case involving the sale of goods, as the consumer will normally want the goods delivered to his home address. However, as regards contracts for the provision of services, particularly in cases where the supplier's contractual performance is effected by the online transmission of electronic data to the buyer's computer, the location of which is not known to the supplier, a consumer might misrepresent his home address in order to be able to contract with the supplier.

[79] PA Stone (2002: 125); JST Øren (2003: 691–4); S van der Hof (2003: 171–2); Z Tang (2007: 45).

[80] See, eg, PR Motion (2001).

member state in the consumer's home forum is not really contentious. Even in the United States, which is less pro-consumer than the European Union, US consumers are normally entitled to sue out-of-state e-traders in their home state with regard to disputes arising out of contracts concluded via the Internet; if a supplier directly solicits a contract from an individual in a particular state, a single transaction is sufficient to require the supplier to respond to litigation arising out of that transaction in that state.[81]

4.43 Furthermore, when one puts together the fact that litigation arising out of cross-border consumer contracts is extremely rare with the ring-fencing measures that a supplier can take to avoid transacting with consumers from 'unacceptable' countries, the jurisdictional risk which suppliers assume when marketing their goods and services on a global scale is really very small. Against this background, it is reasonable to conclude that the fuss generated by article 15(1) of the Brussels I Regulation was somewhat disproportionate—all the more so when one remembers that, as regards contracts in general, article 5(1)(b) of the Regulation allocates jurisdiction to the courts for the place of performance of the supplier's obligation; if the supplier's obligation is to deliver goods to the consumer at the consumer's home address (or to perform services there), the courts for the place where the consumer is domiciled would have jurisdiction in any event—even if the Brussels I Regulation contained no provisions relating specifically to consumer contracts.

4.44 It is sometimes suggested that 'unpredictability of jurisdiction makes it difficult for companies with websites to limit their legal liability and inhibits the growth of e-commerce.'[82] While this type of assertion is fairly common,[83] it is based on questionable premises—at least as far as the consumer context is concerned. First, as has been seen, the operation of jurisdiction rules in relation to online consumer contracts is, for the most part, relatively straightforward in both the European Union and the United States. Secondly, even if the courts of the country in which the consumer resides are able to assume jurisdiction over disputes arising from online consumer contracts, the idea that e-traders run a serious risk of being sued by consumers in the courts of the various countries in which they sell goods or provide services is largely fanciful.

4.45 Imagine that a German e-trader sells books, CDs, and DVDs over the Internet to consumers who reside in each of the 27 member states of the European Union. By virtue of the consumer contract provisions of

[81] EF Scoles and P Hay (1992: 298).

[82] C Chen (2004: 423).

[83] See, eg, BL Smith (2000: 333); AM Sachdeva (2007: 257).

the Brussels I Regulation, as regards each online sale, the courts of the consumer's home forum have jurisdiction over any contractual disputes. In such circumstances, it has to be conceded that, in theory, the e-trader runs the risk of being sued in each of the member states. But, in reality, what is the extent of the e-trader's jurisdictional risk? How likely is it that an English consumer would incur the costs of both suing the German e-trader in England and then, if successful, seeking to enforce the judgment in Germany? Not surprisingly, ECC-Net noted in its e-commerce report of 2005 that 'not a single ECC office has ever had a consumer, or even heard of one, that has initiated litigation against a foreign webtrader'.[84]

Many of the hypothetical examples used by commentators to illustrate the perceived strengths or weaknesses of the jurisdiction rules are extremely implausible (normally, because they involve low-value transactions in relation to which litigation is almost inconceivable). Within this sort of context, the supposed litigation risks generated by pro-consumer jurisdiction rules (such as those set out in Section 4 of Chapter II of the Brussels I Regulation) are very largely confined to the realm of theory. **4.46**

[84] ECC-Net (June 2006: 29). See, also, European Commission, COM (98) 198, p 5.

5

Improving Civil Justice: European Developments

I. INTRODUCTION

Although the Brussels I Regulation and the Lugano Convention tackle jurisdictional questions relating to consumer contracts—and include provisions which are designed to 'protect' the interests of consumers—they do not address consumers' access-to-justice problems. Jurisdiction rules designed to benefit consumers are meaningful in cross-border cases only if the underlying procedural framework provides a truly accessible avenue through which consumers are able to vindicate their legal rights. **5.01**

Notwithstanding legislative efforts at the national level to make legal processes more user-friendly, it has been acknowledged by the European Commission that the judicial systems of the member states 'are too expensive, too slow and too difficult to deal with'.[1] Whatever problems consumers face at the domestic level, these problems are more pronounced in the cross-border context: 'The costs are higher, the delays are longer, and the relevance and effectiveness of the courts for resolving such disputes, especially when the value of the disputed product is low, is not obvious.'[2] Furthermore, if what is being contemplated is litigation in a foreign country, there may be not only the added time and expense of travelling to another country, but also unfamiliarity with the foreign legal system and **5.02**

[1] European Commission, COM (2002) 746, p 49. See also K Viitanen (2000: 315).

[2] M Wilikens, A Vahrenwald, and P Morris (April 2000: 2).

language differences.[3] Not surprisingly, in the cross-border context, '[m]any people, faced with the expense of the proceedings, and daunted by the practical difficulties that are likely to ensue, abandon any hope of obtaining what they believe is rightfully theirs.'[4]

5.03 It is against this background that the attention of legislators at the European level has been directed at the reform of civil procedure. As regards developments which may possibly have an impact in the consumer context, the most significant reform concerns the introduction of a European Small Claims Procedure (ESCP).[5] It is also possible that a European class action procedure will be introduced at some point.

II. SMALL CLAIMS

1. Background

General

5.04 As regards small claims procedures, there is a very wide variety of solutions under the national laws of the member states. Whereas some member states (including the United Kingdom) have specific small claims procedures, others do not; however, some of the countries which do not have small claims procedures as such, provide for a simplification of the ordinary procedure in cases involving small claims.[6] As regards those countries which do have specific small claims procedures, there is no uniformity as to what counts as a 'small claim': for example, in Germany the monetary threshold for small claims is €600, whereas in England, the limit is £5,000.[7] In some member states (such as France and Portugal) oral hearings are usually required and the claimant is expected to attend in person.[8] In others (such as Germany and Sweden) a purely written procedure is possible; in Germany, written procedure is the rule in practice.[9] Although in England a judgment may be based on a written procedure alone if the judge thinks it appropriate and the parties agree, such cases are rare.

[3] Organisation for Economic Co-operation and Development (2006: 28).

[4] European Commission, COM (2002) 746, p 49.

[5] Developments with regard to the European Enforcement Order (EEO) and the European Order for Payment Procedure (EOPP) are considered in ch 6.

[6] Study Centre for Consumer Law (January 2007: 196–9). See also European Commission, COM (2002) 746, p 52.

[7] COM (2002) 746, p 53.

[8] Organisation for Economic Co-operation and Development (2006: 28).

[9] COM (2002) 746, p 57.

Notwithstanding the variations between different legal systems, small claims procedures tend to share some common characteristics: (i) such procedural models apply only to claims which have a monetary value below a certain threshold; (ii) there is a simplified method of commencing such proceedings (normally by the completion of a relatively simple form, which can be filled in by a layperson without legal knowledge); (iii) rules concerning the taking of evidence are relaxed; and (iv) litigants are normally expected to present their own cases and the participation of professional lawyers at small claims hearings, if not entirely eliminated, is much reduced.[10]

Most small claims procedures were designed to deal with domestic disputes. **5.05**
One of the significant problems with such procedures is that they may be wholly unsuited to dealing with cross-border cases. For example, the Irish Small Claims Court is, in practical terms, not structured in a way that enables non-resident claimants to use it—as it requires the claimant to be present at the hearing.[11] Similar problems exist in the English legal system; for example, the online small claims procedure requires the defendant to have an address in England.[12] A report written by the ECC (Dublin) refers to a case in which an Irish consumer attempted to commence proceedings against an English supplier in England: the consumer sent his application and the fee to the county court, but they were returned on the basis that the claimant was not resident in the United Kingdom; the ECC (Dublin) contacted the court once again and was told that the court employee did not understand the system; the consumer was left frustrated and confused.[13]

The extent to which consumers litigate small claims varies substantially **5.06**
from one country to another.[14] For example, in Sweden, which has a well-developed system of ADR through consumer complaints boards, small claims litigation in the consumer context is very unusual: in 2004 only six court cases were initiated by a consumer against a supplier.[15] By contrast, in England, the annual number of small claims cases involving claims by consumers against suppliers runs into the thousands.[16] (It is not recorded

[10] See, generally, CJ Whelan (1990); Study Centre for Consumer Law (January 2007: 210–29).

[11] ECC (Dublin) (June 2004: 6); JP Cortes Dieguez (2008: 88).

[12] Civil Procedure Rules, PD 7E, para 4(6).

[13] ECC (Dublin) (June 2004: 10–11).

[14] See Study Centre for Consumer Law (January 2007: 226).

[15] Study Centre for Consumer Law (January 2007: 30, n 7).

[16] In 2005, there were 47,512 small claim cases in England: *Judicial Statistics 2005* (Cm 6799); research indicates that the proportion which involves a claim by an individual against

how may, if any, are cross-border cases.) Nevertheless, it needs to be noted that the majority of small claims litigation is commenced by businesses and other commercial organizations (rather than by individuals).[17]

Small Claims in England[18]

5.07 When a claim is brought in the county court, an important first stage is the allocation of the case by a District Judge to the appropriate 'track': if the value of the claim does not exceed £5,000 the claim is normally allocated to the small claims track:

> The small claims track is supposed to provide a simple and informal way of resolving disputes in comparison to the multi track or fast track, where as a general rule, the winning party would normally expect to recover their costs, including their legal costs, from the losing party.[19]

5.08 A significant factor in the accessibility of the small claims procedure is the so-called 'no costs' rule. The court may normally award to the successful party in a small claim only: (i) court fees and fixed commencement costs;[20] and (ii) limited loss of earnings for parties and witnesses plus their expenses. The use of lawyers is not prevented, but lawyers' fees cannot be claimed. This means that, because legal aid is not normally available, parties who wish to have legal representation must pay for it themselves. The 'no costs' rule deters most litigants involved in small claims from hiring a lawyer.[21] It is also a significant factor in reducing the financial risk involved in the pursuit of a small claim through the courts; in a case where the

a business is something between 15 per cent (J Baldwin (December 1997: 94)) and 21 per cent (Touche Ross (1986: 21)). It is interesting to note that, in Israel, the percentage of consumer claims in the Small Claims Court is around 16 per cent: S Deutsch (2004: 180).

17 In England, a business is the claimant in around 60 per cent of cases: J Baldwin (1997: 30). The position in several other European countries is similar: see Study Centre for Consumer Law (January 2007: 229). See also M Cappelletti and B Garth (1978: 71, 78).

18 For detailed consideration of small claims in England, see J Baldwin (1997) from which much of the data considered in this section is derived.

19 Constitutional Affairs Committee (December 2005: para 6).

20 For claims within the small claims limit, the county court fees are low—but not negligible: the fee for the issue of a claim form starts at £30 (where the claim is for a sum of money not exceeding £300) and rises in steps to £108 if the value of the claim is more than £3,000 but does not exceed £5,000; however, there are other fees which, depending on the circumstances, may also be payable—such as an allocation fee or a hearing fee (which may be as much as £300): see <http://www.hmcourts-service.gov.uk/courtfinder/forms/ex50.pdf> [14/17/08].

21 Research has found that neither party is legally represented in more than four-fifths of cases and that both parties are legally represented in only around 2 per cent of cases: J Baldwin (1997: 39).

defendant opts for legal representation, the claimant, if unsuccessful, does not have to reimburse the fees charged by the defendant's lawyer.

There is, however, a downside to the fact that litigants in small claims procedures tend not to be legally represented. Notwithstanding the relative simplicity of the small claims track, there is evidence to suggest that litigants in person still find it complicated and difficult to negotiate.[22] Research has revealed that 'lay litigants, since they lack legal expertise, experience difficulty in establishing the legal validity of their claims and defences and in arguing a coherent case in court'.[23] Although some of these problems could be addressed if litigants obtained legal advice, it seems that, in practice, few take the trouble to do so.[24] **5.09**

One of the most significant problems with the small claims process is that, not infrequently, litigants obtain a judgment which they are not able to enforce; only a minority of claimants who succeed at small claims hearings receive payment from the other party in full; a substantial minority receive nothing at all.[25] Research in the 1990s made the following findings: **5.10**

> [W]hile 58 per cent of successful plaintiffs recovered all or part of the money from defendants, two-fifths of them had to take steps to enforce the court's judgment. But only about a third of those who said that they had taken such action . . . managed to recover even a part of their claim. . . . Six months after the event, only half of successful plaintiffs said that they had received full payment from the defendant without having to take further legal and other measures. A substantial proportion had received no payment at all. . . . With less than a third of the plaintiffs in the sample receiving full payment on time, the inescapable conclusion is that enforcement poses major problems for the small claims regime.[26]

Given that there are certain types of defendant who always satisfy judgments (such as insurance companies), there appears to be 'a core of individuals or companies who either cannot, or will not, pay judgments which have been entered against them'.[27] Part of the problem is that enforcement of a judgment is the responsibility of the litigant, rather than the court (which can only provide advice on the avenues available to a successful claimant): 'it remains the case that any defendant who is prepared to brazen things out and knows how to avoid the predatory eyes of the bailiffs **5.11**

[22] Constitutional Affairs Committee (December 2005: para 15).
[23] J Baldwin (1997: 19).
[24] J Baldwin (1997: 10).
[25] Constitutional Affairs Committee (December 2005: para 29).
[26] J Baldwin (1997: 131–3).
[27] Constitutional Affairs Committee (December 2005: para 30).

can evade payment without too much difficulty'.[28] Steps have been taken in the Tribunals, Courts and Enforcement Act 2007 to try to improve enforcement methods, but it remains to be seen whether these reforms will assist consumers who obtain a judgment in their favour.[29]

2. The European Small Claims Procedure Regulation

5.12 In 2005 the Commission made a proposal for the creation of a European small claims procedure. The objective was 'to simplify and speed up litigation concerning small claims, and to reduce costs'.[30] The European Small Claims Procedure Regulation (ESCP)[31] was adopted in the summer of 2007 and applies as from 1 January 2009.[32] The material scope of the Regulation mirrors that of the Brussels I Regulation[33] but it applies only where 'the value of the claim does not exceed €2000 at the time that the claim form is received by the court or tribunal with jurisdiction, excluding all interest, expenses and disbursements'.[34] In addition, the ESCP is available only in cross-border cases[35]—which are defined as those 'in which at least one of the parties is domiciled or habitually resident in a Member State other than the Member State of the court or tribunal seised'.[36] However, the ESCP does not displace national procedural law in cross-border cases; it provides a separate procedural avenue which claimants may pursue as an alternative to the national procedure.[37] So, in a cross-border case involving a claim within the ESCP limit, a claimant who proposes to initiate small claims litigation in England can choose between the procedure provided by the Civil Procedure Rules and the procedure set out in the Regulation.

5.13 The ESCP is commenced by completing the claim form set out in Annex 1 to the Regulation and lodging it with the relevant court.[38] Member states

[28] J Baldwin (1997: 139).

[29] The provisions of the 2007 Act relating to enforcement (in particular, Parts 3 and 4) have yet to be brought into force.

[30] See art 1 of the proposal: European Commission, COM (2005) 87.

[31] Reg (EC) No 861/2007 [2007] OJ L199/1.

[32] Art 29.

[33] Art 2.

[34] Art 2(1). This financial limit is significantly lower than the limit for proceedings allocated to the small claims track under the Civil Procedure Rules (which currently stands at £5,000).

[35] The original proposal was that the ESCP should be available in both domestic and cross-border cases: see European Commission, COM (2005) 87. However, this proved controversial and many argued that the ESCP should be limited to cross-border cases: see, eg, Constitutional Affairs Committee (December 2005: para 63).

[36] Art 3(1).

[37] Art 1.

[38] Art 4(1).

are required to ensure that the claim form is available at all courts and tribunals at which the ESCP can be commenced.[39] The procedure envisages that the court will play an active role in the process; it is provided not only that the parties cannot be required to be represented by a lawyer or another legal professional,[40] but also that the court 'shall not require the parties to make any legal assessment of the claim'.[41] In the typical case in which one or more of the parties is unrepresented, the ESCP requires the court to translate the parties' factual assertions into legally relevant claims and defences. It is also provided that '[w]herever appropriate, the court or tribunal shall seek to reach a settlement between the parties.'[42]

In cross-border cases, a wholly written procedure is likely to be more attractive for the consumer (and for witnesses). Where court procedures are based on oral hearings, some of the costs of the proceedings result from the fact that the consumer has to take time off work and, if the proceedings are abroad, travel to wherever the court sits. These are major obstacles which reduce the number of cases in which a consumer might consider that it is worthwhile pursuing litigation. Not surprisingly, therefore, the ESCP is envisaged as a written procedure. However, article 5(1) provides that the court 'shall hold an oral hearing if it considers it necessary'; furthermore, a party may request an oral hearing—though the court may refuse such a hearing if 'an oral hearing is obviously not necessary for the fair conduct of the proceedings'. If a hearing is necessary, the court may hold the hearing 'through video conference or other communication technology if the technical means are available'.[43] In those countries which normally require an oral hearing under their national small claims procedures, it will be interesting to see whether a wholly written procedure under the Regulation becomes the norm (as envisaged by the drafters of the Regulation) or the exception. Although the ESCP is intended as a uniform procedure throughout the European Union, there must be a significant possibility that the operation of article 5(1)—which turns on what the court 'considers . . . to be necessary'—will differ from one member state to another, depending on the procedural traditions of the country in question. 5.14

An important element of the ESCP concerns the question of costs. If, for example, the recovery of costs does not extend to the expenses incurred in 5.15

[39] Art 3(5). It is also provided that 'Member States shall ensure that the parties can receive practical assistance in filling in the forms': art 11.

[40] Art 10.

[41] Art 12(2).

[42] Art 12(3).

[43] Art 8.

hiring a lawyer—so that even a successful claimant has to bear his lawyer's fees—potential litigants (especially consumers) will tend to be deterred from employing a lawyer to assist in the presentation of their claim (or defence). Whereas the Civil Procedure Rules adopt the 'no costs' rule, the general rule under the Regulation is that 'the unsuccessful party shall bear the costs of the proceedings'.[44] On the one hand, this rule may have the effect of not discouraging consumers from hiring a lawyer—because, if successful, the consumer can recover his costs from the losing party. On the other hand, the 'loser-pays' principle exposes litigants to considerable financial risk in cases where the other party to the proceedings retains a lawyer to handle his case. A potential consumer-claimant who, if unsuccessful in his claim, faces the prospect of having to reimburse the supplier's legal costs may well be worried about running the economic risks which legal proceedings entail. The Regulation's only qualification to the 'loser-pays' principle is that the court 'shall not award costs to the successful party to the extent that they were unnecessarily incurred or are disproportionate to the claim'.[45] What this means in practical terms is hard to assess in the abstract as this provision appears to give courts considerable discretion over the awarding of costs.

5.16 Where a consumer (in reliance on articles 15 to 17 of the Brussels I Regulation) brings proceedings in his home forum, there is still the question of cross-border enforcement of any judgment which the consumer obtains in his favour. This is a stage of the litigation process which is liable to involve added expense and delay. Chapter III of the Regulation seeks to facilitate the cross-border enforcement of small claims judgments, largely through the elimination of intermediate measures as a prerequisite for enforcement in another member state.[46]

III. COLLECTIVE ACTIONS FOR DAMAGES

5.17 In the commercial context, where the loss resulting from a breach of contract is reckoned to be, say, £100,000, the party suffering the loss has a strong financial incentive to seek compensation—if necessary by litigating the claim. In the consumer context, however, a supplier may cause the same loss (by selling a defective product which costs £5 to repair to 20,000 different consumers), but no individual whose interests have been

[44] Art 16.

[45] Art 16. See also recital 29.

[46] European Commission, (2002) COM 159, p 3. For further discussion, see paras 6.20–6.24.

adversely affected by the supplier's conduct would seriously consider bringing (or threatening to bring) legal proceedings against the supplier. Even if a legal system adopts consumer-friendly procedures which enable a consumer to take individual action against a supplier in the consumer's home forum, in practice, few consumers make use of such procedures, because of the practical obstacles which render cross-border litigation such an unattractive option.[47] The net result of consumers not being able, in practical terms, to enforce their rights when small sums of money are at stake is that suppliers 'enrich themselves at the expense of those with whom they contract'.[48]

If consumer rights are to be upheld by legal action, one possible approach **5.18** to consumer protection is to re-conceptualize little injustices as collective harms.[49] It has been observed that, although consumer claims frequently represent individual losses, in the absence of collective procedures, consumers have grave difficulty obtaining a remedy for the loss they have suffered.[50] In theory, collective action can be useful in cases where large numbers of consumers have each suffered small losses.[51] This partly explains the development of the second 'wave' of the access-to-justice movement[52]—whereby legal standing has been given to bodies, such as consumer organizations, to act on behalf of the collective interests of consumers in general.[53]

In addition to the role played by public bodies and consumer organiza- **5.19** tions in taking action to bring unfair commercial practices to an end ('public interest collective litigation'[54]), there are two models of collective litigation ('private interest collective litigation'[55]) which aim at compensating consumers for wrongful conduct which inflicts a small amount of harm on a large number of consumers. The first model—which is the one to be found in the United States and has been adopted elsewhere—is the class action (or group action), which is the collective exercise of individual rights of action; an individual consumer initiates the claim in the name of a group of consumers. The second possibility is to give consumer organizations or public authorities the power to bring representative actions on

47 G Howells and R James (2002: 50).
48 PD Carrington (1998: 226).
49 L Nader (1979: 1021).
50 G Howells and R James (2002: 7).
51 Organisation for Economic Co-operation and Development (2006: 30).
52 See M Cappelletti (ed) (1981: vi–vii).
53 See ch 8.
54 G Howells and R James (2002: 31).
55 G Howells and R James (2002: 31).

behalf of consumers each of whom has suffered individual harm as a result of the same wrongful conduct. The purpose of both class actions and representative actions is the same—namely, to provide compensation for a group of consumers who have been harmed by the conduct of a supplier. The difference between the two approaches is institutional or organizational, rather than in terms of objective or outcome. Where consumer organizations may file representative actions the procedure operates in broadly the same way as other models of private interest collective litigation.[56]

5.20 Various legal systems both in Europe and elsewhere have introduced the possibility of class or representative actions for the enforcement of consumer rights. In England, notwithstanding the theoretical attractions of private interest collective litigation and the fact that the Civil Procedure Rules make some attempt to facilitate collective procedures,[57] it seems that the legal and practical problems surrounding such litigation have meant that, in the context of disputes arising out of consumer contracts, group litigation in England is rare to the point of being virtually non-existent.[58] It has been concluded that, as far as England is concerned, the legal system has failed to provide effective solutions to the challenge of finding mechanisms whereby consumers who individually have suffered small losses can group together so that litigation becomes a viable option.[59]

5.21 The position in most other EU member states is similar. For example, under French law consumer organizations may sue on behalf of consumers who have 'suffered individual harm caused by an act of one and the same professional and having a common origin'.[60] This is a true representative action—in the sense that it is not an action to protect a collective interest but rather the collective exercise of individual rights of action.[61]

[56] Organisation for Economic Co-operation and Development (2006: 33).

[57] C Hodges (2001: chs 2–9); C Scott and J Black (2000: 120–9). See CPR Pt 19.

[58] To the extent that group litigation has been initiated in recent years in England, it has tended to involve the following areas: personal injuries (including pharmaceutical product liability and accidents and illness suffered while on holiday); taxation; pension schemes; public authorities (including government departments); health care; and environmental cases. See the case studies discussed in C Hodges (2001: chs 16–32). There appear to have been few, if any, cases concerned with group litigation relating to anything that might reasonably be described as straightforward consumer contract disputes.

[59] G Howells and R James (2002: 33).

[60] Law 92/60 of 18 January 1992, art 8 (cited by European Commission, COM (93) 576, p 54).

[61] European Commission, COM (93) 576, p 54.

However, the French legislation has been of limited practical use.[62] Similar legislation has been introduced in several other member states.[63] In most EU countries, very few cases have been handled under the relevant legislation and the practical impact of the legislation has been very limited.[64] There is a view that the Swedish experience with the Group Proceedings Act of 2003 (under which provision is made not only for private collective actions, but also for the consumer ombudsman to file a 'public group action') has been a little more positive;[65] nevertheless, very few claims are brought under this legislation.[66]

Because few legal systems within the EU have introduced an effective framework for class actions, it has been suggested that 'there is a need to bring the legal process more in line with modern society and introduce group action at Community level'.[67] In view of the fact that cross-border transactions are on the increase and consumers across Europe will face the same problems, national solutions risk being ineffective when businesses can easily shift from country to country; the ability of consumers from different member states to act together against a business may also have a preventative effect[68] and deter potential offenders.[69] Areas where group action may be of particular importance include the telecommunications and financial service sectors and situations where consumers have paid too high a price as a result of price cooperation between businesses.[70] **5.22**

62 European Consumer Law Group (February 2005: 5). Experience of other countries with consumer class actions has also been disappointing. For example, in Israel, although a number of class actions are commenced, the courts have dismissed the majority of them and, as regards those which are approved, few reach a final decision or settlement: see S Deutsch (2004).

63 At the end of 2006, a minority of EU member states (namely, Austria, Estonia, France, Germany, Lithuania, Netherlands, Portugal, Spain, Sweden, and the United Kingdom) made provision for class, group, or representative actions: Study Centre for Consumer Law (January 2007: 271).

64 See Study Centre for Consumer Law (January 2007: 264).

65 European Consumer Law Group (February 2005: 5–6).

66 In the first three years of the Act's operation there were fewer than 10 collective actions (whether initiated by groups of consumers or by the consumer ombudsman): see <http://ec.europa.eu/consumers/redress/out_of_court/adr/abyhammar_intervention_adr2006.pdf> [11/1/08].

67 European Consumer Law Group (February 2005: 3). But compare C Hodges (2001a: 346): 'A case of practical need for a multi-party rule of procedure in Europe remains to be made out.'

68 European Consumer Law Group (February 2005: 4).

69 Study Centre for Consumer Law (January 2007: 264). For criticism of the view that class actions play a significant deterrent role (at least, in the context of heavily regulated industries, such as the manufacture of pharmaceuticals), see C Hodges (2001a: 341).

70 European Consumer Law Group (February 2005: 7–8).

5.23 The European Commission has indicated that it intends to look into the possibility of enabling 'collective redress mechanisms for consumers both for infringements of consumer protection rules and for breaches of EU anti-trust rules'.[71] Presumably, one of the motivations for this policy initiative is the fact that research has shown that between two-thirds[72] and three-quarters[73] of European consumers say that they would be more willing to defend their rights through litigation if they were able to join with other consumers who have experienced the same problem. Although some preparatory work has been undertaken,[74] it is still unclear whether or not European legislation on class actions will be proposed and, if such legislation is enacted, whether it will provide an effective mechanism for enabling groups of consumers to vindicate their contractual rights.

5.24 The creation of even a well-designed procedure for the bringing of group litigation does not necessarily mean that such litigation would become very common. The experience of other legal systems with class actions does not encourage the view that, in practice, the introduction of a European class action would play a very significant role in the context of run-of-the-mill consumer contracts.[75] However, the existence of such a procedure might strengthen the hand of ombudsmen and other public authorities (such as the Office of Fair Trading in the United Kingdom) in their dealings with businesses who have caused small amounts of harm to a significant number of consumers. Even if, in due course, a European-level class action is introduced, it might be expected that group claims would be brought only very occasionally. In most member states, the class action is an alien concept which does not form part of the traditional legal landscape; it is doubtful whether the class action 'can be plucked out of its American environment and transplanted to European soil without considerable modification'.[76] Even if adapted to the European environment,

[71] European Commission, COM (2007) 99, p 11. See also European Commission, COM (2005) 672, p 8. The idea of introducing a European group action has been mooted for nearly a decade; see European Commission, COM (99) 396; COM (2000) 167.

[72] Eurobarometer (October 2004: 36).

[73] Eurobarometer (September 2006: 100).

[74] For example, the Commission organized a brainstorming event on collective redress in June 2007 (see <http://ec.europa.eu/consumers/redress_cons/docs/summary_leuven_event.pdf> [27/2/08]) and a conference on collective redress was held in Lisbon in November 2007: <http://ec.europa.eu/consumers/redress_cons/collective_redress_en.htm> [27/2/08].

[75] For example, the class action was introduced in Israel by legislation in 1994 (since replaced by a new law in 2006); however, the first (and so far only) decision in which the Supreme Court has given a final judgment in favour of the plaintiff in a class action was not until 2006: see R Plato-Shinar (2007: 540).

[76] H Kötz (1981: 114). See also R Faulk (2003: 335–45).

how likely is it that such an alien procedure, grafted onto national procedural systems, will flourish? Perhaps the most that can be said is that, if there were an effective European procedure for collective litigation (and this is a big 'if'), businesses whose conduct causes damage to consumers' interests, might be more willing to settle group claims.

IV. CONCLUSION

Recognition of the fact that the Brussels I Regulation in itself does nothing **5.25** to solve consumers' access-to-justice problems has led the European legislature to attempt to address questions of civil procedure in cross-border cases. As these developments are very recent (or, in the case of collective actions, not even at the stage of a formal proposal), it is impossible to say what, if anything, the (proposed) reforms will achieve. Nevertheless, one is entitled to be sceptical. First, it is doubtful whether, on the assumption that a European collective action for damages is introduced, such a procedure will take root in member states' systems of civil procedure. Secondly, although there is a possibility that the European Small Claims Procedure Regulation will have a positive impact on European consumers' access to justice, there are serious question marks surrounding the ESCP in the context of consumer claims. It is perhaps more likely that the ESCP will assist small businesses who have low-value claims against consumers or other business entities domiciled in other member states than that it will significantly enhance consumer access to justice.

It is not difficult to see what has motivated the introduction of the ESCP. **5.26** Even if it is accepted that cross-border consumer litigation will remain exceptional, this is not a good reason for failing to attempt to make small claims litigation as user-friendly and accessible as possible. And it would be churlish to suggest that there is nothing to be said in favour of the Regulation; the procedure established by the Regulation has several advantages when compared to traditional small claims procedures under the laws of the member states. To the extent that the obstacles to consumer-initiated litigation are related to questions of cost and legal complexity, the Regulation might be thought to take a step in the right direction. Although the ESCP does not completely remove the obstacles facing consumers who wish to vindicate their contractual rights through litigation, the Regulation has the potential to make litigation against a foreign supplier (whether in the country of the consumer's domicile or the supplier's domicile) a less daunting prospect than has hitherto been the case. Furthermore, if cross-border small claims litigation is made a more viable option, suppliers may feel under more pressure to respond reasonably to consumers' legitimate complaints. As the Irish experience shows, one of the problems which flows from the absence of a truly accessible small claims procedure for cross-border claims is that there is less incentive for businesses to treat foreign consumers fairly; in the absence of a credible threat of small claims litigation, the consumer's leverage is greatly reduced.[77]

5.27 Nevertheless, there are potential problems with the ESCP at two levels. First, the potential impact of the European procedure is limited in a number of ways.

(i) Because the financial threshold for the ESCP has been fixed at €2,000—and research suggests that, across the member states of the European Union, it does not make economic sense to pursue a cross-border claim if the value of the claim is less than €2,500[78]—it may be doubted whether many consumers will be willing to litigate claims whose value falls under the Regulation's upper limit.[79] From the UK perspective, the limit of €2,000 is simply too low.[80]

(ii) As regards costs, the 'loser-pays' principle in article 16 is a significant disincentive for a potential consumer-claimant (who fears the economic consequences of his claim being unsuccessful). In the original proposal, the financial risk was reduced by an important proviso to the 'loser-pays' principle: an unsuccessful litigant would not have been obliged to reimburse the fees of a lawyer or legal professional retained by the other party if the unsuccessful party was a natural person (such as a consumer) and had not been represented in the proceedings.[81] As has been seen, this protective provision was significantly watered down in the final version of the Regulation. From the point of view of a consumer who is contemplating cross-border litigation, the general rule according to which the losing party is obliged to reimburse the other party's costs (including lawyers' fees), represents a significant deterrent to the commencement of litigation.

(iii) It is recognized that, if means of redress are to be effective, potential users need to have a sufficient degree of familiarity with the procedure.[82]

[77] ECC (Dublin) (June 2004: 4).

[78] See ch 2.

[79] Although survey data based on what respondents *say* they would do in a particular situation suggests that a significant proportion of European consumers would be prepared to litigate both domestic and cross-border claims for values even lower than €1,000 (see Eurobarometer (October 2004: 28–31, 53–5)), it appears that far fewer consumers who have experienced problems with goods or services purchased from abroad *actually* initiate cross-border litigation.

[80] Citizens Advice (October 2005). See also JP Cortes Dieguez (2008: 89).

[81] See art 14(2) of the proposal: European Commission, COM (2005) 87.

[82] Study Centre for Consumer Law (January 2007: 229).

Because the ESCP can apply only in cross-border cases, it will take many years for courts and advice agencies to develop any kind of experience of the procedure. As regards the public at large, the position is far worse: 'The fact that most consumers will only very rarely be confronted with cross-border disputes may indeed have a negative influence on the familiarity of consumers with [the ESCP].'[83] If the ESCP were available in domestic cases as an alternative to the national procedure—as advocated in the original proposal—a higher level of familiarity could have been established more swiftly.

(iv) There is a danger that the co-existence of two small claims procedures for different types of claim will lead to confusion.[84]

(v) The position on the ground, as it were, is unlikely to change unless consumers are made aware of the possibilities offered by the ESCP. Lack of public awareness is a general problem: because there is little money to be made from consumer law, the legal profession does not solicit dispute-resolution business relating to consumer problems; furthermore, advice agencies have limited funds and are often overstretched.[85]

Secondly, and more fundamentally, it may simply be that the European legislator, by seeking to solve access-to-justice issues by reforming civil procedure, is barking up the wrong tree. It is interesting that many of the documents prepared by the European Commission relating to consumer redress seem to be based on the premise that procedural changes will remove barriers which prevent consumers taking court action against suppliers. There are several cultural assumptions underlying the European Commission's approach: (i) litigation is the natural and proper way to settle disputes that cannot be resolved by the parties themselves; (ii) to the extent that litigation does not provide an effective channel of redress, the problems can be solved by changing the law (for example, by procedural changes aimed at making the conduct of litigation easier); and (iii) lack of uniformity across Europe is a significant barrier to consumer litigation. All of these assumptions are questionable. Although procedural changes can reduce the legal barriers which prevent consumers seeking to vindicate their rights, the most fundamental obstacles are social and economic and cannot be removed simply by new legislation. Accordingly, it is more than likely that, as regards consumer access to justice, the impact of legal reforms at the European level will be extremely marginal. **5.28**

[83] Study Centre for Consumer Law (January 2007: 229).

[84] Citizens Advice (October 2005).

[85] Citizens Advice (October 2005).

5.29 Even in the United States, which is generally regarded as a highly litigious society, it is recognized that, for economic reasons, a small claims court may not provide a satisfactory forum for the resolution of disputes arising from consumer contracts, particularly in cross-border cases.[86] Attempts to channel low-value claims into litigation are almost bound to fail. A more positive strategy is to accept that certain types of dispute are not well suited to resolution by court procedures and to try to find alternative answers to consumer access-to-justice questions.[87] While one should try to avoid the temptation of extreme pessimism, there is a real possibility that the European Small Claims Procedure Regulation will turn out to be something of a damp squib. Time will tell.

[86] See, eg, MS Donahey (2003: 475).

[87] See chs 9 to 11.

6

Recognition and Enforcement of Judgments

I. INTRODUCTION

It has already been seen that, in a case involving a protected consumer **6.01** contract under the Brussels I Regulation, a consumer who decides to litigate a claim against a supplier domiciled in another EU member has a choice between: (a) bringing the claim in the supplier's home forum and (if necessary) proceeding to enforce the judgment in that country; or (b) commencing proceedings in the consumer's home forum and, then seeking to enforce the judgment in the member state where the supplier's assets are located, typically the country of the supplier's domicile. This chapter is concerned with the issues raised by the second of these two scenarios—where proceedings are brought in one country and enforcement is required in another country. These issues may also arise (in theory) in cases not governed by the Brussels I Regulation—for example, where a US consumer, having obtained a judgment against an English e-trader in California, applies to enforce the judgment in England. This type of case would be governed by the traditional English rules on the recognition and enforcement of judgments.

6.02 Enforcement may also be a relevant issue in cases where the claimant is the supplier and the defendant is the consumer. In terms of the potential for this type of litigation, there are competing factors which pull in different directions. On the one hand, research (at the domestic level) has consistently found that consumer litigation is significantly more likely to involve the consumer as defendant and the supplier as claimant than vice versa.[1] On the other hand, as regards protected consumer contracts under the Brussels I Regulation, cross-border enforcement cannot normally arise as an issue in cases where the defendant is a consumer—because the jurisdiction rules channel litigation to the courts of the member state in which the consumer is domiciled;[2] if, in such a case, the supplier obtains a money judgment in his favour, there is no international dimension to the enforcement of the judgment as the consumer's assets from which the judgment will have to be satisfied will invariably be found in the country in which the proceedings took place. Of course, not all consumer contracts are protected consumer contracts under the Brussels I Regulation; claims against consumers may be brought in a country in which the consumer does not have assets; in such cases, a supplier who obtains a judgment in its favour against an English consumer, whether in another EU member state or a third state, may apply to enforce the judgment in England.

6.03 As regards cases in which the consumer is the claimant, the European Commission's rather bland comment that the costs and delays of cross-border enforcement, 'especially in the event of a small claim, can be a disincentive to litigation where enforcement is to be sought against an adversary or assets in another country'[3] significantly underestimates the seriousness of the problems facing consumers in cross-border cases. Not surprisingly, there seems to be no reported case involving a b2c contract in which a consumer has taken steps to enforce a judgment under the Brussels I Regulation (or the Brussels Convention). The problems surrounding cross-border enforcement in consumer cases are part of the background to recent European legislation—in particular, the Regulation establishing the European Small Claims Procedure (ESCP)[4]—which makes provision for the simplification of the enforcement of judgments in certain types of case.

[1] See, eg, Touche Ross (1986: 20); National Consumer Council (1989: 277); H Genn (1999: 151, 153); J Baldwin (1997: 26).

[2] Art 16(2).

[3] COM (97) 609, p 6.

[4] Reg (EC) No 861/2007 [2007] OJ L199/1. See also the European Enforcement Order Regulation (Reg (EC) No 805/2004 [2004] L143/15) and the European Order for Payment Procedure Regulation (Reg (EC) No 1896/2006 [2006] L399/1)—which are discussed at paras 6.25–6.34.

After the entry into force of the European Small Claims Procedure Regulation (in 2009), there will be three regimes for the cross-border enforcement of consumer judgments. First, as regards a claim which exceeds €2,000, the cross-border enforcement of judgments between EU member states is governed by Chapter III of the Brussels I Regulation.[5] Secondly, with regard to claims whose value does not exceed €2,000 and which are resolved through the ESCP, simplified rules set out in the European Small Claims Procedure Regulation apply. Thirdly, as regards judgments granted by the courts of third countries, the traditional rules[6] are relevant; in such cases the fact that the underlying cause of action arose out of a consumer contract rather than a commercial contract is of limited relevance. **6.04**

II. THE BRUSSELS I REGULATION

In relation to the recognition and enforcement of judgments granted by the courts of member states, there are few issues specific to cases involving consumer contracts—as opposed to contracts in general.[7] This section considers only issues which are specific to consumer contracts. **6.05**

1. The Defence Based on Jurisdictional Error by the Court of Origin

As a general rule, under the Brussels I Regulation, the court addressed cannot review the assumption of jurisdiction by the court of origin. Even though a judgment shall not be recognized 'if such recognition is manifestly contrary to public policy in the Member State in which recognition is sought,'[8] it is expressly provided that the jurisdiction of the court of origin cannot be reviewed and that '[t]he test of public policy . . . may not be applied to the rules relating to jurisdiction.'[9] However, the general rule is subject to an exception; according to the 'jurisdiction defence', a judgment shall not be recognized under the Brussels I Regulation 'if it conflicts with **6.06**

[5] Title III of the Lugano Convention applies to the enforcement in England of judgments granted by the courts of Iceland, Norway, and Switzerland.

[6] ie, the common law, the Administration of Justice Act 1920, and the Foreign Judgments (Reciprocal Enforcement) Act 1933.

[7] See J Hill (2005: ch 13).

[8] Art 34(1).

[9] Art 35(3).

Sections 3, 4 or 6 of Chapter II'.[10] Of course, the jurisdiction defence applies to cases involving enforcement in the same way as to cases concerning only recognition.[11]

6.07 The operation of the jurisdiction defence can be illustrated by the following example. C, a consumer domiciled in England, buys goods on instalment credit terms from S, a supplier domiciled in Germany. C fails to pay the instalments; S sues C in Germany and the court, relying on article 5(1), exercises jurisdiction on the basis that Germany is the place of performance of the obligation in question. When S applies to enforce the judgment in England, C invokes the jurisdiction defence. C's argument is that, as the contract is a protected consumer contract (under article 15(1)(a) of the Brussels I Regulation), article 16(2)[12] requires that S's claim against C should have been brought in England; if the German court misapplied the jurisdiction provisions of Section 4, the German judgment should be refused recognition and enforcement in England.[13]

6.08 Not all cases are as straightforward as this example and the scope of the jurisdiction defence is, in some respects, uncertain. The nature of the problem emerges from the opinion of the Advocate General in *Mietz*.[14] Consider the following situation: C, an English consumer, buys goods from S, a French supplier; the circumstances are such that the contract falls within the scope of article 15(1)(c) of the Brussels I Regulation; because of C's failure to pay for the goods, S commences proceedings in France and, although C defends the claim, S obtains a judgment in its favour. When S applies to have the judgment enforced in England, can S rely on the jurisdiction defence?

6.09 C might seek to resist enforcement of the French judgment by arguing that Section 4 is mandatory. According to this line of argument, notwithstanding the fact that C submitted to French jurisdiction, the French court assumed jurisdiction in contravention of article 16(2) of the Brussels I Regulation, which requires proceedings against the consumer to be brought in the member state where the consumer is domiciled. The literal wording of Section 4 would appear to support C's position: article 15 provides that,

10 Art 35(1). Sections 3, 4, and 6 apply to matters relating to insurance, consumer contracts, and exclusive jurisdiction under art 22.

11 Art 45(1).

12 As supplemented by sched 4 to the 1982 Act, r 8(2).

13 Arts 35(1) and 45(1). The same analysis applies in cases where the court of origin misapplied either the jurisdiction provisions dealing with matters relating to insurance or art 22 of the Brussels I Regulation.

14 Case C-99/96 [1999] ECR I-2277, 2287–90 (paras 28–37).

in matters relating to protected consumer contracts, jurisdiction shall be determined by Section 4 (without prejudice to article 4 and article 5(5)); article 35(1) provides that a judgment shall not be recognized if it conflicts with Section 4; there is nothing in Section 4 itself to suggest that the defendant's submission can override the provisions of Section 4.

Nevertheless, it is widely assumed that, if the defendant submits to the original court's jurisdiction, Section 4 yields to article 24.[15] According to the text of article 24, the submission rule is subject to only two exceptions: (i) where the defendant enters an appearance to contest the court's jurisdiction or (ii) where another court has exclusive jurisdiction under article 22; article 24 is not expressly made subject to any other provision. If, within the hierarchy of jurisdiction rules established by the Brussels I Regulation, the defendant's submission overrides the special rules governing protected consumer contracts (even if the defendant is a consumer), it would be contrary to principle if a consumer were able to rely on the jurisdiction defence in a case where the court of origin exercised jurisdiction on the basis of a rule which is hierarchically superior to Section 4. **6.10**

The principle of party autonomy points in the same direction. Although it is legitimate to limit party autonomy in order to protect the weaker party from oppressive or unfair contractual terms in the context of standard-form contracts, there is no reason to prevent the weaker party from waiving the benefit of protective jurisdiction rules after the contract between the parties has been concluded and a dispute has arisen.[16] So, if the English consumer submits to the French court's jurisdiction, the consumer should not be able to rely on the jurisdiction defence to resist recognition or enforcement of the French judgment in England. **6.11**

A question arises whether the same conclusion should be reached in a case where C, while accepting the notion that article 24 takes priority over Section 4, denies that his conduct amounts to submission to the French court's jurisdiction. The arguments in this type of case are finely balanced. On the one hand, article 24 is not one of the provisions listed in article 35(1); the text of the Regulation does not support the view that a misapplication of article 24 (even in the context of proceedings concerning a consumer contract) can give rise to a jurisdiction defence at the stage of recognition or enforcement. On the other hand, the policy of the Brussels I Regulation is to provide jurisdictional protection for consumers in certain **6.12**

[15] See paras 3.125–3.126.

[16] This is why, although jurisdiction clauses in protected consumer contracts are not normally enforceable, a jurisdiction agreement between a supplier and a consumer is binding if it is concluded after the dispute has arisen: see art 17(2).

types of situation. From the point of view of this policy, a case where the French court wrongly concludes that the consumer-defendant submitted to its jurisdiction poses as much of a problem as a case where the French court wrongly exercises jurisdiction under article 5(1) when it should have declined jurisdiction on the basis that the courts of another member state had jurisdiction under article 16(2); in each case the consumer is deprived of the right to be sued in the member state of his domicile. It would be perfectly possible to give effect to the policy of protecting consumers by interpreting article 35(1) as authorizing the court addressed to review the exercise of jurisdiction by the court of origin not only in a case where there was a misapplication of the provisions of Section 4 but also in a situation involving a protected consumer contract where the court of origin purported to exercise jurisdiction on the basis of a rule which takes priority over the provisions of Section 4 (such as article 24).

6.13 To the extent that this issue might be thought to have arisen in *Mietz*, the Court of Justice was not required to deal with it.[17] The issue was, however, discussed by the Advocate General. Notwithstanding the desirability of the underlying policy of Section 4 being upheld, Advocate General Léger took the view that, in the context of the jurisdiction defence, the court addressed is not entitled to verify that the court of origin correctly applied jurisdiction provisions other than those expressly identified in the jurisdiction defence itself.[18] This opinion is, however, in direct conflict with a decision of the German courts. *Re Jurisdiction in a Consumer Contract*[19] concerned an application under the Brussels Convention for the enforcement of an English judgment granted against a consumer domiciled in Germany. The English court had purported to exercise jurisdiction on the basis of the defendant's submission. The German court considered that, in deciding whether the defendant could invoke the jurisdiction defence, it was entitled to review the international jurisdiction of the English court under what is now article 24 of the Brussels I Regulation. The German court reasoned that, if the jurisdiction defence allows the court addressed to examine whether there has been a breach of the provisions on jurisdiction in relation to consumer contracts, 'it is necessary to investigate at the same time whether the entry of an appearance in the proceedings has displaced the consumer contract jurisdiction'.[20] The German court's reasoning is convincing. Although it is not difficult to understand the importance of not allowing national courts to extend the scope of the jurisdiction defence,

[17] Case C-99/96 [1999] ECR I-2277, 2315 (para 45).
[18] Case C-99/96 [1999] ECR I-2277, 2290 (para 36).
[19] [2002] ILPr 157 (Regional Court of Appeal, Koblenz).
[20] [2002] ILPr 157, 162 (para 19).

the proper application of the jurisdiction defence requires the court addressed to consider the operation of other jurisdiction rules when those rules interact with the provisions of Section 4.

The jurisdiction defence is limited by the fact that, when examining the ground of jurisdiction with which it is alleged that the judgment conflicts, the court addressed is 'bound by the findings of fact on which the court of the . . . State of origin based its jurisdiction'.[21] So, if the court of origin decides that a party claiming to be a consumer bought and sold 20 vintage cars for profit over a five-year period, the court addressed cannot re-evaluate the evidence and decide that the party in question actually bought and sold 40 vintage cars during the period in question or that 20 vintage cars were sold over a two-year period. Having said that, the court addressed is not bound by the legal conclusions drawn from the facts by the court of origin. Accordingly, it is possible for the court of origin to conclude that the sale of a particular vintage car is a b2c contract (within Section 4)—because the seller's buying-and-selling activities amount to carrying on a trade—but for the court addressed to conclude that the contract is a c2c contract (outside the scope of Section 4)—on the basis that the volume of sales amounts only to the pursuit of a hobby rather than carrying on a trade.[22] **6.14**

There is some doubt over whether the court addressed must take into account new factual evidence which is relevant to the question whether the court of origin breached Section 4 (and which was not presented to or considered by the court of origin). Although this issue was raised by the third question submitted by the German Federal Supreme Court in *Mietz*,[23] the Court of Justice decided that it was not necessary for it to examine whether, and under what circumstances, the court addressed might take account of new facts in the context of the jurisdiction defence.[24] However, the Advocate General considered the issue and thought that the court addressed should not be able to take into account factual matters which could have been put before the court of origin.[25] This approach seems the right one; it is consistent with the principle that litigants should not **6.15**

[21] Brussels I Regulation, art 35(2).

[22] This is the kind of situation which arose—albeit at the jurisdictional stage—in *Standard Bank London Ltd v Apostolakis*: the English court ([2000] ILPr 766) decided that a contract was a protected consumer contract (and, as a result, the Greek courts had jurisdiction) and the Greek court ([2003] ILPr 499) decided that the contract was a b2b contract (and, on the basis of a contractual jurisdiction clause, that the English courts had jurisdiction). See ch 3.

[23] See Case C-99/96 [1999] ECR I-2277, 2308 (para 20).

[24] Case C-99/96 [1999] ECR I-2277, 2319 (para 57).

[25] Case C-99/96 [1999] ECR I-2277, 2295 (para 63).

normally be able—at the enforcement stage—to rely on matters which could have been raised at the merits stage.[26]

6.16 The defence based on jurisdictional error can, depending on the circumstances, be invoked either by a consumer or by a supplier. Where, for example, an English consumer is sued in another member state, enforcement of the judgment will be refused in England if the consumer had a right under article 16 of the Regulation to be sued in England and the court of origin erroneously assumed jurisdiction.[27] Similarly, in cases where an English supplier has been sued by a consumer in another member state, if the consumer, having obtained a judgment abroad seeks to enforce the judgment in England, the English court must refuse enforcement if the contract was not a protected consumer contract—as a consequence of which the foreign claimant was not entitled to sue in his home forum on the basis of article 16(1). In these types of case, the fact that the court of origin decided that it had jurisdiction does not preclude the English court from refusing to enforce the judgment on the basis that the court of origin assumed jurisdiction in contravention of the provisions of Section 4.

2. Public Policy

6.17 In cases involving foreign judgments, recognition or enforcement will be refused if the substance of the judgment is contrary to public policy. Article 34(1) of the Brussels I Regulation provides that a judgment granted by the courts of a member state shall not be recognized 'if such recognition is manifestly contrary to public policy in the Member State in which recognition is sought'. Although, in the commercial context, the public policy defence can be successfully invoked very infrequently, there may be greater potential for the operation of public policy in the context of consumer contracts. Consumer policy is one of the areas in which legislators (both at the national and the European levels) have laid down mandatory rules. Although there is a general principle that the court addressed will not seek to review the substance of the judgment of the court of origin,[28] recognition and enforcement will be refused if the foreign judgment

[26] See *Ellis v M'Henry* (1871) LR 6 CP 228; *Israel Discount Bank of New York v Hadjipateras* [1984] 1 WLR 137; *Interdesco SA v Nullifire Ltd* [1992] 1 Lloyd's Rep 180.

[27] See *Weber v SA Eurocard Belgium-Luxembourg* [1993] ILPr 55 (Court of Appeal, Luxembourg). See also *Bertrand* Case 150/77 [1978] ECR 1431 (although, on the facts, the contract was not a consumer contract and the jurisdictional defence was not available).

[28] Brussels I Regulation, arts 36, 45(2).

involves a breach of a fundamental principle or of a rule of law regarded as essential in the legal order of the state addressed.[29]

In *Renault*,[30] for example, it was held that the fact that the court of origin made a mistake in the application of EU law is not enough to justify non-recognition of the judgment. In this case, it was alleged that the judgment was defective because of a failure by the court of origin to apply EU competition law properly. The Court of Justice did not consider the relevant rule of EU law to be either a fundamental principle or an essential rule of law. The question arises whether it would be legitimate for the courts to take a different view if the proceedings in the state of origin had failed to uphold key consumer rights. Consider, for example, the situation where French proceedings are brought by a foreign supplier against an English consumer for breach of contract; suppose that, notwithstanding the fact that the consumer, relying on the rights conferred by the French legislation which implements the Distance Selling Directive, had purported to exercise his right to withdraw from the contract during the statutory cooling-off period, the French court handed down a judgment ordering the consumer to pay damages. This situation is not obviously distinguishable from that which arose in the *Renault* case. There is, however, an argument for saying that—in view of the protective policy underlying the cooling-off period and the mandatory nature of the rule in question—the English court should be entitled to refuse to enforce the French judgment on grounds of public policy in such circumstances. **6.18**

One area where it is acknowledged that public policy has a role to play is where the law of the state of origin has failed to prevent a manifest breach of the defendant's rights under the European Convention on Human Rights. If, in the context of legal proceedings in the state of origin, the defendant's right to a fair trial under article 6 of the ECHR is infringed, the ensuing judgment will not be entitled to recognition or enforcement in other countries.[31] If, for example, an English consumer were barred from participating in proceedings in another member state as a result of being unable to lodge funds with the foreign court, this would be inconsistent with his article 6 rights and the consumer would be able to resist enforcement of the judgment in England on grounds of public policy. **6.19**

[29] Case C-7/98 *Krombach* [2000] ECR I-1935; Case C-38/98 *Renault* [2000] ECR I-2973.

[30] Case C-38/98 [2000] ECR I-2973.

[31] Case C-7/98 *Krombach* [2000] ECR I-1935.

III. ENFORCEMENT UNDER THE EUROPEAN SMALL CLAIMS PROCEDURE REGULATION

6.20 Once the European Small Claims Procedure Regulation[32] has entered into force, a consumer or supplier who, in a cross-border case, has a contractual claim whose value does not exceed €2,000 will be able to rely on the ESCP (as an alternative to the national procedure of the court in question).[33] Chapter III of the Regulation makes provision for the simplified cross-border recognition and enforcement of judgments which result from the ESCP. There are several ways in which the Regulation seeks to streamline the process of enforcement.

6.21 First, a judgment given in the ESCP 'shall be recognised and enforced in another Member State without the need for a declaration of enforceability and without any possibility of opposing its recognition'.[34] This should speed up the enforcement process by avoiding the *exequatur* stage of the usual procedure for enforcement in most member states. As regards the enforcement in England of a judgment obtained in another member state through the ESCP, the judgment-creditor does not have to apply to register the judgment.[35]

6.22 Secondly, the judgment-creditor is not required to have an authorized representative or a postal address in the member state of enforcement.[36] Notwithstanding the fact that cross-border enforcement of ESCP judgments has been simplified, it seems highly unlikely that litigants will have the confidence to attempt the cross-border enforcement of a judgment without professional help or that even a well-informed consumer would be able to undertake the enforcement process without such assistance. The extent to which the enforcement process will entail costs in terms of lawyer's fees will depend in part on the availability and effectiveness of free advice and assistance from organizations such as the network of European Consumer Centres (ECC-Net).

6.23 Thirdly, the grounds on which a judgment which results from the ESCP can be refused recognition or enforcement are reduced to one (as opposed to the five grounds which exist under the Brussels I Regulation[37]). It is

[32] Reg (EC) No 861/2007 [2007] OJ L199/1.

[33] Art 1.

[34] Art 20(1).

[35] For the usual procedure for the registration of foreign judgments, see CPR Pt 74.

[36] Art 21(3).

[37] Art 34(1) (public policy); art 34(2) (lack of opportunity to defend); arts 34(3) and (4) (irreconcilability); art 35(1) (jurisdictional conflict with Sections 3, 4, or 6).

provided that an ESCP judgment shall be refused enforcement only if it conflicts with an earlier judgment (whether given by another member state or a third country) involving the same cause of action and the same parties.[38] Moreover, even this ground for non-enforcement is limited by the fact that it is only available if 'the irreconcilability was not and could not have been raised as an objection in the court or tribunal proceedings in the Member State where the judgment in the European Small Claims Procedure was given'.[39] This means that, in practice, a litigant who obtains a judgment under the ESCP in one member state can be more or less certain that the judgment will be entitled to enforcement in other member states.

It should be noted that, after the entry into force of the Regulation, not all claims whose value does not exceed €2,000 will necessarily be conducted according to the ESCP; claimants have a choice whether to proceed under the Regulation or in accordance with the civil procedure of the court seized. If the value of the claim does not exceed the monetary threshold, questions of enforcement have the potential to be a factor which influences the claimant's decision to opt for one procedure rather than the other. As the enforcement process under the European Small Claims Procedure Regulation is intended to be significantly quicker, simpler, and cheaper than the procedure under the Brussels I Regulation, this may incline a claimant to choose the ESCP in preference to the relevant national procedure.[40] **6.24**

IV. UNCONTESTED CLAIMS AND ORDERS FOR PAYMENT

For the sake of completeness, brief mention should also be made of developments in the field of uncontested claims and orders for payment—though reforms in this area were not motivated by a desire to correct weaknesses in relation to consumer redress and they are unlikely to have much of a role to play in the context of cross-border consumer contracts. The starting point for legislative action is the recognition that most civil litigation in the lower courts is not directed at the resolution of disputed questions of fact or law; the majority of small claims procedures focus on attempts by creditors to collect sums due from debtors in cases where the **6.25**

[38] Art 22(1).

[39] Art 22(1)(c).

[40] By contrast, different costs rules might incline a consumer-claimant towards the national procedure. See ch 5.

debtor is simply unwilling to pay. Research has revealed that, in the European Union, the percentage of uncontested claims ranges from around 50 per cent (Ireland) to more than 80 per cent (Austria, Germany, and Sweden).[41] The evidence from England suggests that, as regards small claims, the great majority of judgments are entered without any court hearing—because the court has received no response from the defendant within 14 days of service of the summons.[42] To simplify the handling of uncontested claims and the enforcement of judgments which issue from such proceedings, two instruments have been adopted: the European Enforcement Order Regulation[43] and the European Order for Payment Procedure Regulation.[44]

6.26 Where the claimant obtains a European Enforcement Order (EEO) under the Regulation, cross-border enforcement of the EEO does not need to follow the enforcement procedure laid down by the Brussels I Regulation. Article 5 of the European Enforcement Order Regulation provides:

> A judgment which has been certified as a European Enforcement Order in the Member State of origin shall be recognized and enforced in the other Member States without the need for a declaration of enforceability and without any possibility of opposing its recognition.

This is effectively the same rule which is applied to judgments given within the framework of the European Small Claims Procedure Regulation.[45]

6.27 At first sight, it might appear that the EEO procedure offers a convenient (and cheaper) mechanism whereby a supplier domiciled in one member state can collect sums due from consumers domiciled in other member states—for example, in cases where consumers have failed to pay for goods. In a situation where the contract is not a protected consumer contract under the Brussels I Regulation, it might well be more straightforward for the supplier to obtain an EEO through proceedings in the country in which the supplier is domiciled and then have the EEO enforced in the country of the consumer's domicile. However, the EEO procedure is not available for the cross-border enforcement of judgments against consumers. The Regulation provides that, where (i) the claim relates to 'a contract concluded by a person, the consumer, for a purpose which can be regarded as being outside his trade or profession'[46] and (ii) 'the debtor is the consumer',

[41] COM (2002) 746, p 8, n 2.
[42] J Baldwin (1997: 21–2).
[43] Reg (EC) No 805/2004 [2004] L143/15.
[44] Reg (EC) No 1896/2006 [2006] L399/1.
[45] Art 20(1).
[46] For interpretation of this phrase, see ch 3.

a judgment on an uncontested claim cannot be certified as an EEO unless the judgment was given in the member state of the consumer's domicile.[47] Even where the case is not within Section 4 (ie, the dispute arises out of a transaction which is a consumer contract, but not a protected consumer contract), a supplier domiciled in state A cannot use the EEO procedure to obtain an EEO in member state A against a consumer domiciled in state B.

There is no problem, in principle, with the EEO procedure being used by consumers in their claims against suppliers; the procedure might be useful in a case where the consumer (relying on the jurisdiction provisions of the Brussels I Regulation) brings proceedings in the consumer's home forum and the supplier does not contest the claim. In these circumstances, if the court of origin makes an EEO under the terms of the Regulation, the costs of enforcement of the order should be quite modest. Of course, if the supplier contests the claim (for example, by appearing in the original proceedings to defend the claim on the merits), the EEO procedure is not available[48] and the costs of the legal process (in the county of origin and in the country where enforcement of the ensuing judgment is sought) are likely to be prohibitive for the vast majority of consumer claims. **6.28**

Standing alone, the European Enforcement Order Regulation does nothing to harmonize the legal procedures whereby creditors may recover unpaid sums from debtors; it leaves such processes to be regulated by the national procedural law of the country of origin. However, the European Commission also made a proposal for the establishment of a harmonized procedure[49] and this led to the enactment, in 2006, of the European Order for Payment Procedure Regulation.[50] **6.29**

The purpose of the Regulation is to simplify, speed up, and reduce the costs of litigation in cross-border cases concerning uncontested pecuniary claims and to provide for the free circulation of European Orders for Payment (EOPs) throughout the member states.[51] Like the European Small Claims Procedure Regulation, the Regulation does not supersede national procedural rules; it provides an alternative procedure in cross-border cases for the collection of pecuniary claims for a specific amount that have fallen due. The procedure is based on an application which has to be made **6.30**

[47] Art 6(1)(d).

[48] See art 3(1).

[49] COM (2004) 173. See also the opinion of the European Economic and Social Committee: [2005] OJ C221/77.

[50] Reg (EC) No 1896/2006 [2006] L399/1.

[51] Art 1.

on a standard form.[52] As long as the conditions laid down in the Regulation are satisfied, the court issues the EOP,[53] which is then served on the defendant.[54] If the defendant does not lodge a statement of opposition,[55] the court of origin makes a declaration that the EOP is enforceable and sends the enforceable EOP to the claimant.[56] Article 19 is in the same terms as article 20(1) of the European Small Claims Procedure Regulation and article 5 of the European Enforcement Order Regulation: an EOP is entitled to recognition and enforcement throughout the member states 'without the need for a declaration of enforceability and without any possibility of opposing its recognition'. As with the ESCP, there is only one basis on which enforcement of an EOP can be resisted: irreconcilability with an earlier decision involving the same cause of action between the same parties.[57]

6.31 Although it is possible to imagine the EOPP being used in the consumer context, in cases where the defendant is a consumer, only the courts of the member state in which the consumer is domiciled have jurisdiction.[58] So, the Regulation cannot be used as a simplified procedure whereby a supplier established in member state A can initiate the EOPP in member state A and then have the EOP enforced against the consumer in member state B.[59] However, the procedure may be used by the consumer domiciled in member state B to commence the EOPP in member state B against a supplier domiciled in member state A (as long as the courts of member state B have jurisdiction under the rules set out in articles 15 to 17 of the Brussels I Regulation) and, then, have the EOP enforced in member state A.

6.32 There are not many contexts in which this possibility might arise since, as a general rule, consumer contracts involve payment by the consumer to the supplier rather than vice versa. However, consumers are sometimes faced with problems where they have exercised their right to cancel the contract within the statutory cooling-off period, but the supplier, having taken payment through a credit or debit card, fails to refund the payment as required by the Distance Selling Directive. In these cases, it may be that the supplier does not actively deny the consumer's right to a refund, but

52 Art 7.
53 Art 12.
54 Arts 13–15.
55 Art 16.
56 Art 18.
57 Art 22.
58 Art 6.
59 Of course, if the claim is for no more than €2,000, the supplier may use the ESCP in whichever EU member state courts have jurisdiction under the Brussels I Regulation.

simply fails to respond to the consumer's legitimate demand. In this type of case—at least where the supplier is domiciled in a member state and the courts of the member state in which the consumer is domiciled have jurisdiction (as will normally be the case if the consumer has entered a distance contract for the purchase of goods or services)—the consumer may consider the EOPP to be an effective mechanism for the recovery of his money.

Of course, there are significant limits to the operation of the European Order for Payment Procedure Regulation in the field of consumer redress. First, it has no value in cases where the supplier is not domiciled in a member state. Secondly, the supplier can easily thwart the procedure—simply by lodging a statement of opposition. This statement does not have to specify any reasons for contesting the claim.[60] If an opposition is lodged, the claim continues in the form of ordinary civil proceedings (though the claimant can indicate that if an opposition is lodged he wants the proceedings to be terminated).[61] So, in a case where the value of the claim justifies a consumer initiating the EOPP, but is not sufficiently large to justify the costs of ordinary litigation (even small claims proceedings), it may be doubted whether the EOPP will lead to a successful conclusion from the consumer's perspective. **6.33**

V. TRADITIONAL RULES

The potential for foreign judgments in consumer cases to be enforced in England under the traditional rules is quite limited—at least, as long as English consumers and suppliers do not submit to the jurisdiction of the original court. This proposition can be illustrated relatively simply. **6.34**

1. The Consumer as Claimant

Consider the situation where a US consumer (resident in New York) purchases goods from an English supplier; the transaction may be entered either through in-person shopping (in England) or through some method of distance communication (such as the Internet). If the consumer starts proceedings in New York and obtains a judgment in his favour, the judgment will not be entitled to enforcement in England unless the New York court is a court of competent jurisdiction for the purposes of English private international law—which will be the case only if the supplier either **6.35**

[60] Art 16(3).
[61] Art 17(1).

submitted to the New York court's jurisdiction or has a place of business in New York.[62] For the purposes of this rule the place of business must be a physical location. So, as long as the supplier does not submit, it will only be in exceptional cases—for example, where the supplier has a business presence in New York—that the New York court's judgment will be enforceable in England.

2. The Consumer as Defendant

6.36 The position is largely the same in cases in which an English consumer is sued abroad: the consumer will not normally be present in the foreign country when the proceedings are initiated and, assuming that the consumer does not submit to the foreign court's jurisdiction, the foreign judgment will have no effect in England.

6.37 What, however, is the situation if the contract contains a jurisdiction clause in favour of the supplier's home forum—for example, where an online contract between an English consumer and a US e-trader includes a jurisdiction clause in favour of the New York courts? If the clause is valid and binding, the chosen forum is, in principle, a court of competent jurisdiction for the purposes of the enforcement in England of any ensuing judgment in the supplier's favour.[63] However, if the jurisdiction agreement is not binding on the consumer (from the perspective of English private international law), the New York court cannot be regarded as a court of competent jurisdiction. By virtue of the Unfair Terms in Consumer Contracts Regulations 1999[64] a jurisdiction clause in a cross-border consumer contract which purports to confer exclusive jurisdiction on the courts of the supplier's home forum will normally be regarded as unfair and, therefore, unenforceable against the consumer.[65] Accordingly, even if an online consumer contract purports to confer jurisdiction on the courts of New York, a judgment which results from proceedings brought in New York against an English consumer will not qualify for enforcement in England (unless the consumer submits to the jurisdiction of the New York court).

6.38 In view of the foregoing, further discussion of the recognition and enforcement of judgments under the traditional rules is unnecessary.

[62] *Adams v Cape Industries plc* [1990] Ch 433.

[63] *Emanuel v Symon* [1908] 1 KB 302, 309.

[64] SI 1999 No 2083. The 1999 Regulations implement the Directive on unfair terms in consumer contracts (Dir 93/13/EEC [1993] L95/29).

[65] See ch 7.

VI. CONCLUSION

To date, questions surrounding the cross-border enforcement of judgments in consumer cases have been even less prominent in the law reports than jurisdictional issues. Nevertheless, although there are no reported English cases which discuss such questions, other member states have had some experience with consumer cases involving enforcement under the Brussels Convention.[66] As regards situations which are not within the scope of the Brussels I Regulation, the cross-border enforcement in England of judgments granted by the courts of third countries in consumer matters is, for reasons considered above, almost always completely out of the question. **6.39**

In most situations, the complexities of the enforcement regime under the Brussels I Regulation are one of the factors which operate as a disincentive to the cross-border litigation of consumer complaints. The intention is that the Regulations relating to the ESCP, the EEO, and the EOPP should make cross-border enforcement a more viable option. It is too early to tell whether these Regulations will have the desired effect.[67] However, it is not implausible to suggest that, with regard to disputes arising from b2c contracts, the cross-border enforcement of judgments, to the extent that it arises at all, is more likely to involve cases in which the supplier (rather than consumer) is the judgment-creditor. For example, the European Enforcement Order Regulation and the European Order for Payment Regulation are more directed to the interests of businesses including SMEs (who are in a position to benefit from streamlined procedures for recovering money that is owed to them) than the interests of consumers (who tend to be debtors, rather than creditors). Similarly, if experience in domestic cases is a reliable guide as to what may happen in the cross-border context, the ESCP is likely to facilitate the collection of debts by suppliers from consumers more than it will either ameliorate consumer access to justice or promote consumer redress through the courts. **6.40**

66 See *Weber v SA Eurocard Belgium-Luxembourg* [1993] ILPr 55 (Court of Appeal, Luxembourg); *Re Jurisdiction in a Consumer Contract* [2002] ILPr 157 (Regional Court of Appeal, Koblenz).

67 The EOPP came into force in June 2008; the ESCP takes effect in January 2009. Although the EEO has applied since October 2005, there is, as yet, no evidence of its operation in practice.

7

Dispute-Resolution Agreements

I. INTRODUCTION

As a general rule, the principle of party autonomy permits contracting **7.01** parties to determine the content of their bargain according to their wishes. Failure to comply with a freely entered agreement is a civil wrong; courts uphold such agreements either by ordering contracting parties to act in accordance with the terms of the agreement or by awarding damages for breach. The application of the principle of party autonomy in the field of cross-border contracts means that courts should normally enforce dispute-resolution agreements: 'Today the freedom of the parties to an international contract to choose . . . the forum, judicial or arbitral, for the settlement of their disputes is almost universally acknowledged.'[1] Although dispute-resolution agreements may take a number of different forms, there are three main types of contractual clause (albeit with numerous variants). First, contracting parties may include a jurisdiction clause in their contract. In its simplest form, this type of agreement provides that any dispute arising out of a contract shall be referred to the jurisdiction of the courts of a particular place or country. In a typical commercial contract, there are very

[1] PE Nygh (1999: 13).

strong arguments in favour of the courts upholding contractual clauses which purport to grant exclusive jurisdiction to a specific forum and preventing litigants from bringing proceedings other than in the contractual forum. It is only in exceptional circumstances that a jurisdiction agreement in a b2b contract will not be enforced.[2] Secondly, parties may, instead of agreeing to the jurisdiction of particular courts, agree to refer any disputes that arise out of their legal relationship to arbitration. In the commercial context, such arbitration agreements are normally strictly enforced; article II of the New York Convention 1958 (which is in force in well over 100 countries throughout the world[3]) provides that, with regard to matters which the parties have, by means of an agreement in writing, agreed to submit to arbitration, the court of a contracting state, if seized of such a matter, is obliged to refer the parties to arbitration (unless the agreement is null and void, inoperative, or incapable of being performed).[4] Thirdly, parties may agree to seek to resolve their contractual disputes by means of a dispute-resolution process which is neither litigation nor arbitration. In principle, an ADR clause[5] is entitled to be enforced in the same way as other dispute-resolution agreements.[6]

7.02 It is far from obvious that dispute-resolution clauses in consumer contracts should be enforced so readily. Common features of the vast majority of consumer contracts, whether concluded offline or online, are that they involve parties of very different bargaining power and that they are standard-form contracts; their terms and conditions are dictated by the supplier and are not the subject of negotiation by the parties.[7] Anecdotal evidence strongly suggests that consumers are normally ignorant of the non-essential terms of contracts for goods and services that they enter; more systematic empirical studies also support the view that consumers

[2] See, eg, Brussels I Regulation, art 23; *The Eleftheria* [1970] P 94; *The El Amria* [1981] 2 Lloyd's Rep 119. For recent international efforts to promote the enforcement of jurisdiction agreements see the Hague Convention on Choice of Court Agreements: <http://www.hcch.net/index_en.php?act=conventions.pdf&cid=98> [4/2/08]. The convention, which does not apply to agreements to which a consumer is party (art 2), is not yet in force; there is currently only one contracting state (Mexico): <http://www.hcch.net/index_en.php?act=conventions.status&cid=98> [15/4/08].

[3] See<http://www.uncitral.org/uncitral/en/uncitral_texts/arbitration/NYConvention_status.html> [2/12/07].

[4] Art II. For implementation of this provision in England, see Arbitration Act 1996, s 9.

[5] For the purposes of this chapter, the expression 'ADR clause' is used to signify a contractual provision whereby disputes arising from a particular contractual relationship are referred to an alternative dispute resolution process other than arbitration.

[6] *Cable & Wireless plc v IBM United Kingdom Ltd* [2002] 2 All ER (Comm) 1041.

[7] Although some commentators discuss the legal implications of individually negotiated e-contracts (see, eg, Z Tang (2007a: 129)) such contracts are rarely encountered in practice.

are largely unaware of the terms of their contracts.[8] Consumers generally enter into contracts without having obtained legal advice; before entering a contract few consumers read the detailed terms and conditions (the 'small print') or apply their mind to issues relating to dispute resolution; even if consumers do read the small print, they may well not fully understand its significance. Accordingly, if a standard-form consumer contract contains a dispute-resolution clause, the consumer is not likely to be aware of it.

For the purposes of the current discussion, nothing of substance turns on whether the contract containing the dispute-resolution clause was concluded in the real world or in cyberspace; it makes no difference whether the contract was concluded face-to-face, by post, or via the Internet. In the context of e-commerce, the method of contacting may pose doctrinal questions about when exactly an e-contract is concluded, what exactly are the terms to which the consumer is taken to have agreed, and whether a dispute-resolution clause which forms part of the supplier's standard terms is to be regarded as an agreed contractual term. The answer to some of these questions may depend, in part, on whether the contract is a 'click-wrap' or 'browse-wrap' agreement;[9] indeed, some of the American cases in which the courts have had to decide whether a consumer arbitration agreement is binding and enforceable have involved so-called 'click-wrap' agreements. However, these are doctrinal questions of contract law in general—rather than questions which relate specifically either to dispute-resolution clauses or to cross-border contracts—and fall outside the scope of the current work. In any event, these questions are not significant for the purposes of the current discussion for, as will be seen, as far as English law is concerned, dispute-resolution clauses in consumer contracts rarely have any legal significance. **7.03**

From the supplier's point of view, a dispute-resolution clause—if routinely upheld by the courts—can, in theory, play a significant role in managing risk. In a world in which e-traders are potentially amenable to the **7.04**

[8] See L Goldman (1992: 716 n 88). There do not appear to be significant differences in consumer behaviour whether the contract is concluded offline or online: see RA Hillman (2005).

[9] See C Coteanu (2005: 53–62). A 'click-wrap' agreement arises where the structure of the e-trader's website is such that the consumer has to go through a page which sets out the e-trader's terms and conditions before clicking on a 'buy' or 'accept' icon which is intended to signify that the consumer has read the terms and conditions and consents to them; contracts which are concluded via a website which enables the consumer to click on a link in order to see the e-trader's terms and conditions (rather than being channelled through a webpage containing those terms and conditions) is a 'browse-wrap' agreement.

jurisdiction of the courts of any country in which they sell goods or services,[10] a dispute-resolution clause which purports to direct claims arising from consumer contracts to a single forum may play a role in limiting the supplier's costs. A mandatory dispute-resolution clause would ensure not only that any claims brought by consumers against the supplier would have to be brought in the contractual forum, but also that the supplier would be able to pursue claims for non-payment against a consumer in the chosen forum (rather than in the country in which the consumer is resident).

7.05 Because dispute-resolution clauses in standard-form consumer contracts are drafted solely by or on behalf of suppliers, such clauses seek to refer disputes to a forum which is convenient for, or advantageous to, the supplier. It is not uncommon for e-traders to include within their standard terms and conditions a compulsory dispute-resolution clause. For example, one of the terms may be an exclusive jurisdiction clause in favour of the courts of the country in which the e-trader is established or a clause referring disputes to arbitration in that country. As regards jurisdiction clauses, a supplier might select as the contractual forum the courts of any country which is convenient for the supplier and/or whose legal system is thought to be sympathetic to the supplier's interests; however, jurisdiction clauses in consumer contracts which identify a forum other than that in which the supplier is established are very uncommon, though such clauses are occasionally found in practice.[11] A few years ago, an international comparative study of e-commerce found that, to the extent that e-contracts are concluded by reference to terms and conditions which include a jurisdiction clause, the chosen forum is invariably the country in which the supplier is established.[12] In the event of a dispute arising, if a jurisdiction agreement is upheld, two consequences follow. First, if it is the consumer who is seeking redress against the supplier, the enforcement of the jurisdiction clause places a further access-to-justice obstacle in the consumer's path; in all probability, the enforcement of a jurisdiction clause in a cross-border consumer contract will be tantamount to depriving the consumer of any redress through the courts. As already noted, the disincentives

[10] See ch 4.

[11] See, eg, the terms and conditions of the website of *PlayUSA.com*: <http://www.playusa.com>. Although the owner of this website is a company registered in Jersey, the terms and conditions include a clause purporting to refer disputes to the exclusive jurisdiction of the courts of the British Virgin Islands: <http://www.playusa.com/DVD/Region_1/ABOUT/4-/AboutUs.html?page=terms_conditions> [13/7/07].

[12] Consumers International (September 2001: 26). It should be noted that the findings of this report are difficult to disentangle as it is not clear whether the relevant passage of the report is referring to jurisdiction clauses or choice-of-law clauses (or both).

for a consumer to sue a foreign supplier in the consumer's home forum are formidable enough; the prospect of having to sue a foreign supplier in a foreign court is enough to deter all but the most determined of potential consumer-claimants.[13] Secondly, if the supplier is the claimant, the consumer will face the added complication of having to defend the claim in a foreign forum. In such proceedings, there is a real possibility that the consumer will be deprived of the shield provided by the substantive legal provisions which would apply were the litigation conducted in the country of the consumer's habitual residence and on which the consumer may legitimately expect to be able to rely.[14] So, a jurisdiction clause in a consumer contract is likely to make it procedurally much harder for a consumer to vindicate his rights through civil litigation and/or may adversely affect the consumer's substantive rights. These factors suggest that dispute-resolution clauses in consumer contracts should not be treated in the same way as similar provisions in commercial contracts.

There is a question as to the theoretical basis for the policy of not enforcing dispute-resolution clauses in consumer contracts. When looking at dispute-resolution clauses in b2c contracts and whether or not they are unfair, there are two possible approaches; the issue of unfairness may be seen from either a 'procedural' or a 'substantive' perspective. The 'procedural' approach asks the question whether, before entering the contract, the consumer had a reasonable opportunity of knowing that the terms of the contract included the dispute-resolution clause in question. This approach starts from the premise that the inequality which consumer protection legislation should seek to redress is the consumer's information deficit. According to this approach, a dispute-resolution clause—even if its practical effect is to impose further burdens on a consumer whose rights have been infringed—is not unacceptable as long as the supplier has taken proper steps to bring the existence of the clause to the consumer's attention. By contrast, a 'substantive' approach would tend to strike down an onerous dispute-resolution clause in a consumer contract whether or not the consumer is made aware of such a clause before entering the contract. Because the consumer is powerless in the contractual relationship and has no opportunity to bargain over the contract's terms and conditions, a dispute-resolution clause which deprives the consumer of any effective means of redress (by requiring him to pursue any claim against the supplier in an alien forum) may be thought to be substantively unfair, even if it has not **7.06**

13 See *Yoder v Heinold Commodities Inc* 630 F Supp 756, 759 (ED Va, 1986): 'where the clause requires the filing of a suit in a distant state it can serve as a large deterrent to the filing of suits by consumers against large corporations'.

14 See ch 12.

been imposed on the consumer by the supplier in an unfair way. Obviously, a 'substantive' approach to dispute-resolution clauses is likely to be more interventionist than a purely 'procedural' approach.

II. JURISDICTION CLAUSES

1. Common Law Failures

7.07 One of the features of a common law system is that, as a general rule, doctrines developed by the courts apply equally to all legal relationships of a particular type; courts tend to be reluctant to try to distinguish consumer contracts from commercial contracts with a view to fashioning specific doctrines to deal with the problems posed by consumer contracts (as opposed to contracts in general). As a result, contract law doctrines developed by the courts normally apply equally to commercial contracts and consumer contracts. In view of the fact that there seems to be no authority in the Commonwealth on the question whether or not contractual dispute-resolution clauses in consumer contracts are subject to the same rules as such agreements in b2b contracts,[15] it is legitimate to conclude that, in the absence of specific legislation to the contrary, dispute-resolution clauses in consumer contracts are not subject to special rules. It is, however, difficult for the courts to formulate common law doctrines that can provide satisfactory solutions to both b2b and b2c contracts; a common law rule which provides a satisfactory solution in the commercial context may produce unacceptable results in the consumer context and vice versa. That the common law approach may cause considerable hardship for consumers is graphically illustrated by the position in the United States.

7.08 The leading US case concerned with the enforceability of jurisdiction clauses in consumer contracts is *Carnival Cruise Lines Inc v Shute*.[16] Prior to the decision in this case, some commentators had assumed (on the basis of the Supreme Court's decision in the *Bremen* case,[17] in which it was held that a freely negotiated forum-selection clause should be given full effect) that jurisdiction clauses in standard-form consumer contracts were unenforceable.[18] Nevertheless, in the *Carnival Cruise* case the Supreme

[15] In England, there is no reported litigation which concerns the enforceability at common law of a jurisdiction clause in a consumer contract.

[16] 111 S Ct 1522 (1991).

[17] *Bremen v Zapata Off-Shore Co* 407 US 1 (1972).

[18] L Goldman (1992: 706).

Court upheld a jurisdiction clause in the consumer context. The plaintiffs, who were resident in Washington state, purchased a cruise from the defendant, which was a company incorporated in Panama, but based in Florida. The tickets issued by the defendant set out the terms and conditions of the Passage Contract Ticket which included the following clause:

> It is agreed by and between the passenger and the Carrier that all disputes and matters whatsoever arising under, in connection with or incident to this Contract shall be litigated, if at all, in and before a Court located in the State of Florida USA to the exclusion of the Courts of any other state or country.

Although the ticket was sent to the plaintiffs only after they had made full **7.09** payment for the cruise, clause 3(a) stated that 'acceptance of this ticket by the person or persons named hereon as passengers shall be deemed to be an acceptance and agreement by each of them of all of the terms and conditions of this Passage Contract Ticket'. The plaintiffs boarded the vessel in Los Angeles and, while the vessel was in international waters off the Mexican coast, one of the plaintiffs suffered personal injury when she slipped on a deck mat. When the plaintiffs started proceedings in Washington state (in which they claimed damages for the injuries which, it was alleged, had been caused by the defendant's negligence), the defendant sought to rely on the Passenger Contract Ticket's exclusive jurisdiction clause in favour of the courts of Florida.

The dispute over forum ascended through the judicial hierarchy to the **7.10** Supreme Court which, by a majority, decided that the plaintiffs were bound by the jurisdiction clause in the contract and that they were not entitled to litigate their claim in the Washington courts. The fact that the jurisdiction clause was part of a standard-form contract (rather than a specifically negotiated agreement) was not fatal to its enforceability. Justice Blackmun, who delivered the opinion of the court, gave three reasons in support of upholding the clause: first, in view of the fact that cruise passengers may be resident in a variety of different states and countries, the defendant had a special interest in limiting the fora in which it could be sued; secondly, the clause had the effect of dispelling any confusion about where disputes arising from the contract could be litigated, thereby sparing litigants time and expense and conserving judicial resources; and thirdly, 'it stands to reason' that passengers benefit from the jurisdiction clause 'in the form of reduced fares reflecting the savings that [the defendant] enjoys by limiting the fora in which it may be sued'.[19]

[19] 111 S Ct 1522, 1527 (1991).

7.11 This reasoning has not convinced all commentators and the decision was greeted with a torrent of criticism.[20] Even though the Supreme Court sought to justify its conclusion on the basis that the enforcement of jurisdiction clauses is desirable for reasons of economic efficiency—by reducing the supplier's costs consumers benefit from a reduced price—this strand of the decision is merely asserted; there are no factual findings or empirical evidence to support it.[21] Furthermore, it has been strongly argued that the non-enforcement of jurisdiction clauses in consumer contracts is more likely to yield economically efficient outcomes than their enforcement.[22] Notwithstanding the fact that the decision was widely criticized by commentators—and there was a failed attempt to reverse the ruling by legislation[23]—a few years later it was followed in *Effron v Sun Line Cruise Inc*,[24] a similar case (involving a South American cruise) in which the contract contained a jurisdiction clause in favour of the Greek courts. Although Judge Calabresi, like some of the academic commentators who were so critical of the *Carnival Cruise* case, considered that 'upholding forum-selection clauses like the one involved in this case makes very little economic sense',[25] the Court of Appeals decided that the application of previous authority to the facts of the case dictated enforcement of the Greek jurisdiction clause.

2. Legislative Solutions in Europe

7.12 In Europe, to the extent that the law has tried to deal with the questions raised by dispute-resolution clauses in standard-form consumer contracts, legislation has sought to provide the answers.

Brussels I Regulation

7.13 As regards protected consumer contracts falling within the scope of Section 4 of Chapter II of the Brussels I Regulation,[26] article 17 is designed to make sure that suppliers are not normally able to rely on jurisdiction clauses which confer exclusive jurisdiction on the supplier's home forum (or some other forum which is convenient for the supplier, but inconvenient for the consumer). The reasons for this approach are fairly obvious: a clause which

[20] See, eg, PJ Borchers (1992); EP Gilbert (1992); L Goldman (1992); LS Mullenix (1992).
[21] LS Mullenix (1992: 343).
[22] L Goldman (1992).
[23] See A Gehringer (2001: 650).
[24] 67 F 3d 7 (2nd Cir, 1995).
[25] 67 F 3d 7, 11 (2nd Cir, 1995).
[26] See chs 3 and 4.

confers exclusive jurisdiction on a court other than the consumer's home forum makes it more difficult or onerous for the consumer to litigate a claim.[27] In the context of a cross-border consumer contract, a consumer who is denied access to the courts of his own country and drawn to the courts of another country will have to deal with foreign lawyers, possibly in a foreign language, and he may well have to travel abroad. All of this involves additional time and expense.

Under the Brussels I Regulation there are only three types of situation in **7.14**
which a jurisdiction agreement in a protected consumer contract is enforceable against a consumer domiciled in a member state.[28] First, a jurisdiction agreement which is entered into after the dispute has arisen is enforceable between the parties. This exception can be justified on theoretical grounds; a post-dispute agreement will be individually negotiated, rather than imposed by the supplier's standard terms and conditions, and, once the dispute has arisen, the consumer will necessarily be in a better position to understand the implications of agreeing to the jurisdiction of particular courts. However, some consider that the first exception in article 17 is objectionable on the basis that consumers do not become more equal with suppliers just because a dispute has arisen.[29] Be that as it may, it is doubtful whether this exception has much practical significance; there can be hardly any cases in which, after the emergence of a dispute between the parties, a consumer intentionally agrees to the jurisdiction of the courts of a country in which he is not domiciled—as there is no possible incentive for a consumer to make such an agreement. Secondly, a jurisdiction clause which gives the consumer an opportunity to bring proceedings in fora other than those identified by other provisions of the Brussels I Regulation is enforceable. As there are good theoretical arguments for upholding

[27] B Dahl (1977: 110).

[28] Art 17. The approach to jurisdiction clauses in insurance contracts (in Section 3) is basically the same as the approach to jurisdiction clauses in consumer contracts (in Section 4) see F Seatzu (2003: 62–4). Under multilateral conventions which address questions of international jurisdiction in relation to specific subject-matters, there is a lack of uniformity. The approach to jurisdiction agreements may be largely the same as that to be found in the Brussels I Regulation: see, eg, art 17(2) of the 1974 Athens Convention relating to the Carriage of Passengers and their Luggage by Sea (implemented in the United Kingdom by means of the Merchant Shipping Act 1995, s 183). Alternatively, a completely different approach may be adopted: for example, the 1999 Montreal Convention for the Unification of Certain Rules for International Carriage by Air (implemented into UK law by SI 2002 No 263, which makes various amendments to the Carriage by Air Act 1961 and the Carriage by Air (Supplementary Provisions) Act 1962) allows for disputes to be referred to arbitration (art 34), but does not make provision for the parties to depart by agreement from the jurisdictional rules set out in art 33.

[29] B Dahl (1977: 107).

contractual clauses which are for the consumer's benefit, the second exception is entirely unobjectionable. But, in practice, it is almost certainly irrelevant. Given that standard-form consumer contracts are invariably drafted by the supplier, the practical significance of this exception is extremely limited; there is no reason why a supplier would choose to give the consumer the possibility of litigating in fora other than those provided by article 16(1) (ie, the courts of the member state in which the supplier is domiciled or for the place in which the consumer is domiciled); even if a consumer were allowed such a choice, in view of the problems associated with cross-border litigation, it is hard to see why a consumer would elect to bring proceedings in a court which was neither his home forum nor the forum in which the supplier is domiciled (and in which any judgment in the consumer's favour would need to be enforced). The third exception gives effect to a jurisdiction clause if, at the time of the conclusion of the contract, both parties were domiciled or habitually resident in the same member state and agreed to the jurisdiction of the courts of that member state.[30] This exception, which has been described as 'on the whole superfluous',[31] deals with the situation where, following the conclusion of a domestic consumer contract, one of the parties moves to another member state. In a case where the contract includes a jurisdiction clause in favour of the courts of the member state of the parties' common domicile or residence at the time of contracting, if the consumer moves to another member state between the conclusion of the contract and the emergence of the dispute, the supplier's reasonable expectations are protected. From the supplier's perspective, the contract is like any other domestic consumer contract and the supplier has no reason to think that cross-border issues are relevant. For reasons of equity[32] the consequences of the third exception are: first, if the supplier needs to sue the consumer for non-payment, the contractual forum has jurisdiction, notwithstanding the fact that the consumer is no longer living in that country; and, secondly, the consumer is not able to bring proceedings against the supplier in the member state to which he has moved. The circumstances in which the exceptions might come into play are unlikely to arise and, not surprisingly, there seem to be no reported cases in which article 17 of the Brussels I Regulation (or the equivalent provision of the Brussels Convention) has been part of the jurisdictional equation.[33] In practical terms, the effect of the Brussels I

[30] This exception has a proviso: 'provided that such an agreement is not contrary to the law of that Member State'.

[31] B Dahl (1977: 107).

[32] Jenard Report [1979] OJ C59/33.

[33] Note that, in B Hess, T Pfeiffer, and P Schlosser, (September 2007), the review of member states' experience with the provisions of the European jurisdiction regime does not refer at all to art 17 or to jurisdiction clauses in consumer contracts.

Regulation is that jurisdiction clauses in protected consumer contracts are unenforceable.

In broad terms, there are two types of situation in which the unenforceability of a jurisdiction clause under the Brussels I Regulation may be a relevant issue. The paradigm cases are where the contract contains a clause which purports to confer exclusive jurisdiction on the courts of the country in which the supplier is established. The first situation is where proceedings are brought in the contractual forum, but the defendant-consumer argues that, as the contract is a protected consumer contract, the jurisdiction clause is not binding. This situation is illustrated by *Standard Bank London Ltd v Apostolakis*.[34] The defendants, a Greek couple, had entered into foreign exchange contracts with the claimant, the English subsidiary of a South African bank. The primary document signed by the parties was headed 'Terms and Conditions for Foreign Exchange and Precious Metals Margin Trading'; as regards claims brought by the bank against its customers, clause 17 of this agreement provided for the non-exclusive jurisdiction of the English courts. However, the Preamble to the agreement also referred to another document ('terms of business') which the parties signed. This document, which stated that the terms of business were incorporated into the terms and conditions of the primary agreement, provided that 'the courts of England shall have exclusive jurisdiction of [sic] any claim or dispute hereunder'. When the defendants started proceedings against the bank in Greece, the claimant started English proceedings with a view to obtaining an anti-suit injunction to restrain the defendants from continuing with the Greek proceedings.[35] The defendants successfully argued that the contract was a protected consumer contract for the purposes of Section 4 as a result of which the jurisdiction agreement was not enforceable. **7.15**

The second situation is where the contractual forum assumes jurisdiction (on the basis of the clause in the contract) and gives judgment in the supplier's favour; when the supplier applies to enforce the judgment in the defendant's home forum, the defendant resists enforcement by seeking to rely on the defence in article 35(1) of the Brussels I Regulation which provides that a judgment shall not be recognized if it conflicts with, inter alia, Section 4 of Chapter II.[36] This second situation is illustrated by *Weber v SA* **7.16**

[34] [2000] ILPr 766.

[35] Note that this case was decided before the Court of Justice's ruling in Case C-159/02 *Turner* [2004] ECR I-3565 that, in civil and commercial matters, the courts of one member state may not issue an anti-suit injunction aimed at preventing a litigant from proceeding in another member state.

[36] See Case 150/77 *Bertrand* [1978] ECR 1431 and the discussion in ch 6.

Eurocard Belgium-Luxembourg,[37] a decision of the Court of Appeal of Luxembourg. The judgment-creditor, a Belgian credit card company, had obtained a Belgian judgment ordering the defendant to pay various sums due under a credit card agreement. The contract between the parties had purported to confer exclusive jurisdiction on the Belgian courts. The defendant successfully resisted enforcement of the judgment in Luxembourg on the basis that: (i) he was domiciled in Luxembourg; (ii) the contract was a protected consumer contract; and (iii) the Belgian court had wrongly assumed jurisdiction on the basis of the jurisdiction clause in the contract.[38]

7.17 As regards cases which are internal to the United Kingdom (for example, where a dispute arises between a consumer domiciled in Scotland and a supplier domiciled in England), a contractual clause in a protected consumer contract is unenforceable against the consumer (except in the types of situation identified by article 17 of the Brussels I Regulation).[39] Consider the situation where an e-trader domiciled in Northern Ireland enters an online contract for the sale of goods with an English consumer. Such a contract is a protected consumer contract because the e-trader directs commercial activities to England and the contract falls within the scope of such activities.[40] If the terms and conditions of the e-trader's website include a clause purporting to confer exclusive jurisdiction on the courts of Northern Ireland that clause cannot be enforced against the consumer. Were the e-trader to start proceedings against the consumer in Northern Ireland, the court would, notwithstanding the jurisdiction clause, have to decline jurisdiction (unless the consumer submitted to the court's jurisdiction[41]); if the consumer were to start proceedings in England,[42] the e-trader would not be able to rely on the jurisdiction clause in order to have the proceedings stayed or dismissed.

Unfair Terms in Consumer Contracts Regulations 1999

7.18 The provisions of Section 4 (and the equivalent provisions of schedule 4 to the Civil Jurisdiction and Judgments Act 1982) apply only if the defendant

[37] [1993] ILPr 55.

[38] The result would be the same (but for different reasons) in a case where a contract between an English consumer and a US supplier includes a jurisdiction clause in favour of, say, the New York courts. See paras 6.37 and 7.27–7.30.

[39] Civil Jurisdiction and Judgments Act 1982, sched 4, r 9.

[40] Civil Jurisdiction and Judgments Act 1982, sched 4, r 7(1)(c).

[41] Civil Jurisdiction and Judgments Act 1982, sched 4, r 13.

[42] On the basis of Civil Jurisdiction and Judgments Act 1982, sched 4, r 8(1).

is domiciled in a member state. So, in a case where an English consumer enters an online contract with a US e-trader via a website whose terms and conditions include an exclusive jurisdiction clause in favour of the Californian courts, if the consumer seeks to sue the supplier in England (under the traditional rules), neither the Brussels I Regulation nor schedule 4 to the 1982 Act comes into the picture. Furthermore, article 17 applies only in cases where the conditions of article 15 are satisfied. Where, for example, an English consumer purchases goods from a French supplier while on holiday in France, the conditions of article 15 are not satisfied and the contract is not a protected consumer contract. This does not mean, however, that jurisdiction clauses in consumer contracts which fall outside the scope of Section 4 are entitled to be enforced in accordance with the principles that apply to jurisdiction agreements in commercial contracts. That is because, in cases not governed by the provisions of the Brussels I Regulation, the Unfair Terms in Consumer Contracts Regulations 1999[43] (which implement the Unfair Terms in Consumer Contracts Directive[44]) are potentially relevant.

In *Océano Grupo Editorial and Salvat Editores*[45] the defendants, Spanish consumers who resided in various parts of Spain, entered into a contract for the purchase by instalments of encyclopaedias from the claimant, a Spanish company whose principal place of business was in Barcelona. The terms of the contract provided that, in the event of a dispute, the Barcelona court would have exclusive jurisdiction. When the defendants failed to pay the instalments allegedly due under the contract, the claimant started proceedings in Barcelona. One of the questions facing the Spanish court was whether the jurisdiction clause was 'unfair' for the purposes of the Unfair Terms in Consumer Contracts Directive. **7.19**

According to article 3 (1) of the Directive: **7.20**

> A contractual term which has not been individually negotiated shall be regarded as unfair if, contrary to the requirement of good faith, it causes a significant imbalance in the parties' rights and obligations arising under the contract, to the detriment of the consumer.

Clauses 'excluding or hindering the consumer's right to take legal action or exercise any other legal remedy'[46] are among the types of clause which are prima facie regarded as unfair for the purposes of the Directive. A jurisdiction clause of the type under consideration in *Océano Grupo Editorial*

[43] SI 1999 No 2083.

[44] Dir 93/13/EEC [1993] L95/29.

[45] Joined Cases C-240/98 to C-244/98 [2000] ECR I-4941.

[46] Art 3(3); Annex 1, para 1(q).

and Salvat Editores 'obliges the consumer to submit to the exclusive jurisdiction of a court which may be a long way from his domicile. This may make it difficult for him to enter an appearance. In the case of disputes concerning limited amounts of money, the costs relating to the consumer's entering an appearance could be a deterrent and cause him to forego any legal remedy or defence.' [47] According to the Court of Justice:

> where a jurisdiction clause is included, without being individually negotiated, in a contract between a consumer and a seller or supplier within the meaning of the Directive and where it confers exclusive jurisdiction on a court in the territorial jurisdiction of which the seller or supplier has his principal place of business, it must be regarded as unfair within the meaning of Article 3 of the Directive in so far as it causes, contrary to the requirement of good faith, a significant imbalance in the parties' rights and obligations arising under the contract, to the detriment of the consumer.[48]

7.21 The result in *Océano Grupo Editorial and Salvat Editores* indicates that a jurisdiction clause will fall foul of the Directive in cases where consumer-defendants are required to litigate 'in the courts of a city other than that of their domicile but still in the country of their domicile'.[49] So, where a contract between an English supplier and a Scottish consumer includes an exclusive jurisdiction clause in favour of the English courts, even if the case is not determined by the provisions of schedule 4 to the Civil Jurisdiction and Judgments Act 1982 (which largely replicates the provisions of the Brussels I Regulation with regard to jurisdictional disputes which involve more than one part of the United Kingdom), that jurisdiction clause will not be enforceable by the supplier against the consumer.[50]

7.22 By the same token, the effect of the 1999 Regulations is to render unenforceable jurisdiction clauses in consumer contracts which do not fall within the scope of Section 4 (by virtue of their not satisfying the requirements of article 15(1) of the Brussels I Regulation). In *Standard Bank London Ltd v Apostolakis (No 2)*[51] David Steel J, having decided that, under the Brussels Convention, the contractual jurisdiction clause was not binding on the Greek defendants, went on to consider *obiter* the significance of the 1999 Regulations. To decide whether or not a clause was 'unfair' for the

[47] Joined Cases C-240/98 to C-244/98 [2000] ECR I-4941, 4972 (para 22).

[48] Joined Cases C-240/98 to C-244/98 [2000] ECR I-4941, 4973 (para 24).

[49] C Withers (2002: 58).

[50] The Court of Justice also emphasized that the Directive ought to be raised by the court of its own motion. This poses questions for the English courts, which according to the traditional model of civil litigation in common law systems is heavily dependent on the relevant issues being raised by the parties to the dispute: see S Whittaker (2001).

[51] [2001] Lloyd's Law Reports Banking 240.

purposes of the 1999 Regulations, David Steel J had regard both to the decision of the Court of Justice in *Océano Grupo Editorial and Salvat Editores* and the following passage taken from the academic literature:

> I suspect that good faith has a double operation. First, it has a procedural aspect. It will require the supplier to consider the consumer's interests. However, a clause which might be unfair if it came as a surprise may be upheld if the business took steps to bring it to the consumer's attention and to explain it. Secondly, it has a substantive content: some clauses may cause such an imbalance that they should always be treated as being contrary to good faith and therefore unfair.[52]

David Steel J held that, even had the jurisdiction clause in the document signed by the defendants not been rendered unenforceable by the Brussels Convention, it would have fallen foul of the 1999 Regulations: the jurisdiction clause requiring the defendants to litigate in England involved 'potential cost and inconvenience'; any litigation in England would be 'conducted in a language that [the defendants] do not speak'; the defendants were 'taken . . . by surprise' by a jurisdiction clause 'calling for translation and careful explanation' which 'was not forthcoming'.[53] **7.23**

The approach adopted in *Standard Bank London Ltd v Apostolakis (No 2)* and the factors which David Steel J considered to be relevant lead to the conclusion that a jurisdiction clause in a cross-border consumer contract will normally be 'unfair' for the purposes of the 1999 Regulations. It is not usual for suppliers to explain the significance of the small print of a consumer contract to consumers; in the context of most distance contracts (such as mail order contracts and those concluded via the Internet), there is no opportunity for such an explanation to be given. Furthermore, in the cross-border context, if the contractual forum is the supplier's home forum, upholding the clause would involve cost and inconvenience for the consumer. The argument which won the day in the *Carnival Cruise* case in the United States—that an apparently harsh term is acceptable because it leads to a lower price—is not likely to succeed in the context of the 1999 Regulations.[54] **7.24**

In cases such as *Océano Grupo Editorial and Salvat Editores* and *Standard Bank London Ltd v Apostolakis (No 2)* there is no doubt that the case fell within the territorial scope of the Directive; all elements of the situation were connected with one or two member states. There are, however, questions surrounding the applicability of the Directive in cases where the **7.25**

52 H Beale (1995: 245). This passage had been cited with approval by the Court of Appeal in *Director General of Fair Trading v First National Bank plc* [2000] 2 WLR 1353, 1365.

53 [2001] Lloyd's Law Reports Banking 240, 250.

54 See H Beale (1995: 243).

connecting factors are not so densely grouped in a member state (or member states)—especially if the contract in question is not governed by the law of a member state. What would be the proper solution in a case where an English consumer enters an online contract with a US company and the contract includes both an exclusive jurisdiction clause in favour of the New York courts and a choice-of-law clause selecting New York law as the applicable law?

7.26 Consider the situation in which the US supplier, first, brings proceedings against the consumer for non-payment in New York and, then, having obtained a judgment from the New York courts, applies to enforce the judgment in England. If, on the one hand, the jurisdiction clause is binding on the consumer, the New York court is a court of competent jurisdiction for the purposes of English private international law and the judgment is prima facie enforceable in England; if, on the other hand, the agreement on jurisdiction is not enforceable against the consumer, the New York court is not a court of competent jurisdiction (as long as the consumer does not submit to the New York proceedings) and the judgment is not entitled to enforcement in England.[55]

7.27 A key aspect of the Directive—as implemented by the 1999 Regulations—is an anti-avoidance provision. Regulation 9 (which gives effect to article 6(2) of the Directive) provides that the 1999 Regulations apply 'notwithstanding any contract term which applies or purports to apply the law of a non-Member State, if the contract has a close connection with the territory of the Member States'. Although this aspect of the 1999 Regulations has yet to receive judicial exegesis, it seems clear that, where a contract is concluded with a consumer who is habitually resident in one of the member states or performance by the supplier (such as physical delivery of goods) takes place in one of the member states, the contract has a close connection with the territory of the member states.[56]

7.28 The significance of regulation 9 can be illustrated by the *Ingmar* case,[57] which involved the applicability of the Commercial Agents (Council Directive) Regulations 1993[58] (which contains an anti-avoidance provision

[55] See ch 6. The same basic issue would also arise in the unlikely event of the consumer bringing proceedings in England against the US supplier for breach of contract. The question would be whether the English court should uphold the jurisdiction clause (and dismiss the consumer's claim on jurisdictional grounds) or declare the jurisdiction clause to be unenforceable (on the basis of the Unfair Terms in Consumer Contracts Regulations 1999) and, if the circumstances were such that the English court was entitled to assume jurisdiction (such as if the supplier had a place of business in England), allow the claim to proceed in England.

[56] See L Collins *et al* (2006: para 33–48).

[57] Case C-281/98 *Ingmar GB Ltd v Eaton Leonard Technologies Inc* [2000] ECR I-9305.

[58] SI 1993 No 3053 which implements Dir 86/653/EEC [1986] OJ L382/17.

similar to the one to be found in the 1999 Regulations). The claimant, a UK company, had been employed by the defendant, a Californian company, as the defendant's exclusive agent in the United Kingdom and Ireland. The agency contract between the parties contained an express choice of Californian law. When the defendant terminated the contract, the claimant started English proceedings with a view to recovering payments to which it claimed to be entitled under the 1993 Regulations. The High Court rejected the claim on the basis that the contract was governed by Californian law. However, the Court of Appeal made a reference to the Court of Justice which ruled that the 1993 Regulations, the purpose of which is to guarantee certain rights to commercial agents after the termination of agency contracts, are applicable in cases where the contract has a close connection with the territory of the member states regardless of the law governing the contract. Accordingly, a commercial agent who carries on his activity in a member state can rely on the 1993 Regulations, even though the principal is not established in a member state and the contract contains a choice-of-law clause selecting the law of a non-member state.

The same approach is applicable in cases concerning a consumer contract **7.29** concluded between a consumer who is domiciled or habitually resident in a member state and a supplier established in a non-member state. The fact that the consumer is domiciled or resident in a member state means that the contract has a close connection with the territory of that member state for the purposes of the Unfair Terms in Consumer Contracts Regulations 1999. Accordingly, regardless of the law governing the contract, the rule which renders the jurisdiction clause unfair (and, therefore, unenforceable against the consumer) takes precedence over the chosen law. It follows that, notwithstanding the inclusion of a choice of New York law and jurisdiction in the supplier's standard terms and conditions, the judgment granted by the New York courts against the consumer would not be enforceable in England.

III. ARBITRATION CLAUSES

1. Introduction

In the consumer context, there is a broad range of potential arbitration **7.30** agreements.[59] At one end of the spectrum, one finds pre-dispute compulsory arbitration agreements (ie, the equivalent of traditional contractual arbitration clauses). If the parties refer a dispute to an arbitrator who is

[59] See CR Drahozal and RJ Friel (2002: 361–2).

authorized to make a binding determination, a party who is unhappy with the manner in which the arbitration is conducted cannot simply opt to litigate his claim instead; he is bound by the arbitrator's award—unless it is set aside by the court with supervisory jurisdiction over the arbitration.[60] At the other end of the spectrum, there is post-dispute non-binding arbitration (ie, where neither party is bound by the arbitrator's award).[61] In between, there are many possibilities. One which has a certain appeal in the consumer context is post-dispute asymmetrically binding arbitration: after a dispute has arisen from a b2c contract, the parties agree to refer the dispute to arbitration, but only the supplier is bound by the decision of the arbitrator; in theory, the consumer has the option of litigating the dispute after the award has been made.[62]

7.31 Consumer arbitration agreements are intrinsically problematic and raise several of the issues which have already been considered with regard to jurisdiction agreements. The effect of a compulsory arbitration agreement is to prevent a consumer seeking legal redress against a supplier by means of litigation in his home forum. Although private international law cannot resolve the access-to-justice problems generated by national systems of civil procedure, one of its objectives in the field of consumer protection is to try to avoid further diminishing the opportunities for consumers to vindicate their legal rights. An arbitration clause in a standard-form consumer contract normally favours the supplier rather than the consumer; it selects a seat of arbitration which is convenient for the supplier (and, in a cross-border case, which may be very inconvenient for the consumer). In the

[60] Supervisory jurisdiction is normally exercised by the courts of the seat of arbitration. See Arbitration Act 1996, s 2.

[61] For example, in the US, in addition to its more formal arbitration scheme, the Better Business Bureau (BBB) operates 'informal dispute settlement' for disputes arising out of consumer contracts. Although the hearing officer's decision is not binding, by participating in the scheme, suppliers agree to act in good faith. See <http://www.dr.bbb.org/programs/ids.asp> [12/7/07].

[62] See, eg, the dispute-resolution scheme of the Financial Services Ombudsman: <http://www.financial-ombudsman.org.uk>. Under the rules of the FOS—whose remit includes assisting in the settlement of cross-border financial disputes—if the consumer accepts the ombudsman's decision both parties are bound by the decision; a consumer who does not accept the decision remains free to take court proceedings against the business. Note, however, that, as regards complaints which are referred to the FOS, very few cases result in a formal decision by the ombudsman; the vast majority are handled informally at an earlier stage of the process. See <http://www.financial-ombudsman.org.uk/publications/consumer_advisers_handbook.pdf> [12/7/07]. There are other dispute-resolution schemes which also provide that the arbitrator's award is binding only on the supplier. See, eg, *Qualitas* ('the Furniture ombudsman') <http://www.adrnow.org.uk/go/SubPage_43.html#pro> [12/7/07].

vast majority of cases, the process of arbitration will be wholly unfamiliar to the consumer—who would be at a significant disadvantage vis-à-vis a supplier which has greater financial resources and easier access to legal advice. Furthermore, the costs of arbitrating a low-value dispute normally exceed the costs associated with a court-based small claims procedure. So, if the courts routinely enforce arbitration agreements in consumer contracts (by staying court proceedings brought in breach of the terms of the arbitration agreement), the effect would be to place a further barrier in the way of a consumer who was seeking redress for breach of contract. It would, therefore, not be unreasonable to conclude that arbitration is not suitable for consumer disputes.[63] Indeed, under the laws of some countries, parties to a consumer contract are not permitted to submit their contractual disputes to arbitration.[64]

2. The New York Convention 1958

One of the objectives of the New York Convention of 1958 is the enforcement of international arbitration agreements (by requiring national courts to decline jurisdiction in cases where one party commences litigation in breach of the terms of an arbitration agreement). In principle, there is no reason why the Convention cannot apply to consumer arbitration as well as to commercial arbitration. However, because of the dangers that arbitration will operate only to exacerbate the effects of the socio-economic inequality between suppliers and consumers, article I.3 of the Convention provides that any state may 'declare that it will apply the convention only to differences arising out of legal relationships, whether contractual or not, which are considered as commercial under the national law of the State making such declaration'. As regards those countries making this reservation,[65] if they do not regard consumer disputes as commercial, the New York Convention does not apply. In addition, there is a question whether, in the context of e-commerce, an online arbitration agreement (concluded for example, by an exchange of e-mails or by a 'click-wrap' agreement) satisfies the requirement that the arbitration agreement should be 'in writing' for the purposes of article II of the New York Convention. **7.32**

[63] C Coteanu (2005: 92).

[64] For example, consumer disputes are not capable of settlement by arbitration in Finland, Italy, and Switzerland: see G Kaufmann-Kohler and T Schultz (2004: 172). See also A Vahrenwald (October 2000: 211–13).

[65] By the beginning of the 21st century 51 states had made the commercial reservation: K Stewart and J Matthews (2002: 1133).

7.33 In terms of the implementation of the New York Convention in England, it is clear that an arbitration agreement in an e-contract satisfies the requirement of writing for the purposes of section 5 of the Arbitration Act 1996, which provides that the formality requirements are fulfilled if the arbitration agreement is 'recorded by any means'.[66] Even without the broad definition of writing in the 1996 Act, there is an argument for saying that, as '[t]he drafters of the New York Convention could hardly have desired to freeze commercial practices into the straightjacket of immediate post-war technology',[67] 'writing' for the purposes of the Convention extends to an exchange of e-mails or an affirmative mouse-click. Even as regards those countries which have implemented the New York Convention without glossing the words of article II, many commentators consider that the requirement of writing is satisfied by an agreement concluded through electronic means.[68]

7.34 The fact that the New York Convention may enable arbitration to be used as a means of dealing with consumer disputes does not mean that arbitration is appropriate. As will be seen, different legal systems take different approaches to the enforceability of arbitration agreements in consumer contracts. As with other questions addressed in this chapter, there is a significant divergence between the United States and the European Union.

3. The US Approach

7.35 In the United States, mandatory arbitration clauses in consumer contracts have a particular attraction for suppliers as arbitration can be used to avoid some of the economic risks which are part and parcel of civil litigation in the United States. In a world of class actions, jury trials, and punitive damages, there are strong incentives for businesses to seek to take consumer disputes out of the courts.[69] The Federal Arbitration Act (FAA), originally enacted in 1925, applies to 'any maritime transaction or a contract evidencing a transaction involving commerce'.[70]

7.36 There is a view that, having regard to its legislative purpose, the FAA should apply only to b2b contracts and not to b2c contracts. Nevertheless, when interstate commerce is involved and the FAA is relevant, a compulsory

[66] R Hill (1999: 202–3).
[67] LJ Gibbons (2002: 52).
[68] See, eg, J Arsic (1997: 216); R Hill (1999: 200–3); G Kaufmann-Kohler and T Schultz (2004: 140); M Wahab (2004a: 154).
[69] See CR Drazohal and RJ Friel (2002: 389–91).
[70] 9 USC s 2 (2001).

arbitration clause in a consumer contract is, in principle, enforceable.[71] In the 1980s the Supreme Court decided that a pre-dispute arbitration clause in a contract between a brokerage house and its customers could be enforced against the customers.[72] Notwithstanding the fact that this approach arguably pushed the scope of the FAA beyond that which had been envisaged for it in 1925, the Supreme Court confirmed the efficacy of pre-dispute arbitration clauses in b2c contracts in the 1995 case of *Allied-Bruce Terminix Companies Inc v Dobson*.[73] Although there is relatively little discussion of the consumer dimension of the case, the Supreme Court proceeded on the basis that arbitration clauses in consumer contracts are to be treated on the same footing as arbitration agreements in commercial contracts. In *Hill v Gateway 2000 Inc*[74] the Court of Appeals went so far as to uphold an arbitration clause although it had not been made available to the customer until it arrived as part of the warranty brochure provided (along with many other documents) in the boxes containing a new computer which the consumer had ordered by telephone.

There are, however, circumstances in which common law or equitable doctrines have been held to limit the extent to which arbitration clauses will be enforced. For example, arbitration agreements are subject to general contractual doctrines according to which enforcement may be refused—such as on the basis of unconscionability. However, the cases indicate that only the most obviously unfair arbitration clauses will be held by lower courts to be unenforceable due to unconscionability or similar reasons.[75] **7.37**

Where federal statutory claims are involved, if the consequence of upholding an arbitration clause would be to prevent the claimant from effectively vindicating his statutory rights in the arbitral forum, a claimant may be allowed to litigate the claim instead. So, the court may refuse to uphold an arbitration agreement in a situation where the costs of arbitration are prohibitive—with the consequence that the consumer is effectively prevented from vindicating his rights.[76] For example, in *Comacho v Holiday* **7.38**

[71] If the FAA does not apply (because interstate commerce is not involved), state law governs; many US state arbitration laws make consumer arbitration agreements enforceable: CR Drazohal and RJ Friel (2002: 375).

[72] *Shearson/American Express Inc v McMahon* 482 US 220 (1987); *Rodriguez de Quijas v Shearson/American Express Inc* 490 US 477 (1989).

[73] 513 US 265; 115 S Ct 834 (1995). See J Senderowicz (1999: 288–94).

[74] 105 F3d 1147 (7th Cir, 1997).

[75] JR Sternlight (2002: 836).

[76] *Green Tree Fin Corp-Ala v Randolph* 531 US 79 (2000). However, it was held that the very limited evidence submitted by the consumer had failed to show that the costs of the arbitration were prohibitively high.

Homes Inc[77] an arbitration clause in a contract for the purchase of a pre-fabricated house was held to be unenforceable because the arbitral forum was inaccessible to the purchaser. Similarly, in *Mendez v Palm Harbour Homes*,[78] a case involving a dispute arising from the sale of a mobile home, the court refused to compel arbitration because the administrative costs of the American Arbitration Association (AAA) were prohibitively high. Also, in *Brower v Gateway 2000 Inc*,[79] an arbitration clause in a consumer contract for the sale of a personal computer providing for ICC arbitration was not enforced on the basis that the clause was unconscionable; in view of the low value of the claim, the costs of ICC arbitration were excessive.

7.39 In response to these developments, there have been rule changes by arbitral institutions with a view to keeping the costs of consumer arbitration within more reasonable limits. For example, as regards AAA arbitration, for a claim of less than $10,000, the fees payable by the consumer will not exceed $125; if the value of the claim is between $10,000 and $75,000, the consumer's cost is set at $375; the supplier is responsible for all other arbitration costs in these cases.[80] Similar changes to fee structures have been made by other American arbitral institutions.[81] Of course, the arbitration fees are on top of the costs which the consumer may incur by engaging a lawyer to pursue (or defend) the claim on his behalf. So, institutional arbitration remains a relatively expensive option—and it is difficult to see how arbitration along traditional lines can solve consumer access-to-justice issues. One of the major defects of the private litigation model is the fact that the cost of the process will often exceed the amount of the claim; arbitration suffers from exactly the same defect—but more so: in the consumer context, the costs of arbitration are normally substantially higher than the costs of litigation.[82] Some of these problems are partially addressed by the US Better Business Bureau (BBB) which offers an arbitration service for consumer disputes which, from the consumer's perspective, is free.[83] The BBB handles hundreds of thousands of complaints a year, though disputes

[77] 167 F Supp 2d 893 (WD Va, 2001).

[78] 45 P 3d 594 (Wash Ct App, 2002).

[79] 676 NYS 2d 569 (NY App Div, 1998).

[80] See the AAA's *Consumer-Related Disputes Supplementary Procedures* (effective 15 September 2005): <http://www.adr.org/sp.asp?id=22014> [2/12/07], replacing the 2003 version of the rules: <http://www.adr.org/sp.asp?id=26412> [21/7/06]. For consumer claims, the filing fee of the National Arbitration Forum is only $49: EC Thornburg (2003: 318).

[81] See D Bates (2004: 835–8).

[82] JA Scarpino (2002: 681).

[83] See BBB's dispute resolution website: <http://www.dr.bbb.org>.

are referred to arbitration in only a very small percentage of these cases. An obvious limitation of the BBB scheme is that it is only available in cases where the supplier is a member of the BBB.[84]

Overall, the practice of the US courts towards consumer arbitration is not consistent and it is not always easy to predict whether or not an arbitration clause in a consumer contract will be upheld. For example, as regards a particular dispute-resolution clause in a shrink-wrap agreement or a click-wrap agreement, some courts may uphold the clause,[85] while others declare it to be unenforceable.[86] Although the majority of commentators are opposed to the enforcement of arbitration clauses in consumer contracts,[87] the trend in the hundreds of cases in which the US courts have considered arbitration clauses in consumer contracts is towards upholding them. In *Rollins Inc v Foster*,[88] for example, an arbitration clause in a consumer contract was upheld: even though the consumer had been long-term unemployed and in receipt of social security and disability benefits, the court considered that she had failed to prove that she was without recourse by reason of being unable to afford the costs of the arbitration (which the court thought would be likely to be in excess of $1,000).[89] Similarly, in the e-commerce context, most US courts faced with a dispute between an e-trader and a consumer reach the conclusion that an arbitration clause in the contract between the parties is enforceable.[90] Although there are some consumer cases in which the courts have refused to uphold arbitration agreements, there is a general judicial approval of arbitration clauses in standard-form contracts;[91] most courts require consumers to arbitrate under most clauses.[92] **7.40**

4. Legislative Solutions in Europe

Part of the background to the European approach to arbitration clauses in consumer contracts is the European Convention on Human Rights, **7.41**

[84] For further discussion of 'embedded' ADR schemes, see ch 11.

[85] *Hill v Gateway 2000 Inc*, 105 F3d 1147 (7th Cir, 1997).

[86] *Brower v Gateway 2000 Inc*, 676 NYS 2d 569 (NY App Div, 1998).

[87] See, eg, JR Sternlight (2002), H Arfazadeh (2002); but, compare CR Drahozal (2001).

[88] 991 F Supp 1426 (MD Ala, 1998).

[89] See also *N Am Van Lines v Collyer* 616 So 2d 177 (Fla Dist Ct Ap, 1993); *Delta Funding Corporation v Harris* 466 F3d 273 (3rd Cir, 2006); *Dale v Comcast Corporation* 453 F Supp 2d 1367 (ND Ga, 2006).

[90] JK Winn and M Webber (2006: 225).

[91] J Senderowicz (1999: 297).

[92] JR Sternlight (2002: 843). Compare C Coteanu (2005: 49–62), who considers that, in general, US courts have been unwilling to enforce arbitration agreements in consumer contracts.

in particular Article 6, which is designed to protect an individual's right to a fair trial.[93] According to the European Commission:

> use of the out of court alternative may not deprive consumers of their right to bring the matter before the courts unless they expressly agree to do so, in full awareness of the facts and only after the dispute has materialised.[94]

7.42 In policy terms, jurisdiction agreements, arbitration agreements, and other ADR agreements raise similar issues. It would, therefore, be surprising if a pre-dispute arbitration agreement in a b2c contracts were enforceable, given that pre-dispute jurisdiction agreements in consumer contracts are not. As already noted, the Unfair Terms in Consumer Contracts Directive[95] (implemented in the United Kingdom by the Unfair Terms in Consumer Contracts Regulations 1999[96]) seeks to make sure that consumers are not prejudiced by inter alia onerous dispute-resolution clauses in standard-form contracts. Even if a consumer fails to raise the unfairness of an arbitration clause under the Directive within the context of arbitration proceedings, the issue must be considered by the court (if necessary, of its own motion) if there are subsequent court proceedings relating to the annulment or enforcement of the award.[97]

7.43 Although the enforceability of arbitration clauses in consumer contracts has not been expressly considered by the Court of Justice,[98] its approach in *Océano Grupo Editorial and Salvat Editores*,[99] a case concerning a jurisdiction clause in a domestic Spanish contract, is equally applicable to cases involving arbitration clauses. Under the 1999 Regulations, clauses 'excluding or hindering the consumer's right to take legal action or exercise any other legal remedy, particularly by requiring the consumer to take disputes exclusively to arbitration not covered by legal provisions'[100] are expressly identified within the illustrative list of terms 'which may be regarded as unfair'.[101] In England, to a large extent, questions surrounding the interaction of arbitration clauses and the Unfair Terms in Consumer Contracts

[93] See S Schiavetta (2004).

[94] Commission Recommendation 98/257/EC on the principles applicable to the bodies responsible for out-of-court settlement of consumer disputes [1998] OJ L115/31.

[95] Dir 93/13/EEC [1993] OJ L95/29.

[96] SI 1999 No 2083.

[97] See Case C-168/05 *Mostaza Claro* [2006] ECR I-10421.

[98] In Case C-168/05 *Mostaza Claro* [2006] ECR I-10421 the referring court, the Madrid Provincial Court, had established that the arbitration clause contained in the consumer contract in question was unfair.

[99] Joined Cases C-240/98 to C-244/98 [2000] ECR I-4941.

[100] Sched 2, para (q).

[101] Reg 5(5).

Regulations 1999 are expressly dealt with by section 91 of the Arbitration Act 1996, which provides that an arbitration agreement is automatically unfair for the purposes of the 1999 Regulations if it relates to a claim for a pecuniary remedy which does not exceed a certain figure (which is currently set by secondary legislation at £5,000[102]). According to the Office of Fair Trading, a compulsory arbitration clause forbidden by the 1996 Act 'is both legally ineffective and open to regulatory action in all cases'.[103]

Only a tiny fraction of cross-border consumer contracts for the purchase of goods or services involve sums greater than £5,000. Research in 2000, based on an analysis of 12,000 consumer complaints across 10 member states over a four-month period, found that the contract value of 96 per cent did not exceed €5,000; as regards the higher value claims (with a value of more than €5,000), the transactions tended to be domestic, rather than cross-border in nature.[104] A more recent Europe-wide survey of consumer behaviour published in 2006 found that, although 26 per cent of the sample had made at least one cross-border purchase during the previous 12-month period, only 2 per cent of this group (ie, about 0.5 per cent of the sample) had made cross-border purchases whose *total* value was more than €5,000.[105] From this data it is reasonable to conclude that, in Europe, the number of cross-border consumer contracts whose value exceeds £5,000 is very small indeed: research conducted in the United Kingdom found that only 4 per cent of the 25 per cent of consumers who are cross-border shoppers (ie, no more than 1 per cent of all shoppers) had spent more than £5,000 on purchases from abroad in the previous 12 months.[106] This is not very surprising: because, as regards cross-border shopping, there is a lack of consumer confidence, the likelihood of consumers buying domestically increases as the value of the contract rises. **7.44**

Even where the claim exceeds the financial limit under the 1996 Act, a contractual clause in a cross-border b2c contract providing for compulsory arbitration will generally be unenforceable against the consumer by virtue of the 1999 Regulations. According to the Office of Fair Trading, any clause whereby a company attempts to restrict the legal remedies of consumers by referring all disputes to compulsory arbitration is potentially unfair for the purposes of the Unfair Terms in Consumer Contracts **7.45**

[102] Unfair Arbitration Agreements (Specified Amount) Order 1999, SI 1999 No 2167.

[103] OFT *Unfair Contract Terms Guidance*, para 17.2: <http://www.oft.gov.uk/advice_and_resources/resource_base/legal/unfair-terms/guidance#named1> [2/12/07].

[104] See European Commission (2000).

[105] Eurobarometer (September 2006: 5).

[106] Department for Trade and Industry (November 2002).

Regulations 1999[107] and the Office of Fair Trading has exercised its statutory powers to require suppliers to delete or modify inappropriate arbitration clauses in their standard terms and conditions—even with regard to contracts for high-value goods (such as motor cars[108] and computer equipment[109]) and potentially expensive services (such as holidays[110] and home improvements[111]).

7.46 There is, however, an argument for saying that, as regards cases where the value of the claim exceeds £5,000, a compulsory arbitration clause which identifies the supplier's place of establishment as the seat of arbitration is not necessarily unenforceable. This argument starts from the wording of paragraph (1)(q) of schedule 2 to the 1999 Regulations which refers to a clause which excludes or hinders the consumer's right to take legal action 'particularly by requiring the consumer to take disputes to arbitration not covered by legal provisions'. There are various problems with this phrase and its precise meaning is far from clear.[112] One possibility is that an arbitration clause is unfair for the purposes of the 1999 Regulations if the agreement does not provide a satisfactory legal framework.[113] Another interpretation is that the reference to 'legal provisions' concerns substantive rather than procedural matters. According to this view, in order not to fall foul of the Regulations, a dispute-resolution scheme which prevents a consumer from pursuing his claim by means of litigation must provide legal safeguards similar to those applicable in the court system.[114] This would mean that an 'equity clause' (ie, an agreement making provision for arbitration *ex aequo et bono* or *amiable composition*) or an arbitration agreement purporting to exclude the right to appeal to the courts on a point of law would be unenforceable against a consumer.

7.47 The most convincing interpretation is that the effect of the 1999 Regulations is to render traditional arbitration clauses in consumer contracts unenforceable against consumers. The key part of paragraph (1)(q) is the

[107] A Vahrenwald (May 2000: 12). This view may not be shared in all member states: A Vahrenwald (May 2000: 12).

[108] See Office of Fair Trading (October 1998: 105); Office of Fair Trading (December 2003: 43).

[109] See Office of Fair Trading (August 2003: 44).

[110] See Office of Fair Trading (August 2003: 53).

[111] See Office of Fair Trading (April 1999: 52); Office of Fair Trading (August 2003: 68).

[112] Possible interpretations identified by WW Park (1998: 21 n 49) include the following: (i) arbitration agreements are per se invalid in all consumer transactions; (ii) equity clauses in consumer contracts are prohibited; and (iii) consumer contracts cannot exclude the right of appeal to the court on questions of law. Compare also the conflicting views of M Odams de Zylva (2001: 10) and A Vahrenwald (October 2000: 149).

[113] A Vahrenwald (October 2000: 149).

[114] C Kuner (2000).

phrase 'excluding or hindering the consumer's right to take legal action'. These words are apt to cover all clauses making provision for binding arbitration; the fact that the legislation goes on to identify a specific type of arbitration (namely, 'arbitration not covered by legal provisions'—whatever that may be) which is 'particularly' likely to be unfair, does not undermine the validity of the general proposition.

The issues raised in the preceding three paragraphs are primarily of theoretical interest. In the context of private litigation, potential doubts about the enforceability of an arbitration clause in a consumer contract could only arise where not only the amount of the claim exceeds £5,000 but also either a consumer starts legal proceedings against a supplier who seeks to obtain a stay of those proceedings under section 9 of the Arbitration Act 1996 (by relying on a compulsory arbitration clause in the contract) or where a supplier, having obtained an arbitral award in its favour, seeks enforcement of the award against the consumer. Such cases are so rare as to be almost unheard of. So, the likelihood is that the precise significance of the words 'arbitration not covered by legal provisions' in paragraph (1)(q) of the 1999 Regulations will remain a matter of conjecture for some time to come. **7.48**

There is, however, another category of case which can raise the question of the enforceability of consumer arbitration clauses—namely, where a public or quasi-public body brings proceedings with a view to establishing that a particular clause in a supplier's standard terms and conditions falls foul of the Unfair Terms in Consumer Contracts Directive. Although such litigation has not taken place in England,[115] there are instances of such actions in other European countries (for example, with regard to arbitration clauses in timeshare contracts);[116] the case law from other EU countries confirms that a binding pre-dispute arbitration clause will normally be regarded as infringing the Directive (regardless of the amount of money at stake). **7.49**

It should be emphasized that arbitration clauses in b2c contracts will not fall foul of the 1999 Regulations if they are drafted in the appropriate way.[117] **7.50**

[115] This is largely because, when the Office of Fair Trading has exercised its statutory powers to police unfair terms (see ch 8), the businesses concerned have given appropriate assurances or undertakings—as a result of which it has not been necessary for the case to go to court.

[116] See the European Database on Case Law Concerning Unfair Contract Terms: <https://adns.cec.eu.int/CLAB/SilverStream/Pages/pgHomeCLAB.html> [8/11/07]. This database collects summaries of judicial decisions and decisions taken by consumer protection organizations (such as the Office of Fair Trading).

[117] See OFT *Unfair Contract Terms Guidance*, para 17.3: <http://www.oft.gov.uk/advice_and_resources/resource_base/legal/unfair-terms/guidance#named1> [2/12/07].

There are two ways of ensuring that an arbitration agreement is not regarded as 'unfair' from the legal point of view. First, a term which is individually negotiated cannot be 'unfair' for the purposes of the 1999 Regulations.[118] Accordingly, it is perfectly possible for parties to a consumer contract to agree to refer their dispute to mandatory arbitration after the dispute has arisen. In a situation where bilateral negotiations fail to produce a satisfactory solution to a consumer's complaint, the parties may agree to refer the dispute to arbitration (normally under a designated dispute-resolution scheme which is part of a code of practice to which the supplier subscribes[119]). In these circumstances, it is legally permissible for the arbitration agreement to be drafted in such a way that the possibility of the claim being litigated is excluded. Secondly, a contractual term is not incompatible with the Regulations if it makes provision for voluntary or non-binding arbitration; because, in this situation, the consumer is free (in theory) to litigate his claim against the supplier, the arbitration clause does not have the effect of 'excluding or hindering the consumer's right to take legal action'.

IV. ADR CLAUSES[120]

7.51 In the commercial context, a question arises as to whether a contractual ADR clause—by which the parties agree, at the time of contracting, that any dispute arising out of the contract shall be settled by means of a particular ADR mechanism—is legally enforceable in the same way as arbitration agreements or jurisdiction agreements. In *Cable & Wireless plc v IBM United Kingdom Ltd*[121] Colman J upheld an ADR clause in a commercial contract: one of the parties sought to bypass the ADR clause by starting litigation in England; on the other party's application, the court granted a stay of proceedings—thereby effectively forcing the claimant to pursue the claim through the agreed dispute-resolution process.

7.52 In the consumer context, however, the general practice throughout the developed world appears to be that pre-dispute contractual clauses which bind parties to ADR will be regarded as an 'unfair' contract term or

[118] Reg 5(1).

[119] See ch 11.

[120] Although the literature distinguishes 'ADR' (alternative dispute resolution) from 'ODR' (online dispute resolution), ODR is nothing other than ADR facilitated by the Internet and other web- and computer-based technologies. Accordingly, the expression ADR necessarily incorporates extra-judicial ODR.

[121] [2002] 2 All ER (Comm) 1041.

contrary to public policy.[122] It has already been seen that, in relation to a standard-form contract, the Unfair Terms in Consumer Contracts Regulations 1999[123] provide that a contractual term is unenforceable if it is not individually negotiated and, 'contrary to the requirement of good faith, it causes a significant imbalance in the parties' rights and obligations arising under the contract, to the detriment of the consumer'.[124] Compulsory jurisdiction and arbitration clauses contained in contracts of adhesion almost invariably fall foul of the 1999 Regulations;[125] such clauses are not individually negotiated and they have the effect of 'excluding or hindering the consumer's right to take legal action'.[126] However, in the consumer context, ADR agreements, to the extent that they are found in practice, are normally made by the parties after the dispute has arisen and after attempts by the parties to deal with the dispute without the intervention of a third party have failed. Accordingly, for the purposes of the 1999 Regulations, such agreements are 'individually negotiated'. Furthermore, in the consumer context, some ADR agreements provide that the consumer is not bound by the outcome of the ADR process and retains the right to pursue his claim through the courts. ADR agreements of this type do not exclude or hinder the consumer's right to take legal action and cannot be unfair for the purposes of the 1999 Regulations.[127]

Conversely, a pre-dispute compulsory ADR clause in a consumer contract **7.53** will normally be rendered unenforceable against the consumer by the Unfair Terms in Consumer Contracts Regulations 1999, in the same way as pre-dispute mandatory jurisdiction and arbitration agreements.[128] If a consumer starts legal proceedings against a supplier in England, the supplier is not entitled to a stay of the proceedings on the basis of a seemingly mandatory ADR clause in the contract. By virtue of regulation 9 of the 1999 Regulations, it makes no difference whether the law governing the contract is English law or the law of another country which does not provide consumers with an equivalent level of protection against unfair contract terms.

However, the 1999 Regulations provide only that '[a]n unfair term in a **7.54** contract concluded with a consumer by a seller or supplier shall not be

[122] Organisation for Economic Co-operation and Development (July 2002: 8).

[123] Implementing the Unfair Contract Terms Directive.

[124] Unfair Terms in Consumer Contracts Regulations 1999, reg 5(1).

[125] Joined Cases C-240/98 to C-244/98 *Océano Grupo Editorial and Salvat Editores* [2000] ECR I-4941.

[126] Unfair Terms in Consumer Contracts Regulations 1999, sched 2, para 1(q).

[127] LA Mistelis (2001: 194).

[128] See European Commission, COM (2002) 196, p 25 (para 67).

binding on the consumer';[129] 'unfair' terms continue to bind the supplier if they are relied upon by the consumer. So, in a case where the contract contains an ADR clause, if the supplier sues the consumer in England for breach of contract (such as for non-payment), the consumer is entitled to rely on the clause and to apply for a stay of proceedings on the ground that the dispute should be referred to the agreed ADR mechanism. In such cases, there is every reason to think that, as long as the ADR clause is sufficiently certain, the court should follow the *Cable & Wireless* case[130] and refer the parties to the agreed ADR process.

7.55 During the legislative process which led to the Brussels I Regulation, the European Parliament proposed that, in certain circumstances, pre-dispute ADR clauses in online consumer contracts should be binding on both parties.[131] The amendment was premised on the terms of the contract specifying a 'recognised out-of-court dispute-settlement system with binding effects'. This amendment was not accepted for a number of reasons, not least the fact that the ADR schemes which were presupposed by the proposal were not yet in operation.[132] Although there can be little doubt that, when the amendment was proposed, the practical objections to it were overwhelming, this episode is a good illustration of the growing recognition that litigation is not the best solution to consumer disputes and that ADR has the potential to be a better alternative. However, one can only realistically think about using ADR for the resolution of disputes arising out of b2c contracts (whether concluded online or offline) if a proper institutional framework exists. As things currently stand, a Europe-wide system of ADR schemes with comprehensive coverage of disputes arising from cross-border consumer disputes is not in place.[133]

V. CONCLUSION

7.56 The weaknesses of the American approach to dispute-resolution clauses in consumer contracts are obvious. First, although there are general contractual doctrines (such as unconscionability, fraud, undue influence, and overweening bargaining power) which may prevent a dispute-resolution clause being enforced in the circumstances of a particular case, the general trend is to enforce such clauses against consumers as long as the consumer

[129] Unfair Terms in Consumer Contracts Regulations 1999, reg 8(1).

[130] [2002] 2 All ER (Comm) 1041.

[131] See European Parliament, Report (18 September 2000) A5-0235/2000.

[132] European Commission, COM (2002) 196, p 20.

[133] See chs 10 and 11.

had sufficient notice of the clause. This means that there are certain types of case (such as the *Carnival Cruise* case itself) in which consumers, as a result of being unable to bring proceedings in their local forum, have no realistic prospect of vindicating their rights through the courts. Secondly, because the US courts police dispute-resolution clauses on a case-by-case basis and the operation of general contractual doctrines is very fact-specific, whether or not a dispute-resolution clause in a consumer contract is enforceable is unpredictable. Even in the commercial context, satellite litigation in which parties litigate over the question where their dispute is going to be resolved is seen as being fundamentally wasteful. As regards disputes arising out of consumer contracts, uncertainty as to venue is even more undesirable; such uncertainty presents yet another disincentive for a consumer who is considering whether to attempt to vindicate his legal rights through litigation. As regards consumer contracts, an approach to the enforceability of dispute-resolution clauses which turns on the precise contextual circumstances of each individual case is fundamentally unsatisfactory. A more consistent approach is to decide whether—as a matter of policy—dispute-resolution clauses in certain *types* of contract are acceptable or not. In practice, dispute-resolution clauses in consumer contracts, if upheld, are likely to be detrimental to the interests of consumers. From this perspective, when compared to the American position, the European approach has much to recommend it and, unsurprisingly, is widely supported by European commentators.[134]

One of the consequences of the fact that the United State and Europe take **7.57** differing approaches to dispute-resolution clauses in consumer contracts is that an e-trader may well use a pre-dispute compulsory arbitration clause for online sales to consumers in the United States (as such clauses are, in general, enforceable), but include a different type of dispute-resolution clause (or no dispute-resolution clause at all) in contracts with European consumers.[135] This differential approach can be illustrated by the *Amazon* websites. The terms and conditions of the US website (*amazon.com*) provides that '[a]ny dispute relating in any way to your visit to Amazon.com or to products you purchase through Amazon.com shall be submitted to confidential arbitration in Seattle, Washington.... Arbitration under this agreement shall be conducted under the rules then prevailing of the American Arbitration Association....'[136] By contrast, the terms and conditions of the website which UK consumers are encouraged to use

[134] For a contrary view, see S Schiavetta (2004).

[135] See CR Drazohal and RJ Friel (2002: 377–83).

[136] See <http://www.amazon.com/gp/help/customer/display.html/103-0034287-1566216?ie=UTF8&nodeId=508088> [13/7/07].

(*amazon.co.uk*) include the following non-exclusive jurisdiction clause: 'You agree, as we do, to submit to the non-exclusive jurisdiction of the courts of the district of Luxembourg City.'[137]

7.58 A similar approach is adopted by *Dell*, the computer manufacturer. Clause 12 of the US 'terms and conditions of sale' provides as follows:

ANY CLAIM, DISPUTE, OR CONTROVERSY (WHETHER IN CONTRACT, TORT, OR OTHERWISE, WHETHER PREEXISTING, PRESENT OR FUTURE, AND INCLUDING STATUTORY, COMMON LAW, INTENTIONAL TORT AND EQUITABLE CLAIMS) BETWEEN CUSTOMER AND DELL, its agents, employees, principals, successors, assigns, affiliates (collectively for purposes of this paragraph, 'Dell') arising from or relating to this Agreement, its interpretation, or the breach, termination or validity thereof, the relationships which result from this Agreement (including, to the full extent permitted by applicable law, relationships with third parties who are not signatories to this Agreement), Dell's advertising, or any related purchase SHALL BE RESOLVED EXCLUSIVELY AND FINALLY BY BINDING ARBITRATION ADMINISTERED BY THE NATIONAL ARBITRATION FORUM (NAF) under its Code of Procedure then in effect (available via the Internet at http://www.arb-forum.com, or via telephone at 1-800-474-2371). In the event of any inconsistency or conflict between NAF Code of Procedure and this Agreement, this Agreement shall control. The arbitration will be limited solely to the dispute or controversy between customer and Dell. NEITHER CUSTOMER NOR DELL SHALL BE ENTITLED TO JOIN OR CONSOLIDATE CLAIMS BY OR AGAINST OTHER CUSTOMERS, OR ARBITRATE ANY CLAIM AS A REPRESENTATIVE OR CLASS ACTION OR IN A PRIVATE ATTORNEY GENERAL CAPACITY. The individual (non-class) nature of this dispute provision goes to the essence of the parties' arbitration agreement, and if found unenforceable, the entire arbitration provision shall not be enforced. This transaction involves interstate commerce, and this provision shall be governed by the Federal Arbitration Act 9 U.S.C. sec. 1-16 (FAA). Any award of the arbitrator(s) shall be final and binding on each of the parties, and may be entered as a judgment in any court of competent jurisdiction. Dell will be responsible for paying any arbitration fees to the extent such fees exceed the amount of the filing fee for initiating a claim in the small claims or similar court in the state in which you reside. Each party shall pay for its own costs and attorneys' fees, if any. However, if any customer prevails on any claim that affords the prevailing party attorneys' fees, or if there

[137] See <http://www.amazon.co.uk/gp/help/customer/display.html/026-8561277-7345236?ie=UTF8&nodeId=1040616> [13/7/07]. As regards consumers domiciled in EU member states, it would appear that this jurisdiction clause is either otiose or unenforceable. From the point of view of the consumer-claimant, the clause is otiose: given that the *amazon.co.uk* website is operated by companies based in Luxembourg (*Amazon EU SàrL* and *Amazon Services Europe SARL)*, the Luxembourg court has jurisdiction in any event by virtue of art 16(1) of the Brussels I Regulation. From the point of view of the supplier-claimant, a pre-dispute jurisdiction clause purporting to confer jurisdiction on the Luxembourg court is unenforceable (by virtue of art 17 of the Brussels I Regulation) against a consumer domiciled in a member state other than Luxembourg.

is a written agreement providing for fees, the Arbitrator may award reasonable fees to the prevailing party, under the standards for fee shifting provided by law. Information may be obtained and claims may be filed with the NAF at P.O. Box 50191, Minneapolis, MN 55405.[138]

The drafting of this clause is driven by a number of concerns—other than the obvious one of trying to keep disputes between the suppliers and its US customers out of the US courts. First, the use of capital letters is meant to demonstrate that the clause was reasonably communicated to the customer. Secondly, the clause seeks to prevent the joining of individual claims or the bringing of class actions.[139] Thirdly, it seeks to head off any argument that the dispute-resolution process imposes excessive financial burdens on the customer by limiting the consumer's costs to the equivalent of small claim proceedings. **7.59**

This clause is not used in contracts with European customers. In its website directed at UK consumers, *Dell*'s 'Terms & Conditions of Sales & Services—UK' includes a jurisdiction clause: **7.60**

This Agreement is to be interpreted in accordance with English Law but may be subject for Consumers to the jurisdiction of the English, Welsh, Northern Irish or Scottish courts at the claimant's choice. For Business Customers the English courts shall have exclusive jurisdiction.[140]

Although this clause recognizes that the legal position of jurisdiction clauses in consumer contracts differs from that in relation to commercial contracts, it is, nevertheless, poorly drafted. The clause makes reasonable sense (and is compatible with the Brussels I Regulation) in a case where the consumer is the claimant. However, what about cases in which the supplier is the claimant? In such cases the clause is unenforceable to the extent that it would require the consumer to defend in a forum (chosen by the claimant) other than the part of the United Kingdom in which the consumer is domiciled.

It has been observed that many dispute-resolution clauses in online contracts have been badly drafted with little appreciation of the legal context in which they are intended to operate: **7.61**

Frequently [online contracts] regulate in minute detail technical aspects but seem to attribute little attention to dispute settlement. Contract provisions in this respect

[138] See <http://www.dell.com/content/topics/global.aspx/policy/en/policy?c=us&l=en&s=gen&~section=012> [13/7/07].

[139] See also the terms and conditions of *Hallmark*, the US greeting card manufacturer (<http://www.hallmark.com>) and *Toshiba* (<http://www.toshibadirect.com>).

[140] See <http://www1.euro.dell.com/content/topics/topic.aspx/emea/topics/footer/terms?c=uk&l=en&s=gen&~lt=popup> [13/7/07].

are at best standard clauses which . . . not infrequently show little, if any, understanding of the law and practice of international commercial dispute settlement.[141]

7.62 As has been seen, the combined effect of the Brussels I Regulation, schedule 4 to the Civil Jurisdiction and Judgments Act 1982, and the Unfair Terms in Consumer Contracts Regulations 1999 is that, in cases involving consumers who are closely connected with any part of the United Kingdom (or another member state), pre-dispute compulsory dispute-resolution clauses in consumer contracts are rarely, if ever, enforceable against consumers. The position is essentially the same under the laws of the other EU member states.[142] Notwithstanding this non-enforceability of dispute-resolution clauses in consumer contracts, it is surprising that many e-traders attempt to use such clauses in their standard terms and conditions.

7.63 Among UK websites, there are some which indicate that the drafter had thought about the legal implications of choice-of-law and jurisdiction clauses and had some inkling of what some of the legal problems might be. For example, the terms and condition of *IKEA*'s UK website provide:

> This agreement is governed by English law unless you live in Scotland in which case it will be governed by Scots law. Each of us agrees to bring legal actions relating to these Terms of Sale and the Returns Policy only in a UK court.[143]

7.64 However, as regards UK websites through which e-traders sell goods or services throughout the United Kingdom (and beyond), if questions of jurisdiction are addressed at all, it is much more common to find a clause purporting to refer disputes to the exclusive jurisdiction of the English courts—even in the websites of well-known suppliers who might be expected to be in receipt of sound legal advice.[144] A good example is provided by the website of a company which sells television services. The following clauses are included within its terms and conditions:

> 15. Geographical Status
> This Agreement will be accepted by [the supplier] only if it is submitted by a Subscriber who is resident in the United Kingdom of Great Britain and Northern Ireland, the Republic of Ireland, the Channel Islands and the Isle of Man.

[141] ME Schneider and C Kuner (1997: 18).

[142] A Vahrenwald (May 2000a: 7).

[143] See <http://www.ikea.com>.

[144] Among the countless examples, see the websites of the following companies: *Apple* (<http://store.apple.com/Catalog/uk/Images/salespolicies_consumer.html>); *Early Learning Centre* (<http://www.elc.co.uk/page-5>); *Expedia* (<http://www.expedia.co.uk/daily/service/legal.asp>); *Penguin* (<http://www.penguin.co.uk/nf/Ecommerce/ShoppingCart#store_terms>); *Marks & Spencer* (<http://www.marksandspencer.com/gp/node/n/43712031/202-9177569-7227845?ie=UTF8&mnSBrand=core#law>); *Staples* (<http://www.staples.co.uk/eng/static/wrapper.asp?param=help_policie_sale.htm>).

16. Law
These Conditions and this Agreement are governed by English Law and the English courts shall have exclusive jurisdiction.[145]

In the event of a dispute between the supplier and a consumer domiciled in Scotland or Ireland, clause 16 would neither confer jurisdiction on the English courts nor be enforceable against the consumer in the event of proceedings being brought against the supplier by an Irish consumer in Ireland[146] or a Scottish consumer in Scotland.[147]

In cases where the supplier brings proceedings against a consumer (typically, for payment of the purchase price), the non-enforcement of a jurisdiction clause in the contract prevents the consumer having to defend the claim in an alien forum; this can be of real value to the consumer. This is the context in which the European approach presents major advantages over any alternative regime which allows suppliers to require consumers to defend legal proceedings in the supplier's home forum. Although it is not a cross-border case, *Océano Grupo Editorial and Salvat Editores*[148] is the perfect illustration of the appropriateness of not upholding onerous dispute-resolution clauses in consumer contracts. **7.65**

It is important not to exaggerate the practical significance of the legal principles considered in this chapter. As a general rule, consumer contracts are simple in nature. The supplier has to deliver goods or provide services; the consumer has to pay for them. Accordingly, the prospect of a supplier contemplating litigation against a consumer arises only in cases where the supplier has not secured payment from the consumer before performing its side of the bargain. The reason for the litigation in *Océano Grupo Editorial and Salvat Editores* was that the consumers, having agreed to buy goods by instalments, failed to make the necessary payments. As regards consumer e-commerce, in the vast majority of cases the e-trader is able to structure its website in such a way that the consumer is required to pay for the goods or services (by credit card or debit card) before the goods are dispatched or the services provided. Accordingly, the circumstances in which suppliers may have the need to enforce payment by litigation are quite limited. It is not unreasonable to conclude that some of the cries of anguish from the e-commerce lobby—railing against the unfairness of the fact that, in Europe, dispute-resolution clauses in consumer contracts are unenforceable against consumers—are somewhat disproportionate. **7.66**

145 See <http://www.televisionx.co.uk/tvx_redhot_terms.html> [13/7/07].
146 Brussels I Regulation, art 17.
147 Civil Jurisdiction and Judgments Act 1982, sched 4, r 9.
148 Joined Cases C-240/98 to C-244/98 [2000] ECR I-4941.

7.67 In theory, the non-enforcement of pre-dispute mandatory dispute-resolution clauses benefits consumers who seek to vindicate their contractual rights by means of court action—by permitting consumers to seek redress in their home forum. For reasons already considered, such litigation hardly exists.[149] Consequently, looked at from the perspective of the vindication of consumers' contractual rights in the cross-border context, the regulation of dispute-resolution clauses in consumer contracts is largely symbolic, rather than being of major practical significance.

[149] See ch 2.

8

Litigation in the Public Interest

I. INJUNCTIONS

8.01 In view of the fact that, from the consumer's perspective, private litigation is an extremely unattractive solution to the vast majority of contractual disputes, it is hardly surprising that attention has turned to other mechanisms for dealing with the problems arising out of consumer contracts. One technique for trying to advance collective consumer interests (rather than the interests of individual consumers) is by giving public authorities and consumer organizations the right to litigate on behalf of consumers in general.[1] One of the ideas underlying this strategy is that if market standards are improved (by suppliers being discouraged or prevented from engaging in unfair practices), the scope for disputes between suppliers and consumers will be reduced.

8.02 Until relatively recently there was no European framework for enabling public authorities and consumer organizations to respond to the problems posed by cross-border commerce. This gap was exposed in the *Home Vertrieb* case.[2] A German firm had distributed advertisements in France; these advertisements were in breach of the French law on unfair advertising.

[1] In the early 1980s it was argued that 'statutory standing for consumer groups is the single most needed reform in consumer law': RHS Tur (1982: 167).

[2] See C Joustra (1992: 433–4).

The advertisements were also in breach of German law, but they were not distributed in Germany. The question arose how this illegal advertising could be brought to an end. Although the relevant French consumer organization could bring criminal proceedings in France, there is no way of enforcing a French criminal judgment in Germany. Furthermore, the French organization did not have the right to act before the German courts and the German consumer organizations could not litigate in France. Although both countries allowed consumer organizations to bring proceedings in the consumer interest, there was no mechanism which provided for such organizations to take cross-border action.

1. EC Directives and the Implementing Legislation

8.03 At the European level, the policy of enabling public authorities and consumer organizations to play a role in the enforcement of the rights which EC directives purport to confer on consumers has been advanced in two stages. The first step was taken in the Directive on unfair terms in consumer contracts.[3] One of the objectives of this Directive was to enable public authorities and consumer organizations to take legal proceedings with a view to outlawing the use of unfair terms by suppliers. Article 7 provides that member states 'shall ensure that . . . adequate and effective means exist to prevent the continued use of unfair terms in contracts concluded with consumers' and that such means shall include 'provisions whereby persons or organizations, having a legitimate interest under national law in protecting consumers, may take action . . . before the courts or before competent administrative bodies for a decision as to whether contractual terms drawn up for general use are unfair'. In the United Kingdom, the Unfair Terms in Consumer Contracts Regulations 1999[4] provide that the Office of Fair Trading (and, in certain circumstances,[5] a number of other public bodies and organizations[6]) 'may apply for an injunction (including an interim injunction) against any person appearing . . . to be using, or recommending use of, an unfair term drawn up for general use in contracts concluded with consumers'.[7] A similar provision was included in the Distance Selling Directive,[8] and the implementing legislation in the

[3] Dir 93/13/EEC [1993] OJ L95/29.

[4] SI 1999 No 2083.

[5] Reg 12(2).

[6] Including the Information Commissioner, the Office of Rail Regulation, every weights and measures authority in Great Britain, and the Financial Services Authority. See sched 1 to the 1999 Regulations.

[7] Reg 12(1).

[8] Dir 97/7/EC [1997] OJ L144/19. See art 11.

United Kingdom, the Consumer Protection (Distance Selling) Regulations 2000,[9] provides that the Office of Fair Trading (or any other enforcement authority[10]) 'may apply for an injunction . . . against any person who appears . . . to be responsible for a breach'.[11]

There are two ways in which the provisions of these Directives are limited. First, obviously, the Directives (and the implementing legislation) deal only with injunctions which seek to prevent breaches of those particular instruments—rather than commercial practices which are inconsistent with any of the consumer rights granted by other EC legislation. Secondly, these Directives do not address the cross-border dimension. In the United Kingdom's legislation implementing the Directive on unfair terms in consumer contracts, for example, the power to bring proceedings for an injunction (to prevent the continued use of unfair contractual terms) is conferred only on UK bodies and organizations; the 1999 Regulations do not provide for the bringing of English proceedings by public bodies or consumer organizations from other member states. **8.04**

Both of these deficiencies were tackled in 1998 by the adoption of the Directive on injunctions for the protection of consumers' interests.[12] The Directive was based on the European Commission's *Green Paper on Access to Justice*,[13] in which it was noted that '*actions for an injunction* are provided for in all the Member States, in respect of certain commercial practices which can prejudice the good functioning of the market'.[14] The problem, however, was that this regulatory mechanism was conceived by each member state from its own national perspective. As a result, national legislation failed to make provision for the cross-border nature of the problem.[15] One of the examples given by the European Commission referred to English consumers being victims of frauds connected with the purchase of alcoholic drinks in France. In this type of case, the Office of Fair Trading had no standing to bring proceedings against the supplier in the French courts (because it is not a 'registered association' for the purposes of the domestic French legislation); nor does the relevant French authority have an interest (in the legal sense) in bringing an action. **8.05**

[9] SI 2000 No 2334.

[10] Enforcement authorities include 'every weights and measures authority in Great Britain': reg 3(1).

[11] Reg 27.

[12] Dir 98/27/EC [1998] OJ L166/51.

[13] European Commission, COM (93) 576.

[14] European Commission, COM (93) 576, p 65.

[15] See H-W Micklitz (1993).

8.06 The Directive seeks to overcome these obstacles. The key element of the Directive is that it makes provision for 'qualified entities' (typically, consumer organizations and public bodies) to bring actions for an injunction against sellers who act in breach of a whole range of EC directives in the field of consumer law.[16] The framework of the Directive is based around two types of institution: first, the courts or administrative authorities which are designated by member states to rule on issues relating to the infringement of consumer rights;[17] secondly, 'qualified entities' which, under national law, are competent to litigate on behalf of consumers in a particular member state.[18] The Directive requires that a qualified entity must, in principle, be able to take action against suppliers who infringe EC consumer law in *any* of the member states. That is to say, the principle of mutual recognition applies: member state A cannot deny standing to a body which is a qualified entity under the law of member state B—even if it does not satisfy the criteria to be a qualified entity under the law of member state A.[19] Article 4(1) of the Directive provides that each member state 'shall take the measures necessary to ensure that, in the event of an infringement originating in that Member State, any qualified entity from another member state where the interests protected by that qualified entity are affected by the infringement, may seize the [relevant] court or administrative authority'. So, if French consumers are adversely affected by an infringement of EC consumer law by a German supplier, the French 'qualified authority' must, in principle, be able to take legal action in Germany (or, if appropriate, in any other member state).

8.07 The Directive was originally implemented in the United Kingdom by the Stop Now Orders (EC Directive) Regulations 2001,[20] which came into force in June 2001. Subsequently, the 2001 Regulations were replaced by provisions of Part 8 of the Enterprise Act 2002 which introduced a new regime which draws a distinction between 'domestic infringements' and 'Community infringements'.[21] A domestic infringement is an act or omission which has been specified by the Secretary of State and which harms the collective interests of consumers in the United Kingdom.[22] A Community infringement is an act or omission which harms the collective interests of

[16] Listed in the Annex to the Directive. See also Study Centre for Consumer Law (January 2007: 328–9).

[17] Art 2.

[18] Art 3.

[19] See P Rott (2001: 405).

[20] SI 2001 No 1422. For consideration of the implementation in the United Kingdom through the 2001 Regulations, see P Rott (2001).

[21] See, generally, G Howells and S Weatherill (2005: 591–600).

[22] Enterprise Act 2002, s 211.

consumers and which contravenes a listed Directive as given effect by the laws, regulations, or administrative provisions of another EEA State.[23] Under section 215 of the 2002 Act, the Office of Fair Trading is entitled to bring proceedings in England with a view to obtaining an enforcement order in respect of both domestic and Community infringements.[24] The English court has jurisdiction to make an enforcement order against a trader who carries on business or has a place of business in England.[25]

The cross-border dimension is addressed by sections 215 and 221 of the 2002 Act. Section 215(4) provides that a 'Community enforcer' (ie, a qualified entity for the purposes of the Injunctions Directive which is listed under article 4(3)[26]) 'may make an application for an enforcement order in respect of a Community infringement'. So, if an English trader, in breach of, say, the Timeshare Directive, engages in commercial activities which are considered to harm the collective interests of Irish consumers, the Irish Director of Consumer Affairs may apply to the English court for an enforcement order under the 2002 Act. It is also provided that an enforcer (such as the Office of Fair Trading) 'has power to take proceedings in EEA States other than the United Kingdom for the cessation or prohibition of a Community infringement'.[27] **8.08**

It seems clear that if the Injunctions Directive is going to achieve its objectives, a high degree of cooperation between consumer protection agencies across the European Union will be required. The provisions of the Enterprise Act 2002 seem to envisage such cooperation between national authorities in cross-border cases. Where an enforcer seeks to bring proceedings in another member state, the enforcer 'may co-operate with **8.09**

[23] Enterprise Act 2002, s 212. The relevant directives, which are listed in sched 13, include the Directives on package holidays (Dir 90/314/EEC [1990] OJ L158/59), unfair terms in consumer contracts (Dir 93/13/EEC [1993] OJ L95/29), timeshares (Dir 94/47/EC [1994] OJ L280/83), distance selling (Dir 97/7/EC [1997] OJ L144/19), and consumer guarantees (Dir 99/44/EC [1999] OJ L171/12).

[24] The same (or similar powers) are also conferred on other 'enforcers' (such as the Information Commissioner and the Gas and Electricity Markets Authority). See Enterprise Act 2002, s 213.

[25] Enterprise Act 2002, s 215(5).

[26] Enterprise Act 2002, s 213(5). An updated list should be published every six months (see Dir 98/27/EC, art 4(3)); the list in the Official Journal dating from February 2006 (see [2006] OJ C39/2) was not updated until March 2008: see *Commission communication concerning Article 4(3) of Directive 98/27/EC of the European Parliament and of the Council on injunctions for the protection of consumers' interests, concerning the entities qualified to bring an action under Article 2 of this Directive* [2008] OJ C63/5. Community enforcers include, for example, the Danish Consumer Ombudsman, the Irish Director of Consumer Affairs, and the Cypriot Consumer Association. The full list runs to more than 35 pages of the Official Journal.

[27] Enterprise Act 2002, s 221(2).

a Community enforcer' for the purpose of bringing proceedings for the cessation or prohibition of a Community infringement in another member state.[28]

8.10 Proceedings for an injunction should be seen as a last resort.[29] This approach seems to have been adopted by most member states—albeit by different routes. One approach is derived directly from article 5 of the Injunctions Directive which gives member states the option of imposing consultation requirements before proceedings for an injunction can be initiated. In the United Kingdom, proceedings for an enforcement order can be brought only when other attempts at achieving compliance have failed; under the provisions of the Enterprise Act 2002 which implement article 5, an enforcer may not make an application for an enforcement order unless he has engaged in appropriate consultation with the trader and the Office of Fair Trading (if it is not the enforcer).[30] The objective is for the trader to agree to desist from the harmful conduct without there being a need for court proceedings. In a situation where the enforcer has the power to apply for an enforcement order, the enforcer may accept an undertaking from the trader to bring any infringement to an end.[31] If, however, the supplier refuses to make appropriate undertakings, litigation is left as the only avenue for seeking compliance.[32] Most other member states, although they have not built meaningful consultation requirements into their national implementing legislation, have adopted a procedure (whether formally or informally) which first aims at achieving voluntary compliance.[33]

2. Jurisdictional Issues

8.11 Although the Injunctions Directive makes provision for qualified entities to take legal action against infringing suppliers—whether in their home country or in other member states—it does not refer specifically to jurisdictional questions. Accordingly, the Directive has to be read in conjunction with the Brussels I Regulation.

[28] Enterprise Act 2002, s 221(4).

[29] H Kötz (1981: 112): 'One must keep in mind . . . that [government agencies'] main tool of administering and enforcing the law is not litigation, but the refusal of licences and permits required by law, the imposition of fines, the initiation of criminal proceedings and, last but not least, the subtle art of persuasion.'

[30] Enterprise Act 2002, s 214.

[31] Enterprise Act 2002, s 219.

[32] See, eg, *Office of Fair Trading v Officers Club Ltd* [2005] EWHC 1080 (Ch) (concerning a Community infringement relating to misleading advertising).

[33] See Study Centre for Consumer Law (January 2007: 336–9).

8.12 The jurisdictional aspects of legal proceedings in the collective interests of consumers are illustrated by the decision of the Court of Justice in *Henkel*.[34] The proceedings were initiated in Austria by the claimant, an Austrian consumer organization, against a businessman domiciled in Germany. The basis of the claim was the Austrian legislation implementing the Directive on unfair terms in consumer contracts.[35] Under that legislation, the claimant has *locus standi* to apply for injunctions to prevent businesses from employing unfair terms in standard-form contracts which they use in their commercial dealings. The claimant alleged that the defendant had used general terms and conditions in his contracts with several consumers in Austria and that those terms and conditions infringed Austrian consumer protection law. The defendant denied that the Austrian courts had jurisdiction over the proceedings and various jurisdictional questions under the Brussels Convention were referred to the Court of Justice.

8.13 A preliminary issue was whether the proceedings fell within the material scope of article 1 of the Brussels Convention. In its submissions, the UK government argued that the proceedings did not concern 'civil and commercial matters'; the claimant was a public authority and the right to obtain an injunction of the type sought in the Austrian proceedings was a public power. The Court of Justice rejected this argument; the claimant was not an organ of the state, but a non-profit-making private organization, and the subject-matter of the proceedings was not an exercise of public powers; in the Court's view, the proceedings were seeking 'to make relationships governed by private law subject to review by the courts'.[36] Accordingly, even if the claimant had been a public authority (such as the Office of Fair Trading), rather than a consumer organization, the case would have fallen within the scope of article 1.

8.14 The main question was whether the proceedings were within the scope of one of the following provisions of the Brussels Convention: article 13[37] (on the basis that the proceedings concerned a consumer contract); article 5(1) (on the basis that the claim concerned matters relating to a contract); or article 5(3) (on the ground that the claim concerned matters relating to tort). In view of the Court of Justice's interpretation of article 13 of the Brussels Convention in *Shearson Lehman Hutton*[38] it was clear that the case was not covered by the provisions relating to consumer contracts: these

[34] Case C-167/00 [2002] ECR I-8111.

[35] Dir 93/13/EEC [1993] OJ L195/29.

[36] Case C-167/00 [2002] ECR I-8111, 8138 (para 30). See also the opinion of Advocate General Jacobs: Case C-167/00 [2002] ECR I-8111, 8118 (para 22).

[37] The equivalent of art 15 of the Brussels I Regulation.

[38] Case C-89/91 [1993] ECR I-139.

provisions apply only to the extent that the proceedings are between a private final consumer and a supplier; they cannot apply to proceedings brought by a consumer organization on behalf of consumers in general.[39]

8.15 As regards the question whether the proceedings were within the scope of article 5(1) or article 5(3), the Court noted that, although the defendant had entered into contracts with a number of consumers, there was no contractual relationship between the claimant and the defendant; the purpose of the proceedings was to prevent damage to consumers in the future by preventing the defendant from including unfair clauses in his standard terms and conditions. Accordingly, the proceedings concerned matters relating to tort, rather than matters relating to a contract.

8.16 The final question was whether article 5(3) was effective to confer jurisdiction on the Austrian courts. As article 5(3) of the Brussels Convention allocated jurisdiction to courts for 'the place where the harmful event occurred', the defendant argued that the Austrian courts could only claim jurisdiction if a wrong had already been committed and the harmful event had taken place in Austria; in view of the fact that the consumer organization's application for an injunction was to prevent harm occurring in the future, the defendant argued that article 5(3) did not allocate jurisdiction at all.

8.17 The Court of Justice rejected this argument and ruled that article 5(3) extended to purely preventative actions which are brought before any actual damage has occurred.[40] This interpretation was consistent with the view expressed in the Schlosser Report[41] and it anticipated the express terms of the Brussels I Regulation, article 5(3) of which refers to 'the place where the harmful event occurred *or may occur*'.[42] The change of wording in article 5(3) of the Brussels I Regulation was designed to remove an ambiguity in the interpretation of article 5(3) of the Convention[43] and not to extend its scope.[44]

3. Choice of Law

8.18 Choice-of-law issues will not normally be significant as the relevant law on which the claim for an injunction is based derives from European legislation which applies throughout the member states. However, harmonization

[39] Case C-167/00 [2002] ECR I-8111, 8138–9 (para 33).
[40] Case C-167/00 [2002] ECR I-8111, 8142–3 (para 48).
[41] [1979] OJ C59/111 (para 134).
[42] Emphasis added.
[43] European Commission, COM (99) 348, p 14.
[44] Case C-167/00 *Henkel* [2002] ECR I-8111, 8123–4 (para 49) (Jacobs AG).

is incomplete because most of the consumer protection legislation is in the form of directives rather than regulations. As the directives lay down a minimum level of harmonization, member states are generally free to impose a higher level of consumer protection than that required by the directives. So, where a German consumer organization takes action against a German supplier in respect of its activities in France, if German law is more stringent than French law, it might be significant whether the applicable law is French or German.

It is clear that the Directive on injunctions for the protection of consumer interests does not lay down any choice-of-law rules: its provisions are 'without prejudice to the rules of private international law, with respect to the applicable law'.[45] However, it is stated that, in the context of an application for an injunction within the terms of the Directive, the applicable law will normally be 'either the law of the Member State where the infringement originated or the law of the Member State where the infringement has its effects'.[46] **8.19**

For the last decade or so, English choice-of-law rules for tortious obligations have been found in Part III of the Private International Law (Miscellaneous Provisions) Act 1995. However, following a legislative process spanning several years, a set of European choice-of-law rules for non-contractual obligations was introduced by the so-called Rome II Regulation.[47] Whether the matter is governed by the 1995 Act or the Rome II Regulation (which applies to events which take place after its entry into force on 11 January 2009[48]) will rarely make any practical difference. **8.20**

A claim for an injunction under the Directive should be regarded as tortious for the purposes of both the Private International Law (Miscellaneous Provisions) Act 1995[49] and the Rome II Regulation.[50] Under the 1995 Act, the general choice-of-law rule for cases which do not involve either personal injury or property damage stipulates that the applicable law is the law of the country in which the events constituting the tort occur (in cases where all those elements occur in the same country)[51] or the country in which the most significant element or elements of the events constituting **8.21**

[45] Art 2(2).

[46] Art 2(2).

[47] Reg (EC) No 864/2007 on the law applicable to non-contractual obligations (Rome II) [2007] OJ L199/40. For the background to the Regulation, see European Commission, COM (2003) 427; COM (2006) 83; COM (2006) 566.

[48] Arts 31–2.

[49] S 9(6).

[50] Art 1(1).

[51] S 11(1).

the tort occur (in cases where the elements of the events constituting the tort occur in more than one country).[52] The general rule under the Rome II Regulation refers to the law of the country in which the damage occurs 'irrespective of the country in which the event giving rise to the damage occurred and irrespective of the country or countries in which the indirect consequences of that event occur'.[53] Accordingly, in a simple case such as *Henkel*, the applicable law is Austrian law—the law of the country in which the consumers whose interests are adversely affected by the defendant's wrongful conduct are resident.

8.22 The position may be different where, for example, a supplier targets groups of holiday-makers—such as where an English company markets timeshares to English tourists while they are on holiday in Spain. Where the supplier and the targeted consumers come from the same country, the law of that country will normally be the applicable law.[54] What is the position, however, if the supplier is a German company, rather than an English company? Under the Rome II Regulation, there is a good argument for saying that the law of Spain, as the country where the damage occurs, should apply.[55] The position under the 1995 Act is probably the same.

II. COOPERATION BETWEEN NATIONAL AUTHORITIES FOR THE ENFORCEMENT OF CONSUMER PROTECTION

1. Europe: The CPC Regulation

8.23 In the 1990s it was suggested that 'European integration is dominated by legal technicalities, by language barriers, and by misunderstandings which make joint efforts of consumer organizations difficult.'[56] Some attempts have been made to establish a framework which reduces these difficulties. The key legislation is the Regulation on consumer protection co-operation (the 'CPC Regulation').[57] The aim of the Regulation is to link up national enforcement authorities and enable them to take coordinated

[52] S 11(2)(c).
[53] Art 4(1).
[54] Private International Law (Miscellaneous Provisions) Act 1995, s 12; Rome II Regulation, art 4(2).
[55] Art 4(1).
[56] H-W Micklitz (1993: 418).
[57] Reg (EC) No 2006/2004 on cooperation between national authorities for the enforcement of consumer protection laws [2004] OJ L364/1. See G Betlem (2007: 685–700).

action against rogue traders established in one member state who target consumers resident in other member states.[58] The CPC Regulation has two specific objectives:

- to provide for cooperation between enforcement authorities in dealing with intra-Community infringements that disrupt the internal market;
- to contribute to improving the quality and consistency of enforcement of consumer protection laws and to the monitoring of the protection of consumer economic interests.[59]

The Regulation removes barriers to information exchange and cooperation, empowers enforcement authorities to seek and obtain action from counterparts in other member states, and obliges each member state to enforce EU law in its territory on behalf of EU consumers. Article 8(1) provides: **8.24**

> A requested authority shall, on request from an applicant authority, take all necessary enforcement measures to bring about the cessation or prohibition of the intra-Community infringement without delay.

If, for example, there is a rogue trader operating in the United Kingdom who is targeting Irish consumers, the Irish Office of the Director of Consumer Affairs should liaise with the UK Office of Fair Trading with a view to tackling the problem. The general principle under the Regulation is that 'competent authorities can act against traders within their jurisdiction regardless of the location of the consumers involved'.[60] **8.25**

In 2007 the European Commission suggested that the CPC Regulation would 'bring about a sea change in the way enforcement authorities in the Member States cooperate amongst themselves and with the Commission'.[61] The Commission also considered that '[t]he main challenge for the coming years will be to ensure that the considerable legal, institutional and administrative measures already taken are implemented effectively and lead to effective cooperation on the ground, to the benefit of consumers and honest businesses.'[62] **8.26**

It remains to be seen how beneficial the CPC Regulation will prove to be in practice. It is clear that, in the context of the current work, its significance (if any) is preventative (rather than remedial)—in the sense that the **8.27**

[58] See, generally, European Commission, COM (2003) 443.
[59] European Commission, COM (2003) 443, p 5.
[60] European Commission, COM (2003) 443, p 9.
[61] European Commission, COM (2007) 99, p 10.
[62] European Commission, COM (2007) 99, p 10.

Regulation does nothing to resolve specific disputes that have arisen (or may arise) between consumers and foreign suppliers. The most that can be said is that, if the Regulation proves to be effective in enabling and encouraging national consumer authorities to cooperate in tackling rogue traders, the number of consumers who find themselves in dispute with a supplier who is established in another member state may be reduced. Even if the Regulation proves to be a success, it does not do away with the need for effective dispute-resolution mechanisms designed to deal with those disputes that do arise between individual consumers and suppliers.

2. Other Initiatives

8.28 In situations not falling within the scope of the CPC Regulation, it is much more difficult for administrative action to be taken against suppliers who deal with consumers across borders. If, for example, a US e-trader sells goods in Europe, there is no obvious channel of communication whereby consumers who find themselves the victim of unfair marketing practices can complain to a relevant authority who can take action against the e-trader in question.

8.29 Some attempt has been made to fill this gap by various initiatives. For example, the *econsumer.gov* website,[63] which is allied to the International Consumer Protection Enforcement Network (ICPEN),[64] is a collaborative venture by the governmental agencies of more than 20 countries (including many of the EU member states). The website, which was established in 2001 and is maintained by the US Federal Trade Commission, enables consumers from anywhere in the world to complete an online form giving details of their complaint and the supplier involved. The idea is that, if patterns of fraudulent behaviour and other unfair commercial practices come to light, the relevant governmental agency (or agencies) can take appropriate action against the trader in question. As the website states: 'Because the Internet marketplace is a borderless one, sharing your complaint with governmental agencies in different countries will help to keep the Internet safe. It will also prevent others from experiencing the problem you did.'[65]

8.30 The extent to which this venture is successful is very difficult to assess; there is no information on the website to suggest that information provided

[63] <http://www.econsumer.gov>. The project also includes an ADR element to link consumers to ADR providers; it is unlikely, however, that this link is very significant in practice.

[64] See <http://www.icpen.org/>.

[65] <http://www.econsumer.gov/english/> [3/8/07].

by consumers has led to any specific governmental action against rogue traders. Furthermore, it is unclear how widely the *econsumer.gov* website is known about by consumers. The number of participating countries has increased (from 12 in 2001 to more than 20 by the end of 2007) and the number of complaints has been steadily rising (from fewer than 2,000 in the first six months of 2003,[66] to 5,000 in the first half of 2005[67] and, more recently, to around 6,000 in the first six months of 2007[68]). Although the scheme is meant to be international, usage of the website is primarily by US consumers. The majority of complaints (more than 80 per cent) are lodged by US consumers; in the first half of 2007, whereas there were more than 5,300 complaints by US consumers, no other country lodged more than 400 complaints (with only three countries, other than the United States, lodging more than 100). It seems likely that awareness of the *econsumer.gov* website is higher in the United States because it largely mirrors, on the international level, the US domestic system of reporting fraud and identity theft through the *Consumer Sentinel* website[69] (which also operates under the auspices of the Federal Trade Commission). It does not seem that other countries have made much of an effort to promote awareness of the *econsumer.gov* initiative.

These figures illustrate a strand which runs through much of the material **8.31** discussed in this book: lack of consumer awareness of options available to them. The cross-border consumer environment is extremely complex and highly fragmented. There are numerous agencies, both domestic and international—each with its own website and each taking initiatives which aim to advance consumer interests. There is, however, a lack of coordination and consumer awareness of new developments appears to be low. As a result, it is hardly surprising that consumers seem not to know where to turn and do not make as much use as they might of the services on offer.

III. CONCLUSION

In view of the access-to-justice problems faced by consumers, there is much **8.32** to be said in favour of giving public bodies and consumer organizations the power to police unfair commercial practices which are detrimental to

[66] <http://www.econsumer.gov/english/contentfiles/pdfs/PU15JanJun2003.pdf> [15/4/08].

[67] See<http://www.econsumer.gov/english/content/pdfs/pu15percent20Jan-Decpercent 202005.pdf > [17/7/06].

[68] <http://www.econsumer.gov/english/contentfiles/pdfs/econsumer_stats.pdf> [3/8/07].

[69] <http://www.consumer.gov/sentinel/>.

consumer interests. Simply leaving consumers to challenge unfair terms in private litigation, for example, is not an effective means of stopping the use of such terms.[70] As Lord Steyn noted in *Director General of Fair Trading v First National Bank plc*: 'the system of pre-emptive challenges is a more effective way of preventing the continued use of unfair terms and changing contracting practices than *ex casu* actions'.[71] In recent years, there have been various investigations by the Office of Fair Trading which have led to businesses being warned about different aspects of their business practices or their standard terms and conditions.[72] For example, in 2006, following concerns raised by the Office of Fair Trading, Dell Corporation Ltd was encouraged to make changes to the terms and conditions which apply to its online sales.[73] However, the Office of Fair Trading's most high-profile case to date ended in failure—as it was ultimately decided that the contracts in question were not covered by the arguably relevant legislation: in the *easyCar* case,[74] the Office of Fair Trading sought to prevent the defendant from refusing consumers the right to withdraw from online car-hire contracts during the seven day cooling-off period laid down by the Consumer Protection (Distance Selling) Regulations 2000.[75] However, the Court of Justice accepted the defendant's argument that self-drive car-hire contracts are outside the scope of the relevant part of the Regulations as they fall within the exclusion which refers to 'contracts for the provision of . . . transport . . . services'.[76]

8.33 Whether the current framework—particularly that established at the European level—is effective is open to question. It has been cogently argued that the Injunctions Directive displays various weaknesses,[77] not least the fact that it 'is not linked to any mechanism to grant redress to consumers and put them back in the same economic position as they were before the relevant consumer protection rules were infringed'.[78] In any event, it is perhaps too early to tell whether the Injunctions Directive and

[70] E Macdonald (2004: 72).

[71] [2001] 3 WLR 1297, 1312 at [33].

[72] See Office of Fair Trading (June 2007: 106 n 214).

[73] See <http://www.oft.gov.uk/news/press/2006/111-06> [8/11/07].

[74] C-336/03 *easyCar (UK) Ltd v Office of Fair Trading* [2005] ECR I-1947. See E Hall (2007).

[75] SI 2000 No 2334.

[76] Reg 6(2)(b), implementing art 3(2) of the Distance Selling Directive (Dir 97/7/EC [1997] OJ L144/19).

[77] Study Centre for Consumer Law (January 2007: 347–8).

[78] Study Centre for Consumer Law (January 2007: 348). In Swedish law there is a theoretical possibility of consumers joining a claim for damages to the application for an injunction; there seems to be no example of this actually being done in practice: Study Centre for Consumer Law (January 2007: 340).

CPC Regulation are bearing fruit. It is also very difficult to test scientifically whether a system of public enforcement reduces the incidence both of bad commercial practices and of consumer disputes.[79] As public authorities will normally attempt to deal with unfair practices without having to go to court, the absence of reported litigation tells us very little about the effectiveness of the system.[80] There are, however, signs that the system is able to tackle cases of inappropriate behaviour by suppliers who fail to cooperate with national enforcing authorities: for example, in the early 2000s the Office of Fair Trading took the initiative with a view to putting an end to fraudulent practices relating to timeshares and similar holiday contracts by traders in southern Europe (particularly Spain).[81] Similarly, in recent years there have been instances in which the Office of Fair Trading has obtained undertakings and assurances from companies based in other member states which have been engaging in unfair commercial practices (in particular, misleading advertising and bogus prize draws).[82] **8.34**

[79] For a review of the current state of play in the United Kingdom, see Office of Fair Trading (June 2007: ch 8).

[80] Some indication of the enthusiasm with which the Office of Fair Trading embraced its powers to bring a stop to commercial practices which infringe consumer protection legislation can be gleaned from various issues of its 'Fair trading magazine' (which, since July 2006, is no longer published): see <http://www.oft.gov.uk/advice_and_resources/publications/corporate/fair_trading/> [22/11/07].

[81] See <http://www.oft.gov.uk/shared_oft/fair_trading/ft33news.pdf> [22/11/07]. See also ECC-Net (December 2002: 25). The ECC-Net report of December 2002 details various fraudulent practices which have bedevilled the European timeshare industry since the 1990s. The Timeshare Directive (Dir 94/47/EC) was passed in response to fraudulent trading in the timeshare market. However, the result of the Directive was that aggressive traders simply developed a new product—the holiday club—to avoid the impact of the legislation; the net result has been that consumers are still open to abuse in this market: Euroconsumer (December 2005: 5). In 2006 the European Commission launched a review of the Timeshare Directive with a view to tackling some of these problems. See the consultation paper (European Commission (June 2006)) and the proposed directive (European Commission, COM (2007) 303). There is a reasonable prospect that the new directive will be enacted in 2008 or 2009.

[82] For example, in 2005, a Dutch marketing company (misleading mailings), see <http://www.oft.gov.uk/news/press/2005/95-05> [27/11/07]; in 2006, an Irish company (misleading premium rate prize promotions), see <http://www.oft.gov.uk/news/press/2006/125-06> [27/11/07]; and in 2007 a Belgian mail order company (misleading advertising in the form of prize draw mailings), see <http://www.oft.gov.uk/news/press/2007/137-07> [27/11/07].

9
Alternative Dispute Resolution: Introduction

I. PRELIMINARY ISSUES

9.01 One of the important strands in the development of consumer protection over the course of the last half century concerns access to justice. It has been widely recognized that an absence of quick, simple, and cheap mechanisms whereby consumers are able to vindicate their legal rights results in consumers being poorly served by the legal system. However, there is little agreement on what should be the answer to this problem. There is a tendency among lawyers to think that the answer lies in fine tuning legal rules and procedures with a view to trying to make the courts more accessible to consumers. This approach seems to be premised on the notion that private litigation should be the main avenue for the resolution of consumer disputes.[1] Many lawyers are inclined to be rather obsessive about the vindication of legal rights and very focused on what happens (or fails to happen) in the courtroom. Such lawyers see the disinclination of consumers to litigate their claims against suppliers as evidence of a defect in the civil justice system. However, in view of the value of many consumer contracts,[2] it is far from obvious that, in an ideal world, consumers would see the courts as their primary avenue for dispute resolution; a narrow focus on individual justice through litigation seems misdirected. Although it may be perfectly rational to attempt to make civil litigation a more effective means of redress for consumers (for example, through the development of suitable small claims procedures), as far as cross-border cases are concerned it may be questioned whether reforms in the areas of private international law and civil procedure are capable of producing changes on the ground (as opposed to merely in the statute book).

[1] See, eg, EA O'Hara (2005: 1941–2).

[2] Various studies have suggested that the average value of online consumer contracts is something in the region of £50. See para 1.35.

9.02 A different starting point is found among commentators who remain to be convinced that private litigation provides a meaningful solution to consumer problems. Their focus is on alternatives to private litigation and attempts to make alternative dispute resolution (ADR) a more effective means of resolving consumer disputes. The reasons why ADR is potentially important are easy enough to see: 'Out-of-court dispute settlement mechanisms are particularly valuable in the context of low-value transactions where one party is significantly more powerful than the other. In these cases, the prospect of expensive and time-consuming court action may intimidate those with limited resources and prevent the resolution of the dispute.'[3] It has been observed that any form of ADR will be worth considering where the cost of court proceedings is likely to equal or exceed the amount of money at stake.[4]

9.03 Because of the problems associated with consumer litigation—and the question marks over whether it is an effective way of enforcing consumers' contractual rights—there is a good case for saying that the most practical, consumer-friendly form of dispute resolution for cross-border cases is extra-judicial rather than judicial.[5] Accordingly, the encouragement of alternative mechanisms for dealing with the problems generated by consumer contracts has been a major theme in consumer policy in recent years. As the European Commission noted in 2001: 'It is clear . . . that the use of alternative extra-judicial methods for resolving disputes has a key role to play in improving access to justice for individual consumers.'[6] The same point is made in the European Commission's *Proposal for a directive . . . on certain aspects of mediation in civil and commercial matters*: 'The concept of access to justice should . . . include promoting access to adequate dispute resolution processes for individuals and business, and not just access to the judicial system'.[7] The question whether or not consumers litigate disputes with suppliers is, therefore, something of a red herring. What is important is that, as far as possible, consumer complaints are handled in a satisfactory way.

9.04 As noted by the Organisation for Economic Co-operation and Development, ADR 'is widely regarded as holding great promise for the low-cost and efficient resolution of consumer disputes, especially cross-border disputes'.[8] Accordingly, one of the ways of attempting to tackle consumers'

[3] P Naarajärvi and JV Koivisto (2002: 91).

[4] LA Mistelis (2001: 183). See also HH Perritt Jr (2000: 675); Y Farah (2005: 124).

[5] ECC (Dublin) (June 2004: 12).

[6] COM (2001) 161, p 2.

[7] COM (2004) 718, p 2.

[8] Organisation for Economic Co-operation and Development (2006: 6).

access-to-justice issues has been through the establishment of different kinds of ADR bodies.[9] The aim of ADR mechanisms is to attempt to bridge 'the gap, if any, between a consumer . . . deliberately deciding not to take any action and a consumer . . . wishing to take action but refraining from doing so because of the perceived disadvantages of an ordinary court procedure'.[10]

In terms of analysis of these developments, one of the problems is that there is a wide range of different types of dispute-resolution mechanism: **9.05**

> ADR procedures may include . . . arbitration, early neutral evaluation, expert determination, mediation and conciliation. Accordingly, the mechanisms for resolving disputes may vary from binding decisions to recommendations or agreements between the parties. Also the organisation and the management of ADR procedures may vary: they may be publicly or privately organised and take the form of an ombudsman scheme, consumer complaint board, private mediator, trade association etc . . . . It is often unhelpful and confusing to group them together under one heading.[11]

At one end of the spectrum of possible ADR mechanisms, there are relatively formal processes, albeit processes which take place outside the courtroom (such as arbitration, which involves a decision made by a third party); at the other end, there are very informal processes (such as third-party-assisted negotiation which only reaches a definitive conclusion to the dispute if the parties can reach agreement). At the more formal end of the spectrum, many of the legal and practical problems encountered mirror those which bedevil private litigation. At the more informal end (such as complaints assistance), law in general (and private international law in particular) often has little or nothing to say; if such informal processes do not lead to a satisfactory resolution of the dispute, an aggrieved consumer may, in practical terms, have little choice but to put it down to experience. **9.06**

Before the discussion takes a closer look at ADR in relation to cross-border consumer contracts, it is important, in the context of this introduction, to say something about ADR in general. In the literature there is a lack of consensus on what constitutes ADR.[12] Indeed, there is disagreement over what exactly ADR is alternative to. Although the most widespread view is that ADR is alternative to court-based procedures,[13] others—who **9.07**

[9] K Viitanen (2000: 315).
[10] Study Centre for Consumer Law (January 2007: 6).
[11] European Commission, COM (2001) 161, pp 3–4.
[12] See A Redfern and M Hunter (2005: 42–3).
[13] See, eg, C Rule (2002: 13).

take a broader view—regard ADR as referring to dispute-resolution processes which are different from 'normal' private litigation; this extended definition encompasses phenomena such as small claims procedures and class actions.[14] Traditionally, a fundamental distinction between court-based processes and ADR was the fact that the court's jurisdiction was derived directly from the law, whereas ADR processes were possible only with the consent of both parties. Although this distinction still holds good in most contexts, it has broken down in others; there are, for instance, ombudsman schemes in which suppliers are bound to participate—although the commencement of the procedure depends on the consent of the consumer.[15]

9.08 Some of the definitional problems surrounding ADR stem from the fact that, in terms of classification, dispute-resolution mechanisms can be divided by reference to two different types of distinction. On the one hand, there is a functional distinction: whereas some dispute-resolution mechanisms seek to help the parties to a dispute reach a solution (such as third-party-assisted negotiation or mediation), others involve 'umpiring'—that is, the intervention of a third party who makes a determination of the parties' rights.[16] On the other hand, distinctions can be drawn along institutional lines: some methods of dispute resolution are court-based; others are extra-judicial. There is a large degree of overlap between the classification of ADR on the basis of these two criteria: court-based procedures traditionally involve umpiring, whereas many extra-judicial processes do not. However, the overlap is not complete. In particular, although arbitration is an extra-judicial process, a central feature of arbitration is that the arbitrator plays a judicial role and makes a decision (an award) as to the parties' legal rights and obligations—in the same way that a judge reaches a judgment.

9.09 Because of the relative formality of arbitration and the fact that many ADR mechanisms provide an alternative to 'umpiring', some commentators do not treat arbitration as a type of ADR at all.[17] Such an approach leads to the conclusion that the term ADR should be reserved for methods of attempting to resolve disputes by informal procedures, without resort to the courts or to arbitration.[18] However, from an institutional point of view,

[14] See M Cappelletti (1993).

[15] For example, the UK Financial Ombudsman Service (<http://www.financial-ombudsman.org.uk>) has compulsory jurisdiction over firms that are regulated by the Financial Services Authority.

[16] See, generally, S Roberts and M Palmer (2005: ch 4).

[17] See, eg, LA Mistelis (2001: 169).

[18] A Redfern and M Hunter (2005: 43).

ADR is alternative to litigation; it encompasses both private arbitration and other extra-judicial mechanisms for the resolution of private disputes. Notwithstanding the parallels between the role of the judge in civil proceedings and the role of the arbitrator in private arbitration, for the purposes of the current work, 'alternative dispute resolution' is used to mean methods of dispute resolution other than court-based procedures. In the consumer context, at least, there is a feature that is common to both arbitration and more informal facilitative processes: the fact that all of these extra-judicial dispute-resolution mechanisms can be seen as having the potential to overcome the obstacles which effectively deter or prevent consumers from seeking to vindicate their legal rights through the civil courts. What is important in the consumer context is that ADR mechanisms take place outside the courtroom.

The next question is whether, in definitional terms, all extra-judicial processes should be regarded as falling within the scope of ADR. According to one typology, dispute resolution processes can be divided into three broad types: (i) bilateral negotiation; (ii) facilitated negotiations (such as mediation or conciliation); and (iii) umpiring processes (such as arbitration and litigation).[19] Given that the first category—bilateral negotiation—does not involve anyone other than the parties to the dispute and is fundamentally unregulated, it is tempting to treat processes such as a supplier's internal complaints-handling procedure as not falling under the ADR umbrella at all. However, consumers who have a complaint about goods or services they have bought are invariably advised to approach the supplier directly[20] (and may effectively be required to do so before seeking to invoke an ADR process which involves the intervention of a third party[21]); moreover, the internal procedures of businesses play an important role in dealing with consumer complaints by preventing their escalating into **9.10**

[19] S Roberts and M Palmer (2005: 87). See also Consumers International (December 2000: 9).

[20] See, for example, the advice of *Euroconsumer*, which, until it closed in March 2007, operated as the UK European Consumer Centre: 'Whatever solution you want for your consumer problem, the best approach is for you first to try to negotiate with the trader' <www.euroconsumer.org.uk/index/where_to_start.htm> [14/5/06]. The website of the relaunched ECC (UK) contains similar advice: 'First contact the retailer or service provider (the trader) to seek a solution' <http://www.ukecc.net/sub.asp?id=156> [10/8/07]. See also Organisation for Economic Co-operation and Development (June 2002: 3): 'When you have a problem with a purchase you have made online, try to resolve the problem with the company directly, as a first step.'

[21] See, for example, the FSA Handbook (which sets out the procedure for complaints handled by the Financial Ombudsman Service); it provides that a complaint can be handled by the FOS only if, inter alia, the firm has 'failed to resolve the complaint to the satisfaction of the complainant within eight weeks of receiving it': DISP 2.2.1(5).

full-blown disputes. Accordingly, it makes sense, in the context of the present work, to use 'ADR' to encompass all extra-judicial dispute-resolution processes, whether or not they entail the participation of a third party (or third parties).

9.11 Although, conceptually, there is a clear distinction between cases where a decision is taken by a third party and cases which lead to an agreed solution, in practice, a dispute-resolution process may combine different elements. It is, for example, possible to establish a hybrid procedure whereby a third party, first, attempts to mediate a solution, but if the parties fail to reach an agreement, then, makes a decision ('med-arb'). Similarly, in the context of 'neutral evaluation', a neutral third party suggests a solution to the parties' dispute (which is based on the strengths and weaknesses of the parties' respective positions). To this extent, the third party plays a role not unlike that of a judge or arbitrator. However, the solution is not binding on the parties; the function of the third party's decision is to guide the parties to a negotiated solution.

9.12 At this juncture, certain terminological questions need to be addressed. First, a distinction should be drawn between ADR processes which are 'voluntary' and those which are 'compulsory' or 'mandatory'. From the consumer's perspective, an ADR process is voluntary if the consumer is free to pursue either that ADR process or litigation instead. (This freedom may, of course, be more theoretical than practical and akin to the consumer's freedom to dine at the Ritz.) By contrast, the process is mandatory (or compulsory) if the consumer cannot choose to litigate his claim instead of pursuing the contractually designated ADR process. Secondly, there is a distinction between 'binding' and 'non-binding' processes. An ADR process is 'non-binding' if the decision of the third party involved in assisting the resolution of the dispute is not legally enforceable. So, in the consumer context, an ombudsman scheme may be, as far as the consumer is concerned, both voluntary and non-binding; in the United States, consumer arbitration is normally compulsory and binding; in the United Kingdom and other European countries, however, consumer arbitration is normally voluntary (because an arbitration clause in a consumer contract is usually unenforceable against the consumer[22]). In the consumer context, the extent to which 'umpiring' processes lead to legally binding outcomes is highly variable: (i) the decision may be no more than a recommendation (ie, not binding on either party);[23] (ii) the decision may be binding on the

[22] See ch 7.

[23] See, eg, the US Better Business Bureau's 'informal dispute settlement' process: <http://www.dr.bbb.org/programs/ids.asp> [12/7/07].

supplier, but not the consumer (who can, theoretically, decide to ignore the decision and commence litigation against the supplier instead);[24] (iii) the decision may be binding on both parties.[25]

As regards consumer disputes, it is possible to attach too much significance to the question whether the outcome of the ADR process is legally binding or not. In consumer cases, ADR is likely to be used in situations where, having regard to the value of the claim, the costs of litigation would be disproportionate. Whether or not the outcome of the ADR process is legally binding, if the supplier does not comply with the ADR decision, the process has failed to achieve its objective—because the obstacles which discourage consumers from seeking to litigate their claims in the first place also stand in the way of consumers trying to enforce ADR outcomes through the courts. So, from the consumer's point of view, whether an ADR outcome is legally enforceable is largely irrelevant; much more important is the question whether, in cases where there is an ADR decision in the consumer's favour, the supplier will comply with that decision without the involvement of the courts. This is where codes of practice and trustmarks can play an important role.[26] Membership of a trustmark scheme (or the organization which oversees the code of practice)—and the risk of being ejected from the scheme for non-compliance with the code—may provide a strong economic incentive for a supplier to comply with an adverse ADR decision even though the chances of a consumer seeking to enforce such a decision through the courts if it is not complied with voluntarily are extremely slim. **9.13**

The received wisdom is that the availability of ADR can play a positive role in promoting confidence in cross-border economic activity by providing assurance that, if things go wrong, consumers can obtain redress;[27] there is a danger that both suppliers and consumers will be reluctant to become involved in cross-border commerce unless there are effective means of redress if problems arise.[28] The existence of effective ADR mechanisms can also help to forestall serious problems by encouraging **9.14**

[24] See, eg, the dispute-resolution scheme of the Financial Services Ombudsman: <http://www.financial-ombudsman.org.uk>.

[25] See, eg, art 6.1 of the *Rules of the Independent Arbitration Scheme for the Travel Industry* (2003 edn): <http://www.idrs.ltd.uk/ABTA/Rules.asp> [3/8/07].

[26] See ch 11.

[27] See, eg, C Rule (2002: 92–3, 97–100); E Katsh (2006: 6–7); E Katsh and L Wing (2006: 26).

[28] HH Perritt Jr (2000: 675). Recently, however, a small empirical study has cast some doubt on whether, in practice, the easy availability of ADR mechanisms has a significant role in building consumer trust: see L Edwards and A Theunissen (2007).

parties to settle their differences without the intervention of a third party.[29]

9.15 Although there are important legal questions surrounding consumer ADR in the cross-border context, to a large extent these issues are not specifically related to private international law. The development of consumer ADR results from recognition that, if the practical enforcement of consumers' contractual rights is the objective, the private litigation model is seriously defective; consumer litigation is a realistic option in only relatively unusual circumstances. Accordingly, for practical purposes, the 'hard law' of civil procedure and contract law is replaced by the 'soft law' of codes of practice, ADR, ombudsman schemes, and the like.

9.16 In recent years, quite a lot of attention has been devoted to ODR (online dispute resolution) and some commentators have made rather extravagant claims on its behalf. In essence, the relationship between ADR and ODR is no different from the relationship between commercial activity which occurs in the real world and e-commerce. For some commentators, ODR means online arbitration;[30] for others ODR encompasses any alternative dispute resolution mechanism which is operated online.[31] For the purposes of the current work, ODR is 'the use of the Internet and other web- and computer-based technologies for facilitating alternative dispute resolution'.[32] Accordingly, the term 'ADR' includes extra-judicial online dispute resolution; this work draws a distinction between ADR and ODR only to the extent that it is necessary to assist a discussion of particular aspects of ODR.[33]

II. COMPLAINTS HANDLING

9.17 There has been a lot of encouragement given to suppliers to adopt consumer-friendly policies in terms of providing clear information, having effective consumer complaints-handling mechanisms, taking a generous approach to returns (beyond the seven day cooling-off period required by the Distance Selling Directive[34]), and offering a high quality

[29] European Commission COM (2001) 161, p 3.

[30] See LJ Gibbons (2002).

[31] See J Hörnle (2002).

[32] American Bar Association (2002: 15). An even broader view, which is not adopted in this work, is that ODR includes not only online ADR but also 'cybercourts': G Kaufmann-Kohler and T Schultz (2004: 7).

[33] See ch 11.

[34] Dir 97/7/EC [1997] OJ L144/19.

after-sales service. Many of the codes of guidance allied to particular trade associations lay down quite stringent requirements on all of these matters.

In general terms, there are economic incentives for suppliers to respond effectively to consumer complaints; success in the consumer market depends upon building customer loyalty—so that consumers become repeat customers. It has become common practice for many suppliers to adopt a 'no questions asked' policy in cases where a consumer changes his mind and does not want to be bound by the contract. If a consumer buys a couple of CDs from an e-trader which does not respond to consumer disputes in the way that the consumer reasonably expects, the next time that the consumer decides to buy CDs, he is likely to purchase them from another supplier. Even where a particular consumer may not be likely to make a specific type of purchase on a regular basis, good PR is beneficial—so that satisfied customers will be more inclined to recommend a particular supplier to other potential customers. By not taking consumer complaints seriously, a supplier runs the risk of getting a bad reputation and losing potential business from new consumers entering the marketplace. Accordingly, it makes sense to regard the consumer market as shaped by the economic advantages to be gained from persuading consumers to become regular customers. There is a view that, in the world of e-commerce, most online merchants are eager to resolve consumer complaints in order to encourage repeat business.[35] **9.18**

Empirical research shows that direct negotiation between consumers and suppliers is by far the most prevalent method whereby consumers register complaints.[36] It is generally recognized that relatively few consumer complaints get beyond the supplier's internal complaints procedure; most disputes over consumer transactions are resolved within the supplier's internal customer care systems and never reach a stage requiring third-party involvement.[37] However, it should not be thought that the relative paucity of cases in which third parties become involved in consumer disputes signifies that consumer complaints are always resolved in a way in which consumers find satisfactory or that there is no need for effective dispute-resolution mechanisms for problems arising from b2c contracts. **9.19**

In the domestic context, it appears that, in around three-quarters of cases, consumers who have problems with faulty goods or services **9.20**

[35] MS Donahey (2003: 475).
[36] Study Centre for Consumer Law (January 2007: 9).
[37] International Chamber of Commerce (July 2002: 9).

contact the supplier.[38] According to the English research, agreement is reached between the parties in more than half these cases (56 per cent), but in a significant minority of cases (40 per cent) no resolution of the problem is ever achieved.[39] In the e-commerce context, as many as two-thirds of those who complain achieve a satisfactory resolution of the problem.[40] A similar picture emerges from recent European studies. A study into the effectiveness of the European Commission's Consumer Complaint Form revealed that, in cases where consumers used the form, consumers obtained complete or partial satisfaction in 53 per cent of cases[41] and, in a 2006 survey, 54 per cent of consumers who complained to the supplier about goods or services were satisfied with the way in which their complaint had been dealt with.[42]

9.21 It is important not to read too much into these data. Although the research measures rates of dispute resolution, it does so without attempting to assess the strength of consumer claims. It is obvious that it does not follow from the fact that a consumer has a complaint that he has a legally valid claim;[43] consumers' perceptions that they have a serious complaint does not necessarily correlate with their rights having been infringed. It must be the case that, in a proportion of cases, although the consumer has a sense of grievance, no legal wrong has been committed by the supplier. There seems to be no research which attempts to find out what that proportion may be.

9.22 Furthermore, it should not be thought that consumer complaints are less likely to be resolved than other sorts of legal problems. The overall

[38] H Genn (1999: 39). In a recent survey of Internet shoppers who had experienced a problem, 79 per cent complained to the supplier: Office of Fair Trading (June 2007: 66).

[39] H Genn (1999: 156). A 1988 OFT report estimated that, in cases where the consumer took some form of action to secure redress, around one-third of consumer complaints remained unresolved: R Thomas (1991: 160). A later OFT report on the e-commerce market showed that 20 per cent of dissatisfied consumers had given up pursuit of their complaint and another 17 per cent were still trying to achieve redress: Office of Fair Trading (June 2007: 67). Similarly, in cases where problems are encountered with transactions concluded via online auctions, the 'clear-up' rate is poor: a 2007 survey indicated that in 52 per cent of cases the problem was resolved to the consumer's satisfaction; in 10 per cent of cases, the consumer was still trying to resolve the problem; and in 38 per cent of cases the consumer had given up: Office of Fair Trading (June 2007: 142).

[40] Office of Fair Trading (June 2007: 66).

[41] European Commission (2000: 8).

[42] Eurobarometer (September 2006: 34). See also a 1975 US study which found that, in cases where a dissatisfied consumer made a complaint to the supplier, a conclusion satisfactory to the consumer was reached in 56.5 per cent of cases: A Best and AR Andreasen (1977: 726).

[43] HL Ross and NO Littlefield (1978: 203).

picture is that about half of all members of the public who experience 'non-trivial justiciable problems' are unable to achieve any resolution of those problems.[44] So, the problems in the consumer context are not significantly worse than (indeed, they are not as bad as) the difficulties experienced in other areas of dispute (such as employment, housing, neighbour, injury etc).

It seems clear that bilateral negotiation between the consumer and the supplier is the most important mechanism for the resolution of consumer complaints.[45] Accordingly, direct approach to the supplier should be 'the first port of call for discontented consumers'.[46] For this reason, it has been argued that one of the most successful ways of advancing consumer interests is by fostering conditions under which complaining is likely to be successful.[47] One way to increase the proportion of consumer complaints leading to a positive outcome would be to raise consumer awareness of the importance (and the art) of complaining about defective goods and services in an effective way. **9.23**

There is also a good case for requiring suppliers to provide information to the public about their complaints-handling procedures (and to keep a record of complaints received and their resolution).[48] The E-Commerce Directive,[49] however, does not require European e-traders to provide information on their websites about their complaints-handling processes and the number of websites which provide such information is low (less than 50 per cent).[50] **9.24**

Notwithstanding the importance of encouraging (or requiring) businesses to adopt effective complaints-handling procedures, it is important to recognize that there are limits to what can be achieved through such procedures. First, bilateral dealings between consumer and supplier are not at all meaningful in cases where the supplier is fraudulent or uncooperative; **9.25**

44 H Genn (1999: 176).

45 I Ramsay (1981: 125).

46 Office of Fair Trading (June 2007: 66).

47 HL Ross and NO Littlefield (1978). It has been suggested that '[o]ne way of giving incentives to consumers and (to a lesser extent) merchants to negotiate with each other, could be to impose direct negotiations as a first step should any of them intend to commence legal procedures through ordinary legal procedures or ADR procedures': Study Centre for Consumer Law (January 2007: 74). It is not clear how such a proposal could be made to work in practice.

48 A Best and AR Andreasen (1977: 731).

49 Dir 2000/13/EC [2000] L178/1.

50 Office of Fair Trading (June 2007: 85).

indeed, in such cases, only some form of legally enforceable process would be likely to produce a satisfactory solution for the consumer.

9.26 Secondly, it is difficult to see how, outside certain heavily regulated sectors (such as the financial services industry), it would be possible to introduce a legal requirement that businesses should have a complaints-handling process which complies with appropriate best-practice standards.[51] The imposition of such a requirement and any sort of policing of it would run the risk of creating an expensive bureaucratic nightmare. Furthermore, one has to be realistic about what small businesses can be expected to do: for example, although it is not unreasonable that small businesses should formulate a procedure for dealing with complaints, it is not practical to expect them to employ a specialized complaints handler.

[51] For a discussion of the characteristics of a high quality complaints-handling scheme, see Study Centre for Consumer Law (January 2007: ch 2).

10

The Promotion of Alternative Dispute Resolution in Europe

Over the course of the last decade, there has been quite a lot of work undertaken at the European level to promote the use of ADR (including ODR) for disputes arising from b2c contracts: **10.01**

> The growing interest by the European Commission in ODR is motivated by the need to enhance consumers' rights of access to justice through effective means of cross border dispute resolution at a low cost and by the need to ensure a fair balance between the different interests in the internal market . . .[1]

Notwithstanding the various initiatives of the European Commission, whether these efforts have borne much fruit is debatable. To the extent that ADR has been developed as an effective mechanism for resolving consumer disputes, developments have operated largely at the national level and have done relatively little to facilitate the resolution of cross-border consumer disputes. **10.02**

I. CONSUMER COMPLAINT FORM

In view of the weaknesses of private litigation as a method of resolving cross-border consumer disputes—and the fact that it is widely recognized **10.03**

[1] C Coteanu (2005: 89).

that, in practical terms, most consumer disputes are resolved by informal means (if they are resolved at all)—the European Commission has taken various steps to promote ADR in the consumer context. One such development towards the end of the 1990s was the drafting of a Consumer Complaint Form.[2] The purpose of this form is to assist the resolution of consumer disputes, in the first instance, without the intervention of a third party. It was intended that the form would be used primarily by consumers to help them, first, formulate the nature of the complaint in question (such as non-delivery of goods or delivery of goods which were not ordered) and, secondly, to particularize the redress being sought (such as cancellation of an invoice). The Commission also launched a pilot project in which the Consumer Complaint Form was employed by consumer organizations in the context of their case-work. The form was used in a total of 12,000 cases over the period May 1999 to August 2000.[3] The results of the pilot project were mixed. On the one hand, there was some evidence that the form was useful in producing a successful resolution of consumer complaints; on the other, some national consumer organizations did not think that the form was well drafted and various suggestions were made as to how it could have been made more effective.

10.04 For present purposes, the details of the form and how it might have been improved are not significant. The important points are these. First, although the form was designed for use in cross-border cases as well as domestic cases, only 0.5 per cent of the sample comprised cross-border disputes.[4] One possible explanation for the low proportion of cross-border cases is that the consumer organizations considered that the form was not well adapted for such situations. This explanation seems, however, unlikely. In view of the fact that the form is available in a wide variety of European languages, it is extremely easy for someone in, say, France to complete a German version of the form—even if the person filling in the form knows no German—simply by comparing the two language versions of the form and ticking the appropriate boxes. Indeed, one of the objectives behind the drafting of the form was to assist the resolution of

[2] See <http://ec.europa.eu/comm/consumers/redress/compl/cons_compl/acce_just03_en.pdf> [3/8/07]. General guidance on how to fill in the form is provided on the European Commission's website: <http://ec.europa.eu/comm/consumers/redress/compl/cons_compl/acce_just03_en.htm> [3/8/07]. There is also a 'Guide Concerning the Types of Consumer Problems and Requests': <http://ec.europa.eu/comm/consumers/redress/compl/cons_compl/acce_just03_en_guide.pdf> [3/8/07].

[3] See European Commission (2000).

[4] European Commission (2000: 4 n 6).

cross-border disputes in cases where the consumer and the supplier do not speak the same language:

> The multiple-choice design, and the fact that the form is available in the 11 languages of the European Union, should facilitate the problem of translation in cases of cross-border disputes where the parties speak different languages.[5]

Therefore, it seems far more likely that the low proportion of cross-border cases is a reflection of the fact that, even though it is easier than ever for consumers to engage in cross-border economic activity, the vast majority of consumer contracts are still essentially domestic (in the sense that either the consumer and the supplier are domiciled in the same country or the supplier, though domiciled in a country other than that of the consumer's domicile, has a branch or other place of business in the consumer's country) and that consumers are less likely to seek redress—even by informal means—in cross-border cases than in domestic cases. **10.05**

Secondly, although the evaluation of the pilot project suggested various ways in which the form could be improved, it seems that very little further work has been undertaken by the European Commission since the publication of the report.[6] The form—which is still available for downloading from the *Europa* website[7]—appears not to have been re-drafted and there is no evidence that steps have been taken to promote use of the form. Notwithstanding the development of a network of European Consumer Centres (ECC-Net),[8] promotion of the Consumer Complaint Form through these centres is uneven. For example, the ECC (Dublin)'s website[9] does not make any reference to the form and the ECC (Dublin) employs its own online complaint form.[10] By contrast, the ECC (Denmark), in its step-by-step guide to making a complaint, states that the consumer 'must complete the complaint form prepared by the EU Commission';[11] similarly, since the **10.06**

[5] <http://ec.europa.eu/comm/consumers/redress/compl/cons_compl/acce_just03_en.htm> [25/3/08].

[6] Notwithstanding the enlargement of the European Union, the relevant webpage of the Commission's website (see n 5) still refers to 'the 11 official languages of the European Union'.

[7] See <http://ec.europa.eu/consumers/redress/compl/cons_compl/acce_just03_en.pdf> [25/3/08].

[8] See <http://ec.europa.eu/comm/consumers/redress/ecc_network/index_en.htm> [3/8/07].

[9] See <http://www.eccdublin.ie>.

[10] See <http://www.eccdublin.ie/about_us/contact.html> [22/11/07]. See also ECC (Finland) (<http://www.webropol.com/P.aspx?id=174909&cid=31869321> [3/12/07]) and ECC (Latvia) (<http://www.ecclatvia.lv/?menu=21>). Many other ECC websites do not alert consumers to the existence of the Consumer Complaint Form.

[11] See <http://www.forbrugereuropa.dk/english/how/step/> [3/12/07]. Although a few other ECCs include reference to the form, they do not necessarily do so in a way which

end of 2007, the United Kingdom's ECC has suggested that, when first making contact with a supplier with a complaint, 'you may find the Consumer Complaint Form provided by the European Commission's services useful in laying out your complaint and providing the trader with all the relevant information'.[12] These examples illustrate one of the findings of the research relating to the pilot study: opinion as to the usefulness of the form among the ECCs is mixed.[13] One view is that the form is too complicated for simple complaints, but too limited to deal properly with complex matters and disputes.[14] To the extent that the Consumer Complaint Form is employed in relation to the attempted resolution of cross-border consumer disputes, its use is very patchy. Furthermore, knowledge of the form among consumers is extremely limited: in a fairly recent survey, only 5 per cent of European consumers had heard of the form.[15]

10.07 It seems, therefore, that the European Commission's attempt to promote the resolution of cross-border consumer complaints consensually—by the use of a Consumer Complaint Form—has had no more than limited success. The story here is a typical one in the field of consumer redress: an idea is formulated; an attempt is made to put the idea into practice; some problems are noted; the pursuit of the idea loses momentum. It is often unclear why a particular initiative runs into the sand: it may be that the basic idea is shown to be defective; alternatively the basic idea may be sound, but further work is needed to make it fully effective. In some cases the impression is that those who initiated the idea either have no funds to take the matter forward or simply lose interest and turn their attention elsewhere. It is very difficult to tell whether the apparent failure of the Consumer Complaint Form is explained by one or more of these reasons.

II. RECOMMENDATIONS

10.08 In view of the broad range of ADR mechanisms, harmonization of procedures and mechanisms either regionally or globally is an unrealistic objective. However, the establishment of minimum standards and the identification of shared principles and values is a desirable and more plausible goal. In the context of its work on ADR, the European Commission

makes the information very accessible; see, eg, ECC (Austria): <http://www.europakonsument.at/Europakonsument/ek_detail.asp?lang=EN&category=&id=10054> [3/12/07].

[12] See <http://www.ukecc.net/sub.asp?id=156> [22/11/07].

[13] European Commission (2000: 2).

[14] European Commission (2000: 3).

[15] Eurobarometer (October 2004: 61).

has made two Recommendations. The distinction between the sphere of application of each Recommendation is based on the distinction between 'umpiring', on the one hand, and assisting the parties to reach a settlement, on the other: which Recommendation is relevant turns on whether 'the third party formally adopts a position on the possible resolution of the dispute or merely helps the parties to reach an agreement'.[16] Notwithstanding the fact that each Recommendation is directed at a different type of ADR process, in terms of substance, the two Recommendations have a number of principles in common.

The first Recommendation, dating from 1998, is directed at ADR which involves decision-making by a third party, but does not apply to mediation procedures.[17] In this type of ADR, certain requirements should be met with regard to the third party's independence, the procedure etc. There are seven basic principles: independence, transparency, adversarial proceedings, effectiveness, legality, liberty, and representation. In the context of the current discussion, it is not necessary to set out the precise content of each of these principles; to a large extent, they are principles which almost everyone would endorse as providing a framework for a fair dispute-resolution process. **10.09**

There are, however, aspects of the principles which seem rather optimistic and potentially out of touch with reality. One of the stipulated criteria is the legality principle, which provides that, in the case of cross-border disputes, the decision taken by the third party may not result in the consumer being deprived of the protection afforded by the mandatory provisions applying under the law of the member state in which he is normally resident in the instances provided for under article 5 of the Rome Convention on the law applicable to contractual obligations.[18] There is a danger that this principle is in conflict with both the ethos of ADR and the practicalities of its operation in the consumer context. First, one of the perceived advantages of ADR is that it can take an approach based on fairness rather than the strict letter of the law.[19] Secondly, in the consumer context, ADR is intended to provide consumers with 'simple, swift, effective and inexpensive **10.10**

[16] European Commission, COM (2002) 196, p 27 (para 74).

[17] Commission Recommendation on the principles applicable to the bodies responsible for out-of-court settlement of consumer disputes (98/257/EC) [1998] OJ L115/31.

[18] For further consideration of choice of law in relation to consumer contracts, see ch 12.

[19] M Doyle, K Ritters, and S Brooker (January 2004: 75). For example, under the Spanish system of consumer arbitration the decision is made on the basis of equity unless the parties expressly agree that the arbitration should be conducted on the basis of the law: A Vahrenwald (October 2000: 199).

dispute resolution channels'.[20] The desired characteristics of effective ADR are hard to square with a requirement that decision-makers—who may not be lawyers, let alone private international lawyers—engage in the complicated choice-of-law process which is envisaged by the European Commission's principle of legality.

10.11 The second Recommendation of 2001 is concerned with facilitative processes in which the third party seeks to assist the parties in reaching an agreed settlement.[21] Because, in cases coming within the scope of the second Recommendation, the third party does not formally intervene in the process, the requirements are less stringent. There are only four basic principles which need to be adhered to: impartiality, transparency, effectiveness, and fairness.

10.12 The terms of the Recommendations are not binding—in the sense that an ADR service provider which fails to comply with the relevant guiding principles does not commit a breach of European law and there are no sanctions for non-compliance. As ADR service providers do not have to comply with the European Commission's principles, the Recommendations create a system of regulation at a very low level. This does not mean, however, that the Recommendations are wholly irrelevant.

10.13 So that consumers have easy access to reliable ADR services the member states were called upon to draw up an inventory of bodies responsible for the out-of-court resolution of consumer disputes which they consider to be in line with the Commission's Recommendations; an organization which has been certified as meeting the relevant criteria appears on a list of 'nominated' ADR service providers. The national lists have been communicated to the Commission which is responsible for publishing them.[22] This means that, in principle, both consumers and businesses know which ADR service providers are expected to operate according to the appropriate professional standards. In effect, the European Commission has sought to establish a kind of accreditation system—which some commentators have advocated.[23]

10.14 However, this system falls a long way short of establishing a comprehensive network of ADR service providers or of ensuring that European ADR service providers, in general, satisfy the criteria which, according to the European Commission, ought to be adhered to: in several member states

[20] European Commission, COM (2001) 161, p 2.

[21] Commission Recommendation on the principles for out-of-court bodies involved in the consensual resolution of consumer disputes (2001/310/EC) [2001] OJ L109/56.

[22] See <http://ec.europa.eu/consumers/redress/out_of_court/adrdb_en.htm> [25/3/08].

[23] See, eg, Y Farah (2005: 127).

very few ADR service providers have been nominated[24] and some of the nominated ADR service providers do not, in fact, comply with the relevant principles.[25] Furthermore, although the list of nominated ADR service providers is meant to be kept up-to-date, the list published on the European Commission's website[26] is inaccurate in a number of respects; for example, the website lists some ADR service providers which no longer exist.

III. ECC-NET

The European Commission has established networks of national bodies aimed at helping consumers access out-of-court procedures for the resolution of cross-border disputes, in particular in cases where the consumer is domiciled in one member state and the supplier is domiciled in another: **10.15**

> The European Consumer Centres Network (ECC-Net) aims to promote consumer confidence by advising citizens on their rights as consumers and providing easy access to redress in cross border cases.[27]

The ECC (Dublin) has described its role in the following terms: **10.16**

> The primary function of the [ECC] is the provision of advice and assistance to consumers with cross border consumer disputes. Irish consumers are helped to resolve disputes with European businesses and European consumers are helped to resolve disputes with Irish businesses. . . . The ECC aims to resolve disputes amicably, by intervening with the business where there has been a communication breakdown or the business needs to be reminded (and sometimes educated) of their obligations under consumer protection legislation. In order to achieve an amicable resolution a variety of dispute mechanisms are used. These may include writing to the business directly; contacting professional bodies or requesting the assistance of Inspectors from the Office of the Director of Consumer Affairs. Regrettably it is not always possible to come to an amicable resolution in a consumer dispute . . . . At this stage the [ECC] will consider the applicability of nominated ADR bodies; non-nominated ADR bodies and the Small Claims Court.[28]

[24] As regards several of the newer member states, there are no nominated ADR service providers.

[25] See the response of BEUG, the European Consumer Organisation, to the European Commission's *Green Paper on alternative dispute resolution in civil and commercial law* (COM (2002) 196), cited by M Doyle, K Ritters, and S Brooker (January 2004: 79–80).

[26] For the list of nominated ADR service providers in the United Kingdom, see: <http://ec.europa.eu/consumers/redress/out_of_court/ecc_united_kingdom_en.htm> [25/3/08]. Somewhat confusingly, there is a slightly different list at a different web address: <http://ec.europa.eu/consumers/redress/out_of_court/database/index_en.htm> [25/3/08].

[27] European Commission, COM (2007) 99, p 11.

[28] ECC (Dublin) (June 2004: 3).

10.17 At the beginning of 2008, there were 27 ECCs in total; among the EU member states only Bulgaria and Romania had not yet set up an ECC; in addition to the 25 ECCs in EU member states, there are ECCs in Iceland and Norway.[29] Between 2005 and April 2007 the United Kingdom's ECC, which operated through the *Euroconsumer* website,[30] fell under the umbrella of Citizens Advice (which also oversees Citizens Advice Bureaux).[31] However, as a result of restructuring, the office ceased to operate after the end of March 2007 and the *Euroconsumer* website was closed down in April of that year. A new ECC (UK), which is co-financed by the European Commission and the Department for Business, Enterprise and Regulatory Reform, was officially launched on 14 November 2007 (under the auspices of the Trading Standards Institute) and operates from a new web address.[32]

10.18 This network originally comprised two separate groups. First, there was a network of '*Euroguichets*', the creation of which was started in 1991 and whose role was to provide advice and information to consumers who had problems with goods or services bought from suppliers established in other member states. Secondly, the European Extra-Judicial Network (EEJ-Net), which was given the role of helping consumers resolve their disputes through alternative dispute resolution schemes, was launched in 2001. The European Commission described the EEJ-Net in the following terms:

> [It] is a consumer support and information structure which consists of national contact points (or 'Clearing Houses') located in each Member State and in Iceland and Norway. Each of the contact points relays information to the 400 bodies which the Member States consider as having met the requirements of the two Commission recommendations concerning the principles applicable to bodies responsible for the out-of-court resolution of consumer disputes.[33]

10.19 In 2005, EEJ-Net and the *Euroguichets* were effectively merged to create the European Consumer Centres Network (ECC-Net), which combines both roles: the centres advise consumers on cross-border problems and seek to provide access to redress through ADR. The aim of ECC-Net is 'to create consumer confidence in the internal market by providing consumers with information on their rights within the European Union and giving advice

[29] See <http://ec.europa.eu/consumers/redress/ecc_network/ecc_network_centers.pdf> [25/3/08]. Romania set up its EEC in June 2008.

[30] <http://www.euroconsumer.org.uk>.

[31] <http://www.citizensadvice.org.uk>. All Citizens Advice Bureaux in England, Wales, and Northern Ireland are members of Citizens Advice, the national charity which sets standards for advice and equal opportunities and supports bureaux with an information system, training, and other services.

[32] <http://www.ukecc.net>. The telephone advice service started in August 2007 and the new website went live at the same time.

[33] COM (2002) 196, p 17.

and assistance in the resolution of their cross-border complaints and disputes'.[34] Furthermore, ECC-Net seeks to counteract the excessive fragmentation of ADR mechanisms in certain member states. The objective of the network is to enable consumers to approach a single contact point in their member state to obtain information and, in cross-border cases, to facilitate uncomplicated and swift access to a relevant out-of-court dispute resolution scheme in the supplier's country. Within this system, the national ECC is designed as a one-stop shop for consumers resident in that member state.

The basic idea is that a consumer from member state A who has a complaint **10.20** in relation to a supplier established in member state B can approach the ECC in member state A (route 1). The ECC in member state A (ECC-A) assists the consumer in the preparation of his complaint before transmitting it to the ECC in member state B (ECC-B). When ECC-A has forwarded the complaint, ECC-B will contact the supplier. ECC-B can play an important role in trying to resolve the consumer's complaint without there being a need to refer the dispute to an ADR body. If, however, ECC-B's intervention does not result in the dispute being resolved by agreement between the parties, ECC-B is able to recommend to which ADR body, if any, the complaint should be referred. Alternatively, the consumer may approach directly ECC-B (route 2), which will provide appropriate advice to the consumer and, if necessary, refer the dispute to the relevant ADR body in member state B.

It was envisaged that, in the standard case, a typical consumer (who is not **10.21** particularly well informed about ADR in Europe) would adopt route 1. However, in practice, about a quarter of the cases handled by the ECC (UK) come directly from non-British consumers who have a complaint concerning a British supplier. In 2005 ECC (UK) fielded more than 1,800 consumer queries.[35] More than half of the queries were made by British consumers: 47 per cent directly from the consumers themselves; 8 per cent via CABx. More than a third of the enquiries came from other EU member states: 16 per cent were referrals from other members of ECC-Net, but 23 per cent came directly from consumers based in other EU member states. A small number of enquiries (5 per cent) were made by consumers and traders resident in non-member states. The European Commission's factsheet on ECC-Net gives some typical examples of how intervention by ECC-Net can provide a solution to cross-border disputes:

A French consumer ordered a digital camera from a German internet trader. He paid in advance and the trader told him that the item had been sent—but it

[34] ECC-Net (June 2006: 3).

[35] Euroconsumer (April 2006). The ECC (UK)'s website is also quite extensively used: for the year 2005, there were nearly 200,000 visits to the website.

never arrived. The consumer contacted the French ECC, which transferred the documents to the centre in Germany. Thanks to the centre's intervention, another camera was dispatched.

An Italian consumer bought a product from a Lithuanian trader over the Internet. He paid in advance, but did not receive his product. The customer got in touch with the ECC in Lithuania, which ensured that the Italian finally received his goods.[36]

10.22 The extent to which these examples are typical is unclear as ECC-Net does not systematically report on the outcomes of matters that are referred to the various ECCs. There is, however, some evidence that ECC-Net's 'clear-up' rate may be quite low. For example, ECC-Net's report on airline complaints indicates that significantly less than half of complaints referred to one of the European Consumer Centres relating to matters such as lost and damaged luggage, delays, and cancellations result in the complaint being satisfied in full.[37]

10.23 As part of their work, the ECCs undertake various activities other than answering consumers' questions about their rights under European legislation and assisting them in the resolution of cross-border disputes: they carry out information campaigns designed to educate consumers of their rights; they publish information materials and websites; they give presentations and talks; and they provide feedback information to the European Commission based on their practical experiences of case handling.[38]

10.24 In theory, the ECC-Net system is an attractive solution to many of the access-to-justice problems which European consumers face in cross-border cases. There are, however, a number of weaknesses with the system.

10.25 The first is the fact that the ECC has very limited leverage over a reluctant supplier:

Although the ECC offices do manage to resolve many e-commerce cases successfully, some disputes are simply not possible to resolve amicably. One problem is that many webtraders simply choose not to communicate with the relevant ECC. A webtrader that does not care if it has a good relationship with the ECC can safely

[36] 'Factsheet: The European Consumer Centres Network: ECC-Net' <http://ec.europa.eu/consumers/publications/factsheet-ECC-Net_en.pdf> [12/7/07]. See also ECC (Dublin) (July 2007).

[37] See ECC-Net (October 2006: 9). The overall picture is hard to discern accurately since, when the report was published, the outcome of more than a quarter of complaints was unknown.

[38] ECC-Net (June 2006: 3).

ignore any correspondence or complaints since there is no obligation to respond.[39]

Suppliers are much more likely to take ADR processes seriously (and make an effort to help find a reasonable solution to consumer complaints) if there is some kind of sanction if they do not. For example, where the ADR process is embedded within a code of practice which the supplier is required to observe (by virtue of its subscription to a trustmark scheme or its membership of a professional or trade association[40]) or where a public authority has the power to impose sanctions on a non-complying business, there is a greater likelihood that ADR will lead to a successful conclusion and that a decision in the consumer's favour will be complied with voluntarily. However, without these types of incentives, suppliers can effectively ignore not only attempts to resolve disputes by out-of-court mechanisms but also, even if they participate in the ADR process, any decision given against them. **10.26**

Secondly, the coverage provided by national ADR service providers is very patchy. Although some legal systems have ADR bodies which cover all (or nearly all) consumer disputes, others have a much less extensive system of ADR. The national ECC is not able to provide a solution in cases where, the ECC having failed to facilitate a settlement between the parties, there is no relevant ADR body to which the complaint can be referred. If, for example, an English consumer has a dispute with an Irish e-trader, there is limited help that the ECC (Dublin) can provide: there are relatively few ADR bodies in Ireland and the Small Claims Court is inherently problematic for consumers who are not resident in Ireland; as a result many consumers with complaints give up pursuing the case because there are no other options open to them.[41] **10.27**

Thirdly, ECC-Net's impact is less significant than it might be because public awareness of its role is quite limited. In a Europe-wide survey in 2006, 11 per cent of the sample (but only 6 per cent in the United Kingdom) said that they knew of ECC-Net's existence.[42] Furthermore, in an earlier survey, in response to the question whether, if they had a dispute about **10.28**

[39] ECC-Net (June 2006: 28).

[40] See, further, ch 11.

[41] ECC (Dublin) (June 2004: 3).

[42] Eurobarometer (September 2006: 72). Although the figure is still low, it seems that public awareness of the ECC's role is gradually increasing (at least in other parts of Europe, if not in the United Kingdom); an earlier survey in 2004 had shown that only 5 per cent of the sample had heard of EEJ-Net (which was absorbed into ECC-Net in 2005): Eurobarometer (October 2004: 66).

something purchased abroad, they would use the network to gain information and/or to make a complaint and follow it up, 25 per cent of European consumers answered in the negative and 17 per cent said that they did not know.[43] These figures are symptomatic of a general problem in the field of consumer redress—at both domestic and European levels—namely, widespread ignorance of consumer rights and means of redress. Much more could be done to promote awareness of the services that ECC-Net provides and to encourage consumers to understand that ECC-Net is helpful, trustworthy, and reliable.

10.29 Notwithstanding these weaknesses, there has been a gradual increase in the workload of ECC-Net in recent years. The number of complaints and disputes (arising from offline as well as online contracts) handled by the ECC (UK) in a four-year period in the early 2000s rose steadily year on year: 291 (2002); 492 (2003); 776 (2004); and 1,880 (2005).[44]

IV. FIN-NET

10.30 A network similar to ECC-Net exists in relation to disputes arising out of contracts for financial services. The Financial Services Complaints Network (FIN-Net) was developed as part of the drive to help consumers who buy financial services across borders to obtain redress if things go wrong; it deals with problems experienced by consumers in relation to services provided by banks, building societies, insurance companies, and financial advisers. The network comprises the competent national ADR bodies which meet the requirements of the Commission's 1998 Recommendation. In the United Kingdom, the relevant ADR mechanism is the ombudsman scheme run through the Financial Ombudsman Service (FOS).[45]

10.31 In the case of a financial dispute between a consumer and a financial service provider based in another member state (or in Iceland or Norway, whose ADR bodies are also part of FIN-Net), the consumer can contact the out-of-court complaints body in his own country of residence. This body will give him all the necessary information about FIN-Net and about the relevant foreign complaints scheme and its procedure. If the consumer decides to file a complaint, he can normally do so by registering the

[43] Eurobarometer (October 2004: 63).

[44] See <http://www.euroconsumer.org.uk/index/publications/other_reports/activity_apr06_cross_border_queries_2005.htm> [12/06/06]. More recent figures are not available.

[45] <http://www.financial-ombudsman.org.uk>. See R James and P Morris (2003); G Howells and S Weatherill (2005: 626–31).

complaint with the FIN-Net member in the consumer's home country. So, an English consumer who has a complaint concerning a German insurance company can file his complaint with the FOS. The FIN-Net member of the consumer's home country then transfers the complaint to the relevant body in the country in which the supplier is established. In some cases, however, the consumer may be asked to lodge the complaint directly with the foreign scheme.[46]

10.32 The FOS dispute-resolution process is free for consumers; the scheme, which is limited to complaints where the sum in dispute does not exceed £100,000, is funded by a levy on the relevant financial institutions. Although the decision of the ombudsman is binding on the financial institution, the decision is not binding on the consumer, who may choose to litigate his claim if he is not satisfied with the outcome of the FOS process. The figures provided on the European Commission's website indicate that the FOS process is reasonably quick and efficient: 95 per cent of claims are handled within a year; 50 per cent are resolved within only three months, and 25 per cent within six months.[47]

10.33 Nevertheless, somewhat surprisingly, although the FSA Handbook makes it clear that a complaint can be dealt with under the FOS irrespective of whether the complainant lives or is based in the United Kingdom, it seems that the FOS is used almost exclusively by consumers resident in the United Kingdom. The FOS's annual reports do not suggest that other members of FIN-Net referred any cases to the FOS.[48] A similar picture emerges from other countries. For example, the annual report for 2004/05 of the French *Médiateur de l'Association Française des Sociétés Financières* states that during the course of the year under review no requests for intervention were received through FIN-Net.[49]

[46] For an overview of FIN-Net, see 'Settling cross-border financial disputes out of court: Consumer guide': <http://ec.europa.eu/internal_market/finservices-retail/docs/finnet-guide/unitedkingdom-light_en.pdf > [3/8/07].

[47] See <http://ec.europa.eu/internal_market/finservices-retail/docs/finnet-addresses/ukingdom/ukingdom-secur_en.pdf> [8/3/07].

[48] The statistics set out in the annual reviews for 2002/03 to 2006/07 suggest that all complaints handled by the FOS were made by UK residents: see <http://www.financial-ombudsman.org.uk/publications/annual-reviews.htm> [25/8/06]. Although the FOS does receive some complaints from consumers who live outside the United Kingdom, the figure is such a small proportion (less than 1 per cent) of the total number of new cases (94,392 in 2006/07) that, when the percentages have been rounded up (and down), the complaints from non-UK residents fail to appear in the statistics: e-mail from the Technical Advice Desk of the FOS [3/8/07].

[49] <http://www.asf-france.fr/asfcommunication/indexoui/commediateur2005.pdf> [25/8/06].

10.34 What is the reason for the fact that FIN-Net handles so few cross-border cases? Although it may be a consequence of serious weaknesses within FIN-Net, this explanation is not convincing. On the face of it, the FOS dispute-resolution process seems relatively efficient and effective and it is designed to be user-friendly for consumers who are not from the United Kingdom. The FOS invites consumers who wish to complain to telephone and state the language in which they would like to discuss their complaint; in such a case, the FOS will 'get an interpreter on the line straight away'.[50] In addition, the FOS provides information and publications in a range of different languages.

10.35 More plausible explanations for the lack of complaints referred to the FOS concerning cross-border transactions are the relative non-integration of the European market for retail financial services and a lack of awareness on the part of consumers of the availability of FIN-Net. Within the European Union, the market for financial services is still, to a large extent, divided according to national boundaries. According to a recent Europe-wide survey of consumer behaviour, only 3 per cent of the sample had even thought about taking out insurance or obtaining a mortgage in another member state[51] and the cross-border dimension of contracts for financial services which consumers had entered into during the previous twelve months was negligible: only 1 per cent had bought from suppliers based in another EU member state and another 1 per cent from non-EU suppliers.[52] In addition, very few European consumers have heard of FIN-Net. Of the various initiatives of the European Commission in the field of consumer ADR, none of which have a made a significant impact on the consciousness of European consumers, FIN-Net seems to have a particularly low profile. A 2006 survey indicated that, across the EU member states, only 2 per cent of the sample (1 per cent in the United Kingdom) was aware of FIN-Net's existence.[53]

10.36 However, these explanations do not tell the whole story as a significant proportion of the enquiries fielded by the ECC (UK) concern problems with financial services.[54] Why do these problems not generate disputes under the FOS scheme? There are two possibilities: first, the existence of the FOS may provide a sufficient incentive for suppliers to make a genuine effort to settle disputes consensually (thereby avoiding having to participate

[50] <http://www.financial-ombudsman.org.uk/faq/index.htm> [25/8/06].

[51] Eurobarometer (September 2006: 107).

[52] Eurobarometer (September 2006: 108).

[53] Eurobarometer (September 2006: 72).

[54] For example, in 2005, 17 per cent of the cases handled by the ECC (UK) were related to questions concerning financial services: Euroconsumer (April 2006).

in the ADR procedure of the FOS); and secondly, consumers based in other member states may simply decide to drop the matter if direct negotiations with the supplier fail to produce a satisfactory solution.

V. TRUSTMARKS AND ODR

At various points, the European Commission has sought to promote self-regulation of the e-commerce market through the development of trustmarks. In 2000 the *Web Trader* scheme was launched in Europe; it emerged from a private international project aimed at regulating commercial sites and awarding quality labels. This project included consumer organizations from ten countries, eight of them EU member states. The project, which involved the development of codes of conduct and the creation of ADR systems, received support from the European Commission and was managed by it.[55] Although, in the United Kingdom, the scheme—which was operated by the *Which?* consumer organization—had a measure of success,[56] the project failed to get off the ground in other participating states. After the European Commission stopped providing financial assistance, the project folded; *Which?* could no longer afford to operate the scheme in the United Kingdom and the scheme closed in January 2003. The European Commission has also been involved in the financing of the *Euro-Label* trustmark scheme.[57] This scheme is small scale and largely concentrated in Germany and Austria.[58] **10.37**

In addition, the European Commission has dipped its toe in the waters of online dispute resolution (ODR). The Electronic Consumer Online Dispute Resolution (ECODIR) project,[59] which was (partly) funded by the European Commission, was set up by a consortium of academic and industry partners. The aim of the project was 'to provide consumers with the possibility to see their disputes solved through the network: as the dispute arises from the use of the network, the consumer will be able to find a solution directly from the network'.[60] The project involved setting up a website through which, during a trial period, consumers were able to file claims which ECODIR's dispute resolution service attempted to resolve (either by **10.38**

55 See European Commission, COM (2002) 196, p 18, n 92.
56 J Trzaskowski (2006: 63).
57 For further discussion, see ch 11.
58 Office of Fair Trading (June 2007: 154).
59 See <http://www.ecodir.org> and L Caplin (2004).
60 L Caplin (2004: para 3.2.2).

encouraging direct negotiation between the parties or by mediation).[61] The ECODIR pilot project ran from 2002 to 2004 and it would be fair to describe its achievements as modest. Since the end of the pilot period it has not been possible to file disputes with ECODIR and, although the website is still accessible, the system's future is, at best, uncertain.[62]

VI. MEDIATION

10.39 As a dispute-resolution method, mediation puts the accent on dialogue between parties to a dispute. Mediation appears to be most useful in cases where the parties have to solve a problem within a relationship that is continuing (such as family cases).[63] In view of the fact that consumer sales are typically one-off transactions, it may be thought that mediation is not a dispute-resolution process which is particularly well suited to consumer disputes. Nevertheless, if adapted to the particular characteristics of consumer disputes, mediation can play a useful role in this context—particularly as part of a dispute-resolution mechanism allied to a code of practice or a trustmark scheme.[64]

10.40 It has been observed that, as it does not follow a strict legal procedure, international mediation and/or conciliation is hardly subject to any form of regulation at all.[65] In 2004 the European Commission presented a proposal for a directive on certain aspects of mediation in civil and commercial matters.[66] Although the proposed measure is not specifically directed at consumer mediation, the scope of the proposal is very wide ('civil and commercial matters'[67]) and covers the mediation of consumer disputes. The 2004 proposal was the subject of significant criticism[68] and, during the course of the legislative process, it underwent substantial revision. The proposed directive completed its first reading in the European Parliament

[61] Between March 2002 and July 2004 a total of 87 cases were filed, of which 39 were presumed to be 'genuine', with the remaining 48 being presumed to be 'test cases': L Caplin (2004: para 3.4).

[62] Although it has been suggested that ECODIR became a commercial service in 2003 (G Kaufmann-Kohler and T Shultz (2004: 87)), this suggestion is not consistent with the information provided by the ECODIR website which states that its 'processes are entirely free of charge on a pilot basis': <http://www.ecodir.org/odrp/fees.htm> [6/2/08].

[63] European Consumer Law Group (November 2004: 2).

[64] See, further, ch 11.

[65] M Wilikens, A Vahrenwald, and P Morris (April 2000: 5).

[66] European Commission, COM (2004) 718.

[67] Art 1.

[68] European Consumer Law Group (November 2004).

in 2007 and the Directive was finally accepted by the Council and published in the *Official Journal* in May 2008.[69] It will, however, be some time before the directive is translated into the legal systems of the member states; Article 12 provides that member states are required to pass the domestic legislation needed to comply with the Directive by May 2011.

It may be doubted whether the Directive will have much of an impact on **10.41** the resolution of consumer disputes. The main points of the Directive are that a settlement agreement reached as a result of a mediation must be capable of being rendered enforceable—typically, through a court-based process—and that rules on the limitation of actions should not have the effect of preventing parties from going to court or to arbitration if the attempted mediation fails to reach a settlement. Neither of these issues is very significant in the consumer context. First, the whole point of ADR is to avoid litigation; if the only way in which a consumer can obtain redress is by having to commence court proceedings with a view to enforcing a settlement agreement, the ADR process has failed. From the perspective of a consumer-claimant, a rule which states that a settlement agreement is enforceable in the same way as a judgment is something of a Pyrrhic victory. Secondly, while a rule that suspends the running of the limitation period while parties to a dispute are trying to resolve it by mediation makes perfect sense, such a rule is hardly needed in the consumer cases which, even without the rule, will hardly ever give rise to limitation issues.

VII. CONCLUSION

What is to be concluded from these various initiatives taken at the **10.42** European level? One view is that 'the EU has made great progress on developing a proper dispute resolution system to protect consumers in the Community'.[70] This view is consistent with the self-assessment of the European Commission, which tends to be upbeat about its achievements in the field of consumer protection in general. For example, in 2001 the European Commission predicted that its 1998 Recommendation[71] and the creation of the network which has evolved into ECC-Net would 'go a long way to making ADR work in the Internal Market'.[72] Although it would

[69] [2008] OJ L136/3. See also European Commission, COM (2008) 131 .

[70] Z Tang (2007: 52).

[71] Commission Recommendation on the principles applicable to the bodies responsible for out-of-court settlement of consumer disputes (98/257/EC) [1998] OJ L115/31.

[72] European Commission, COM (2001) 161, p 4.

be unduly harsh to suggest that ECC-Net has not been a success, its penetration into the consciousness of consumers is very limited. Furthermore, the range of national ADR bodies which satisfy the requirements of the 1998 Recommendation is not very extensive. Accordingly, there are huge gaps in the provision of effective ADR services for the resolution of cross-border consumer complaints. So, a more realistic assessment would be that, rather than 'go[ing] a long way to making ADR work in the Internal Market', the work to date has made some progress but that 'much work needs to be done to turn the theory into reality'.[73] There are some signs that the European Commission is acknowledging how much more needs to be done. Having referred to some of the recent developments (including the establishment of ECC-Net) as 'a solid start', the Commission goes on to note that, in terms of the creation of a truly effective internal market, 'significant obstacles remain, notably in the area of consumer contracts and redress'.[74]

10.43 The ADR picture in the European Union is extremely fragmented and it would not be unfair to suggest that some initiatives appear to have been pursued rather half-heartedly. No doubt there is a financial dimension here; how much can be achieved partly depends on how much money is available for the implementation of desired policies. Nevertheless, for all the work that the European Commission has done in the field of consumer redress, public awareness of its efforts is very limited: a survey in 2006 of consumers across the (then) 25 member states revealed that 69 per cent of the sample indicated that they had heard of none of the services provided by the European Union to help consumers; in the United Kingdom the figure was 77 per cent.[75] These data highlight one of the areas in which much more needs to be done: even if an appropriate institutional framework is established, ADR schemes will not be able to achieve the desired aim of providing access to 'simple, swift, effective and inexpensive dispute resolution channels'[76] unless consumers are properly educated about what services are available and how they can be used.

[73] Consumers International (September 2001: 11).
[74] European Commission, COM (2007) 99, p 5.
[75] Eurobarometer (September 2006: 72).
[76] European Commission, COM (2001) 161, p 2.

11

Alternative Dispute Resolution and Online Dispute Resolution

I. GENERAL CHARACTERISTICS

In the field of ADR, different legal systems have adopted different institutional solutions—although it should be noted that, in many countries (even in Europe), ADR is not at all common or widespread.[1] Within Europe there are several different models.[2] For instance, the Nordic model (and the similar model to be found in the Baltic states) is mainly based on public complaints boards, established and financed by the state.[3] In Denmark, for example, there are consumer complaints boards for various sectors of the economy (such as the building, travel, insurance, and tourism industries). Notwithstanding the non-binding nature of the boards' decisions, compliance rates are generally quite high: for example, in Denmark, the decisions of the complaints boards are complied with in 80 to 85 per cent of cases.[4] **11.01**

[1] See ECC (Dublin) (April 2004).

[2] See K Viitanen (2000).

[3] See M Cappelletti and B Garth (1978: 96–9).

[4] ECC (Dublin) (April 2004: 41). The position in Sweden appears to be similar: M Cappelletti and B Garth (1978: 98).

Some of the problems of enforcement are mitigated by the fact that the consumer ombudsman may give assistance to consumers in bringing court cases and that a blacklist of businesses which refuse to honour decisions is published.[5]

11.02 The Dutch model is similar, but the complaints boards are run jointly by trade organizations and consumer organizations under the auspices of an umbrella body, the Foundation for Consumers Complaints Commissions. There are over 30 commissions which deal with consumer complaints in various economic sectors and the Foundation actively encourages sectors which do not come under one of the existing commissions to establish a commission to cover their area of activity.[6]

11.03 By contrast, the Iberian model is based on consumer arbitration.[7] The arbitration process leads to a decision more quickly than court procedures, is free of charge, and the arbitral award has the same legal status as a judgment. In Spain, consumer arbitration boards include representatives from consumer organizations and businesses. However, a supplier is bound to participate only if it has formally accepted the consumer arbitration system (as a result of which it is entitled to use the system's logo).[8]

11.04 This very brief picture is potentially misleading as very few legal systems display institutional homogeneity. For example, within the United Kingdom, ADR services are provided in different sectors through codes of practice sponsored by trade associations and by ombudsman schemes, one of the most prominent of which is the Financial Services Ombudsman. Notwithstanding the fact that there are some ombudsman schemes which have a statutory basis and whose costs are borne, at least in part, by the public purse, in the United Kingdom there is a tendency to regard ADR services as something which are provided primarily by the private sector (rather than by the state)—typically by industry-centred bodies as a measure of self-regulation.

11.05 Notwithstanding this very broad institutional and procedural diversity, in the context of disputes arising out of cross-border consumer contracts, there are several problems which are common to many of these different ADR models.

[5] European Consumer Law Group (March 2001: 19).

[6] Study Centre for Consumer Law (January 2007: 93–4).

[7] For details of the Portuguese and Spanish models, see A Vahrenwald (October 2000: 192–9).

[8] It seems that, although a relatively small proportion of businesses participate in the scheme, the number of participating businesses is gradually rising: see the statistics cited by A Vahrenwald (October 2000: 99).

11.06 First, some of the perceived problems with ADR are similar to those which can be found in relation to small claims litigation. As a general rule, the more experienced supplier has various advantages over the less experienced consumer. Suppliers may be better educated and articulate than consumers and may, therefore, be in a better position than consumers to present their point of view clearly; suppliers may have a better understanding of which aspects of the case are legally relevant and which are irrelevant. Accordingly, there are good arguments for seeking to find procedural solutions which try to establish as level a playing field as possible. Although ADR mechanisms cannot address socio-economic inequalities at a profound level, the significance of such inequalities can be reduced by a dispute-resolution process which is either free to the consumer or whose costs are very low, does not require the involvement of lawyers and, when compared to litigation, is relatively informal.

11.07 Secondly, most ADR schemes are primarily designed to deal with domestic disputes and these more informal methods of providing redress for consumers often do not take cross-border complaints into account. This basic point can be illustrated by a few examples. A recent survey of ADR provision in the United Kingdom reported that, of the 29 ADR schemes examined, only 14 said that they were available to non-UK consumers.[9] In many countries, consumer complaints boards are organized nationally[10] and may not be adapted to deal with cross-border disputes: for example, the Austrian Internet consumer ombudsman is competent to deal only with claims by consumers resident in Austria.[11] One commentator writing in the early 1990s, states:

> If, for instance, a Dutch consumer has a complaint against a German furniture retailer, he will not be able to bring his case before the 'Geschillencommissie Woninginrichting' ('Tribunal for consumer disputes about furniture'), because according to the tribunal's rules the firm has to have its place of business in the Netherlands.[12]

Furthermore, in relation to cross-border consumer contracts, it may not be clear whether the consumer complaint system at the place where the supplier is established or at the place where the consumer is habitually resident should deal with the complaint.[13] The absence of cooperation at

[9] M Doyle, K Ritters, and S Brooker (January 2004: 16).

[10] M Schellekens and L van der Wees (2002: 292).

[11] Study Centre for Consumer Law (January 2007: 158, n 475).

[12] C Joustra (1992: 433). See also L Gibson (1992: 410–11).

[13] M Wilikens, A Vahrenwald, and P Morris (April 2000: 6). See also A Vahrenwald (May 2000b: 7, 11).

the international level makes it very difficult for informal mechanisms of dispute resolution to deal adequately with disputes arising out of cross-border contracts.[14]

11.08 Thirdly, in many legal systems, the ADR picture is very fragmented. This generates various problems. For example, ADR bodies do not provide complete coverage of all types of consumer dispute.[15] Moreover, even in situations where the dispute does not fall within one of the gaps in ADR provision, it may be difficult for consumers to find the appropriate ADR body.[16] In the words of a recent comparative report: 'the wide variety of [ADR] schemes has not always contributed to the coherency and transparency of the dispute resolution mechanisms available'.[17]

11.09 A good example of the inadequate coverage of ADR bodies is provided by ECC-Net's recent report on complaints against airlines.[18] In 2005, around 1,500 air travellers contacted ECC-Net with complaints about airlines.[19] The majority of problems (around 70 per cent) related to lost and damaged luggage, delays, and cancellations. Although, as regards lost or damaged luggage, consumers have various rights under the Montreal Convention,[20] there are real problems with claims under the Convention as there are very strict limitation periods for such claims (seven days for damaged luggage; 21 days for delayed baggage) and it is very difficult to prove that various items have been lost in luggage which has gone missing and to prove their value. Consumers also have rights to compensation or assistance under Regulation (EC) No 261/2004[21] in certain cases where flights are delayed for long periods or cancelled. There is, however, widespread misunderstanding of consumers' rights under the Regulation—which is not very surprising as the rules are complicated and it is difficult to set them out succinctly in a leaflet.[22]

[14] In 2005, the Dutch Foundation for Consumer Complaints Commissions dealt with only 156 complaints (out of a total of roughly 13,000) by consumers resident in other member states: Study Centre for Consumer Law (January 2007: 158, n 475).

[15] See M Doyle, K Ritters, and S Brooker (January 2004: 57–9).

[16] Study Centre for Consumer Law (January 2007: 157).

[17] Study Centre for Consumer Law (January 2007: 78).

[18] ECC-Net (October 2006).

[19] ECC-Net (October 2006: 6). There were also 1,200 approaches to ECC-Net in the form of requests for information.

[20] 1999 Montreal Convention for the Unification of Certain Rules for International Carriage by Air 1999, implemented into UK law by SI 2003 No 262.

[21] Reg (EC) No 261/2004 on denied boarding, cancellation, or long delay of flights [2004] OJ L46/1 (implemented in the United Kingdom by Civil Aviation (Denied Boarding, Compensation and Assistance) Regulations 2005, SI 2005 No 975).

[22] ECC-Net (October 2006: 20).

At the time of the publication of ECC-Net's report towards the end of 2006, the outcome of more than a quarter (27 per cent) of the 1,500 or so complaints was unknown. As regards 12 per cent, the consumer did not in fact have a valid claim; 4 per cent were referred to a relevant ADR body and these cases were still ongoing when the report was published. Nearly a quarter of cases (24 per cent) were solved by the carrier satisfying the consumer's claim, but the striking statistic is that, in 33 per cent of all complaints handled through ECC-Net, the problem was either not resolved at all or was only partially resolved.[23] **11.10**

The ECC-Net report shows not only that airline legislation is failing air travellers, but also that national enforcement bodies (NEBs) are not helping the situation. Although the Regulation stipulates that '[e]ach Member State shall designate a body responsible for the enforcement of this Regulation as regards flights from airports situated on its territory and flights from a third country to such airports',[24] in practice, the NEBs are not carrying out their role of compelling compliance with the Regulation.[25] In addition, most member states do not have appropriate ADR bodies for dealing with consumers' claims against airlines. For example, there is no designated ADR body for air travel-related problems in the United Kingdom.[26] **11.11**

ECC-Net concludes that, if the NEBs are failing to ensure that airlines comply with the legislation and suitable ADR is not available, the consumer's only remaining option is to pursue the complaint through the courts: 'This is not a practical course of action, however.'[27] When small amounts of money are involved, consumers will decide that it is 'not worth the hassle'[28] and will not seek to recover the reimbursement to which they are entitled. **11.12**

Fourthly, in many cases, there are major problems in terms of enforcement if the supplier fails to comply voluntarily with the outcome of the ADR process (whether in the form of an award pronounced by an arbitrator or ombudsman or a negotiated or mediated settlement). As regards non-binding ADR systems, such as the Scandinavian countries' consumer complaints boards, rates of compliance are variable (anything from below **11.13**

[23] ECC-Net (October 2006: 9). This figure is not, however, significantly out of line with 'clear-up' rates for consumer disputes in general: see para 9.20.

[24] Art 16. In the United Kingdom, the designated enforcement body is the Civil Aviation Authority: reg 5(1).

[25] ECC-Net (October 2006: 27–9).

[26] ADR under the *ABTA* code of practice is possible only for disputes relating to holidays purchased through a travel agent which is a member of *ABTA*.

[27] ECC-Net (October 2006: 27).

[28] ECC-Net (October 2006: 21).

30 per cent to as much as 85 per cent, depending on the sector of the economy in question). The compliance rate of the similar—but by no means identical—ADR mechanisms in the Baltic states appears to be higher (even as much as 90 per cent or more). This may be because, in the Baltic states, public authorities can impose administrative sanctions on suppliers who do not comply with the decisions of the consumer complaints boards.[29]

11.14 This last point illustrates the need for there to be some kind of leverage over suppliers so that the outcome of an ADR process does not end up being a *brutum fulmen*. If one of the rationales of providing ADR for the resolution of consumer disputes is the fact that litigation is not a practical option for the resolution of such disputes, an ADR process achieves very little—particularly in the cross-border context—if a consumer who has obtained, say, an arbitral award in his favour is faced by the prospect of having to try to enforce that award through the courts. To be truly effective, a system of consumer ADR needs to operate within an environment where, as a general rule, suppliers voluntarily comply with ADR outcomes. Such an environment may be established through, for example, ADR schemes that operate as part of a code of practice to which the supplier subscribes and which allows the code owner to impose sanctions for non-compliance or legal systems which enable public authorities to impose penalties on non-complying businesses. While there are some contexts in which the right sort of environment has been established, few legal systems have found overarching solutions to the practical problems surrounding enforcement in cases which are referred to ADR.

11.15 Fifthly, ADR mechanisms, no less than litigation, may not be cost effective for low-value disputes. For example, even in the Baltic states, where consumer complaints are handled by consumer protection boards, the expenses of the procedure (which may be no more than €40) may exceed the monetary amount involved (for example, as regards complaints involving footwear).[30]

II. ONLINE DISPUTE RESOLUTION

1. Introduction

11.16 In recent years there has been a huge interest in 'online dispute resolution' (ODR). This interest results from the idea that, as regards disputes which arise from e-commerce transactions, there is a certain logic in employing

[29] K Viitanen (2000: 336).
[30] K Viitanen (2000: 335).

the technology which was used for concluding the contract also for resolving any dispute arising from that contract. In the field of ODR there has been a 'surfeit'[31] of initiatives from various international bodies (such as the United Nations, the Organisation for Economic Co-operation and Development, and the International Chamber of Commerce). One of the major themes of these initiatives is self-regulation. The product of all this endeavour has been conferences, codes of practice, action plans, policy statements, and guidelines for consumer protection in e-commerce—rather than any specific legislative proposals.[32] Although these various efforts display differences in terms of detail, it seems to be universally accepted that an important objective is the establishment of easy and cost effective extra-judicial means of resolving disputes which arise out of b2c e-contracts.

To a large extent the distinction between ADR and ODR is, from a legal point of view, illusory; as regards arbitration and mediation, the perceived originality of online dispute resolution is more technological than anything else. Indeed, ODR started out as the administration of ADR processes online.[33] Even at the start of the Internet revolution, some commentators doubted whether, in view of the large variety of different dispute-resolution mechanisms in existence, there was any need to try to invent a new dispute-resolution system for electronic commerce.[34] According to this view, the only requirement for disputes arising out of e-commerce is some adaptation of existing ADR techniques to take account of the new technology. Whether a mediator communicates with the parties to a dispute by post, telephone, or e-mail is, in principle, unimportant. Of course, in practical terms, certain advantages may flow from the use of communication by electronic means—especially in the cross-border context.[35] **11.17**

There remains, however, a huge gap between ODR's potential and its actual use. This gap is at least partly attributable to lack of confidence on the part of potential users. Some see this lack of confidence as a consequence of the fact that ODR is not heavily regulated and argue that more government regulation is required as the means of increasing confidence in ODR.[36] While issues of confidence are not insignificant, whether governmental intervention is the answer is debatable; increased regulation **11.18**

[31] M Wahab (2004: 132).
[32] See, eg, G Kaufmann-Kohler and T Schultz (2004: 83–108).
[33] C Rule (2002: 44).
[34] ME Schneider and C Kuner (1997: 25).
[35] See C Rule (2002: ch 3).
[36] See T Schultz (2004).

involves a cost and, in the current economic climate, governments seem unwilling to devote public money to civil justice in general[37] and specifically to areas which many believe should be left largely to self-regulation.

11.19 Within the literature, there are some commentators who make exaggerated claims on behalf of ODR and some of the discussion has a rather utopian feel to it.[38] While, for several years, there have been rather extravagant predictions about the inevitable rise of ODR as a method of resolving e-commerce disputes and about the role that ODR is destined to play within the world of alternative dispute resolution, evidence suggests neither that ODR plays a central role with regard to disputes arising out of b2c e-contracts nor that ODR in the consumer context is on the increase. In fact, the evidence seems to point in the opposite direction—as it appears that some of the pioneering providers of ODR services have withdrawn from the consumer market in recent years. As regards the resolution of contractual disputes, the practical achievements of ODR appear to be quite limited.

11.20 There is a strong element of 'Emperor's new clothes'[39] about ODR—just as there is a lot of hype about the distinctiveness of e-commerce in general. The only distinctive aspect of ODR (as opposed to ADR in general) is that communication between the parties to the dispute and any third parties involved in assisting its resolution is by e-mail or other computer-based systems of communication. Any method of computer-assisted dispute resolution can be replicated in the real world[40] and the legal issues raised

[37] For example, in the United Kingdom, 2005 saw 'stringent financial cuts across the whole of the justice system': S Prince (2007: 330).

[38] See, eg, Y Zhao (2005: chs 5 and 6); G Kaufmann-Kohler and T Schultz (2004: 67): 'ODR is not a passing trend, it is not some legal or business fad and is not simply a new tool of dispute resolution. It is a movement.' See also A Patrikios (2008: 67).

[39] See J Hörnle (2003).

[40] Automated settlement systems provide an example of how ODR can display a degree of distinctiveness—although even these systems can be largely replicated in the real world without the involvement of computer technology. Indeed, some automated settlement systems have been operated in parallel, both online and offline: for example, *Settlement Online Systems*: <http://settlementonlinesystems.com.au> (an Australian dispute resolution service which seems to have been operative only for a couple of years early in the 2000s). Automated settlement systems are computer-based mechanisms designed to encourage the settlement of monetary claims through a system of blind bidding. If and when the bids of the disputing parties are sufficiently close together the computer software proposes a solution. One of the best known of these systems is *cybersettle* (<http://www.cybersettle.com>) which plays a significant role in the settlement of insurance disputes; it has handed more than 100,000 cases since1998:<http://www.cybersettle.com/info/about/company/overview.aspx>[8/11/07]. Under a system of blind bidding, if the parties fail to agree, the position is no different from that which arises when any other attempted mediation fails to produce an agreed solution. See E Clark, G Cho, and A Hoyles (2003: 11–14).

by ODR are not very different from those arising from real-world ADR. This is particularly true with regard to ODR in the consumer context. For example, the fact that mediation is conducted in cyberspace (rather than in the real world) appears to be largely irrelevant from the legal point of view; similarly, there is very little difference between a documents-only arbitration conducted by post and a documents-only arbitration conducted online; the practical advantages and problems inherent in online arbitration parallel those which apply to any documents-only consumer arbitration. The obvious conclusion is that, if ODR is simply ADR carried out over the Internet, the rules that apply to real-world ADR should also apply to ODR.[41]

As regards b2c contracts, it seems generally to be accepted that, to a large extent, the problems surrounding ODR are technical and practical rather than legal.[42] As a result, most of the discussion of ADR in the context of e-commerce focuses on issues of practicalities; if the right practical solutions are found, ODR can offer consumers the possibility of fast, inexpensive, and effective remedies. In the context of ODR, the brave new world of cyberspace boils down to little more than making provision for electronic communication within well-recognized systems of mediation or arbitration. **11.21**

The vast literature on the subject of ODR[43] is almost certainly disproportionate to either its legal interest or its practical significance; the reality is that the potential market for ODR services for e-commerce disputes is quite limited.[44] A typical assertion is that ODR has 'introduced more complexity both from the point of view of legal questions and conflict of laws as well as the issue of jurisdiction'.[45] However, it is far from clear that this is true—at least in the consumer context. This is not to say that there are no legal questions surrounding ODR. Is an ODR agreement binding on the parties—so that the courts will stay any proceedings brought in breach of **11.22**

41 S Schiavetta (2004).

42 See, eg, E Clark, G Cho, and A Hoyle (2003); J Hörnle (2002); J Hörnle (2003); E Katsh and J Rifkin (2001); LM Ponte (2005); M Schellekens and L van der Wees (2002); M Wahab (2004); H-L Yu and M Nasir (2003). Compare L Biukovic (2002: 346): 'the practice of online arbitration is more limited by the strict formal requirements of the New York Convention than by software'.

43 See the 50-page bibliography compiled and updated by M Conley Tyler and E Gasson (2006).

44 International Chamber of Commerce (July 2002: 9). One author suggests that, by 2006, one of the most successful providers of online binding arbitration (the Chartered Institute of Arbitrators) had handled approximately 400 cases (presumably mainly domestic rather than cross-border in nature), primarily in the field of b2c contracts: T Schultz (2004: 75).

45 E Clark, G Cho, and A Hoyle (2003: 22).

the ODR agreement?[46] Does an award which is delivered by e-mail or via a webpage qualify for enforcement under the New York Convention of 1958?[47] To the extent that such questions may arise at all, they are more likely to do so in relation to b2b contracts than in relation to b2c contracts. For example, there seems to be no example of reported litigation in England involving an attempt to enforce a consumer arbitration award, let alone an e-award. Notwithstanding the range of potentially interesting doctrinal questions surrounding consumer ODR, these questions—like so many of the legal issues surrounding cross-border consumer contracts—are, in practical terms, rarely of significance. Much of the literature which discusses the legal issues relating to consumer arbitration is excessively theoretical in nature[48] and appears to have little connection with anything that might reasonably be expected to happen.

2. Stand-alone ODR

11.23 From a practical point of view, it is important to distinguish 'stand-alone' ADR from what might be termed 'embedded'[49] ADR schemes. An ADR scheme is 'embedded' if it forms part of a code of practice (whether voluntary or imposed by law) to which suppliers subscribe. Such schemes normally involve a trustmark—a logo which the supplier can display on its website and other promotional material to inform potential customers that the supplier subscribes to the scheme and adheres to a particular code of practice. In contrast to embedded ADR schemes, there are organizations which offer stand-alone ADR services. In principle, these services are available (for a fee) for the resolution of any dispute, but there is no formal link between the supplier and the ADR service provider.

11.24 One significance of the distinction is that, as regards stand-alone ADR, the pressure that can be brought to bear on the supplier is strictly limited.

[46] Whether the proposed arbitration is to be conducted online or offline, pre-dispute compulsory arbitration agreements in consumer contracts will normally fall foul of the Unfair Terms in Consumer Contracts Regulations 1999: see paras 7.41–7.50. Accordingly, for ODR to be legally effective in the consumer context 'it would be in the best interests of an e-business to adopt an optional, post-dispute ODR program': LM Ponte (2002: 464).

[47] It has been suggested that, in the case of arbitration proceedings which were conducted entirely online, a successful claimant would be unable to enforce the award as he would be unable to produce the original award in writing or a duly authenticated copy of it: ME Schneider and C Kuner (1997: 18); L Buikovic, (2002: 349–50). The consensus is that awards should be sent to the parties using conventional (ie, non-electronic) methods of communication; the arbitrators should print out the award, sign it, and pass it on to the parties: see, eg, J Arsic (1997: 217); M Wahab (2004a: 164).

[48] See, eg, A Vahrenwald (October 2000: 200–20).

[49] See M Schellekens and L van der Wees (2002: 298).

This problem exists at two levels. First, as involvement in stand-alone ADR processes is voluntary, suppliers may have little interest in participating in cases referred by dissatisfied consumers; if the supplier does not respond to the consumer's complaint, there is little that the ADR service provider can do about it.[50] Secondly, even if the supplier does participate in the ADR process, obtaining an award in his favour may well not be the end of the consumer's problems; there is still the question of the enforceability of the award if the supplier decides not to comply with it voluntarily.[51] As regards stand-alone ODR, there is normally nothing that can be done to promote compliance by a recalcitrant supplier[52] and providers of stand-alone ODR services normally do not assist consumers with uncooperative e-traders.[53]

In the world of online dispute resolution, it would appear that, subject to one significant exception (which is discussed below), stand-alone ODR has very little to offer in the consumer context. In the late 1990s a number of ODR service providers set up online. In 2000 *Consumers International* conducted a review of 30 ADR service providers which were available (i) online (ii) to consumers in dispute with suppliers and (iii) regardless of the location of the parties.[54] (Purely national schemes were outside the scope of the study.) In 2002 the ICC ran its *Business-to-Consumer and Consumer-to-Consumer Alternative Dispute Resolution (ADR) Inventory Project*. The result of the widespread circulation of a detailed questionnaire was a total of 37 responses from ADR providers in 16 countries, of which 28 offered some form of online service. Most of the organizations which responded were located in the United States and Europe.[55] **11.25**

There is some evidence that stand-alone ODR schemes have not been as widely used as those who set up the schemes had imagined. For example, the Virtual Magistrate Project (VMAG)[56] in the United States was used far less than its creators had hoped or anticipated.[57] It has been **11.26**

[50] See L Caplin (2004).

[51] HH Perritt Jr (2000: 676).

[52] J Hörnle (2003a: 829).

[53] Consumers International (December 2000: 22).

[54] Consumers International (December 2000).

[55] See International Chamber of Commerce (July 2002). Only 10 ODR service providers appear in both *Consumers International*'s report of 2000 and the ICC's 2002 report.

[56] <http://www.vmag.org>.

[57] See HH Perrett Jr (2000). VMAG was set up to deal with various types of cyberspace dispute, although not with disputes arising out of e-contracts; in its first 15 years of operation only one dispute was determined by arbitration under the scheme (Tierney and Email America): E Katsh and J Rifkin (2001: 56). Even this case is unsatisfactory as the sole defendant (Email America) was absent from the proceedings: Y Zhao (2005: 158).

suggested that, despite the early promise of ODR, the uptake in the consumer context (except in relation to disputes arising from transactions effected through the *eBay* auction website) has been modest.[58] Several of the ODR providers which emerged in the late 1990s alongside the birth of e-commerce have since disappeared. According to one author, of the 76 ODR websites established in the late 1990s and early 2000s[59] only 57 were still active by 2006.[60] Similarly, in 2000 *Consumers International* found that, during the three months of its study, new services came online and existing services ceased to operate or changed significantly.[61] Of the 30 ODR providers which were reviewed, the majority either no longer exist or do not operate services for disputes arising out of b2c contracts or have changed their name and/or their web address; by early 2007 fewer than half were still seeking to offer ODR services that were at all suitable for the resolution of disputes arising out of b2c contracts.[62]

11.27 One of the major problems with stand-alone ODR is that of cost. In view of the fact that governments are unwilling to provide public money to support the development of ODR services,[63] a large proportion of ODR service providers charge fees that exceed the amount which is in dispute in a typical consumer case.[64] In this kind of environment 'the profitability of effective stand-alone ODR for small value consumer disputes is questionable'.[65] There are major problems in finding a business model which enables the ODR service provider to offer low-cost or free services to consumers while, at the same time, establishing an appropriate degree of independence from business interests (which are, in practice, the major source of funding). The evidence suggests that, in the context of consumer disputes, ODR service providers have found it very difficult to carve out a viable niche within the e-commerce market;[66] if ODR services are not financed through the membership fees of a trustmark scheme or trade

[58] E Clark, G Cho, and A Hoyle (2003: 10).

[59] M Coney Tyler and D Bretherton (2003).

[60] R Morek (2006: 172). See also M Conley Tyler (2004).

[61] Consumers International (December 2000: 8).

[62] Similarly, only two of the four services reviewed by T Puurunen (2003a) were still in operation early in 2008; interestingly, the two services which were thought to be promising examples of how ODR service providers have remedied the various problems afflicting ODR are the services which are no longer operational.

[63] One exception is the ECODIR (Electronic Consumer Dispute Resolution) project, which was funded by the European Commission and the Irish government: see para 10.38.

[64] Consumers International (December 2000: 22). See also JW Goodman (2003: 26).

[65] Consumers International (December 2000: 23).

[66] Some of early experiments with ODR in North America started as university-based research projects. See, for example, *Cybertribunal* (<http://www.cybertribunal.org/>) and *Virtual Magistrate* (<http://www.vmag.org/>).

association the ODR service will almost invariably be too costly for most consumer claims.[67] Following the retrenchment of the stand-alone ODR market, there are few easily accessible providers of stand-alone ODR services for the resolution of disputes arising out of cross-border b2c contracts.[68]

As already noted, the other major problem surrounds questions of enforcement. Although there is an international system for the cross-border recognition and enforcement of arbitral awards,[69] as the process of enforcement is through the ordinary courts, it is largely inaccessible to consumers—for the same reasons which render litigation an impractical mechanism for the vindication of consumers' contractual rights. As regards settlements achieved through mediation and other ADR processes, there is no simplified system for cross-border enforcement. In legal terms, a settlement is no more (and no less) than a contract between the parties. In the event that there is not voluntary compliance with the terms of the settlement agreement, the only means of enforcement is through the ordinary courts. So, once again, the consumer is faced by all the problems associated with cross-border litigation. Having said that, it is worth noting that there is some limited evidence that mediation has a beneficial impact on compliance; where mediation leads to a settlement, there is an increased likelihood that sums owed under the agreement will be paid voluntarily.[70] **11.28**

Overall, stand-alone ODR has not been viewed favourably. It has been suggested that the ODR industry is still in its infancy and, in addition to the problem of costs and enforcement, ODR is subject to a number of failings in terms of transparency, proper safeguards, oversight, and securing that consumers enjoy certain procedural rights.[71] This view is supported by the study conducted on behalf of *Consumers International* in 2000, which provides an assessment of whether ODR service providers actually meet the appropriate standards—in terms of impartiality, transparency, legality, and oversight. The study found, inter alia, that: (i) there are significant weaknesses in the services provided (such as inadequate assurance of impartiality, insufficient information to users about the service provider, lack of transparency, and inadequate incentives for compliance with the results of the ODR process); (ii) most services are, in practice, available only to English-speakers; and (iii) most ODR services are disproportionately **11.29**

67 J Hörnle (2003a: 829).

68 M Schellekens and L van der Wees (2002: 292).

69 New York Convention on the recognition and enforcement of foreign arbitral awards (1958).

70 S Prince (2007: 340).

71 T Puurunen (2003a: 244–53).

costly for typical retail transactions.[72] The report concluded that, in the context of disputes which arise from b2c contracts, stand-alone ODR does not provide the answer to consumers' access-to-justice problems: 'consumers at present cannot and should not trust that alternative dispute resolution systems available online can offer adequate redress'.[73] This assessment is pretty damning and there is little evidence to suggest that matters have improved since the report was published.

11.30 There is, however, an exception to this general assessment. One area where stand-alone ODR seems to play a significant role is in relation to disputes arising from transactions concluded via online auction websites, in particular *eBay*.[74] Of course, many of these transactions are not consumer contracts; they are c2c sales. Nevertheless, quite a lot of *eBay* transactions involve sales by suppliers to consumers[75] and fixed price sales are becoming increasingly important; for example, in 2005 'normal' sales (rather than online auctions) accounted for 38 per cent of sales transacted via the *eBay.co.uk* website.[76] One of the features of the *eBay* website is the fact that it is linked to *SquareTrade*,[77] an online dispute-resolution service. Notwithstanding this linkage, it could not be said that *SquareTrade* is a truly embedded ADR system;[78] those who buy and sell through *eBay* do not thereby agree to use *SquareTrade*'s dispute-resolution services. The position is simply that *SquareTrade* is *eBay*'s preferred dispute-resolution provider and that any consumer with a complaint who looks through the *eBay* website may find himself being directed towards *SquareTrade*.[79]

11.31 The services of *SquareTrade* are provided either free or, if a mediator becomes involved, for a low cost.[80] The ADR process is broken down into

[72] Consumers International (December 2000: 5).

[73] Consumers International (December 2000: 5).

[74] See <http://www.eBay.com>. The UK website is <http://www.ebay.co.uk/>.

[75] According to a recent UK survey 5 per cent of SMEs that sell online use *eBay*: Office of Fair Trading (June 2007: 25).

[76] Office of Fair Trading (June 2007: 137).

[77] <http://www.squaretrade.com>.

[78] There is, however, a 'SquareTrade Seal Program' to which *eBay* users can subscribe (for a fee); this program shares some of the features of other e-commerce trustmark schemes.

[79] *EBay*'s UK site (*ebay.co.uk*) includes a 'Dispute Console' (<http://feedback.ebay.co.uk/ws/eBayISAPI.dll?ViewDisputeConsole&DisputeType=1> [8/1/08]) which encourages parties to a (potential) dispute to reach a settlement without there being any need to involve an outside dispute-resolution service provider. Recent research in the United Kingdom suggests that only a very small number of eBayers who experience problems take their problem 'all the way' to *SquareTrade*: L Edwards and A Theunissen (2007).

[80] The standard fee for mediation is $29.95, but, in certain circumstances the fee is discounted to $19.95: <http://www.squaretrade.com/odrsvcs/odr_pricing.jsp?vhostid=bliss&stmp=squaretrade&cntid=fj9vyh3fa2> [10/8/07]. For information on how the funds required

four phases.[81] (1) The claimant files a claim, using the online complaint form. The structure of the form requires the claimant to identify the problem and its possible solutions. (2) The other party is notified that a dispute has been filed. (3) The parties engage in direct negotiation. According to the wishes of the parties, a mediator can be brought into the process at this stage. (4) The parties reach a settlement agreement (either with or without the involvement of a '*SquareTrade* Mediator').

According to its website, *SquareTrade* has handled over two million cases since its inception in 1999 and '[o]ver 80 per cent of buyers and sellers who have completed *SquareTrade*'s Online Dispute Resolution Service said they would use the service again.'[82] Apart from this statistic, the website does not contain any information about 'clear-up' rates and whether or not settlement agreements are complied with. 11.32

Although *SquareTrade* dispute resolution is an example of apparently successful stand-alone ODR, it has to be recognized that the environment in which *SquareTrade* operates has particular characteristics which have the effect of encouraging parties to participate in the dispute-resolution process in good faith. In view of the fact that an important aspect of the *eBay* system is that users of the site can give feedback on the reliability of their contractual partners, it is reasonable to think that there are significant incentives for suppliers who sell via *eBay* to avoid getting into disputes with consumers (with a view to avoiding an adverse reliability rating); *a fortiori*, if a dispute does arise from a b2c contract concluded via *eBay*, the supplier has the same incentives to try to settle the dispute swiftly and without antagonizing the consumer.[83] 11.33

III. EMBEDDED ADR: CODES OF PRACTICE AND THE ROLE OF TRUSTMARKS

One of the most potentially significant developments in promoting consumer confidence and self-regulation involves codes of practice and the use of trustmarks or seals of approval. The process works very simply: organizations (code owners) establish standards (codes of practice) for 11.34

for setting up the scheme were raised, see: <http://www.squaretrade.com/cnt/jsp/prs/vcj0600.jsp> [3/12/07].

81 See <http://www.squaretradedisputeresolution.com/step-by-step.html> [10/8/07].

82 See <https://www.squaretrade.com/odr/jsp/fil/filing_start_a.jsp?vhostid=bliss&stmp=squaretrade&cntid=wmfjrj3012> [10/8/07].

83 See E Katsh and J Rifkin (2001:114–15).

conducting business and certify that particular suppliers (code subscribers) have met those standards; the code owner includes code subscribers on the list of businesses which satisfy the standards laid down by the code and, once certified, the code subscribers are permitted to display the code owner's seal or trustmark on their promotional material or on their website. In the United Kingdom, for example, numerous trade associations have developed private codes of practice, many of which are focused solely on the domestic market.

11.35 The same approach has also been adopted in the world of e-commerce. Whereas some codes of practice focus on a single issue such as privacy and data collection[84] or web accessibility,[85] others are multi-faceted and deal with a wide range of issues relating to reliability (such as advertising, provision of information about products or services for sale, security of computer systems, dealings with children, and complaints handling). From the point of view of the current discussion, one of the most important features of such codes of practice is that they normally incorporate ADR mechanisms for the resolution of disputes between consumers and suppliers. Although it is important not to paint too rosy a picture of embedded ADR schemes, ADR within the context of a trustmark scheme holds out one of the better prospects for the effective resolution of consumer disputes.[86]

1. General Characteristics

11.36 Because there are many codes of practice governing various types of consumer contract, the overall picture is far from uniform and it is difficult to provide a clear overview which is not potentially misleading. There are, however, a number of threads which are common to a large number of trustmark schemes which incorporate ADR mechanisms.[87]

11.37 (i) The possibility of referring a contractual dispute to arbitration normally arises only after the consumer has pursued the matter through the supplier's internal complaints procedure and it has not been possible for the parties to reach an agreed settlement through informal processes. A typical ADR scheme within a multi-faceted code of practice comprises three layers.

[84] See A Endeshaw (2001). See, eg, the *BBBonline* Privacy Seal Program: <http://www.bbbonline.org/privacy/>; the *TRUSTe* Web Privacy Seal scheme: <http://www.truste.org/businesses/web_privacy_seal.php>.

[85] See, eg, *Segala* <http://segala.com/>.

[86] See J Hörnle (2003a: 829).

[87] Most e-commerce trustmark schemes in Europe display considerable similarities in terms of the level of consumer protection they aim to provide: see J Trzaskowski (2006: 39–43).

First, the supplier is required to have an internal complaints handling service and undertakes to deal with consumer complaints within a reasonably short time frame. Secondly, if the supplier's internal mechanism fails to produce an agreed solution to the consumer's complaint, the consumer may invoke the assistance of the code owner which will seek to facilitate a settlement of the dispute between the parties.[88] Thirdly, if 'assisted' negotiation or mediation by the code owner does not lead to a settlement, the complaint may be referred to an arbitration scheme, typically provided by a specialized dispute-resolution service specified in the code of practice.

In cases where the complaint progresses to this third stage, the decision of the arbitrator is normally binding; depending on the terms of the code of practice the arbitral award may either be binding on both parties or may be binding only on the supplier, thereby allowing (in theory) the consumer to ignore the result of the ADR process and litigate the claim in the relevant civil courts. An agreement to refer a dispute to arbitration within the context of this type of embedded ADR scheme does not fall foul of the Unfair Terms in Consumer Contracts Regulations 1999. Any such agreement is concluded by the parties after the dispute has arisen; as a post-dispute arbitration agreement is 'individually negotiated' it cannot be 'unfair' for the purposes of the 1999 Regulations.[89] **11.38**

(ii) Embedded ADR schemes are normally cheaper for the consumer than litigation; the majority operate on a no-cost basis.[90] The major source of funding is provided by the subscriptions paid by the code subscribers. In England, the general pattern is that consumer arbitration within the context of an embedded ADR scheme is either free for the consumer (with the costs of the arbitration being borne either by the supplier or by the trade organization of which the supplier is a member[91]) or the potential costs to the consumer are low (typically less than £100).[92] **11.39**

[88] See, eg, art 5.4 of *SafeBuy*'s Code of Practice: <http://www.safebuy.org.uk/code-of-practice.html> [20/7/07].

[89] See ch 7.

[90] Study Centre for Consumer Law (January 2007: 126).

[91] For example, in the context of the Independent Consumer Arbitration Service (which operates under the auspices of IDRS Ltd, a wholly-owned subsidiary of the Chartered Institute of Arbitrators) the filing fee of £500 has to be paid by the business involved in the dispute; the consumer has no costs other than costs incurred in pursuing the claim.

[92] See, eg, the schedule of fees under the *Rules of the Independent Arbitration Scheme for the Travel Industry* (2003 edn): <http://www.abta.com/arbitration.shtml> [18/8/07]. Even in America some of the embedded ADR schemes provide free or low-cost services for consumers: see, eg, the dispute resolution services of the Better Business Bureau: <http://www.dr.bbb.org>.

11.40 (iii) The procedure is generally written. Under some schemes a hearing is not possible in any circumstances; others provide for a hearing to be held if one of the parties specifically requests it. Such written procedures are frequently conducted by e-mail—as regards disputes arising from both online and offline transactions.

11.41 (iv) In the cross-border consumer context, if the system of enforcement depends upon the consumer commencing (or having to threaten to commence) litigation, the dispute-resolution process has failed. As a general rule, in a case where a consumer feels that it is not worth litigating a dispute which arises from a cross-border contract, it would also not be worth seeking to enforce an arbitral award or mediated settlement through the courts—particularly if enforcement proceedings would have to be brought in a country which is not the consumer's home forum. In practice, if the solution achieved by ADR is not complied with voluntarily, that is likely to be the end of the matter.

11.42 The importance of an embedded ADR scheme is that it takes disputes out of the strictly legal sphere. One of the reasons for the development of such schemes is to provide a dispute-resolution process which avoids the need for consumers to incur the costs which legal proceedings entail. An embedded arbitration scheme can go some way towards addressing enforcement problems: there is a greater degree of compulsion than exists in relation to stand-alone ADR and the consumer can be more confident that the result achieved by the ADR process will be honoured. There are two possible aspects to this.

11.43 First, where ADR is embedded within a code of practice, the code owner will typically have disciplinary powers—and, normally after a series of warnings, may expel a member which breaches the code (for example, by failing to honour an arbitral award in the consumer's favour):

> [B]usinesses that fail to comply with the results of an ODR within a trustmark program risk the loss of their right to use the trustmark, and may be subject to adverse publicity. Thus, there is an inherent incentive for businesses to comply with ODR when it is part of a trustmark program.[93]

If suppliers value their membership of the particular trustmark scheme, there are good reasons for them to comply with the terms of the code of practice and to abide by the result of the code's dispute-resolution processes.

[93] Consumers International (December 2000: 11).

Secondly, there are some schemes which go further and, in certain cases, ensure that a dissatisfied consumer will at least get his money back. For example, under the US *WebAssured* scheme,[94] members who have had a clean track record for at least six months are covered by the scheme's 'On-line Purchase Protection' programme under which, if a consumer files a complaint about a member and the e-trader does not resolve the matter, the *WebAssured* organization guarantees to refund the purchase price paid by the consumer.[95] A similar solution is provided by *TrustedShops*.[96] This trustmark scheme appears to be focused mainly on the German e-commerce market, although there are English, French, and German versions of the website and a few of the *TrustedShops* subscribers are UK businesses. As well as providing a mediation service, the *TrustedShops* scheme offers an effective money-back guarantee for consumers who buy from e-traders who are entitled to use the *TrustedShops* trustmark. This applies both where goods that have been ordered are not delivered and in cases where the consumer cancels the contract, but does not receive a refund after returning the goods. The guarantee is provided through the *Atradius* insurance group and the insurance scheme is funded from the subscriptions of the e-traders which are members of *TrustedShops*.[97] Although the money-back guarantee is free of charge for the consumer, the cost of goods purchased from *TrustedShops* subscribers will reflect, in part, the fact that the insurance is paid for out of the e-traders' subscriptions. However, so far, these schemes have failed to make a big impact on the market. As regards *WebAssured*, relatively few US e-traders are members of the scheme[98] and a similar venture called *Word&Bond*[99] was fairly short-lived.[100] The *TrustedShops* scheme has not been able to attract many subscribers from EU member states other than Germany and currently it has only about 2,000 active members. 11.44

[94] <http://www.webassured.com>.

[95] See <http://www.webassured.com/faq/consumerfaq.cfm> [25/8/06].

[96] See < http://www.trustedshops.com/en/home/index.html> [19/7/07].

[97] Subscribers to the *TrustedShops* scheme pay a monthly subscription, which varies from £29.90 per month if turnover is not more that £25,000 to £79.90 if turnover exceeds £200,000.

[98] For example, on 15 November 2006, the *WebAssured* database listed 1,772 e-traders under the heading 'Jewelry'; only five subscribed to the *WebAssured* scheme; similarly, although there were over 5,000 businesses under the heading 'Computers', only two were subscribers.

[99] The *Word&Bond* scheme worked in a similar way to *WebAssured*—in the sense that its decisions were executed against sums deposited with the code owner by code subscribers: see M Odams de Zylva (2001: 10).

[100] The *Word&Bond* website started early in 2001, but the domain name <www.wordand-bond.com> expired on 23 October 2006; it has since been taken over by another business.

11.45 Notwithstanding the limited success of trustmarks which offer a money-back guarantee, the same result may be achieved through a different avenue. For example, where an online purchase is made through the *PayPal*[101] payment system, there are many circumstances in which the buyer is able to recover the purchase price if (i) the seller does not perform his side of the bargain and (ii) *PayPal*'s online dispute-resolution process does not result in the buyer's complaint being satisfactorily resolved.[102] Although *PayPal* is not promoted as a trustmark scheme (and the scheme does not purport to certify the general reliability of e-traders who accept payment through *PayPal*), in effect, *Paypal*'s online dispute-resolution process and buyer protection programmes operate as an embedded ADR system in cases where goods are purchased using *PayPal*.

2. Problems with Trustmarks

11.46 Although trustmark programmes incorporating embedded ADR elements have various positive features, there are also several potential problems with such schemes, particularly when looked at from the perspective of cross-border transactions. These include: (1) fragmentation; (2) patchiness; (3) lack of transparency; (4) lack of public awareness; (5) cross-border issues; (6) lack of guaranteed enforcement; (7) lack of independence; and (8) technical issues. Although several of these problems are interrelated, it is necessary, for the purposes of exposition, to try to separate the various issues.

Fragmentation

11.47 It has been noted that none of the members of the Organisation for Economic Co-operation and Development has 'an overarching regulatory framework for B2C ADR . . . . Rules have been developed for different types of ADR depending on the subject matter of the dispute . . . or the underlying transaction.'[103] As regards the United Kingdom, the overall picture is very incoherent (notwithstanding the fact that there have been some attempts at promoting greater simplicity and transparency[104]). For example, there are several dozen consumer arbitration schemes (each applicable to a specific

101 <http://www.paypal.co.uk/>. *PayPal* is used, for example, in a large proportion of sales conducted through the *eBay* website.

102 See para 13 of the 'User Agreement for PayPal Service': <https://www.paypal.com/uk/cgi-bin/webscr?cmd=xpt/UserAgreement/ua/EUUA-outside> [7/2/08].

103 Organisation for Economic Co-operation and Development (July 2002: 13).

104 In the United Kingdom, some simplification was achieved in the field of financial services when the various sectoral ADR schemes were replaced by the Financial Ombudsman

retail sector) operated through IDRS Ltd (which is a wholly-owned subsidiary of the Chartered Institute of Arbitrators).[105] In addition, the Independent Consumer Redress Service (ICRS), which is part of IDRS, operates both an arbitration scheme and a conciliation scheme for a number of organizations and businesses.[106] It is hard enough for a lawyer who is a native English-speaker to navigate his way through the IDRS website and to find the relevant information;[107] it must be immeasurably more difficult for a layperson whose first language is not English to do so. There are also many other ADR schemes which are operated by trade associations rather than by IDRS. Notwithstanding the fact that these schemes were established from the perspective of domestic transactions, some of them also apply, in principle, to disputes arising from cross-border transactions.[108] Unless appropriate assistance is provided (for example, by ECC (UK)), these consumer ADR schemes must be almost wholly inaccessible to non-UK residents who find themselves in dispute with English suppliers.

The same type of problem exists as regards e-commerce trustmarks: in **11.48** several countries of the European Union there is more than one scheme.[109] For example, in the United Kingdom, there are three e-commerce trustmarks which have a reasonable degree of prominence: *ISIS* (Internet Shopping is Safe),[110] *SafeBuy*,[111] and *WebTraderUK*.[112] Across Europe, there is a plethora of different schemes. A report in 2002 found that, in the world of e-commerce, there were more than 25 different seals of approval.[113]

Service—a one-stop shop for complaints relating to businesses regulated by the FSA. See R James and P Morris (2003).

105 See the list of schemes on the IRDS website: <http://www.idrs.ltd.uk/business/servicelist.asp> [3/8/07]. Furthermore, in some sectors there are several 'competing' trade associations, each with its own code of practice. For example, as regards the provision of funeral services in the United Kingdom, there are three trade associations: Funeral Standards Council, National Association of Funeral Directors, and National Society of Allied and Independent Funeral Directors.

106 See <http://www.idrs.ltd.uk/consumer/ICRS.asp> [4/12/07].

107 In fact, the IDRS website is extremely poorly organized; it is very difficult or impossible to access some important information (such as the rules which govern some of the dispute resolution schemes and their schedule of fees) and not all of the links work as they should.

108 See M Doyle, K Ritters, and S Brooker (January 2004: 16), who reported that almost half the UK code of practice schemes (14 out of 29) covered cross-border as well as domestic cases.

109 See J Trzaskowski (2006: 29).

110 See <http://www.internetshoppingissafe.co.uk>.

111 See <http://www.safebuy.org.uk>.

112 See <http://www.webtrader.org.uk>. *WebTraderUK* was set up by the Direct Marketing Association following the withdrawal of the *Which?Webtrader* scheme (see para 10.37) which was closed in January 2003. See also *TrustedWebTraders*: <https://www.trustedwebtraders.com/>.

113 E Delgado (2002).

A more recent report dealing with trustmarks in Europe identified more than 30 different logos.[114] Although the principle of non-discrimination on grounds of nationality requires that all these schemes must be available to subscribers from any EU member state, most trustmark schemes give the impression of being mainly national in scope.[115] As trustmark schemes have invariably been set up by public and private bodies within a single member state, the focus is primarily on domestic e-commerce.[116] As a result, most trustmark schemes lack 'European sensitivity'[117] (for example, information is generally not provided in more than one language[118]).

11.49 To date, attempts to develop international trustmarks have had very little success. The European *WebTrader* scheme only operated in any meaningful sense for four years (1999–2003) and cannot be regarded other than as a failure.[119] There is also a scheme called *Euro-Label*,[120] which originated in Austria and is supported by the European Commission. This scheme, which is designed to foster the growth of national and cross-border e-transactions within Europe, operates as an 'umbrella trustmark'[121] for national certification bodies; the *Euro-Label* seal of approval incorporates the trustmark of the national organization into the *Euro-Label* logo. *Euro-Label* operates along similar lines to other trustmark schemes: there is a code of practice[122] (with which certified e-traders must comply) and allied dispute-resolution mechanisms. Although the aim is for the *Euro-Label* trustmark to be available in all the EU member states, national certifying bodies from only seven of the member states (Austria, France, Germany, Italy, Malta, Poland, and Spain) participate in the scheme.[123] As with many such ventures, the website is poorly maintained. Although a Maltese certifying body has joined the *Euro-Label* scheme, this fact is not revealed on the website. The website appears not to be updated very frequently;

[114] J Trzaskowski (2006: 25–8).

[115] J Trzaskowski (2006: 47).

[116] ECC-Net (May 2001: 27).

[117] R de Bruin, E Keuleers, C Lazaro, Y Poullet, and M Viersma (February 2005: 9).

[118] A report published in 2003 suggests that, in Europe, only about a quarter of subscribers to trustmark schemes offer information about the trustmark in more than one language: ECC-Net (May 2003: 27).

[119] See para 10.37.

[120] <http://www.euro-label.com>.

[121] J Trzaskowski (2006: 18).

[122] See <http://www.euro-label.com/euro-label/ControllerServlet;jsessionid=A2C5B757694238B03510D241F3978284?lg=en&to=welcome&tc=classic2&z2Page=eurococ&z3Page=blank&tradersQueryParam2=1> [28/6/07].

[123] Research revealed that a few national trustmark schemes, when asked whether they had considered becoming part of the *Euro-Label* scheme, replied that they had never heard of it: J Trzaskowski (2006: 35).

the most recent 'news' item is dated November 2005. This gives a strong impression that the scheme has not made a lot of progress in recent years; the number of certified e-traders does not seem to be rising and some of the links are to non-existent websites.

The extreme fragmentation of the ADR picture has another negative consequence. It is almost impossible for a consumer to build up any experience of specific ADR schemes. Consumer complaints leading to disputes are reasonably rare; the majority of consumer transactions give rise to no problems at all. But, a significant minority may give rise to problems which cannot be resolved amicably. If there were a one-stop shop for consumer complaints and a uniform procedure for dealing with those complaints, consumers would be able to build up some experience of that process. Even if a dissatisfied consumer had never used the ADR scheme before, he might know people who had done so and there could be a certain amount of sharing of experience. **11.50**

Patchiness

Whereas civil courts are competent to deal with all types of civil dispute, ADR mechanisms do not achieve such complete coverage. There are two main reasons for this. **11.51**

First, there are some sectors of the retail market in relation to which there are no codes of practice and relevant ADR bodies are lacking. For example, although more than half the EU member states have at least one e-commerce trustmark scheme, there are several European countries which have none.[124] In the offline context, even a country which has a well-developed system of consumer complaints boards does not necessarily provide ADR mechanisms covering all types of consumer disputes and all geographical locations in that country.[125] **11.52**

Secondly, one of the problems with self-regulation is the fact that participation by suppliers is voluntary: 'Trade associations can be ineffective in particular because they have inadequate coverage of the industry—and those traders that are not members are likely to be less willing to comply with a Code and probably less likely to have good complaints-handling procedures.'[126] Code owners cannot force traders to subscribe to the **11.53**

[124] J Trzaskowski (2006: 29). In general, e-commerce trustmark schemes are found less frequently in smaller countries and in countries which have joined the European Union relatively recently.

[125] Such as Sweden: Study Centre for Consumer Law (January 2007: 103).

[126] M Doyle, K Ritters, and S Brooker (January 2004: 16).

relevant code of practice; each business decides for itself whether the advantages of participating in the scheme outweigh the disadvantages. Even in areas where an appropriate scheme exists, the proportion of suppliers participating in the relevant code of practice may be low. For example, with regard to the timeshare industry, *OTE* (Organisation for Timeshare in Europe[127]) was established in 1998; it promotes a code of ethics[128] which includes a low-cost arbitration scheme, the European Timeshare Arbitration Scheme, under the auspices of IDRS.[129] However, the existence of *OTE* did little to prevent the widespread complaints surrounding the timeshare industry in the 1990s and early 2000s. A relatively small proportion of operators within the timeshare market are members of *OTE*[130] and the vast majority of the problems generated by the mis-selling of timeshares and similar holiday products were caused by traders who were not *OTE* members.[131] As regards disputes arising in relation to non-*OTE* members, effective ADR mechanisms are not available.

11.54 Similarly, in the world of e-commerce, the existing trustmark schemes have yet to achieve significant success. In order to be truly effective, a trustmark needs to reach a critical mass;[132] to date, e-commerce trustmarks have not been able to generate a climate in which enough e-traders feel that it is sufficiently beneficial to be able to display a seal of approval on their website. This is partly because many e-traders (more than one-fifth[133]) are not aware that such schemes exist. Furthermore, if consumers are not aware of accreditation schemes—and do not favour accredited e-traders over unaccredited ones—there is less pressure than there might be on e-traders to subscribe to a code of practice. There are only three trustmark schemes in Europe which have more than 1,000 subscribers: *TrustedShops*, a German-based scheme established in January 2000, which has some subscribers from countries other than Germany, and the two largest UK trustmark schemes: *SafeBuy* and *ISIS* (Internet Shopping is Safe). Even the

[127] See <http://www.ote-info.com/index.php?option=com_frontpage&Itemid=1> [18/3/07].

[128] The current version of the *OTE* Code of Ethics, which dates from March 2005, can be found at: <http://www.ote-info.com/dmdocuments/OTE%20Code%20of%20Ethics%20&%20ADR%20Scheme%202005%20English.pdf> [18/3/07]. For critical comments on a previous version the *OTE*'s code of ethics, see ECC-Net (December 2002: 35–47).

[129] <http://www.idrs.ltd.uk/business/sevices.asp> [10/8/07].

[130] One suggestion is that *OTE* represents only 10 per cent of the firms operating in the timeshare industry: M Doyle, K Ritters, and S Brooker (January 2004: 2). More recently, it has been estimated that 30 per cent of the timeshare market is in the hands of *OTE* members: European Commission (June 2006: 20 n 23).

[131] ECC-Net (December 2002: 35).

[132] C Rule (2002: 107).

[133] Office of Fair Trading (June 2007: 92).

only international trustmark in Europe, *Euro-Label*, has fewer than 500 subscribers from the seven participating member states (mostly from Austria and Germany).[134] Many of the other schemes have fewer than 100 certified e-traders and there are some national schemes which have no more than a (small) handful of subscribers.[135] It has been estimated that fewer than 10 per cent of commercial websites are part of an accredited e-commerce trustmark scheme.[136] Although this estimate may be slightly wide of the mark (one e-commerce code owner, for instance, estimates that the scheme has only 2 per cent to 2.5 per cent of the market[137]), there can be no doubt that, at the moment, an overwhelming majority of e-traders operate outside any code of practice. The position is not likely to change significantly in the near future as, to the extent that e-commerce trustmark schemes are growing, they are doing so only slowly.[138]

These figures reveal one of the weaknesses of a market-based system **11.55** (which, in theory, should drive consumers away from e-traders who fail to comply with high standards of customer care, thereby providing strong economic motivation for suppliers to join a trustmark scheme). In order for the market model to work, consumers need to be sufficiently well-informed to understand how the system operates and, before entering a transaction, to think about how potential problems arising from that transaction might be resolved. However, this is not how things work out in practice; evidence suggests that most consumers do not take steps to check the other party's reliability before they make a purchase. Research indicates that most consumers do not anticipate disputes when they are about to enter an online contract and only tend to look to an e-trader's track record *after* a dispute has arisen.[139] Accordingly, whether or not a supplier displays a seal of approval will normally not affect consumers' purchasing decisions.

By contrast, in some sectors, the economic pressures are such that large **11.56** numbers of traders within a particular sector subscribe to a code of practice. But, these are the exceptions. For example, a majority of travel agents in the United Kingdom are members of *ABTA*. Although the overall number of consumer disputes that are dealt with by ADR is quite low, the dispute-resolution scheme under the *ABTA* code of practice is one area where consumer arbitration is relatively common. In recent years, the *ABTA*

134 T Scharmacher in ECC (Denmark) (November 2006: 18).
135 See J Trzaskowski (2006: 30–1).
136 ECC-Net (May 2003: 27).
137 Office of Fair Trading (June 2007: 91).
138 Office of Fair Trading (June 2007: 91).
139 K Stewart and J Matthews (2002: 1142).

system has dealt with between 15,000 and 17,500 complaints per year.[140] While the majority of complaints are settled, more than 1,000 complaints are referred to arbitration annually,[141] notwithstanding the fact that the fee which the consumer has to pay is often more than the cost of starting proceedings in the small claims court.[142] The arbitration rules which regulate such cases[143] make provision for a documents-only procedure (which may be conducted either online or offline); awards are made in around 70 per cent of cases, with the average sum awarded rising in recent years from £600 to £750.[144]

11.57 As things stand at the moment, the overall picture is not very encouraging: 'provision of ADR for consumer problems is patchy and presents a lottery for the consumer. The nature of the lottery depends either on the type of problem faced or where the problem arises.'[145] Although this assessment was made in relation to the situation in the United Kingdom, the same could be said for most countries in Europe as well.[146]

Lack of Transparency

11.58 Another facet of the fragmented landscape of embedded ADR schemes is that there are different sorts of organization which act as code owners. Trustmark schemes may be operated by three different types of body: private organizations (such as *SafeBuy* or *WebTraderUK* in the United Kingdom), trade associations (such as *ABTA*), and consumer organizations (such as the Better Business Bureau in the USA). Also, the various bodies involved operate (mainly) at two different levels. At the lower level,

[140] One of the reasons for there being so many arbitrations under the *ABTA* scheme is that, where services (rather than goods) are involved, defective performance by the supplier cannot be resolved by the cancellation of the contract. In cases involving the online purchase of goods, many consumer problems can be resolved by the consumer returning the goods and obtaining a refund. By contrast, in a case where a holiday-maker considers that the quality of the holiday is unacceptable, the only meaningful form of redress is compensation.

[141] *ABTA*'s statistics do not reveal how many of the claims related to cross-border contracts.

[142] If the amount claimed does not exceed £3,000, the registration fee is £72.85; if the amount claimed is between £3,000 and £5,000, the fee is £98.70: <http://www.abta.com/arbitration.shtml> [18/8/07]. The filing fee for small claims proceedings starts at £30 (for a claim of up to £300) and rises to £120 (for a claim of between £1,000 and £5,000). See <http://www.hmcourts-service.gov.uk/infoabout/fees/county.htm> [14/4/08].

[143] See the *Rules of the Independent Arbitration Scheme for the Travel Industry* (2003 edn): <http://www.idrs.ltd.uk/ABTA/Rules.asp> [15/4/08].

[144] See Association of British Travel Agents (June 2005: 28); M Doyle, K Ritters, and S Brooker (January 2004: 48).

[145] M Doyle, K Ritters, and S Brooker (January 2004: 59).

[146] Study Centre for Consumer Law (January 2007: 114).

there are the code owners which formulate the code of practice and run the trustmark scheme. At a higher level, there may be a body (such as a governmental or quasi-governmental agency) which runs a trustmark accreditation scheme, which approves and promotes b2c codes of practice. Within such a structure a website might display both the trustmark logo of the code owner and the trustmark logo of the accrediting organization.

The lack of a clear regulatory framework—and the absence of a suprana- **11.59**
tional accreditation scheme—means that the overall picture is very confusing. This problem is graphically illustrated by the UK situation. *TrustUK* was established in 2000 (with support from the Department for Trade and Industry) and was overseen by the Direct Selling Association (DSA). *TrustUK* was a non-profit organization set up with the purpose of providing a framework for the accreditation of code owners in the field of e-commerce. *TrustUK* gave its approval to four organizations which operate e-commerce trustmark schemes: *ABTA*, *DSA*, *SafeBuy*, and *WebTraderUK*. One of these four schemes (the one operated by the *DSA*) is also accredited by the Office of Fair Trading under its Consumer Codes Approval Scheme[147] (along with several others which do not relate to e-commerce[148]). In addition, by the summer of 2006, *SafeBuy* had successfully completed the first stage of the Office of Fair Trading's Consumer Codes Approval Scheme.[149] As for *TrustUK*, it has ceased to operate and its website is closed, though the *TrustUK* logo can still be found on the websites of some e-traders who subscribe to trustmark programmes which received accreditation from *TrustUK*. (Rather confusingly, there is also the totally separate *TrustMark* scheme,[150] which is supported by the government, the building industry, and consumer groups; its purpose is to help consumers find reliable and trustworthy tradesmen to make home improvements and repairs.)

The point of this narrative is not to elucidate the state of trustmark scheme **11.60**
accreditation in the United Kingdom for its own sake. Rather the objective is to illustrate the complexity of the system and to suggest that, as not only are there overlaps between accreditation schemes but also accreditation can operate at different levels, even a well-informed consumer is likely to be unaware whether a code of practice has been approved by a governmental or quasi-governmental body and what significance attaches to the

[147] See <http://www.oft.gov.uk/oft_at_work/consumer_initiatives/codes/> [14/4/08].

[148] See <http://www.oft.gov.uk/advice_and_resources/resource_base/approved-codes/codes-search/cons_trade_search.aspx> [14/4/08].

[149] See <http://www.safebuy.org.uk/press-release-28-02-2006.html> [4/12/07].

[150] <http://www.trustmark.org.uk/>.

level of accreditation that a particular e-trader has obtained.[151] It is hard to believe that such a degree of complexity is either necessary or helpful; it seems obvious that from the perspective of the consumer (whom these trustmark schemes are primarily designed to benefit) a simpler and more transparent system would be far preferable.

11.61 As long ago as 2001 it was argued that there was a need to find solutions to the increasing confusion generated by the proliferation of trustmarks in the field of e-commerce.[152] The continued introduction of new trustmarks in recent years means that this need has become all the more pressing. A mushrooming of different seals of approval works against the interests of consumers. In its 2001 report, *Consumers International* found that some websites display numerous symbols showing that the website belongs to more than one certification scheme:

> The large number of these schemes means it is difficult for consumers to know what to make of them. The implication is that they offer a promise of good service, yet the scope, standards and quality of these schemes varies greatly.[153]

If one of the goals of accreditation schemes is to build consumer confidence, complexity and lack of stability are bound to have negative effects; a constantly shifting picture—with no clear framework—is more likely to generate confusion in the minds of consumers than instil them with confidence.

Lack of Public Awareness

11.62 One of the problems with ADR schemes in general is that they have 'low visibility to the public eye'.[154] A recurrent theme among commentators is that public awareness of bodies (other than courts) that are responsible for settling consumer disputes remains limited;[155] in the United Kingdom, apart from a few well-known ADR schemes (notably the *ABTA* and *Qualitas* schemes) few of the ADR options are known even to those who offer advice to consumers (such as CABx).[156] There appears to be little knowledge among consumers of the existence of ADR procedures and of the circumstances in which such procedures are available; a consumer

[151] Among EU member states, the United Kingdom is not alone in having a complex trustmark landscape; Germany has five trustmark schemes accredited through Initiative D21 (a public-private partnership): J Trzaskowski (2006: 17).

[152] A Endeshaw (2001: 204).

[153] Consumers International (September 2001: 11). See also J Hörnle (2002).

[154] G Howells and R James (2002: 11).

[155] See, eg, Study Centre for Consumer Law (January 2007: 156).

[156] M Doyle, K Ritters, and S Brooker (January 2004: 63).

who complains to a supplier, but does not obtain satisfactory redress through the supplier's complaints-handling procedure, may be unaware that there are further steps short of going to court that can be taken. In 1993 the European Commission noted in its *Green Paper on Access to Justice* that, although a number of low-cost arbitration schemes have been set up, the main problem with them is ignorance of their existence.[157]

In order for a trustmark scheme to have success, the 'brand' has to be established in such a way that consumers are able to recognize it and understand what it signifies. To date, trustmarks have not been able to achieve brand recognition by consumers.[158] Public consciousness of trustmark schemes is very limited.[159] A consumer may see a logo in a shop window or on a website, but have no idea what it means—although some consumers will probably assume that the logo is a sign of a better than average quality of service. Before entering a contract, most consumers do not know (or seek to find out) whether the particular supplier is a member of a trade association or trustmark scheme or whether there is a code of practice (incorporating an ADR mechanism) which would be relevant to disputes arising out of that transaction. A recent survey in the United Kingdom found that only 24 per cent of consumers look to see whether the supplier is a member of any code when shopping online; 75 per cent are unaware of such codes and their role.[160] When shown the logos of the main UK e-commerce trustmarks, 21 per cent of consumers recognized *ISIS*, 9 per cent recognized *Safebuy*, and 8 per cent recognized *WebTraderUK*.[161] In addition, a consumer cannot easily find out whether a particular supplier which does not display a trustmark logo either has never applied to subscribe to a trustmark scheme or has been a member of a scheme but has been ejected for some reason.[162] Accordingly, the absence of a trustmark logo is largely neutral. **11.63**

The Cross-border Dimension

Although many embedded ADR schemes in the United Kingdom are, in principle, available for the resolution of cross-border disputes as well as domestic disputes, it is more difficult for foreigners than for UK residents **11.64**

157 COM (93) 576, p 51.

158 R de Bruin, E Keuleers, C Lazaro, Y Poullet, and M Viersma (February 2005: 5).

159 ECC-Net (May 2003: 30).

160 Office of Fair Trading (June 2007: 92).

161 Office of Fair Trading (June 2007: 92).

162 However, e-traders whose membership of the *ISIS* trustmark has been revoked are listed on the *ISIS* website: <http://www.internetshoppingissafe.co.uk/>.

to navigate their way, unaided, through the complexities of the system. To some extent, this problem can be addressed by advice agencies. In the cross-border context, consumers have access to relevant advice and information through ECC-Net.[163] For example, a French consumer who has a dispute arising out of a purchase from an English supplier may seek assistance either from the ECC (France)—which would be likely to refer the matter to the ECC (UK)—or directly from the ECC (UK). In such a case, the ECC (UK) would normally contact the supplier and seek to assist the parties in reaching an amicable settlement. If the parties were unable to reach agreement, the ECC (UK) would be in a position to advise the French consumer which ADR scheme (if any) was appropriate for the dispute in question. Of course, a consumer will only contact ECC-Net if he knows of its existence and, unfortunately, public awareness is relatively low. A 2006 survey found that only 6 per cent of UK residents had heard of ECC-Net[164] and 65 per cent stated that they did not know where to get information and advice about cross-border shopping.[165]

11.65 Even if embedded ADR schemes are available to residents from other countries, many of them were formulated to serve a local or national base with local markets in mind.[166] In cross-border cases, there may, for example, be problems with language; many of the ADR schemes in England operate only in English. Notwithstanding the fact that English is widely spoken and understood as a second language, the fact that an ADR process is conducted in English may operate as a major disincentive for people for whom English is not their first language.[167]

Lack of Guaranteed Enforcement

11.66 Although embedded ADR processes score more highly than stand-alone procedures, a system of self-regulation cannot guarantee that the consumer's legal rights will be fully vindicated. For example, a subscriber to an e-commerce code of practice may refuse to cooperate in the code owner's attempts to mediate a solution and, if an award is made in the consumer's favour, may refuse to honour the award. Of course, such conduct runs the

[163] See paras 10.15–10.29.

[164] Eurobarometer (September 2006: 72). British consumers seem less well informed than residents of other EU member states: the average across the 25 EU member states which were surveyed was 11 per cent.

[165] Eurobarometer (September 2006: 73).

[166] SL Donegan (2003: 159).

[167] It has been said that almost 70 per cent of ODR providers offer their services solely in English, whereas less than one-third of Internet users speak English: M Conley Tyler and D Bretherton (2003: 13).

risk that the code owner will expel the supplier from the trustmark scheme and there have been instances of expulsions for non-compliance with the specified code of practice.[168]

In theory, the risk of being expelled from a trustmark scheme should be sufficient to encourage suppliers to comply with the code of practice. However, in a world where there is a multitude of different seals of approval, the supervisory powers of the code owner may not be sufficiently draconian to produce compliance. It has been suggested that: **11.67**

it is doubtful that revocation of a trustmark would be a powerful enough incentive to force a business to comply with a decision of an online arbitrator that it found unacceptable. This is because a wide variety of symbols already exist and the standards and quality of each varies greatly.[169]

An e-trader who is unable or unwilling to satisfy the standards of a stringent code owner can simply allow that trustmark to be revoked and join another scheme with lower standards. A recent study of ADR in the United Kingdom reported that there have been concerns expressed about suppliers leaving their trade association in order to avoid having to comply with awards.[170] In the current situation, this would be unlikely to have negative economic consequences for the trader. Although consumers could (in theory) 'punish' a supplier for losing its trustmark (by ceasing to buy from that supplier and buying from another supplier who benefits from the trustmark), as has already been noted, consumers are generally poorly informed about trustmarks and their significance. A model in which a supplier is likely to suffer a significant downturn in business if it loses its trustmark status (thereby providing the strongest incentive for the supplier to take part in ADR processes and abide by their outcomes) requires consumers to be much better informed than they are at present.

Lack of Independence

Even though the fact that ADR schemes are either low-cost or free (to the consumer), this may be a double-edged sword. A consumer may think that, if the ADR process is paid for by the supplier (or the supplier's trade association), the decision-maker is more likely to see the dispute from the supplier's perspective.[171] Within the system there are factors which might cause the decision-makers to favour businesses over consumers: businesses are repeat-players, whereas consumers are normally one-shotters; **11.68**

[168] J Trzaskowski (2006: 64).
[169] K Stewart and J Matthews (2002: 1140–1).
[170] M Doyle, K Ritters, and S Brooker (January 2004: 3).
[171] M Cappelletti and B Garth (1978: 94).

the costs of the ADR process will normally be borne by the business and it has regularly been observed that, in the field of ADR, he who pays the piper calls the tune. These problems are not insoluble. One possible solution to concerns about (potential) bias on the part of ADR service providers is through money-back guarantees by the trustmark owner to consumers who have been unable to recover directly from the subscribing e-trader.[172] However, it has already been seen that trustmark schemes that provide a money-back guarantee have been unable to penetrate the market beyond a superficial level. A more common way of trying to address such concerns is by code owners taking steps to put the final stage of the ADR process (typically, an arbitration stage) into the hands of an independent ADR service provider; in England, dozens of sectoral schemes make use of the Chartered Institute of Arbitrators (through IDRS Ltd).

11.69 In terms of consumer confidence, whether or not ADR processes favour suppliers over consumers is not the only issue. Even assuming that ADR service providers are scrupulously impartial, there is still a problem if consumers think that they are not (or may not be). If consumers do not have faith in the impartial nature of the process, they will be less inclined to use it—regardless of whether it actually operates fairly and impartially. A survey in 2004 revealed that a majority of European consumers (59 per cent) had heard of ADR bodies and that two-thirds of this group would be prepared to take a complaint to such a body.[173] But, it also indicated that consumer confidence in ADR is quite low—only 10 per cent of the people surveyed considered that ADR bodies are the institutions best placed to resolve cross-border disputes.[174]

Technical Matters

11.70 Although ADR is meant to be more flexible and less formal than litigation, ADR procedures are often quite complicated. For example, the ADR process may involve more than one phase (such as conciliation and arbitration). The process is obviously 'legal' in nature—which tends to be off-putting for consumers: the rules which provide the framework for consumer arbitrations are often written in technical language which may be difficult for a layperson to understand; even if the words themselves are comprehensible, it is not always easy for a layperson to understand their significance. At first glance, many consumer ADR schemes appear no less technical and daunting than court proceedings.

[172] Consumers International (December 2000: 11).
[173] Eurobarometer (October 2004: 13–17).
[174] Eurobarometer (October 2004: 57).

IV. AN ADR STRATEGY FOR CROSS-BORDER CONSUMER CONTRACTS?

1. General Observations

Regardless of the pros and cons of the available consumer arbitration systems, the reality is that very few consumer disputes—either domestic or cross-border—ever reach the final stages of an ADR process (ie, where a decision is taken by a third party). At the domestic level, resort to ADR across Europe is almost as uncommon as consumer litigation; a 2006 Europe-wide survey indicated that 6 per cent of those consumers who had made a formal complaint about faulty goods or services and were dissatisfied with the way in which the complaint was handled—this was 1.5 per cent of the total sample—referred the matter to an ADR body.[175] As far as the United Kingdom is concerned, it is suggested that outside the financial service sector, there are few effective industry-based ADR schemes.[176] At the domestic level, apart from the *ABTA* and *Qualitas* schemes, each of which has a case load of more than a thousand per year,[177] most ADR schemes allied to a trade association's code of practice are used very infrequently, if at all.[178] **11.71**

Resort to ADR in the cross-border context is even more unusual. In a 2004 European survey, only 3 per cent of the sample had reason to complain **11.72**

[175] Eurobarometer (September 2006: 30). Whether use of ADR in the United Kingdom is above or below the European average is hard to discern as research data is inconsistent. On the one hand, a recent report examining consumer ADR in the United Kingdom found that 'for each sector [in which ADR is offered] the number of cases going to an existing relevant ADR service is a microscopically small fraction of the total number of complaints. While recorded complaint levels are in the thousands, use of ADR schemes is in the double digits only for most ADR schemes, and lower for many others': M Doyle, K Ritters, and S Brooker (January 2004: 2). On the other hand, research conducted in England in the 1990s suggests that ADR procedures are invoked reasonably frequently; as regards non-trivial consumer problems relating to faulty goods or services, 2 per cent of consumers took the problem to an ombudsman: H Genn (1999: 39).

[176] G Howells and R James (2002: 11).

[177] M Doyle, K Ritters, and S Brooker (January 2004: 62).

[178] Over the four year period 1983–86, a couple of hundred complaints concerning cars were referred to consumer arbitration, but during the same period, three disputes involving furniture and one involving the servicing of electrical goods were referred to arbitration; there were no arbitrations under the applicable code of practice concerning photographic equipment, funerals, vehicle body repairs, or motorcycles: R Thomas (1991: 163).

about something bought from abroad; fewer than 1.5 per cent of this group (ie, 0.0002 per cent of the sample) got in touch with an ADR body.[179]

11.73 This does not necessarily mean that embedded ADR mechanisms are not working properly.[180] As regards dispute resolution, the aim of a code of practice is to settle the dispute by agreement (whether directly between the consumer and the supplier or with the assistance of the code owner or some other third party); reference of the dispute to a third-party decision-maker is normally seen as a last resort. Indeed, one of the purposes of an accessible mechanism for resolving consumer disputes is to encourage suppliers to respond reasonably to consumer complaints and/or attempts by the code owner to mediate a solution. There is an argument for suggesting that, as regards embedded ADR schemes, because there is the possibility that, if a consumer complaint is not resolved informally, a more formal process will be initiated under the rules of the code of practice, suppliers recognize that it is in their interests to try to find an agreed solution to the consumer's complaint.[181] Although the possibility of arbitration is in the background, if the code of practice works as intended, the vast majority of consumer complaints should be dealt with satisfactorily at either the first stage of the ADR process (direct negotiation between the parties) or the second stage (mediation by the code owner). Indeed, there is quite a lot of evidence to suggest that a large proportion of consumer disputes are settled by negotiation (whether or not within the context of a code of practice to which the supplier subscribes). However, for the reasons already considered, in cases where no informal settlement is reached and the ADR process is not supported by a third party (such as a code owner or ombudsman), consumers tend not to bother to take the matter further.

11.74 It is difficult to provide an accurate assessment of the current state of play in the field of consumer ADR. Part of the difficulty stems from the fact that opinion is very much divided as to the effectiveness of ADR schemes in providing redress for consumer complaints. For example, the Organisation

[179] Eurobarometer (October 2004: 55–6).

[180] See, eg, the views of the Finance and Leasing Association, cited by M Doyle, K Ritters, and S Brooker (January 2004: 37).

[181] For example, in 2005, there were around 4 million orders from e-traders which subscribe to the *SafeBuy* trustmark scheme. There were fewer that 550 mediated disputes; the vast majority were based on misunderstandings and, once the misunderstanding was sorted out, the parties agreed on a solution; there were 20 or so cases in which the consumer litigated the claim under the small claims procedure; no claims went to arbitration under the code of practice: data provided in a telephone interview by Richard Jones, managing director of Software Research Ltd, the company which runs *SafeBuy*.

for Economic Co-operation and Development seems quite upbeat about the provision of ADR in member countries. In a recent report it is stated that:

> A common theme . . . is the importance Member countries attach to informal ADR. In the majority of countries, policy initiatives recognising the potential benefits of ADR have been developed. These initiatives aim at increasing the availability of effective, timely and cheap mechanisms as an alternative to formal court-based dispute resolution.[182]

However, there appears to be a gulf between the rhetoric and the reality. A recent report in the United Kingdom suggested that there is a significant gap between the promotion of ADR at the level of governmental policy and the day-to-day reality of consumer access to effective ADR mechanisms.[183]

One potential response to the weaknesses of ADR in the cross-border consumer context is a call for regulation at the international level. There are some commentators who advocate international cooperation—with the aim of there being a new international convention on the enforcement of ODR awards (whether in the form of arbitral awards or negotiated/ mediated settlements).[184] While calls for such developments are not intrinsically unreasonable and it is tempting to see international conventions as the solution to cross-border problems, there is a fundamental practical problem behind any proposed solution which is premised on consumers initiating court proceedings to enforce their rights. As has been seen in earlier chapters, in the vast majority of cases, private litigation is ill-suited to the resolution of cross-border consumer disputes. Unless backed by appropriate enforcement mechanisms—that is, enforcement mechanisms which do not depend upon consumers being expected to commence litigation to secure their rights—legal regulation is very unlikely to achieve its objective. Accordingly, a solution to enforcement has to be found primarily in what might be termed 'soft law'. **11.75**

2. Realizable Goals

Notwithstanding efforts to promote ADR, achievements to date are relatively modest. At the European level, there is too much fragmentation and too little coordination; there is no coherent, Community-wide strategy for establishing effective dispute-resolution procedures so that consumers **11.76**

182 Organisation for Economic Co-operation and Development (July 2002: 4).
183 M Doyle, K Ritters, and S Brooker (January 2004: 1).
184 See, eg, LM Ponte (2002); V Heiskanen (1999).

have access to a forum through which they can obtain redress for their legitimate grievances.[185] Although there have been repeated calls for governments to make a coordinated response to the ongoing access-to-justice issues in the ADR context[186] and an interest has been expressed at the international level (through the Organisation for Economic Co-operation and Development) of 'promoting fair and effective ODR as a way to resolve small value B2C disputes, particularly cross-border disputes',[187] there is no effective international strategy for ODR procedures, no common standards, and no overarching framework.[188]

11.77 There are two competing pressures. On the one hand, there is a view that it would not be beneficial to attempt to impose a centralized model of ADR for consumer disputes. According to the European Commission, 'a "one size fits all" approach will not be appropriate to encouraging diverse, innovative, flexible and effective ADR solutions for consumer disputes'.[189] Even in terms of ADR schemes for the resolution of disputes arising out of cross-border consumer contracts there seems to be general agreement that 'a distributed architecture' (rather than a centralized approach) is the preferred solution.[190]

11.78 On the other hand, a lack of coordination has led to excessive fragmentation, thereby creating a situation in which consumers (particularly those who are less able to look after their own interests) may be incapable of navigating their way through the labyrinthine complexities of the system (which comprises a myriad of publicly-organized and private industry-based extra-judicial systems). Although some measure of rationalization and simplification is needed so that ADR systems are more accessible and comprehensible, it seems clear that the creation of a unitary, global (or even regional) system of ADR provision is both undesirable and wholly unrealistic. Even if diverse countries with different legal traditions could agree on a common institutional framework, the creation of such a system would be a mammoth undertaking.

[185] L Gibson (1992: 411).

[186] See, eg, C Coteanu (2005: 91).

[187] C Coteanu (2005: 90).

[188] But, see the efforts of the American Bar Association Task Force on E-Commerce and Alternative Dispute Resolution. This taskforce started up a website (<http://law.washington.edu/aba-eadr>) in June 2002. After the publication of its final report in October 2002, the taskforce and its website were largely inactive—though the website was not finally closed until January 2007.

[189] European Commission, COM (2001) 161, p 5.

[190] M Wilikens, A Vahrenwald, and P Morris (April 2000: 15).

Nevertheless, in the consumer context, when a dispute arises out of a cross-border e-commerce transaction an EU-wide system of alternative dispute resolution is needed.[191] The highly fragmented nature of ADR systems across Europe is a serious obstacle to consumers seeking to take advantage of national ADR processes: 11.79

> To date, despite the initiatives taken by the Commission in the last few years, consumers do in practice NOT have the possibility to pursue a cross-border complaint through ADR systems. Where national ADR bodies exist, they are not equipped to deal with complaints from foreign consumers and consumers themselves often would not be able to pursue their rights without institutionalised assistance.[192]

In order for ADR systems to provide a real solution to access-to-justice problems in the cross-border context, there has to be as near universal coverage as possible. If the objective is to produce a framework of ADR systems which has comprehensive coverage of consumer transactions, there are four strands which need to be pursued.

A European Trustmark

The aim of a trustmark system is to improve the standards of suppliers, to encourage them to comply with the law (or even provide a level of consumer protection which goes further than the law requires[193]), to avoid the occurrence of disputes and, if disputes arise, to provide a quick and cheap way of resolving them. Although hard empirical data is thin on the ground, there are good reasons for thinking that a code of practice, with sanctions for non-compliance, is more likely than any other dispute-resolution model both to prevent consumer complaints escalating into serious disputes and, when disputes do arise, to secure effective redress for consumers. 11.80

However, the existence of a multiplicity of trustmarks (and a lack of international harmonization) poses major problems. Unless there is a major input of effort and resources, it seems unlikely that, for the immediate future, trustmark schemes will be a significant feature of Internet shopping.[194] Although some have suggested that there is no pressing need for a Community-wide scheme,[195] as far back as 2002, the European 11.81

[191] European Consumer Law Group (December 2000: 17).

[192] European Consumer Law Group (December 2000: 17).

[193] In fact, the codes of practice of most trustmark schemes in Europe are based on EU legislation and do not provide a level of consumer protection significantly above that legislation: J Trzaskowski (2006: 47).

[194] Office of Fair Trading (June 2007: 155).

[195] A Vahrenwald (May 2000b: 17).

Commission suggested that '[c]onsideration might be given to the possibility for the various actors in ADR of preparing common codes of conduct applying on the regional or global levels and offering a number of procedural guarantees in ADR schemes'[196] and there seems to be an emerging consensus that '[t]here is a need for a symbol which stands for safe and reliable shopping which is recognisable internationally so that consumers can shop with confidence both in their own countries and internationally.'[197] On the one hand, agreement on a global scale would be extremely difficult to achieve; on the other, notwithstanding the failure of the European *WebTrader* project, the establishment of a Europe-wide trustmark scheme really should not be beyond the capabilities of the European Union. To enhance consumer confidence in Europe—and to provide an effective mechanism for the resolution of cross-border disputes—one of the first objectives should be the creation of a pan-European trustmark scheme for e-commerce. Given that there is already a range of trustmarks throughout Europe, the most plausible way forward would be though a European-level scheme for the accreditation of 'national' trustmarks—something along the lines of the *Euro-Label* scheme.

11.82 How can one ensure that a sufficient number of suppliers subscribe to the scheme? There are some contexts in which participation in a code of practice is compulsory. For example, as regards regulated economic activities which require a licence, membership of a professional body, or some other form of registration, it is relatively easy to impose a code of practice. So, a person cannot practice as a solicitor without being bound by the solicitors' code of conduct;[198] businesses which provide financial services are bound by the FSA Handbook and come under the jurisdiction of the Financial Ombudsman Scheme. However, this type of arrangement cannot be replicated in other economic areas (such as e-commerce in general) without the imposition of an unacceptable level of red tape. Given that, currently, among European business organizations 'the level of knowledge of and enthusiasm about trustmark schemes for online shops seems low',[199] the establishment of a truly effective European trustmark scheme would be a major undertaking. It seems that the only way in which such a scheme could take off is if it were thoroughly promoted through advertising and a vigorous public information campaign—directed both at e-traders and consumers. Even measures of this type are not going to produce overnight success; for this type of project, a long-term view is needed.

[196] COM (2002) 196, p 24.

[197] Consumers International (September 2001: 11).

[198] See <http://www.sra.org.uk/code-of-conduct.page> [3/8/07].

[199] R de Bruin, E Keuleers, C Lazaro, Y Poullet, and M Viersma (February 2005: 6).

As regards disputes arising from a contract between a consumer and a supplier who subscribes to a code of practice, one would normally expect either that the dispute would be settled (with or without the assistance of the code owner) or that any decision taken by a third party in the context of the designated ADR scheme would be complied with voluntarily. However, it is possible to go further and effectively guarantee that any award in the consumer's favour will be honoured; in cases where a supplier blatantly fails to comply with the code of practice to which it subscribes, there is a case for saying that, at the very least, the dissatisfied consumer should be protected by a money-back guarantee.[200] This could be achieved in one of a number of ways: for example, by the code owner taking out insurance against non-compliance by subscribers; alternatively, the code of practice could require subscribers to deposit a certain sum with the code owner and any awards in favour of consumers could be satisfied from this deposit. **11.83**

Ultimately, a European trustmark scheme could be made self-financing—by subscriptions paid by e-traders to the code owners; but in the short- to medium-term the costs of promoting such a scheme are high. It has been plausibly estimated that the minimum cost per year for an e-commerce trustmark scheme covering all the member states would be €26 million.[201] To put this figure into some sort of context: in recent years, the total amount which the European Commission has had available annually for spending on consumer policy is less than €20 million.[202] So, whatever advantages would flow from a Europe-wide trustmark scheme, such a scheme will not have a realistic chance of survival unless and until a viable business model can be found.[203] It is difficult to see how the start-up costs of a coordinated European trustmark can be borne other than by the governments of the EU member states. If governments are not willing to assume this burden, there is little likelihood that any new initiative to establish a European trustmark will fare any better than the failed *WebTrader* scheme and the underdeveloped *Euro-Label* scheme. **11.84**

A European Network of ADR Bodies

To date, many governments have tended to prefer to rely on industry self-regulation, particularly in the field of e-commerce.[204] So, even though the **11.85**

200 A Endeshaw (2001: 225).
201 T Wagemans in ECC (Denmark) (November 2006: 16).
202 D Mair in ECC (Denmark) (November 2006: 8–9).
203 T Wagemans in ECC (Denmark) (November 2006: 17).
204 See Y Zhao (2003: 49–51).

E-Commerce Directive[205] provides that member states must 'ensure that their legal system permits the use of ADR mechanisms by electronic means',[206] national governments have not been required to put in place institutional solutions for the resolution of e-commerce disputes. Similarly, the proposal for a new Timeshare Directive provides only that 'Member States shall *encourage* the setting up or development of adequate and effective out-of-court complaints and redress procedures for the settlement of consumer disputes under this Directive'.[207] Presumably, reliance on self-regulation is partly motivated by questions of funding; the cost of an industry-based regulatory framework does not impose a burden on the public purse.

11.86 It has been seen that one of the problems with this approach is that the coverage of industry-promoted codes of practice and trustmark schemes is far from comprehensive:

> Often those who cause the most problems for consumers do not choose to join [a trustmark scheme]; sometimes respectable businesses also choose not to join, knowing that their reputation does not need the boost of adherence to what may be a half-baked scheme. Where membership is voluntary, a business which does not want to adhere to the code can simply resign membership.[208]

This problem is particularly evident in the field of e-commerce; as things currently stand, only a small proportion of e-traders are members of a trustmark scheme. Even if it is assumed that a successful pan-European scheme for e-commerce can be established, there will continue to be a need for ADR to deal with disputes arising out of offline and online transactions which are not covered by an appropriate code of practice.

11.87 In situations where litigation is not a realistic option, if there is no suitable ADR mechanism, a supplier can effectively enrich itself at the expense of the consumer. The importance of easily accessible and inexpensive ADR mechanisms is illustrated by ECC-Net's report on airline complaints. Because ADR for such disputes is not available in many member states:

> some air carriers adopt a cynical approach to complaint handling, especially with the cross-border consumer, because they suspect that the consumer won't ultimately take legal action against them. The resources required in time, effort and finance when taking legal action against big companies are not commensurate with the amount that passengers might receive.[209]

[205] Dir 2000/31/EC [2000] OJ L178/1. See recital 51 and art 17. See also the policy statements cited by A Vahrenwald (May 2000: 20).

[206] European Commission, COM (2002) 196, p 19 (para 43).

[207] European Commission, COM (2007) 303 (art 10(2)) (emphasis added).

[208] European Consumer Law Group (March 2001: 12).

[209] ECC-Net (October 2006: 32).

To overcome this type of problem, each legal system would need to provide adequate ADR mechanisms for dealing with disputes arising out of consumer transactions. One of the weaknesses of the European Union's strategy is that, while it has sought to promote ADR, it has done nothing to *require* member states to establish an effective institutional framework which covers the whole range of consumer transactions. **11.88**

As a consequence, there continue to be many gaps in the availability of ADR mechanisms for the resolution of consumer disputes and, as regards the mechanisms that do exist, much more could be done to make consumers aware of them. In a recent survey of European consumers, nearly four-tenths of the sample indicated that they had not even heard of ADR bodies. There were, however, very considerable national variations: at one end of the scale 90 per cent of Finnish consumers knew about ADR bodies (which is hardly surprising given the well-established system of consumer complaints boards in the Nordic countries); at the other extreme, only a quarter of Greek consumers were aware of bodies providing out-of-court dispute-resolution services.[210] **11.89**

In its report on the E-Commerce Directive the Economic and Social Committee recommended the rapid establishment of a cross-border network of consumer protection agencies or ombudsmen to act as conduits and possibly arbitrators in the event of disputes between consumers in one country and e-traders based in another.[211] As has been seen, by setting up ECC-Net, which can assist consumers in cross-border cases and direct consumers to appropriate ADR bodies, the European Commission has attempted to deal with some of the problems that result from the fact that many informal dispute-resolution mechanisms are premised on consumer contracts being domestic, rather than international. However, whether ECC-Net provides a sufficiently broad institutional solution is doubtful. As things currently stand, the availability of ADR for the resolution of consumer disputes remains extremely patchy.[212] **11.90**

An obvious solution to the patchiness of ADR provision would be to establish 'a general ADR scheme as a fall back position'.[213] There is a need for 'an ADR scheme with general competence and guaranteed geographical coverage' as a complement to sector-specific mediation and arbitration schemes: 'Such a "fall back" scheme can plug gaps in ADR provision and **11.91**

[210] Eurobarometer (October 2004: 13).

[211] European Economic and Social Committee, [1999] OJ C169/36 (para 3.6.4).

[212] This patchiness of the provision of ADR services is a feature not only of the legal systems of EU member states: Organisation for Economic Co-operation and Development (2006: 6).

[213] Study Centre for Consumer Law (January 2007: 33).

at the same time it does not interfere with the need to ensure flexibility.'[214] To make ADR a reality for cases not governed by an online trustmark scheme or another sector-specific ADR scheme, national ADR bodies need to have either *de jure* or *de facto* compulsory jurisdiction (such as the Financial Services Ombudsman scheme in the United Kingdom)—otherwise there is no reason why a supplier should participate in the ADR process or comply with the outcome of that process.[215] There are, however, potential problems. For example, if an ADR mechanism is compulsory, its compliance with article 6 of the ECHR becomes an important issue. Not all ADR schemes will automatically comply with the requirement that the tribunal should be 'independent and impartial'.[216] These difficulties are not insuperable, but any 'fall back' ADR scheme would need to address them.[217]

11.92 There is a good argument for saying that, although member states have different legal and cultural traditions, they should be required to ensure that appropriate ADR service providers are available for the resolution of any dispute arising out of a cross-border consumer contract. As there is no need for each member state to adopt the same institutional solution, this is the type of issue that could be addressed by a European directive.

11.93 The point is not that it is anticipated that a large number of complaints arising from cross-border consumer contracts would be referred to ADR bodies; rather it is that, if ADR mechanisms exist, suppliers have more incentive to respond reasonably to legitimate consumer complaints: 'the mere presence of [ADR] procedures may motivate the prevention of problems'.[218] However, whether a system of ADR can be made fully effective without some measure of compulsion is doubtful. In order to encourage suppliers either to participate in the ADR process or to comply with a decision in the consumer's favour (or a settlement agreement) which results from such a process, it would be possible to establish a system of sanctions to be imposed on recalcitrant businesses. Although this scheme may sound bureaucratic (and potentially expensive), it would not be as difficult to implement as it may appear at first glance. There are two

[214] Study Centre for Consumer Law (January 2007: 160).

[215] See, eg, the evidence of ECC (Dublin) (April 2004). See also the views of the Timeshare Consumers' Association, which considers that '[i]f ADR is to work in the timeshare industry in Europe then it needs to be "imposed" as it will never happen voluntarily': M Doyle, K Ritters, and S Brooker (January 2004: 47).

[216] It has even been questioned whether the Financial Ombudsman Service complies with art 6 ECHR: Study Centre for Consumer Law (January 2007: 124).

[217] See Study Centre for Consumer Law (January 2007: 34).

[218] European Commission, COM (2001) 161, p 3.

institutions which already have a role to play in the field of consumer redress which, if properly resourced, should be able take on this task.

First, it is reasonable to attempt to channel all cross-border disputes arising from a b2c contract through the relevant ECCs. In cases where the consumer deals with one or more of the ECCs, these bodies would be aware whether or not a dispute had reached a satisfactory conclusion. So, the ECCs in each member state would be able to gather data about which local suppliers were not complying with appropriate standards in the field of dispute-resolution and consumer redress. **11.94**

Secondly, each member state also has 'qualified entities' (under the Injunctions Directive[219]) authorized to take legal action (if necessary) to require compliance by suppliers with EU consumer legislation. It would not be difficult to formulate a set of standards in the field of dispute resolution with which suppliers are expected to comply (participation in the relevant ADR process invoked by a consumer and compliance with the outcome of that process, be it an arbitral award or a negotiated settlement) and to add these standards to the list of matters in relation to which qualified entities may take remedial action against suppliers who fall short of the required standards. **11.95**

The ECCs would be in a good position to collect the necessary information about non-complying businesses and to pass it on to the relevant qualified entities which could then take appropriate action either to encourage compliance or, in appropriate cases, to take legal action with a view to the imposition of sanctions for non-compliance (such as the levying of administrative fines). Within such a system, qualified entities would not need to initiate litigation very often. The whole structure of the Injunctions Directive—and its implementation in the United Kingdom—is for enforcement actions to be initiated as a last resort. The possibility of such litigation would, it might be supposed, provide sufficient incentive for legitimate businesses to adopt appropriate dispute-resolution practices and to cooperate in cases where their non-compliance with the applicable dispute-resolution standards had been referred to the qualified entity. One of the advantages of using the framework established by the Injunctions Directive is that national qualified entities are entitled to initiate enforcement proceedings in relation to not only suppliers in their own country, but also those established in other member states. So, in a case involving an English consumer and an Irish supplier, if the Irish supplier failed to participate in the ADR process stipulated by the Irish legal system or to **11.96**

[219] Dir 98/27/EC [1998] OJ L166/51. See ch 8.

comply with an award in the consumer's favour, the Office of Fair Trading, as the United Kingdom's principal qualified entity, would be able to take appropriate remedial action. Furthermore, the CPC Regulation[220] provides a framework through which the Office of Fair Trading could call upon the relevant Irish qualified entity to take action.

11.97 This type of system would have another advantage. As it would apply only in cases where the supplier does not subscribe to a certified trustmark scheme or other code of practice, it would be an inducement for suppliers to subscribe to such schemes. In this way, the pressure on the 'fall back' ADR system—and the burden imposed on ECC-Net and national qualified entities which would be largely responsible for enforcing the system—would be lessened.

11.98 To be successful, such a scheme would require a measure of public investment (in addition to a funding mechanism which would enable the bulk of the costs to be covered by private funds—in particular a levy on businesses). Although the European Commission has stated that 'ADR is a political priority, repeatedly declared by the European Union institutions, whose task it is to promote these alternative techniques',[221] the EU institutions have yet to put their money where their mouth is. If an effective and comprehensive ADR system for consumer complaints really is a political priority, its realization requires not only a clear, coherent, and coordinated plan but also an appropriate level of funding to turn the plan into reality. To date, policy initiatives have been both too disparate and too half-hearted. The preceding paragraphs suggest a potential model, which is coherent and, because it builds on existing institutions, is not excessively utopian or unrealizable.

Promotion; Consumer Education

11.99 The long-term objective of an e-commerce trustmark scheme must be the attainment of the kind of coverage and effectiveness of the *ABTA* scheme in the United Kingdom. Business conducted by travel agents which are members of *ABTA* accounts for 90 per cent of the UK package holiday market;[222] as a result, consumers expect a UK travel agent to be a member of *ABTA* (and may be wary of dealing with a travel agent which is not a member).[223] It is possible to imagine a situation in which,

[220] See ch 8.

[221] COM (2002) 196, p 5.

[222] M Doyle, K Ritters, and S Brooker (January 2004: 48).

[223] Whereas fewer than 10 per cent of consumers recognize the *SafeBuy* logo, more than three-quarters of consumers recognize the *ABTA* logo: Office of Fair Trading (June 2007: 92).

for economic reasons, any supplier which trades online needs to be part of an effective trustmark scheme. If there are clear advantages to consumers when they transact with e-traders which are members of such a scheme (rather than suppliers who are not) and, if those advantages are widely known to and understood by consumers, it is possible that, over time, e-traders which remain outside the scope of the scheme will suffer loss of business to such an extent that membership of the trustmark scheme will become an economic imperative. For such a scheme to be able to evolve, public awareness of the scheme and a real appreciation of the benefits of the scheme needs to be raised to a level such that consumers expect e-traders (in Europe) to subscribe to the scheme and avoid making purchases from e-traders who do not do so. But, raising public awareness is not easy—and cannot be done on the cheap; it is not enough simply to set up a website and hope that consumers will visit it and inform themselves of the relevant issues. The European Commission acknowledges that raising consumer awareness is an important aspect of any consumer strategy. Part of the Commission's strategy for the period 2007–13 is to assist in the education of consumers: 'In particular the European Consumer Centre network should develop further as the EU's interface with consumers.'[224]

The enormity of the task needs to be understood—as well as the very **11.100** low baseline from which any strategy for consumer education would be starting. Although the European Commission tends to be optimistic in how it describes its various initiatives in the field of consumer protection and likes to suggest that it is making a lot of progress, it is worth noting that most European consumers are completely unaware of the Commission's efforts. In a recent Europe-wide survey, 69 per cent of the sample taken from the (then) 25 EU member states said they had not heard of *any* of the services provided by the EU to help consumers.[225] An effective network of ADR mechanisms for the resolution of disputes arising from b2c contracts requires not only that there is an appropriate institutional framework, but also that consumers are sufficiently educated about the channels of redress which are available to them and how to make the most of them. In many ways, the major challenge is to find a way of providing public information to consumers about how to set about seeking redress in cases where something has gone wrong. The fact that advice agencies (such as ECC-Net) exist and operate a website is not enough;

[224] European Commission, COM (2007) 99, p 8.

[225] Eurobarometer (September 2006: 72). In the United Kingdom, consumers appear to be even less well informed: 77 per cent said that they were wholly unaware of the European Union's services in the field of consumer protection.

a much more proactive strategy is needed for there to be any chance of public awareness being significantly increased.

International Cooperation

11.101 Even if the three strands discussed in the preceding sections were pursued successfully, this would deal only with one part of the cross-border dimension. Cooperation at the European level can only tackle problems within the European Union; it cannot address the difficulties which European consumers may face when buying goods from e-traders based in non-European counties, particularly the United States.

11.102 If real solutions can be found to European issues, the broader international dimension can, to a certain extent, be left to look after itself. If, for example, there were established an effective trustmark system in Europe and European consumers were properly educated as to the significance of a trustmark logo and the advantages it provides in cases where problems arise, one might reasonably hope that European consumers would take the trouble to look for a reliable trustmark when dealing with e-traders from outside Europe and check that the applicable code of practice provides a satisfactory level of consumer protection.

11.103 At the global level, there is an organization known as the Global Trustmark Alliance (GTA), whose organizing committee was launched in November 2004. The members of the GTA are national trustmark organizations:

> Once fully operational, participating businesses in these member trustmark organizations will agree to abide by an international code of conduct for cross-border transactions, to participate in out-of-court dispute resolution procedures based on code standards, and to display an international seal on their website signaling their participation in the GTA.[226]

If the state of the GTA website is a fair indication of the organization's level of activity, one should probably not hold out too much hope for major achievements to come from this quarter. The website has only recently stopped being described as a 'demonstration site'; there have been only two press releases since the launch of the organizing committee in 2004; one of the organizations listed as a member of this committee (*TrustUK*), no longer exists, having closed in April 2007. According to the Office of Fair Trading, the GTA has 'made little recent progress'.[227]

226 See <http://www.globaltrustmarkalliance.org> [26/3/08].

227 Office of Fair Trading (June 2007: 154).

To a significant extent, the potential problems arising from consumer e-contracts would be dealt with quite satisfactorily if, in each of the European and US e-commerce markets, a single trustmark were to become dominant in that market and to achieve brand recognition. In such an environment, it should not be too difficult to establish a degree of harmonization between the European and US code owners, so that consumers who dealt with certified e-traders based either in the European Union or in the United States would know that the code of practice would ensure that the e-trader complied with certain standards and that, in the event of a dispute arising out of a cross-border online contract, there would be a good chance that the dispute would be resolved in a satisfactory way. **11.104**

This picture is, admittedly, somewhat optimistic. However, it is not obvious that, with concerted and coordinated effort, it is unattainable. If the political will were there—and governments decided to devote appropriate funds to enable this vision to be turned into reality—there is no reason why progress should not be made. To date, there is little evidence that the creation of an effective ADR system for e-commerce has really been, in political terms, a high priority. It also seems that, to the extent that governments want something to be achieved in this area, they want someone else to achieve it and, more significantly, someone else to pay for it. Until this changes it is unlikely that the embryonic (and highly fragmented and complex) system that currently exists will develop into a fully-functioning and effective system of self-regulation. **11.105**

V. CONCLUSION

It is widely acknowledged that as regards ADR and redress, 'much work needs to be done to turn the theory into reality'.[228] A recent report notes that 'a number of surveys . . . indicate that ADR has not yet fulfilled its potential as a low cost and efficient mechanism for the resolution of business to consumer disputes'.[229] For the vast majority of disputes arising from consumer contracts, the solution offered by appropriate ADR mechanisms is more promising than private litigation. Even a less-than-perfect ADR scheme is likely to be better than a court-based process which, in practical terms, is entirely beyond the consumer's reach. **11.106**

Self-regulation can go part of the way towards providing an answer to questions of consumer redress. However, self-regulation can only be truly **11.107**

[228] Consumers International (September 2001: 11).

[229] Organisation for Economic Co-operation and Development (2006: 23).

seen as a mechanism for the vindication of consumer rights if: (i) it is either a legal or a practical necessity for suppliers to subscribe to an appropriate code of practice and (ii) the code of practice is fully effective. Some of the key elements in the establishment of an effective ADR system are already in place—albeit in embryonic form. For example, through the principles set out in the European Commission's Recommendations,[230] work has been undertaken on the development of international standards for alternative dispute resolution. Within member states there are bodies (such as the Office of Fair Trading) which play a role in providing third-party accreditation (and oversight) of codes of practice and trustmarks. What is needed is focused international effort—either at the regional or global level—to develop these elements into a truly effective international system. Nevertheless, under current conditions, self-regulation cannot deliver a comprehensive system of redress—and it is difficult to see how it could ever do so. One has to recognize that a functioning trustmark scheme can never directly address the problems of rogue traders (who would not voluntarily subscribe to any scheme); as regards rogue traders, the most one can hope for is that a widely recognized trustmark may help to marginalize them.[231] Because of the inherent limitations of self-regulation, if consumer access to justice is to be taken seriously, there is effectively no alternative to a 'fall back' ADR system which can pick up those problems which fall through the (loose) net of embedded ADR schemes. There remains, however, the question whether the development of ADR solutions to cross-border consumer disputes is a sufficiently high priority for governments (at national and European levels) to be prepared to spend public money so that effective ADR mechanisms can be established. There is also the question whether the public at large wants tax revenue to be diverted to issues relating to consumer redress from other policy areas.

11.108 Although, as has been seen, the European Union has taken some steps to facilitate ADR in Europe—for example, through ECC-Net—it seems that too much of the European Commission's efforts have been directed at trying to reform the private litigation model in the (largely forlorn) hope that it might deal more effectively with cross-border small claims and insufficient attention has been given to promoting effective ADR within the European Union. However worthy attempts to reform small claims procedures may be, such reforms are unlikely to bring about changes other than at the margins. A widely known trustmark scheme operating throughout the European Union and a 'fall back' ADR system would have a more

[230] See paras 10.08–10.14.

[231] Office of Fair Trading (June 2006: 89).

positive impact on both consumer confidence (particularly in the context of cross-border Internet shopping) and the satisfactory resolution of consumer disputes than any amount of tinkering with private international law rules or small claims procedures. The efforts which have been directed at legislative developments (such as the European Small Claims Procedure Regulation) might have been much more profitably directed at promoting and establishing a fully effective ADR framework for consumer disputes (in particular, those arising out of e-commerce).

It has to be conceded that the channelling of consumer disputes into ADR **11.109** mechanisms involves some degree of compromise. Justice available through ADR may, in practice, be a form of 'rough justice';[232] it may, for example, not be realistic to expect ADR decision-makers to apply accurately the choice-of-law rules set out in the Rome Convention or the Rome I Regulation or the substantive laws of foreign countries in cases where the choice-of-law rules point to a law other than the *lex fori* as the applicable law. However, criticisms directed at ADR on the basis that ADR does not guarantee that its outcomes are always legally accurate seem to be premised on the idea that there is a meaningful choice between, on the one hand, an ADR outcome which (potentially) gives the consumer less than he is legally entitled to and, on the other, the full vindication of the consumer's contractual rights through a court judgment which is legally unimpeachable. Such a premise is totally false; in the real world, even if one puts aside the possibility that court-based small claims procedures may not be legally reliable in every case, the choice may well be between a (potentially) inaccurate ADR decision and nothing. Without suggesting that one should turn a blind eye to situations in which ADR processes fail to uphold high standards of procedural and substantive justice, there is nevertheless a good case for saying that half a loaf really is better than no bread. Or to put it another way: 'Imperfect justice for A is better than no justice for A at all.'[233]

[232] Of course, the same criticism may be levelled at court-based small claims procedures: see J Baldwin (1997).

[233] AJ Duggan (2003: 51).

12

Consumers' Substantive Rights and Choice of Law

I. BACKGROUND

One of the objectives of consumer law is to find an appropriate balance **12.01** between the rights of consumers and suppliers. The superior economic power of suppliers means that consumer contracts are invariably contracts of adhesion which are offered to consumers on a 'take it or leave it' basis. Such contracts are, obviously, drafted to reflect the interests of suppliers and can impose contractual terms which favour the supplier and fail to give effect to consumers' reasonable expectations; for example, through the use of contractual exclusion clauses and the like, consumer contracts may be drafted in a way that takes advantage of the consumer's weak position and seeks to limit or exclude the supplier's liability in the event of the supplier failing to perform the contract in the way that the consumer would reasonably anticipate. Accordingly, for several decades, it has been recognized that, in the consumer context, it is wholly inappropriate to allow full rein to freedom of contract. Because individual consumers are unable to bargain over the terms of contracts into which they enter, the law has had to intervene—to outlaw certain types of contractual practice and to confer various substantive rights on consumers.

12.02 In recent decades there have been various legislative initiatives—both at national and European levels—with the objective of creating a fair balance of rights and obligations between suppliers and consumers. One of the earliest efforts in England to restrict the use by suppliers of exclusion clauses was the Unfair Contract Terms Act 1977. Since the United Kingdom's accession to the European Community, there has been a succession of directives in the field of consumer protection.[1] Each of these directives has had to be translated into domestic law either by primary or secondary legislation.

12.03 The level of protection provided by EC law (as implemented into national law) is different from the level of protection offered by the law of non-member states. Accordingly, in terms of legal theory, where an English consumer purchases goods from a Californian supplier, the extent of the consumer's contractual rights may well turn on whether the contract is governed by English law, Californian law, or the law of some other country. Similar issues may arise within the European Community. Although, as regards issues which are significant to consumers (such as guarantees, price information, and cooling-off periods) there is a high degree of harmonization,

[1] See, eg, Dir 85/577/EEC to protect the consumer in respect of contracts negotiated away from business premises [1985] OJ L372/31; Dir 90/314/EEC on package travel, package holidays, and package tours [1990] OJ L158/59; Dir 93/13/EEC on unfair terms in consumer contracts [1993] OJ L95/29; Dir 94/47/EC on the protection of purchasers . . . of a right to use immovable properties on a timeshare basis [1994] OJ L280/83; Dir 97/7/EC on the protection of consumers in respect of distance contracts [1997] OJ L144/19; Dir 98/6/EC on consumer protection in the indication of the prices of products offered to consumers [1998] OJ L80/27; Dir 98/27/EC on injunctions for the protection of consumer interests [1998] OJ L166/51; and Dir 1999/44/EC on certain aspects of the sale of consumer goods and associated guarantees [1999] OJ L171/12.

uniformity has not been attained. Even though all member states are required to implement directives into national law, most of the directives in the field of consumer protection have been 'minimum harmonization' measures. That is to say, the directive lays down the minimum level of protection which national law must attain, but each member state is free to lay down a more extensive level of protection if it so wishes. This can clearly be seen in relation to the implementation of the Distance Selling Directive[2] (which applies to purchases made by mail order, by telephone, or via the Internet). The Directive lays down a minimum cooling-off period (of seven days) in which the consumer can withdraw from the contract, but national legislation of the member states varies considerably because the Directive gives member states the freedom to enact more stringent rules which provide a higher level of consumer protection under their national law.[3] Whereas several member states (including the United Kingdom) have adopted a cooling-off period of seven working days, there are other member states which have set the period at eight, 10, 14, or 15 days.

So, even in an area where there is quite a high measure of harmonization, **12.04** the precise nature and extent of the contractual rights enjoyed by a European consumer may depend on whether the contract is governed by the law of one member state, rather than another. Where, for example, an English consumer makes an Internet purchase from a German supplier, if English law applies, the consumer enjoys a cooling-off period of seven working days, whereas if German law is the governing law, the consumer has two weeks in which to change his mind and to withdraw from the contract.

Within the European Community, the rules for determining the law appli- **12.05** cable to an international contract are to be found in the Rome Convention on the law applicable to contractual obligations of 1980[4] and the Rome I Regulation.[5] The Rome Convention applies not only to contracts concluded prior to the commencement of the Rome I Regulation—that is,

[2] Dir 97/7/EC [1997] OJ L144/19. For detailed consideration of how the Directive has been transposed into the national laws of the various member states, see European Commission, COM (2006) 514.

[3] See European Commission, COM (2006) 514, p 19; ECC-Net (May 2003: 31); Euroconsumer (December 2005: 14).

[4] Implemented in the United Kingdom by the Contracts (Applicable Law) Act 1991.

[5] See Reg (EC) No 593/2008 [2008] OJ L177/6. For further discussion of the background to the European choice-of-law regime, see para 1.93.

17 December 2009[6]—but also, in any member state which is not bound by the Regulation, to contracts concluded after that date.[7]

II. INTRODUCTION TO CHOICE-OF-LAW RULES

1. Approaches to Choice of Law

12.06 Just as in relation to jurisdiction issues, there is a basic question in the field of choice of law: pro-consumer or pro-supplier? Arguments over what the appropriate approach to choice of law should be in the consumer context have tended to focus on distance contracts (in particular, online consumer contracts).[8] On the one hand, it has been argued that, because consumers are unwilling to enter into online transactions with 'unknown' suppliers (even if such suppliers offer the same or substantially similar goods more cheaply than better-known suppliers), it makes sense in economic terms to have a choice-of-law regime which favours consumers over suppliers—at least in the online situation.[9] The basic premise appears to be that choice-of-law rules which seek to guarantee levels of consumer protection can have a beneficial role in enhancing trust in online transactions. The factual assumptions on which this premise is based are, however, questionable. There is a lot of evidence to suggest that consumers are not well informed about legal questions in general.[10] In view of the fact that, until formally introduced to private international law, most law students are not normally aware of choice-of-law questions or their implications, it seems inherently unlikely that the purchasing decisions of the public at large are influenced in any way by questions such as whether a contract with a foreign supplier is governed by the law of the country in which the consumer is habitually resident or the law of another country. This is not to

[6] See art 28.

[7] Denmark is not bound by the Regulation and, at the time of writing, the UK government had not decided to participate in the adoption of the Regulation. On the question of whether the UK government will change its mind and opt in, see para 1.93. It seems likely that, by the time the Regulation starts being applicable in other member states, the UK government will have decided to opt in.

[8] It seems to be accepted that, as regards in-person cross-border shopping, the chosen law or, in the absence of choice, the supplier's law should be the applicable law. See paras 12.18–12.21.

[9] See EA O'Hara (2005).

[10] See, eg, National Consumer Council (September 1979: 13–16); M Cappelletti and B Garth (1978: 68). Note also the view of the Public Legal Education and Support Task Force that, among the public at large, there is an 'extraordinary lack of understanding' of legal issues: PLEAS Task Force (July 2007: 7).

deny that many consumers feel less confident about buying goods or services from suppliers established in other countries.[11] There is, however, no evidence to suggest that choice-of-law issues play a significant role in that equation.

On the other hand, there is an argument that, in order to promote e-commerce and to avoid imposing excessive burdens on e-traders, contracts concluded online ought to be governed by the law of the country in which the e-trader's place of business is located. That is to say, a 'country-of-origin' approach should be applied to choice of law for e-contracts. It has been suggested that, if this approach is not adopted, economic operators will refuse to involve themselves in e-commerce and the potential macroeconomic benefits of the Internet will not be maximized. For example, it is argued that the legal risks which arise from uncertainties surrounding choice of law—and the possibility that online consumer contracts are governed by the law of the country in which the consumer is habitually resident (rather than the law of the country where the supplier is established)—can be prohibitive, particularly for small businesses which are aiming to establish an online presence.[12] In the European context, the argument is that, without a 'country-of-origin' approach to choice of law for e-contracts, competitive advantage will be conceded to the United States and the development of e-commerce in Europe will be impeded. **12.07**

Quite a lot of the literature discussing choice of law in the context of consumer contracts has a tendency to be extremely abstract. This is not only a consequence of the fact that the law reports do not contain any instances of choice-of-law problems arising out of consumer contracts; it is also the case that some discussions of the relevant principles appear to have little connection with anything that might plausibly take place in the real world. For example, it is unrealistic to approach choice of law in the consumer context on the assumption that consumers in general think very much about legal questions (including choice-of-law questions)—and might seek to find answers to them—before they enter into contracts with suppliers. So, while it is perfectly true that, before entering a contract with a foreign supplier, an average consumer would face severe difficulties in obtaining legal advice about levels of consumer protection available under the law of the country in which the supplier is established, there is an air of unreality surrounding any discussion which seeks to attach significance to this fact.[13] **12.08**

[11] See Eurobarometer (September 2006: 44).
[12] R Andrews (2005: 82).
[13] See, eg, Z Tang (2007a).

12.09 In the consumer context, the arguments between those who favour a pro-consumer approach and those who prefer a country-of-origin approach are, of course, premised on the notion that whether a consumer contract is governed by the law of country X or the law of country Y may have a significant bearing on the substantive rights of the parties to the contract. Whether, in practical terms, choice-of-law rules have much of a role to play in the consumer context is debatable. However, before an attempt is made to assess the practical importance (or lack of importance) of choice-of-law rules, the following sections consider different potential choice-of-law models and set out a brief account of the current framework for choice of law as regards consumer contracts.

2. Different Choice-of-law Models

12.10 In broad terms there are four different choice-of-law models which could be adopted (in various combinations) in the consumer context.[14] The first option is the principle of free choice; contracting parties could be allowed complete freedom to choose the governing law (with the law providing a default rule in cases where no choice is made). In practice, this would enable the supplier (who formulates the terms of the contract) to select the applicable law. Choice-of-law clauses are less widespread in consumer e-commerce than might be imagined; e-traders may decide that it is not good marketing policy to provide overly detailed terms and conditions[15] and websites which contain very little explicit information about contractual terms are very common. In a 1999 survey by *Consumers International* relating to international business websites it was found that only 10 per cent of sites visited mentioned the applicable law; where the applicable law was mentioned it was always the law of the e-trader's home country.[16] More recent research suggests that choice-of-law clauses may be becoming a less uncommon feature of online contracts—at least, in Europe. According to the findings of a worldwide survey conducted in 2001, around a quarter of the e-traders which conducted cross-border business included a choice-of-law clause in the website's terms and conditions.[17] This figure masks, however, significant regional variations: choice-of-law clauses were more frequently encountered in European websites (36 per cent) than in US websites (12 per cent). This finding is consistent with the survey conducted by ECC-Net in 2003, which indicated that 38 per cent of

[14] See Z Tang (2007a).
[15] J Dickie (1999: 87).
[16] See A Vahrenwald (May 2000a: 14).
[17] Consumers International (September 2001: 26).

European e-traders made use of choice-of-law clauses. In common with the earlier research, ECC-Net reported that, if there is a choice of law, the law of the e-trader's country is the preferred choice.[18]

Allowing the principle of party autonomy full rein in the consumer context opens up the possibility that suppliers will choose a law (perhaps wholly unconnected with the contractual situation) which provides the lowest possible level of consumer protection. Accordingly, there is a view that, as regards consumer contracts, a choice-of-law clause in standard terms and conditions should not be allowed.[19] Be that as it may, it appears that 'abusive' choices (of a law unconnected with the contract) do not occur very frequently; as already noted, if a website's terms and conditions contain a choice of law, the law of the e-trader's country is almost invariably the chosen law.[20] In practical terms, the free choice approach is, in most cases, the same as the second approach—the principle of limited choice, according to which there must be a reasonable connection between the chosen law and the contract. Nevertheless, where the supplier's law provides a lower level of protection than the consumer's law, giving full effect to a supplier's choice of law has the effect of reducing the level of consumer protection below that which consumers would have been entitled to expect. **12.11**

These problems with the first and second models, suggest a third option—the 'preferential law' approach according to which the parties are free to select the applicable law, but this choice cannot have the effect of reducing the level of consumer protection provided by the rules of the consumer's law that cannot be derogated from by contract (normally referred to as 'mandatory rules'). So, under the 'preferential law' approach, provisions of the chosen law are superseded by the mandatory rules of the consumer's law to the extent that those rules provide a higher level of protection than the chosen law. **12.12**

[18] ECC-Net (May 2003: 22).

[19] European Consumer Law Group (2000: 17).

[20] There are, however, instances of clauses which select a law which is wholly unconnected with the contract. A good example is provided by the *PlayUSA* website: <http://www.playusa.com>; the owner of this website is a company registered in Jersey. The website appears to be designed primarily for customers in the USA, although the site allows the consumer to choose between four different currencies (US$, Can$, €, £), which strongly suggests that the supplier also accepts orders through this website from consumers outside the USA (notwithstanding the fact that there is also a sister website <http://www.play.com>, which seems designed for European consumers—as it offers goods for sale either in € or £.) The *PlayUSA* website includes the following choice-of-law clause: 'These terms and conditions are subject to the laws . . . of the British Virgin Islands': <http://www.playusa.com/DVD/Region_1/ABOUT/4-/AboutUs.html?page=terms_conditions> [13/7/07].

12.13 The 'preferential law' approach, which provides consumers with the highest level of protection, can be supported in terms of principle as well as policy. As regards cases involving distance contracts, the consumer has not entered the international arena and would have a reasonable expectation of receiving the level of consumer protection provided by his own law.[21] Equally, the supplier has no grounds for complaint if the consumer has the benefit of a more generous level of protection provided by the chosen law—for the simple reason that the supplier has chosen this law to govern the contract.

12.14 Nevertheless, the 'preferential law' approach is open to a number of objections. First, it is more complicated than the other options—since, instead of applying a single law, it may require the blending of rules originating in two different legal systems: in cases where there is a choice of the supplier's law, the parties' legal rights and obligations are determined by a mixture of the chosen law and the (more protective) mandatory rules of the law of the country in which the consumer is habitually resident. Secondly, as the chosen law is superseded only by the mandatory rules of the law of the country in which the consumer is habitually resident, the 'preferential law' approach is premised on there being a clear dividing line between rules that cannot be derogated from by contract and other rules. Many commentators have drawn attention to the fact that this dividing line between mandatory rules and other rules is not always obvious in practice.[22] Thirdly, it may be difficult to determine whether the chosen law or the consumer's law provides a higher level of protection. In simple situations, there is little problem: for example, there can be no doubt that Maltese law, which provides a 15-day cooling-off period for distance contracts, offers more protection than English law, which lays down a period of seven working days. However, the position is more difficult where multi-faceted rules are involved. Which system of rules is the more protective where, on the one hand, the law of the country in which the consumer is habitually resident makes provision for a cooling-off period of seven days and requires the supplier to send the consumer an annulment form (which informs the consumer of the right of withdrawal and a simple mechanism for exercising that right) and, on the other, the chosen law stipulates a cooling-off period of 14 days, but provides only that information on the right of withdrawal must be given in a clear and intelligible manner?[23]

[21] Nevertheless, not all commentators consider that, where a consumer contract contains a choice-of-law clause in favour of the supplier's law, the chosen law should yield to the mandatory rules of the law of the consumer's habitual residence. See, eg, R Schu (1997: 228).

[22] See, eg, LE Gillies (2007: 98); C Riefa (2004: 68–9).

[23] This example is given by Z Tang (2007a: 125).

The final option is to deny the parties the right to choose the governing law. This 'no choice' approach starts from the notion that the purpose of the choice-of-law regime in the consumer context is not necessarily to achieve the highest level of consumer protection (which is one of the aims of the 'preferential law' approach), but to ensure that the consumer's legitimate expectations are not confounded. Accordingly, the 'no choice' approach provides for the application of the law of the country in which the consumer is habitually resident. According to this approach, the consumer's law would, of course, also apply in cases where the contract does not contain a choice of law. **12.15**

3. The General Approach of the European Choice-of-law Regime

With regard to protected consumer contracts, the Rome Convention of 1980 adopted the 'preferential law' approach.[24] However, the European Commission's original proposal for a Community instrument relating to choice of law for contractual obligations[25] (which ultimately evolved into the Rome I Regulation) advocated the 'no choice' approach: it was proposed that protected consumer contracts should be governed by the law of the consumer's habitual residence. The advantage of the 'no choice' approach is that it achieves a measure of simplicity; only one law is relevant (the consumer's law), rather than two (the chosen law and the mandatory rules of the consumer's law), thereby avoiding any complex interplay between them. Under the original proposal, the law of the country of the consumer's habitual residence would be applicable even if the contract contained a clause choosing a law which provided a greater degree of consumer protection than the consumer's law. However, this proposal was subject to criticism from various quarters[26] and, as will be seen, the final version of the Regulation followed the approach of Rome Convention, rather than the original proposal. **12.16**

It has already been noted that cross-border consumer contracts can be divided into two categories: (i) in-person purchases (where the consumer travels from the country of his habitual residence to another country and buys goods or services from a supplier established in that other country); and (ii) distance contracts (where a consumer purchases goods from a supplier who is established in a country other than that in which the consumer is resident and the contract is concluded via some form of **12.17**

[24] See art 5.
[25] COM (2005) 650.
[26] See, eg, O Lando and PA Nielsen (2007: 39–40).

long-distance communication, such as post, telephone, or the Internet). This distinction is relevant in the choice-of-law context as, in terms of the applicable law, these two types of situation are treated differently.

In-person Shopping

12.18 If a consumer resident in country X purchases goods or services while visiting country Y, the law governing the contract is normally determined by the choice-of-law rules which apply to contracts in general (rather than by the choice-of-law rules which apply to protected consumer contracts). The application of these rules has the result that, in the vast majority of cases, the applicable law is the law of country Y. There are four points to consider.

12.19 First, since the terms of the contract are determined by the supplier, any choice-of-law clause in the contract will almost invariably select the law of the country in which the supplier is established. Such an express choice of law is valid under both the Rome Convention and the Rome I Regulation.[27] Secondly, if the contract does not include a choice of law, the supplier's law will apply. Under the Rome Convention, article 4(2) presumes that a contract is most closely connected with the country in which the characteristic performer has its principal place of business; in a contract for the supply of goods or services, the supplier is the characteristic performer. Similarly, under the Rome I Regulation, the supplier's law applies on the basis of the rules set out in article 4(1): a contract for the sale of goods (or for the provision of services) is governed by the law of the country where the seller (or the service provider) has his habitual residence.[28] Thirdly, if the supplier is based in country Z, but the contract is closely connected with a branch or other place of business in country Y (for example, if the supplier's performance is to be effected through that other place of business), the law of country Y will normally be the applicable law.[29] Fourthly, although the choice-of-law rules provide for the possibility of the applicable law being the law of another country—that is, in cases where the contract is more closely connected[30] or manifestly more closely connected[31]

[27] Art 3(1).

[28] Art 4(1)(a) and (b). The supplier's habitual residence will normally be its central administration or principal place of business: art 19.

[29] The relevant provisions of the Rome Convention (art 4(2)) and the Rome I Regulation (arts 4(1) and 19(2)) are drafted somewhat differently. Nevertheless, their overall objective is the same and, in the majority of scenarios, they produce the same results.

[30] Rome Convention, art 4(5).

[31] Rome I Regulation, art 4(3).

with that other country—this possibility is very unlikely to arise in a case of in-person shopping. Where a contract concluded in country Y between, on the one hand, a consumer resident in country X and, on the other, a supplier established in country Y (or a supplier established in country Z who performs its side of the bargain through a place of business located in country Y), it would be only in the most exceptional of circumstances that the contract could be thought to be more closely connected with a country other than country Y.

The fact that a cross-border contract entered into by a consumer who is visiting another country (while on holiday or on a business trip) should be governed by the supplier's law, rather than by the consumer's law, is not very surprising. In cases of in-person cross-border shopping, it is the consumer, rather than the supplier, who has entered the international arena. Accordingly, a supplier established in country Y has a legitimate expectation that his contractual relationships—not only with consumers resident in country Y, but also with consumers resident in other countries—should be governed by the law of country Y. By the same token, the 'active' consumer who, having travelled from country X to country Y, enters a contract with a supplier in country Y does not have a reasonable expectation that the contract would be governed by the law of country X. **12.20**

There is, however, one type of in-person cross-border shopping which attracts the choice-of-law rules applicable to protected consumer contracts. Under the Rome Convention, the 'preferential law' approach applies to cases of 'cross border excursion selling'—a phenomenon which is defined as a situation where 'the contract is for the sale of goods and the consumer travelled to another country and there gave his order, provided that the consumer's journey was arranged by the seller for the purpose of inducing the consumer to buy'.[32] Although the Rome I Regulation does not legislate specifically for cross-border excursion selling, the formula used for determining which contracts qualify as protected consumer contracts is broad enough to include consumer sales which result from this marketing method.[33] **12.21**

Distance Contracts

As regards distance contracts which qualify as protected consumer contracts, the European choice-of-law regime adopts the 'preferential law' approach. This is achieved through two basic choice-of-law rules. First, if **12.22**

[32] Art 5(2).
[33] See art 6 (which is discussed at paras 12.53–12.54).

the contract does not contain a choice of law, the contract is governed by the law of the country in which the consumer is habitually resident.[34] Secondly, any choice of law (which will almost invariably select the law of the country in which the supplier is established) may not have the result of depriving the consumer of the protection afforded to him by the mandatory rules—that is, the rules that cannot be derogated from by contract—of the law of the country which would have applied in the absence of choice.[35] In cases where the law chosen by the supplier provides a higher level of protection than the law of the country of the consumer's habitual residence, the chosen law applies; the mandatory rules of the consumer's law prevail over the chosen law only if the former enhance the consumer's legal rights.[36]

12.23 The intended operation of these rules can be illustrated by the following example: a supplier established in the US sells goods via its website to a consumer in England; the website's terms and conditions include a choice of New York law (which does not provide for a cooling-off period after the goods have been delivered); a few days after delivery of the goods, the consumer purports to cancel the contract, returns the goods, and asks for a refund; the supplier refuses to refund the purchase price. From the perspective of English (private international) law, the consumer is entitled to cancel the contract and obtain a refund, because, notwithstanding the choice of New York law, the relevant provisions of the Distance Selling Directive (as implemented in England by the Consumer Protection (Distance Selling) Regulations 2000[37]) cannot be derogated from by contract.[38] Article 12 of the Distance Selling Directive provides:

> Member States shall take the measures needed to ensure that the consumer does not lose the protection granted by this Directive by virtue of the choice of the law of a non-member country as the law applicable to the contract if the latter has a close connection with the territory of one or more Member States.[39]

[34] Rome Convention, art 5(3); Rome I Regulation, art 6(1).

[35] Rome Convention, art 5(2); Rome I Regulation, art 6(2).

[36] See CGJ Morse (1992: 8–9); R Plender and M Wilderspin (2001: para 7-21); L Collins *et al* (2006: para 33-014).

[37] SI 2000 No 2334 (as amended by the Consumer Protection (Distance Selling) Regulations 2005, SI 2005 No 1689).

[38] See the analysis of the Court of Justice in Case C-381/98 *Ingmar* [2000] ECR I-9305, which concerned the mandatory nature of analogous provisions under the Commercial Agents (Council Directive) Regulations (SI 1993 No 3053), implementing Dir 86/653/EEC [1986] OJ L382/17.

[39] This provision is implemented in English law by reg 25(3) of the Consumer Protection (Distance Selling) Regulations 2000 which closely follows the wording of the Directive.

As the requirement of a close connection is satisfied in cases where the consumer is habitually resident in a member state,[40] it follows that, when selling to consumers habitually resident in member states, a US-based seller cannot escape the Directive by including in its terms and conditions a choice-of-law clause which selects the law of a country which is not an EU member state as the applicable law.[41] At least, this is the theoretical position.[42] **12.24**

As already noted, although the 'preferential law' approach can be supported in policy terms, it has to be conceded that, in cases where a law has been chosen, it potentially produces a more complex situation than other approaches. This may be particularly so in England as, in the consumer context, the position with regard to mandatory rules is complicated by the fact that there are two significant pieces of legislation: the Unfair Contract Terms Act 1977 and the Unfair Terms in Consumer Contracts Regulations 1999. The two sets of provisions apply different tests, have different spheres of operation, and are completely unrelated to each other. Neither piece of legislation is particularly easy to understand and the relationship between them gives rise to considerable complexities; with regard to legislation which is intended to protect consumer interests, these features might be thought to be significant defects.[43] The Law Commission (together with the Scottish Law Commission) has worked on the integration of the two legislative schemes and a final report (including a draft bill) was published in 2005.[44] Although the government accepted the Law Commissions' recommendations (subject to a regulatory impact assessment), legislation to implement the recommendations has yet to be introduced. **12.25**

III. THE E-COMMERCE DIRECTIVE

Before the discussion turns to consider the scope of the European choice-of-law regime, there is a more general question which needs to be addressed: as regards choice-of-law issues arising out of consumer **12.26**

[40] Although 'close connection' is not defined by the Distance Selling Directive, the Court of Justice has held that Spain failed properly to transpose the Directive into national law by equating 'close connection' with the cumulative conditions as to residence and conclusion of the contract referred to in art 5 of the Rome Convention: Case C-70/03 *Commission v Spain* [2004] ECR I-7999.

[41] J Dickie (1999: 94).

[42] It may be doubted, however, whether the rights of consumers under the Distance Selling Directive can be vindicated in practice in this type of case. See the discussion at paras 12.94–12.101.

[43] See E Macdonald (2004).

[44] Law Com No 292.

contracts, what is the significance of the E-Commerce Directive?[45] This is a field in which commentators have adopted polarized positions and confusion seems to have been generated by there being a widespread failure to appreciate certain fundamental distinctions.

12.27 The most important distinction is between, on the one hand, the legal regulation of Internet service providers and, on the other, the law applicable to transactions which take place via the Internet.[46] As regards the regulation of Internet service providers, it is generally accepted that the best approach is the adoption of the 'country-of-origin' principle. In the European context, the E-Commerce Directive provides that an information society service provider (ISSP) which complies with the law of the country in which it is established is free to engage in e-commerce throughout the European Union.[47] So, the law of the country in which an ISSP is established determines questions such as whether—and in what circumstances—an ISSP is obliged to inform the competent public authorities of alleged illegal activities and what sanctions (if any) should be imposed on an ISSP which fails to comply with the requirements of the Directive. The Directive also makes it clear that it does not determine either which courts have jurisdiction in relation to transactions concluded via the Internet or which law governs such contracts: it is expressly provided that the Directive 'does not establish additional rules on private international law nor does it deal with the jurisdiction of Courts'.[48] Notwithstanding the express terms of the Directive, some commentators have taken the view either that the E-Commerce Directive does in fact lay down a private international law rule[49] or that, as regards choice of law, the impact of the E-Commerce Directive (in general) is uncertain.[50]

12.28 According to some commentators, the E-Commerce Directive and the European choice-of-law regime are inconsistent: the E-Commerce Directive supports the 'country-of-origin' approach, while the Rome Convention and the Rome I Regulation give primacy to the law of the country in which the consumer is habitually resident (which could be said to be

[45] Dir 2000/31/EC [2000] OJ L178/1.

[46] See J Hörnle (2005: 353–4).

[47] This rule is supported, in part, by the fact that it would be prohibitively expensive for SMEs to ensure that their activities complied with the laws of all the member states. In 1999 it was suggested that '[t]he legal fees to make their services compatible with the laws of 15 Member States could amount to several million Euro': European Telecommunications Network Operators' Association (1999: 5).

[48] Dir 2000/31/EC, art 1(4). See also recital 23.

[49] See, eg, M Ortino (2004), BD Boone (2006: 281), and the authors cited by M Schaub (2004: 49 n 111).

[50] See M Lehmann (2000).

a 'country-of-destination' approach).[51] There are two possible forms which the argument can take—and, as regards some discussions, it is not always clear which form of the argument is being pursued.[52]

The first line of argument is that there is an inconsistency *in approach* between the E-Commerce Directive and the contractual choice-of-law rules. In essence, this form of the argument postulates that the choice-of-law rule which applies to regulatory questions *should also apply* to online transactions—and that the choice-of-law rules which determine the law governing private law relations should be amended accordingly. In support of this position, it is suggested that a country-of-destination approach to choice of law in the consumer context places excessive burdens on businesses (by requiring them to comply with the laws of all countries in which they do online business); to minimize such burdens and to encourage suppliers to become involved in e-commerce, the country-of-origin approach should be extended to transactions concluded (and torts committed) via the Internet. Nevertheless, the majority view (in Europe, at least) remains that alignment between the law which governs regulatory questions and the law which governs online transactions is unnecessary, and that it is better that the consumer's law (rather than the supplier's law) should govern consumer contracts.[53] **12.29**

The second line of argument is that there is a *legal* incompatibility between the E-Commerce Directive, on the one hand, and the contractual choice-of-law rules, on the other, and that the effect of the E-Commerce Directive is to introduce a new choice-of-law rule for contracts concluded via the Internet. This form of the argument is that, by virtue of the E-Commerce Directive, the country-of-origin rule applies to online transactions.[54] This argument cannot be accepted as the country-of-origin rule is primarily addressed to the public authorities of the member states; it is 'a rule of European administrative law and as such does not apply to private law disputes'.[55] **12.30**

Once it is appreciated that the E-Commerce Directive and the choice-of-law rules applicable to consumer contracts are operating at different levels and are directed at different types of legal question, any apparent incompatibility between the Directive and the European choice-of-law regime is revealed to be wholly illusory.[56] Even if, in the context of **12.31**

[51] See, eg, MD Powell and PM Turner-Kerr (2000: 26).

[52] See, eg, W Roebuck (2002).

[53] This view has also found favour with some commentators in North America: EA O'Hara (2005).

[54] See G Pearce and N Platten (2000: 375, 376).

[55] J Hörnle (2004: 363).

[56] PA Stone (2000: 16). See also S Dutson (2000): JST Øren, (2003: 668).

contracts in general, there were some legal incompatibility between the E-Commerce Directive and the European choice-of-law regime, as regards consumer contracts, the E-Commerce Directive could not be clearer. It is expressly stated that the Directive 'does not affect the law applicable to contractual obligations relating to consumer contracts'.[57] The implementing legislation in the United Kingdom—the Electronic Commerce (EC Directive) Regulations 2002[58]—makes the same point.[59] Accordingly, further discussion of the choice-of-law implications (real or imagined) of the E-Commerce Directive and the 2002 Regulations is unnecessary.[60]

IV. THE SCOPE OF THE EUROPEAN CHOICE-OF-LAW REGIME

12.32 The scope of the choice-of-law rules which apply to protected consumer contracts is determined by two elements: (a) the nature of the contract and (b) the circumstances in which the contract was concluded. If both elements are satisfied, the 'preferential law' approach applies and, in the absence of a choice of law, the law of the country in which the consumer is habitually resident governs. Although these rules apply to contracts concluded by post and by telephone as well as to online contracts, it is in the context of e-commerce that their operation has been thought to pose most problems. It is for this reason that the Rome I Regulation adopts a different form of words from the Convention—and, as one might expect, follows the same approach as article 15 of the Brussels I Regulation. Nevertheless, in terms of its objectives the Rome I Regulation is consistent with the Convention and, notwithstanding various differences between the two texts, it is not intended that the scope of the two instruments should be significantly different; in reality, it will rarely make any difference whether the Rome Convention or the Rome I Regulation applies.[61]

1. The Nature of the Contract

The Parties

12.33 As regards the parties to the contract, article 6 of the Regulation expressly provides that one party must be a consumer—that is, a person who

[57] Dir 2000/31/EC, recital 55.
[58] SI 2002 No 2013.
[59] Reg 4(4) and sched, para 3.
[60] For further discussion, see A Halfmeier (2003).
[61] PA Stone (2002: 126).

concludes a contract for a purpose which is outside his trade or profession—and the other party must be acting in the exercise of his trade or profession. Although article 5 of the Convention is less explicit—in that it refers to one party being a consumer, but does not articulate the characteristics of the other party, there is no substantive difference between the two provisions in this regard; it is generally assumed that article 5 of the Convention applies to b2c contracts only and not to cases where neither party to the contract is acting in the course of his trade or profession.[62] The phrase 'for a purpose . . . outside his trade or profession' has already been considered in the context of article 15 of the Brussels I Regulation[63] and there is no reason to think that its interpretation in the context of the choice-of-law regime should be any different.

The Subject-matter

Article 5 of the Rome Convention

Article 5 applies to contracts 'the object of which is the supply of goods or services'.[64] There has been some discussion in the literature on the question whether digitized products (such as computer programs) should be regarded as 'goods' or 'services' (or neither).[65] Although there may be situations in which the question whether digitized products are to be treated as goods or services is relevant (for example, for the purposes of the Sale of Goods Act 1979[66]), this question does not really arise in the context of article 5 of the Rome Convention. The classificatory question would be relevant only if there were a plausible case in support of the argument that contracts involving digitized products should be regarded as *neither* contracts for the sale of goods *nor* contracts for the provision of services—in which such contracts would fall wholly outside the scope of article 5.[67] **12.34**

Some commentators have suggested that a consumer credit agreement is neither a contract for the sale of goods nor a contract for the provision of services.[68] However, such a view is unconvincing and is contradicted by the case law of the Court of Justice;[69] a consumer credit agreement should **12.35**

[62] Giuliano-Lagarde Report [1980] OJ C282/23.

[63] See paras 3.46–3.63.

[64] Some types of contract are, however, expressly excluded. See paras 12.55–12.68.

[65] See, eg, M Chissick and A Kelman (2002: 69–71); R Debusseré (2002: 350); JL Goldsmith (1998: 1224); M Foss and LA Bygrave (2000: 109); S Green and D Saidov (2007).

[66] See *St Albans City and District Council v International Computers Ltd* [1996] 4 All ER 481.

[67] For further discussion, see ch 1.

[68] B von Hoffman (1992: 378).

[69] 'The grant of a credit facility is indeed the provision of a service. . .': Case C-45/96 *Dietzinger* [1998] ECR I-1199, 1221 (para 18).

be classified as a contract for the provision of services for the purposes of article 5. Indeed, with the exception of situations considered in the next paragraph and of those types of contract which are expressly excluded from the scope of article 5, the most rational interpretation is that article 5 covers all types of consumer purchase—with contracts for the provision of services being the category of consumer purchases which are not contracts for the sale of goods.

12.36 The category of cases which are not covered by article 5 is contracts for the purchase of property other than goods. It seems reasonably clear that a contract for the sale of land or a tenancy of land is neither a contract for the sale of goods nor a contract for the provision of services. The same must be true for the sale (but not the licence) of an intellectual property right (such as a patent, a trade mark, or copyright)—though such transactions must be extremely rare in the consumer context. It would also seem that a contract for the sale of a chose in action is outside the scope of article 5: in the context of schedule 4 to the Civil Jurisdiction and Judgments Act 1982, it has been held that a contract relating to units in a unit trust is not a contract for the sale of goods.[70]

Article 6 of the Rome I Regulation

12.37 Whatever problems of classification may arise under article 5 of the Convention, they are largely sidestepped by article 6 of the Regulation which refers simply to 'a contract' (rather than to a contract, 'the object of which is the supply of goods or services'). It should be noted, however, that there are a number of express exclusions.[71]

2. The Circumstances in which the Contract was Concluded

12.38 Article 5 of the Rome Convention was drafted long before the emergence of the Internet and e-commerce. Not surprisingly, therefore, the verbal formula used to define the circumstances in which a consumer can rely upon the consumer choice-of-law rules does not fit with the phenomenon of online shopping as comfortably as it might. In essence, when translated into the online world, article 5 of the Rome Convention reveals the same uncertainties as article 13 of the Brussels Convention. Accordingly, the drafting of article 6 of the Rome I Regulation, like that of article 15 of the

[70] *Waverley Asset Management Ltd v Saha* 1989 SLT (Sh Ct) 87 (Sheriff Court, Lothian and Border).

[71] See paras 12.55–12.68.

Brussels I Regulation, attempts to take account of developments in marketing techniques, in particular marketing through the Internet.

The Rome Convention

Under article 5 of the Convention, the 'preferential law' approach applies to a consumer contract only if certain criteria relating to the circumstances in which the contract was concluded are satisfied. First, the conduct of the supplier must satisfy one of the 'marketing' criteria—either the 'invitation' criterion or the 'advertising' criterion. The text of article 5(2) refers to the conclusion of the contract having been 'preceded by a specific invitation addressed to [the consumer] or by advertising'. Secondly, the conduct of the consumer must satisfy the 'contracting' criterion, which requires that the consumer took 'all the steps necessary on his part for the conclusion of the contract' in the country in which he has his habitual residence. These criteria were also to be found in article 13 of the Brussels Convention (as amended by the 1978 Accession Convention) and, to the extent that there has been any reported case law dealing with the question of how the criteria should be understood, it has arisen in relation to jurisdictional questions and not in the context of choice of law. **12.39**

The invitation criterion

The Giuliano-Lagarde Report which accompanied the Rome Convention gives little indication of what constitutes a 'specific invitation', though it does suggest that the consumer contract rules are intended to cover 'mail order and door-step selling' and that the supplier 'must have made business proposals individually through a middleman or by canvassing'.[72] As regards offline contracts, common techniques for marketing consumer goods are the use of prize draws, competitions, and other forms of direct marketing to named consumers. Where a supplier sends several personalized letters to a consumer along with a sales catalogue and an order form, with a view to persuading the consumer to contract on the basis of the supplier's proposals, the invitation criterion is satisfied.[73] While it seems reasonably clear that the invitation criterion would be satisfied where an e-trader solicits business from consumers by means of personalized e-mail messages,[74] the maintenance of a website (which is accessible from anywhere in the world by anyone who has a computer linked to the Internet) cannot constitute a 'specific invitation'. **12.40**

[72] [1980] OJ C282/24. See *Standard Bank London Ltd v Apostolakis (No 2)* [2001] Lloyd's Rep Banking 240.

[73] See Case C-96/00 *Gabriel* [2002] ECR I-6367, 6402 (para 52).

[74] M Chissick and A Kelman (2002: 118). See also T Puurunen (2002: 158).

12.41 A question arises whether the invitation criterion can be satisfied in a case where the consumer approaches the supplier rather than vice versa. In *Standard Bank London Ltd v Apostolakis (No 2)*[75] the claimant, the English subsidiary of a South African bank, had marketed its financial products in Greece through an 'introducer' whose role was to introduce to the claimant clients who might wish to enter into foreign exchange transactions. The defendants had concluded a foreign exchange agreement with the claimant through the 'introducer'. David Steel J held that the invitation criterion had been satisfied in this case, even though the defendants had made the initial approach to the 'introducer'.[76]

12.42 However, a different result was reached in *Rayner v Davies*.[77] In this case, the claimant (who lived in England) purchased a yacht which, at the time of the sale, was berthed in Italy. The defendant, a marine surveyor, was domiciled in Italy. Prior to the sale, the claimant contacted the defendant and, after the claimant had inspected the yacht and met the defendant in Italy, the parties concluded a contract under the terms of which the defendant undertook to carry out a survey of the yacht. Following the meeting in Italy, the defendant faxed terms to the claimant in England and the claimant signed the fax and returned it to the defendant. A dispute arose when the claimant alleged that the survey had been carried out negligently. As the defendant was the offeror and the claimant was the offeree, it could be argued that the literal wording of the invitation criterion had been satisfied: the conclusion of the contract had been preceded by a specific invitation addressed to the consumer. Nevertheless, as Morison J pointed out, such an argument 'loses sight of the wood for the trees';[78] the important question was whether the defendant had taken steps to market his services in England. As he had not, the invitation criterion had not been satisfied. The Court of Appeal dismissed the claimant's appeal. According to Waller LJ, the invitation criterion 'seems to contemplate some positive conduct on the part of the seller of goods or services preceding the contract, and (. . . normally) preceding the involvement of the consumer'.[79] This condition was not satisfied in the present case: 'If one stood back from the factual situation in this case and asked the question who invited whom to do business, the answer would be that the claimant invited the defendant.'[80] Accordingly, the invitation criterion was not satisfied.

[75] [2001] Lloyd's Rep Banking 240.
[76] [2001] Lloyd's Rep Banking 240, 248 (at [41]).
[77] [2003] ILPr 258.
[78] [2003] ILPr 258, 255 (at [12]).
[79] [2003] ILPr 258, 267 (at [24]).
[80] [2003] ILPr 258, 267 (at [26]).

As for the relationship between these two cases, the Court of Appeal said nothing. However, two points emerge from the judgment of the first instance judge: first, the decision in the earlier case 'was, on the facts of the case, obviously right';[81] secondly, if David Steel J had been saying that it was irrelevant whether the business was initiated by the supplier or the consumer, Morison J did not agree with him. The cases are obviously distinguishable and there is every reason to think that both cases were correctly decided; in *Standard Bank London Ltd v Apostolakis (No 2)* the claimant had marketed its investment products (through the 'introducer') in Greece, where the defendants were domiciled, whereas the defendant in *Rayner v Davies* had taken no such steps to market his services in England. **12.43**

The invitation criterion requires only that the contract should be preceded by a specific invitation addressed to the consumer; it does not require that the contract between the supplier and the consumer should be based on that invitation.[82] This does not mean, however, that the invitation criterion is satisfied in a case where a supplier specifically offers to supply apples, but the consumer rejects the offer and contracts to buy pears instead. The invitation criterion requires there to be 'substantial identity' between the goods or services proposed in a specific invitation and the subject-matter of the contract between the supplier and the consumer.[83] So, if a car dealer makes a specific offer to sell a *Toyota Corolla 1.6i* car, but the consumer decides to buy a *Toyota Corolla 1.4i*, there can be no doubt that the invitation criterion would be satisfied. There is a good argument for saying that the same should be true if the consumer purchases a different *Toyota* model (such as a *Toyota Yaris*) or, indeed, another make of car (such as a *Honda* or a *Nissan*). It is less obvious that there would be sufficient identity between the goods proposed and the goods purchased if the supplier offered to sell a car, but the consumer purchased a motorbike. **12.44**

The advertising criterion

The Giuliano-Lagarde Report suggests that, in order for this criterion to be satisfied, the supplier 'must have done certain acts such as advertising in the press, or on radio or television, or in the cinema or by catalogues aimed specifically at that country'.[84] The following contrasting situations (based on examples provided in the Giuliano-Lagarde Report[85]) should clarify what is intended by the requirement that the advertising should be **12.45**

[81] [2003] ILPr 250, 255 (at [13]).
[82] See C-464/01 *Gruber* [2005] ECR I-439, 454 (para 65) (Jacobs AG).
[83] See C-464/01 *Gruber* [2005] ECR I-439, 454–5 (para 67) (Jacobs AG).
[84] [1980] OJ C282/24.
[85] See [1980] OJ C282/24.

specifically aimed at a particular country: (i) if a Swiss consumer makes a contract in response to an advertisement published by an English company in a Swiss publication, the advertising criterion is satisfied; (ii) if the Swiss consumer replies to an advertisement in an English publication, even if it is sold in Switzerland, the advertising criterion is not normally satisfied; (iii) however, if the Swiss consumer replies to an advertisement in a special edition of an English publication intended for mainland European countries (including Switzerland) the advertising criterion is satisfied.

12.46 Does there have to be a connection between the advertising and the conclusion of the contract? Although the question (in the context of article 13 of the Brussels Convention) has been referred to the Court of Justice on several occasions, the Court has left the question unanswered.[86] It has been suggested that it is more natural to read the advertising criterion as requiring not only that the advertising came to the consumer's attention but also that it played a role in inducing the consumer to enter into the contract.[87] This approach has not, however, been adopted by the Advocates General. In the *Shearson Lehman Hutton* case, Advocate General Darmon considered that 'the consumer is not required to prove that he was actually affected by the advertising or that there was a causal link between the advertising and the conclusion of the contract';[88] the advertising criterion 'lays down a species of irrebuttable presumption that there is a link between the appearance of the advertising and the conclusion of the contract where the former preceded the latter'.[89] In *Gruber* this view was accepted as correct by Advocate General Jacobs; the text refers to a contract being '"preceded"—not "brought about"—by advertising'.[90] Accordingly, as long as the supplier has previously advertised products in the country of the consumer's domicile, the advertising criterion is satisfied even if the specific goods or services supplied to the consumer have not been the subject of cross-border advertising.[91]

12.47 Nevertheless, common sense suggests that there must be some degree of proximity between the advertising and the conclusion of the contract in order for the contract to fall within the scope of article 5. It would be strange, to say the least, if the advertising criterion were satisfied, as

[86] Case C-89/91 *Shearson Lehman Hutton* [1993] ECR I-139; Case C-318/93 *Brenner and Noller* [1994] ECR I-4275; Case C-464/01 *Gruber* [2005] ECR I-439.

[87] PA Stone (2000: 7).

[88] Case C-89/91 [1993] ECR I-139, 175 (para 83).

[89] [1993] ECR I-139, 176 (para 85).

[90] Case C-464/01 *Gruber* [2005] ECR I-439, 453 (para 60) (Jacobs AG).

[91] See Case C-464/01 *Gruber* [2005] ECR I-439, 454 (para 63) (Jacobs AG).

regards a contract concluded in 2009, simply because the supplier had run a short cross-border advertising campaign in 1990. A national court would be wrong to conclude that the advertising criterion was satisfied in a case where the advertising was too remote in time from the conclusion of the contract.[92]

The operation of the advertising criterion in the context of online contracts is uncertain as whether a website constitutes 'advertising' is not uncontroversial.[93] Whereas traditional advertising requires active steps to be taken by the supplier (for example, placing advertisements in newspapers or magazines), a website owner does not have to take any such steps to bring information to the attention of people in other countries; the nature of the Internet is that a customer who surfs the world wide web visits the supplier's website without the supplier having to take active steps to bring the site's existence to the attention of the potential customer. Accordingly, there is an argument for saying that, because web pages are never 'directed' at a particular jurisdiction, but are passively visible across the world, a website is not advertising for the purposes of the Rome Convention. If this analysis is correct, consumer contracts concluded via a website would not fall within article 5—and the law governing such contracts would be determined by articles 3 and 4, according to which the supplier's law would invariably be the applicable law. Nevertheless, most commentators consider that a website does constitute 'advertising'[94] and this interpretation is the most rational in policy terms. One of the advantages is that this interpretation achieves a greater degree of symmetry and continuity between the Rome Convention and the Rome I Regulation (and ensures that, as far as possible, the choice-of-law regime of the Convention runs in parallel with the jurisdictional regime of the Brussels I Regulation). **12.48**

The contracting criterion

One of the purposes of the contracting criterion is to help to identify contracts which are sufficiently closely connected with the country of the consumer's habitual residence to justify departing from the choice-of-law rules that apply to contracts in general. The combined effect of the marketing and **12.49**

[92] See Case C-89/91 *Shearson Lehman Hutton* [1993] ECR I-139, 175 (para 84) (Darmon AG); Case C-464/01 *Gruber* [2005] ECR I-439, 452–3 (para 57) (Jacobs AG).

[93] See M Chissick and A Kelman (2002: 118); F Debusseré (2002: 352–3); M Foss and LA Bygrave (2000: 114–17).

[94] See, eg, PA Stone (2000: 8); P Naarajärvi and JV Koivisto (2002: 115); J Dickie (1999: 85, 86); A Lopez-Tarruella (2001: 252); S Rawson (2002: 166); R Plender and M Wilderspin (2001: para 7-18); S van der Hof (2003: 171). But see the more equivocal position of R Schu (1997: 214).

contracting criteria is to distinguish 'passive' consumers (who have not entered the international arena and should not be deprived of the level of consumer protection provided by the law of their habitual residence) from 'active' consumers (who have entered the international arena and do not merit special protection). By focusing on where the consumer takes 'the steps necessary for the conclusion of the contract', the drafters deliberately avoided the tricky question of where an international contract is concluded.[95] The term 'steps' includes 'writing or any action taken in consequence of an offer or advertisement'.[96] So, where a consumer sends an order form from the country in which he is habitually resident to a supplier in another country, the requirements of the contracting criterion are met.[97] In addition, in the context of online contracting, the term 'steps' covers actions which consumers typically carry out when buying goods or services via a website—such as completing an online form or clicking on an 'accept' icon.

12.50 The contracting criterion does not require all the stages of the contracting process to take place where the consumer is resident. For example, a situation does not fall outside the scope of article 5 simply because negotiations prior to the conclusion of the contract took place in the country in which the supplier is established.[98] In the typical case, where the consumer makes an offer (in response to the supplier's invitation to treat) and the supplier accepts it, what matters is where the consumer was when he made the offer. The mode of communication used by the consumer is irrelevant.[99]

12.51 As regards online contracts, it may be difficult to say with accuracy where the consumer 'took . . . the steps necessary for the conclusion of the contract'. In the context of e-commerce, the supplier may not know where the consumer was located when he took the relevant steps. Unless it could be proved to the contrary, it would be natural to presume that the consumer took the relevant steps in the country of his habitual residence. Nevertheless, in principle, where it is established that a consumer who is habitually resident in country X orders goods from the supplier's website while visiting country Y, the contracting criterion is not satisfied.[100]

Conclusion

12.52 Notwithstanding the potential difficulties surrounding the application of article 5 of the Convention to online consumer contracts, it can be seen that those difficulties are far from insoluble. Once it is accepted that a website

[95] See Giuliano-Lagarde Report [1980] OJ C282/24.
[96] Giuliano-Lagarde Report [1980] OJ C282/24.
[97] See, eg, Case C-96/00 *Gabriel* [2002] ECR I-6367, 6402 (para 52).
[98] Case C-464/01 *Gruber* [2005] ECR I-439, 456 (para 74) (Jacobs AG).
[99] Case C-464/01 *Gruber* [2005] ECR I-439, 456 (para 75) (Jacobs AG).
[100] M Foss and LA Bygrave (2000: 125–6).

constitutes advertising, the vast majority of online consumer contracts are protected consumer contracts for the purposes of article 5; except in a case involving an e-contract concluded by a 'mobile' consumer (ie, where a consumer habitually resident in country X enters the contract while physically in country Y), online consumer contracts fall within the scope of article 5 and the governing law is determined by the 'preferential law' approach.[101] If this analysis is correct, the substantive differences between the Convention and the Regulation in the field of consumer contracts are really very limited.

The Rome I Regulation

Under the Rome I Regulation, a contract between a consumer and a supplier falls within the scope of the consumer choice-of-law rules if the supplier '(a) pursues his commercial or professional activities in the country where the consumer has his habitual residence, or (b) by any means, directs such activities to that country or to several countries including that country, and the contract falls within the scope of such activities'.[102] The aim of this formula is, first, to iron out arbitrary distinctions in terms of scope between the jurisdiction regime of the Brussels I Regulation and the choice-of-law regime and, secondly, to resolve some of the perceived problems in the Rome Convention—in particular, by making it clear that the consumer choice-of-law rules apply to online contracts concluded between a consumer who is habitually resident in one country and a supplier based in another.[103] **12.53**

It should be noted that, whereas article 5 of the Convention requires that the consumer took the steps necessary for the conclusion of the contract in the country of his habitual residence, the requirement of article 6 of the Regulation is simply that the contract falls within the scope of the supplier's activities which are directed towards the country in which the consumer is habitually resident. Where the consumer takes the steps necessary to conclude the contract is irrelevant. **12.54**

3. Exclusions

Both the Rome Convention and the Rome I Regulation exclude certain types of contract from the scope of the choice-of-law regime which applies to protected consumer contracts. In addition, contracts of insurance—in **12.55**

[101] There may also be circumstances in which an online consumer contract also falls within the second indent of art 5(2) which refers to cases where 'the other party or his agent received the consumer's order in that country'. See L Collins *et al* (2006: paras 33-021–3-023).

[102] Art 6(1).

[103] For further discussion, see the relevant sections of chs 3 and 4.

relation to which different choice-of-law rules apply[104]—are covered neither by article 5 of the Convention nor by article 6 of the Regulation. Although there is a substantial overlap between the two instruments, some of the exclusions are not coterminous.

Services Supplied Outside the Consumer's Country

12.56 The first exclusion covers contracts for the provision of services 'where the services are to be supplied to the consumer exclusively in a country other than that in which he has his habitual residence'.[105] So, a holiday contract concluded between an English consumer and a Spanish holiday company via the company's website would, in principle, be a protected consumer contract; however, it is excluded if the services provided by the Spanish company are supplied wholly in Spain (or another country other than England). In this type of case the consumer 'cannot reasonably expect the law of his State of origin to be applied in derogation from the general rules of Articles 3 and 4'.[106] There is a question whether this exception could be interpreted to exclude contracts for the provision of electronic services (such as database access or the online provision of software).[107] In textual terms, it is plausible to take the view that, where the consumer accesses services from his home country, the services are not performed exclusively in a country other than that in which the consumer is habitually resident. A teleological approach leads to the same conclusion: the purpose of this exception is primarily to protect the legitimate expectations of a supplier who contracts to perform services (in his own country) for a consumer who has physically travelled to the supplier's country. This rationale does not apply when the consumer is habitually resident in a country other than that in which the supplier is established.

Contracts of Carriage

12.57 The 'preferential law' approach does not apply to contracts of carriage[108] (other than contracts for package holidays). For the purposes of article 5 of the Convention, package holidays are defined as contracts which, for an inclusive price, provide for a combination of travel and accommodation.[109] Article 6 of the Regulation takes the same basic approach, but is more specific;

[104] See paras 12.70–12.75.
[105] Rome Convention, art 5(4)(b); Rome I Regulation, art 6(4)(a).
[106] Giuliano-Lagarde Report [1980] OJ C282/24.
[107] R Schu (1997: 217–18).
[108] Rome Convention, art 5(4)(a); Rome I Regulation, art 6(4)(b).
[109] Art 5(5).

the contracts of carriage which are *not* excluded from the Regulation are contracts 'relating to package travel within the meaning of Council Directive 90/314/EEC of 13 June 1990 on package travel, package holidays and package tours'.[110] Notwithstanding the technical difference in the way in which the Convention and the Regulation frame this particular exception, it seems likely that, were it ever necessary for the issue to be decided, the package holiday exception in article 5 of the Convention would be interpreted so that its scope is identical to the equivalent exception in article 6 of the Regulation.

In the context of the Rome Convention, the reason for this exclusion is not very clear, in view of the fact that contracts for services which are supplied to the consumer in a country other than that in which he is habitually resident are covered by the first exception. The Giuliano-Lagarde Report states simply that: 'The exclusion of contracts of carriage is justified by the fact that the special protective measures for which provision is made in Article 5 are not appropriate for governing contracts of this type.'[111] As regards the Rome I Regulation, the exclusion of contracts of carriage makes more sense as, unlike the Convention, the Regulation contains a separate article dealing solely with such contracts.[112] **12.58**

Contracts Relating to Immovable Property

As already noted, article 5 of the Rome Convention does not apply to contracts relating to immovable property, as such contracts are neither contracts for the sale of goods nor contracts for the supply of services. However, without an express exception, article 6 of the Rome I Regulation would cover a contract for the sale of land or a tenancy which displayed the general characteristics of a consumer contract. As there is no intention **12.59**

[110] Art 6(4)(b). Art 2 of the 1990 Directive ([1990] OJ L158/59) provides that a 'package' is: 'the pre-arranged combination of not fewer than two of the following when sold or offered for sale at an inclusive price and when the service covers a period of more than twenty-four hours or includes overnight accommodation: (a) transport; (b) accommodation; (c) other tourist services not ancillary to transport or accommodation and accounting for a significant proportion of the package'. There have been references to the Court of Justice relating to the proper interpretation of the Directive: see, eg, Case C-237/97 *AFS Intercultural Programmes Finland* [1999] ECR I-825; Case C-400/00 *Club Tour Viagens e Turismo SA* [2002] ECR I-4051. Several questions under the Directive have yet to receive an authoritative answer (such as whether a cruise qualifies as a package holiday for the purposes of the Directive). Such uncertainties were considered by the European Commission in a 1999 report which suggested a number of ways in which the Directive could be clarified and amended: see S Weatherill (2005: 100–1). However, no formal proposals have been put forward.

[111] [1980] OJ C282/24.

[112] Art 5.

that the Regulation should depart from the Convention on this issue, the Regulation expressly excludes contracts relating to a right *in rem* in immovable property or a tenancy of immovable property.[113]

12.60 There are good reasons for excluding such contracts from the choice-of-law rules that apply to protected consumer contracts; the country where the immovable is situated has the predominant interest in how disputes arising from contracts relating to immovable property and tenancies of such property should be resolved. For example, most countries have detailed rules on the regulation of tenancies and it seems self-evident that the rights of a tenant of a flat situated in Bristol should normally be determined by English housing law, whether or not the tenant is English, French, or Japanese.

12.61 Where the subject-matter of the contract is a right *in rem* in immovable property, contracting parties are free to select the governing law under article 3. In the absence of choice by the parties, the governing law is the *lex situs*.[114] However, under the Rome I Regulation, there is a special rule for tenancies of immovable property 'concluded for temporary private use for a period of no more than six consecutive months'; the applicable law is the law of the country in which the landlord is habitually resident 'provided that the tenant is a natural person and has his habitual residence in the same country'.[115] So, if a French landlord lets a cottage in the Lake District to a French resident for two months, French law is the governing law (unless the contract contains a clause choosing another law). The position would probably be the same under the Rome Convention: the *lex situs* yields to the law of another country if the contract is more closely connected with that other country;[116] the Giuliano-Lagarde Report—which uses the example of a holiday letting of property in Elba between two Belgians—suggests that, in this type of case, the residence of the parties is more significant than the location of the property and that the governing law should be the law of the country in which both parties are resident (rather than the *lex situs*).[117]

12.62 The only type of contract concerning rights *in rem* in immovable property which is within the scope of article 6 of the Regulation is 'a contract relating to the right to use immovable properties on a timeshare basis within

[113] Art 6(4)(c).
[114] Rome Convention, art 4(3); Rome I Regulation, art 4(1)(c).
[115] Art 4(1)(d).
[116] Art 4(5).
[117] [1980] OJ C282/21.

the meaning of Directive 94/47/EC'.[118] Unlike most other contracts relating to immovable property, timeshare contracts display many of the characteristics of consumer contracts in general—in terms of marketing, unfair terms, and the like. Accordingly, it make sense for the choice-of-law rules for consumer contracts to apply to such transactions.

As the Rome Convention contains no counterpart to the timeshare proviso in article 6 of the Regulation, the position of timeshare contracts under article 5 of the Convention is uncertain. Depending on their exact form, timeshare contracts may look like leases for discontinuous periods or contracts for services (or some mixture of the two). On the basis of the Court of Justice's approach in the *Klein* case[119] (in the context of the Brussels Convention), a timeshare contract which obviously takes the form of a tenancy of immovable property (albeit a lease for discontinuous periods) would fall outside the scope of article 5 of the Convention, particularly if the majority of the purchase price paid by the consumer relates to the right to use the property in question. In such cases, the applicable law has to be determined in accordance with the rules set out in articles 3 and 4. **12.63**

However, many contracts for various timeshare-like products (which were developed with a view to side-stepping the Timeshare Directive's provisions[120]) take the form of a contract for services. For example, holiday club contracts specify neither the property in relation to which the consumer acquires a right of use nor where it is located; some contracts also fail to specify the week or weeks to which the right of use applies.[121] Although contracts of this type fall outside the scope of the Timeshare Directive, they are clearly contracts for services which are capable of falling within the scope of article 5 of the Rome Convention or article 6 of the Rome I Regulation. **12.64**

Contracts Relating to Certain Financial Instruments

The final two exclusions, which are to be found in article 6 of the Rome I Regulation and which have no direct counterpart in the Rome Convention, concern contracts relating to certain types of financial instrument (such as unit trusts and bearer bonds). The purpose of these exclusions is to ensure that the same law applies to a particular financial instrument, regardless of the territorial connections of the consumers subscribing to the instrument **12.65**

118 Art 6(4)(c).
119 Case C-73/04 *Klein v Rhodos Management Ltd* [2006] ILPr 29.
120 See ECC-Net (December 2002).
121 See ECC-Net (December 2002: 11).

in question. Without these exceptions, there would be a danger that the precise nature of the rights and obligations under a particular financial instrument would turn on where the consumer was habitually resident; this could have a detrimental effect on the 'fungible trading' of such instruments.[122]

12.66 Article 6 does not apply to 'rights and obligations which constitute a financial instrument and rights and obligations constituting the terms and conditions governing the issuance or offer to the public and public take-over bids of transferable securities, and the subscription and redemption of units in collective investment undertakings in so far as these activities do not constitute provision of a financial service'.[123] The rights and obligations covered by this exception include 'the terms governing . . . the allocation of securities or units, rights in the event of over-subscription, withdrawal rights and similar matters in the context of the offer . . .'.[124] The purpose of this exception is to 'ensur[e] that all relevant contractual aspects of an offer binding the issuer or the offeror to the consumer are governed by a single law'.[125]

12.67 Finally, it is provided that article 6 does not apply to 'a contract concluded within a multilateral system which brings together or facilitates the bringing together of multiple third-party buying and selling interests in financial instruments, as defined by Article 4(1), point (17) of Directive 2004/39/EC'.[126] For the purposes of this exception the important distinction is between, on the one hand, contracts relating to 'financial services such as investment services and activities and ancillary services provided by a professional to a consumer'[127] (which, assuming the relevant conditions are satisfied, are covered by the consumer contract choice-of-law rules) and, on the other, 'rights and obligations which constitute a financial instrument'[128] (which fall within the scope of the choice-of-law rules which apply to contracts in general).[129] Again, the purpose of the exception is to ensure that a single law governs contracts relating to certain

[122] Recital 28.
[123] Art 6(4)(d).
[124] Recital 29.
[125] Recital 29.
[126] Art 6(4)(e), which cross-refers to art 4(1)(h).
[127] Recital 26.
[128] Recital 28.
[129] In *Waverley Asset Management Ltd v Saha* 1989 SLT (Sh Ct) 87 (Sheriff Court, Lothian and Border) it was held, in the context of sched 4 to the Civil Jurisdiction and Judgments Act 1982, that a contract relating to units in a unit trust is not a protected consumer contract for jurisdictional purposes.

types of financial contract as defined in the Markets and Financial Instruments Directive.[130] The effect of this final exclusion is that if a consumer becomes involved in the more sophisticated end of the investment market (through, for example, contracts relating to money-market instruments, swaps, forward rate agreements, or derivative instruments for the transfer of credit risk[131]), the law applicable to such contracts will be determined by the law applicable to contracts in general.

Although these last two exclusions have no direct counterpart in the Rome Convention, contracts for certain financial instruments also fall outside the scope of article 5. It must be remembered that article 5 applies only to contracts for the sale of goods and for the supply of services. If the subject-matter of the contract is neither goods nor services, the contract cannot be a protected consumer contract under the Convention. There is, for example, authority for the view that a contract for units in a unit trust is not a contract for the supply of goods or services.[132] Accordingly, with regard to financial instruments, the substantive difference between the Convention and Regulation may be narrower than it appears at first sight. **12.68**

V. SPECIFIC CONTRACTS

In relation to contracts of insurance and contracts of carriage, there are significant differences between the position under the Rome Convention and that under the Rome I Regulation. As already noted, the Regulation applies only with regard to contracts concluded more than 18 months after the publication of the Regulation in the Official Journal and only in member states which are bound by the Regulation. **12.69**

1. Insurance Contracts[133]

The Rome Convention

Contracts of insurance relating to risks which are located within the European Economic Area fall outside the scope of the Rome Convention.[134] **12.70**

[130] Dir 2004/39/EC [2004] OJ L145/1.

[131] A full list of the financial instruments covered by this exception is set out in Section C of Annex I of Dir 2004/39/EC.

[132] *Waverley Asset Management Ltd v Saha* 1989 SLT (Sh Ct) 87 (Sheriff Court, Lothian and Border).

[133] See F Seatzu (2003: chs 9–10).

[134] Art 1(3).

For these contracts, the choice-of-law rules from the relevant European directives,[135] transposed into national law, apply. However, as regards contracts of insurance which deal with risks located outside the EEA, the Rome Convention applies.

12.71 As far as English law is concerned, the special choice-of-law rules for insurance contracts dealing with risks located within the EEA are to be found in the Financial Services and Markets Act 2000 (Law Applicable to Contracts of Insurance) Regulations 2001.[136] The general rule broadly mirrors that to be found in article 5 of the Rome Convention—that is to say, in the absence of choice by the parties, the law of the country in which the policyholder is habitually resident governs.[137] Although contracts of insurance may include a choice of law, the parties' freedom of choice (which, in the context of consumer insurance, invariably means the freedom of the insurer to choose the governing law) is strictly limited: indeed, the choice of another law will usually be without effect.[138]

The Rome I Regulation

12.72 The Regulation attempts to simplify the position with regard to choice of law for insurance contracts by replacing the choice-of-law rules derived from the insurance directives with article 7 of the Regulation. In the consumer context, the potentially relevant choice-of-law rules are those which apply to risks other than so-called 'large risks'.[139] As regards insurance contracts which do not concern large risks, article 7 applies if the risk is situated in a member state; if the risk is not situated in a member state, the applicable law is determined in accordance with the choice-of-law rules which apply to contracts in general (in particular, articles 3 and 4).[140]

12.73 In relation to insurance contracts which cover risks (other than 'large risks') which are situated within the territory of the member states, article 7 adopts the principle of limited choice coupled with a simple fall-back

[135] Second Non-Life Insurance Directive, Dir 88/357/EC [1988] OJ L172/1; Third Non-Life Insurance Directive, Dir 92/49/EC [1992] OJ L228/1; Second Life Insurance Directive, Dir 90/619/EC [1990] L330/50.

[136] SI 2001 No 2635, amended by SI 2001 No 3542.

[137] Regs 2(1), 4(2), and 8(2).

[138] J Basedow (2001: 499).

[139] As defined by Dir 73/239/EEC, art 5(d).

[140] In cases not involving life insurance, the country in which the risk is situated is determined in accordance with Dir 88/357/EEC, art 2(d); in the case of life insurance, the country where the risk is situated is the country of the commitment within the meaning of Dir 2002/83/EC, art 1(1)(g): art 7(6).

rule in cases where the applicable law has not been chosen. Article 7(3) provides that the parties may choose one of the following laws:

(a) the law of any member state where the risk is situated at the time of conclusion of the contract;
(b) the law of the country where the policy holder has his habitual residence;
(c) in the case of life insurance, the law of the member state of which the policy holder is a national;
(d) for insurance contracts covering risks limited to events occurring in one member state, other than the member state where the risk is situated, the law of that member state . . .[141]

It is also provided that, in a case within paragraphs (a) or (b), if the law of the member state in question is more liberal than article 7—in the sense that it permits the parties to the contract in question a wider freedom to choose the law applicable to the insurance contract—the parties may take advantage of that freedom. So, where a French national who lives in England enters a contract of life insurance with an English insurance company, if French law permits the parties to choose the law of the country in which the policyholder resides, a contractual clause choosing English law is valid. **12.74**

The fall-back rule—for cases where the contract does not include a choice of law—states that the contract 'shall be governed by the law of the Member State in which the risk is situated at the time of conclusion of the contract'.[142] This marks a departure from the previous rules—which provide that, in the absence of choice by the parties, the applicable law is the law of the country in which the policy holder is habitually resident.[143] Nevertheless, in the consumer context, this change in the rules is not intended to produce a huge change in practice;[144] in the majority of cases, the risk will be situated where the consumer is habitually resident. **12.75**

[141] It should be noted that there is also a fifth paragraph which applies only in the commercial context: it covers cases where 'the policy holder . . . pursues a commercial or industrial activity or a liberal profession' and the insurance contract relates to those activities.

[142] Art 7(4).

[143] Financial Services and Markets Act 2000 (Law Applicable to Contracts of Insurance) Regulations 2001, regs 2(1), 4(2), and 8(2).

[144] In a Declaration by the Council and the Commission relating to the law applicable to insurance contracts (of 7 April 2008), the Council and the Commission 'note that the rules contained in Article 7 essentially reflect the legal situation as regards applicable law as presently included in the insurance Directives': <http://register.consilium.europa.eu/pdf/en/08/st07/st07689-ad01.en08.pdf> [14/4/08].

2. Contracts of Carriage

12.76 Contracts relating to package holidays are within the consumer contract choice-of-law regime; if an English consumer buys a package holiday from a Swedish travel company via the company's website, the applicable law is determined in accordance with the choice-of-law rules which apply to protected consumer contracts.[145] However, as a general rule, contracts of carriage are excluded. As regards contracts of carriage which are not subject to the choice-of-law rules applicable to consumer contracts, the Rome Convention and the Rome I Regulation adopt different approaches. Under the Convention, the applicable law is determined by the choice-of-law rules which apply to contracts in general (in particular, articles 3 and 4).[146] By contrast, article 5 of the Regulation sets out specific choice-of-law rules for contracts of carriage.

12.77 With regard to contracts for the carriage of goods, the applicable law will normally be the law of the country of the carrier's habitual residence—either by virtue of a choice-of-law clause in the contract or the default rule which applies in the absence of choice.[147] However, the default rule provides for the application of the carrier's law only if the country of the carrier's habitual residence is also the place of receipt or the place of delivery or the country in which the consignor is habitually resident. If the country of the carrier's habitual residence does not coincide with one of these three other connecting factors, the applicable law is the law of the country where the place of delivery as agreed by the parties is situated.

12.78 The position is slightly more complicated with regard to contracts for the carriage of passengers. First, although the parties may choose the applicable law, the principle of limited choice applies. The parties may choose only the law of the country where:

(a) the passenger has his habitual residence; or
(b) the carrier has his habitual residence; or
(c) the carrier has his place of central administration; or

[145] Unless the services are to be supplied to the consumer exclusively in a country other than that in which he has his habitual residence, in which case the choice-of-law rules which apply to contracts in general are relevant: Rome Convention, art 5(4)(b); Rome I Regulation, art 6(4)(a).

[146] Note, however, that, in the absence of a choice-of-law clause, a contract for the carriage of goods will normally be governed by the law of the country in which the carrier has its principal place of business: art 4(4). Although structured slightly differently, a very similar rule is also to be found in art 5(1) of the Regulation.

[147] Art 5(1).

(d) the place of departure is situated; or
(e) the place of destination is situated.[148]

Secondly, to the extent that the applicable law is not chosen by the parties, the applicable law is the law of the country where the passenger has his habitual residence, provided that either the place of departure or the place of destination is situated in that country. If these requirements are not met, the law of the place where the carrier has his habitual residence applies. Thirdly, the default rule is subject to the general proviso that, where it is clear from all the circumstances of the case that the contract is manifestly more closely connected with another country, the law of that other country governs.[149] **12.79**

The net result of these rules—when applied in the consumer context—is that contracts of carriage are more likely to be governed by the carrier's law than by the consumer's law. If the pattern of choice-of-law clauses in consumer contracts in general is replicated in relation to contracts of carriage in particular, a choice-of-law clause will normally rely on paragraphs (b) and (c) and select the law of the country in which the carrier is based (either where the carrier is habitually resident or has its central administration). As a result, consumers will not retain the benefit of the mandatory rules of the law of the country in which they are habitually resident—even if the contract of carriage satisfies the requirements of article 6 (such as where a consumer purchases flights to and from a foreign destination via the carrier's website). **12.80**

VI. THE IMPACT OF HARMONIZATION ON CHOICE-OF-LAW RULES

It goes without saying that the potential significance of choice-of-law rules is a consequence of the fact that the law varies from one country to another. If the law of every country were the same, choice-of-law rules would become entirely redundant. Although there are international bodies (such as UNCITRAL) whose aim is to achieve, through international conventions, the harmonization of the world's commercial laws, there has been no progress to date towards the harmonization of consumer contract law at a global level. However, at the regional level, the position within Europe is different. In recent decades, differences between the national consumer laws of EU member states have been significantly eroded by the **12.81**

[148] Art 5(2).
[149] Art 5(3).

legislative programme of the European Community. It has already been noted that much of this development has been by means of minimum harmonization measures. So, although there should be a minimum level of consumer protection across all the member states, differences between national laws persist.

12.82 As things currently stand, even within the narrow field of cooling-off periods and cancellation rights, the situation is extremely complicated and there is plenty of scope for confusion and misunderstanding: in addition to the fact that the implementation of directives is far from uniform, there are different legislative schemes for doorstep selling, distance selling, timeshares, and so on. All this may change. It seems obvious that it would be in everyone's interests if the existing rules were reformed in order to make cancellation rights throughout the member states and across all consumer legislation more consistent.[150]

12.83 In 2006 the European Commission launched a consultation on a review of the Community *acquis* in the field of consumer protection. In its *Green Paper*,[151] the European Commission identified differences in the way in which the consumer directives have been transposed into national law as a factor which contributes to the general unwillingness of European consumers to buy goods and services from suppliers established in other member states:

> Different rules resulting from minimum harmonisation may have a negative impact on the internal market. One reason for consumers being reluctant to make cross-border purchases is that consumers cannot be sure that the level of protection that they enjoy at home will apply when they buy cross-border.[152]

12.84 One of the main questions is whether the length of cooling-off periods should be harmonized across the consumer *acquis*.[153] The objective of the review is to reach a situation in which it is possible to say to EU consumers: 'wherever you are in the EU or wherever you buy from it makes no difference: your essential rights are the same'.[154] Although it is still unclear what will flow from this review, one of the options under consideration is the replacement of the existing minimum harmonization measures with full harmonization measures (according to which the law applicable in all the member states would be the same) and it is clear that 'full harmonisation of consumer protection rules at an appropriately high level will tend

[150] Euroconsumer (December 2005: 17).
[151] European Commission, COM (2006) 744.
[152] European Commission, COM (2006) 744, p 7.
[153] European Commission, COM (2006) 744, p 21.
[154] European Commission, COM (2006) 744, p 3.

to be the Commission's approach'.[155] If further work within the context of the review confirms the preliminary findings, the Commission will make proposals in 2008.[156] Notwithstanding the fact that the review of the consumer *acquis* will not affect EC rules on the conflict of laws,[157] if the review results in legislation designed to achieve full harmonization—replacing the current set of directives which promote minimum harmonization—the sphere of application of choice-of-law rules in the European consumer context will be further reduced.[158]

VII. CONTEXTS

1. Supplier Behaviour

It has been argued that a choice-of-law regime which adopts the 'preferential law' approach of the Rome Convention and the Rome I Regulation (or the 'no choice' approach which was advocated in the European Commission's original proposal for the Regulation[159]) imposes excessive compliance burdens on suppliers.[160] If an e-trader sells goods online to consumers resident in 10 different EU member states, the supplier has to comply with the mandatory rules of 10 different laws. This burden is said to discourage suppliers from selling goods and services to consumers resident in other member states, especially with regard to banking and other financial services.[161] Although it has to be conceded that a supplier which attempted to discover the laws of the various countries to which it sells goods and then adapted its contractual behaviour in order to comply with all these laws would incur some costs, it is important that the problem should be kept in proportion. There are several angles to consider. **12.85**

First, an e-trader can simply choose not to sell goods or services to consumers who are resident in certain countries. During the conduct of a 1999 survey of Internet shopping (both domestic and cross-border), researchers **12.86**

[155] European Commission, COM (2007) 99, p 7.

[156] European Commission, COM (2007) 99, p 9.

[157] COM (2006) 744, p 5.

[158] *A fortiori*, the same would be true if there were ever to be introduced a European Civil Code or a European code of contract law. Notwithstanding the European Commission's *Communication . . . on European Contract Law* (COM (2001) 398), the chances of such a measure being introduced in the foreseeable future appear to be very slim.

[159] COM (2005) 650.

[160] See EMOTA (September, 2003: 4); EuroISPA (September 2003: 2). See also Y Zhao (2005: 141).

[161] See European Banking Federation (September 2003: 6); LIBA (2003: 14).

wasted a lot of time trying to place orders through websites, only to be told when the order was being submitted that the website would not accept orders from the country from which the researcher was operating.[162] Similarly, a survey conducted by ECC-Net in 2003 reported that the researchers had problems locating e-traders that actually sold to foreign consumers.[163] A 2007 survey of UK websites found that 63 per cent were not aiming to sell abroad and that sales by UK e-traders to UK consumers averaged 93 per cent of all online sales.[164]

12.87 Secondly, in view of the fact that disputes arising from consumer contracts are limited in scope, the rights of parties under a consumer contract will not usually turn on whether the applicable law is the law of country X or the law of country Y. Whatever law is the governing law, a supplier will normally fail to comply with his contractual obligations only if: (i) he misrepresents the nature of the goods or services which are the subject-matter of the contract; or (ii) he fails, within a reasonable time, to perform his side of the bargain (for example, by failing to deliver goods which are of satisfactory quality and fit for the purpose or to perform services of an appropriate standard). The consumer's obligation is even simpler: to pay the agreed price. Furthermore, because of harmonization at the European level, the consumer protection laws of the member states are highly convergent.[165]

12.88 It is not being suggested that all legal systems are the same or that there is no potential for choice-of-law issues to arise in the context of consumer contracts. The point is rather that one should be aware of the relatively narrow range of situations in which such issues may be relevant. The simplicity of the vast majority of consumer contracts, coupled with the fact that some fundamental contractual principles are almost universal,[166] means that the contexts in which choice-of-law questions can become of practical significance are severely circumscribed.

12.89 Thirdly, in the consumer context, it is generally unlikely that a contractual dispute will turn on complex questions of law.[167] It is much more likely that there will be disagreements over questions of fact (such as whether

[162] Consumers International (September 2001: 20).

[163] ECC-Net (May 2003: 17).

[164] Office of Fair Trading (June 2007: 151).

[165] T Puurunen (2003: 790).

[166] In their discussion of 'Contract', K Zweigert and H Kötz (1992: 546–7) note that 'attentive readers will repeatedly have noticed that the practical results in the legal systems under investigation are much more often in agreement than one would expect in view of their theoretical starting-points'.

[167] M Rutherford (2003: 638).

goods were delivered on time) and questions of judgment or evaluation (such as whether the goods were as described by the supplier or of satisfactory quality). Again, this does not mean that legal disputes cannot arise. Consider, for example, the case where a European consumer buys goods online from a New York supplier. The consumer may expect to be able to return the goods within the cooling-off period (and obtain a full refund) in accordance with the law of the country of his habitual residence, whereas there may be no such right under New York law. In the online context, it is more than likely that the consumer will have had to pay in advance (typically by credit card or debit card). Accordingly, in a dispute over the alleged right to cancel the contract, the supplier is in the stronger position—having already obtained the consumer's money—and, if the supplier refuses to give a refund, the onus is on the consumer to take action to try to recover it. It has already been observed that it is extraordinarily unlikely that the consumer will start proceedings in his home forum to enforce his rights under the Distance Selling Directive (and, if successful, seek to enforce the judgment in the United States). Accordingly, the risk to e-traders of their non-compliance with foreign laws is extremely small.

The position may be more difficult for the supplier in cases where the **12.90** consumer has not already paid. If the consumer's home law provides the consumer with a self-help remedy (such as withdrawing from a contract during the cooling-off period) in a situation in which the consumer has not made payment due under the contract (for example, where the consumer cancels a long-term contract which provides for periodic payments and stops making the payments), the risk shifts to the supplier. Even if the supplier is entitled to the payments due under the contract according to the law chosen to govern the contract, if the consumer can rely on the right to withdraw from the contract under the law of the country of his habitual residence, the supplier may have little prospect of being able to recover the unpaid sums.[168] So, while it is important not to exaggerate the potential burden placed on suppliers by a choice-of-law regime which gives priority to the (mandatory rules of the) law of the country in which the consumer is habitually resident, one should not go to the other extreme and conclude that such a choice-of-law regime can impose no burden at all on suppliers.

[168] For an illustration, albeit in the domestic context, of the problem faced by a supplier in a case where the consumer, who has not already made payments due under the contract, exercises his right to withdraw from the contract (relying on Dir 85/577/EEC to protect the consumer in respect of contracts negotiated away from business premises [1985] OJ L372/31), see Case C423/97 *Travel-Vac SL v Sanchis*, [1999] ECR I-2195.

12.91 Perhaps more significant than the legal regime that governs cross-border consumer contracts is the actual practice that is followed by the parties to such contracts. Not surprisingly, it seems that, in the e-commerce context, there is widespread flouting of laws providing for consumer protection.[169] Surveys conducted within the last decade indicate that the information requirements of the Distance Selling Directive (which imposes an obligation on the supplier, 'in good time prior to the conclusion of any distance contract', to provide the consumer with information on, inter alia, the existence of a right of withdrawal, the identity and address of the supplier, the price of the goods and delivery costs[170]) are frequently ignored: for example, one survey found that only 55 per cent of e-traders based in the European Union made any reference to whether the consumer could cancel an order or withdraw from the contract;[171] a more recent survey found that 32 per cent of websites failed to give information about the cooling-off period that applies to distance sales.[172] Notwithstanding such breaches, there is hardly any litigation arising from e-commerce in the consumer context (and no reported cases in this area in England).

12.92 Furthermore, the system of sanctions for non-compliance is relatively weak. The Injunctions Directive[173] (which is transposed into English law by Part 8 of the Enterprise Act 2002) authorizes public authorities to take action against traders who do not comply with the requirements of European legislation in the field of consumer protection.[174] However, legal action is very much a last resort and, in the United Kingdom, there are no instances of reported litigation in which the Office of Fair Trading (or any other qualified entity) has brought proceedings against e-traders for failure to abide by the requirements of the Distance Selling Directive (or, indeed, any other directive).[175] If an enforcement order is made under the Enterprise Act 2002 it does not involve the imposition of a financial penalty on the supplier.

12.93 Finally, the risks imposed on suppliers by a pro-consumer choice-of-law regime can be further reduced by the supplier adopting a flexible approach to issues which are of concern to consumers (for example, by having a generous returns policy). There are non-legal factors which might encourage

[169] Consumers International (September 2001: 8)
[170] Dir 97/7/EC, art 4.
[171] Consumers International (September 2001: 26).
[172] ECC-Net (May 2003: 17).
[173] Dir 98/27/EC [1998] OJ L166/51.
[174] See ch 8.
[175] This lack of litigation does not mean that the Office of Fair Trading is not tackling inappropriate trader behaviour. See ch 8.

e-traders to take a more sympathetic approach to the legitimate interests of consumers and make a virtue out of providing a service which goes beyond the minimum that is required by the law of the country in which the supplier is established. There seems little doubt that an extensive after-sales service can go a long way towards preventing problems arising; if complaints do arise, a clear and comprehensive refund policy nips most problems in the bud.[176] Such an approach will normally ensure that the supplier will not fall foul of the mandatory rules of even the most exacting systems of consumer protection. The business success of many online suppliers (which are involved in the sale of relatively low value goods—such as books, CDs, posters, software, clothes, etc) depends on establishing an environment in which consumers become repeat customers and recommend e-traders to their friends and family. Such an environment requires the supplier to behave in a way which consumers consider to be reasonable—otherwise they will take their custom elsewhere.[177] Even if the consumer's complaint has no legal basis and the supplier is legally entitled to disregard it, the supplier may choose to go beyond the bare minimum of the consumer's legal rights. There is research which suggests that, in sectors where suppliers depend on repeat business, most suppliers respond positively to consumer complaints—for example, by allowing consumers to return or exchange goods in situations where they do not have a legal right to do so.[178] This practice, which—for commercial reasons—has become almost universal among high street stores, is equally applicable in the online context.

2. Bargaining Situations

Only a tiny proportion of disputes are resolved by the intervention of a third party (such as a judge, arbitrator, or ombudsman); far more disputes are solved through bilateral negotiations between the parties than through any other process.[179] The extent to which legal rules play a role within such negotiations is uncertain. There is a theoretical model according to which rules play a significant role—even though they do not necessarily determine the outcome of the dispute in a direct way. The hypothesis is that: **12.94**

> Those involved in negotiation will entertain some picture, however erroneous, of what might happen if they resorted to other modes of decision-making—notably

[176] C Schulze and J Baumgartner (2001: 33). See also M Schellekens and L van der Wees (2002: 299).

[177] A Best and AR Andreasen (1977: 712–13).

[178] I Ramsay (1981: 127).

[179] See ch 9.

lawyer negotiations or adjudication. That picture will necessarily bear significantly on the conduct of negotiations.[180]

12.95 According to this model, the terms of any settlement are a product of an assessment of the strengths and weaknesses of each party's case; in cross-border cases, these strengths and weaknesses include an assessment of the likely outcome of jurisdictional and choice-of-law questions if the case were to go to court. This process of negotiation was famously described by Mnookin and Kornhauser as 'bargaining in the shadow of the law'.[181] Although 'bargaining in the shadow of the law' was presented as a theoretical model (and was not supported by systematic empirical research), the model has been widely assumed to apply to many different kinds of bargaining situation in which litigation might ensue if negotiations fail.[182] Two points are, however, worth noting. First, although subsequent commentators have tended to treat Mnookin and Kornhauser as suggesting a model of negotiating which treats legal norms as central, it is far from clear that Mnookin and Kornhauser actually considered that legal norms are the only (or even the most significant) background factor which shapes how negotiations are conducted.[183] Secondly, a number of empirical studies have shown that social norms may play an equally (or more) important role in certain types of negotiating situation.[184]

12.96 In the commercial context (in which potential litigants have access to and are likely to act upon legal advice), it is not unreasonable to suppose that legal rules are factors which are relevant to how parties evaluate their respective bargaining positions. Furthermore, in cases where the stakes are high enough, there is a real possibility that the party advancing a claim will resort to litigation if an acceptable solution is not reached through negotiation. So, even though neither party wants (or expects) the dispute to be resolved through the courts, the fact that there is a real possibility of litigation ensures that the parties' legal rights (which, in the cross-border context, depend upon the impact of jurisdiction and choice-of-law rules) shape, at least in part, the way in which the dispute is settled. This analysis suggests that there are two factors which produce 'bargaining in the shadow of the law': first, the parties are able, as a result of obtaining relevant

[180] M Palmer and S Roberts (2005: 114).

[181] R Mnookin and L Kornhauser (1979).

[182] H Jacob (1992: 565). For an example of this assumption, see BGM Main and A Park (2000). An illustration of how the theory presented by Mnookin and Kornhauser has become integrated into lawyers' modes of thought is provided by the fact that a search via *Google Scholar* for the phrase 'in the shadow of the law' generates well over 1,500 hits [20/6/07].

[183] See R Mnookin and L Kornhauser (1979: 973).

[184] See H Jacob (1992: 566).

legal advice, to assess the range of outcomes which might be reached if the dispute were decided by a court of law; secondly, if negotiations fail, there is a real (as opposed to merely theoretical) possibility that the claim will be litigated.

Such evidence as there is strongly suggests that the law plays a very limited role in the resolution of consumer disputes. Even in the domestic context, there is no evidence that 'bargaining in the shadow of the law' occurs in consumer cases. For example, following a study in Canada in the 1970s, the Ontario Law Reform Commission noted that the law appeared to have at best a marginal impact on consumer complaint handling.[185] Further research in Canada led to the conclusion that consumers' rights at the level of bilateral negotiation are 'dependent on norms generated by sellers partly in response to market forces rather than in response to legal rules'.[186] A similar picture emerges from research into small claims procedures in England.[187] If the law plays a very limited role in the resolution of domestic disputes, it seems safe to assume that, in the cross-border context, choice-of-law issues are unlikely to play a significant role in the resolution of disputes by means of bilateral negotiation between suppliers and consumers. **12.97**

If one considers a situation in which a US e-trader refuses to grant a refund to an English consumer who has sought to cancel a contract for the sale of goods concluded via the e-trader's website, is it realistic to imagine the consumer replying to the supplier's refusal by drawing attention to the primacy given to the consumer's law and the mandatory nature of the consumer's right to cancel the contract under the Consumer Protection (Distance Selling) Regulations 2000? The idea of 'bargaining in the shadow of the law' evokes an image of a consumer who knows his rights and the potential outcomes of litigation and who rationally calculates its impact on his bargaining position: 'The most casual empiricism suggests that this is not an accurate picture of consumer market disputing.'[188] **12.98**

One might surmise that at least three reasons underlie the fact that the law plays such a limited role in the resolution of consumer disputes. First, consumers in general are profoundly ignorant of their legal rights.[189] Consumer organizations consider that consumers' awareness of their rights generally when shopping is relatively low, and that awareness of **12.99**

[185] I Ramsay (1981: 123).
[186] I Ramsay (1981: 129). See also the findings of HL Ross and NO Littlefield (1978).
[187] J Baldwin (1997: 18).
[188] I Ramsay (2003: 30).
[189] See M Cappelletti and B Garth (1978: 68); PLEAS Task Force (July 2007: 7).

their rights when shopping online is lower still.[190] There is also evidence to suggest that consumers are actually less aware of their rights than they think they are.[191] Although it seems that there is some correlation between experience of buying online and knowledge of consumer rights, research suggests that even the most experienced Internet shoppers are still largely unaware of their rights.[192] If consumers do not know of their rights under the domestic law of the country in which they are habitually resident, it can be safely assumed that they know nothing at all about the private international law framework which is (potentially) relevant in cross-border situations.

12.100 Secondly, evidence suggests that consumers with complaints rarely seek legal advice before contacting the supplier. Research conducted in England in the 1990s revealed that people seek advice in relation to consumer problems less frequently than in relation to any other type of justiciable problem.[193] In a Europe-wide survey conducted a few years ago, 8 per cent of the sample admitted to having had, during the previous five years, a problem with a product or service that they had been unable to resolve with the supplier amicably. However, only a quarter of these individuals (ie, 2 per cent of the sample) sought advice either from a lawyer or a consumer organization.[194] A similar picture emerged from an equivalent survey two years later: 15 per cent of the sample had made a formal complaint to a supplier in the previous year; although 41 per cent of this group (ie, 6 per cent of the sample) were dissatisfied with the way in which their complaint was handled, only 23 per cent of these dissatisfied consumers (ie, less than 1.5 per cent of the sample) sought advice either from a consumer organization or from a lawyer.[195] These figures relate to domestic contracts, rather than cross-border contracts, but they show the extent to which consumers with complaints seem unwilling to seek out legal advice. A further significant point is that, to the extent that consumers seek advice and assistance, they normally do so only *after* their own efforts to obtain redress through bilateral negotiations have failed.[196]

12.101 Thirdly, 'bargaining in the shadow of the law' is premised on the idea that, if negotiations do not lead to a settlement, there is a credible threat that the claimant will decide to pursue his claim by more formal means.

[190] Office of Fair Trading (June 2007: 77).
[191] Office of Fair Trading (June 2007: 78).
[192] Office of Fair Trading (June 2007: 79).
[193] H Genn (1999: 107).
[194] Eurobarometer (October 2004: 23–6).
[195] Eurobarometer (September 2006: 30–3).
[196] H Genn (1999: 108).

However, litigation arising out of cross-border consumer contracts is so rare[197] that any threat of litigation (if there is no negotiated settlement) is almost entirely illusory.

3. ADR Mechanisms Involving the Intervention of a Third Party

Some commentators have asserted that: **12.102**

> It is generally agreed that ADR occurs 'in the shadow of the law,' meaning that negotiation, mediation and arbitration take place with the parties being somewhat aware that law, looming in the background, is a force that should enter into any calculations in how one develops and pursues a strategy for resolution.[198]

There are, however, factors which cast doubt on this hypothesis in the consumer context, especially as regards disputes arising out of online cross-border contracts.

One of the reasons for the relative unimportance of legal questions (includ- **12.103** ing choice-of-law questions) in the consumer context is the existence of systems of self-regulation.[199] A study of the resolution (by mediation) of disputes arising from transactions concluded via the *eBay* auction site noted that, during the dispute resolution process, law or recourse to any court system was rarely mentioned.[200] Many ADR schemes are allied to trustmark schemes or trade associations which promote a code of practice. In such cases, the rights and obligations of the parties are primarily determined by the standards of the code of practice, rather than the law applicable to the contract. This will often be to the consumer's advantage as such codes of practice frequently require suppliers to comply with standards that go further than the local law in terms of consumer protection. Alternatively, the code may adopt a 'preferential law' approach; for example, the *Rules of the Independent Arbitration Scheme for the Travel Industry* (2003 edn) provide that 'the Arbitrator shall have regard to ABTA's Code of Conduct' and that '[i]n the event of conflict between a rule of law and a provision of the code, the interpretation most favourable to the customer shall prevail'.[201]

Furthermore, there is a tendency for ADR schemes to play down the sig- **12.104** nificance of formal legal rules, particularly if the application of such rules

[197] See ch 2.
[198] E Katsh, J Rifkin, and A Gaitenby (2000: 707–8). See also C Rule (2002: 13).
[199] PP Swire (2005: 1976).
[200] E Katsh, J Rifkin, and A Gaitenby (2000: 731).
[201] Art 1.8: <http://www.idrs.ltd.uk/ABTA/Rules.asp> [15/4/08].

would result in a denial of justice (for example, because of a failure to comply with certain formalities).[202] For instance, under the Spanish system of consumer arbitration, the decision is made on the basis of equity unless the parties expressly agree to arbitration on the basis of the law; under this system, the parties opt for arbitration on the basis of the law in only a tiny proportion of cases.[203] The rules of the US Better Business Bureau state that, in consumer cases, '[a]rbitrators are not bound to apply legal principles in reaching what the arbitrator considers to be a fair resolution of the dispute.'[204] Similarly, in the United Kingdom, it is provided that, as regards cases which fall within the compulsory jurisdiction of the Financial Ombudsman Service, complaints are to be determined 'by reference to what is, in the opinion of the ombudsman, fair and reasonable in all the circumstances of the case'.[205] These factors have the effect of reducing the significance of the law and, *a fortiori*, choice-of-law rules in the ADR context.

12.105 Of course, where an English consumer buys from an e-trader established in another country there is no guarantee that a code of practice to which the supplier subscribes imposes a higher level of consumer protection than English law. Accordingly, it is possible that the application of the standards of a code of practice will give the consumer a lower level of protection than would (theoretically) be provided if the dispute were resolved by English litigation (in which case the consumer would be entitled to rely on rights conferred by the mandatory provisions of English law). There is little choice but to accept that this kind of problem is an inevitable feature of extra-judicial dispute-resolution processes. This is one of the reasons why, in the consumer context, decisions taken within the framework of an ADR scheme, although binding on the supplier, are often not binding on the consumer;[206] should the consumer's formal legal rights not be upheld through the ADR process, the consumer retains the right to litigate the claim.

12.106 Most extra-judicial systems for the resolution of consumer disputes (such as ombudsman schemes) have been established to deal primarily with domestic (rather than cross-border) complaints. If, for example, an English

[202] Study Centre for Consumer Law (January 2007: 142).

[203] Less than 1 per cent of the 8,000 awards rendered in 1999 were decided on the basis of law: A Vahrenwald (October 2000: 199).

[204] BBB Rules of Arbitration (Binding), para 28. See <http://www.us.bbb.org/WWWRoot/SitePage.aspx?site=113&id=21f49e22-ff8f-474b-8f92-caddd41adfb2> [7/1/08].

[205] Financial Services and Markets Act 2000, s 228(2).

[206] See, eg, *Safebuy*'s Code of Practice, art 5.6 <http://www.safebuy.org.uk/code-of-practice.html> [27/6/07].

consumer has a complaint against a French e-trader which is referred to an ADR scheme in France, the decision-maker will normally start from the assumption that French law applies: in general, the rules of ADR bodies do not consider the application of a foreign law relating to consumer protection.[207] Although, in theory, the consumer is entitled to rely on mandatory rules of English law, it can hardly be expected that, even if the procedural rules allow for the application of foreign law, the decision-maker will undertake research into English law and apply its mandatory rules of consumer protection of its own motion. The onus would be on the English consumer to raise any questions of English law which he considered relevant.

Some consumer arbitration schemes provide that, if the parties fail to agree, the law to apply shall be determined by the arbitrator.[208] Such a provision suggests that, in cases where the parties agree (which, in the consumer context, signifies cases where the supplier's standard terms and conditions include a choice of the supplier's law), the arbitrator will apply that law (without reference to any mandatory rules of any other law). There is, however, little evidence of how arbitrators actually decide cases in which they are empowered to select the governing law (because the parties have not agreed on the matter). **12.107**

In the consumer context, ADR mechanisms are designed to enable the consumer to advance his claim in person (without incurring the costs associated with legal representation). The fact that members of the public rarely seek legal advice in relation to consumer complaints has already been noted. In the context of a dispute-resolution process in which there is very limited participation by lawyers, choice-of-law issues—even if potentially relevant—will hardly ever be raised; it is almost impossible to imagine an unrepresented consumer averting to such issues. **12.108**

Although detailed information about ADR decision-making in individual cases is very hard to come by, one can be fairly confident that, in practice, to the extent that consumer disputes are not resolved by the application of the standards of the relevant code of practice (if there is one) or by reference to what the decision-maker considers to be fair, decisions will normally be made without any reference to choice-of-law issues and without choice-of-law rules being considered or applied. **12.109**

[207] A Vahrenwald (2000b: 13–14). It is worth noting, however, that the Consumer Complaints Boards in Denmark, Finland, and Sweden have considered themselves bound by the European choice-of-law regime: T Puurunen (2003a: 268).

[208] See, eg, art 9.1 of *Rules of the Independent Arbitration Scheme for the Travel Industry* (2003 edn): <http://www.idrs.ltd.uk/ABTA/Rules.asp> [15/4/08].

4. Litigation

Small Claims Procedures

12.110 Several of the factors considered with regard to ADR are also relevant in the context of small claims procedures. As regards small claims in England, litigants have been encouraged to present their own cases; legal representation is not prohibited but, since legal aid is not normally available, consumers who wish to be represented by a lawyer have to incur these costs themselves. Furthermore, the 'no costs' rule means that, even a successful litigant in the small claims procedure cannot recover the costs of legal representation from the losing party. It is, therefore, no surprise that lawyers do not figure prominently in small claims hearings in England. Research conducted in the 1990s shows that in more than four-fifths of cases neither party is legally represented and in only 2 per cent do both parties employ a lawyer.[209] As regards individuals (as opposed to businesses), only about one-in-six claimants have legal representation and significantly fewer than one-in-ten defendants.[210] When this is put together with the fact that most consumers do not seek legal advice—even in relation to disputes that are going to court—the chances of choice-of-law questions being raised in small claims procedures are extremely thin: research shows that, because they lack legal expertise, litigants in person find it difficult to establish the legal validity of their claims and defences and to argue a coherent case in court.[211]

12.111 Indeed, the research suggests that, in the domestic context, the law does not always feature prominently in cases which are resolved by the small claims procedure. First, lay litigants in the small claims procedure do not normally present their case by reference to legal arguments:

> Most litigants trust to luck and common sense, prepare their own cases as best they can, and arrive at court armed with little more than a strong conviction that right is on their side.[212] . . . Many litigants fail fully to appreciate that, although they feel an acute sense of injustice about their claim and are in no doubt whatever about the moral rectitude of their position, it is still necessary for them to establish that it has legal validity.[213]

[209] J Baldwin (1997: 39).
[210] J Baldwin (1997: 40).
[211] J Baldwin (1997: 19).
[212] J Baldwin (1997: 109–10).
[213] J Baldwin (1997: 121–2).

Lay litigants tend to imagine that their dispute will be resolved by the application of common sense; it comes as something of a surprise to them that a straightforward common-sense argument may be legally irrelevant in court proceedings[214] and that the outcome of small claims litigation may turn on legal argument and an application of legal rules or principles to the facts of the case.[215]

Secondly, district judges do not apply the law in a rigid way. Research has shown that only a minority take the view that it is their unequivocal duty strictly to apply legal principles in reaching decisions in dealing with small claims.[216] In interviews many district judges admitted that, in the context of small claims, they feel that it is more important for them to decide cases by reference to a standard of justice that the parties can understand and are likely to regard as fair than in strict accordance with the law.[217] **12.112**

These findings of the research into the small claims procedure have been set out at some length in order to illustrate the extent to which small claims in England operate in a relatively 'law-free' environment and to highlight a fundamental contradiction within the system—at least as far as the English legal system is concerned. On the one hand, the effect of the Rome Convention and the Rome I Regulation is that EU member states have adopted a quite complex choice-of-law model for consumer contracts; in cases where the contact includes a choice of law, the 'preferential law' approach of the Rome Convention and the Rome I Regulation requires a melding of the chosen law and the mandatory rules of the law of the country in which the consumer is habitually resident. Appreciation of the existence and significance of choice-of-law rules and an understanding of the distinction between mandatory rules and other legal rules are high-level legal skills. On the other hand, in cases where the amount in dispute is no more than £5,000, consumer disputes which are litigated in England are channelled into a procedure which discourages the participation of lawyers and in the context of which district judges do not feel constrained to apply the law strictly if such application would not be consistent with their conception of what justice requires. The result of this contradiction is that, to the extent that cross-border consumer litigation takes place in England under the small claims procedure, it is hard to imagine that choice-of-law questions can be a prominent feature of such litigation. **12.113**

[214] M Doyle, K Ritters, and S Brooker (January 2004: 21).
[215] J Baldwin (December 1997: 61–3).
[216] J Baldwin (1997: 71).
[217] J Baldwin (1997: 71–2).

'Ordinary' Litigation

12.114 In cases where the amount in dispute is more than £5,000, the claim will not normally be allocated to the small claims track; it will be assigned to the fast track or the multi-track. In essence, this means that the claim will be litigated in broadly the same way as other civil claims. In such cases, the parties will normally be represented by lawyers. This is probably the only context in which, in cases involving disputes which arise out of cross-border consumer contracts, the system can operate in accordance with the theoretical model which is postulated by the private international law system. Instead of the court automatically applying English law (or some version of English law tempered by the district judge's conception of justice)—which is what tends to happen in the small claims procedure—the court must apply the relevant rules of foreign law which the English choice-of-law rules determine to be applicable to the case and which one or other of the parties has pleaded and, if necessary, proved to the satisfaction of the court.

12.115 It goes without saying that circumstances giving rise to such a situation would be truly exceptional. There has yet to be a case reported in England involving choice-of-law questions arising from a cross-border consumer contract.

VIII. CONCLUSION

12.116 The aim of this chapter is to inject some sense of reality into the discussion of choice-of-law issues in relation to cross-border consumer contracts. The principal point is not that choice of law is irrelevant, but rather that its practical significance is rather less than some accounts of the topic might suggest. It is for this reason that the foregoing analysis, although addressing the most important theoretical concerns, does not examine in detail all the questions surrounding the interpretation of article 5 of the Rome Convention and article 6 of the Rome I Regulation.

12.117 There are a lot of factors which have the effect of limiting the role that choice of law can play. Not only are there matters which prevent choice-of-law questions from arising at all (even as a matter of theory): harmonization of the laws of different countries; the fact that many legal systems—even from different legal traditions—share common principles in the field of contract law; the fact that consumer contracts are usually quite simple and that disputes arising from consumer contracts tend to turn on factual issues. But also, in the limited circumstances in which it is possible for choice-of-law issues to arise, an examination of various contexts shows that, in practice, choice-of-law issues do not have a major impact on the way in which cross-border consumer disputes are resolved: consumers in dispute with suppliers do not 'bargain in the shadow of the law'; ADR mechanisms either operate according to extra-legal standards or result in cases being decided by reference to the local law; the small claims procedure (at least, in England) encourages the informal resolution of disputes in ways which make it almost inconceivable that (potentially relevant) choice-of-law issues will be addressed.

The implication of this analysis is that, notwithstanding the fact that seri- **12.118** ous legislative effort has been directed (particularly at the European level) not only at conferring a range of contractual rights on consumers but also at establishing a choice-of-law regime which is designed to ensure that consumers cannot be deprived of these rights, it seems clear that the legislation is unable to guarantee the vindication of consumers' strict legal rights. The nature of the practical issues is such that one might reasonably question whether choice-of-law rules can provide a very effective way of addressing the problem.

If the strict legal framework of choice-of-law rules does not achieve its **12.119** objective, there is an argument for trying an alternative approach. One of the most radical solutions is expressly to allow judges in small claims procedures (and ADR decision-makers) to step outside the framework of strict legal rights. For example, section 15(4) of the Small Claims Tribunals Act 1976 (NZ) provides:

> The Tribunal shall determine the dispute according to the substantial merits and justice of the case, and in doing so shall have regard to the law but shall not be bound to give effect to strict legal rights and obligations or to legal forms or technicalities.

This approach is consistent with what many district judges in England say **12.120** they do in any event. There are several advantages to explicitly conferring on judges and arbitrators the power to decide by reference to the justice of the case (rather than the strict law). First, in view of the fact that consumers seem to imagine that the outcome of their claim will turn on a common-sense view of the merits, a process which does not slavishly follow the strict letter of the law is likely to operate in a way that consumers can both understand and participate in with a degree of confidence. Secondly, if consumer claims are decided on the basis of the equity of the case, suppliers are encouraged to act reasonably in response to consumers' understandable (even if not legally justified) complaints.

13
Conclusions

Each of the earlier chapters contains some conclusions on specific topics **13.01** considered in this work and it is not intended to repeat them all in this final chapter. However, there are several broad themes which should be emphasized by way of conclusion.

I. PROBLEMS WITH LITIGATION

The problem with cross-border litigation as a solution to consumer disputes **13.02** is that, although consumers in general know that civil courts exist and that they are available for the resolution of legal disputes, the litigation process is intimidating, time-consuming, potentially expensive, and generally not well-adapted to the resolution of the low-value disputes that typically arise from consumer contracts. Although this problem can impact on suppliers as well as consumers, difficulties surrounding access to justice are more likely to affect consumers for several reasons. First, by and large, suppliers have a deeper pocket than consumers, are better able to take the financial risks that litigation entails and, as a general rule, are more geared up for litigation.[1]

[1] See M Cappelletti and B Garth (1978: 17–18).

Secondly, in the majority of situations, suppliers can avoid almost all economic risks by securing payment from the consumer in advance of performing their side of the bargain:

> In practice, the complicated rules of jurisdiction and choice of law will not be very important for the trader in consumer cases. Usually the trader will ask pre-payment from the consumer, including the use of modern payment instruments like credit cards, debit cards, electronic money and so on. Only with regard to larger transactions will it potentially be necessary to enforce outstanding payments . . . .[2]

13.03 Accordingly, except in relation to transactions which involve deferred payment or payment by instalments, the risks of non-performance are borne by the consumer, rather than the supplier. Thirdly, there is a discernable (and entirely understandable) reluctance by consumers to take claims to court:

> Many consumer disputes have a 'why bother' factor that may not be the case for other types of dispute . . . . As a result consumers will be less likely to pursue a resolution of the dispute if it is costly, inconvenient, time consuming or difficult to access.[3]

13.04 From the consumer's perspective, private international law rules designed to 'protect' consumers in the context of cross-border contracts are incapable of resolving the access-to-justice issues which are inherent within national legal systems. If the applicable procedural rules do not provide effective small claims procedures (including enforcement mechanisms) which, in practical terms, enable consumers to vindicate their rights through the legal process, a jurisdiction rule which allows a consumer to sue a foreign supplier in the consumer's home forum (rather than in the country in which the supplier is domiciled) is little more than an irrelevance.

13.05 The weaknesses of traditional small claims procedures are clear. In 2004, the European Consumer Centre (Dublin) produced a paper which outlined some of the problems which foreign consumers faced when seeking to make use of the Irish Small Claims Court.[4] Having noted all the difficulties, including the fact that the procedure did not work for cross-border cases, the authors concluded that the most practical and consumer-friendly form of dispute resolution in cross-border cases is extra-judicial rather than judicial.[5]

13.06 Although a streamlined small claims procedure can deal with some of the technical obstacles which confront consumers who are contemplating

[2] European Consumer Law Group (April 1998: para 21). See also EA O'Hara (2005: 1915).
[3] M Doyle, K Ritters, and S Brooker (January 2004: 4).
[4] ECC (Dublin) (June 2004).
[5] ECC (Dublin) (June 2004: 12).

cross-border litigation, such a procedure can do nothing to address the fundamental economic and social realities of most consumer disputes. Even if a small claims procedure is cheap and involves little financial risk, legal proceedings involve cost in terms of time, effort, stress etc. So, even where a consumer has an unanswerable claim, it does not follow that starting legal proceedings is either a rational or an appealing course of conduct. The ECC (Dublin), in its 2004 paper on the small claims procedure, gives the following example:

> While in Ireland on business, an English based consumer purchased a suit from a retailer in Dublin at a cost of €120. When the consumer returned to his accommodation he realised that the suit did not fit him and returned it to the shop the next day. The retailer agreed to replace the suit for a larger size, but as they did not have any in stock they agreed to send it by post to England.
>
> After several months of waiting for the suit to arrive the consumer contacted the ECC for assistance. The ECC made numerous attempts to resolve the dispute through direct contact with the retailer . . . . The unresolved dispute was then forwarded to the [Clearing House]. However as there was no nominated ADR body to deal with the complaint, the case was closed unresolved.
>
> The option of the Small Claims Court was outlined to the consumer; however it was felt that the value of the claim (€120) would not justify the trip to attend a Court Hearing.[6]

Although this example is given in the context of a criticism of the Irish **13.07** small claims procedure which requires the claimant to appear in person, it is questionable whether changes in procedure—which would obviate the need for the consumer to incur travel costs—would make a significant difference to the attractiveness of litigation as an option. If the consumer values his time, there is a monetary threshold below which a claim is simply not worth pursing by legal action, however well the procedure has been conceived. In these cases, unless the dispute can be resolved by negotiation—whether bilateral or assisted by a neutral third party—the consumer's only rational decision is to put the matter down to experience and resolve to take greater care in future. If informal dispute resolution mechanisms fail, the dispute remains unresolved and the consumer normally elects to 'lump it'—rather than investing time and effort in pursing court proceedings (or other formal dispute resolution processes).

The European Small Claim Procedure (ESCP) holds out the prospect **13.08** that litigation may become a potential solution for a wider range of consumer disputes. Nevertheless, it seems inevitable that, in view of the low value of so many consumer claims, it would still be irrational in

[6] ECC (Dublin) (June 2004: 4–5).

most cases for consumers to contemplate the commencement of legal proceedings—even if a streamlined and cheaper small claims procedure is available. Although the new procedure has some positive features (such as simplified cross-border enforcement), the costs rule potentially exposes a consumer whose claim fails to having to reimburse the defendant for expenditure on lawyers' fees[7] and, in its fundamentals, the procedure is not very different from the existing procedures in some member states. One is entitled to be sceptical about whether the ESCP will make a significant difference to the landscape of small claims litigation (at least in those member states which already have a small claims procedure); as a leading expert on the small claims procedure in England has made clear: 'any hopes that the small claims context might provide an avenue through which the poor might find redress for their grievances seem to have no empirical support whatever.'[8] If experience with national small claims procedures is replicated at the European level, there is every chance that the ESCP, rather than being of particular benefit to private individuals bringing consumer disputes to the courts, will be used more by other groups and for other purposes.[9]

13.09 It has been observed that little has been done to make court procedures more accessible to claimants who are resident in other countries (for example, through the use of information technology).[10] This criticism can legitimately be levelled at the European Union: although the European Small Claims Procedure Regulation pays lip-service to technological questions by providing that an oral hearing may be held 'through video conference or other technology', such a hearing can take place only 'if the technical means are available'[11] and there is no obligation on member states to provide appropriate technical facilities.[12]

13.10 The ultimate conclusion here is that, regardless of steps to improve consumers' access to court (by the reform of small claims procedures), the private litigation model cannot provide a satisfactory solution to the vast majority of cross-border consumer disputes. In relation to low-value claims there is nothing that can be done to make cross-border litigation a plausible option. Unless the consumer is interested in litigating a claim on a point of principle, the personal cost (in terms of time and effort) involved

[7] See ch 5.

[8] J Baldwin (1997: 15).

[9] See J Baldwin (1997: 30), writing about the small claims procedure in England.

[10] Organisation for Economic Co-operation and Development (2006: 44).

[11] Art 8.

[12] For the suggestion that the Regulation should impose the use of ICT into legal procedure, see JP Cortes Dieguez (2008: 95).

in pursuing legal proceedings is almost invariably going to be worth more than the amount of money in dispute. In practice, consumers are more likely to get what they want from their transactions if steps are taken to improve standards among suppliers in general and to make alternatives to court-based procedures more widespread and accessible. This requires a change of focus—away from the idea of the vindication of rights on an individual basis through the courts and towards dispute avoidance on a collective basis and alternative dispute resolution.

From this point of view, the priorities of the European institutions—as revealed by their legislative programme—are controversial. There seems to be a belief in the European Commission that, as a result of the establishment of the internal market, issues such as international jurisdiction and cross-border enforcement of judgments are of increasing significance. For example, writing in 1997, the Commission stated that '[t]he Brussels Convention and the rules relating to civil procedure are of ever increasing importance in relations between citizens and businesses in an increasingly integrated internal market.'[13] This bald assertion looks more like an article of faith than a conclusion based on empirical evidence; the Commission certainly fails to provide any evidence to support it. **13.11**

There appears to be a strongly ideological aspect to the European Commission's position—a position which is heavily influenced by what might be termed the 'lawyer's perspective'—namely, the idea that litigation is the primary (or a natural) means of settling disputes. However, in the foreseeable future, there is no realistic prospect of litigation becoming the dominant mechanism for handling cross-border consumer complaints—and it is hard to see how anything can be done in terms of either procedural law or the conflict of laws to render litigation a suitable mechanism for resolving low-value consumer claims. Accordingly, there is strong case for saying that developments at the European level as regards small claims procedures are largely irrelevant—in the sense that they are looking for a solution to access-to-justice problems in the wrong place. **13.12**

It is hard to disagree with the views of the European Parliament, which concluded—in the context of its deliberations over the Rome I Regulation—that, while the introduction of a European instrument dealing with small claims in cross-border cases is a step forward: **13.13**

> [T]he protection afforded to consumers by conflict-of-laws provisions is largely illusory in view of the small value of most consumer claims and the cost and time consumed by bringing court proceedings. It is therefore considered that,

[13] European Commission, COM (97) 609, p 9.

particularly as regards electronic commerce, the conflicts rule should be backed up by easier and more widespread availability of appropriate online alternative dispute resolution (ADR) systems.[14]

II. PROBLEMS WITH ADR

13.14 One of the main problems with ADR mechanisms is that they are difficult for consumers to access, not because they are unsuitable or expensive, but because consumers often do not know that they exist. ADR service providers are not very visible; they have a low profile and even a reasonably sophisticated, well-educated consumer is unlikely to be aware of either codes of practice and their implications or the various ADR schemes and other channels that they might pursue in order to obtain redress. In addition, European consumers who are aware of ADR mechanisms do not seem to have a lot of confidence in ADR as a way of reaching a satisfactory solution to their disputes.[15]

13.15 The fact that ADR is viewed so negatively and plays such a limited role is remarkable when one considers the emphasis which has been placed on ADR by non-governmental bodies, by national governments, and by the European Union. Even though various non-governmental organizations have issued recommendations concerning ADR in the context of e-commerce,[16] these bodies have not been able to make much progress towards establishing an international framework for the operation of ADR in the consumer context.

13.16 At the EU level, the European Commission has recognized that '[c]onsumer disputes require tailored mechanisms that do not impose costs and delays disproportionate to the value at stake'[17] and it is claimed that the promotion of ADR for consumer disputes is an important policy objective:

> ADR is a political priority, repeatedly declared by the European Union institutions, whose task it is to promote these alternative techniques, to ensure an environment propitious to their development and to do what it can to guarantee quality.

[14] See 'Compromise Amendments 2-44' (PE393.856v01-00): <http://www.europarl.europa.eu/meetdocs/2004_2009/documents/am/681/681958/681958en.pdf> [2/11/07]. A similar proposed amendment during the legislative process leading to the Brussels I Regulation was not accepted by the Council. See Joint Declaration of the Council and the Commission concerning Articles 15 and 73 of the Brussels I Regulation: <http://ec.europa.eu/civiljustice/homepage/homepage_ec_en_declaration.pdf> [2/11/07].

[15] See, eg, Eurobarometer (October 2004: 49, 57).

[16] European Commission, COM (2002) 196, pp 11–12.

[17] European Commission, COM (2007) 99, p 11.

This political priority was specifically asserted in the context of the information society.[18]

If ADR has been such a political priority in recent years, it is disappointing that the EU institutions have achieved so little in terms of establishing ADR in Europe as a truly effective mechanism for the resolution of disputes arising out of cross-border consumer contracts. Although the Commission has produced consultation documents, these consultations have not yet led to much in the way of concrete developments. At the EU level, there have been a lot of statements about the significance attached to ADR, but very little has been achieved in terms of tangible measures to support the use of ADR in practice. A provision such as article 17 of the E-Commerce Directive[19] (which states that member states 'shall ensure that . . . their legislation does not hamper the use of out-of-court schemes, available under national law'[20]) is extremely weak in terms of promoting ADR as it imposes no obligation on member states to make adequate provision for the settlement of disputes by ADR. **13.17**

An inventory of EU achievements in the broad field of ADR[21] includes: (i) the Injunctions Directive;[22] (ii) the two Recommendations on standards in ADR; (iii) the Consumer Complaint Form (which few consumers have ever heard of and which is not used very frequently); (iv) ECC-Net (which is also not known about by many consumers); (v) ECODIR (an online dispute resolution system, which after the initial pilot project appears to have become dormant); and (vi) the *Webtrader* trustmark scheme (which, after an initial period of support from the European Commission, folded).[23] In terms of durable outcomes, this is not a very impressive list. Furthermore, proposals by the European Parliament which attempted to give greater prominence to ADR in the consumer context have not been adopted: the Parliament's proposed amendment to the proposal for the Brussels I Regulation[24] was rejected by the Council;[25] a similar proposed amendment to the Rome I Regulation[26] shared the same fate. **13.18**

[18] COM (2002) 196, p 5.

[19] Dir 2000/31/EC [2000] OJ L178/1.

[20] See also recital 51 and the policy statements cited by A Vahrenwald (May 2000: 20).

[21] See European Commission, COM (2002) 196, pp 17–18.

[22] See ch 8.

[23] See ch 10.

[24] See [2001] OJ C146/98–99.

[25] See Joint Declaration of the Council and the Commission concerning Articles 15 and 73 of the Brussels I Regulation: <http://ec.europa.eu/civiljustice/homepage/homepage_ec_en_declaration.pdf> [2/11/07].

[26] See 'Compromise Amendments 2-44' (PE393.856v01-00): <http://www.europarl.europa.eu/meetdocs/2004_2009/documents/am/681/681958/681958en.pdf> [2/11/07].

13.19 It seems as though the European Commission imagines that, somehow, ADR will take care of itself—without serious measures being adopted to guarantee its efficient operation within the internal market. This contrasts with the legislative attempts to reduce the obstacles to cross-border litigation (such as the European Enforcement Order Regulation and the European Small Claims Procedure Regulation). Notwithstanding the exhortations and protestations about the importance of ADR, the practical measures taken by the European Commission suggest that, in Brussels, litigation is still seen as the primary route whereby legal rights should be protected.

13.20 As a result, consumers with claims which are not, in economic terms, worth pursuing through litigation are faced with a very unattractive vista. The ADR map is extremely fragmented and consumers remain largely unaware of the (often limited) ADR options which are open to them.

III. LACK OF CONSUMER AWARENESS

13.21 One of the themes which runs through many of the discussions relating to consumer redress is the need for consumers to be better informed—often presented as the need for consumers to inform themselves better. Governmental agencies seem agreed that any meaningful e-commerce strategy designed to increase consumer confidence and promote online shopping must give prominence to raising public awareness of a range of issues (such as trustmarks, codes of practice, and ADR).[27] This is an area where progress seems to be terribly slow. In the context of e-commerce, it has been observed that 'the image of the active and resourceful e-consumer . . . is yet a distant aspiration'.[28]

13.22 There are several ways in which increased levels of consumer awareness could have a positive impact on consumer disputes.

1. Sensible Shopping

13.23 Perhaps, most fundamentally, the incidence of consumer problems would be significantly reduced if consumers were more aware of mechanisms which can provide valuable information about suppliers (for example, trustmark schemes and 'Howard', ECC-Net's online 'shopping assistant'[29])—so that they are better able to make sensible purchasing decisions. If consumers

[27] See Office of Fair Trading (June 2007: 45, 62, 69, 87, 160). The same objective has also been identified in the United States: see Federal Trade Commission (November 2000: 11).

[28] T Puururen (2003a: 237).

[29] See, eg, <http://www.ukecc.net/sub.asp?id=209> [20/4/08].

had a balanced view of the risks involved in cross-border shopping and knew how to minimize those risks, they could choose to avoid purchasing goods and services from unreliable suppliers who fail to maintain high standards of customer care (including responsive complaints-handling procedures).

2. Awareness of Legal Rights

If consumers (and suppliers) were more aware of their rights (and obliga- **13.24**
tions) under consumer protection legislation, the kinds of dispute which arise from misunderstandings and unreasonable expectations could be avoided. However, the idea that, in practice, there is very much that can be done to make the public in general more legally aware of consumer issues may be little more than wishful thinking. To the extent that there have been attempts, in the past, at public information campaigns in the consumer field, the achievements have been very limited.[30] Some initiatives, however well intentioned, are patently incapable of achieving their objective. For example, in 2003 the European Commission and the Council of Europe established a European Civil Justice Day to take place on 25 October each year, in order to bring civil justice to the attention of the European public. This day is 'an opportunity for the public to familiarise themselves with the civil justice system, which should make it easier for them to access it' and it is said that it 'will also help to raise awareness among Europeans of the emerging area of justice which they share'.[31] But, when one looks to see what the European Civil Justice Day means in terms of concrete activity, the gulf between the rhetoric and the reality is truly astonishing. For example, it appears that, in the United Kingdom, European Civil Justice Day 2007 amounted to no more than a one-day conference organized by the Law Society with the title 'Dispute resolution across borders—a new toolkit for practitioners'.[32] So, although the intended objective of relevant events taking place on 25 October is 'to make civil justice more comprehensible to the *public*'[33] the organized activity involved *lawyers* talking to each other. It would be interesting to know how many members of the public (not only in the United Kingdom but also in other member states) are aware of the significance which the European Commission attaches to 25 October.

[30] National Consumer Council (September 1979: 13–16).

[31] See <http://ec.europa.eu/civiljustice/news/ecjd_2007_en.htm#national_events> [10/1/08].

[32] For the programme of the event, see <http://ec.europa.eu/civiljustice/docs/ecjd_2007/law_society_programme_en.pdf> [28/3/08].

[33] See <http://ec.europa.eu/civiljustice/news/ecjd_2007_en.htm#national_events> [10/1/08]. Emphasis added.

13.25 In recent years, public legal education has begun to feature more explicitly on the policy agenda and a consensus has emerged that a strategy on consumer education is needed.[34] In 2004 the Office of Fair Trading announced a new consumer education strategy[35] and in January 2006 the government established the Public Legal Education and Support (PLEAS) Task Force,[36] whose remit was to develop proposals for how to promote and improve public legal education (PLE). In its report, published in July 2007, the Task Force recommended the setting up of a new independent agency to implement a PLE strategy and the creation of a new PLE centre (to be funded by central government for five years) with seven key tasks (in its first year): (i) to promote a coherent identity for PLE; (ii) to establish partnerships; (iii) to create a practitioner and resources network, including online; (iv) to develop good practice in PLE; (v) to commission early pilot projects; (vi) to undertake research; and (vii) to work to establish a statutory remit for the PLE Centre.[37] Whether such developments at the strategic level (and any practical initiatives which may ultimately be spawned by them) can make significant inroads into the general public's 'extraordinary lack of understanding'[38] of legal issues remains to be seen. Without in any way wishing to question either the importance of attempts to raise public awareness of the ways in which the law is relevant to people's lives or the sincerity of those who are working in this field, a sceptical observer might be inclined to think that, for the foreseeable future, levels of public ignorance of the law are likely to remain fairly constant. Moreover, it has to be accepted that the capacities of typical consumers (and, indeed, their interest in learning about legal issues) are not limitless:

> Trying to reach the consumer through different media imposes information providers a challenging task in moulding the consumer more in the direction of a quasi-lawyer. There are limits to what consumers can and should be required to understand

[34] See M Coppack (November 2003). Many commentators allude to the need to educate consumers on various legal matters; see, eg, L Edwards and C Wilson (2007: 328).

[35] See Office of Fair Trading (October 2004).

[36] See <http://www.pleas.org.uk/>. The task force was the government's response to a joint initiative of the Advice Services Alliance, Citizenship Foundation, and the Legal Action Group. The first step was a discussion paper in September 2004 ('Towards a national strategy for public legal education'): see <http://www.advicenow.org.uk/fileLibrary/pdf/PLE_Consultation_paper.pdf> [29/11//07]. The discussion paper was widely circulated and the response was collated in 'Public Legal Education: A Proposal for Development', which was published in March 2005: see <http://www.pleas.org.uk/uploads/Publicpercent20Legalpercent20Educationpercent20-percent20percent20apercent20Proposalpercent20forpercent20Development.pdf > [29/11/07].

[37] PLEAS Task Force (July 2007: 29).

[38] PLEAS Task Force (July 2007: 7).

and perform, and governments and consumer protection organisations have a major task in getting pertinent information to the consumer in a digestible form.[39]

At the day-to-day level, there seem to be real problems in directing publicly available information to those who would benefit from it. For example, research conducted in the 1990s in England concluded that leaflets produced by the Lord Chancellor's Department had failed to raise public awareness of issues in small claims procedures; most litigants that reach the court have not even seen the leaflets, let alone read them.[40] Moreover, advice agencies report that, as regards those consumers who do obtain relevant leaflets, such leaflets are sometimes very difficult to understand.[41] This is symptomatic of a general problem—both as regards ADR mechanisms and small claims procedures. While there are many organizations which have established websites and produce leaflets and brochures dealing with aspects of consumer rights and access to justice, it seems that few consumers know of their existence. The fact that information can be obtained from a website does not mean that consumers either know how to find it or, if they do, are able to make effective use of the information contained in it.[42] The same type of problem exists in relation to the myriad of leaflets and factsheets produced by numerous organizations; the relevant leaflets may not find their way to those who would benefit from them and, even if they do, there is no guarantee that the recipients either take the trouble to read them or can fully understand their significance. For example, in the context of small claims procedures, research suggests that: **13.26**

> The problem is that while some courts . . . have information (brochures or leaflets) available on the procedure, they play no active role in its distribution. Consequently this information often does not reach the parties in general, and even less defendants.[43]

[39] T Puurunen (2003a: 237).

[40] J Baldwin (1997: 110).

[41] Citizens Advice (October 2005).

[42] In the United Kingdom, advice and assistance is available through the *ConsumerDirect* website (<http://www.consumerdirect.gov.uk>) which also provides a telephone service through which consumers may speak to regional advisers. There seems to be no research into the extent to which consumers know about and make use of this service. See also <http://www.dolceta.eu/>, which was established by a consortium of universities with the financial assistance of the European Commission. This website contains a huge amount of information about consumer rights throughout the EU member states. However, this website is primarily intended for use in the context of adult education (rather than simply as a public source of information) and the information is presented in a way that a non-lawyer may well find difficult to process. For a more optimistic view of the positive role played by public information posted on websites, see Y Zhao (2005: 80).

[43] Study Centre for Consumer Law (January 2007: 231).

3. Awareness of ADR Mechanisms

13.27 Consumers would be more likely to be able to obtain redress in cross-border cases if they knew about available ADR avenues:

> Increasing consumer awareness of ADR bodies and, more importantly, assisting consumers in finding the best way to obtain redress in the patchwork of existing possibilities for consumer redress, seems one of the most important action points on which to work.[44]

Within the European Union, a significant (and not wholly unrealizable) step forward would be to promote awareness among consumers of the existence of ECC-Net and the ways in which it can assist in the resolution of cross-border problems.

13.28 Viewed in the round, the problem is not so much that sources of advice and information are not available, but that consumers are not aware of them or do not use them. Nevertheless, there is much more that could be done to promote public awareness of advice agencies and the like. But, any system of public advice (as opposed to individual advice by legal professionals) involves costs. Unless these costs are borne by the inadequately funded and hopelessly stretched voluntary sector, public education and advice shifts the costs from the parties in dispute to the state.[45] This raises serious questions about how much money governments are (and should be) prepared to spend on improving consumer access to justice.

IV. THE ROLE OF THE LAW AND POTENTIAL REFORMS

13.29 To some extent, as regards low-value transactions, suppliers can afford to adopt a generous approach to consumer complaints. To a supplier, the costs of arguing the toss with a consumer will often exceed the cost of satisfying the consumer's demand in full. In addition, responding positively to consumer complaints is good PR and helps to establish goodwill and encourage repeat business. For these reasons, many retailers who sell low-value items adopt a 'no questions asked' return policy—which allows the consumer simply to change his mind, return the goods, and obtain a full refund.[46] In this kind of environment, the way in which disputes are

[44] Study Centre for Consumer Law (January 2007: 157).
[45] Study Centre for Consumer Law (January 2007: 232).
[46] See I Ramsay (1981: 395–408).

resolved depends largely on economic considerations; the legal rights of the parties are secondary (or even irrelevant). Accordingly, it is important for lawyers not to see court-based small claims procedures as the key solution to consumers' access-to-justice problems.

These comments should not be thought to suggest that the fine tuning of small claims procedures is inappropriate; there can be no argument for the retention of procedural models that fail to work properly and are amenable to improvement. A small claims procedure should be as responsive to the needs of consumers as possible and should take into account the cross-border dimension. However, it has to be recognized that the development of better small claims procedures is only a very small part of the answer to consumers' problems; the economics are such that court-based remedies are going to play no more than a very minor role in the disputes which arise out of the vast majority of consumer contracts. **13.30**

It is also worth noting that, from the perspective of private international law and civil procedure, subject to one exception, there is probably not a lot more that can be done in Europe to improve consumer access to the courts for small claims.[47] In terms of private international law, the Brussels I Regulation, the Rome Convention, and the Rome I Regulation tilt the balance—both as regards jurisdiction and choice of law—in the consumer's favour. The only potential change would be to extend the scope of the protective rules to include cross-border consumer contracts which result from in-person shopping. There is, however, no justification for such a change; where, for example, an English consumer purchases goods from a French supplier's store in Paris, the supplier—who has not entered the international arena—has a legitimate expectation that, if litigation were to arise, it would take place in France and English law would be irrelevant to the resolution of the dispute. **13.31**

Similarly, following the entry into force of the European Small Claims Procedure Regulation, an EU consumer can use the ESCP in any of the member states. There are various ways in which the procedure could have been made more consumer-friendly; for example, the final version of the Regulation adopted the 'loser-pays' principle (rather than the 'no costs' rule, as found in England) as a result of which the ESCP is more financially risky than it could have been; also, the Regulation could have taken **13.32**

[47] As regards the Brussels I Regulation, see the statement of B Hess, T Pfeiffer, and P Schlosser (September 2007: 144) that '[m]ost national reporters agree that Section 4 is satisfactory and that no additional consumer protection is needed' and their conclusion (at 148) that '[t]he materials found and the information brought to our knowledge do not indicate that an amendment of the Regulation's drafting [of Section 4] should be suggested.'

a stronger lead in terms of requiring that modern technology be available to facilitate cross-border small claims litigation. However, these potential weaknesses probably do not make the ESCP significantly less attractive to consumers than it might have been. As argued already, the most significant obstacles to cross-border consumer litigation result from social and economic factors unconnected with the small claims procedure itself.

13.33 The one area in which there is still scope for procedural reform is in relation to procedures for collective actions for damages. It remains to be seen whether the European institutions decide to introduce such a procedure at the EU level. Even if they do, whether such a reform would achieve very much with regard to disputes arising from consumer contracts is perhaps doubtful.

13.34 Although steps have been taken with the (largely unrealizable) objective of making litigation a mechanism whereby consumers may vindicate their contractual rights, there is much more that could be done in the field of ADR. In the overall landscape of ADR in Europe, on top of the general public ignorance of the extent of ADR provision, there are several areas of concern: (i) although different EU member states have a different 'mix' of the available ADR avenues (which is not necessarily a problem in itself), there are significant gaps in terms of coverage; (ii) there are insufficient incentives for bilateral negotiation; and (iii) payment card protection schemes are not very widespread.[48]

13.35 If one starts from the premise that, to the extent that there will be a significant increase in cross-border economic activity involving consumers, this increase is likely to take place mainly as a result of the expansion of e-commerce, a rational strategy would focus on the problems posed by disputes arising from online contracts. Although there are no simple answers—and there is no dispute-resolution mechanism which is going to be perfect—the development of codes of practice and trustmarks is likely to be as good a way forward as any. So, rather than focusing on the barriers which prevent consumers from seeking to litigate their claims (which legislators can do very little to remove), governments at all levels would be more likely to achieve something positive in the field of consumer redress if they made a concerted effort to: (i) create and promote an effective Europe-wide code of practice for European e-traders; (ii) establish a Europe-wide network of ADR bodies—with complete coverage of disputes which arise from consumer contracts; and (iii) take meaningful steps to promote consumer awareness of ADR mechanisms and to foster consumer

[48] Study Centre for Consumer Law (January 2007: 43).

confidence in ADR as an appropriate solution to consumer disputes. Of course, the implementation of such a strategy would involve significant costs—which governments may well be unwilling to incur.

V. E-COMMERCE AND ODR

One of the themes of this book is that, from a legal point of view, there is much less to e-commerce and ODR than meets the eye. Although it has been (and, in certain quarters, remains) fashionable to oppose 'real space' with 'cyberspace', it has to be remembered that cyberspace is not a place and events do not happen there. The idea that e-commerce 'happens in virtual space' and that 'events on the Net occur everywhere but nowhere in particular'[49] cannot be accepted; an online contract, no less than an offline one, is concluded between natural or legal persons who have a physical existence (in real space) and results from decisions taken by human beings in the real world. Whether a contract is concluded offline or online, a consumer contract is invariably a standard-form contract, the value of the subject-matter of the contract is normally low, and the access-to-justice problems faced by the consumer are very largely the same. In addition, with regard to the questions considered in this work, most of the legal issues are the same—or very similar. In terms of getting to grips with the e-commerce dimension of cross-border consumer contracts, one of the real problems is that, in the published literature, there are many accounts of the relationship between e-commerce and the law which both display misunderstandings about the workings of private international law and place undue weight on technical factors (such as the fact that, in the world of e-commerce, 'messages can travel along networks anywhere on the globe'[50]) which, in the context of b2c contracts, are legally irrelevant. **13.36**

The advent of the Internet means that it is easier than ever before for consumers to conclude contracts with foreign suppliers. As has been seen, this has not, in fact, brought private international law into centre stage—mainly because the low value of consumer transactions means that litigation does not provide a realistic solution to consumer disputes. As a result, ADR and ODR become potentially relevant; ADR offers, in the majority of cases, the only realistic prospect of resolving a dispute which cannot be settled by the parties through bilateral negotiation. In view of the fact that, in practice, **13.37**

[49] DR Johnson and DG Post (1996: 1376).
[50] Y Zhao (2005: 152).

the differences between ADR and ODR boil down to little more than different modes of communication between the parties and any third parties who participate in the dispute-resolution process, it is difficult to know why, in the literature, so much attention has been lavished on ODR. Any attempt to provide an explanation is necessarily somewhat speculative.

13.38 One possibility is that when ODR first became a practical option, communication by electronic means had not yet become ubiquitous in the commercial world. In such an environment, ODR may have appeared more distinctive than it really is. Now that the Internet plays such an important role in people's working and non-working lives and that e-mail is the dominant form of communication in so many areas of modern life, the idea of online mediation or arbitration is entirely unremarkable. Another factor is that discussion of e-commerce and related topics has tended to be conducted by technophiles. There is a strand in the literature which reveals a fascination with, and revels in, the technological aspects of the topic. Much of this discussion masks the fact that, from a legal point of view, there is relatively little that is distinctive about e-commerce and ODR.

VI. POLICY AND COSTS

13.39 The issue of consumer redress seems to have been the subject of endless discussion at the European and international levels. There has been a plethora of workshops, conferences, forums, and task forces which have sought to produce guidelines and strategies. Some of these initiatives have been considered in previous chapters, but by no means all of them—largely because several initiatives have produced very little (if anything) of value. It seems that, although consumer redress is something which governments and international bodies say is very important, progress towards the establishment of an environment in which a consumer who has a complaint arising from a cross-border contract can be confident of having access to an appropriate and effective mechanism for the resolution of that dispute is painfully slow.

13.40 The material discussed in the previous chapters raises various policy questions—about what type of dispute-resolution landscape is wanted and about how much public money should be spent on it. Notwithstanding the numerous statements at national, European, and international levels about the economic importance of consumers being empowered,[51] there seems to be an unwillingness by governments to spend public money on

[51] See, eg, European Commission, COM (2007) 99, p 5.

making consumer access to justice a reality. This observation should not be seen as a suggestion that governments should necessarily spend more on consumer redress. In the end, it is a question of political priorities; if governments put more public money into consumer policy either there will be less money to spend on other areas of governmental concern (such as education, health, and defence) or more tax revenue will need to be raised. The point is rather that a fully functioning system of consumer redress cannot be achieved at no cost; but many governments seem to be wedded to the idea that much of the answer can be found through self-regulation and to imagine that a solution to access-to-justice problems can be found without a major investment of public money. Within the context of EU policy relating to the internal market, there is an argument for saying that European governments should be prepared to establish some sort of public legal framework for ADR mechanisms—at least to deal with disputes which arise from e-commerce. If an important policy objective is making the internal market a reality for EU consumers, something meaningful with regard to cross-border consumer redress needs to be achieved in order for an appropriate level of consumer confidence to be attained.

VII. A BROADER QUESTION

This work has focused mainly on issues surrounding consumer redress in **13.41** situations where a dispute has arisen. There is a case for saying that this takes too narrow a view of the problem; it has been argued that, in terms of the development of a dispute, there are three stages: naming (identifying a particular experience as injurious), blaming (attributing an injury to someone else's fault), and claiming (seeking a remedy from the person responsible).[52] Although a very large proportion of injurious events do not generate legal disputes, the focus of legal reformers centres on legal questions—such as the reform of jurisdiction rules or small claims procedures. Such reforms have the potential to assist those who have articulated their grievance in legal terms and seek legal redress. However, such reforms do nothing to address the earlier stages of the process (ie, naming and blaming). There is evidence to support the conclusion that consumer redress mechanisms are used primarily by middle-class consumers; research in England in the 1990s found that, as regards small claims proceedings, most claimants were both relatively well-off and well-educated:

> Over two-thirds of those in paid employment were in professional or managerial occupations and the same applied to well over half of all defendants . . . . Very few

[52] W Felsteiner, R Abel, and A Sarat (1980–81).

litigants were from ethnic minority groups. The genuinely 'poor' make few appearances at small claims hearings, and, when they do, it is typically as defendants to face landlords or money lenders.[53]

There is similar evidence that middle-class consumers make more use of internal complaints procedures and are more likely than other social groups to obtain redress by informal means.[54]

13.42 The reform of legal processes does nothing to assist less privileged socio-economic groups to identify their injuries as potential disputes or to attribute responsibility to another person. As a result, the access-to-justice movement may, in part, be expending its energy in the wrong place:

> Access to justice is supposed to reduce the unequal distribution of advantages in society; paradoxically it may amplify these inequalities. The ostensible goal of these reforms is to eliminate bias in the ultimate transformation: disputes into lawsuits. If, however, as we suspect, these very unequal distributions have skewed the earlier stages by which injurious experiences become disputes, then current access to justice efforts will only give additional advantages to those who have already transformed their experiences into disputes. That is, these efforts may accentuate the effects of inequality at the earlier, less visible stages, where it is harder to detect, to diagnose and to correct.[55]

13.43 This is one of the reasons why any consumer redress strategy needs to be multi-faceted, combining private action (whether through litigation or ADR processes) with both consumer education and public mechanisms whereby government authorities and consumer organizations can police the consumer market, take action against rogue traders, and provide a deterrent against sharp practices—for the benefit of all consumers. Although public collective action does not provide redress for individual consumers who have suffered loss as a result of unlawful behaviour by suppliers, such actions, if successful, have the effect of reducing the chances that consumers will suffer such losses in the future.[56] Other methods of driving up standards—such as codes of practice—can also play an important role in reducing the incidence of consumer problems.

[53] J Baldwin (1997: 166). See also I Ramsay (2003: 37). In the words of H Kötz (1981: 89): 'Stimulating lawsuits by consumers . . . will typically benefit middle class interests rather than the interest of the citizens below the poverty line.'

[54] See I Ramsay (1981: 121–34).

[55] W Felsteiner, R Abel, and A Sarat (1980–81: 637).

[56] See European Consumer Law Group (April 1998: para 8 n 3). For further discussion, see ch 8.

VIII. FINAL COMMENTS

The overarching theme of this work is the legal system's failure to provide a framework in which a consumer who has a legitimate complaint arising from a cross-border contract can obtain redress against a supplier which has failed to comply with its obligations. Not only is litigation an inappropriate redress mechanism for all but a tiny proportion of cross-border consumer disputes, but also ADR processes are insufficiently developed and promoted. Within such an environment, is it any wonder that a majority of consumers who run into problems ultimately decide to 'lump it'? **13.44**

So, the question is whether anything should be done to improve this state of affairs—and if so, how much? It is easy to suggest that there needs to be a sophisticated multi-pronged strategy for the advancement of consumer interests: enhanced access to justice through improved small claims procedures; better public enforcement of consumer legislation against rogue traders; and effective ADR mechanisms which are both accessible and easy to understand. However, such a strategy would be difficult and costly to implement. It is not self-evident that society as a whole (as opposed to the consumer-rights lobby) wants more tax revenue to be devoted to improved consumer access to justice (whether judicial or extra-judicial). Furthermore, in the final analysis, one has to be realistic. There will always be some cases where suppliers fail to comply with their contractual obligations and consumers fail to obtain redress. Whether one likes it or not, this is a fact of life. How much public resource should be devoted to addressing this issue? **13.45**

Bibliography

I. BOOKS AND JOURNAL ARTICLES

G Alpa, (2001) 'Trading On-line and the Protection of the Consumer' [2001] European Business Law Review 244.

M Andenas, (2006) 'National Paradigms of Civil Enforcement: Mutual Recognition or Harmonization in Europe?' [2006] European Business Law Review 529.

R Andrews, (2005) 'Electronic Commerce: Lessons Learned from the European Legal Model' 9(2) Intellectual Property Law Bulletin 81.

H Arfazadeh, (2002) 'In the Shadow of the Unruly Horse: International Arbitration and the Public Policy Exception' 13 American Review of International Arbitration 43.

J Arsic, (1997) 'International Commercial Arbitration on the Internet' 14(4) Journal of International Arbitration 209.

R August, (2002) 'International Cyber-Jurisdiction: A Comparative Analysis' 39 American Business Law Journal 531.

J Baldwin, (1997) *Small Claims in the County Courts in England and Wales: the Bargain Basement of Civil Justice* (Oxford: Clarendon Press).

RA Bales and S van Wert, (2001) 'Internet Web Site Jurisdiction' 20 John Marshall Journal of Computer and Information Law 21.

J Basedow, (2001) 'The European Insurance Market, Harmonization of Insurance Contract Law, and Consumer Policy' 7 Connecticut Insurance Law Journal 495.

DM Bates, (2004) 'A Consumer's Dream or Pandora's Box: Is Arbitration a Viable Option for Cross-Border Consumer Disputes?' 27 Fordham International Law Journal 823.

H Beale, (1995) 'Legislative Control of Fairness: The Directive on Unfair Terms in Consumer Contracts' in J Beatson and D Friedman, *Good Faith and Fault in Contract Law* (Oxford: Clarendon Press) pp 231–61.

J Bell, S Boyron, and S Whittaker (1998) *Principles of French Law* (Oxford: Oxford University Press).

M Berliri, (2003) 'Jurisdiction and the Internet, and European Regulation 44 of 2001' in D Campbell and S Woodley (eds), *E-commerce: Law and Jurisdiction* (The Hague: Kluwer Law International) pp 1–12.

—— (2003a) 'Jurisdiction and Choice of Law in Cyberspace in Europe' 16 International Law Practicum 48.

PS Berman, (2002) 'The Globalization of Jurisdiction' 151 University of Pennsylvania Law Review 311.

——(2005) 'Choice of Law and Jurisdiction on the Internet' 153 University of Pennsylvania Law Review 1819.

A Best and AR Andreasen, (1977) 'Consumer Response to Unsatisfactory Purchases: A Survey of Perceiving Defects, Voicing Complaints, and Obtaining Redress' 11 Law & Society Review 701.

G Betlem, (2007) 'Public and Private Transnational Enforcement of EU Consumer Law' [2007] European Business Law Review 683.

L Biukovic, (2002) 'International Commercial Arbitration in Cyberspace: Recent Developments' 22 Northwestern Journal of International Law and Business 319.

PA Bonner and EJ Metzen, (1992) 'Small Claims Court: Factors Influencing a Successful Outcome for the Individual Plaintiff' 26 Journal of Consumer Affairs 1.

BD Boone, (2006) 'Bullseye!: Why a "Targeting" Approach to Personal Jurisdiction in the E-Commerce Context Makes Sense Internationally' 20 Emory International Law Review 241.

PJ Borchers, (1992) 'Forum Selection Agreements in the Federal Courts after *Carnival Cruise*: A Proposal for Congressional Reform' 67 Washington Law Review 55.

A Briggs, (2002) *The Conflict of Laws* (Oxford: Oxford University Press).

——(2006) Book Review [2006] Lloyd's Maritime and Commercial Law Quarterly 127.

——and P Rees, (2005) *Civil Jurisdiction and Judgments* (London: LLP, 4th edn).

JH Bruch, (1992) 'Forum Selection Clauses in Consumer Contracts: An Unconscionable Thing Happened on the Way to the Forum' 23 Loyola University of Chicago Law Journal 329.

JJA Burke, (2004) 'Brussels I Regulation (EC) 44/2001: Application to Financial Services under Article 5(1)(b)' 10 Columbia Journal of European Law 527.

JS Burns and RA Bales, (2001) 'Personal Jurisdiction and the Web' 55 Maine Law Review 29.

M Cappelletti (ed), (1981) *Access to Justice and the Welfare State* (Alphen aan den Rijn: Sijthoff and Noordhoff).

——(1993) 'Alternative Dispute Resolution Processes within the Framework of the Worldwide Access-to-Justice Movement' 56 Modern Law Review 282.

——and B Garth, (1978) 'Access to Justice: The World-Wide Movement to Make Rights Effective. A General Report' in M Cappelletti and B Garth (eds), *Access to Justice Vol 1 A World Survey (Book 1)* (Alphen aan den Rijn: Sijthoff and Noordhoff).

D Capps, (2004) 'Electronic Mail and the Postal Rule' 15(7) International Company and Commercial Law Review 207.

PD Carrington, (1998) 'Regulating Dispute Resolution Provisions in Adhesion Contracts' 35 Harvard Journal on Legislation 225.

C Chen, (2004) 'United States and European Union Approaches to Internet Jurisdiction and Their Impact on E-Commerce' (2004) 25 University of Pennsylvania Journal of International Economic Law 423.

B Cheng, (2004) 'A New Era in the Law of International Carriage by Air: From Warsaw (1929) to Montreal (1999)' 53 International and Comparative Law Quarterly 833.

M Chissick and A Kelman, (2002) *Electronic Commerce: Law and Practice* (London: Sweet & Maxwell, 3rd edn).

S Christensen, (2001) 'Formation of Contracts by Email—Is it Just the Same as the Post?' 1 Queensland University of Technology Law & Justice Journal 22.

E Clark, G Cho, and A Hoyle, (2003) 'Online Dispute Resolution: Present Realities, Pressing Problems and Future Prospects' 17 International Review of Law, Computers & Technology 7.

CMV Clarkson and J Hill, (2006) *The Conflict of Laws* (Oxford: Oxford University Press, 3rd edn).

L Collins, (1983) *The Civil Jurisdiction and Judgments Act 1982* (London: Butterworths).
——*et al*, (2006) *Dicey, Morris and Collins on the Conflict of Laws* (London: Sweet & Maxwell, 14th edn).
A Colman, (2003) 'ADR: An Irreversible Tide?' 19 Arbitration International 303.
M Conley Tyler, (2004) '115 and Counting: The State of ODR 2004' <http://www.odr.info/unforum2004/ConleyTyler.htm> [26/2/08].
——and D Bretherton, (2003) 'Seventy-Six and Counting: An Analysis of ODR Sites' <http://www.odr.info/unece2003/pdf/Tyler.pdf> [7/11/07].
M Cordera, (2001) 'E-Consumer Protection: A Comparative Analysis of EU and US Consumer Protection on the Internet' 27 Rutgers Computer and Technology Law Journal 231.
JP Cortes Dieguez, (2008) 'Does the Proposed European Procedure Enhance the Resolution of Small Claims?' 27 Civil Justice Quarterly 83.
C Coteanu, (2005) *Cyber Consumer Law and Unfair Trading Practices* (Aldershot: Ashgate).
B Dahl (1977), 'Consumer Protection and the Provisions on Jurisdiction in the 1968-EEC Judgments Convention' 46 Nordisk Tidsskrift for International Ret 104.
L Davies, (1997) 'Contract Formation on the Internet: Shattering a Few Myths' in L Edwards and C Waelde (eds), *Law and the Internet: Regulating Cyberspace* (Oxford: Hart Publishing) pp 97–120.
M de Boisseson, (1999) 'Thoughts on the Future of ADR in Europe: A Critical Approach' 15 Arbitration International 349.
F Debusseré, (2002) 'International Jurisdiction over E-Consumer Contracts in the European Union: Quid Novi Sub Sole?' 10 International Journal of Law and Information Technology 344.
E Delgado, (2002) 'E-Commerce and Trustmarks: Results from SATURN' <http://hosteddocs.ittoolbox.com/Delgado022004.pdf> [19/7/07].
F Dessemontet, (2000) 'The European Approach to E-Commerce and Licensing' 26 Brooklyn Journal of International Law 59.
S Deutch, (2004) 'Consumer Class Actions: Are They a Solution for Enforcing Consumer Rights? The Israeli Model' 27 Journal of Consumer Policy 179.
HA Deveci, (2005) 'Personal Jurisdiction: Where Cyberspace Meets the Real World—Part I Computer Law & Security Report 464.
——(2006) 'Personal Jurisdiction: Where Cyberspace Meets the Real World—Part II' 22 Computer Law & Security Report 39.
N de Witt, (2001) 'Online Transnational Arbitration: Nine Issues Crucial to Its Success' 12 American Review of International Arbitration 441.
J Dickie, (1998) 'When and Where Are Electronic Contracts Concluded?' 49 Northern Ireland Legal Quarterly 332.
——(1999) *Internet and Electronic Commerce Law in the European Union* (Oxford: Hart Publishing).
A Dickinson, (2007) 'Third-Country Mandatory Rules in the Law Applicable to Contractual Obligations: So Long, Farewell, Auf Wiedersehen, Adieu?' 3 Journal of Private International Law 53.

M Dogauchi, (2002) 'Judicial Jurisdiction in the Era of E-Commerce' in T Kono *et al* (eds), *Selected Legal Issues of E-Commerce* (The Hague/London/New York: Kluwer Law International) pp 127–44.

MS Donahey, (1998) 'Dispute Resolution in Cyberspace' 15(4) Journal of International Arbitration 127.

——(2003) 'The UDRP Model Applied to Online Consumer Transactions' 20(5) Journal of International Arbitration 475.

SL Donegan, (2003) 'Alternative Dispute Resolution for Global Consumers in E-Commerce Transactions' in D Campbell and S Woodley (eds), *E-commerce: Law and Jurisdiction* (The Hague: Kluwer Law International) pp 117–64.

CR Drahozal, (2001) '"Unfair" Arbitration Clauses' 2001 University of Illinois Law Review 695.

——and RJ Friel, (2002) 'Consumer Arbitration in the European Union and the United States' 28 North Carolina Journal of International Law and Commercial Regulation 357.

AJ Duggan, (2003) 'Consumer access to justice in common law countries: a survey of the issues from a law and economics perspective' in CEF Rickett and TGW Telfer, *International Perspectives on Consumers' Access to Justice* (Cambridge: Cambridge University Press) pp 46–67.

S Dutson, (2000) 'International E-Commerce' 6(3) Computer and Telecommunications Law Review 76.

L Edwards and A Theunissen, (2007) 'Creating Trust and Satisfaction Online: How Important Is ADR?: The UK eBay Experience' [2007] 5 Web Journal of Current Legal Issues <http://webjcli.ncl.ac.uk/2007/issue5/edwards5.html> [20/12/07].

L Edwards and C Wilson, (2007) 'Redress and Alternative Dispute Resolution in EU Cross-Border E-Commerce Transactions' 21 International Review of Law, Computers & Technology 315.

A Endeshaw, (2001) 'The Legal Significance of Trustmarks' 10 Information & Communications Technology Law 203.

Y Farah, (2005) 'Critical Analysis of Online Dispute Resolutions: The Optimist, the Realist and the Bewildered' 11(4) Computer and Telecommunications Law Review 123.

RO Faulk, (2003) 'Armageddon through aggregation? The use and abuse of class actions in international dispute resolution' in CEF Rickett and TGW Telfer, *International Perspectives on Consumers' Access to Justice* (Cambridge: Cambridge University Press) pp 330–55.

W Felsteiner, R Abel, and A Sarat, (1980–81) 'The Emergence and Transformation of Disputes: Naming, Blaming and Claiming . . .' 15 Law and Society Review 631.

G Finocchiaro, (2003) 'European Law and Consumer Protection in the Information Age' 12 Information & Communications Technology Law 111.

M Foss and LA Bygrave, (2000) 'International Consumer Purchases through the Internet: Jurisdictional Issues pursuant to European Law' 8 International Journal of Law and Information Technology 99.

TS Fried, (2005) 'Maintaining the Home Court Advantage: Forum Shopping and the Small Business Client' 6 Transactions: the Tennessee Journal of Business Law 419.

HD Gabriel, (2004) 'The Fear of the Unknown: The Need to Provide Special Procedural Protections in International Electronic Commerce' 50 Loyola Law Review 307.

E Gambaro and N Landi, (2006) 'Consumer Contracts and Jurisdiction, Recognition and Enforcement of Judgments in Civil and Commercial Matters' [2006] European Business Law Review 1355.

A Gehringer, (2001) 'After *Carnival Cruise* and *Sky Reefer*: An Analysis of Forum Selection Clauses in Maritime and Aviation Transactions' 66 Journal of Air Law and Commerce 633.

MA Geist, (2001) 'Is There a There There? Toward Greater Certainty for Internet Jurisdiction' 16 Berkeley Technology Law Journal 1345.

H Genn, (1999) *Paths to Justice: What People Do and Think about Going to Law* (Oxford: Hart Publishing).

LJ Gibbons, (1998) 'Rusticum Judicium? Private "Courts" Enforcing Private Law and Public Rights: Regulating Virtual Arbitration in Cyberspace' 24 Ohio Northern University Law Review 769.

——(2000) 'Private Law, Public "Justice": Another Look at Privacy, Arbitration, and Global E-Commerce' 15 Ohio State Journal on Dispute Resolution 769.

——(2002) 'Creating a Market for Justice: A Market Incentive Solution to Regulating the Playing Field; Judicial Deference, Judicial Review, Due Process, and Fair Play in Online Consumer Arbitration' 23 Northwestern Journal of International Law and Business 1.

L Gibson, (1992) 'Access to Justice and Consumer Redress Within a Single Market' 15 Journal of Consumer Policy 407.

EP Gilbert, (1992) 'We're All in the Same Boat: *Carnival Cruise Lines, Inc v Shute*' 18 Brooklyn Journal of International Law 597.

LE Gillies, (2001) 'A Review of the New Jurisdiction Rules for Electronic Contracts within the European Union' 2001(1) Journal of Information, Law and Technology <http://www2.warwick.ac.uk/fac/soc/law/elj/jilt/2001_1/gillies> [29/11/07].

——(2001a) 'Jurisdiction for Consumer Contracts—European Union: Modified Rules of Jurisdiction for Electronic Consumer Contracts' 17 Computer Law & Security Report 395.

——(2002) 'The Impact of the Hague Conference's Proposed Judgments Convention for Electronic Commerce and Intellectual Property Disputes' 16 International Review of Law, Computers & Technology 233.

——(2003) 'Adapting International Private Law Rules for Electronic Consumer Contracts' in CEF Rickett and TGW Telfer, *International Perspectives on Consumers' Access to Justice* (Cambridge: Cambridge University Press) pp 359–83.

——(2007) 'Choice-of-Law Rules for Electronic Consumer Contracts: Replacement of the Rome Convention by the Rome I Regulation' 3 Journal of Private International Law 89.

D Girsberger and D Schramm, (2002) 'Cyber-Arbitration' 3 European Business Organization Law Review 605.

A Gkoutzinis, (2003) 'Online Financial Services in the European Internal Market and the Implementation of the E-Commerce Directive in the UK' 17 International Review of Law, Computers & Technology 323.

L Goldman, (1992) 'My Way and the Highway: The Law and Economics of Choice of Forum Clauses in Consumer Form Contracts' 86 Northwestern University Law Review 700.

JL Goldsmith, (1998) 'Against Cyberanarchy' 65 University of Chicago Law Review 1199.

JW Goodman, (2003) 'The Pros and Cons of Online Dispute Resolution: An Assessment of Cyber-Mediation Websites' 2003 Duke Law and Technology Review 0004.

S Green and D Saidov, (2007) 'Software as Goods' [2007] Journal of Business Law 161.

F Greggio and A Platania, (2000) 'The Competent Jurisdiction in B2C Contracts' 11(6) International Company and Commercial Law Review 193.

A Halfmeier, (2003) 'Waving Goodbye to Conflict of Laws? Recent Developments in European Union Consumer Law' in CEF Rickett and TGW Telfer, *International Perspectives on Consumers' Access to Justice* (Cambridge: Cambridge University Press) pp 384–406.

E Hall, (2007) 'Cancellation Rights in Distance-selling Contracts for Services: Exemptions and Consumer Protection' [2007] Journal of Business Law 683.

H Haloush, (2007) 'Enforcement, Recognition, and Compliance with OADR Outcome(s)' 21 International Review of Law, Computers & Technology 81.

TC Hartley, (1984) *Civil Jurisdiction and Judgments* (London: Sweet & Maxwell).

S Hedley, (2006) *The Law of Electronic Commerce and the Internet in the UK and Ireland* (London: Cavendish).

V Heiskanen, (1999) 'Dispute Resolution in International Electronic Commerce' 16(3) Journal of International Arbitration 29.

CAJFM Hensen, (1992) 'Consumers and the Conflict of Laws in Dutch Legal Practice' 15 Journal of Consumer Policy 355.

K Hertz, (1998) *Jurisdiction in Contract and Tort under the Brussels Convention* (Copenhagen, DJØF Publishing).

J Hill, (2005) *International Commercial Disputes in English Courts* (Oxford: Hart Publishing, 3rd edn).

R Hill, (1997) 'The Internet, Electronic Commerce and Dispute Resolution: Comments' 14(4) Journal of International Arbitration 103.

——(1999) 'Online Arbitration: Issues and Solutions' 15 Arbitration International 199.

SWB Hill, (2001) 'Flogging a Dead Horse—The Postal Acceptance Rule and Email' 17 Journal of Contract Law 151.

C Hodges, (2001) *Multi-Party Actions* (Oxford: Oxford University Press).

——(2001a) 'Multi-Party Actions: A European Approach' 11 Duke Journal of Comparative and International Law 321.

J Hörnle, (2002) 'Online Dispute Resolution in Business to Consumer E-commerce Transactions' 2002(2) Journal of Information, Law and Technology <http://www2.warwick.ac.uk/fac/soc/law/elj/jilt/2002_2/hornle> [29/11/07].

——(2003) 'Online Dispute Resolution: The Emperor's New Clothes?' 17 International Review of Law, Computers & Technology 27.

——(2003a) 'Online Dispute Resolution' in J Tackaberry and A Marriott (eds) *Bernstein's Handbook of Arbitration and Dispute Resolution Practice* (London: Sweet & Maxwell, 4th edn) pp 779–835.

——(2004) 'The UK Perspective on the Country of Origin Rule in the E-commerce Directive—A Rule of Administrative Law Applicable to Private Law Disputes?' 12 International Journal Law and Information Technology 333.

G Howells and R James, (2002) 'Litigation in the Consumer Interest' 9 ILSA Journal of International and Comparative Law 1.

G Howells and S Weatherill, (2005) *Consumer Protection Law* (Aldershot: Ashgate, 2nd edn).

H Jacob, (1992) 'The Elusive Shadow of the Law' 26 Law & Society Review 565.

R James and P Morris, (2003) 'The New Financial Ombudsman Service in the United Kingdom: Has the Second Generation Got It Right?' in CEF Rickett and TGW Telfer, *International Perspectives on Consumers' Access to Justice* (Cambridge: Cambridge University Press) pp 167–95.

S Jawahitha, (2004) 'Negligent Liability and E-Consumers in Malaysia' 10(8) Computer and Telecommunications Law Review 200.

——(2005) 'Cyberjurisdiction and consumer protection in e-commerce' 21 Computer Law & Security Report 153.

DR Johnson and DG Post, (1996) 'Law and Borders: The Rise of Law in Cyberspace' 48 Stanford Law Review 1367.

S Jones, (2000) 'Forming International Contracts in the United Kingdom' 11(9) Electronic Company and Commercial Law Review 301.

C Joustra, (1992) 'Cross-Border Consumer Complaints in Private International Law' 15 Journal of Consumer Policy 431.

E Katsh, (2006) 'Online Dispute Resolution: Some Implications for the Emergence of Law in Cyberspace' 10(3) *Lex Informatica.*

——(2007) 'Online Dispute Resolution: Some Implications for the Emergence of Law in Cyberspace' 21 International Review of Law, Computers & Technology 97.

——and J Rifkin, (2001) *Online Dispute Resolution: Resolving Conflicts in Cyberspace* (San Fransisco: Jossey-Bass).

——J Rifkin, and A Gaitenby, (2000) 'E-Commerce, E-Disputes, and E-Dispute Resolution: In the Shadow of "eBay Law"' 15 Ohio State Journal of Dispute Resolution 705.

——and L Wing, (2006) 'Ten Years of Online Dispute Resolution (ODR): Looking for the Past and Constructing the Future' 38 University of Toledo Law Review 19.

L Katz, (2000) 'Jurisdiction and E-Commerce Disputes' 3 Journal of World Intellectual Property 289.

G Kaufmann-Kohler and T Schultz, (2004) *Online Dispute Resolution: Challenges for Contemporary Justice* (The Hague: Kluwer Law International).

P Kaye, (1987) *Civil Jurisdiction and Enforcement of Foreign Judgments* (Abingdon: Professional Books Limited).

——(1999) *Law of the European Judgments Convention* (Chichester: Barry Rose).

M Keller, (2004) 'Lessons for The Hague: Internet Jurisdiction in Contract and Tort Cases in the European Community and the United States' 23 John Marshall Journal of Computer and Information Law 1.
I Kilbey, (2005) 'Consumer Protection Evaded via the Internet' 30 European Law Review 123.
S Knöfel, (1998) 'EC Legislation on Conflict of Laws: Interactions and Incompatibilities between Conflicts Rules' 47 International and Comparative Law Quarterly 439.
U Kohl, (1999) 'Legal Reasoning and Legal Change in the Age of the Internet—Why the Ground Rules are Still Valid' 7 International Journal of Law and Information Technology 123.
——(2002) 'Eggs, Jurisdiction and the Internet' 51 International and Comparative Law Quarterly 555.
——(2005) 'The Rule of Law, Jurisdiction and the Internet' 13 International Journal of Law and Information Technology 365.
H Kötz, (1981) 'Public Interest Litigation: A Comparative Survey' in M Cappelletti (ed), *Access to Justice and the Welfare State* (Alphen aan den Rijn: Sijthoff and Noordhoff) pp 85–117.
C Kuner, (2000) 'Legal Obstacles to ADR in European Business to Consumer Electronic Commerce' 5 Electronic Commerce & Law Report 773 [also at <http://www.kuner.com/data/pay/adr.pdf> [21/7/06]].
O Lando and PA Nielsen, (2007) 'The Rome I Proposal' 3 Journal of Private International Law 29.
M Lehmann, (2000) 'Electronic Commerce and Consumer Protection in Europe' 17 Santa Clara Computer and High Technology Law Journal 101.
TD Leitstein, (1999) 'A Solution for Personal Jurisdiction on the Internet' 59 Louisiana Law Review 565.
TP Lester, (2003) 'Globalized Automatic Choice of Forum: Where Do Internet Consumers Sue?' 9 New England Journal of International and Comparative Law 431.
I Lloyd, (1993) 'Shopping in Cyberspace' 1 International Journal of Law and Information Technology 335.
——(2004) *Information Technology Law* (Oxford: Oxford University Press, 4th edn).
AR Lodder, (2006) 'The Third Party and Beyond. An Analysis of the Different Parties, in Particular the Fifth, Involved in Online Dispute Resolution' 15 Information & Communications Technology Law 143.
A Lopez-Tarruella, (2001) 'Cross-Border Disputes on On-line Consumer Contracts in the European Union: The Brussels Convention, the Brussels Regulation and the Role of Alternative Dispute Resolution Systems' 2 Journal of Network Industries 231.
E Macdonald, (2004) 'Unifying Unfair Terms Legislation' 67 Modern Law Review 69.
——(2005) 'Unfair Terms in Consumer Contracts' 121 Law Quarterly Review 38.
BGM Main and A Park, (2000) 'The British and American Rules: An Experimental Examination of Pre-trial Bargaining in the Shadow of the Law' 47 Scottish Journal of Political Economy 37.
J Meuser, (2005) 'Germany: Electronic Commerce—Distance Selling' 11(2) Computer and Telecommunications Law Review N13.

MI Meyerson, (1990) 'The Efficient Consumer Form Contract: Law and Economics Meets the Real World' 24 Georgia Law Review 583.

H-W Micklitz, (1993) 'Cross-Border Consumer Conflicts—A French-German Experience' 16 Journal of Consumer Policy 411.

FL Miller, (1999) 'Arbitration Clauses in Consumer Contracts; Building Barriers to Consumer Protection' 78 Michigan Bar Journal 302.

LA Mistelis, (2001) 'ADR in England and Wales' 12 American Review of International Arbitration 167.

R Mnookin and L Kornhauser, (1979) 'Bargaining in the Shadow of the Law: The Case of Divorce' 88 Yale Law Journal 950.

R Morek, (2006) 'The Regulatory Framework for Online Dispute Resolution: A Critical View' 38 University of Toledo Law Review 163.

CGJ Morse, (1992) 'Consumer Contracts, Employment Contracts and the Rome Convention' 41 International and Comparative Law Quarterly 1.

PR Motion, (2001) 'The Brussels Regulation and E-Commerce—A Premature Solution to a Fictional Problem' 7(8) Computer and Telecommunications Law Review 209.

LS Mullenix, (1992) 'Another Easy Case, Some More Bad Law: *Carnival Cruise Lines* and Contractual Personal Jurisdiction' 27 Texas International Law Journal 323.

AD Murray, (2000) 'Entering Into Contracts Electronically: The Real WWW' in L Edwards and C Waelde (eds), *Law and the Internet: A Framework for Electronic Commerce* (Oxford: Hart Publishing, 2nd edn) pp 17–35.

P Naarajärvi and JV Koivisto, (2002) *Which Law, Which Forum? Jurisdiction and Applicable Law in International Electronic Commerce* (Helsinki: Werner Söderstöm Corporation).

L Nader, (1979) 'Disputing Without the Force of Law' 88 Yale Law Journal 998.

D Naylor and C Ritter, (2005) 'French Judgment Condemning AOL Illustrates EU Consumer Protection Issues Facing US Businesses Operating in Europe' 1 New York University Journal of Law and Business 881.

JP Nehf, (1999) 'Borderless Trade and the Consumer Interest: Protecting the Consumer in the Age of E-Commerce' 38 Columbia Journal of Transnational Law 457.

L Niglia, (2006) 'The "Rules" Dilemma—The Court of Justice and the Regulation of Standard Form Consumer Contracts in Europe' 13 Columbia Journal of European Law 125.

PM North and JJ Fawcett, (1999) *Cheshire and North's Private International Law* (London: Butterworths, 13th edn).

Note, (2003) 'No Bad Puns: A Different Approach to the Problem of Personal Jurisdiction and the Internet' 116 Harvard Law Review 1821.

PE Nygh, (1999) *Autonomy in International Contracts* (Oxford: Oxford University Press).

M Odams de Zylva, (2001) 'Effective Means of Resolving Distance Selling Disputes' <http://206.130.104.53/paperfree/015_odamas_distance.pdf> [2/10/06].

KH Offerman (ed), (2001) *Working Paper: Private International Law—Electronic Commerce—Country of Destination Principle* Legal Affairs Series JURI 105 A XX.

EA O'Hara (2005) 'Choice of Law for Internet Transactions: The Uneasy Case for Online Consumer Protection' 153 University of Pennsylvania Law Review 1833.
PJ Omar, (1999) 'Consumer Litigation: An International Perspective' 10(5) International Company and Commercial Law Review 148.
R Ong, (2004) 'Consumer Based Electronic Commerce: A Comparative Analysis of the Position in Malaysia and Hong Kong' 12 International Journal of Law and Information Technology 101.
M Ortino, (2004) 'EC Law on Cross-border On-line Financial Services' [2004] European Business Law Review 367.
D Oughton and J Lowry, (2000) *Textbook on Consumer Law* (London: Blackstone Press, 2nd edn).
WW Park, (1998) 'The New English Arbitration Act' 13 Mealey's International Arbitration Report 21.
A Patrikios, (2008) 'The Role of Trasnational Online Arbitration in Regulating Cross-border E-business—Part I' 24 Computer Law & Security Report 66.
——(2008a) 'The Role of Trasnational Online Arbitration in Regulating Cross-border E-business—Part II' 24 Computer Law & Security Report 129.
G Pearce and N Platten, (2000) 'Promoting the Information Society: The EU Directive on Electronic Commerce' 6 European Law Journal 363.
HH Perritt Jr, (2000) 'Dispute Resolution in Cyberspace: Demand for New Forms of ADR' 15 Ohio State Journal on Dispute Resolution 675.
R Plato-Shinar, (2007) 'Israel: The New Law on Class Actions' [2007] Journal of Business Law 527.
P Plender and M Wilderspin, (2001) *The European Contracts Convention* (London: Sweet & Maxwell, 2nd edn).
LM Ponte, (2002) 'Boosting Consumer Confidence in E-Business: Recommendations for Establishing Fair and Effective Dispute Resolution Programs for B2C Online Transactions' 12 Albany Law Journal of Science and Technology 441.
MD Powell and PM Turner-Kerr, (2000) 'Putting the E- in Brussels and Rome' 16 Computer Law & Security Report 23.
S Prince, (2007) 'Mediating Small Claims: Are we on the Right Track?' 26 Civil Justice Quarterly 328.
JEJ Prins, (2003) 'Consumer Protection in an Information Society' 12 Information & Communications Technology Law 91.
T Puurunen, (2002) 'The Judicial Jurisdiction of States over International Business-to-Consumer Electronic Commerce from the Perspective of Legal Certainty' 8 UC Davis Journal of International Law and Policy 133.
——(2003) 'Choice of Law in European Business-To-Consumer Electronic Commerce—A Trail Out of a Political Impasse' [2003] Zeitschrift für Europaisches Privatrecht 789.
——(2003a) 'International Online Dispute Resolution—Caveats to Privatizing Justice' 14 Finnish Yearbook of International Law 233.
I Ramsay, (1981) 'Consumer Redress Mechanisms for Poor-Quality and Defective Products' 31 University of Toronto Law Journal 117.
——(2003) 'Consumer Redress and Access to Justice' in CEF Rickett and TGW Telfer, *International Perspectives on Consumers' Access to Justice* (Cambridge: Cambridge University Press) pp 17–45.

S Rawson, (2002) 'Mobility and Liability: The Hazards of Handhelds' 18 Computer Law & Security Report 164.

A Redfern and M Hunter, (2004) *Law and Practice of International Commercial Arbitration* (London: Sweet & Maxwell, 4th edn).

LA Reich, (2003) 'Potentials, Pitfalls, and Policy Implications of Electronic Consumption' 12 Information & Communications Technology Law 93.

N Reich, (2005) 'A European Contract Law, or an EU Contract Law Regulation for Consumers?' 28 Journal of Consumer Policy 383.

——and A Halfmeier, (2001) 'Consumer Protection in the Global Village: Recent Developments in German and European Union Law' 106 Dickinson Law Review 111.

JR Reidenberg, (2005) 'Technology and Internet Jurisdiction' 153 University of Pennsylvania Law Review 1951.

A Reynolds, (2002) 'E-auctions: Who Will Protect the Consumer?' 18 Journal of Contract Law 75.

DT Rice, (2001) 'A Cyberspace Odyssey through US and EU Internet Jurisdiction over E-Commerce' 661 Practising Law Institute/Patent 421.

CEF Rickett and TGW Telfer, (2003) *International Perspectives on Consumers' Access to Justice* (Cambridge: Cambridge University Press).

C Riefa, (2004) 'Article 5 of the Rome Convention on the Law Applicable to Contractual Obligations of 19 June 1980 and Consumer E-contracts: The Need for Reform' 13 Information & Communications Technology Law 59.

S Roberts and M Palmer, (2006) *Dispute Processes: ADR and the Primary Forms of Decision Making* (Cambridge: Cambridge University Press, 2nd edn).

W Roebuck, (2002) 'Jurisdiction and E-Commerce' 8(2) Computer and Telecommunications Law Review 29.

AS Rosenberg, (2006) 'Better than Cash? Global Proliferation of Payment Cards and Consumer Protection Policy' 44 Columbia Journal of Transnational Law 520.

HL Ross and NO Littlfield, (1978) 'Complaint as a Problem Solving Mechanism' 12 Law & Society Review 199.

P Rott, (2001) 'The Protection of Consumers' Interests After the Implementation of the EC Injunctions Directive Into German and English Law' 24 Journal of Consumer Policy 401.

G Rühl, (2007) 'Common Law, Civil Law, and the Single European Market for Insurance' 55 International and Comparative Law Quarterly 879.

C Rule, (2002) *Online Dispute Resolution for Business: B2B, E-commerce, Consumer, Employment, Insurance, and Other Commercial Conflicts* (San Francisco: Jossey Bass).

M Rutherford, (2003) 'Documents-only Arbitrations in Consumer Disputes' in J Tackaberry and A Marriott (eds), *Bernstein's Handbook of Arbitration and Dispute Resolution Practice* (London: Sweet & Maxwell, 4th edn) pp 624–50.

AM Sachdeva, (2007) 'International Jurisdiction in Cyberspace: A Comparative Perspective' 13(8) Computer and Telecommunications Law Review 245.

S Saxby, (2006) 'Court of Appeal Increases UK Consumer Protection for Overseas Credit Purchases' 22 Computer Law & Security Report 181.

JA Scarpino, (2002) 'Mandatory Arbitration of Consumer Disputes: A Proposal to Ease the Financial Burden on Low-Income Consumers' 10 American University Journal of Gender, Social Policy and the Law 679.

M Schaub, (2004) *European Legal Aspects of E-Commerce* (Groningen: Europa Law Publishing).

M Schellekens and L van der Wees, (2002) 'ADR and ODR in Electronic Commerce' in JEJ Prins *et al*, *Trust in Electronic Commerce* (The Hague: Kluwer Law International) pp 271–300.

S Schiavetta, (2004) 'The Relationship Between e-ADR and Article 6 of the European Convention of Human Rights Pursuant to the Case Law of the European Court of Human Rights' 2004(1) Journal of Information, Law and Technology <http://www2.warwick.ac.uk/fac/soc/law/elj/jilt/2004_1/schiavetta/> [29/11/07].

——(2004a) 'Does the Internet Occasion New Directions in Consumer Arbitration in the EU?' 2004(3) Journal of Information, Law and Technology <http://www2.warwick.ac.uk/fac/soc/law/elj/jilt/2004_3/schiavetta> [29/11/07].

ME Schneider and C Kuner, (1997) 'Dispute Resolution in International Electronic Commerce' 14(3) Journal of International Arbitration 5.

R Schu, (1997) 'The Applicable Law to Consumer Contracts Made Over the Internet: Consumer Protection Through Private International Law?' 5 International Journal of Law and Information Technology 192.

T Schultz, (2004) 'Does Online Dispute Resolution Need Governmental Intervention? The Case for Architecture of Control and Trust' 6 North Carolina Journal of Law and Technology 71.

C Schulze and J Baumgartner, (2001) *Don't Panic! Do E-Commerce* <http://europa.eu.int/ISPO/ecommerce/books/dont_panic.pdf> [6/07/06].

EF Scoles and P Hay, (2004) *Conflict of Laws* (St. Paul, Minnesota: Thomson/West, 4th edn).

C Scott and J Black, (2000) *Cranson's Consumers and the Law* (London: Butterworths, 3rd edn).

F Seatzu, (2003) *Insurance in Private International Law* (Oxford: Hart Publishing).

J Senderowicz, (1999) 'Consumer Arbitration and Freedom of Contract: A Proposal to Facilitate Consumers' Informed Consent to Arbitration Clauses in Form Contracts' 32 Columbia Journal of Law and Social Problems 275.

A Shah, (2004) 'Using ADR to Resolve Online Disputes' 10 Richmond Journal of Law and Technology 25.

BL Smith, (2000) 'The Third Industrial Revolution: Law and Policy for the Internet' 282 Receuil des cours 229.

H Snijders, (2003) 'The Moment of Effectiveness in E-mail Notices' in H Snijders and S Weatherill (eds), *E-commerce Law: National and Transnational Topics and Perspectives* (The Hague/London/New York: Kluwer Law International) pp 79–88.

JH Sommer, (2000) 'Against Cyberlaw' 15 Berkeley Technology Law Journal 1145.

B Sookman, (2001) 'Legal Framework for E-Commerce Transactions' 7(4) Computer and Telecommunications Law Review 85.

AR Stein, (2005) 'Parochialism and Pluralism in Cyberspace Regulation' 153 Pennsylvania Law Review 2003.

JR Sternlight, (2002) 'Is the US Out on a Limb? Comparing the US Approach to Mandatory Consumer and Employment Arbitration to that of the Rest of the World' 56 University of Miami Law Review 831.

M Sterpi, (2003) 'Unfair Terms in E-Contracts: The European Viewpoint' in D Campbell and S Woodley (eds), *E-commerce: Law and Jurisdiction* (The Hague: Kluwer Law International) pp 271–86.

R Stevens, (2003) 'E-commerce and Private International Law' in H Snijders and S Weatherill (eds), *E-commerce Law: National and Transnational Topics and Perspectives* (The Hague/London/New York: Kluwer Law International) pp 111–16.

K Stewart and J Matthews, (2002) 'Online Arbitration of Cross-Border, Business to Consumer Disputes' 56 University of Miami Law Review 1111.

P Stone, (2000) 'Internet Consumer Contracts and European Private International Law' 9 Information & Communications Technology Law 5.

——(2002) 'The Treatment of Electronic Contracts and Torts in Private International Law under European Community Legislation' 11 Information & Communications Technology Law 121.

J Struyck, E Terryn, and T van Dyck, (2006) 'Confidence through Fairness? The New Directive on Business-to-Consumer Commercial Practices in the Internal Market' 43 Common Market Law Review 107.

D Svantesson, (2001) 'What Should Article 7—Consumer Contracts, of the Proposed Hague Convention, Aim to Accomplish in Relation to E-Commerce?' 17 Computer Law & Security Report 318.

——(2002) '*Kanitz v Rogers Cable Inc*—Time to Rethink Article 4 of the Proposed Hague Convention' 18 Computer Law & Security Report 340.

PP Swire, (2005) 'Elephants and Mice Revisited: Law and Choice of Law on the Internet' 153 University of Pennsylvania Law Review 1975.

Z Tang, (2005) 'Exclusive Choice of Forum Clauses and Consumer Contracts in E-Commerce' 1 Journal of Private International Law 237.

——(2007) 'An Effective Dispute Resolution System for Electronic Consumer Contracts' 23 Computer Law & Security Report 42.

——(2007a) 'Parties' Choice of Law in E-Consumer Contracts' 3 Journal of Private International Law 113.

DE Tellini, (2005) 'Applicable Law and Electronic Contracts: A European Perspective' 16(1) International Company and Commercial Law Review 1.

R Thomas, (1991) 'Consumer Protection: Strategies for Dispute Resolution' in KJ Mackie (ed), *A Handbook of Dispute Resolution: ADR in Action* (London/New York: Routledge and Sweet & Maxwell) pp 157–71.

EG Thornburg, (2000) 'Going Private: Technology, Due Process, and Internet Dispute Resolution' 34 UC Davis Law Review 151.

——(2003) 'Privatisation and Power: Dispute Resolution for the Internet' in CEF Rickett and TGW Telfer, *International Perspectives on Consumers' Access to Justice* (Cambridge: Cambridge University Press) pp 303–29.

A Thünken, (2002) 'Multi-state Advertising over the Internet and the Private International Law of Unfair Competition' 51 International and Comparative Law Quarterly 909.

M Traynor and L Pirri, (2002) 'Personal Jurisdiction and the Internet: Emerging Trends and Future Directions' 712 Practising Law Institute/Patents 93.

MJ Trebilcock, (1971) 'Consumer Protection in the Affluent Society' 16 McGill Law Journal 263.

——(2003) 'Rethinking Consumer Protection policy' in CEF Rickett and TGW Telfer, *International Perspectives on Consumers' Access to Justice* (Cambridge: Cambridge University Press) pp 68–98.

RHS Tur, (1982) 'Litigation and the Consumer Interest: The Class Action and Beyond' 2 Legal Studies 135.

M Turner and D Callaghan, (2006) 'Is Shopping Online Now Risk Free for UK Consumers?' 22 Computer Law & Security Report 333.

A Vahrenwald, (1994) 'Futures Contracts: Choice of Law' 5(5) International Company and Commercial Law Review C93.

S van der Hof, (2003) 'European Conflict Rules Concerning International Online Consumer Contracts' 12 Information & Communications Technology Law 165.

K Vasiljeva, (2004) '1968 Brussels Convention and EU Council Regulation No 44/2001: Jurisdiction in Consumer Contracts Concluded Online' 10 European Law Journal 123.

K Viitanen, (2000) 'The Baltic Model for the Settlement of Individual Consumer Disputes' 23 Journal of Consumer Policy 315.

HJ Vogel, (2003) 'E-Commerce: Directives of the European Union and Implementation in German Law' in D Campbell and S Woodley (eds), *E-commerce: Law and Jurisdiction* (The Hague: Kluwer Law International) pp 29–78.

B von Hoffmann, (1992) 'Consumer Contracts and the 1980 Rome EC Convention on the Law Applicable to Contractual Obligations' 15 Journal of Consumer Policy 365.

M Wahab, (2004) 'Globalisation and ODR: Dynamics of Change in E-Commerce Dispute Settlement' 12 International Journal of Law and Information Technology 123.

——(2004a) 'The Global Information Society and Online Dispute Resolution: A New Dawn for Dispute Resolution' 21(2) Journal of International Arbitration 143.

I Walden, (2001) 'Regulating Electronic Commerce: Europe in the Global E-conomy' 26 European Law Review 529.

J Watson Hamilton, (2006) 'Pre-Dispute Consumer Arbitration Clauses: Denying Access to Justice?' 51 McGill Law Journal 693.

S Weatherill, (2005) *EU Consumer Law and Policy* (Cheltenham: Edward Elgar, 2nd edn).

CJ Whelan, (1987) 'The Role of Research in Civil Justice Reform: Small Claims in the County Court' 6 Civil Justice Quarterly 237.

——(1990) *Small Claims Courts: A Comparative Study* (Oxford: Clarendon Press).

S Whittaker, (2001) 'Judicial Interventionism and Consumer Contracts' 117 Law Quarterly Review 215.

C Wild, S Weinstein, and C Riefa, (2005) 'Council Regulation (EC) 44/2001 and Internet Consumer Contracts: Some Thoughts on Article 15 and the Futility of Applying "In the Box" Conflict of Law Rules to the "Out of the Box" Borderless World' 19 International Review of Law, Computers & Technology 13.

JK Winn and BH Bix, (2006) 'Diverging Perspectives on Electronic Contracting in the US and EU' 54 Cleveland State Law Review 175.

JK Winn and M Webber, (2006) 'The Impact of EU Unfair Contract Terms Law on US Business-to-Consumer Internet Merchants' 62 Business Lawyer 209.

C Withers, (2002) 'Jurisdiction Clauses and the Unfair Terms in Consumer Contracts Regulations' [2002] Lloyd's Maritime and Commercial Law Quarterly 56.

H-L Yu and M Nasir, (2003) 'Can Online Arbitration Exist Within the Traditional Arbitration Framework?' 20(5) Journal of International Arbitration 455.

GI Zekos, (2007) 'State Cyberspace Jurisdiction and Personal Cyberspace Jurisdiction' 15 International Journal of Law and Information Technology 1.

RS Zembek, (1996) 'Jurisdiction and the Internet: Fundamental Fairness in the Networked World of Cyberspace' 6 Albany Law Journal of Science and Technology 339.

Y Zhao, (2005) *Dispute Resolution in Electronic Commerce* (Leiden: Martinus Nijhoff Publishers).

K Zweigert and H Kötz, (1992) *An Introduction to Comparative Law* (Oxford: Oxford University Press, 2nd edn).

JST Øren, (2003) 'International Jurisdiction over Consumer Contracts in e-Europe' 52 International and Comparative Law Quarterly 665.

II. REPORTS, WORKING PAPERS, THESES ETC

American Bar Association, (2002) 'Addressing Disputes in Electronic Commerce' <http://www.abanet.org/dispute/documents/FinalReport102802.pdf> [2/12/07].

Association of British Travel Agents, (June 2005) 'ABTA Travel Statistics and Trends 2005' <http://www.abtamembers.org/research/abtastatstrends2005.pdf> [6/7/06].

J Baldwin, (December 1997) 'Monitoring the rise of the small claims limit: Litigants' experiences of different forms of adjudication' (Lord Chancellor's Department: Research Series No 1/97).

L Caplin, (2004) *Online Cross-Border Consumer Dispute Resolution: An Assessment of its Potential and Analysis of the ECODIR Project* (LLM Thesis, Faculty of Law, University College Dublin).

Citizens Advice, (October 2005) 'Establishing a European Small Claims Procedure' <http://www.citizensadvice.org.uk/print/index/campaigns/policy_campaign_publications/consultation_responses/cr_legalaffairs/establishing_a_european_small_claims_procedure.htm?x=12&y=14> [2/11/07].

M Conley Tyler and E Gasson, (2006) 'Online Dispute Resolution Library' <http://www.odr.info/library.php> [9/1/08].

Constitutional Affairs Committee, (December 2005) 'The courts: small claims' HC 519 <http://www.dca.gov.uk/majrep/smallclaim/casc_smallclaim.pdf> [4/5/07].

Consumers International, (December 2000) 'Disputes in Cyberspace: Online dispute resolution for consumers in cross-border disputes—an international survey' <http://www.consumersinternational.org/Shared_ASP_Files/UploadedFiles/3E2E907D-FC8C-4951-AC9B-B6A4CCE903D9_Doc35> [25/1/07].

Consumers International, (September 2001) 'Should I buy? Shopping on line 2001: An international comparative study of electronic commerce'
<http://www.consumersinternational.org/Shared_ASP_Files/UploadedFiles/C0F98C93-3556-4E09-B903-CAE2C957C74F_Doc33.pdf> [18/3/07].

M Coppack, (November 2003) 'It all adds up: A consensus for a national strategy for consumer education' (National Consumer Council) <http://www.ncc.org.uk/nccpdf/poldocs/NCC046_it_all_adds_up.pdf> [29/11/07].

R de Bruin, E Keuleers, C Lazaro, Y Poullet, and M Viersma, (February 2005) 'Analysis and Definition of Common Characteristics of Trustmarks and Web Seals in the European Union: Final Report' <http://ec.europa.eu/consumers/cons_int/e-commerce/e-commerce_final_report_en.pdf> [20/7/07].

Department for Trade and Industry, (November 2002) 'Internet and cross border shopping' <http://www.berr.gov.uk/files/file8464.pdf> [23/8/07].

M Doyle, K Ritters, and S Brooker, (January 2004) 'Seeking Resolution: the availability and usage of consumer-to-business alternative dispute resolution in the United Kingdom' (Department for Trade and Industry) <http://www.dti.gov.uk/files/file11557.pdf> [10/8/07].

ECC (Denmark), (November 2006) 'Got what you ordered? Conference Report: E-Commerce Trustmarks in Europe' <http://www.trustmarkconference.dk/Report/Rapport%20Report%20-%20E-commerce%20-%20final.pdf> [13/7/07].

ECC (Dublin), (April 2004) 'Alternative Dispute Resolution (ADR): The need to develop ADR in Ireland' <http://www.eccdublin.ie/publications/reports/ecc_reports/adr_development_in_ireland.pdf> [10/8/07].

ECC (Dublin), (June 2004) 'The Small Claims Court and its Use in Cross Border Dispute Resolution' <http://www.eccdublin.ie/publications/reports/ecc_reports/small_claims_court_report_june_2004.pdf> [8/3/07].

ECC (Dublin), (July 2007) 'Annual Report 2006' <http://www.eccdublin.ie/publications/reports/annual_reports/annual-report-2006.pdf> [7/4/08].

ECC-Net, (December 2002) 'Report: Timeshare in Europe—"The experience of European Consumer Centres (ECCs)"' <http://ec.europa.eu/comm/consumers/redress/compl/euroguichet/timeshare_report_en.pdf> [18/3/07].

ECC-Net, (May 2003) 'Realities of the European Online Marketplace: A cross-border e-commerce project by the European Consumer Centre's Network' <http://ec.europa.eu/comm/consumers/redress/compl/euroguichet/e-commerce_report.pdf> [18/3/07].

ECC-Net, (May 2005) 'The European Online Marketplace: Consumer Complaints 2004' <http://www.euroconsumer.org.uk/eur_online_marketplace_2004.pdf> [18/3/07].

ECC-Net, (June 2006) 'The European Online Marketplace: Consumer Complaints 2005' <http://www.euroconsumer.org.uk/eur_online_marketplace_2005.pdf> [18/3/07].

ECC-Net, (October 2006) 'Air Passenger Rights: Consumer Complaints 2005'
<http://www.eccdublin.ie/publications/reports/ecc_reports/ECC-Net_Airline_Complaints_05.pdf> [30/3/07].

EMOTA, (September 2003) 'Comments on the Green Paper on the conversion of the Rome Convention of 1980 on the law applicable to contractual obligations into a Community instrument and its modernisation COM (2002) 654' <http://ec.europa.eu/justice_home/news/consulting_public/rome_i/doc/emota_en.pdf> [15/11/07].

Eurobarometer, (October 2004) 'European Union Citizens and Access to Justice' <http://ec.europa.eu/comm/consumers/redress/reports_studies/eurobarometer_11-04_en.pdf> [8/3/07].

Eurobarometer, (September 2006) 'Consumer protection in the Internal Market' <http://ec.europa.eu/consumers/topics/eurobarometer_09-2006_en.pdf> [22/3/07].

Euroconsumer, (May 2005) 'The European Online Marketplace: Consumer Complaints, A summary and analysis of consumer complaints reported to the European Consumer Centre Network 2004' <http://www.euroconsumer.org.uk/eur_online_marketplace_2004.pdf> [9/3/07].

Euroconsumer, (December 2005) 'Can you cancel it?' <http://www.euroconsumer.org.uk/can_you_cancel_it_final.pdf> [9/3/07].

Euroconsumer, (April 2006) 'UK European Consumer Centre Cross Border Queries 2005' <http://www.euroconsumer.org.uk/index/publications/other_reports/activity_apr06_cross_border_queries_2005.htm> [9/3/07].

Euroconsumer, (June 2006) 'The European Online Marketplace: Consumer Complaints, A summary and analysis of consumer complaints reported to the European Consumer Centre Network 2005' <http://www.euroconsumer.org.uk/eur_online_marketplace_20052.pdf> [8/3/07].

EuroISPA, (September 2003) 'EuroISPA Position Paper: Green Paper on the Conversion of the Rome Convention into a Community instrument COM (2002) 654' <http://ec.europa.eu/justice_home/news/consulting_public/rome_i/doc/euroispa_en.pdf> [15/11/07].

European Banking Federation, (September 2003) 'FBE Observations on the European Commission's Green Paper Com (2002) 654 final' <http://ec.europa.eu/justice_home/news/consulting_public/rome_i/doc/federation_european_banking_en.pdf> [15/11/07].

European Commission (May 1976), 'European Consumers: Their Interests, Aspirations and Knowledge on Consumer Affairs' <http://ec.europa.eu/public_opinion/archives/ebs/ebs_007_en.pdf> [20/12/07].

European Commission, COM (93) 576 'Green Paper on Access to Justice: The Settlement of Consumer Disputes in the Single Market'.

European Commission, COM (96) 13 'Action Plan on consumer access to justice and the settlement of consumer disputes in the internal market'.

European Commission, COM (97) 609 'Towards greater efficiency in obtaining and enforcing judgments in the European Union'.

European Commission, COM (98) 198 'Communication from the Commission on "the out-of-court settlement of consumer disputes"'.

European Commission, COM (98) 586 'Proposal for a European Parliament and Council Directive on certain legal aspects of electronic commerce in the internal market'.

European Commission, COM (99) 348 'Proposal for a Council Regulation (EC) on jurisdiction and the recognition and enforcement of judgments in civil and commercial matters'.

European Commission, COM (99) 396 'Green paper: Liability for defective products'.

European Commission, COM (2000) 167 'Scoreboard to review progress on the creation of an area of "Freedom, Security and Justice" in the European Union'.

European Commission, COM (2000) 689 'Amended proposal for a council Regulation on jurisdiction and the recognition and enforcement of judgments in civil and commercial matters'.

European Commission, COM (2001) 161 'Communication from the Commission on widening consumer access to alternative dispute resolution'.

European Commission, COM (2001) 398 'Communication from the Commission to the Council and the European Parliament on European Contract Law'.

European Commission, COM (2002) 159 'Proposal for a Council Regulation creating a European enforcement order for uncontested claims'.

European Commission, COM (2002) 196 'Green Paper on alternative dispute resolution in civil and commercial law'.

European Commission, COM (2002) 654 'Green Paper on the conversion of the Rome Convention of 1980 on the law applicable to contractual obligations into a Community instrument and its modernisation'.

European Commission, COM (2002) 746 'Green Paper on a European order for payment procedure and on measures to simplify and speed up small claims litigation'.

European Commission, COM (2003) 427 'Proposal for a Regulation of the European Parliament and the Council on the Law Applicable to Non-Contractual Obligations ("Rome II")'.

European Commission, COM (2003) 443 'Proposal for a Regulation of the European Parliament and of the Council on cooperation between national authorities responsible for the enforcement of consumer protection laws ("the regulation on consumer protection cooperation").

European Commission, COM (2004) 173 'Proposal for a Regulation of the European Parliament and of the Council creating a European order for payment procedure'.

European Commission, COM (2004) 718 'Proposal for a Directive of the European Parliament and of the Council on certain aspects of mediation in civil and commercial matters'.

European Commission, COM (2005) 87 'Proposal for a Regulation of the European Parliament and of the Council establishing a European Small Claims Procedure'.

European Commission, COM (2005) 650 'Proposal for a Regulation of the European Parliament and the Council on the law applicable to contractual obligations (Rome I)'.

European Commission, COM (2005) 672 'Green Paper—Damages actions for breach of the EC antitrust rules'.

European Commission, [2006] OJ C39/2 'Commission communication concerning Article 4(3) of Directive 98/27/EC of the European Parliament and of the Council on injunctions for the protection of consumers' interests, concerning the entities qualified to bring an action under Article 2 of this Directive'.

European Commission, COM (2006) 83 'Amended proposal for European Parliament and Council Regulation on the Law Applicable to Non-Contractual Obligations ("Rome II")'.

European Commission, COM (2006) 514 'Communication from the Commission . . . on the implementation of Directive 1997/7/EC of the European Parliament and of the Council of 20 May 1997 on the Protection of Consumers in respect of Distance Contracts'.

European Commission, COM (2006) 566 'Communication from the Commission to the European Parliament pursuant to the second subparagraph of Article 251(2) of the EC Treaty concerning the common position of the Council on the adoption of a Regulation of the European Parliament and of the Council on the law applicable to non-contractual obligations ("Rome II")'.

European Commission, COM (2006) 744 'Green Paper on the review of the consumer acquis'.

European Commission, COM (2007) 99 'EU Consumer Policy strategy 2007–2013'.

European Commission, COM (2007) 303 'Proposal for a Directive of the European Parliament and of the Council on the protection of consumer in respect of certain aspects of timeshare, long-term holiday products, resale and exchange'.

European Commission, COM (2007) 387 'Proposal for a Council Decision concerning the signing of the Convention between the European Community and the Republic of Iceland, the Kingdom of Norway, the Swiss Confederation, and the Kingdom of Denmark on jurisdiction and the recognition and enforcement of judgments in civil and commercial matters'.

European Commission, COM (2008) 131 'Communication from the Commission to the European Parliament pursuant to the second subparagraph of Article 251(2) of the EC Treaty concerning the common position of the Council on the adoption of a Directive of the European Parliament and of the Council on certain aspects of mediation in civil and commercial matters'.

European Commission, (2000) 'Evaluation of the pilot project on use of the European consumer complaint form for consumer disputes' <http://ec.europa.eu/comm/consumers/redress/compl/cons_compl/acce_just13_en.pdf> [10/8/07].

European Commission, (June 2006) 'Consultation Paper: Review of the Timeshare Directive (94/47/EC)' <http://ec.europa.eu/consumers/cons_int/safe_shop/timeshare/consultation_paper010606_en.doc> [10/8/07].

European Consumer Law Group, (April 1998) 'Jurisdiction and Applicable Law in Cross-Border Consumer Complaints. Socio-Legal Remarks on an Ongoing Dilemma Concerning Effective Legal Protection for Consumer-Citizens in the European Union' ECLG/157/1998 <http://www.europeanconsumerlawgroup.org/Content/Default.asp?pageID=500> [8/3/07]; also published in 21 Journal of Consumer Policy 315.

European Consumer Law Group, (2000) 'Consumer Transactions on the Internet' ECLG/194/2000 <http://www.europeanconsumerlawgroup.org/Content/Default.asp?pageID=500> [25/1/07].

European Consumer Law Group, (March 2001) 'Soft Law and the Consumer Interest' ECLG/071/2001 <http://www.europeanconsumerlawgroup.org/Content/Default.asp?pageID=500> [25/1/07].

European Consumer Law Group, (October 2004) '"Rome I"—Law Applicable to Consumer Transactions' ECLG/096/2004 <http://www.europeanconsumerlawgroup.org/Content/Default.asp?PageID=488> [25/1/07].

European Consumer Law Group, (November 2004) 'Commission Proposal for a Directive on Mediation' ECLG/122/2004 <http://www.europeanconsumerlawgroup.org/Content/Default.asp?PageID=488> [25/1/07].

European Consumer Law Group, (November 2004a) 'Timesharing' ECLG/127/2004 <http://www.europeanconsumerlawgroup.org/Content/Default.asp?PageID=488> [29/1/08].

European Consumer Law Group, (February 2005) 'The need for group action for consumer redress' ECLG/033/05 <http://www.europeanconsumerlawgroup.org/Content/Default.asp?PageID=488> [25/1/07].

European Consumer Law Group, (February 2005a) 'Protecting the Rights of Passengers and Holidaymakers' ECLG/039/05 <http://www.europeanconsumerlawgroup.org/Content/Default.asp?PageID=488> [29/1/08].

European Economic and Social Committee, [1999] OJ C169/36 'Opinion on the Proposal for a Directive on Certain Aspects of Electronic Commerce in the Internal Market'.

European Economic and Social Committee, [2005] OJ C211/77 'Opinion on the Proposal for a Regulation of the European Parliament and of the Council Creating a European Order for Payment Procedure'.

European Parliament, A5-0253/2000 'Report on the proposal for a Council regulation on jurisdiction and the recognition and enforcement of judgments in civil and commercial matters' <http://www.europarl.europa.eu/sides/getDoc.do?pubRef=-//EP//NONSGML+REPORT+A5-2000-0253+0+DOC+PDF+V0//EN> [1/11/07].

European Telecommunications Network Operators' Association, (1999) 'ETNO Reflection Document on the Draft Directive on Certain Legal Aspects of Electronic Commerce in the Internal Market' (ETNO Reflection Document RD 092(1999/01) <http://www.etno.be/DesktopModules/Popup.DocumentsIndex/docs/RD092%20-%20E-commerce.pdf> [1/2/08].

Federal Trade Commission, (November 2000) 'Summary of Public Workshop: Alternative Dispute Resolution for Consumer Transactions in the Borderless Online Marketplace, June 6–7, 2000' <http://www.ftc.gov/bcp/altdisresolution/summary.pdf> [10/12/07].

B Feldtmann, H von Freyhold, and EL Vial, (June 1998) 'The Cost of Legal Obstacles to the Disadvantage of Consumers in the Internal Market' <http://europa.eu.int/comm/dgs/health_consumer/library/pub/pub03.pdf> [17/8/07].

A Fielder, (May 2007) *Making the European internal market work for consumers* (National Consumer Council) <http://www.ncc.org.uk/nccpdf/poldocs/NCC158ft_european_internal_market.pdf> [29/11/07].

M Giuliano and P Lagarde, (1980) 'Report on the Convention on the law applicable to contractual obligations' [1980] OJ C282/1.

B Hess, T Pfeiffer, and P Schlosser, (September 2007) 'Report on the Application of Regulation Brussels I in the Member States' <http://ec.europa.eu/civiljustice/news/docs/study_application_brussels_1_en.pdf> [2/11/07].

RA Hillman, (2005) 'On-line Consumer Standard-Form Contracting Practices: A Survey and Discussion of Legal Implications' (Cornell Law School Legal Studies Research Paper Series: Paper 29) <http://lsr.nellco.org/cgi/viewcontent.cgi?article=1028&context=cornell/lsrp> [3/8/07].

International Chamber of Commerce, (July 2002) 'Business-to-Consumer and Consumer-to-Consumer Alternative Dispute Resolution (ADR) Inventory Project' <http://www.iccwbo.org/home/ADR/ADR%20PROJECT%20REPORT%20final.pdf> [5/4/07].

P Jenard, [1979] OJ C59/1 'Report on the Convention on jurisdiction and the enforcement of judgments in civil and commercial matters'.

Law Commission and Scottish Law Commission, (2005) 'Unfair Terms in Contracts' (Law Com No 252).

LIBA, (2003) 'LIBA response to European Commission Green Paper on the conversion of the 1980 Rome Convention on the law applicable to contractual obligations into a Community instrument, and its modernisation' <http://ec.europa.eu/justice_home/news/consulting_public/rome_i/doc/london_investment_banking_association_en.pdf> [15/11/07].

Lord Chancellor's Department, (1986) 'Civil Justice Review; Consultation Paper No 2: Small Claims'.

S Lott, MH Beaulieu, J Desforges, (November 2004) 'Mandatory Arbitration and Consumer Contracts' (Public Interest Advocacy Centre & Option consommateurs) <http://www.piac.ca/consumers/mandatory_arbitration_and_consumer_contracts> [3/8/07].

National Consumer Council, (September 1979) 'Simple Justice: A consumer view of small claims procedures in England and Wales'.

National Consumer Council, (1989) 'Ordinary Justice' (London: HMSO).

New Zealand Law Commission, (1998) 'Electronic Commerce Part 1: A Guide for the Legal and Business Community' (NZLC R50).

New Zealand Law Commission, (1999) 'Electronic Commerce Part 2: A Basic Legal Framework' (NZLC R58).

New Zealand Law Commission, (2000) 'Electronic Commerce Part 3: Remaining Issues' (NZLC R68).

Office of Fair Trading, (October 1998) 'Unfair contract terms bulletin 5' <http://www.oft.gov.uk/shared_oft/reports/unfair_contract_terms/oft246.pdf> [8/11/07].

Office of Fair Trading, (April 1999) 'Unfair contract terms bulletin 6' <http://www.oft.gov.uk/shared_oft/reports/unfair_contract_terms/oft262.pdf> [8/11/07].

Office of Fair Trading, (August 2003) 'Unfair contract terms bulletin 22' <http://www.oft.gov.uk/shared_oft/reports/unfair_contract_terms/oft669.pdf> [8/11/07].

Office of Fair Trading, (December 2003) 'Unfair contract terms bulletins 24 and 25' <http://www.oft.gov.uk/shared_oft/reports/unfair_contract_terms/oft686.pdf> [8/11/07].

Office of Fair Trading, (October 2004) 'Consumer education: A strategy and framework'<http://www.oft.gov.uk/shared_oft/consumer_education/oft753.pdf> [29/11/07].

Office of Fair Trading, (June 2007) 'Internet Shopping: An OFT market study' <http://www.oft.gov.uk/shared_oft/reports/consumer_protection/oft921.pdf> [3/8/07].

Organisation for Economic Co-operation and Development, (1997) 'Sacher Report' <http://www.oecd.org/dataoecd/54/25/1893999.pdf> [20/11/07].

Organisation for Economic Co-operation and Development, (December 1999) 'Recommendation of the OECD Council concerning Guidelines for Consumer Protection in the Context of Electronic Commerce' <http://www.oecd.org/dataoecd/18/13/34023235.pdf> [5/4/07].

Organisation for Economic Co-operation and Development, (March 2001) 'Consumers in the Online Marketplace; OECD Workshop on the Guidelines: One Year Later' <http://www.oecd.org/dataoecd/34/36/1864439.pdf> [5/4/07].

Organisation for Economic Co-operation and Development, (June 2002) 'Resolving E-Commerce Disputes Online: Asking the Right Questions about ADR' <http://www.olis.oecd.org/olis/2002doc.nsf/43bb6130e5e86e5fc12569fa005d004c/7f89b52192b7f8d5c1256bce00389cc6/$FILE/JT00127493.PDF> [5/4/07].

Organisation for Economic Co-operation and Development, (July 2002) 'Legal Provisions Related to Business-to-Consumer Alternative Dispute Resolution in Relation to Privacy and Consumer Protection' <http://www.olis.oecd.org/olis/2002doc.nsf/43bb6130e5e86e5fc12569fa005d004c/0fc99306e60c98bec1256bf900565f0c/$FILE/JT00129724.PDF> [5/4/07].

Organisation for Economic Co-operation and Development, (February 2003) 'Consumers, in the Online Marketplace: The OECD Guidelines Three Years Later' <http://www.olis.oecd.org/olis/2002doc.nsf/43666130e5e86e5fc12569fa005d004c/af6ec39d8631ca3ac1256cc2005c0edf/$FILE/JT00138646.PDF> [5/4/07].

Organisation for Economic Co-operation and Development, (2006) 'Consumer Dispute Resolution and Redress in the Global Marketplace' <https://www.oecd.org/dataoecd/26/61/36456184.pdf> [10/7/08].

PLEAS (Public Legal Education and Support) Task Force, (July 2007) 'Developing Capable Citizens: the role of public legal education' <http://www.pleas.org.uk/uploads/PLEAS%20Task%20Force%20Report.pdf> [29/11/07].

T Puurunen, (2005) *Dispute Resolution in International Electronic Commerce* (Helsinki: Helsinki University Printing House) <http://ethesis.helsinki.fi/julkaisut/oik/julki/vk/puurunen/disputer.pdf> [21/7/06].

P Schlosser, [1979] OJ C59/71 'Report on the Convention on the Accession of the Kingdom of Denmark, Ireland and the United Kingdom of Great Britain and Northern Ireland to the Convention on jurisdiction and the enforcement of judgments in civil and commercial matters and to the Protocol on its interpretation by the Court of Justice'.

Scottish Consumer Council, (March 2001) 'E-commerce and Consumer Protection' <http://www.scotconsumer.org.uk/publications/reports/reports01/rp03ecomm.pdf> [29/11/07].

Study Centre for Consumer Law (Katholieke Universiteit Leuven), (January 2007) 'An analysis and evaluation of alternative means of consumer redress other than redress through ordinary judicial proceedings' <http://ec.europa.eu/consumers/redress/reports_studies/comparative_report_en.pdf> [3/8/07].

Touche Ross, (1986) 'Civil Justice Review: Study of the Small Claims Procedure' (London: Touche Ross).

J Trzaskowski, (October 2006) 'E-Commerce trustmarks in Europe—an overview and comparison of Trustmarks in the European Union, Iceland and Norway' <http://www.forbrugereuropa.dk/fileadmin/Filer/Forbrugereuropa_-_pdf/Trustmarkconference/trustmarks-report.pdf> [3/12/07].

A Vahrenwald, (May 2000) 'Out-of-court dispute settlement systems for e-commerce, Report on legal issues, Part I: The Parties to the Dispute' (Joint Research Centre of the European Commission) <http://www.vahrenwald.com> [2/10/06].

——(May 2000a) 'Out-of-court dispute settlement systems for e-commerce, Report on legal issues, Part II: The Protection of the Recipient' (Joint Research Centre of the European Commission) <http://www.vahrenwald.com> [2/10/06].

——(May 2000b) 'Out-of-court dispute settlement systems for e-commerce, Report on legal issues, Part III: Types of Out-of-court Dispute Settlement' (Joint Research Centre of the European Commission) <http://www.vahrenwald.com> [2/10/06].

——(October 2000) 'Out-of-court dispute settlement systems for e-commerce, Report on legal issues, Part IV: Arbitration' (Joint Research Centre of the European Commission) <http://www.vahrenwald.com> [2/10/06].

H von Freyhold, V Gessner, EL Vial, and H Wagner, (October/November 1995) 'The Cost of Judicial Barriers for Consumers in the Internal Market' <http://www.freyvial.de/Publications/egi-2.pdf> [17/8/07].

M Wilikens, A Vahrenwald, and P Morris, (April 2000) 'Out-of-court dispute settlement systems for e-commerce, Report of an exploratory Study' (Joint Research Centre of the European Commission) <http://www.federcomin.it/sviluppo/Produzio.nsf/all/AB130AEEEE4848C7C125690E00393B4C/$file/Reportv20apr.pdf> [2/10/06].

Index